Eastern Turkey

the Bradt Travel Guide

Diana Darke

edition
I

www.bradtguides.com

Bradt Travel Guides Ltd, UK
The Globe Pequot Press Inc, USA

C000241592

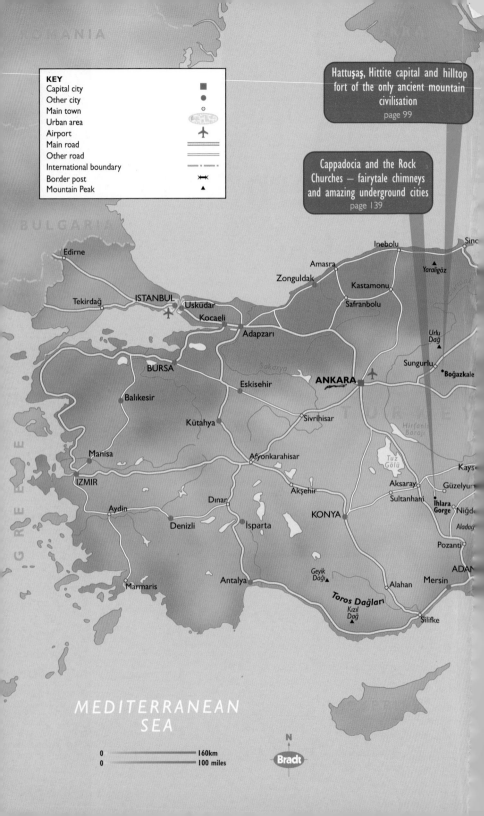

KEY
Capital city ■
Other city ●
Main town ○
Urban area
Airport ✈
Main road
Other road
International boundary
Border post ⋈
Mountain Peak ▲

Hattuşaş, Hittite capital and hilltop fort of the only ancient mountain civilisation
page 99

Cappadocia and the Rock Churches — fairytale chimneys and amazing underground cities
page 139

ROMANIA

BULGARIA

GREECE

Edirne

Tekirdağ

ISTANBUL

Üsküdar

Kocaeli

Adapzarı

BURSA

Eskisehir

Balıkesir

Kütahya

Manisa

İZMIR

Afyonkarahisar

Aydin

Dınar

Denizli

İsparta

Akşehir

Marmaris

Antalya

Geyik Dağı ▲

Toros Dağları

Kızıl Dağ ▲

Alahan

Inebolu

Amasra

Zonguldak

Kastamonu

Safranbolu

Sakarya

ANKARA

Sivrihisar

Hirfanlı Baraji

Tuz Gölü

Aksaray

Sultanhani

KONYA

Sungurlu

Boğazkale

Urlu Dağ ▲

Yaralıgöz ▲

Sinc

TURKEY

Kays

Güzelyur

Ihlara Gorge

Niğd

Aladag

Pozantı

ADAN

Mersin

Silifke

MEDITERRANEAN SEA

0 ——— 160km
0 ——— 100 miles

N

Bradt

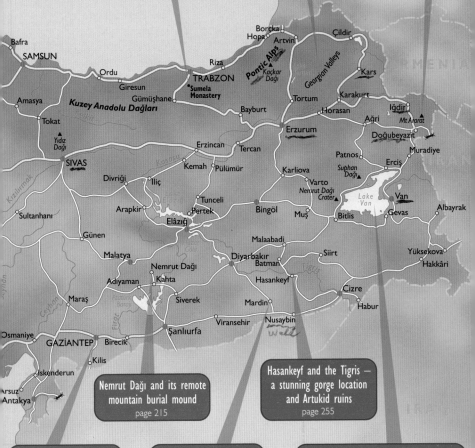

Sumela Monastery, clinging Tibetan-style to a high cliff-face above deep evergreen forests
page 359

The Georgian Valleys and Pontic Alps
page 325

Mt Ararat, Turkey's highest peak at 5,165m
page 295

BLACK SEA

GEORGIA

RUSSIA

ARMENIA

Bafra
SAMSUN
Ordu
Giresun
Amasya
Gümüşhane
Tokat
Yıldız Dağı
SIVAS
Divriği
İliç
Arapkir
Pertek
Elâzığ
Sultanhanı
Günen
Malatya
Nemrut Dağı
Adıyaman
Kahta
Maraş
Siverek
Osmaniye
GAZİANTEP
Birecik
Kilis
İskenderun
Arsuz
Antakya
Şanlıurfa
Viranşehir

Kuzey Anadolu Dağları
TRABZON
Sumela Monastery
Riza
Bayburt
Erzincan
Tercan
Kemah
Pülümür
Tunceli
Bingöl
Malaabadi
Diyarbakır
Batman
Hasankeyf
Mardin
Nusaybin

Borçka
Hopa
Artvin
Cildir
Pontic Alps
Kaçkar Dağı
Tortum
Georgian Valleys
Kars
Karakurt
Horasan
Erzurum
Ağrı
Doğubeyazit
Patnos
Suphan Dağı
Varto
Nemrut Dağı Crater
Muş
Bitlis
Karliova
Iğdir
Mt Ararat
Muradiye
Erciş
Lake Van
Van
Gevas
Albayrak
Yüksekova
Hakkâri
Siirt
Cizre
Habur

SYRIA

IRAQ

Nemrut Dağı and its remote mountain burial mound
page 215

Hasankeyf and the Tigris — a stunning gorge location and Artukid ruins
page 255

Gaziantep and the Zeugma Mosaics, the most impressive and complete Roman mosaics in the world
page 205

Mardin and the Tûr Abdin — stunning architecture and excellent Syrian cuisine
page 245

Lake Van and Akdamar Island — tiny islands graced with Armenian churches in a vast, mountain-ringed lake
page 263

Eastern Turkey Don't miss...

Işak Paşa Sarayı
This pleasure palace of a 19th-century local chieftain, complete with sybaritic harem, has a dramatic mountain setting
(SS) page 300

Ani
Now entirely deserted, this Armenian ghost town with its near-complete cathedral once had a population in excess of **100,000**
(M/DT) page 319

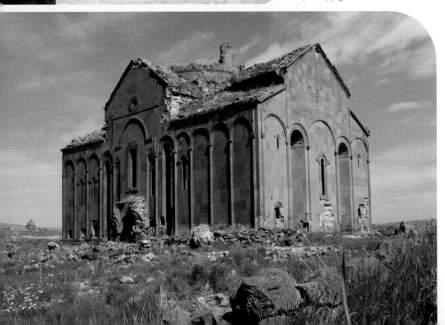

Hoşap Castle
Perched above the Hoşap
River, this remote
Kurdish fortress dates
back to the 17th century
(IS/A) page 289

Konya
The Mevlâna Tekke is the
atmospheric burial place
of the poet Rumi, founder
of the mystic Whirling
Dervishes, and its famous
turquoise dome is a
symbol of the town
(IS/A) page 168

Safranbolu
A near-perfect town of
Ottoman mansions built of
wood, now preserved as a
UNESCO World Heritage Site
(AR/DT) page 370

left Mount Ararat towers over the Anatolian Plateau; at 5,165m, its summit is snow-capped all year round (RHPL/A) page 295

below Göreme Valley holds Cappadocia's best collection of painted cave-churches. Medieval Orthodox Christian monks carved the caves from the soft volcanic stone and decorated them with elaborate Byzantine frescoes (E/DT) page 149

bottom The Bendamahi Falls near Lake Van are an impressive sight in spring, when the river carries the greatest snowmelt down from the mountains (DD) page 296

right Süphan Dağı's summit is atop a massive volcanic plug lying in a beautiful grassy bowl (DD) page 271

below The Kaçkar Mountains offer hikers fantastic views, with high Alpine meadows, mountain lakes and jagged peaks (H/DT) page 333

extinct volcano

above   **Nemrut Dağı is astonishing for its sheer scale; the gigantic stone heads on top of a mountain were a vast funeral monument to the ruler of a small local dynasty with delusions of grandeur** (TW/DT) page 215

below   **The ruined city of Hasankeyf, on the banks of the Tigris, was once the capital of the Artukid dynasty and the Kurdish Ayyubid kings** (SS) page 255

AUTHOR

Diana Darke's fascination with Turkey began by chance when she crossed it from east to west alone in 1979. She has been visiting both western and eastern regions regularly ever since, as well as Istanbul. After taking her undergraduate degree in Arabic at Oxford, she worked initially for the British government and then in British business as a freelance Arabic translator/interpreter. While devising bilingual keyboards and kit for Racal Electronics during the day, she began writing about Turkey as a hobby at night, wondering why no-one else was doing so. She has now authored five books on Turkey, for three different
publishers, whilst watching the country change and develop over the last 30 years. In spite of her Arabist roots, Turkey has always been her first love, and she recently completed an MA in Islamic Architecture, focusing on the Ottoman period. This Ottoman link complements her other main interest, Syria, once also part of the Ottoman Empire before today's arbitrarily imposed boundaries. She is married with two children and divides her time between London, the Kent coast and Damascus, with visits to Turkey as often as possible. She is currently doing research for her PhD at London University's School of Oriental and African Studies.

AUTHOR'S STORY

Most people only know one face of Turkey – Istanbul and the western Mediterranean shores. My motive in writing this book is to lift the veil a little on Turkey's other face, east of Ankara, the two-thirds of the country where 55 of its 81 provinces are to be found. In many ways this is the real Turkey, closer to the original roots of its own civilisations, the Hittites, the Urartians and the Seljuks.

I discovered Turkey backwards. The Lebanese Civil War had broken out, forcing the closure of the government-sponsored Arabic course I had been attending in Shemlan. It would take six weeks to reassemble itself in London, so here was my chance to explore Turkey properly on full evacuation expenses. The other students, eager to return to Europe, got on ferries from Beirut to Marseilles, while I headed north in my Citroën 2CV, entering Turkey from the Syrian Bab Al-Hawa border post. Where was the demonic, dangerous place I had been warned about? I never found it. Instead I meandered through empty landscapes of power and intensity scattered with the remnants of civilisations previously unknown to me. Mt Ararat took my breath away and I vowed to climb it one day. Thirty years later this book provided the chance. To explore this highly complex region of Turkey properly will take another 30 years, and even then I know I will only be scratching the surface.

PUBLISHER'S FOREWORD   *Adrian Phillips, Publishing Director*

If there's a guidebook that embodies the Bradt philosophy, this is surely it. You'll find no shortage of books covering Turkey on the shop shelves. However, this one takes the road significantly less travelled – leaving behind the tourist crowds in Istanbul and the Mediterranean resorts – and introduces a wilder and more exotic land. Diana Darke is well-qualified to be your guide. She first fell in love with this region 30 years ago, and revisits regularly from her home in Damascus. There's little she can't tell you about Ottoman architecture, and she is a fluent Arabic speaker. And, most importantly, she climbed mountains to ensure her research was the best it could be... well, one mountain to be precise – Mount Ararat. You can read her inspiring account of the ascent in *Chapter 10*.

First published February 2011

Bradt Travel Guides Ltd, 23 High Street, Chalfont St Peter, Bucks SL9 9QE, England.
www.bradtguides.com
Published in the USA by The Globe Pequot Press Inc, PO Box 480, Guilford, Connecticut
06437-0480.

Text copyright © 2011 Diana Darke
Maps copyright © 2011 Bradt Travel Guides Ltd
Photography copyright © 2011 Individual photographers (see below)

ISBN-13: 978 1 84162 339 9
British Library Cataloguing in Publication Data
A catalogue record for this book is available from the British Library

Photographs Alamy: Robert Harding Picture Library Ltd (RHPL/A), Hemis (H/A), Images &
Stories (IS/A), Richard Lim (RL/A), mauritius images GmbH (MI/A), Edward Parker (EP/A);
Dreamstime: Array (AR/DT), Ayaltun (AY/DT), Bülent Cengiz (BC/DT), Kobby Dagan
(KD/DT), Emicristea (E/DT), Hugoht (H/DT), Mjunsworth (M/DT), Shanin (SH/DT),
Sinandurdu (SI/DT), Tomwang (TW/DT), Toneimage (TI/DT); Diana Darke (DD); Nicolas
Guyot (NG); SuperStock (SS)
Front cover Stone heads at Nemrut Dağı, Eastern Anatolia (H/A)
Back cover Akdamar Island, Lake Van (IS/A)
Title page Göreme Valley, Cappadocia (SS); Mosaic tiles in the Sırçalı Medrese, Konya (IS/A);
Göreme National Park, Cappadocia (SS)

Maps David McCutcheon, Malcolm Barnes (colour)
Text maps based on original sketch maps from the *Discovery Guide to Eastern Turkey* by Diana
Darke, published by Michael Haag

Typeset from the author's disk by Wakewing
Production managed by Jellyfish Print Solutions and manufactured in India

Acknowledgements

The author would like to thank Zafer Onay and his team of Kurdish helpers – Ibrahim, Ahmet, Juma, Kobe and Ali – for their invaluable support during two mountaineering summers and the ascents of Mt Nemrut, Mt Süphan and Mt Ararat.

DEDICATION

To my mother, with gratitude

Contents

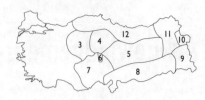

LIST OF MAPS

Introduction

Covering everything from Ankara and Cappadocia eastwards, this guide extends over a vast region which accounts for some 70% of Turkey's land mass, yet has less than 45% of its population. Eastern Turkey remains for most people an unknown, a complete blank, with many convinced that it is totally out of bounds to travellers. Until 2000 this was largely true, with whole tracts under martial law and designated as military zones. Travel for sheer interest or pleasure's sake was difficult to arrange. Now you can travel freely anywhere you are likely to go. Permits are no longer required to visit places close to sensitive borders, such as Ani, the Armenian ghost town. The only thing for which a permit is still required is the ascent of Mount Ararat, a highly specialised permit which must be applied for two months in advance, but which is nevertheless simply a formality, guaranteed to be granted when the mountain is open. (See page 305.)

Aimed at adventurous, possibly even eccentric people of all ages and on all budgets, visitors should be aware that pampering is not on offer here. Instead there is the excitement of entering another world, a big black hole beyond Europe, far away from the familiar centres of civilisation. Eastern Turkey is like a country within a country, light years away from the sophistication of Istanbul and the glamour of the Mediterranean coastline. Wild and rugged, the Anatolian Plateau was home to civilisations of an entirely different kind, all of whom have left their relics for exploration. Early Christians escaping persecution carved out churches and entire cities underground; mountain Hittites and Urartians built fairy-tale castles on impossible crags; power-mad chieftains honoured themselves with fantasy palaces and colossal statues. Mountains, lakes and volcanoes dominate the landscape.

The huge surge in popularity of Turkey's well-known tourist spots, like Istanbul and the Aegean/Mediterranean coast, has led to increasing curiosity about the rest of the country, which even most Turks have not visited and know little about. Many British have now bought houses and settled in western parts of Turkey, especially Kaş and Kalkan, and as they become more familiar with their immediate surroundings, they are starting to become intrigued by what the eastern region has to offer. William Dalrymple's widely read book *From the Holy Mountain* has also raised awareness of the many churches and monasteries of the Tûr Abdin (see page 249) in the extreme southeast and their dwindling Christian communities. Press coverage of turbulent conditions in the countries bordering eastern Turkey, notably Georgia, Armenia, Iran and Iraq, intrigue people as to what the region is like, especially as, unlike its neighbours, petty crime is virtually non-existent and travel here is now safe and straightforward.

This book divides eastern Turkey into ten distinct regions, with detailed maps and itineraries for all budgets and timescales, from one week to one month. One option for newcomers to Turkey is to take a two-centre holiday, with one week perhaps on the coast or in cosmopolitan Istanbul, and a second week of total contrast in eastern Turkey. Extensive practical information is given on transport, accommodation and eating for each of eastern Turkey's ten regions. Turkish Airlines has an excellent network of domestic airports offering regular, cheap and reliable flights that link all parts of eastern Turkey with Istanbul and Ankara. These can be tapped into from the many budget and charter airlines that now fly to Turkey, thereby bringing an exotic destination within easy reach, both financially and in travelling time. The road network has been dramatically improved, with new tarmac surfaces transforming journey times. Inter-city coaches provide excellent, cheap and punctual connections between all major cities. Rail travel in eastern Turkey is especially rewarding, if time-consuming, with comfortable trains that pass through spectacular scenery and gorges that cannot be seen by road. Colourful extras like proverbs and quotes from Turkish literature and folklore are liberally scattered throughout the book for entertainment – a unique feature – and a thorough analysis of Turkish is given by the author, a fluent Arabic-speaker, who has studied this perplexing language intensively.

Usually confined to the back pages of general Turkey guides, eastern Turkey is here finally given the attention it deserves. With first-hand descriptions of everything from Kurdish thermal pools to Armenian ghost towns, there are also detailed sections on birdwatching, trekking and mountaineering, including climbing the volcanoes around Lake Van and a chapter devoted to the ascent of Mount Ararat, Turkey's highest peak at 5,165m. The book also covers all practical details on how best to travel and explore this little-known and often misunderstood destination.

UPDATES WEBSITE AND FEEDBACK REQUEST

Tourism in eastern Turkey is just starting to develop, and most sources of information focus on Istanbul and the Aegean and Mediterranean regions. The Turkish Ministry of Tourism produces a few helpful pamphlets and leaflets on Cappadocia, Nemrut Daği, the Black Sea Coast and eastern Turkey in general, but they are very thin on practical details. All the more valuable then is first-hand feedback from visitors to the country, and the author would greatly appreciate any comments and information from readers to help keep the guide as up to date as possible. Please write or email via the publishers at: Bradt Travel Guides, 23 High Street, Chalfont St Peter, Bucks SL9 9QE; e info@bradtguides.com. For the latest travel news about eastern Turkey, please visit the update page on Bradt's website: updates@bradtguides.com.

Part One

GENERAL INFORMATION

Official name Republic of Turkey

Location Between the northeastern corner of the Mediterranean and the southern shoreline of the Black Sea

Neighbouring countries Armenia 268km (length of border), Azerbaijan 9km, Georgia 252km, Iran 499km, Iraq 331km, Syria 822km (to the west Bulgaria 240km, Greece 206km)

Size 546,406km (70% of the country's area of 780,000km)

Climate Very hot dry summers, very cold snowy winters in the interior. Milder winters and more humid summers on the coast.

Status Parliamentary republic

Population 30 million (40% of the country's population of 75 million)

Life expectancy Male 70 years, female 74 years

Capital (and population) Ankara (4.8 million)

Other main towns Adana, Gaziantep, Konya, Kayseri, Mersin, Diyarbakır

Economy Agriculture, forestry, major industries – automotive, textiles, iron and steel, clothing, white goods, natural resources – antimony, coal, chromium, mercury, copper

GDP US$747.7 billion (2008)

Languages Turkish (official), Kurdish

Religion Muslim

Currency Turkish lira (TL)

Exchange rate £1 = TL2.26, US$1 = TL1.40, €1 = TL1.96 (November 2010)

National airline/airport Turkish Airlines (THY). Hub airports: Istanbul, Ankara.

International telephone code +90

Internet domain .tr

Time GMT+2

Electrical voltage 220V

Weights and measures Metric system

Flag Red flag with white crescent moon and star in centre, derived from the Ottoman flag

National anthem Istiklal Marşı 'Independence March' *'Fear not, the crimson flag, waving in these dawns, will never fade'*

National flower Tulip

National sports Greased wrestling and football

Public holidays See pages 63–5

I

Background Information

The tyranny of a Turk is better than the justice of a Bedouin (Arabic proverb)

GEOGRAPHY

Turkey has always been seen as a passage land between Europe and Asia, having nearly half of its land borders with European countries and half with Asian. The western part of Turkey looks towards the Aegean and Mediterranean seas and is very conscious of its links with Europe. But in culture, racial origins and ways of life, there are frequent reminders that Turkey's geographical situation is primarily part of Asia, and these reminders increase as you head into the eastern part of Turkey. Asiatic Turkey is usually called by its traditional name, Anatolia (Turkish *Anadolu*), and forms a huge rectangular peninsula framed to the north and south by chains of fold mountains which merge in the east to form a tangled knot. The geological structure of Turkey is extremely complicated, and rocks of almost all ages occur. In general Turkey consists of a number of old plateau blocks, against which masses of younger rock series have been squeezed to form fold mountain ranges of varying size. As there were several of these plateau blocks, and not just one, the fold mountains run in many different directions, with no simple pattern discernible, making communications difficult. One mountain range gives way abruptly to another, and you can pass suddenly from highland to plain or plateau. This irregular topography also has given rise to many lakes, more than anywhere else in the Middle East, and certainly if you had to sum up eastern Turkey's geography in three words they would be 'mountains, rivers and lakes'.

LANDSCAPES The main feature is the rugged **Anatolian Plateau** which lies at an altitude of 1,000m, and from this baseline rise many far higher mountain ranges like the Taurus and the Kaçkar, as well as individual colossal volcanoes like Mount Ararat, higher than anything in the European Union countries, and Turkey's highest peak at 5,165m, snow-covered all year round. On this plateau whole stretches are vast tracts of bleak wilderness, sheets of lava which are often of such recent occurrence that soil has not yet been formed. As a result wide expanses are still sterile and uninhabited. Cracking and disturbance of the rocks has taken place on an enormous scale, and the eastern part of Turkey, especially around Erzurum and Erzincan, is still subject to severe earthquakes, though the volcanoes have been dormant for many centuries. Combine this unforgiving landscape with climatic extremes of heat and cold, and you have a country which produces toughness in its people. The sheer scale and roughness of the place lends a power that is almost demonic.

Most surreal of all is Lake Van, its thin piercing blueness ringed with snow-covered peaks, some as high as 4,000m. The **Van region**, once heavily wooded, is now denuded after centuries of man chopping down trees for fuel in the long hard winters and for building material. Though the average altitude of the central plateau is 1,500m you are not aware of it being so high, as the land itself is often flat with distant mountains rimming the horizon. Much of the scenery is therefore far from inspiring, and long drives between towns can be very tedious with little to break the monotony. Lake Van creates a special landscape of its own which, despite the starkness of its shores, has a memorable quality. A few magnificent extinct volcano cones lend majesty to the bleakest of horizons, and in the Hakkâri region in the extreme southeastern corner of the country, the river and gorge scenery is often spectacular in an alpine way.

The most attractive and surprising landscapes of eastern Turkey are to be found in the **Georgian valleys** and the **Pontic Mountains** between Erzurum and the Black Sea. The lush greenness here, in such contrast to the bleakness of the plateau, lends a variety of colour and texture to the landscapes which is often sorely missing elsewhere. The Black Sea coast itself is a shoreline of surprising diversity and prosperity, thanks to its thriving tea plantations which tumble to a narrow coastal strip.

WATER The other remarkable feature of eastern Turkey is the sheer abundance of water. Rarely will you have been in a region so blessed with lakes and rivers. The sound of rushing water becomes something of a constant in many areas. Both the Tigris and the Euphrates have their sources in eastern Turkey, giving the country total control of the headwaters of these rivers and with it, colossal power over its southern neighbours, Syria and Iraq. The Southeast Anatolia Project (known in Turkey as GAP) is a series of dams on the Euphrates, slowly but surely making Turkey self-sufficient in electricity. In addition to these major rivers, there are many lesser-known ones like the Çoruh, popular for white-water rafting, the Murat and the Kızılırmak, along with numerous smaller streams. They run all year round, though are at their most swollen in spring when the winter snows melt.

CLIMATE

Extremes of temperature are the order of the day in eastern Turkey, not just between winter and summer, but also between night and day. This is because of the presence of mountain ranges close to the coast and the great height of the interior plateau ranging from 800m to 2,000m. The most dramatic example of this is Kars, in the northeast, where the highest temperature recorded has been 35°C in the daytime in summer, and the lowest −37°C at night in winter. These enormous seasonal variations are among the widest in the world. Rainfall too is extremely variable. Along the eastern Black Sea coast towards the Georgian border, over 2,500mm fall per year, while parts of the central plateau, shut off by the mountains from the influence of sea winds, are arid, with annual rainfall less than 250mm. Temperatures around the coast are a little more clement, both on the Mediterranean and the Black Sea, but the Anatolian Plateau of the interior, raised up at around 1,500m and exposed to the full harshness of the elements, bears the brunt of the severe weather extremes.

Given the size and extent of the terrain covered in this guide, separate climate entries are given for each chapter, to reflect the huge differences that exist between the areas. See also pages 6–7 for climate charts.

NATURAL HISTORY AND CONSERVATION

Eastern Turkey's rugged terrain is the product of a wide variety of tectonic processes that have taken place over millions of years, and still continue today with frequent earthquakes and even occasional volcanic eruptions. Geologically Turkey is part of the great alpine belt that extends from the Atlantic to the Himalayas. Formed in the Tertiary Period (about 65 million–1.6 million years ago), this belt still has friction points where the African Plate converges with the Eurasian Plate and the Anatolian Plate. Specifically the danger areas are along the North Anatolian Fault zone near the Black Sea coast, and the East Anatolian Fault zone, and the most earthquake-prone part of Turkey is an arc stretching from the Kocaeli (Izmit) area just east of Istanbul near the Black Sea coast to the area north of Lake Van on the border with Armenia and Georgia.

Turkey is well blessed with natural resources. There are abundant coal and lignite deposits, chrome ore, iron ore, copper and petroleum. Even when the Ottoman Empire was known as 'the sick man of Europe' in the 19th century, Turkey's vast territories still held valuable minerals which both European and American industry were keen to exploit. Turkey's first oil discovery was made in southeast Turkey in 1940 and nearly all subsequent discoveries have been made in the same area. The complex geology in the fold mountain areas makes exploration extremely difficult and quite costly.

NATIONAL PARKS Turkey's Ministry of the Environment was established in 1991 in response to the growing awareness of environmental problems in Turkey, notably pollution and conservation of nature. There are 39 national parks scattered throughout Turkey, about half of which are in the eastern region, most of them in forested or mountainous areas where biological diversity is being protected. The Turkish government has also passed special legislation to grant Special Areas of Environmental Protection in places where tourism and construction might damage the habitat of endangered species and the natural beauty of the environment. The Ihlara Gorge in Cappadocia is one such area, and there are national parks in the Rize and Trabzon regions of the Black Sea. Protected animals in these areas include fallow deer, roe deer, northern bald ibis, pheasant, francolin, partridge, wild goat, water fowl, Mediterranean monk seal and mouflon.

WILDLIFE Along the roadsides the large, hairy Bactrian camels are still to be seen in the southern Mediterranean areas, giving way in the central Anatolian regions to the distinctive black water buffalo with their long beards and fierce horns. Both are used as beasts of burden. Sheep and goats abound in many shapes and forms and there are also plentiful cattle. Chickens, geese and ducks are often all over the roads in the villages of the interior.

Further afield in the remoter and more mountainous areas, the game which the Turks shoot includes badger, bear, boar, deer, ibex, jackal and gazelle on the Turkish–Syrian border areas and wild cats and even leopards in the forests. There are also many wolves and wild dogs in the mountains.

Common game birds are wild duck, wild geese, quail, partridge and pheasant.

GOATS IN BRAS

The Anatolian Plateau was not always as barren as it is today: centuries of deforestation by goats and man have transformed the landscape. The government has been trying for some years to encourage people to breed cattle rather than goats, and though they have had some success, old habits die hard. One curiosity still to be seen in some rural areas is goats wearing bras. This is not an attempt at modesty, but purely a practical way of preventing the young from suckling too long.

TEMPERATURES (°C)

	Jan	Feb	Mar	Apr	May	Jun	Jul	Aug	Sep	Oct	Nov	Dec
Adana												
Average	9	10	13	17	21	25	28	28	25	21	15	11
Max	27	26	31	37	42	43	44	46	43	42	34	27
Min	−9	−7	−5	0.1	7	9	11	15	9	3	−4	−4
Ankara												
Average	0	3	5	10	16	20	22	22	16	14	8	3
Max	16	20	28	31	34	36	38	40	35	33	25	20
Min	−25	−24	−16	−7	−1	3	4	5	−1	−5	−17	−24
Antakya												
Average	8	10	13	17	21	24	27	28	25	20	15	10
Max	20	22	27	35	42	42	43	44	41	38	29	22
Min	−15	−7	−4	2	9	12	16	15	10	2	−3	−7
Antalya												
Average	10	12	15	18	20	25	28	29	25	22	16	13
Max	15	15	17	21	25	30	34	34	30	25	20	15
Min	5	5	8	10	15	20	22	22	19	15	10	6
Cappadocia (Kayseri)												
Average	−2	0	4	10	15	19	22	22	17	11	6	1
Max	18	23	28	30	34	37	40	41	36	34	26	18
Min	−32	−31	−26	−11	−7	−1	3	2	−4	−13	−20	−29
Diyarbakır												
Average	4	6	8	16	18	26	32	30	25	15	9	5
Max	17	21	26	33	40	42	46	46	42	35	28	23
Min	−24	−19	−12	−6	1	3	9	8	4	−8	−12	−18
Erzurum												
Average	−9	−7	−3	5	11	15	19	20	15	9	2	−5
Max	8	10	17	23	29	32	34	34	31	27	21	12
Min	−30	−28	−25	−19	−7	−3	1	1	−4	−12	−25	−28
Istanbul												
Average	5	6	7	11	15	21	24	25	21	16	12	7
Max	8	9	11	16	21	25	28	28	24	20	15	11
Min	3	2	3	7	12	16	18	19	16	13	9	5
Izmir												
Average	8	10	13	15	20	24	26	26	24	18	15	10
Max	12	13	16	20	25	30	32	32	28	24	18	14
Min	6	5	7	12	15	20	22	22	18	14	10	7

BIRDWATCHING Travel in eastern Turkey means long distances, sometimes through a spectacular and dramatic landscape, at other times through scenery that is less immediately interesting. But there is one feature as you travel that can always keep you on your toes and which gives every stop an extra dimension and an interest beyond the immediate archaeological, architectural or scenic – the birdlife.

Carrying a pair of binoculars will enhance your trip even if you are totally inexperienced and have never paid any attention to birds before. The best book

TEMPERATURES (°C)

	Jan	Feb	Mar	Apr	May	Jun	Jul	Aug	Sep	Oct	Nov	Dec
Kars												
Average	−12	−10	−4	5	10	13	17	17	13	7	1	−8
Max	5	11	19	24	26	31	35	35	33	26	21	11
Min	−40	−37	−33	−22	−7	−4	2	−2	−6	−18	−30	−35
Konya												
Average	−3	2	5	11	16	20	24	23	18	12	7	2
Max	17	24	28	30	35	36	38	40	35	32	25	22
Min	−28	−26	−16	−7	−2	2	7	5	−3	−9	−19	−26
Malatya (for Nemrut Dağı)												
Average	−1	1	6	13	18	23	27	27	22	16	8	2
Max	15	18	25	30	35	37	42	41	36	35	24	16
Min	−25	−21	−12	−7	2	6	10	9	4	−1	−9	−22
Samsun												
Average	7	7	8	11	15	20	23	23	20	16	13	10
Max	23	26	33	37	38	36	36	39	38	35	32	27
Min	−8	−9	−6	−3	3	8	13	12	7	3	−3	−5
Sivas												
Average	−4	−3	2	8	13	16	20	20	16	11	5	−1
Max	12	17	25	28	31	34	38	37	34	31	24	16
Min	−35	−34	−24	−11	−6	−1	3	3	−3	−9	−24	−30
Trabzon												
Average	7	7	9	12	16	20	24	25	21	17	14	10
Max	26	28	35	37	38	36	33	38	32	34	33	26
Min	−7	−8	−6	−1	4	9	13	13	7	4	−2	−3
Urfa												
Average	5	7	10	15	22	28	32	31	27	20	13	7
Max	22	23	29	34	40	43	47	46	42	38	31	23
Min	−10	−12	−5	−3	3	8	15	16	10	2	−6	−6
Van												
Average	−5	−5	−2	5	11	16	20	19	14	7	2	−3
Max	14	14	20	24	26	33	37	36	32	29	20	14
Min	−28	−28	−20	−18	−7	−3	4	5	3	−14	−20	−21

to have along for reference is *The Birds of Britain and Europe with North Africa and the Middle East* (Collins Pocket Guide) by Heinzel, Fitter and Parslow. Bird identification can at times be a frustrating and disappointing experience if you are not an expert, though it is always challenging and continues to exercise the mind long after the bird in question has disappeared from view.

Inevitably there are the 'big brown birds' of prey and the numerous 'little brown birds' which are aggravatingly difficult to identify because of distance, lack of

Turkey offers a wide range of birdlife in what is a comparatively small area. Just as its geographical position between the land masses of Asia, Africa and Europe laid it open to the movement of peoples and armies from the north, east and south, so too Turkey has elements of the birdlife of all three continents. This diversity is increased by the very wide range of climatic conditions which occur within the compact area of Turkey. There is the semi-desert of the Syrian border and the Mediterranean coastland with its hinterland of scrub-covered mountains. Then there is the bare central Anatolian Plateau ringed and divided by naked mountain ranges, but holding within it natural and artificial lakes, many of them saline. Finally there is the almost temperate, humid Black Sea coast with its own forested mountains. This movement from semi-desert to bare mountain, forested mountain, steppe and wetlands all adds to the diversity of birdlife and makes Turkey an exciting place for the northern European birdwatcher. If you are here in the spring or autumn there is the added attraction that two of the major north–south migration routes cross this land mass. To the east their flight pattern follows the western flanks of the Caucasus and over the passes of the eastern Karadeniz (Black Sea) Mountains. These migrations are on a huge scale: nearly 400,000 birds of prey are routinely recorded passing the northeast coast between mid-August and mid-October. May is the best time, and on a typical three-week holiday in eastern Turkey even the inexperienced birdwatcher can be assured of spotting, if not always identifying with certainty, well over 100 species, nearly 50 of which are not to be seen in Britain.

experience or inability to distinguish birdsong. But all the birds mentioned here are to be seen while travelling from one town to another along the routes you would be following anyway, so do not necessitate any detour. Birdwatching can therefore be easily incorporated to add interest to the long road journeys.

Sticking to the order in which places are covered in this book, the first group of birds to look out for are white storks in meadows by the Kızılırmak River (see page 97) east of Ankara, with grey herons fishing in the river shallows. Stork nests are common on buildings, minarets and telegraph poles. It is along this road from Ankara to the Hittite heartlands that you first notice the crested larks which are, in much of this part of Turkey, the bird which is always running off the tarmac and flying up under the wheels of vehicles. They become less common as you head further east.

The **Hittite sites** are rich with birds: red-backed shrikes and black-eared wheatears in the open spaces of Boğazkale (see page 99), the rocks of Yazılıkaya (see page 103) echoing to the sharp cries of families of rock buntings. After Alacahüyük in the failing light among the hills *en route* to Amasya there are more grey herons and night herons, little egrets, ruddy shelducks and white-winged black terns sweeping across the water.

Birds of the central Anatolian Plateau are many and varied: redshanks, little ringed plovers, rose-coloured starlings and glossy ibises can be seen by flooded fields beside the Sivas to Divriği road. Brightly coloured bee-eaters are the birds of the roadside telegraph wires, swooping down to feed, then back up to look out for the next morsel. At other times cranes, golden orioles, lesser grey shrikes, black-headed buntings and hoopoes are to be seen as well as more familiar birds such as starlings, jays, blackbirds and many magpies.

Overhead, **vultures and birds of prey** are common if not always readily identifiable. The easily distinguished black and white Egyptian vultures circle overhead singly or in groups, but griffon vultures are also to be seen. On the open roads are buzzards and long-legged buzzards. Black kites, seen near Sivas, are often devouring their prey perched on telegraph poles within a few metres of the road. There are also hobbies, kestrels, golden eagles and booted eagles. Just south of the Great Salt Lake (Tuz Gölü) between Ankara and Cappadocia you may spot Montagu's harriers, twisting and turning above a dried-out marsh, with a greylag goose in the distant marshland.

The **Göksu Delta** (see page 181) on Turkey's Mediterranean shore where the Göksu River spreads out into an area of salty marshland on a headland south of Silifke has been designated a national park, thanks to its importance to wildlife. The whole area covers 145km and its two lagoons are home to both **resident and migrating waterbirds**. No transport is laid on to view the birds, so you need your own, but you will be rewarded with sightings of pygmy cormorants, Dalmatian pelicans, grey and purple heron, spoonbills, egrets and wagtails, ospreys and terns, as well as marbled and white-headed ducks. Dawn and dusk in spring and autumn are the best viewing times.

Around Gaziantep and Carchemish near the Syrian border Saker falcons, short-toed larks, black-headed buntings, Upcher's warblers, barred warblers, Montagu's harriers and white-breasted kingfishers can be spotted. On the banks of the Euphrates which flows through Birecik, pied kingfishers can be seen in abundance.

Lake Van (see page 263), always the highpoint of any visit to eastern Turkey, is also the ornithological highpoint. On the northeastern shore there is marshland where, driving past, a smudge of white by the water beyond Adilcevaz and on the eastern shores where the Bendamahi River flows into the lake, can be transformed by binoculars to a large flock of some hundred white pelicans. A short walk from the road across the fields closer to the lake can often reveal a flock of a few dozen flamingoes. Among the reeds there are sometimes black-winged stilts flying overhead trailing their fantastically long red legs, calling as they circle. In the shallow water others step forward like awkward robots, while their long black beaks poke the mud. The reeds conceal both the reed warbler and the greater reed warbler. Also to be seen in spots like this are little-ringed plovers, common sandpipers, redshanks, lapwings, black-headed buntings and corn buntings. On the water are black-necked grebes, great-crested grebes, pochards, ruddy shelducks and shelducks as well as herring gulls and the oddly shaped white-headed duck.

On **Akdamar Island** (see page 273) and at **Hoşap Castle** (see page 289) there are alpine swifts and kestrels, while on the rocky **Van Kalesi** itself there are hoopoes calling, kestrels, bee-eaters and rollers, together with black redstarts and rock nuthatches with their young. In the marshes around the foot of Van Kalesi the rare citrine wagtail thrives, along with the bright yellow feldegg yellow wagtail. On the mountainous road from Van to Hakkâri Lammergeier's vultures can often be seen circling overhead.

On the **bare plains near Erzurum** the roads are sometimes lined with poplars containing extensive rookeries, although the other members of the crow family to be seen are hooded crows, jackdaws and ravens.

The northern mountains and the Black Sea coast are disappointing in comparison with the rest of the country. Cloud-shrouded woods near Borabay Gölü reveal only pied and grey wagtails, dippers and coal tits as well as lots of infuriatingly unidentifiable little brown birds flitting about among the trees. The Black Sea coast itself is not especially rich in birdlife, with mallards, coots and only herring gulls and lesser black-backed gulls. Cormorants can be seen in the water or on the offshore rocks.

In addition to the birds of the countryside there are the birds of the town: apart from the ubiquitous feral pigeons and house sparrows there are the lesser kestrels wheeling round the minarets of the city mosque, but overall is the abiding memory as dusk falls, above the street noises and the cry of the muezzin, of the squeals of the flocks of hundreds of wheeling swifts.

For the serious ornithologist prepared to make specific detours from his itineraries, visits to well-known **birdwatching spots** can be made where some 250 species can be seen. Such sites include Kulu Gölü about 100km south of Ankara and the Sultan Marshes (Aya Gölü) south of Kayseri where immense numbers and varieties of birds can be seen. There are also several bird sanctuaries to visit. At the **Pines National Park** 5km from Yozgat near the Hittite sites of Boğazkale and Yazılıkaya, 13 king eagles reside, said to be over 400 years old. They are found only in the Caucasus Mountains and have a wingspan of 3.5–4m. The nests are on the southwest side of the peaks and the best chance of a sighting is to be concealed near the nests at dawn or sunset. The wild Yozgat tulip is also to be found in the national park. At the **Manyas Bird Sanctuary** 17km from Bandirma on the Sea of Marmara, Lake Manyas is surrounded by a wood of willow trees. Many migratory birds are to be found here nesting each year, arriving in February with the young appearing in April and May. Towards autumn they migrate to India and Africa where they spend the winter months. The common species to be seen here are grey herons, small white herons, cormorants and pelicans. The rarer species include crimson heron, waterfowl, wild duck, falcon, titmouse birds, nightingale and blue crow. Some 180 varieties have been seen in the sanctuary. Finally at **Birecik** (see page 213) near the Syrian border between Gaziantep and Urfa, you can visit the reserve of the bald ibis, a large and extraordinary bird on the verge of extinction and currently the subject of a World Wildlife Fund rescue operation.

For those with a serious interest in the birds of Turkey, contact with or better still membership of the Ornithological Society of the Middle East (*www.osme.org*) is recommended.

MOUNTAINS Eastern Turkey offers a tremendous range of climbing for the mountaineer: from near-tropical landscapes in the Pontic Alps (Kaçkar Mountains) just inland from the Black Sea to arctic peaks with permanent snow covering like Mount Ararat and the Hakkâri range in the extreme southeast. Mountains form an essential part of the landscapes of eastern Turkey. Much of the plateau, though itself already high at a minimum of 1,000m, is very flat and the surrounding countryside is therefore dominated for miles around by any major peaks. This is especially true of the volcanoes which tend to rise up in splendid isolation, their majesty undiluted by a cluster of lesser peaks.

The **Hakkâri range** in Turkey's southeast corner south of Lake Van has Turkey's highest peaks after Ararat, and used to be the most exciting climbing Turkey had to offer the experienced mountaineer. Many well-travelled climbers still consider these mountains, especially the two main peaks of Cilo and Sat, to be among the world's most curious and fascinating, in no small part because of their sheer remoteness. Today and for the foreseeable future they are alas still forbidden to climbers because of possible Kurdish guerrilla activity in the region, but this may change in future.

Since the loss of the Hakkâri area to climbers the **Ala Dağlar range** southeast of Niğde offers the best substitute and has the great advantage of easy access. It is possible to drive in one long day from Istanbul to Niğde and from there up to Çamardı, a small town at 1,500m reachable on tarmac road in a saloon car. Guides and mules can be arranged in Çamardi with no difficulty and no permits are required. About ten days would be needed in total from Istanbul to make a worthwhile trip. The most famous walk is through limestone crags and waterfalls to the stunning Yedigöller (Seven Lakes, 3,500m), and takes two days, starting and

VOLCANO MOUNTAINEERING

There are five volcanoes in eastern Turkey, all of which can be climbed. They are more for the mountain wayfarer than for the real alpinist, though Ararat requires proper equipment and altitude acclimatisation. See pages 12 and 384 for practical information on Mountaineering.

MOUNT ARARAT (5,165M) Turkey's highest mountain and the only one that requires a permit from the authorities to climb it owing to its proximity to the Armenian/Iranian borders. Sometimes compared with Mount Kilimanjaro, it is one of the world's most imposing mountains. Those who have climbed both say that Ararat is the more challenging of the two because of the final assault on the summit which requires crampons and ice axe, even though Kilimanjaro is higher. Also some 15,000 people a year climb Kilimanjaro whereas a maximum of 400 a year climb Ararat. The standard ascent for Ararat takes three days from the base camp of Doğubeyazıt, then one or two days for the descent, but presents no real technical difficulty apart from the glaciers near the top. High winds near the summit can be very unpleasant and even dangerous. July and August are the best months to get as much snow-free terrain as possible, but June has the clearest weather. (For further details, see page 307.)

Winter ascents can also be made by skiers who then ski down. Such ascents are very expensive since no horses, only porters, can be used, and can only be accomplished by very experienced skiers. (For further information, visit the website www.anatolianadventures.com.)

SÜPHAN DAĞI (4,058M) From Adilcevaz there is a fairly straightforward climb, apart from the rock wall of the volcanic plug for the final 200m, with fine views over Lake Van. (For further details, see page 271.)

ERCIYES DAĞI (3,916M) Near Kayseri this is the volcano that created the Cappadocian landscapes. There is a *kayak evi* or mountain hut with 100 beds at the top. Leaving Kayseri by the airport road you take the road to the village of Hisarlik (14km) and then continue to the *kayak evi*. There is good scenery *en route* even if you do not climb.

HASAN DAĞI (3,268M) South of Aksaray near the Ihlara Gorge, the mountain offers a straightforward climb but without spectacular scenery.

NEMRUT DAĞI (3,050M) A walk of several hours from Tatvan, offering the bonus of being able to go down inside the crater to the lakes. Though the outer cone is bleak and denuded of greenery the views over Lake Van compensate. (For further details, see page 267.)

finishing at Demirkazık. (For further details of trekking specialists in the Cappadocia area, see page 142.)

The best climbing in Turkey after the Hakkâri and Ala Dağlar is to be found in the **Kaçkar range**. Also known as the Little Caucasus, this is the range inland from the Black Sea between Rize and Pazar. The approach is either from the coast through Çamlıhemşin and past the hot mineral springs at Ayder Kaplıcaları, or from Parhal via Yusufeli, the less developed side. From the former approach through the lush rainforest the peaks of the Kaçkar (highest 3,932m) offer good rock climbing (mainly granite) and ice and snow climbing, comparable with good second-class alpine peaks of 2,500–3,200m. A total of three weeks should be allowed from Istanbul. For non-mountaineers the approaches through the tea plantations and lush semi-tropical vegetation make interesting walking. The wetness and frequent rainfall are a nuisance but the compensations are the rich and colourful flora, with yellow azaleas, rhododendrons and Pontic lilies, especially in June. All the peaks can also be approached from the south on dry routes which are mountain walks rather than climbs, but which offer bleaker landscapes as most of the vegetation and rainfall is on the northern side. (For further details, see pages 333 and 348–9.)

Located between Erzincan and Tunceli, the **Munzur range** is one of the least explored ranges in Turkey. The peaks rise to between 3,000m and 3,400m. In difficulty they are not in the same league as the Hakkâri or Ala Dag ranges but are well suited to those who are between mountaineer and mountain wayfarer. The range offers fine scenery with many rivers and springs and is genuinely remote. Starting points are either Cağliyan from Erzincan or Ovacık from Tunceli.

With the exception of Ararat no permits are required for climbing. The best procedure is to organise yourself and supplies, drive to the base town and call on the local *veli* (governor) or, if it is a smaller town, the *kaymakam* (mayor), and ask for help in providing guides and if necessary mules. For this reason a knowledge of Turkish is a distinct advantage in making yourself understood, though someone can usually be found to interpret.

Normal mountaineering equipment is required including ice axes, pitons, crampons and ropes. Sun block creams for the face and lips and windproof clothing are needed for peaks higher than 3,000m. Your own food supplies should be taken with you. Suitable supplies to be found locally are limited to tinned sardines, dried apricots, nuts, tea, salt, sugar, bread and margarine. The local chocolate is flimsy and lacking in energy and nutritional value.

HISTORY

Far removed from all European civilisations, eastern Turkey was scarcely touched by the Greek and Roman heritage which so influenced the Aegean and Mediterranean coastlines. Surrounded by unfamiliar cultures like the Hittites, the Urartians and the Armenians, there is much that needs explanation. The policy throughout has been to incorporate such background and historical insights into the text where such relics are being explored, often elucidated by entertaining quotations from earlier travellers, whose comments remain now as apt as they were then. As a handy reference however, the following historical overview is also provided.

INTRODUCTION The land mass which today goes by the name of 'Turkey' has throughout history served as a land-bridge between the two continents of Europe and Asia, and people have moved across it in both directions. The diverse civilisations that blended here almost merit comparison with the Tower of Babel. In pre-classical times this land had no name as its frontiers were not defined by any united political entity. Classical writers referred to it loosely as 'Asia' or 'Asia Minor'. From the 10th century onwards the word Anatolia (Turkish *Anadolu*, from the Greek for 'sunrise' ie: the east as seen from Greece) became the word used to describe the massive central plateau with its mountain chains, 'a bridge with lofty parapets' (Sir William Ramsay). Its indigenous population fused with conquering armies from east and west leaving a complex patchwork of kingdoms and dynasties. Not until the Ottoman Empire, with its sultans ruling from their capital in Istanbul, did the whole of Anatolia come under one rule that was Turkish, extending even beyond into a loosely-knit collection of countries and provinces from Albania to Mecca. It was a Muslim empire with Ottoman Turkish (*Osmanli*) as its official language, but with Arabic as the religious language of Islam, and incorporating disparate elements such as Christian, Jewish, Armenian and even pagan. Since the collapse of the Ottoman Empire in the early 20th century and the phenomenon of Kemal Atatürk (see box pages 90–1), maker of the modern Turkish Republic, this land-bridge has become *Anadolu*, a well-defined state where Turkish nationality and the Turkish language are accepted. To symbolise this change and break from the Ottoman past, he chose his first military headquarters and centre of political administration to be in Ankara, the heart of Anatolia, shifting the whole focus of the country eastwards.

PREHISTORIC ANATOLIA, THE HITTITES AND THE BRONZE AGE The natural fertility of Anatolia attracted man very early and its rivers and the invention of agriculture in the 11th millennium BC led to a fundamental change in human existence, with the beginnings of the first stable settled communities. Artistic creations appeared for the first time, and the emergence of a religious mentality. The site of Çatalhüyük (page 179) dating to the 6th millennium BC is Turkey's earliest such site, where decorative ceramic objects were unearthed in excavations.

The **Bronze Age** (c3000–1200BC) was a hugely important period in Anatolian history, rich as the region was in metals, and the early civilisations here mastered an impressive skill of metallurgy in bronze. The peak of these were the Hatti, whose civilisation occupied a large part of Central Anatolia, and whose royal tombs at Alacahüyük (see page 105) revealed the extraordinary metal finds now on display in the Ankara museum (see page 85), contemporary with the 'Treasure of Priam' found at Troy II. It was the arrival of Assyrian merchants, drawn by Anatolia's wealth of metals at the beginning of the 2nd millennium BC, who introduced the next big change. Installing themselves in the area that corresponds roughly to today's southern Cappadocia (see site of Kültepe page 136), they established commercial counting systems and their tablets written in cuneiform recording their import/export activities undoubtedly introduced **writing** to Anatolia for the first time. The city of Troy in the northwest continued to develop in parallel.

The appearance of the Hittites in Anatolia marked the real entry of Anatolia into the history books. The beginnings of their civilisation are complex and little known (see box page 101) but they are thought to have fused with the native Hatti and invading Indo-Europeans, to form around 1800BC, the **Hittite Empire** with its capital to the north at Hattuşaş (see page 99). Their power spread rapidly to the Near East and they took Babylon in around 1600. The Hittite civilisation also assimilated traits from their oriental neighbours the Hourrites who lived in the Mitanni, western foothills of the Caucasus, and certain Hittite kings even married Hourrite princesses. In the period from 1450 to 1180 the Hittites grew to become one of the greatest powers of the age and the Hittite king was regarded as an equal of the Egyptian pharaoh. Thanks to the discovery of Hittite archives we know that they honoured a Sun goddess and a Moon god as well as quantities of lesser gods (see *Yazılıkaya*, page 103). The collapse of the Hittite Empire around 1200BC after a troubled period remains shrouded in mystery, but coincides with the fall of Troy. Theories revolve around an earthquake or outside invasion, but archaeologists have so far not found the answer and for the next few centuries a veil of oblivion extends over all Anatolia.

THE GREEKS IN WESTERN ANATOLIA AND THE URARTIANS IN EASTERN ANATOLIA The period from 1200 to 800BC is very obscure, the disappearance of the Hittite Empire and the city of Troy leaving a great vacuum, but over the course of these four centuries the human map of Anatolia was to redraw itself in a way that conditioned the course of its history: in the southeast the descendants of the Hittites survived, in the centre indigenous kingdoms emerged, and in the west, between 1200 and 1100BC new arrivals, the Greeks, arriving in small waves, started to settle on the west coast of Anatolia and founded the city of Symrna (Izmir) (and later Ephesus, Miletus and many others). Strangely, the history of Greece in the 2nd millennium BC had a similar evolution to that of Anatolia, and the main civilisation, the Myceneans, also collapsed around 1200BC. While the Greeks were establishing themselves in small colonies along the Aegean coast (the Aeolians in the north, the Ionians in the centre and the Dorians in the south), it was the indigenous civilisations of eastern and central Anatolia, the Urartians and the Neo-Hittites, that took centre stage.

In their native region around Lake Van and Mt Ararat the **Urartians** (see box page 282) built highly advanced systems of dams and canals and rock-carved defensive fortresses on spurs, so impregnable that they were able to hold their own against their powerful neighbours the Assyrians. They developed an exquisite metallurgical skill (see box page 286), exporting their products to Greece in the 8th century BC and greatly influencing as a result the Greek beginnings of metalwork. At the same time (1000–800BC) to the southeast of Anatolia a series of powerful **Neo-Hittite principalities** grew up, still visible today in significant sites such as Aslantepe (see page 134) and Karatepe (see page 213) with impressive bas-reliefs and hieroglyphic inscriptions detailing their history and beliefs. They fell to the Assyrians around 700BC. In central Anatolia the **Phrygians**, a native people speaking an Indo-European language close to Greek, and probably descended from the Balkans after the fall of Troy, emerged from the 8th century BC, with their capital at Gordion (west of Ankara). Their most famous king was Midas 'of the Golden Touch', whose tumulus yielded rich finds now on display at the Istanbul and Ankara archaeological museums. A people called the Cimmerians, linked with the myth of the Amazons (see box page 365), invaded and destroyed the Phrygian kingdom and were in turn destroyed by the **Lydians**, their neighbours to the west, in the course of the 7th century BC. The Lydian kingdom lasted from 700–600BC reaching its apogee under Croesus, their king of legendary wealth ('rich as Croesus'). Their economic prosperity came from the agricultural richness of their territory but also from the particles of gold found in their principal river. It was hardly surprising therefore that the Lydians invented **coinage**. In 546BC Croesus fell to the Persian King Cyrus, who sent his troops to annexe the rest of Asia Minor, which then came under the control of the Persian **Achemenids** for the next two centuries, from 546–334BC. Persian rule was not severe, and apart from the installation of a *satrap*, a type of governor, and the payment of a tribute, life for the indigenous population continued much as before.

Everything changed again with the conquest of Asia Minor by Alexander the Great between 334 and 327BC. Persia, hereditary enemy of the Greeks, had become weak and was easy to conquer, and within three years he had achieved his express goal of conquering the Persian Empire, marching on to take Egypt and even east as far as modern-day Afghanistan. On his sudden death aged 32 in 323BC Alexander's generals divided the empire into different kingdoms, known as 'Hellenistic', with great capital cities like Pergamum for the Attalids and Antioch for the Seleucids. The process of **Hellenisation** in Asia Minor had begun, with Greek becoming the official language and the adoption of Greek institutions. The southeastern regions of Turkey are rich in Hellenistic sites, though most, like Zeugma with its magnificent mosaics, were overlaid with Roman settlements. The victory of Octavius (the future Augustus) over Antony and Cleopatra in 31BC at the Battle of Actium marked the end of the Hellenistic period.

THE ROMAN PERIOD Rome was at first drawn reluctantly into Asia Minor crossing the Hellespont to crush the Seleucid King Antiochus III. With no desire to extend their empire here, they handed over the region they had conquered to the king of Pergamum. The last king of Pergamum, Attulus III, having no heir himself, returned the compliment in 133BC by bequeathing his entire empire to Rome, and in 129BC the Province of Asia was created along Turkey's western region as the first Roman province. Over the next 300 years Rome gradually extended its power eastwards, the period of Pax Romana being the golden age of prosperity for almost all the cities of the province of Asia, with Ephesus as its capital. In today's eastern Turkey the main Roman sites to be visited are Antioch, Hierapolis-Castabala, Zeugma and Edessa. Decline set in from the 3rd century AD after endless disputes and wars had sapped the strength of the empire. This period coincided with the **rise of Christianity** and the resultant struggles between the early Christians and the Roman emperors, until Constantine himself converted to Christianity. St John, the Virgin Mary, St Peter and St Paul all travelled widely across Asia Minor from the Holy Land and Ephesus became one of the major Christian shrines in the world. In 330 Constantine re-founded **Byzantium**, the 'new Rome', under the name of Constantinople. Rome itself was taken by the Goths in 410 and in 476 the last Roman emperor was deposed, leaving Constantinople as the only capital of the Roman Empire. The reign of the Emperor Justinian (527–565) reunited for the last time the Roman Empires of the East and West. The construction of St Sophia in Constantinople marked the appearance of a new artistic form directly associated with the new religion and a bold use of the dome. A symbolic decorative hierarchy gradually evolved, with the placing of certain key figures and motifs in the nave or in the choir of religious buildings. Rome's influence never extended into the extreme east of Turkey and the Lake Van area, which remained as the Kingdom of Armenia.

THE BYZANTINE EMPIRE Spanning nearly a thousand years from 6th to the 15th centuries the complex history of the Byzantine Empire was made up of wars, lost conquests and palace revolutions. The two halves of the former Roman Empire were frequently in conflict, the importance of the Pope in Rome, who filled the vacuum left by the last Roman emperor, frequently disregarded by the emperor of Constantinople who regarded himself as the sole legitimate heir to the former Roman Empire. Between 726 and 843 a row developed over the banning of sacred images, in compliance with the edicts of Leon III (771–741) and Leon IV (813–820), resulting in the Iconoclastic crisis (see box page 152). By 1054 a huge **schism** appeared between the Eastern Orthodox Church and the Roman Church, their mutual incomprehension further compounded by the fact that the Roman Church spoke Latin while the Eastern Orthodox spoke Greek. Between 1000 and 1200 the Byzantine civilisation entered its final throes with the reign of the Comnene dynasty in Trebizond (Trabzon) (see page 352). Christianity extended to all parts of today's eastern Turkey by this time, with extensive communities in Cappadocia (see page 139), and many monasteries and churches belonging to Armenian and Georgian Christians.

THE SELJUK TURKS The history of the Seljuks and the Ottomans began with the arrival in Asia Minor of a nomadic people, neither Semitic nor Indo-European, coming from the confines of Asia, and which wiped out the traces of both the Roman and Byzantine empires. The result was the Turkey of today, as the Seljuks are the origins of the current population of Turkey. In 1055 the Seljuk Empire was founded with its first capital in Baghdad and in the course of the 11th century the Turks seized the holy places and made their first incursions into the edges of Anatolia. The famous victory at the Battle of Manzikert north of Lake Van over the Byzantines in 1071 opened the gates of Anatolia to the Seljuk Turks led by Alp Arslan. The **Turkish language and Islam** were introduced and gradually spread over the region and the slow transition from a predominantly Christian and Greek-speaking Anatolia to a predominantly Muslim and Turkish-speaking one was underway. The Seljuks abandoned their nomadic way of life and over the course of the next century, created various rival Seljuk emirates, till they reached their apogee in the first half of the 13th century establishing the Sultanate of Rum from their capital at Konya (see box page 167) and ruling over the greater part of Anatolia. The Muslim Turks lived peacefully alongside their Christian subjects – especially the Armenians – who accepted their new masters gladly since they had freed them from the burden of heavy Byzantine taxes. Many even converted to Islam to save themselves further taxation.

The Seljuk Empire was greatly influenced by the Persian civilisation which had inspired its art and architecture, its literature and its mysticism (see box page 112). Seljuk architecture was a happy blend of Persian styles with Byzantine and Armenian, whose mosques, *madrasas* and tombs have left a permanent and original mark in towns like Konya (see box page 168), Sivas (see page 116) and Tokat (see page 113). Their series of caravanserais can also be seen across central Anatolia (see pages 112–13). The **Turcomans** on the other hand, who had also swept into Anatolia at the same time as the Seljuks, retained their nomadic ways, keeping their large flocks of sheep and continuing to fight from horseback as accomplished archers, a skill unknown to the Byzantines. They were more numerous than the Seljuks, and rejecting the sedentary lifestyle, adhered to a kind of Islam impregnated with animism and shamanism from their central Asian steppeland origins, which then mixed with new Christian influences. From this popular and syncretist Islam with its mystical and revolutionary aspects, sects such as the Alevis and Bektashis emerged, the **Sufism** of the countryside, expressed in poetry written in Turkish and in the music of dervishes. They also embodied a strange contradiction between the spirit of the *ghazi*, warrior against the Christian Crusader invaders, and the confessional tolerance preached by the great Sufi figures like Mevlâna (see page 173) and Haçı Bektaş (see page 159).

Between 1096 and 1099 the **First Crusade** commenced, with the Crusaders taking Iznik, the first Seljuk capital, then crossing Anatolia and retaking Jerusalem. Driven from Iznik, the Seljuks then established the Sultanate of Rum from their new capital at Konya in 1097. The **Second Crusade** ended in failure in 1148 after internal squabbles among the Crusaders, and in 1190 the **Third Crusade** failed, with Jerusalem staying in the hands of Saladin. In 1202–1204 the **Fourth Crusade** detoured to Constantinople which was sacked and taken by the Latins. In 1243 at the Battle of Köşedağ, the Mongols were victorious over the Seljuks and became the new masters of Anatolia and in 1256 the Second Mongol invasion of Anatolia caused widespread destruction. By 1303 the Seljuk Empire had dispersed into small principalities (*beyliks*).

THE OTTOMAN EMPIRE At the end of the 13th century Anatolia found itself in the hands of three major forces: the Mongols, the Muslims of the cities (heirs to the Seljuk Empire) and the Turcomans. The power and number of the latter continued to grow, and they conquered and founded various small principalities (*beyliks*) on the periphery of the Seljuk Empire, the most powerful of which was Karaman (see page 180) in the western Taurus mountains. It was however Orhan, son of Osman (after whom the Ottoman dynasty was named), whose *beylik* was to provide the future masters of Anatolia. He seized Bursa in 1326 and made it his capital. By the time of Orhan's death in 1362 the Ottomans controlled almost all of the Marmara region, the Dardanelles and eastern Thrace. Murat I seized Edrine and made it the second capital of the Ottomans.

In 1389 the victory at Kosovo over the Serbs and the Bosnians opened the gate of the Balkans to the Ottomans and in 1399–1402 another Mongol invasion led by **Tamerlane** laid waste to Anatolia, taking Sultan Beyazıt prisoner. Tamerlane died shortly afterwards and the Ottomans went on to retake control of their territory.

In 1453 the Ottoman Sultan Mehmet II (the Conqueror) took Constantinople and the city became Istanbul, third and final capital of the Ottomans. The first Ottomans were still semi-nomadic, wintering on the plains and retiring in summer to the freshness of the mountains, but they did not reject urban life either. The Ottoman town offered a synthesis of rural and urban cultures, and the Arabo-Persian civilisation inherited from the Seljuks existed side by side with the popular and heterodox Islam of the nomads. The first *medreses* **and** *tekkes* of the Sufi dervishes were closely connected to the early Ottomans, and the Bektaşi order exerted a strong spiritual authority on the Janissaries, infantry soldiers who were the Sultan's household troops and bodyguards.

In 1462 Bosnia was annexed and in 1511 there was the revolt of the Kızılbaş ('red-heads', ancestors of today's Alevis). These Shi'ites were supported by the Shah of Persia against the Sunni Sultan and their revolt put the stability of the Empire in danger.

The **Ottoman golden age** is generally recognised as being the reign of Selim II (the Grim 1512–1520) who doubled the size of the empire during his eight-year rule, and the reign of Süleyman the Magnificent (1521–1556), when Rhodes was taken in 1522 and the St John Hospitallers fled to Malta. In 1529 they tried to take Vienna and in 1536 Francois I, King of France, signed a commerce treaty with the Ottomans, known by the name of 'capitulations'. Süleyman was a classic 'Renaissance man', composing verses in Persian in his rare moments of leisure, and commissioning the building of many of Istanbul's great buildings, under the supervision of his court architect, Sinan. He also reorganised the secular law of the empire, so that his Turkish surname is *Kanuni,* the Legislator. A huge bureaucracy emerged as a result, directed by the Sultan and his grand *vizir*, with whom he nominated the governors of provinces and other high officials.

After Süleyman's death the Ottoman Empire suffered its first big military setback in 1571 with the **naval defeat of Lepanto** against Spain and over the course of the next centuries the empire began to shrink, abandoning Hungary and part of the Balkans to Austria.

Between 1768 and 1774 war broke out between Russia and the Ottomans, in which the Russians triumphed, taking part of the Black Sea coast, and marking the beginning of the process of the dismemberment of the Ottoman Empire.

The following century saw further **wars and uprisings** and the abolition of the Janissaries and the Sufi Bektashi order. The 1839 Gülhane Edict deeply transformed Ottoman society, giving the same rights to all subjects of the Empire. A wave of liberal reforms (*Tanzimat*) was inaugurated which continued till 1876. In 1840 Egypt acquired its independence under the nominal sovereignty of the Sultan and in 1865 the secret society of Young Ottomans was founded, later the **Young Turks**.

The **Crimean War**, in which the Russians opposed the Turks, the French and the English, raged from 1853 to 1855. It was resolved by the Treaty of Paris (1856), which marked the subservience of the Ottoman economy to the European powers.

By 1876 the Ottoman State was declared officially bankrupt and became known as 'the Sick Man of Europe', and in 1878 Serbia, Rumania and Bulgaria all became independent. Greece obtained its independence in 1830 after nine years of war and in 1897 Crete was re-attached to Greece. In 1908 the

A contemporary of Michelangelo and Christopher Wren, Sinan, a Christian from Kayseri, revolutionised architecture by borrowing from the Byzantine churches with which he was familiar, and applying some of their characteristics to mosques and *madrasas*, adapting them to the requirements of Islamic practice, with ablution fountains in the courtyard or near the entrance, and a *mihrab* niche in the place where the altar would have been placed, to indicate the direction of prayer towards Mecca. He was also an accomplished engineer and designed elaborate water systems for Istanbul and Edirne, conducting meticulous research and carrying out exhaustive surveys of the topography before embarking on his projects. Of his buildings he regarded the Şehzade Mosque in Istanbul as his apprenticeship, the Suleymaniye Mosque in Istanbul as his coming of age, and the Selimiye Mosque in Edirne as his masterpiece. The importance of water to the Ottomans cannot be overstated, as they adhered to the Hanafi sect of Islam which proscribes ablution before prayer under running water, not from stagnant basins like the Shafa'i sect for example. Fountains were a particular passion of the Ottomans, and much attention was lavished on public fountains which provided drinking water to all. Istanbul alone had over 10,000 public fountains at the beginning of the 17th century. Hammams or public baths (see boxes pages 92–3 and 96) were likewise regarded as extremely important institutions on which much architectural attention was bestowed. Both of Istanbul's most famous still-functioning *hammams*, the Çemberlitaş and the Cağlaoğlu, were built by Sinan.

Revolution of the Young Turks took place and Sultan Abdul Hamit II was forced to announce the constitution before being deposed (1909). In 1912–13 in the Balkan wars Turkey lost most of its European territories with the exception of eastern Thrace and Edirne.

During **World War I** (1914–18) the Ottoman Empire allied itself to Germany. Responding to a Russian initiative supported by the Armenians in eastern Anatolia in the winter of 1914–15, a Turkish counter-offensive resulted in the massacre of Armenians in spring 1915 and the deportation of massive numbers of Armenians in the southeast (see page 285) and in 1915–16 the Turks under the command of Mustafa Kemal (later Atatürk see page 20) won a decisive victory at the Battle of the Dardanelles over the Allied Forces who could not hold the straits.

In 1916 a series of Arab revolts began which ended in the detachment of the Arab provinces from the Ottoman Empire (Hijaz, Yemen, Syria, Lebanon, Palestine and Iraq), and after the war in 1920 the Treaty of Sèvres dismantled the Ottoman Empire and put it under European tutelage. The Turks under Mustafa Kemal refused to accept the conditions of the treaty and fought a war of independence against the occupying Greeks from 1920–22, resulting in the abolition of the Sultanate. The 600-year Ottoman Empire had come to an end. In 1923 the Treaty of Lausanne liberated Turkey from foreign tutelage and recognised its independence within the reduced borders of the former Ottoman Empire.

THE TURKISH REPUBLIC The history of modern Turkey began in 1923 when **Mustafa Kemal Atatürk** (1881–1938) founded the Republic of Turkey and became Turkey's first President. From 1923–25 a massive exchange of populations took place between Greece and Turkey in which 1.3 million people were displaced. In 1925 Atatürk ordered that the Gregorian calendar was adopted, and the *fez* was prohibited. Violent ethnic and religious riots erupted in Anatolia, one of the reasons for the abolition of the Sufi orders and banning of pilgrimages to saints' and sultans' tombs.

In 1928 Turkey became secular and the clause retaining Islam as the state religion was removed from the constitution. On Atatürk's orders Turkey adopted the **Latin alphabet**, replacing the Arabic alphabet. Constantinople was officially renamed Istanbul in 1930.

In 1934 every Turkish citizen was obliged to take a surname (see box page 19). Mustafa Kemal became Kemal Atatürk. He died in 1938 from cirrhosis of the liver aged 57.

Between 1939 and 1945 Turkey remained neutral for most of **World War II**, then towards the end declared war on Germany and Japan but did not take part in fighting. It then joined the United Nations.

In 1950 Turkey had its first open elections, won by the opposition Democratic Party, and in 1952 Turkey abandoned Atatürk's neutralist policy and joined NATO.

During the 1960s, 1970s, 1980s and 1990s a series of military coups took control away from the ruling government, as the Turkish military thought they were straying from the principles of Atatürk's legacy. In 1963 Turkey signed an association agreement with the EU, then the EEC. In 1974 Turkish troops took over **Northern Cyprus**.

In the 1980s martial law was imposed after a military coup and remained in place in many eastern provinces in an attempt to curb Kurdish separatist activities. In 1982 a new constitution created a seven-year presidency and reduced parliament to single house. In 1984 Turkey recognised the 'Turkish Republic of Northern Cyprus' and the PKK (Kurdistan Workers' Party) launched a separatist guerrilla war in southeast (see page 233). In 1987 Turkey applied for full EEC membership.

In the 1990s **separatist activities** continued to dominate the eastern provinces and Turkey allowed the US-led coalition against Iraq to launch air strikes from Turkish bases. In 1992 20,000 Turkish troops entered the Kurdish safe havens in Iraq in an anti-PKK operation. The first Turkish woman Prime Minister, Tansu Çiller, was elected in 1993 with veteran politician Süleyman Demirel as President. 1995 was dominated by a major offensive with 35,000 Turkish troops launched

THE SURNAME PHENOMENON

In the 1930s during the Atatürk-led westernising reforms, a decree was issued for a census of all Turkish citizens. Everyone was given the day off work and ordered to stay at home and occupy themselves productively. About nine months later the results of their labours were clear in a population bubble, but the census was abandoned because of confusion in counting the endless Ahmet Son of Alis and Ali Son of Ahmets, as Turks had only ever been given one name plus the name of their father. The realisation came that everyone needed to choose an additional surname for themselves if any future census was to be possible, and a further decree went out stating that families who had failed to give themselves a surname within 18 months would be fined and then issued with a random one anyway. The result was the extraordinary mish-mash of surnames that now exists in Turkey: some simply chose their town name or birthplace, turning it into a suitable adjective. Others were more creative and labelled themselves after what they considered a trait of family beauty such as 'grey-eyed' or 'tall-statured' or went for such puffed up surnames as 'overthrower of mountains' or 'lion-hearted', while many army officers named themselves after battles whose victories they wished to take credit for. This is when Mustafa Kemal chose *Atatürk*, Father of the Turks, as his surname.

against the Kurds in northern Iraq. 1996 saw the signature of a customs union between Turkey and the EU. In 1999 the PKK leader Abdullah Öcalan was captured in Kenya, then sentenced to death, later commuted to life imprisonment. An earthquake with its epicentre at Izmit killed 17,000 people. The Helsinki Accord declared Turkey to be an official candidate for European membership.

In 2001 France recognised the killing of Armenians under the late Ottoman Empire as genocide, leading to a diplomatic row with Turkey. In 2002 a Turkish man was no longer regarded in law as the head of the family. Women were given full legal equality with men. Turkey and Greece agreed to build a gas pipeline for Turkey to supply Greece with gas. The death penalty was abolished except in times of war, and bans on Kurdish education and broadcasting were lifted. The Islamist-based AK Party won a landslide election. Parliament in 2003 decided not to allow US forces to deploy from Turkish bases ahead of war with Iraq, but allowed the use of Turkish airspace. Turkish forces were authorised to dispatch into Kurdish areas of northern Iraq. Three car bombs in Istanbul exploded at the main synagogue, the British Consulate and a British bank. In 2004 the first state TV made broadcasts in the Kurdish language. A car bomb went off in the city of Van, and the PKK denied involvement. Parliament approved reforms for preventing torture and violence against women and the criminalisation of adultery was dropped.

In 2005 the **new lira currency** was introduced (YTL, Yeni Türk Lirası), removing six zeros from the old lira currency, ending the 'millionaire' era. EU membership negotiations were officially launched after intense bargaining. The multi-billion dollar Blue Stream pipeline opened in Samsun, carrying Russian gas to Turkey under the Black Sea. In 2006 an oil pipeline opened between Turkey (Ceyhan), Baku and Tbilisi. Coastal resorts and Istanbul were again targeted by Kurdish separatist groups.

In 2007 the AK Party won elections in spite of secularist rallies in Ankara. Abdullah Gül was elected President. 2008 was the year of the headscarf dispute (see box page 30). Thousands protested at government plans to allow women to wear the Islamic headscarf (*hijab*) at university. A petition was organised to have

ATATÜRK AND HIS REFORMS FOR WOMEN

Among Atatürk's many reforms to modernise Turkey, one of the most far-reaching was improving the position of women. One of his speeches ran:

In the course of my trip I have seen that our women comrades – not in the villages but particularly in the towns and cities – are careful to muffle up their faces and their eyes. I should think this habit must cause them great discomfort, especially now in the hot weather. Men, this is to some extent the result of our selfishness… Let them show their faces to the world and let them have the chance to see the world for themselves. There's nothing to be afraid of in that.

The majority of educated women had in fact discarded the veil years before, many during World War I when they entered the civil service. His speeches, helped by increased interest in Western fashions, did accelerate the disappearance of the veil from the large country towns, but in the rural areas most women continued to be shut off from the equality Atatürk invited them to enjoy, and today still in parts of central and eastern Anatolia, you will see women draw their shawls over their faces when you pass, or cringe towards the walls, just as Atatürk saw them some 80 years ago.

the ruling AK Party banned for undermining the secular constitution of Turkey but failed by a narrow margin. The Ergenekon Trial took place in which 142 were charged over an alleged nationalist coup plot.

In 2009 the governments of Turkey and Armenia agreed to normalise relations, with future opening of the border planned. The government took what it called the **'Kurdish Initiative'**, pledging to introduce measures to increase Kurdish language rights and reduce Turkish military presence in the southeast. In 2010 nearly 70 members of the military were arrested and 33 of them were charged and accused of plotting a coup, code-named Sledgehammer. The head of the Armed Forces insisted that coups were a thing of the past.

On 12 September 2010 a major referendum organised by the ruling AK Party voted in favour of constitutional reform to give parliament more control over the army and the judiciary. The 'yes' vote was 58% of the country, the 'no' vote 42%. Also seen as a vote of confidence in the pro-Islamic AK Party led by Erdoğan, the central and eastern provinces voted overwhelmingly in favour, ignoring PKK calls to boycott the referendum. The 'no' vote was cast mainly in the Aegean and Mediterranean provinces, which were fearful that the government would use the changes to appoint sympathetic judges as part of a back-door Islamic coup. The package of referendum reforms were praised by the EU and by the USA, who see them as necessary steps for Turkey to shed the last remnants of autocratic rule and improve its chances of eventual EU membership. Fittingly, the date of 12 September was the 30th anniversary of the 1980 military coup. The AK Party had been wanting to change the constitution since it first came to power in 2002.

GOVERNMENT AND POLITICS

Since 2002 Turkey has been ruled by the Justice and Development Party (AK Party), founded by Abdullah Gül, who was elected president by parliament in 2007. Originally an Islamist party banned by the courts, it has now renounced the idea that Islam should be a driving force in politics. Turkish secularists, including Turkey's powerful military which sees itself as the guardian of the secular system, opposed Gül's nomination for fear he would try to undermine Turkey's strict separation of state and religion. He is Turkey's first head of state with a background in political Islam. Secularists also feared the effect on Turkey's image of his wife, the First Lady, wearing a headscarf. The president can veto laws, appoint officials and name judges. A referendum held in 2007 approved plans to have future presidents elected by the people rather than by parliament.

Recep Tayyip Erdoğan, leader of the AK Party since 2002 when his party first won elections, also won in 2007, boosting his share of the vote to 47%, in spite of opposition attempts to portray the AK Party as secretly favouring an Iran-style theocracy. In practice, contrary to alarmist fears, Erdoğan's governments have been very pro-business and have pursued reforms faster and more effectively than most of their predecessors. He also pushed for EU membership as a top priority and introduced reforms which paved the way for membership talks to open in 2005. He is from a lowly background, and worked as a street seller to help pay for his education. He attended Koran school and then went on to study economics at university.

THE KURDISH PROBLEM Turkey is home to a sizeable Kurdish minority, maybe as much as 20% of the population. In the past the Turkish government has attempted to deny their ethnic difference, calling them instead 'mountain Turks', a reference to their nomadic tradition of migrating to the mountains in summer with their flocks, thereby banning their Kurdish identity, violating their human rights and ignoring their economic needs. The Kurdistan Workers' Party (PKK) is the best known and most radical of the Kurdish separatist movements, regarded as a terrorist organisation by Turkey, the US and the EU, and in 1984 they launched a guerrilla campaign to establish a homeland in the Kurdish heartlands of the southeast, with Diyarbakır as their capital. Thousands died and hundreds of thousands became refugees in the ensuing clashes between the PKK and the Turkish military, which necessitated whole tracts of eastern Turkey being put under martial law. PKK activity subsided after their leader Abdullah Öcalan was captured in 1999, and martial law was lifted from most eastern provinces by 2002.

Now Prime Minister Erdoğan's government has again taken the initiative, and in 2009 launched its 'Kurdish initiative', acknowledging Kurdish linguistic and cultural rights for the first time since the start of the Turkish Republic in 1922.

JUDICIAL SYSTEM Turkey's judicial system is composed of general law courts, specialised heavy penal courts, military courts and four high courts including the Constitutional Court, the nation's highest court. The court system does not include the concept of a jury: verdicts are reached by a judge or panel of judges. The military courts have jurisdiction to try military personnel for military offences. French administrative law is the main source on which the Turkish system is based, but it has also taken elements of the Swiss Civil Code and the Code of Obligation and the Italian Penal Code and adopted and modified them to fit Turkish customs and traditions. Before the foundation of the Turkish Republic a large part of Turkish civil law – such as laws affecting the family, inheritance, property, obligations, etc – was based on the Koran and administered by special religious (*Sharia*) courts.

ECONOMY

Turkey is a predominantly agricultural country, with about 55% of its population living in the countryside. Main crops are wheat, cotton, tobacco and fruit. The main export earner is cotton, and with abundant sheep, Turkey is Europe's main wool producer. Other main exports are clothing and textiles, fruit and vegetables, iron and steel, motor vehicles and machinery, fuels and oils. Its main trading partners are Russia, Germany, Italy, France and the UK. In recent decades the government's main economic concerns have been to bring down inflation and to privatise the vast state-owned industries. A tough recovery programme was agreed with the IMF in 2002, which has brought strong economic growth and a dramatic drop in inflation, though foreign debt and unemployment remain huge burdens. There has been an ambitious programme of capital infrastructure construction, especially with new highways. Reforestation is also an ongoing process throughout the country. Turkey has oil resources in the southeast but not sufficient to meet its needs. It therefore buys crude oil from Saudi Arabia, Iraq, Iran, Algeria and Russia.

When the IMF three-year US$10 billion loan agreement ended in 2008, the European Bank for Reconstruction and Development agreed to lend money to Turkey for the first time. In pushing through unpopular structural reforms the AK Party had previously maintained tight financial controls, but with the advent of the global economic crisis, it decided, like many other governments, to introduce fiscal stimulus packages. The main challenges of the coming years will be to maintain financial discipline to stop the return of high inflation, and to increase the tax base by decreasing Turkey's large informal economy – big challenges indeed where tax evasion has been the order of the day for so long.

PEOPLE

Even to western and Istanbuli Turks, eastern Turkey remains something of an enigma, with few having travelled there. No familiar Greek and Roman influences are to be seen here, and Europe seems far away. It is home to Turkey's ethnic minorities, such as the Kurds (see page 233), concentrated mainly in the southeast and around Lake Van, and the Georgian Laz (see box page 347), to be found in the northeastern Georgian valleys around Artvin. There used to be many Armenians as well, until the population disappeared in the early 20th century, a

DAMS ON THE EUPHRATES

The ambitious Southeast Anatolia Project consisting of a series of dams on the Euphrates is gradually transforming the wasteland around Urfa and Harran into fertile agricultural land for growing cereals, providing employment and new prosperity for the peasants and semi-nomads (mainly Kurds) in the region. The main dam of the project, the Atatürk Dam, is the sixth-largest dam in the world, and is well on the way to making Turkey self-sufficient in electricity, thereby releasing it from dependence on the Russian grid. The lake created by the dam is so large it will bring with it a change in climate. It began operation in 1994 and the water from the lake is carried to the Harran Plain by the Şanlıurfa Tunnel System, the largest in the world in terms of length at 26.4km and rate of flow through the 7.62m-diameter tunnels. The project is Turkey's largest and most multi-faceted development project, and includes active farming with extensive irrigation systems.

subject of heated debate and much sensitivity (see page 285). The people here are also different, more self-contained and less outward-going than those of western Turkey, and certainly less accustomed to tourists. Armenians, Greeks and Jews are recognised minorities under the Turkish Constitution. Other ethnic minorities include Circassians and Bosnians, both Muslim refugees who had fled from persecution by Russia and the Balkans respectively. Today most of these smaller groups are loosely dispersed in the larger cities.

THE TURKS From their origins in the steppes of Asia the Turks arrived in Asia Minor in the 10th century having adopted the religion of the Arabs *en route*, and for the last six centuries they have lived half in and half out of Europe. Today they are neither Asian nor Middle Eastern nor European, having aspects of all three yet being distinct from them.

In 1970 David Hotham, who spent eight years living in Ankara as *The Times* correspondent, expressed their complexity memorably:

> The Turk is unusually full of contradictions. Not only has he East and West in him, Europe and Asia, but an intense pride combined with an acute inferiority complex, a deep xenophobia with an overwhelming hospitality to strangers, a profound need for flattery with an absolute disregard for what anybody thinks about him. Few people, capable of such holocausts, are at the same time so genuinely kind, helpful, magnanimous and sincere as the Turks. It is as if his nature compensated its capacity for one extreme by a propensity towards the other.

On the whole Turks are not great businessmen. Until the 1920s it was the Greeks and the Armenians who busied themselves with the country's commerce. Even today the Turks are still not naturally adept at selling themselves or their goods, and do not have the 'gift of the gab' that comes so readily for example to the Greeks or the Lebanese. They do, however, have great dignity and great national pride. Atatürk's dictum:

Ne mutlu Türküm diyene (How happy is he who can say he is a Turk) still strikes a chord. After centuries of ruling an empire pride dies hard. Sometimes this can lead to them taking credit to everything in Turkey which was not in fact built by Turks, such as Anamur Castle, built by Armenians, but it can be an endearing habit to equate what you want to believe with the truth.

Throughout history the Turks have shown that, if pushed too far, they will lash out, and live up to their epithet 'terrible'. As Aubrey Herbert (1880–1923), a British diplomat and intelligence officer who was twice offered the throne of Albania, put it:

THE IMPORTANCE OF HONOUR

The Turks' attitude to money is usually one of disdain; it is beneath their dignity to appear preoccupied with it. Correspondingly, trust is very important to a Turk, for whom the most contemptible of crimes is theft, which, except in the big cities, is almost absent. In prison a thief is the lowest form of life and is spat upon by the other prisoners. A murderer, on the other hand, is the elite of the prison. Murder is often a question of honour and is therefore respected. A Turk who returned home to find his wife in bed with another man promptly went out to fetch an axe from the shed, hacked the couple to pieces and then calmly gave himself up to the police, his honour avenged. Crimes of this sort are never, it is important to mention, committed under the influence of drink. Public drunkenness is rare among Turks.

If you see a convoy of cars honking with horns and drums, covered in Turkish flags, it will be the traditional send-off ceremony for a young man about to head to the east of the country on his military service. It is compulsory on reaching the age of 20 and is regarded as an essential part of a man growing up, the final stage of his education, and all employers will want a potential employee to have completed his military service before he is considered ready for the real world of work. Women are exempt. Young men not in full-time secondary education have to complete 15 months as a private soldier, and graduates have to complete either six months as a private soldier or 12 months as a reserve officer. If you have lived and worked abroad for three years or more you are exempt, and just required to complete a symbolic 21 days of military service on returning to Turkey. With 65% of the population under 25, large chunks of the male population are tied up in military service at any given time.

The Turk was unbusiness-like, placid and lazy or long-suffering. But when he turned in his rage he poured out death in a bucket, and guilty and innocent suffered from his blind anger.

This capacity for violent anger showed itself in the massacres of the Kurds and the Armenians, and most recently in 1974 in Cyprus where, having been goaded and maltreated by the Greek Cypriots for years, the EOKA-B guerrilla attacks in support of *Enosis* (union with Greece) were the final straw. The Greeks totally underestimated the Turkish response. Many educated Greek Cypriots admitted that they were wrong to push the Turks so far and that they brought the calamity on themselves.

The Turkish soldier has always been extremely tough – Turkish military service is legendary – but in battle his leaders have often let him down. C B Norman, special correspondent of *The Times* in 1877 during the war with Russia, wrote:

Of the bravery of the Turkish troops it is impossible to speak too highly; of the utter incompetence of their leaders it is equally impossible to speak in terms of sufficient disparagement.

Physically the vast majority of Turks have thick dark hair, and whilst most have brown eyes, a noticeable number have green or less often blue eyes. Some young children, especially the girls, are blond and blue-eyed, but they seem to lose this fairness when they get older. In the Georgian areas north of Erzurum you will still notice a sprinkling of ginger-haired freckly Turks. With the racial mix of Asian, Kurd, Caucasian, Arab and European, there is also enormous variation in features and build, but as a generalisation the Turks are a hirsute nation with paler skins than the Arabs. Some have a noticeable propensity to flatness at the back of the head. The men are often very attractive in a masculine and hirsute way with strong features, while the women, tending to share the strong heavy features of the men, are by and large less attractive.

Virility is prized by the Turks almost more than any other quality and the Turkey of the east is still an essentially male society. A man's most important relationships are with other men, and even in the cities it is surprising how rarely you see a man walking with a woman. When couples meet it is usually the men who embrace and kiss and fall into conversation, while the women stand lamely aside.

WOMEN Despite appearances of submissiveness in eastern Turkey, women have made enormous strides since Atatürk's reforms. Turkish women long ago entered

Background Information PEOPLE

25

the professions and can be found in universities and in parliament – Turkey even had its first woman prime minister, Tansu Çiller, in the early 1990s. Many writers and journalists are women, in the arts there are excellent actresses, ballet dancers, opera singers and musicians. In banks you will be struck by the number of women working behind the counter, many of them very senior, and in the Turkish civil service there are many women in prominent positions. Turkish women got the vote in 1930, years before Greek women got it (1952), and they also achieved this status ahead of the women of Portugal, Spain, Bulgaria, France, Belgium and Switzerland.

Yet in spite of all this there is far less equality between the sexes than might be suggested by these high-profile westernised ladies, especially in the eastern provinces: there, old attitudes die hard, and in cinemas and schools there is still often separate seating for women. As Hotham says, 'You can change a law but not a mentality'.

In hotels and restaurants in the eastern provinces all the staff and waiters are men, whereas in the Aegean and Mediterranean parts there are almost more women than men to be seen behind the reception desks. On the rare occasions in eastern Turkey when you do come into contact with women, you may feel that the remarks of Colonel Frederick Gustavus Burnaby, an English soldier who travelled these parts in the 1870s and recorded his thoughts in his *On Horseback through Asia Minor*, still ring true:

> The faces of the ladies were not pre-possessing, and sadly wanted expression – a defect which I subsequently observed in almost every Turkish woman whose countenance I had the opportunity of seeing. We need not be surprised at this. I have been informed by the Turks themselves that very few women, not one per 1000, can read or write. They amuse themselves with gossip and eating. Their mental faculties become absorbed. They live for the moment, and pine after the coarser and more sensual pleasures.

As the Turkish proverb says: 'The thicker the veil, the less worth lifting.'

Today still, even at sophisticated parties in the cities, the women tend to huddle together in one part of the room leaving the men to talk seriously among themselves, and you will never see a local woman sitting in the coffee shops. These

USELESS ENCUMBRANCES

The views of many men in eastern Turkey today differ remarkably little from those expressed by a Turk whom Burnaby exhorted to educate women as they were educated in Europe.

'It would be difficult to do so,' said the Turk coldly. 'Their women uncover their faces; I have heard that some of them declare that they are the equals of their husbands. What ridiculous creatures they must be,' he continued, 'not at once to accept that inferior position which Allah in His wisdom has awarded to them!'

Again, on the practice of receiving money from future sons-in-law, as opposed to giving their daughters dowries:

> Our daughters are maid-servants; when they marry we lose their services. It is quite right that that the husband should compensate us for our loss. Europeans educate their girls very well, but the latter are utterly useless as cooks or sweepers. When they marry, the fathers lose nothing, but, on the contrary, gain, as they no longer have to pay for their daughters' maintenance and clothes. It is quite proper that you should give a husband something when he saddles himself with such a useless encumbrance, and you have no right to find fault with us for our system.

are packed with men, 'dense oceans of maleness'. As a Western woman you can drink in the coffee shops and tea-houses and eat at the local restaurants. You will be stared at and whispered about, but you should simply ignore it and behave normally and respectfully.

Dress is important in the eastern provinces, and you should always make sure you are not scantily clad. Tight shorts and low-cut T-shirts are not at all appropriate and will cause offence. If you are decently dressed, covering bare flesh above the elbows and knees, and behave sensibly and discreetly, you will cause no offence but will simply be regarded with great curiosity by men and women alike.

ATTITUDES TOWARDS EUROPE Turks today, especially the younger ones, are increasingly regarding themselves as European. Associate members of the EU (previously the EEC) since 1964, they are now intensifying their efforts to gain full membership. Desperately anxious for acceptance by the West, they are anxious to cast off their barbaric image. David Hotham, posing the question, 'Is the Turk a European?' at the beginning of his book *The Turks* (John Murray): ends by concluding that the Turk is 'a potential European', poised to move towards Europe. If however Europe is not welcoming, Turkey increasingly has the confidence to carve its own path, turning east instead, and improving its relations with its eastern neighbours.

LANGUAGE

Turkish is the seventh most widely spoken language in the world, and has very ancient origins going back at least 5,500 years. It belongs to the Ural-Altaic family of languages and is related to Mongolian, Korean and maybe even Japanese. It is therefore fiendishly difficult for Europeans to learn and has strange concepts such as vowel harmony and agglutination, a feature where words get longer and longer by tacking on more and more suffixes to adapt the meaning. For example the two-word sentence: '*Avrupalılastırmadıklarımızdan mısınız?*' means 'Are you one of those whom we could not Europeanise?'

Originally a language of nomadic tribesmen from central Asia, it had a wealth of vocabulary for describing livestock and weather conditions. But this vocabulary was inadequate for coping with the complexities of civilised urban life the Turks discovered in the countries they conquered. So they borrowed the bulk of their abstract and intellectual vocabulary from Arabic (about 40% of the language, similar to the position of French in medieval English), and borrowed from Persian most words to do with crafts, trades and their associated objects. With the Turks' conversion to Islam and their adoption of the Arabic alphabet, their language became increasingly artificial. The Arabic alphabet was never suited to Turkish, being based on three root consonants with vowels generally left out, whereas vowels and vowel harmony are crucial to Turkish grammar.

When Atatürk came to power in the early 1920s he set about removing foreign influences in the language, and tried to find Turkish substitutes for Arabic and Persian words. He also abandoned the Arabic alphabet and adopted the Latin alphabet in use today. Along with many of Atatürk's reforms, the effect was to shift Turkey away from the East and towards Europe. But this led to some problems in communication between generations, where even today there are grandparents who grew up with Arabic and Persian words while their grandchildren at school are taught a new vocabulary. The language reform also had the effect of greatly simplifying the over-elaborate use of language so favoured under the Ottomans. For example the modern Turkish civil servant will now write: 'I have been thinking about your suggestion'. His Ottoman predecessor would have written:

'Your slave has been engaged in the exercise of cogitation in respect of the proposals vouchsafed by your exalted person'.

The amount of English and German spoken east of Ankara is, not surprisingly, far less than in Istanbul and the Aegean and Mediterranean regions. Most hotels and restaurant staff do speak limited English, however, so you will always be able to get by without knowledge of Turkish. For visitors who do speak some Turkish, it is worth mentioning that the kind of Turkish spoken in the east of the country is very different from what you will be used to in Istanbul and the west. The difference is not in dialect but in pronunciation, and the Turkish sounds which are quite soft and pleasant on the ear in the western parts become very harsh and guttural.

One of the most infuriating characteristics of the Turk, as any traveller to Turkey soon discovers, is the way he says no. The famous Turkish negative *yok*, accompanied by an upward movement of the head with eyes half closed, is the negative to end all negatives as it also manages to convey complete indifference on the part of the person using it. When the hotel is full, or there is no orange juice, no fish, no fruit, no vegetables, this upward nod of the head and weary closing of the eyes says, 'No, there isn't any (and who cares anyway)'. Freya Stark described it as: 'that eloquent gesture which is the Turkish equivalent of a blank wall'.

When learning vocabulary be sure to get your consonants exactly right. As a woman you will cause untold mirth by going into a grocer's shop and asking if they have any *erkek*, when you meant to say *ekmek*, as you will have been asking if you can buy a man, instead of bread.

RELIGION

To Western eyes Turkey represents the role model for all Muslim countries – a secular democratic state in which Islam happens to be the dominant religion. Islam is the religion of 95% of the population, yet the country uses the Christian weekend of Saturday and Sunday, and there are also elements of Shamanism, Taoism, Zoroastrianism and fragments of the Chinese and Byzantine cultures. Since Atatürk's reforms in the 1920s non-Muslim religions are tolerated.

The main division in Islam is between Sunnis (from the Arabic meaning 'those following the right path') and Shi'a (from the Arabic meaning 'the party which split off'). This division, which has some parallels with the division in Christianity between Protestants and Catholics, can be traced back to the years immediately following the Prophet Muhammad's death. The Shi'a believed that Muhammad's son-in-law 'Ali and his descendants were the rightful successors to the caliphate, while the Sunnis believed it should pass to the person chosen by the *Ulema* or Islamic clergy. The vast majority of Turks are Sunnis, the orthodox and majority sect within Islam, though a minority are Shi'a, as are almost all Iranians. Shi'a in Turkey are also called Alevis, or partisans of 'Ali. The Sufi and dervish orders with their mystical elements formed another sizeable minority which were very popular in Turkey until Atatürk officially disbanded them in the 1920s.

The Turks as a nation are not especially religious, but in the eastern provinces religious adherence and conservatism is more noticeable than in other parts of Turkey, and so in mosques and generally your dress should be more discreet. It is fine to show bare arms and legs below the elbow and knee in the street but not in a way that exposes too much or is too figure-hugging. In mosques, bare arms and legs are not permitted for men or women, and women should also cover their hair with a scarf.

Ramazan (Arabic *Ramadan*), the month of fasting, is far more strictly observed in the east than it is in the Aegean or Mediterranean areas where you would not even notice it; in the east most restaurants will be closed, and only a very few in the

Superstitions are very much part of Turkish and Islamic culture, most of them pre-dating the advent of Islam. The concept of the evil eye (*nazar boncuk*) appears even in Roman mosaics (see page 202) and generally takes the form of a blue eye, because foreigners, who were more likely to have blue eyes, were also more likely to stare, thereby unwittingly contravening local convention, and, by admiring the children or possessions of their hosts, accidentally casting the evil eye of envy on them. To act as talismans to protect against this, lurid objects often in the form of an evil blue ceramic eye can be found on sale in all markets. They are hung in houses, offices, cars, buses and trucks to protect the occupants from the evil eye. The word *MaSallah*, meaning literally, 'What God wills', has come to mean 'May God preserve you from evil', and is often written on lorries and trucks as protection, and is in fact also the name of the country's largest transportation company. Like the Hand of Fatima (the Prophet Muhammad's daughter) it is used as a good-luck symbol.

biggest hotels will serve alcohol. For this reason it is worth avoiding the east during Ramazan if you are travelling independently as it will seriously affect your ability to get food. (For further information on travelling in Ramazan, see page 39.)

EDUCATION

Young Turks are very keen to be educated and the pressures on them to succeed at university and vocational schools are enormous. Unemployment is a serious problem even in the professions. The only fields which guarantee work are medicine and engineering, so the top students compete for places to study these subjects. A doctor can earn good money in Turkey in private practice in the cities, though only after a period of enforced practical training in the eastern provinces. The less able students study subjects like history, French and English, and as a result the English students often speak English less well than the medical or science students. Children from the state schools who want to fight their way to the coveted medicine and engineering places have a real struggle on their hands, especially if they come from the east, where the standard of teaching is lower, particularly in the villages. Those with wealthier backgrounds whose parents can send them to the private schools of Ankara and Istanbul have a definite advantage. Among schoolchildren it is not unusual to hear of suicides when they can no longer stand the pressure of the intense competition.

Compulsory schooling in Turkey has recently been increased to eight years, from the age of seven to the age of 15, divided into five years at primary level and three years at middle level. The wearing of uniform is compulsory at both levels in all state schools and schooling is free. Religious instruction at school was banned by Atatürk but has been partially reintroduced, resulting in much heated debate between the pro- and the anti-Islamists. At the start of the Turkish Republic in the 1920s the illiteracy rate was 90%, as only a small elite were educated. Today the rate stands at just 15% and falling. The student population has grown by nearly 500% in the last 15 years.

CULTURE

One of the most dominant features of Turkish culture is the need to gather and discuss all aspects of life from religious, through political to literary matters. Regular reunions between friends take place at all levels, and the *kahvehane* (coffee

The right of women to wear the headscarf is one of the most hotly debated issues in Turkish politics, as it strikes directly at the divide between the secularists and the Islamists in Turkey. Since the reforms of Atatürk in the 1920s, when headwear for both men (the *fez*) and women (the *hijab*) was outlawed as backward and religious, the wearing of the headscarf by women has been banned in government and at universities (apart from a brief period in the 1980s when it was permitted under Turgut Özal), meaning that female civil servants and students cannot wear it in public places – what they do at home is another matter and up to them. In early 2008 the Islamist-inclined AK Party which currently governs Turkey introduced constitutional changes aimed at lifting this ban on women's right to wear the headscarf on university campuses, whilst still outlawing the more extreme forms of Islamic dress like the full veil (*niqab* or *burqa*). The secular opposition CH Party challenged these changes in the Constitutional Court, arguing that they threaten the secular character of the state – the challenge was upheld by the court, so the ban on the headscarf in the civil service and the universities remains.

house) or *caybahcesi* (tea-garden) culture so widespread across the country reflects this. In both city and countryside these places were part of the old Ottoman heritage, and traditionally were male-dominated. In recent years however, in the big cities, the form of these kahvehanes has undergone a subtle change. Also known as *kiraathanes* the etymology of the word itself shows the origin of the concept 'reading hall', and among young students there has latterly been a return to what is now called *kafe-kitab*, literally a 'book-café', frequented now by both sexes. As a further development of this, in the last decade there has been an emergence of bars, mainly aimed at a moneyed and Europeanised intellectual elite clientele, known by religious traditionalists as *intell bars*.

The press and TV are the main arena for public debate and Turks have a passion for the written press way beyond anything that exists in the West. The Turkish taste for discussion and polemic on social and political subjects finds its perfect milieu here, and heated televised debates on Turkish television go on for hours, often late into the night. In the press satirical reviews are very popular, and the best known, *Leman* and *Girgir*, are financed by the big national dailies and have a huge circulation. *Hurriyet* is the most influential daily, founded in 1948, taking a centre-right stance. It also publishes daily on-line in English and is a good source for Turkish current affairs. *Zaman,* founded in 1986, was the first Turkish daily to go online in 1995, and is a conservative paper supporting secularism and democracy but regarded by some sources as Islamist. It has a larger circulation than *Hurriyet*. The Ottoman tradition of caricature also continues to play a big social and political role.

MUSIC Music is the most significant indicator of the double culture of the Turks: in effect there are several types of music which co-exist, some inherited from their oriental past, others showing their desire to integrate with the West. The traditional popular folkloric music can be heard in religious *alevi* gatherings across Anatolia, the principal instrument being the *saz*, a kind of lute beloved of mystical poets. Often improvised, the text is often mystical poetry which can be interpreted in a political or social sense. Konya and Sivas are the great centres for this type of music. One of the great contemporary interpreters of this music was an Alevi called Nesimi Çimen who died in 1993.

Classical Ottoman music developed in the Ottoman court at Istanbul and at the *tekkes* (monasteries) of the dervishes, especially the *Mevlevi* dervishes based at Konya. Inspired by the musical traditions of the Byzantine, Arab and Persian worlds, it is a solemn music made by several instruments, notable the *ney*, the reed flute favoured by the **Whirling Dervishes**. Improvisation is again a major principal characteristic and the subtleties of this music cannot be written down in notation. It was learnt orally and passed from master to pupil, perfected through practice. The composers were Turkish, but also Greek, Jewish, Roman and Armenian. It declined after 1925 when Atatürk had the *tekkes* closed down and

SMOKING BAN AND THE *NARGILE*

In summer 2009 a smoking ban was introduced across Turkey in all public places including public transport, restaurants and cafés. This covers the *nargile* or water-pipe (hubble-bubble) as well, which will therefore sadly be a thing of the past except in pavement cafés, on roof terraces and in courtyards. Even smoking a nargile under an outdoor sunshade/umbrella is prohibited – health and safety has descended big time. The original *nargile* came from India, made of coconut shells, from where its popularity spread to Iran and to the Arab world. The word *nargil* means 'coconut' in Persian. In Anatolia it became a very important part of coffee-house culture from the 17th century onwards, and its style has not changed for the last few centuries.

Great ritual was attached to the preparing and lighting of the *nargile* and the ceremony fell to the eldest male in the household. There are four parts: the body, the bowl, the tube and the mouthpiece. The body (*gövde*) is where the bowl is placed and filled with water to cleanse the residue created by the burning tobacco and to absorb the nicotine. The body is usually made of glass, though the fancier ones are made of porcelain or even silver. They are often decorated with floral motifs and are a unique type of Turkish handicraft. The bowl (*lule*) is where the plug of tobacco (*tombeki*) is put and covered with a conical cap to shelter the flame on windy days. Only special dark, strong, very high-nicotine tobacco is used, after being washed several times before use. Oak charcoal is put on top of the tobacco. The tube (*marpuç*) is a long flexible hose connecting the mouthpiece to the body, and might be covered in embroidery or other woven decoration. More than one tube can be attached to the body so that more than one person can smoke at the same time. A small metal tray catches the cinders. The final part is the mouthpiece (*ağızlık*) through which the smoke is inhaled. The technique is to suck the smoke gently, not inhaling deeply, not puffing as strongly as a cigarette. The sucking should make pleasant bubbling sounds in the water (hence hubble-bubble) which is part of the ritual and fun. Separate craftsmen used to make each separate part of the *nargile*, and their trade was named accordingly – hence you can find an area of *marpuççular* in a traditional souk.

The new fashion is for hubble-bubbles to be flavoured with strawberries, apple or even cappuccino. It takes about an hour to smoke a full *nargile* of fruit tobacco, or two hours for the original strong tobacco. The smoke is cooler than cigarette smoke and lightly intoxicating. A Turkish magazine article written when the ban was introduced quoted real *nargile* aficionados as saying that smoking a nargile is nothing like smoking a cigarette: 'Cigarettes are for nervous people, competitive people and people on the run. When you smoke a nargile you have time to think. It teaches you patience and tolerance, and gives you an appreciation of good company. *Nargile* smokers have a much more balanced approach to life than cigarette smokers.'

disbanded, and was then eclipsed by the Western classical music favoured by the regime, before enjoying a revival since the 1970s, thanks to the exceptional ney player Niyaz Siyan, who paved the way for a succession of accomplished players.

Turkish **pop music** has become extremely popular since the 1960s, following the style of Western pop music, and has many talented exponents starting with Bulent Ortacgil, and many others including Baris Manco (died 1999), Sezer Tansu and Tarkan, a kind of Turkish Elvis Presley.

Arabesque music has also become extremely popular in Turkey since the 1980s, when Turgut Özal permitted it and used it to make his government seem more accessible to the people. Inspired by modern Arabic music and accompanied by Western instruments, it was originally beloved of immigrant peasants flooding to the cities. The world of arabesque music dispensed with such divisions as rich and poor, left and right, and used instead such universal themes as nostalgia for birthplace and the breakdown of family values.

FILM When Yilmaz Güney (an 'assimilated' Kurd, as he called himself) won the Cannes Palme d'Or in 1982 with his film *Yol* (*The Road*), Turkish cinema gained international recognition. Conceived and created whilst in prison, he wrote the screenplay and smuggled instructions to his co-director Serif Gören, drawing much publicity to the plight of the dispossessed in Turkey at that time. The film follows the course of five prisoners given one week's home leave. Some of Güney's earlier films, notably *Umut* (*Hope*, 1970), *Sürü* (*The Herd*, 1978) and *Duvar* (*The Wall*, 1983) have now also become recognised, and show the harsh realities of life in eastern Turkey among the working-class poor. His own parents were cotton-farm labourers in Adana. After nearly ten years in prison, he escaped in 1981 and fled to France, where he died aged 47 of gastric cancer in 1987 in exile, stripped of Turkish nationality. Güney said that his film *Sürü* was in fact: 'the history of the Kurdish people, but I could not even use the Kurdish language in this film; if we had used Kurdish, all those who took part in this film would have been sent to jail.'

In 2003 Nuri Bilge Ceylan's film *Uzak* also drew international acclaim, when its two main actors won the Best Actor prize at the Cannes Film Festival, and in 2007 Fatih Akin's film *The Edge of Heaven* (original title in German *Auf der Anderen Seite,* Turkish *Yaşamın Kıyısında*) won the Best Screenplay award at the Cannes Film Festival and at the European Film Awards. If you want to gain a sense of the contrast between the cosmopolitan life of Istanbul and Turkey's Aegean and Mediterranean worlds and the world of eastern Turkey, these films, all now readily available and even cheaply purchasable on Amazon, are a very good starting point for giving you a flavour of Turkey's eastern regions.

LITERATURE

Seljuk times The first decades of Seljuk rule were a time of great chaos for the eastern Islamic world, but by a great stroke of fortune, the Seljuk sultan, Alp Arslan and his son Sultan Malikshah (whose name combines the royal titles of the Turks, Arabs and Persians) found a *vizir* (adviser to the ruler) well up to the task of managing the complicated administrative process of the new sultanate. Persian by birth, he was called Nizam Al-Mulk, his honorific title which means 'regulator of the kingship'. He was a cultured man and clearly saw the need to smooth some of the rough edges of his Turkish overlords, and wrote the remarkable *Book of Government* written in the form of advice to governors. He later added several chapters on 'enemies of the state', and in an unfortunate irony he was himself soon afterwards assassinated by one of the enemies he had identified. Here are a few sample passages:

It is the king's duty to inquire into the condition of his peasantry and army, both far and near, and to know more or less how things are. If he does not do this he is at fault and people will charge him with negligence, laziness and tyranny... Spies must constantly go out to the limits of the kingdom in the guise of merchants, travellers, Sufis, pedlars (of medicines), and mendicants, and bring back reports of everything they hear, so that no matters of any kind remain concealed... Enlightened monarchs and clever ministers have never in any age given two appointments to one man or one appointment to two men, with the result that their affairs were always conducted with efficiency and lustre. When two appointments are given to one man, one of the tasks is always inefficiently and faultily performed; and in fact you will usually find that the man who has two functions fails in both of them, and is constantly suffering censure and uneasiness on account of his shortcomings. And further, whenever two men are given a single post each transfers [his responsibility] to the other and the work remains forever undone. (Translated by Hubert Darke.)

Rumi (1207–73) The greatest mystical poet settled in Konya, though he originally came from Afghanistan and wrote in Persian, the language of the Seljuk court. He is discussed in more detail and parts of his poetry quoted in *Chapter 7, Konya*, page 167.

Ottoman times Sarı Mehmed Pasha, an Ottoman treasurer to Sultan Ahmad III (ruled 1703–30), wrote a fascinating treatise on Ottoman statecraft. Ironically, although he aspired to be grand *vizir*, he never succeeded as he was not sufficiently adept at manipulation and manoeuvring to outwit his rivals, and ended by being disgraced and executed by the government he had served for nearly 50 years. Here is a fragment of what he said on the subject of bribery:

SURPRISING FACTS ABOUT EASTERN TURKEY

- The grape was first cultivated here, making it the home of winemaking (see page 158)
- There are more churches in Cappadocia and eastern Turkey than in Istanbul and western Turkey
- The Hittites of eastern Turkey were contemporary with the ancient Egyptians and the Hittite language is now recognised as the earliest-known Indo-European language, making it the source of all our European languages
- The Southeast Anatolia Project (GAP) of a series of dams on the Euphrates is making Turkey self-sufficient in electricity
- The most valuable silk carpet in the world is in the Mevlâna (Rumi) Museum in Konya
- The world's first cathedral is recognised by the papacy as being in Antakya (ancient Antioch) in the Grotto of Saint Peter, where the apostle is said to have preached after Christ's crucifixion
- King Midas (of the Golden Touch) and Saint Paul were both born in eastern Turkey
- Both the Old Testament and the Koran tell that after the Great Flood, Noah's Ark came to rest on the slopes of Mount Ararat, Turkey's highest mountain
- The Old Testament claims that Abraham was born in Urfa, where a pool of sacred carp now marks the spot as a place of pilgrimage
- Gabled roofs were first seen on Urartian tombs in eastern Turkey, from where the feature passed westward into Greece and the rest of Europe

A 17th-century Turkish writer called Hajji Khalifah wrote a work called *The Balance of Truth*, which included a pair of essays on tobacco and on coffee, both substances whose effects were controversial and which the state periodically attempted to ban, to no avail. He considers, often very amusingly, how to make people give up:

Occasional reprimands from the Throne to smokers have generally been disregarded, and smoking is at present practised all over the globe… Is this tobacco found to be good or bad by the intelligence? If we set aside the fact that addicts think it good, common sense judges it to be bad. […] The fact that it is not used by judges in law courts, at council meetings, in mosques or other places of worship, is a consequence of its being found bad by the criterion of intelligence. […] As to its harmful effects there is no doubt. It ends by becoming a basic need of the addict, who does not consider its evil consequences. Its harmful physical effect too is medically noxious in that it makes turbid the aerial essence… But an evil odour arises in the mouth of the heavy smoker, by comparison with which, in the nostril of the non-smoker, halitosis is as aloes-wood and ambergris… The conclusion must be to recommend abstention… there is no question of interference with those who have the addiction… As most Muslims are addicted to it, they have become inseparably attached to the practice, and will in no circumstance be deterred from it or abandon it, and it has taken hold of the whole world. (Translated by G L Lewis.)

Bribery is the beginning and root of all illegality and tyranny, the source and fountain of every sort of disturbance and sedition, the most vast of evils, and greatest of calamities. …Than this there is no more powerful engine of injustice and cruelty, for bribery destroys both faith and state… The Prophet of God has said: 'May God curse the briber and the taker of bribes. Most tyrannies come from bribes. No position is given justly to the briber.' The Prophet has said: 'The souls of both the briber and bribed are cursed by God. When high officials act in accordance with right and use justice in appointing those who deserve positions, bribery is not necessary… To give office to the unfit because of bribery is a very great sin.' (Translated by Walter Livingstone Wright.)

The novelist Yaşar Kemal (1923–) is the best known of Turkey's contemporary writers, himself of Kurdish origin, his parents coming from Van. He lost his right eye as a young child in a knife accident when his father was slaughtering a sheep for the *Bayram*, and then aged five he had to watch his father being stabbed to death by an adopted son whilst praying in the mosque. The trauma left him with a speech impediment until he was 12. He was employed by rich local farmers on the Çukurova plains near Adana to guard their river water against illicit use by poor local farmers, but ended up instead teaching them how to steal water undetected by night. His village paid for him to go to university in Istanbul and he later worked as a letter-writer, then a journalist and finally as a novelist, describing the living conditions of workers, the exploitation of landless peasants and the forced sedentarisation of nomads from the Taurus mountains by the government. His outspoken criticism of the treatment of Kurds in southeastern Turkey earned him spells in prison. He is still alive and was nominated for the Nobel Prize for Literature for his book *Mehmet, My Hawk* (*İnce Memed*, 1955). His work also stresses the imagination of the rural poor and their ability to create myths to escape the harsh reality of their lives.

Coffee was the subject of another treatise, and he explains how coffee first came to Asia Minor by sea around 1543 and met with a hostile reception, with *fatwas* (religious edicts) being delivered against it. The fact that it was drunk in gatherings and passed from hand to hand suggested loose living, and attempts were made to plunge all cargoes of coffee into the sea.

But these strictures and prohibitions availed nothing. The *fatwas*, the talk, made no impression on the people. One coffee-house was opened after another, and men would gather together, with great eagerness and enthusiasm, to drink… To those of dry temperament, especially to the man of melancholic temperament, large quantities are unsuitable, and may be repugnant. Taken in excess, it causes insomnia and melancholic anxiety. If drunk at all, it should be drunk with sugar. To those of moist temperament, and especially of women, it is highly suited. They should drink a great deal of strong coffee. Excess of it will do them no harm, so long as they are not melancholic. (Translated by G L Lewis.)

Ottoman poetry Often judged harshly because of its use of clichés, Ottoman Sufi poets did compose a few surprising *ghazals* (love poems) such as the following:

Source of being! If a mistress thou should seek,
Then, I pray thee, let thy loved one be a Greek.
Unto her fancies of the joyous bend,
For there's leave to woo the Grecian girl, my friend.
Caskets of coquetry are the Grecian maids,
And their grace the rest of womankind degrades…
(Translated by E J W Gibb.)

Greek Women by Fazil Beg (written at the turn of the 18th century)

Ottoman drama
Karagöz Various forms of popular drama developed across Ottoman times and before, the most popular of which was a classic puppet theatre called *Karagöz* (Black-eyed) after the name of its main protagonist. Possibly of Chinese origin it was known in the Islamic world in the 13th century, becoming popular both in royal courts and in village squares. It was always in the form of a dialogue full of wordplay impossible to translate, between the two characters Karagöz and Hajeivat who appear in an endless variety of disguises. Here are a few sample lines to give the flavour, from one of the enduring favourites, *The Bloody Poplar*, which Karagöz confuses with sweet pumpkin because the Turkish words are very similar. Hadjeivat announces at the start:

This is the performance of shadows. It is an enigma for men of knowledge. You, looking at it with the eye of a spectator, stand amazed by its brilliance and try to understand its meaning; if you cannot understand, they say to you – it is a mystery.

Another character, whose child is about to be snatched, muses:

Your summer is like winter,
You are like a head covered with grief,
Or like a sad drunkard,
You mystically intoxicated mountains!
Mountains, mountains, solitary mountains!
Which make us weep as if in separation from friends;
Let us go…

Let us take evil for good,
Let us go away from death in these mountains,
Where before we enjoyed ourselves,
Which make us weep in separation from friends!'
(Translated by Nicholas Martinovitch.)

Post-Ottoman literature Modern Turkish literature began following the War of Independence, the great turning point in recent Turkish history. With the foundation of the Turkish Republic in 1923 and the reform of the alphabet, in which the Arabic characters – never in any event suited to the phonetics of the Turkish language – were discarded and replaced with the current Latin alphabet, the national culture could express itself for the first time, free from its Ottoman-Islamic heritage. Poetry and prose developed as the preferred genres and two main figures dominated the poetic scene in the early days of the Republic: Yahya Kemal (1884–1958) and Ahmet Haşim (1885–1933). However the key figure in Turkish literature of the 20th century was Nazım Hikmet (1902–1963), a great innovator whose free verse used the rich harmonies of the Turkish language and erased the earlier fixed traditional forms. Sometimes described as a 'romantic revolutionary' and leader of Turkey's *avant-garde*, he was arrested in 1933 for involvement in communism and spent 15 years in prison, where he wrote his masterpiece 'Human Landscapes' (*Memleketimdan İnsan Manzaraları* 1966), an epic novel in verse, before being exiled to Russia just two years before the ban was lifted on his poems. Some of them have been set to music by Zülfü Livaneli. From the 1940s onwards a definite shift took place in Turkish literature. The *Garıp* (Turkish for 'strange') movement began, using vernacular and breaking with the traditional

TURKISH PROVERBS

If you wish to know a people, acquaint yourself with their proverbs

- Ability has no school
- Even if guilt were made of sable, no-one would choose to wear it
- Lower your voice, strengthen your argument
- His brains hang at the top of his fez
- Habits are worse than rabies
- Stretch your feet only as your blanket allows
- For every door God closes, He opens a thousand others
- Every illiterate dreams of being prime minister
- No load is heavier than gratitude
- To give quickly is to give twice
- Listening requires more intelligence than speaking
- The fool praises his wife, the wise man praises his dog
- The man who conceals his pain will never find a cure
- Nine out of ten men are women
- Flatter in Arabic, reprove in Turkish, but argue in Persian [Persian proverb]
- If you want peace in your own house, don't go banging on your neighbour's door
- If you dig a grave for your neighbour, measure it for yourself
- The house with two mistresses remains unswept, with two masters it falls to ruin
- If God wants to make a poor man happy, He makes him lose his ass and then find it again

stereotypical poetry of the past, focussing instead on the intrinsic realities of everyday life for ordinary people, with Orhan Veli (1914–1950) as its main protagonist. In prose the trend towards social realism increased, particularly dealing with the misery of the rural poor in central and eastern Anatolia, social injustice and oppression of wealthy landlords.

Turkey's other famous novelist, Orhan Pamuk (1952–) has had many novels translated into foreign languages. Turkish literature of the earlier part of the 20th century had turned its back on its Ottoman past, but his novels look again at the Ottoman heritage with a questioning and critical eye, in a kind of quest for identity in this double culture which has always looked both East and West for its inspiration.

2

Practical Information

The key to Paradise is patience.

WHEN TO VISIT

The best time to visit the eastern part of Turkey is between May and September, with June probably the best month of all for most places. Even then, you should be prepared for a huge diurnal range, with temperatures between day and night routinely differing by over 20°C, and your clothing needs to take account of this. (See box eastern Turkey *climate charts*, pages 6–7, for details of temperatures across the various regions of eastern Turkey.) The main **tourist season** runs from 1 April to 31 October, and the heavy winter snowfall means that many of the smaller hotels and pensions close from November to March. **Ramazan**, the Muslim month of fasting, is probably best avoided in eastern Turkey, as it is more strictly observed than in the Aegean and Mediterranean parts, and you may find it difficult to find places to eat during the day.

The high-summer months of July and August are extremely hot during the day, with temperatures often reaching 40°C, though it still drops sharply at night. Coastal cities like Adana and Antakya are also very humid in high summer, and air conditioning in your hotel room becomes something that can make a big difference to your night's sleep. The **Black Sea swimming season** is from June to early September, though the weather is not as dependable as the Mediterranean, with far heavier rainfall.

In the **winter** months some parts can be especially attractive, notably Cappadocia and Lake Van, when the snow enhances the landscapes and there are still clear bright days to be had. Temperatures of minus 30–38°C are possible during the daytime up on the Anatolian Plateau and temperatures of minus 20–25°C are normal from December to February, so your clothing needs to reflect that, but the roads are mainly kept clear by snowploughs, with only the highest of passes (above 2,000m) closed for the winter, and even then only on the more minor roads. If you want to avoid the crowds and pretty much guarantee having the place to yourself, the winter may be the time to come, as long as you do not want to climb any of the volcanoes or visit Nemrut Dağı, which, at 2,150m, is inaccessible because of snow from November to April.

HIGHLIGHTS

LAKE VAN AND AKDAMAR ISLAND The eerily blue and other-worldly vast lake ringed with majestic mountains, its tiny islands graced with Armenian churches, especially Akdamar, with its exquisite 10th-century Church of King Gagik (see pages 263–77).

MOUNT ARARAT The highest peak in Turkey and also in any of the European Union countries at 5,165m, a magnificent permanently snow-capped volcano wreathed in legends and famed as the final resting place of Noah's Ark (see pages 304–11).

THE GEORGIAN VALLEYS AND PONTIC ALPS Dramatic heavily forested hills, liberally sprinkled with the ruins of Georgian churches tucked away in beautiful remote green valleys (see pages 325–35).

CAPPADOCIA AND THE ROCK CHURCHES While Göreme is the most famous collection of rock churches, the wild fairy-cone landscapes of Cappadocia are in themselves a highlight, along with many other lesser-known valleys like Ihlara and Soğnali, not to mention the extraordinary underground cities (see pages 139–65).

NEMRUT DAĞI The mountain and its remote hilltop burial royal mound, where the King of Commagene surrounded himself with colossal statues of the gods. Snowbound except from May to October (see pages 215–22).

SUMELA MONASTERY One of eastern Turkey's most visited sites, set in deep evergreen forests and clinging Tibetan-style to a high cliff face, the monastery is reachable only on foot up a steep path, with impressively graffitied wall frescoes (see pages 359–60).

HASANKEYF AND THE TIGRIS Now saved from flooding by the shelving of a dam scheme, Hasankeyf's stunning gorge location and Artukid ruins can be enjoyed while eating freshly caught trout, sprawling on cushions, feet dangling in the Tigris from the shady lunching platforms built out on the river (see pages 255–7).

MARDİN AND THE TÛR ABDİN With stunning architecture in its white limestone houses, mosques and madrasas, Mardin belongs more to Syria and the Arab world, another example of the arbitrary borders of the region. On the nearby plateau lie scattered monasteries and churches, remnants of early eastern Christianity, as featured in William Dalrymple's *From the Holy Mountain* (see pages 245–55).

GAZİANTEP AND THE ZEUGMA MOSAICS The now beautifully restored houses and market areas of Gaziantep are more Syrian in flavour than Turkish, and the magnificent Roman mosaics in the new museum are the most impressive collection in the world (see pages 205–12).

HATTUŞAŞ Hilltop fort and capital of the ancient Hittites, an advanced civilisation rivalling their contemporaries the ancient Egyptians and Babylonians (see pages 99–103).

KONYA AND THE TURQUOISE-DOMED MEVLÂNA TEKKE The atmospheric burial place of the poet Rumi, founder of the mystic Whirling Dervishes (see pages 168–78).

SAFRANBOLU The near-perfect town of wooden Ottoman mansions, preserved as a UNESCO World Heritage Site (see pages 370–1).

SUGGESTED ITINERARIES

The best direction of travel is from Adana or Antakya on the Mediterranean to Lake Van then north on to the Black Sea. The following itineraries show what can be done at a reasonable pace of travel. Those wanting to incorporate a period of rest and recuperation by the sea would be best advised to spend several days at one of the beach hotels near Silifke, before returning from Adana or Ankara.

LONG WEEKEND With only three to four nights at your disposal, the most you can do is to get a taster of one area only, not least because of the travel time, as flying into the airports of eastern Turkey has to be done via Istanbul or Ankara; often this cannot be accomplished the same day, thereby necessitating a stopover of one night on both the outward and return flights. For example:

- Fly into and out of Ankara, stay in one of the simple boutique hotels in Ankara's old citadel, see the Museum of Anatolian Civilisations and do a day trip into the Hittite heartlands (see pages 85–106).
- Fly into Van and base yourself at one of the lakeside hotels while renting a car to explore the sites of the lakeshore (see pages 264–70).
- Fly into Diyarbakır, base yourself at the converted caravanserai, wander round the city's mosques and churches on foot, then venture off by car to explore the monasteries of the Tûr Abdin (see pages 231–53).
- Fly into Nevşehir or Kayseri, then base yourself at one of the rock-cut houses/hotels of Ürgüp, Uçhisar or Ortahisar, while you discover the many surprises of Cappadocia with its underground cities and painted churches (see pages 139–59).

ONE WEEK All four of the long weekend suggestions above lend themselves to being easily expanded to a week, or you can venture a little further afield. One possibility is to combine one week in Istanbul or on the Aegean/Mediterranean coast, with one week exploring a little of eastern Turkey to get the total contrast. Some suggestions for the eastern Turkey week are:

- Fly into Antakya (Hatay Airport) and then head east to Gaziantep to see the world-class Roman mosaics, and further east to the biblical sites of Urfa and Harran (see pages 196–231).
- Fly to Diyarbakır, head north to the colossal mountaintop statues of Nemrut Dağı, and south for a flavour of the Arab world to the beautiful Mardin, its limestone houses overlooking the Plain of Mesopotamia (see pages 215–49).
- Fly into Trabzon, visit its miniature Aya Sofya before heading inland to the lush, green Pontic Alps to see the Sumela Monastery and the ruined Georgian churches tucked away in their valleys (see pages 351–60).
- Fly into Van, explore its lakeshore and island Armenian churches and Seljuk monuments, venture into deepest Kurdish territory in Hakkâri for stunning scenery, castles and Urartian citadels (see pages 264–93).
- Fly into Kayseri or Nevşehir, spend five days exploring the fairy chimney valleys of Cappadocia with lots of walking, then head west to Konya, centre of the Whirling Dervishes (see pages 139–79).

TWO OR MORE WEEKS With two weeks at your disposal you can explore eastern Turkey a little more fully, choosing the area that most appeals. A three-week trip allows you to start to get a proper flavour of the region, but only when you spend four weeks in the area will you feel you are beginning to get below the surface.

Two weeks – Itinerary I Adana–Adıyaman, for Nemrut Dağı (two days)–Urfa–Diyarbakır–Tatvan–Van (two days)–Doğubeyazıt–Kars, for Ani–Erzurum–Trabzon–Samsun–fly to Istanbul

Two weeks – Itinerary 2 Ankara (two days)–Boğazkale–Amasya–Sivas–Elâzığ–Diyarbakır–Urfa–Adıyaman, for Nemrut Dağı–Antakya–Adana–Göreme–Ürgüp

Two weeks – Itinerary 3 Ankara–Boğazkale–Amasya–Ünye–Trabzon (two days)–Artvin–Erzurum–Doğubeyazıt–Van (two days)–Diyarbakır–Adana–fly to Istanbul

Three weeks – Itinerary 4 Ankara–Boğazkale–Amasya–Ünye–Trabzon (two days)–Erzurum–Kars, for Ani–Doğubeyazıt–Van (two days)–Diyarbakır–Adıyaman–Antakya–Silifke (three days)–Konya (two days)–Ankara

Three weeks – Itinerary 5 Adana–Adıyaman–Urfa–Diyarbakır–Mardin–Tatvan (two days)–Van–Hakkâri–Van–Doğubeyazıt–Kars–Sarıkamiş–Erzurum–Hopa–Trabzon (two days)–fly to Istanbul

Four weeks – Itinerary 6 Ankara–Boğazkale–Amasya–Sivas–Elâzığ–Malatya–Kayseri–Ürgüp–Ortahisar–Adana–Adıyaman–Urfa–Diyarbakır–Mardin–Tatvan (two days)–Van–Doğubeyazıt–Kars–Sarıkamiş–Erzurum–Hopa–Trabzon–Samsun–fly to Istanbul

TOUR OPERATORS

There are well over 100 tour operators for Turkey, of which about a third offer holidays to eastern as well as western Turkey. Many of these only extend to Cappadocia and maybe Konya, but some offer a full eastern Turkey experience. There are also specialist activity tour operators offering trekking or rafting holidays.

UK

Andante Travel Salisbury, Wilts; ✆ 01722 713800; www.barebonestours.co.uk. Run by archaeologists & offering archaeological tours of northeast Turkey, Lake Van, Cappadocia & central Anatolia.

Cachet Travel 7 St John's Rd, Isleworth, TW7 6NH; ✆ 020 88478700; www.cachet-travel.co.uk. Offers accommodation & holidays in Cappadocia.

Eldertreks ✆ 0808 234 1714; www.eldertreks.com. Specialising in small group exotic adventures. Offers a 17-day tour of eastern Turkey. Based in the UK & Toronto, Canada.

Interest & Activity Holidays PO Box 59, Ruardean, Glos GL17 TWX; ✆ 0871 8552925; www.iah-holidays.co.uk. Offers ballooning in Cappadocia, with good accommodation provided.

KE Adventure Travel 32 Lake Rd. Keswick, Cumbria CA12 5DQ; ✆ 017687 73966; www.keadventure.com. Offers a range of treks in Cappadocia, the Kaçkar, the Taurus Mountains & an Ararat trek.

McCabe Pilgrimages 11 Hillgate Place, Balham Hill, London SW12 9ER; ✆ 0800 1073107; www.mccabe-travel.co.uk. Offering tours to Konya & Cappadocia to see religious sites.

Naturetrek Ltd Cheriton Mill, Cheriton, Alresford, Hants SO24 0NG; ✆ 01962 733051; www.naturetrek.co.uk. Offering nature & birdwatching tours in eastern Turkey.

Regent Holidays Mezzanine Suite, Froomsgate House, Rupert St, Bristol BS1 2QJ; ✆ 0845 277 3317; www.regent-holidays.co.uk. Offers tailor-made tours in Cappadocia & the eastern region including Diyarbakır.

Savile Tours London; ✆ 020 79233230; www.saviletours.com. This exclusive tour operator runs top-end holidays in Cappadocia.

Tulip Holidays Ltd 9 Grand Parade, Green Lanes, London N4 1JX; ✆ 020 8211 0001; www.tulipholidays.com. Tailor-made holidays all over Turkey. Also offering direct flights to Gaziantep from Stansted for £186 return & to Malatya via Istanbul from London Heathrow for £282.

Water by Nature 3 Wath Rd. Elsecar, South Yorks S74 8HJ; ✆ 01226 740444; www.waterbynature.com. Flying into Erzurum, this company offers white-water rafting on the Coruh River & trekking in the Kaçkar Mountains.

US

Sobek California; www.mtsobek.com. Their Treasures of Turkey tour includes Cappadocia. **Trafalgar Tours** \ 1 866 544 4434; www.trafalgar.com. US-based group founded in 1947, their Best of Turkey tour includes Konya & Cappadocia.

CANADA

Eldertreks 597 Markham St, Toronto, ON M6G 2L7; \ 1 800 741 7956. Specialising in adventure travel for the over-50s.

NEW ZEALAND

Water by Nature PO Box 571, Blenheim 7315; e raft@waterbynature.com; www.waterbynature.com. As above under UK section.

TURKEY

Anatolian Adventures Kadıköy, Istanbul; \ (216) 4185222; www.anatolianadventures.com. Offering a range of trekking throughout eastern Turkey, including Cappadocia, the Kaçkar Mountains & Mount Ararat.
Eastern Turkey Tours Van; \ (432) 2152092; www.easternturkeytour.org. This specialist company offers the biggest range of tours in eastern Turkey & Cappadocia.
Fez Travel Sultanahmet Istanbul; \ (212) 5169024; www.feztravel.com. Offering a 15-day tour of eastern Turkey.
Heritage Travel Göreme; \ (384) 2712687; www.göreme.com. Founded in 2004 by 4 partners

Trekking specialists

Demavend Travel Niğde; \ 388 2327363; www.demavendtravel.com
Middle Earth Travel Nevşehir \ 384 2712559; www.middleearthtravel.com

Water by Nature 2285 South Downing St, Denver, Colorado 80210; \ 1 303 988 5037; www.waterbynature.com. As above under UK section.

native to Göreme & offering tours in Cappadocia & 17-day tours of eastern Turkey.
Insight Travel Turkey Antalya; \ (242) 8363692; www.tour-turkey.com. Offering a 15-day tour of eastern Turkey.
Tur-ISTA Tourism Travel Agency Sultanahmet; \ (212) 5277085; e erdemir@tur-ista.com; www.tur-ista.com. Specialising in ticketing for planes, trains & buses, so a good place to organise (via internet booking) travel across to eastern Turkey or beyond. Tours to Nemrut Dağı & budget but good quality accommodation & tours all over Turkey. Also does car rental.

Sobek Travel Niğde; \ 388 2321507; www.trekkinginturkey.com

For additional information on local tour operators, see the regional chapters.

ℹ TOURIST INFORMATION

There is a good network of tourist information offices in all major cities throughout eastern Turkey which hand out free local maps and leaflets. It is also worth collecting free brochures and maps before your departure from the Turkish Tourist Office in your own country. In the UK this is:

Turkish Tourist Office 4th Floor; St James' St; London SW1A 1HB; \ 020 7839 7778; f 020 7925 1388; www.gototurkey.co.uk

VISAS TO TURKEY Ordinary British passport holders may buy a visa costing £10 on arrival at the Turkish airport which is multiple-entry and valid for three months. Nationals of Australia, Austria, Belgium, Canada, the Netherlands, Norway (one month only), Portugal, Spain and the USA have the same arrangement, though the amount varies from country to country (Americans pay US$20 for example) and it must be paid for in hard currency notes, not coins (US dollars, euros or pounds sterling). You have to queue separately to buy your visa stamp at the separate kiosk before queuing again at passport control. UK citizens can buy visas in advance from the Turkish Consulate General, but it's much more expensive, so it's better to do it at the airport on arrival. Nationals of Denmark, Finland, France, Germany, Ireland, Israel, Italy, Japan, New Zealand, Sweden and Switzerland do not require a visa at all. Tourist visas do not give the right to take up employment, whether paid or unpaid, or to reside or to study (excluding student exchange programmes) or to establish a business in Turkey. Diplomatic passport holders cannot buy tourist visas and must obtain their visa in advance from the Consulate General for the Republic of Turkey in London (for contact information, see page 45). Make sure your passport still has at least six months left to run on it from the time of entry. Visitors of other nationalities should consult the latest regulations on the Turkish Ministry of Foreign Affairs website (*www.mfa.gov.tr*).

VISAS TO NEIGHBOURING COUNTRIES If you plan to travel onward from eastern Turkey to any of its neighbours, the rules vary as follows:

Armenia Armenia's land border with Turkey remains closed for now. See www.armeniaforeignministry.com for the latest information. If you want to travel onwards to Armenia from Turkey you can fly into Yerevan and most nationalities can buy a visa at the airport. Alternatively you can take a bus and travel in via Georgia, then buy your Armenian visa at the border.

Georgia Most nationalities can get a 90-day visa on arrival at any Georgian border. Single entry costs US$30. See www.mfa.gov.ge for full details.

Iran Visas to Iran need to be arranged in advance through the Iranian embassy in your own country and usually take a minimum of ten days. Applications can be made online at www.mfa.gov.ir. Women must arrive wearing full *hijab* (headscarf and full-length robe) though these days a fringe and even jewellery can be showing.

Iraq Visas are currently only issued to people with official business in the country, such as aid workers or journalists, not to tourists. The Kurdish Regional Government in the north however does issue its own ten-day tourist visa at the point of entry. See www.mofa.gov.iq for further information.

Northern Cyprus Tourist visas are available on arrival at the Turkish Republic of Northern Cyprus (TRNC) on the same conditions as those for Turkey. Consult www.cyprus.com. Bear in mind that if you plan to visit mainland Greece or the Greek islands you will be denied entry if you have a TRNC stamp in your passport, so ask for the standard procedure of getting the Turkish Cypriot immigration officials to stamp a separate paper rather than your passport.

Among the items listed as permitted to bring with you on entry are the following: one glider; one two-partitioned camping tent; one boat; one surfboard with sailing equipment; chess set; draughts set; five packs of playing cards; gas mask and protective clothing; toys for child passengers (maximum ten); one 1m x 1.5m prayer rug made from wool, cotton or synthetic fabric; one pair of binoculars (except night binoculars); and one gas stove (not the cylinders).

Syria All non-Syrians need a visa to enter Syria which has to be obtained in advance from the Syrian embassy in your home country. Consult www.syremb.com for online forms and requirements. Alternatively a single-entry visa can be obtained from the Syrian embassy in Ankara for €20, and takes just one day and requires two passport photos. There are no facilities for buying visas at the border.

CUSTOMS REGULATIONS

Duty-free allowances On entry you are allowed to bring in the following items duty free: 200 cigarettes (one box) and 50 cigars, plus 200g tobacco and 200 cigarette papers, or 200g chewing tobacco or 200g tobacco for a *nargile* (water-pipe) or 50g snuff. As well as the above allowances you can also buy at the Turkish duty-free shops on entry to the country a further 200 cigarettes, 100 cigars and 500g pipe tobacco. You may also bring in the following: 1.5kg coffee; 500g tea; 1kg chocolate; 1kg confectionery; one 100cl or two 75cl or 70cl bottles of wine and/or spirits; cologne, lavender water, perfume, essence, lotion (maximum 120ml each).

Antiquities It is strictly forbidden to export antiquities or antiques from Turkey and there are severe penalties for those caught attempting to do so. To export such items legally it is necessary to obtain a certificate from a directorate of a museum; consult www.kultur-turizm.gov.tr.

Drugs Bringing into or out of the country, together with the consumption of, marijuana and other narcotics is strictly forbidden and subject to heavy punishment. If you have prescribed medicine which you have to take on holiday with you, you will need a copy of your prescription or a doctor's note.

Other goods On departure, proof of purchase is necessary for any valuable item such as a Turkish carpet, so receipts need to be kept showing that any currency used in its purchase has been legally exchanged.

E EMBASSIES AND CONSULATES

TURKISH EMBASSIES ABROAD

Australia (Embassy) 60 MuggaWay, Red Hill, Canberra, ACT 2603; ☎ (2) 62950227
Canada (Embassy) 197 Wurtemburg Street, Ottawa, Ontario KIN 8L9; ☎ (613) 7894044
Ireland (Embassy) 11 Clyde Rd, Ballsbridge, Dublin 4; ☎ 01 668 5240, 01 660 1623; f 01 668 5014; e turkembassy@eircom.net
UK (Consulate) Consulate General for the Republic of Turkey, Rutland Lodge, Rutland Gardens, Knightsbridge, London SW7 1BW; ☎ 020 7591 6900/09068 347 348 (visa information line); e turkishconsulate@btconnect.com; www.turkishconsulate.org.uk
UK (Embassy) 43 Belgrave Sq, London SW1X 8PA; ☎ 020 7393 0202; f 020 7393 0066
United States (Embassy) 2525 Massachusetts Ave NW, Washington DC, 20008; ☎ (202) 6126740; www.turkishembassy.org

2

...IGN EMBASSIES IN ANKARA AND EASTERN TURKEY

Australia (Embassy) 7th floor, Uğur Mumcu Caddesi 88, Gaziosmanpaşa, Ankara; \ (312) 4599521; www.embaustralia.org.tr

Canada (Embassy) Cinnah Caddesi 58, Çankaya, Ankara; \ (312) 4092700

France (Embassy) Paris Caddesi 70, Kavalidere, Ankara; \ (312) 4554545; www.ambafrance-tr.org

Georgia (Embassy) Diplomatik Site, Kiliç Ali Sokak 12, Oran, Ankara; \ (312) 4918030

Germany (Embassy) Atatürk Bulvarı 114, Kavalidere, Ankara; \ (312) 4555100

Iran (Embassy) Tahran Caddesi 10, Kavalidere, Ankara; \ (312) 4274320

Iran (Consulate) Alparslan Bulvarı, 201 Sokak, Erzurum; (442) 3159983

Ireland (Embassy) Uğur Mumcu Caddesi no 88, MNG Binasi, B Blok, Kat 3, Gaziosmanpasha, Ankara; \ 312 4466172

Netherlands (Embassy) Hollanda Caddesi 3, Yıldız, Ankara; \ (312) 4091800

New Zealand (Embassy) 4th floor, Iran Caddesi 13, Kavalidere, Ankara; \ (312) 4679054; www.nzembassy.com/turkey

Russia (Embassy) Karyağdi Sokak 5, Çankaya, Ankara; \ (312) 4392122; www.turkey.mid.ru

Russia (Consulate) Sh Refik Cesur Caddesi 6, Ortahisar, Trabzon; (462) 3262728; rusconsultrb@ttnet.net.tr

Syria (Embassy) Abdullah Cevdet Sokak 7, Çankaya, Ankara; \ (312) 4409657

Syria (Consulate) Kemal Koker Caddesi 16, Gaziantep; \ (342) 2326047

UK (Consulate) Çakmak Caddesi, 124 Sokak Mahmut, Tece Is Merkezi A Blok, Kat 4/4, Mersin

UK (Embassy) Şehit Ersan Caddesi no 46/A; Çankaya 06680, Ankara; \ 312 4553344; e britembank@fco.gov.uk; www.britishembassy.org.tr

USA (Embassy) Atatürk Bulvarı 110, Kavalidere, Ankara; \ (312) 4555555

USA (Consulate) Girne Bulvarı 212, Güzelevler Mahallesi, Adana; \ (322) 3466262.

GETTING THERE AND AWAY

✈ **BY AIR** Flights to Istanbul from London take around four hours and arrive at **Atatürk International Airport** (*Yesilkoy, 28km west of Istanbul centre;* \ *(212) 4633000; www.ataturkairport.com*) which is on the European side of the city, with onward domestic flights leaving from the Domestic Terminal, a short taxi ride away. **Sabiha Gökçen International Airport** (*34912 Pendik, 50km from Taksim;* \ *(216) 5855000; www.sgairport.com*) is on the Asian side and therefore less convenient. Eastern Turkey has domestic airports at Adana, Adıyaman, Ağri, Batman, Diyarbakır, Elâzığ, Erzincan, Erzurum, Gaziantep, Hatay (Antakya), Kahramanmaraş, Kars, Malatya, Mardin, Muş, Samsun, Şanlıurfa, Trabzon and Van. All these have flights linking to Istanbul and Ankara, and sometimes in season from Izmir or even Antalya, making two-centre holidays within Turkey entirely feasible. Istanbul's Atatürk International Airport is 30–40 minutes' drive away from Sultanahmet, the tourist centre with the Blue Mosque, the Aya Sofya and the Topkapi Palace.

The most popular scheduled service carriers to Turkey from the UK are the national carrier Turkish Airlines (*www.thy.com*), British Airways (*www.ba.com*), Pegasus Airlines (*www.flypgs.com*) and easyJet (*www.easyjet.com*). These fly from London's airports (Heathrow, Gatwick and Stansted) but Turkish Airlines also operate a direct flight from Birmingham and Jet2 (*www.Jet2.com*) flies to Istanbul from East Midlands, Leeds Bradford, Manchester and Newcastle airports. Germanwings (www.germanwings.com) is a low-cost airline based in Cologne that operates from several German airports to Istanbul (Sabiha Gökçen) and Ankara. Spanair (www.spanair.com) is a Spanish airline that also flies from several Spanish airports to Istanbul's Sabiha Gökçen. Fewer services fly into the newer but smaller Sabiha Gökçen Airport on the Asian shore, though its smallness makes it very user-friendly with fewer queues. Both airports are linked to the city centre at Taksim Square, transport hub of Istanbul, by the bus service Havaş (\ *(212) 4654700; www.havas.com*). Follow the Havaş signs to find the pick-up point in both airports. At Taksim the pick-up/drop/off point is next to the Metropolitan Art Gallery, 20m from the Turkish Airlines office. It takes c40 minutes from Atatürk International Airport costing TL10 and more like an hour from Sabiha Gökçen Airport, costing TL11. The other public transport option is by the new metro line from Atatürk International Airport directly into Sultanahmet, the heart of Istanbul's tourist district. The alternative is the ubiquitous yellow taxis, which are metered with a standard rate across the whole country, and a night rate that applies between midnight and 06.00. Expect to pay about TL40 to Taksim from Atatürk International and TL65 from Sabiha Gökçen.

BY SEA There are no ferry services to eastern Turkey apart from the regular services to and from Girne (Kyrenia) in Northern Cyprus and Tasucu near Silifke, and between Mersin and Gazimağusa (Famagusta) (consult www.fergun.net for details). To arrive in western Turkey there are ferries operating between Ancona in southern Italy, running to Çeşme, near Izmir. They leave Ancona weekly on Saturdays at 22.30, arriving at Çeşme on Tuesdays at 06.30. Car cost €132 return and cabins range from €112–208 return. For further details, see www.ankertravel.net or www.tour-turkey.com/greece-and-turkey-ferries.htm.

BY TRAIN There are direct sleepers running once a day from Serbia (Belgrade, taking 22 hours), Greece (Thessaloniki, taking 11 hours), Bulgaria (Sofia, taking 15 hours) and Romania (Bucharest, taking 19 hours) into Istanbul run by the Turkish State Railway (*www.tcdd.gov.tr*). Fares range from TL50–250 depending on whether you just have a seat or a first-class couchette. For other options consult www.interrailnet.com and www.seat61.com/Turkey.htm. Once a year in August the ultra-luxurious Venice–Simplon Orient Express (*www.orient-expresstrains.com*) runs a six-day trip to Istanbul. This service sells out very quickly so early booking is recommended. All trains coming from the west arrive at Istanbul's historic Sirkeci station on the Golden Horn, just a short distance from Sultanahmet, where Istanbul's main sights are concentrated. From Haydarpaşa station on the Asian side trains also run to Aleppo in Syria once a week on Sundays (Toros Ekspresi, costing TL102 for a first class couchette, the only option available). It runs via Eskişehir, Konya and Adana and takes 30 hours. It was suspended in June 2008 due to the construction of the new high-speed line in Turkey – check with www.seat61.com/syria to get the latest position and other options. The new Gaziantep-Mosul/Baghdad line was also suspended in February 2010 due to long-term engineering work (check www.seat61.com for the current situation). The Trans-Asya Ekspresi to Tabriz in Iran also starts at Haydarpaşa, running weekly on Wednesdays via Ankara, Kayseri and Van, and taking 66 hours. The fare is still only TL112 for a first-class couchette. Consult www.rajatrains.com (the Iranian railways site) for details of these services, both of which also involve a five-hour crossing of Lake Van.

BY BUS Regular coach services run to Turkey from Bulgaria, Romania, Germany, Austria, Italy, Greece and Holland to the west as well as Azerbaijan, Armenia, Georgia, Iran and Syria to the east (see www.eurolines.com). The most comfortable and direct services run from Italy, Germany, Austria and Greece, with a direct route between Vienna and Istanbul taking 27 hours and costing about KK115 one-way, and a direct route from Athens to Istanbul taking 20 hours and costing about KK70. These routes are operated by Ulusoy (\ *(212) 4441888; www.ulusoy.com.tr*) and Varan Turizm (\ *(212) 4448999; www.varan.com.tr*) using large Mercedes coaches which are hard to beat. All buses (both international and domestic intercity) arrive into the colossal Esenler Coach Station (just known as

2

the *otogar*) in the northwest of Istanbul, about 10km from Sultanahmet. The cheapest way into Sultanahmet (for the Blue Mosque, Aya Sofya and the Topkapı Palace) is to catch the LRT (Light Rail Transit) service from its Otogar stop to Aksaray, then catch the metro from the Aksaray stop to the Sultanahmet stop. The whole journey takes 30 minutes and costs TL3. By taxi it costs about TL25 and takes around 20 minutes.

🚗 BY CAR You can drive your own car to Turkey via Bulgaria or Greece, or via Italy (using a ferry from the port of Ancona (see www.marmaralines.com), arriving at the Turkish port of Çeşme on the Aegean coast some two and a half days later (see page 47 for timings.). Your vehicle is allowed to stay in the country for up to six months after entry. At the border you will need to provide a valid passport, international driving licence, vehicle licence, international green card (insurance card) and vehicle registration document. Make sure your vehicle insurance is valid for the Asian side of the country. A **TR** sign can be bought at the border. If you want to keep your car in the country for longer than six months you will have to pay import tax. For further information consult the Turkish Touring and Automobile Club (📞 *+90 212 2828140; www.turkiyeturingveotomobilkurumu.com.tr*). The drive from the UK to Turkey is about 3,000km and the two common routes are a) the northern route via Belgium, Germany, Austria, Hungary, Romania and Bulgaria and b) the southern route via Belgium, Germany, Austria and Italy, with a ferry to Çeşme in Turkey. For route planning you can consult www.viamichelin.com.

⚠ BY PRIVATE YACHT On arrival in Turkish waters yachts must report to the nearest port of entry. In eastern Turkey the possibilities are Iskenderun, Botaş (Adana), Mersin and Tasucu on the Mediterranean coast, or Sinop, Samsun, Ordu, Giresun, Trabzon, Rize or Hopa on the Black Sea coast. Once details of the yacht, yachtsmen, intended route, passports, customs declarations and health clearance have been entered into a transit log, the boat will have permission to remain for two years. On leaving, you need to inform the relevant harbour authority again. For further details, consult www.chamber-of-shipping.org.tr.

➕ HEALTH *with Dr Felicity Nicholson*

With a few sensible precautions most health problems can be avoided, and most people only experience a few minor things which can easily be treated with medicines you can carry with you. Sunstroke is the most likely thing to strike if you are travelling in the summer months, so make sure you always have your head covered with a proper rimmed hat, and keep well hydrated. Use copious amounts of suncream to avoid burning. Stomach upsets are difficult to avoid in eastern Turkey so you should be careful and go prepared with suitable pills; the stronger the better. Lomotil and antibiotics can be bought over the counter from the chemists' shops (*eczane*) in all towns, so check before departure which type you want and buy them as necessary. Always carry a few sachets of oral rehydration salts with you. In central Anatolia and Cappadocia standards of hygiene are higher so you are less likely to pick anything up until you hit the east proper, ie: Adıyaman and eastwards. In the summer months the dust can cause much discomfort to the eyes, with aggravated catarrh in the nose and sore throats. It is a good idea therefore to take eye drops and throat lozenges. Protect yourself from mosquito bites by using whatever type of repellent you prefer, especially important at night to ensure a good night's sleep. The most likely serious incident requiring medical help is a road accident, though the emergency services are good even in rural areas.

WATER Tap water is usually drinkable but often does not taste very ni̅ likely to be heavily chlorinated. Bottled mineral water is readily obtainable, c̅ and usually drunk in preference, even by Turks. Water from a *çeşme* (spring) along the side of the road is drinkable and tastes good; though it may come out of a tap its origin will be from a freshwater spring. If in doubt, ask: *içilir* means 'drinkable', *içilmez* means 'not drinkable'.

VACCINATIONS No vaccinations are stipulated but the WHO (World Health Organization) advises that all travellers should have up-to-date cover for diphtheria, tetanus, measles, mumps, rubella and polio. Hepatitis B protection is also recommended. Rabies is endemic, so if you feel you may be exposed in very rural areas, consider having the course of injections before leaving.

MALARIA There is a slight risk of contracting malaria if you are travelling extensively in southeast Turkey, around Harran for example. Again, prevention is better than cure, so be sure to take with you good supplies of anti-mosquito wipes or sprays to protect exposed skin, and use the anti-mosquito electric plug-in tablets or liquid in your accommodation overnight. These are available in local pharmacies if you have forgotten to buy one in Boots before departure. Malaria tablets need to be taken 24 hours before and for three weeks after your exposure, so you will need to have bought these before departure. Most people would only do this if they are staying for prolonged periods in the southeast.

INSURANCE You will need to pay for any medical treatment you receive in Turkey. For this reason it is advisable to take out medical insurance before travelling. If you are trekking above 2,000m and using ropes or a guide, you will usually need to take out additional special cover. There are foreign-run hospitals in many of the larger cities. You can find a list of hospitals on the British Consulate in Turkey website www.britishembassy.gov.uk.

MEDICAL ADVICE AND CHECKLIST There are pharmacies in most cities and towns with trained pharmacists who can offer advice on minor illnesses. Many medicines which require a prescription in the UK can be bought over the counter, such as antibiotics. Items you could consider taking with you to cover most problems are:

- anti-diarrhoea pills
- anti-inflammatory pills (ibuprofen)
- paracetamol
- antihistamine pills
- antibacterial cream for minor cuts
- plasters to cover minor cuts
- DEET insect repellent wipes or spray
- oral rehydration salts
- insect-bite cream
- iodine tablets to purify water
- high-factor (at least 15) suncream
- eye drops
- sore-throat lozenges

TRAVEL CLINICS A full list of current travel clinic websites worldwide is available on www.istm.org/. For other journey preparation information, consult www.nathnac.org/ds/map_world.aspx. Information about various medications may be found on www.netdoctor.co.uk/travel.

UK

Berkeley Travel Clinic 32 Berkeley St, London W1J 8EL (near Green Park tube station); ☎ 020 7629 6233; ⏰ 10.00–18.00 Mon–Fri; 10.00–15.00 Sat.

The Travel Clinic Ltd, Cambridge 41 Hills Rd, Cambridge CB2 1NT; ☎ 01223 367362; e enquiries@travelclinic.ltd.uk; www.travelcliniccambridge.co.uk; ⏰ 10.00–16.00 Mon, Tue & Sat, 12.00–19.00 Wed & Thu, 11.00–18.00 Fri.

The Travel Clinic Ltd, Ipswich Gilmour Piper, 10 Fonnereau Rd, Ipswich IP1 3JP; ☎ 01223 367362; ⏰ 09.00–19.00 Wed, 09.00–13.00 Sat.

Edinburgh Travel Health Clinic 14 East Preston St, Newington, Edinburgh EH8 9QA; ☎ 0131 667 1030; www.edinburghtravelhealthclinic.co.uk; ⏰ 09.00–19.00 Mon–Wed, 09.00–18.00 Thu & Fri. Travel vaccinations & advice on all aspects of malaria prevention. All current UK prescribed anti-malaria tablets in stock.

Fleet Street Travel Clinic 29 Fleet St, London EC4Y 1AA; ☎ 020 7353 5678; e info@fleetstreetclinic.com; www.fleetstreetclinic.com; ⏰ 08.45–17.30 Mon–Fri. Injections, travel products & latest advice.

Hospital for Tropical Diseases Travel Clinic Mortimer Market Centre, Capper St (off Tottenham Ct Rd), London WC1E 6JB; ☎ 020 7388 9600; www.thehtd.org; ⏰ 09.00–16.30 Mon, Tue, Wed & Fri, 10.00–16.30 Wed. Offers consultations & advice, & is able to provide all necessary drugs & vaccines for travellers. Runs a Travellers Healthline Advisory Service (☎ 020 7950 7799) for country-specific information & health hazards. Also stocks nets, water purification equipment & personal protection measures. Travellers who have returned from the tropics & are unwell, with fever or bloody diarrhoea, can attend the walk-in emergency clinic at the Hospital without an appointment.

InterHealth Travel Clinic 111 Westminster Bridge Road, London, SE1 7HR, ☎ 020 7902 9000; e info@interhealth.org.uk www.interhealth.org.uk; ⏰ 08.30–17.30 Mon–Fri. Competitively priced, one-stop travel health service by appointment only.

Irish Republic

Tropical Medical Bureau 54 Grafton St, Dublin 2; ☎ +353 1 2715200; e graftonstreet@tmb.ie; www.tmb.ie. ⏰ Mon–Fri to 20.00 & Sat mornings.

USA

Centers for Disease Control 1600 Clifton Rd, Atlanta, GA 30333; ☎ (800) 232 4636 or (800)

MASTA (Medical Advisory Service for Travellers Abroad), at the London School of Hygiene & Tropical Medicine, Keppel St, London WC1E 7HT; ☎ 09068 224100 www.masta-travel-health.com; enquiries@masta.org. This is a premium-line number, charged at 60p per minute. For a fee, they will provide an individually tailored health brief, with up-to-date information on how to stay healthy, inoculations & what to take.

MASTA pre-travel clinics ☎ 01276 685040. Call or check www.masta-travel-health.com/travel-clinic.aspx for the nearest; there are currently 50 in Britain. They also sell malaria prophylaxis, memory cards, treatment kits, bednets, net treatment kits, etc.

NHS travel websites www.fitfortravel.nhs.uk or www.fitfortravel.scot.nhs.uk. Provide country-by-country advice on immunisation & malaria prevention, plus details of recent developments, & a list of relevant health organisations.

Nomad Travel Clinics Flagship store: 3–4 Wellington Terrace, Turnpike Lane, London N8 0PX; ☎ 020 8889 7014; e turnpike@nomadtravel.co.uk; www.nomadtravel.co.uk; walk in or appointments ⏰ 09.15–17.00 everyday with late night Thu. Also has clinics in west & central London, Bristol, Southampton & Manchester — see website for further information. As well as dispensing health advice, Nomad stocks mosquito nets & other anti-bug devices, & an excellent range of adventure travel gear. Runs a Travel Health Advice line on ☎ 0906 863 3414.

Trailfinders Immunisation Centre 194 Kensington High St, London W8 7RG; ☎ 020 7938 3999; www.trailfinders.com/travelessentials/travelclinic.htm; ⏰ 09.00–17.00 Mon, Tue, Wed & Fri, 09.00–18.00 Thu, 10.00–17.15 Sat. No appointment necessary.

Travelpharm The Travelpharm website (www.travelpharm.com) offers up-to-date guidance on travel-related health & has a range of medications available through their online mini-pharmacy.

For other clinic locations, & useful information specific to tropical destinations, check their website.

232 6348; e cdcinfo@cdc.gov; www.cdc.gov/travel. The central source of travel information in the

USA. Each summer they publish the invaluable *Health Information for International Travel.*
IAMAT (International Association for Medical Assistance to Travelers): 1623 Military Rd, #279

Niagara Falls, NY 14304-1745; ☏ 716 754 4883; e info@iamat.org; www.iamat.org. A non-profit organisation with free membership that provides lists of English-speaking doctors abroad.

Canada
IAMAT (International Association for Medical Assistance to Travellers) Suite 10, 1287 St Clair Street West, Toronto, Ontario M6E 1B8; ☏ 416 652 0137; www.iamat.org

TMVC Suite 314, 1030 W Georgia Street, Vancouver, BC V6E 2Y3; ☏ (604) 681 5656; e vancouver@tmvc.com; www.tmvc.com. One-stop medical clinic for all your international travel health & vaccination needs.

Australia & New Zealand
TMVC (Travel Doctors Group) ☏ 1300 65 88 44; www.tmvc.com.au. 30 clinics in Australia & New Zealand, including: *Auckland* Canterbury Arcade, 174 Queen St, Auckland 1010, New Zealand; ☏ (64) 9 373 3531; e auckland@traveldoctor.co.nz; *Brisbane* 75a Astor Terrace, Spring Hill, Brisbane, QLD 4000, Australia; (07) 3815 6900; brisbane@traveldoctor.com.au;

Melbourne 393 Little Bourke St, Melbourne, Vic 3000, Australia; ☏ (03) 9935 8100; melbourne@traveldoctor.com.au; *Sydney* 428 George St, Sydney, NSW 2000, Australia; ☏ (2) 9221 7133; e sydney@traveldoctor.com.au. **IAMAT** 206 Papanui Rd, Christchurch 5, New Zealand; www.iamat.org

South Africa
SAA-Netcare Travel Clinics ☏ 011 802 0059; e travelinfo@netcare.co.za; www.travelclinic.co.za. Eleven clinics throughout South Africa.

TMVC NHC Health Centre, Cnr Beyers Naude & Waugh Northcliff; ☏ 0861 300 911; e info@traveldoctor.co.za; www.traveldoctor.co.za. Consult the website for clinic locations.

SAFETY

Eastern Turkey has only recently reopened to tourism after several years of political instability and lack of security. Everywhere is now accessible and can be visited without restriction, and travelling around is very safe and easy. Petty crime rates for such things as pickpocketing and car theft are very low, and there are too few tourists for the habit of overcharging foreigners to have caught on. However, the region has had a history of violence between its various ethnic groups, which resulted in martial law being imposed by the Turkish government throughout the 1980s and 1990s. Very few foreigners get caught up in violent incidents, and if they do, it tends to be by accident. In July 2008 three German tourists were kidnapped by the PKK, a Kurdish separatist group, on the slopes of Mount Ararat, and released unharmed a few days later, an act of protest against the German government for its closure of PKK offices in Germany.

POLICE AND JANDARMA There are two types of police in Turkey – civil police (*polis*) and military police (*jandarma*). In many places you will find that there is just one or the other, and that both fulfil the same function. If you need to report a crime you should go to the nearest police station. You will usually be asked to submit and sign a statement. It is sensible to request a copy in case you need it for your own insurance at a later point. The jandarma or gendarmerie is a branch of the armed forces which polices the rural areas where there are no civilian police. As long as you behave sensibly, dress decently and do not take any photos near military zones, you will have nothing but courtesy from the jandarma and the other arms of the police. Horror stories of people being clapped in prison only apply if you are carrying drugs or have infringed the law. Make sure your passport and any car documents are in order. There are no road blocks on the main roads, and on the minor dirt tracks the only road blocks can be where the road passes very close to the Iranian or Russian borders.

The only other way you can fall foul of the law is if you attempt to export any antiquities from the country without obtaining a permit (see page 45). Buried treasure is an obsession in eastern Turkey and illicitly dug up Urartian bronzes or Byzantine coins are always checked to see if they are gold. Beware that the legislation on antiquities carries severe penalties if you are found with any in your possession.

PASSPORTS Turks have compulsory ID cards which they must carry on them at all times. Foreigners are expected to carry such ID with them, which means that you should keep your passport with you at all times.

WOMEN TRAVELLERS Bus or long-distance coach is the best and safest way for single women to travel round the country. Single women should keep away from traditional male enclaves like the *meyhane* (wine house) and *birahane* (beer house) as their presence there drinking will be taken as an invitation for sexual attention. In cities where there is a university and therefore a student population there may be some Western-style *barlar* (bars) where it is acceptable for women to go for a drink if other female students are present. Otherwise, you should bear in mind that gender segregation is much more prevalent in eastern Turkey than in the western parts of the country, and foreign women who drink too much in public will be regarded as conforming to stereotype and only after one thing. In Turkish baths, *hammams*, there are always separate times for men and women. Etiquette varies from hammam to hammam about whether or not you remove your underwear under your *pestemal* (short cotton sarong you are given), while men keep theirs on at all times. Carry a headscarf to cover your head and shoulders on visiting a mosque and always dress modestly so as not to invite unwanted attention. Body language is very important, especially eye contact. If you make too much direct eye contact with a male stranger it is seen as very forward and again, inviting attention. Try to learn therefore to make only as much eye contact as is necessary when buying tickets, food, etc, so that it is clear you are only interested in carrying out the task. Watch how Turkish women behave and interact with other men in public. Whether or not you get hassled as a female in Turkey (or any Muslim country) has nothing to do with how attractive you are. A blond blue-eyed woman for example will not get hassled if she behaves modestly and dresses and carries herself demurely, because her whole body language is conveying she is not available. The best manner to convey is polite but distant.

FAMILIES AND CHILDREN The family is very important to Turkish people and children of all ages are welcomed everywhere. This does not mean that society is child-centred, as nowhere will you find child menus or toys supplied. It is simply that they are accepted as a normal part of life, so adults can relax and enjoy themselves. Even very young children are taken out to eat in restaurants in the evening with their parents and amuse themselves happily with the forks and spoons on the table, eating small amounts of their parents' food. High chairs are a rarity, as young children either sit on an adult's knee or are big enough to have their own chair. Formula milk and nappies are available now in the eastern regions, either at the budding supermarkets or at the pharmacies. Baby food in jars is not always easy to find, however, but restaurants and hotels will usually be happy to purée food for you. UHT milk is widely available in small cartons with a straw. Some hotels can provide cots if these are requested in advance, but standards vary quite widely, and sides can be lower than those common in the UK, making them fine for a baby but less suitable for a mobile toddler. Child car seats are not regarded as standard, so you should check with the car-hire firm whether they can provide these on request.

GAY/LESBIAN TRAVELLERS Homosexuality is illegal in Turkey (as it is in most countries where Islam is the predominant religion), and whilst it is tolerated in big cities like Istanbul and Ankara, and there are even a few gay bars, in eastern Turkey it is a different story and you will need to be very careful in public, as there is still strong prejudice against both gays and lesbians. There is a Turkish gay and lesbian support group (*www.lambaistanbul.org*) which even publishes a magazine, and there are now a couple of gay-friendly travel agents such as Absolute Sultans (*www.absolutesultans.com*) and Pride Travel (*www.turkey-gay-travel.com*).

DISABLED TRAVELLERS In Turkey's eastern regions, many Turkish cities, hotels and tourist sites have no wheelchair access, though Turks will always try their best to improvise and be helpful. A visit to eastern Turkey will therefore be very challenging to disabled travellers, with virtually no adapted toilets, ramps or wide doorways. Turkish Airlines does however give 25% discount to travellers with minimum 40% disability and their accompanying carer(s), but you need a doctor's letter as proof at the time of booking. Ankara and Cappadocia do have better facilities, but it is best to check in advance via a tour operator. There is one tour operator, Mephisto Voyage (*www.mephistovoyage.com*) based at the İn Pension (see page 142) in Çavuşin, which can arrange special tours of Cappadocia for mobility-impaired people, using the Joelette system, a comfortable wheelchair on one wheel with adjustable treadle, head- and foot-rest.

WHAT TO TAKE

Soap is not always provided at the smaller pensions, though towels usually are. Bring your own suntan potions, toothpaste and medicines as you may not find the brands you want in Turkey. An initial supply of toilet paper is a good idea – amazing how useful it can be and how often it is not there. Bring your own film if your camera is not digital. If you are driving bring a tyre-pressure gauge and use it regularly, especially after going off tarmac. A powerful torch is good for exploring caves, tunnels or the toilet when the light does not work. Bring a sheet sleeping bag if you are travelling on a budget to insulate you from heavily used bedding. A universal sink plug is also useful as hotels rarely provide them in basins or baths.

MAPS A good map is essential. The maps produced by the Turkish Tourist Office are better than nothing, but it is well worth buying a good map. The best ones currently available are *Turkey GeoCenter Euro Map* (2007), *Rough Guide Map Turkey* (2007) and *Turkey Insight Travel Map* (2008).

ELECTRICITY Electricity throughout Turkey is 220V AC. A two-pin round plug is used so a travel plug adapter will be necessary for anyone wishing to use any appliance with the square three-pin UK plug.

$ MONEY

In 2005 the New Turkish Lira (Yeni Türk Lirasi – YTL) was introduced and six zeros were deleted from the existing Turkish lira, which had become impractical – before this about TL2,500,000 was equivalent to one pound sterling. From 2006

2

only the new currency has been in circulation and the lira is now known only as the TL (Turkish lira). There are 100 *kurus* (Kr) to the Turkish lira. Turkish currency is available in the following denominations: TL1, TL5, TL10, TL20, TL50, TL100 (banknotes); and Kr1, Kr5, Kr10, Kr25, Kr50, TL1 (coins).

You can obtain currency before travelling to Turkey or on arrival. Exchange rates are usually slightly better inside Turkey and all international airports have exchange facilities. Cash can usually be exchanged without charging commission in exchange offices, banks or the bigger hotels of category $$$ (see page 60) and above. Scottish notes are not accepted in Turkey. **ATMs** are available in most areas, and they accept major UK credit and debit cards and give instructions in English. It is a good idea to inform your bank in advance that you are travelling to Turkey as some will automatically put a stop on cards after the first usage in an assumption that your card has been stolen.

Avoid **travellers' cheques**, which are cumbersome and time-consuming to change in banks.

Exchange rates are published daily in Turkish newspapers. If you are planning to exchange currency back from TL before leaving the country, or are making a major purchase which may need to be declared in customs, you will need to keep your transaction receipts to show your currency has been legally exchanged. There is no limit to the amount of foreign and Turkish currency to be brought into Turkey. Up to US$5,000 worth of Turkish or foreign currency can be taken out of the country provided it can be shown that the currency has been obtained from authorised banks. You can obtain this proof by requesting a receipt from the bank teller or the ATM.

CREDIT CARDS The bigger hotels ($$$ and upwards), international car-hire agencies like Avis and Europcar and the more expensive shops in cities will usually accept American Express, Diners Club, Visa and MasterCard, though unless you are always staying in the top-class hotels, it is best not to rely on them but rather to take them as a fall back. They are not in general use in the more rural areas, and not in petrol stations, so make sure you always have some cash in reserve.

BUDGETING

The cost of actually getting to Turkey will be by far the biggest element in your holiday budget. After that it is a question of how you travel: car hire is obviously the most expensive way, averaging out at about £30 a day, while travel by bus or train will be more like £10 a day per person. If however you are four people travelling together, car hire starts to become cheaper, as petrol costs in Turkey are still relatively low. Add to that the fact that once you have a car you can also bulk-buy water, olives, cheese and general picnic provisions, and you can again save a bit of money.

Once all travel expenses are settled, the cost of holidaying in Turkey is very low, far lower than in most Mediterranean countries, and at the time of writing the pound sterling had not fallen as badly against the Turkish lira as it had against the US dollar and the euro. A reasonable daily budget for two people including accommodation in a three-star mid-range hotel, meals, drinks and entry fees will be about £40. If you are prepared to spend less on accommodation and eat in more basic places or from snack stalls you can bring the daily budget down to £20–25 a day. If on the other hand you want to stay in the top places and eat in the best restaurants throughout eastern Turkey, then think in terms of a daily budget for two of closer to £150. In many parts of eastern Turkey it will not even be possible to spend that sort of amount as the hotels and restaurants at that level simply do not exist. Doğubeyazıt, at the foot of Mount Ararat, is said cheapest place to eat in the whole of Turkey. You can eat out for break, and dinner and still spend less than £6 a day.

TIPPING Tipping is something which Turks do not generally expect as the automatic right that it has become in the West. It is regarded rather as a gesture of appreciation for good service, and since service in Turkey is usually excellent, most Turks do in practice leave tips. In restaurants 10% is usual, although in smaller basic restaurants, especially in rural areas, tips closer to 5% are fine. In all hotels registered with the Ministry of Culture and Tourism, 10% is added to your bill automatically. Taxis are the exception worth knowing about: Turks never tip taxi drivers.

GETTING AROUND

✈ BY AIR The national carrier Turkish Airlines (Türk Hava Yolları) (*www.thy.com*) flies at very reasonable prices between all the main cities of eastern Turkey, namely Adana, Adıyaman, Ağri, Batman, Diyarbakır, Elâzığ, Erzincan, Erzurum, Gaziantep, Hatay (Antakya), Kahramanmaraş, Kars, Malatya, Mardin, Muş, Samsun, Şanlıurfa, Trabzon and Van. All these cities have flights at least once or twice a day linking them to Istanbul and Ankara (not to each other – for that, you need the intercity buses see page 57). The flights range in time between one and two hours, bringing even the remotest corners of eastern Turkey within easy reach. In the summer high season there are also connecting flights to the eastern airports to and from Izmir and even to and from Antalya, making two-centre holidays within Turkey a realistic option. Consult www.turkishairlines.com for the latest up-to-date timings and prices or their domestic subsidiary Anadolujet at www.anadolujet.com. By way of example, flights to Van from Atatürk International Airport, Istanbul are daily at 07.15 and 12.15, arriving at 09.15 and 14.15 respectively. Both cost TL129 one-way.

Other airlines who fly within Turkey to eastern domestic airports are OnurAir (*www.onurair.com.tr*), Pegasus Airlines (*www.flypegs.com*) and Sun Express (*www.sunexpress.com*). For all internal flights you need only arrive at the airport one hour before departure. Apart from Ankara, all the eastern airports are very small and processing through on arrival and departure is very quick.

The Domestic Terminal (*İç Hatlar*) at Istanbul is about 1km away from Atatürk International Airport (*Dış Hatlar*) on the European side, and a courtesy shuttle bus operates between the two every few minutes. If you are making an onward internal flight from Istanbul, which will usually be the case if you are intending to tour the eastern part of Turkey, you must go out of the International Terminal and wait for the courtesy bus to the Domestic Terminal. Check-in arrangements at the Domestic Terminal can be confusing, and it is best to ask rather than assume, as you can easily waste time standing in the wrong queue. Tickets can be bought online with the usual system of the cheaper tickets available a couple of months in advance. They can also be bought on the spot in the Domestic Terminal, although this is risky as the flights can get full. Tickets for internal flights are not usually issued by Turkish Airlines in advance, and have to be collected from the ticket office in the Domestic Terminal, a procedure for which a strict 'take a number and wait your turn' queuing system applies, so allow at least an extra half hour for that. On the flights themselves a simple snack is served with soft drinks as the flights are never longer than two hours. No alcohol is available.

The pilots on the internal flights are often like bus drivers. They taxi along the runway at great speed to the take-off point while the cabin crew struggle to keep their balance in demonstrating the emergency procedures. On landing they are inclined to slam on the brakes the second the wheels touch the ground, so that they can take an earlier slipway turn-off as a short cut to the docking bay.

BY BOAT There are no domestic boat services between the Turkish Mediterranean ports or along the Black Sea ports. The Turkish Maritime Lines car ferry no longer runs along the Black Sea coast to Istanbul. Travel by sea is therefore only possible in private boats (see page 48).

BY TRAIN All onward travel from Istanbul is from the Asian side at Haydarpasha station, Kadıköy \ (216) 3364470, though tickets for travel eastwards can still be bought at Sirkeci station (see page 47) on the European side. The train stations accept cash only, no credit cards. The rail network was constructed in the late Ottoman period and often follows a mysterious routing system, though newer more direct lines are being laid. A comfortable modern train runs once a week from Istanbul to Tehran called the Trans-Asia Express, and a train from Istanbul to Syria called the Toros Express (see page 47). There is now also a high-speed Istanbul to Ankara express train which takes just six hours. The following towns east of Ankara are all connected to a rail service of some sort: Samsun, Amasya, Sivas, Divriği, Erzincan, Elâzığ, Malatya, Kayseri, Konya, Niğde, Adana, Mersin, Maraş, Gaziantep, Diyarbakır, Tatvan, Van, Kars and Erzurum. The only railway station on the Turkish Black Sea coast is at Samsun. The main train lines are:

Eylül Mavi – Haydarpaşa (Istanbul) to Malatya (via Ankara, Kayseri & Sivas)

Doğu Ekspresi – Haydarpaşa to Kars (via Ankara, Kayseri, Sivas & Erzurum)

Güney Ekspresi – Haydarpaşa to Kurtulan (via Ankara, Kayseri, Sivas, Malatya & Diyarbakır)

İç Anadolu Mavi – Haydarpaşa to Adana (via Malatya)

Meram Ekspresi – Haydarpaşa to Konya

Toros Ekspresi – Haydarpaşa to Gaziantep (via Konya & Adana)

Vangölü Ekspresi – Haydarpaşa to Tatvan (via Ankara, Kayseri & Malatya)

Fares to Ankara range from TL10 to TL70 depending on the train itself and the type of seat chosen.

Full details are given in each regional chapter of the relevant train services and routes. In general the train is suitable for longer journeys, but services are a lot less frequent than intercity bus services with departures just once or twice a day, often slower, and not necessarily any cheaper. For example, the Vangölü Ekspresi from Istanbul to Tatvan on Lake Van takes nearly two days, while the bus takes less than 24 hours for a similar price. Reliability has also been a bit of a problem, when some services are suddenly cancelled with no warning or heavily delayed. If time is not a problem, the pleasure of leisurely train travel through spectacular scenery has a lot to be said for it. The best trains have air conditioning, a restaurant car (limited but adequate – you might want to supplement with your own food a little) and are of the same standard as in western Europe. Consult www.seat61.com/Turkey2 or www.turkeytravelplanner.com. Tickets can be booked and paid for online at the Turkish State Railways website www.tcdd.gov.tr (\ (212) 4448233). There is a 20% discount for children under 16, students, senior citizens and disabled travellers. For further discounts Euro-domino, Inter-Rail and Balkan Flexipasses are valid on the Turkish network, but not Eurail. Places in the sleeper carriages (*yatakli*) need reserving well in advance especially at peak holiday times. They have private sleeping compartments for one to three people complete with all bedding with washbasin. A couchette carriage (*küşetli*) has shelf-like beds in compartments shared with four or six people and no bedding provided, unless they are described as *örtülü küşetli* (covered couchette). The usual system is for a long-distance train to have a mix of carriages, such as one sleeper, one covered couchette, one couchette and three Pullman (reclining seat) carriages and one carriage for unreserved seating. Toilets on board are shared and adequate

🚐 BY COACH/BUS This is by far the most popular and convenient way to travel by public transport inside Turkey. Every town and city has its own bus station (*otogar*) with many routes linking every corner of the country, many frequent services and many companies to choose from, each varying slightly in frequency and comfort. The competition between them means that the system is efficient and cheap. Some of the biggest names are Kamil Koç (*www.kamilkoc.com.tr*), Metro (*www.metroturizm.com.tr*), Ulusoy (*www.ulusoy.com.tr*) and Varan (*www.varan.com.tr/english*). Varan and Metro have an online reservations service so you can even make reservations from the UK, something that is otherwise extremely difficult to do unless you speak Turkish. Tickets can usually be bought on the day at the bus station, where each bus company has its own office, though at weekends or on public holidays it is advisable to book in advance. Seats are reserved, so to ensure the best position on the bus you can buy your ticket a day or two in advance. The middle seats are generally considered to be the best, as the ride can be bumpy towards the front or rear. Bus companies also have central offices in cities and large towns where tickets can be bought. The coaches are clean, modern and air conditioned, with comfortable seating. They make regular stops on longer journeys every two hours or so, at established points, often at restaurants attached to petrol stations, where toilet facilities and refreshments are always available. Complimentary water or soft drinks are usually handed out during the journey, as well as sweets and refreshing splashes of cologne. The *otogar* tends to be situated a little out of the centre, so it is usually necessary to catch a local bus or taxi there. Services always run punctually. Sometimes the bus companies run shuttle minibus services between their town offices and the *otogar*. Journey times are often the same, if not shorter, than the equivalent train journey.

🚕 BY TAXI AND *DOLMUŞ* Taxis are always yellow. Although meters are usually fitted in eastern Turkey, they rarely work, so it is wise to agree on the fare first. If you are travelling outside the city boundaries it is usual to agree a fixed rate in advance. The *dolmuş* is a shared taxi, usually a minibus, sometimes a large car, which follows specific routes within larger towns and cities, picking people up and setting them down anywhere along the route. It is recognisable by its yellow band. The word *dolmuş* means literally 'stuffed', from the fact that they do not follow a set timetable but simply set off when they are full. The fares are fixed by the relevant municipality and each passenger pays according to the distance travelled and can get out at any of the specified stops. Much cheaper than a private taxi, it is often good to take a dolmuş from the airport to the bus station or to the centre of town. As well as linking the city centres with the suburbs, there are also some intercity dolmuş services, but these are more expensive than the bus and often less comfortable.

🚲 BY BICYCLE Eastern Turkey is a good place for cyclists (Bettina Selby did it alone in 1992 and wrote her book *Beyond Ararat* Mountain House Publishing 1993), as roads are often empty and little used. In Cappadocia there are already plenty of places hiring out bicycles (see page 142), a perfect way to explore the lesser-known valleys. It is possible to take your own bicycle on Turkish trains and buses as long as you have notified the train or bus company in advance. On buses they will put it in the baggage compartment underneath with all the other luggage (so beware of possible damage), and on trains they will put it in a baggage compartment, assuming the train has one. Often it is the slower trains that have them, not the faster trains with Pullman seats and couchettes, so check in advance direct with the station concerned if you speak Turkish or else via an agency like Tur-ISTA (see page 43). On ferries you can just wheel it on and off yourself.

BY PRIVATE CAR Travel by car is by far the best way of exploring Turkey. Without one you will be able to see less, or you will need more time (adapting your plans to bus schedules, etc) to see everything. The roads in central Anatolia and eastern Turkey are usually very empty. Many places in eastern Turkey lie off the main roads, making them difficult to reach with public transport. Having your own car is therefore a huge help and saving in time, and sometimes even in cost if you are travelling in a group of four, say. Another saving if travelling by car is that you can stock up with suitable picnic food and drink and keep it in the boot, so that you are not dependent on finding somewhere to eat during the day. You can also keep to your own timetable. The number of private cars on the road is still quite small in relation to the number of buses and trucks, due to the high price of cars in the country. The area where you do get heavy traffic is on the main transit highway from Ankara south through Aksaray and Pozantı to Tarsus, along the coast to Adana, Gaziantep, Urfa and Nusaybin, where the transit route enters the eastern corner of Syria or border crossings to Mosul in Iraq.

The only road hazard for the most part is therefore livestock, large quantities of sheep and cows which frequently stray all over the road and stay there insistently to the total indifference of the shepherds. Their dogs, some with spiked anti-wolf collars, are often quite ferocious and will chase your car as if it is a runaway outsize sheep, snarling at the wheels. One other thing you will learn to ignore is the insistent waving down by men standing in the middle of nowhere. Their frantic waggling hand motion suggests there has been some ghastly accident or that you are being warned about something dreadful round the next corner, when all he wants is a lift.

Driving at night is not recommended as the road markings are usually poor and other vehicles, especially trucks, can often have faulty lights or no lights at all.

When self-driving round eastern Turkey always make sure your petrol tank is at least a third full, as **petrol stations** can be few and far between, routinely about 100km. Unleaded petrol (*kursunuz*) is usually available. Always carry a copy of your driving licence, together with your passport and insurance documents in the car at all times.

Roads between the cities are pleasantly empty on the whole, with traffic consisting of lorries and vans more than other saloon cars. In the cities signposting can be erratic, so try to look at a map before arrival to orient yourself in advance. Traffic behaviour is far more orderly than in the Middle East, though not as orderly as in Europe. The road network is good and well maintained, and driving is on the right, as in continental Europe. The urban speed limit is 50km/h and on rural roads it is 90km/h.

Important **road signs** include:

- DUR: stop
- DIKKAT: attention (warning you, eg: of road works)
- ŞEHİR MERKESİ: town centre
- TEK YOL: one-way

On signs at the entrance to towns you will see figures given for *rakım* (altitude) and *nufus* (population) below the town name. On public bins you can see written *çöp bana at* (throw the rubbish into me). Carved into hillsides or written in slogans above the entrance to military camps you will see *Ne mutlu 'Türküm' diyene* (How happy is he who can say he is a Turk), and *Her şey vatan için* (Everything for the homeland).

CAR HIRE All the major international car-hire agencies, as well as a number of local ones, have offices at airports and all major centres. Europcar (*www.europcar.com*) and Avis (*www.avis.co.uk*) are the ones with the most offices across eastern Turkey (Adana, Ankara, Diyarbakır, Erzurum, Gaziantep, Kayseri, Konya, Samsun, Şanlıurfa, Ürgüp and Van), and arrangements can often be made to pick up in one location and drop off in another. The German car-hire company Sixt (*www.sixt.com*) also has offices in Adana, Ankara and for Cappadocia, the cities of Kayseri and Nevşehir, and Hertz (*www.hertz.co.uk*) has offices in Adana, Ankara, Diyarbakır, Kayseri and Mersin. Rates start at about £30 per day for unlimited mileage in a small saloon car including collision damage waiver, and the minimum driver age is 23. If your driving licence does not have a photo, it would be advisable to get an international driving licence from the AA (*www.theaa*.com) before setting off.

ACCOMMODATION

Standards of accommodation in eastern Turkey have improved dramatically over the last 20 years, so that on the whole you will find the full range from top to bottom. The upper range in particular has seen great leaps forward, with a handful of boutique hotels now available in places like Diyarbakır, Mardin, Gaziantep, Urfa and even Kars. These are usually in restored and converted Ottoman buildings such as caravanserais (Diyarbakır and Antakya), residential mansions (Mardin, Gaziantep, Kars and Urfa), and in Cappadocia there are literally scores of boutique hotels and pensions in imaginatively converted cave-complexes or in old Greek mansions, often restored by cultured ex-professionals or academics from Istanbul seeking a mid-life change of pace. Most are in the 4 and 5 star price bracket given below, and many have excellent restaurants. The big towns like Adana, Antakya and Erzurum also have one or two top-range modern business hotels. The mid-range places are harder to find and tend to be run-down ex-business hotels (as in Van or Doğubeyazıt). In many smaller towns you will still struggle to find anywhere above rock bottom, such as Hasankeyf, Hakkâri, and Bitlis, with only simple family-run establishments, the closest thing to home-stays available in eastern Turkey. The best-provided area is Cappadocia with charming accommodation at all levels, as are Safranbolu and Kastamonu with their restored Ottoman mansions at reasonable prices. Many tourist hotels and pensions in Cappadocia and along the Black Sea close in winter from November to March. Full details and listings are given in each chapter and one additional good source

NO FORBIDDEN ZONES

There is still a widespread belief that much of eastern Turkey is out of bounds and heavily militarised. While this was true until 1960 and for a spell of particular Kurdish activity during the 1990s, it is no longer the case, and the whole of the country can now be travelled with ease and with no necessity for permits. The Turkish for forbidden zone is *Yasak Bölge*, a sign you will only see now in the vicinity of dams, which are regarded as military installations and potential terrorist targets, and at military camps. You can now travel all round eastern Turkey without ever seeing a single soldier.

of mid-range accommodation suitable for independent travellers is the *Little Hotel Book*, published annually and available in bookshops or through www.nisa.nyan.net. Prices in the bigger top-end hotels are often given in US dollars or euros and credit cards are accepted, but in the smaller bottom-end places Turkish liras are the norm and cash is required. In the mid-range it can be either. There are no apartment hotels or youth hostels. Official campsites are to be found in Cappadocia, on the Mediterranean coast, in a few of the Georgian valleys around Artvin and on the way up to Nemrut Dağı, but are few and far between and not the norm. Rough camping is permitted anywhere, though probably not advisable in the Kurdish areas unless you are with a local guide. The following price code has been used throughout:

$$$$$	luxury	£100+	TL240+
$$$$	upmarket	£75–100	TL180–240
$$$	mid-range	£50–75	TL120–180
$$	budget	£25–50	TL60–120
$	shoestring	<£25	up to TL60

Prices refer to the price of a standard double room in high season. Accommodation listings in each chapter are given in price order, starting with the most expensive.

CAMPING There are few campsites in eastern Turkey. Cappadocia and the Nemrut Dağı area have some camping sites of a sort, though the facilities will not be what you would expect in Europe. Rough camping is legal except where notices state otherwise, but it is not generally advisable unless you are on a trek or climb with local guides. If you do decide to camp rough it is best to do so near a local *jandarma* post, after first asking permission.

✖ EATING AND DRINKING

No-one comes to eastern Turkey for the food, and while Turkish cuisine has been praised, even by French gourmets, as one of the finest in the world, sadly such praise rarely applies in eastern Turkey, where food is on the whole far more limited than in the rest of the country. Notable exceptions are in the extreme southern parts close to Syria, heavily influenced by Syrian cuisine, so in towns like Mardin, Gaziantep and Antakya, there awaits you a gastronomic experience of a different order. Make the most of it, for as you head north and east, the food becomes increasingly basic and unvarying. Doğubeyazıt, at the foot of Mount Ararat, is known as the cheapest place to eat in all of Turkey, and quantity outweighs quality by a long way. Hors d'oeuvres or *mezze*, usually the highpoint of Turkish cuisine, are hard to come by except in the areas close to the Syrian border. Soup is usually the only thing on offer as the prelude to the main course. The common **staples** are as follows:

- Hot yoghurt soup with rice and mint (usually quite good)
- Tomato soup (very bland, a Heinz lookalike)
- Potato or lentil soup (variable, and best inspected before deciding)
- Lukewarm or cold green beans cooked in tomato sauce and grease
- Baked beans
- Chips or pilav rice
- Salads with tomatoes, cucumber, onion and green chillies
- Stuffed green peppers with rice and pine nuts (usually cold, and though rather greasy, not at all bad)

When Frederick Burnaby, an English colonel travelling incognito on horseback in eastern Turkey in the 1870s to observe the Russian border just before the Crimean War, had to stay in the private houses of various hosts in the days before any kind of hotel was available, he ranked them in descending order of squalor from Turks, to Armenians, to Kurds, to Nestorian (Christians) at the very bottom:

'The Armenians in their habits of body are filthy to the last degree. Their houses and clothes are infested with vermin. The Turks, on the contrary, are much cleaner, and are most particular about the use of the bath.' Fleas often stopped him sleeping and his English manservant complained to their host: 'There are many fleas; my Effendi cannot sleep.'

'It is true,' replied the Armenian, 'but there are by no means so many here as in a Kurd village a few miles distant. The Kurds have been obliged to abandon their houses in consequence of these insects. They have had to live in tents for several months past.'

A Turkish major staying in a Kurdish house had moved out of the room before Burnaby's arrival, the insects proving too much for him. The Kurdish host had said disparagingly: 'These Turks have thin skins; only think of their being frightened by a few fleas. You Ingliz are much braver people.'

'My Effendi is very particular about these matters,' remarked Burnaby's manservant, 'if he is bitten, there will be no *baksheesh*.'

When there was a choice of spending the night in a Nestorian village, Burnaby says: 'The inhabitants of these hamlets possess the reputation of being dirtier than the Kurds, so the traveller who is wise will invariably elect to spend the night with the mountaineers.'

Burnaby found the Persians cleaner than all these, however, and when he commented to his Turkish escort that the Persian roads and houses were much cleaner than those in Turkey, the captain replied sorrowfully: 'That is true: the little dogs can do some things well, but they are sly and deceitful.'

Burnaby was no shrinking violet. In 1882 he crossed the English Channel by hot-air balloon, sought out active service, and died aged 43 in 1885 in hand-to-hand fighting in the Battle of Abou Klea in Egypt.

Practical Information **EATING AND DRINKING** 2

- Chicken cooked in grease
- Meat (mutton) stew with aubergine and okra
- Meat kebab, lamb or mutton (usually quite grisly)
- Trout (*alabalık*) plainly grilled or fried (available close to rivers)
- Rice pudding (strangely comforting)
- Crème caramel (usually very good)
- Baklava (not one for picnics – too sticky)
- Fresh fruit in season: strawberries (May), oranges and apples (late summer), guavas and green *erik* (a small sharp kind of plum), peaches, cherries (May and June)   *Needs washed*
- Nuts: pistachios are especially good in Gaziantep and Antakya

In the central Anatolian areas and along the Black Sea coast the food is noticeably better than in the east proper, and there is more variety and imagination shown in the preparation. In the cheaper eateries (often called *lokantas* or *tesisleris*) all across the eastern region there is also the widespread habit of bringing your food in a totally random order, so your main course may arrive before your soup. Almost all the food is pre-prepared in large open aluminium tureens in the

THE PICNIC TRADITION

In Ottoman times there was a great tradition on weekends and holidays of the whole family taking food off into the countryside and sitting on carpets beside rivers, lakes and under trees all day, just chatting, enjoying nature and the outdoor life. Many paintings and drawings exist of Ottoman picnics which illustrate this custom well. Modern Turks continue the tradition and like nothing better than a barbecue and a meal taken outdoors sitting on rugs on the ground in natural surroundings. You can in your own small way join in this tradition, buying staples like black olives, white cheese, bread and tomatoes, which you can produce at lunchtime on your travels, sitting on rocks under trees, beside streams whenever possible.

kitchen and is frequently lukewarm when it arrives. Going into the kitchen or to the display counter to choose your food is more common than having a written menu, and waiters and cooks in such places are always men. Alcohol is rarely served in such places. Presentation counts for little and it is definitely a case of eating to live rather than living to eat. In the towns it is the restaurants attached to the best hotels and pensions which most often have the best food in the most salubrious surroundings, in complete contrast to the Aegean and Mediterranean areas, where you are likely to enjoy a far better meal in a restaurant than in a hotel. Hotel restaurants are also far more likely to be licensed. Full and detailed restaurant listings are given in each chapter under each town, according to the following price code, based on the average price of a main course per person:

$$$$$	expensive	£20+	TL48+
$$$$	above average	£12–20	TL28–48
$$$	average	£7–12	TL16–28
$$	cheap and cheerful	£2–7	TL4–16
$	rock bottom	£1–2	TL2–4

Typical opening hours for restaurants and *lokantas* are 08.00 to 22.00 daily.

Like the food, all **drink** in Turkey, alcoholic or not, is very cheap, and some sample prices are listed below. *Ayran* is the non-alcoholic national drink, a chilled unsweetened yoghurt liquid, thirst-quenching and slightly sour. *Rakı* (a clear aniseed spirit similar to the Greek *ouzo*) is the national alcoholic drink, usually mixed with ice and water, which makes it go cloudy white. It goes well with Turkish food and is usually drunk as such, rather than on its own.

As befits the place where it is thought the grape was first cultivated, Turkey today has the fourth-largest area in the world under viticulture, and is the sixth-largest wine producer in the world (see page 158). Very little of this wine is exported. On the red side the best is Buzbağ, a full-bodied red, closest to a Burgundy; other good reds to ask for are Yakut, Villa Doluca, Dikmen and Trakya. The premium whites are Çankaya, Villa Doluca, Kavalidere and white Trakya. The locally brewed beer is the ubiquitous Efes, sold in cans and bottles. It is very refreshing and tastes like a kind of Pilsner lager.

While alcohol – spirits, wine and beer – is available in all the better hotels in the cities, around 70% of the local restaurants never serve it at all, and during Ramazan this percentage may go up to as high as 90%. If you want a drink with your food it is therefore best to check before ordering so that you are not disappointed once it is too late. Of the non-alcoholic drinks available, ayran and water are the commonest, although cola and fizzy orange are usually available as well. Sample costs at the Büyük Kervanseray's courtyard restaurant ($$$) in Diyarbakır are:

Red Kalecik Karasi 2009 Vinkara exp.18 novut special

- *Mezze* for two: TL20 (£8.40); starter, hot or cold (average price): TL5 (£2.10); salads: TL7.50 (£3.15)
- Main courses: TL17.50–20 (£7.35-8.40)
- Sweets: TL6–7 (£2.50-3)
- Wine: 75cl bottle: TL30 (£12.60) for a house red/white, up to TL80 (£33.60) for top quality; glass TL8 (£3.36)
- Rakı: TL18 (£7.50) for 20cl
- Beer: TL7 (£3) bottle of Efes

The standard Turkish breakfast of black olives and white cheese washed down with strong sugared black tea applies in the east as it does in the rest of the country, though the bread, butter and jam varies considerably from town to town. Coffee of the Nescafé variety is extremely expensive, more so than in the south and east, so take your own and ask for hot water if you want it. Some hotels will run to freshly squeezed orange juice and cooked eggs. Thick black Turkish coffee is drunk by itself in tiny cups at cafes or after meals. You need to specify if you want it unsugared (*sade*), medium sweet (*şekerli*) or very sweet (*çok şekerli*). Black tea comes in small glasses with the sugar cubes separate or on the saucer for you to sweeten according to taste.

PUBLIC HOLIDAYS AND FESTIVALS

Turkey follows the Gregorian calendar like Europe and has weekends of Saturday and Sunday in the same way. However, being a predominantly Muslim country it also celebrates the major **Islamic festivals**. The dates for these are not fixed in our Gregorian calendar but are timed according to the lunar system, which is 11 days shorter than our solar one. The dates of Ramazan for example keep moving backwards by 11 days each year, and at the moment it is creeping into the hottest time of year in high summer, when going without water or liquid of any sort is very tough indeed, often in temperatures of over 40°C.

There are two major religious festivals (the equivalents if you like of the Christian Easter and Christmas). The first is **Şeker Bayramı**, literally 'Sugar Festival' **(Eid)**, a three-day national holiday which falls at the end of **Ramazan**, the month of fasting. During Ramazan strict Muslims observe a fast which means that nothing must pass their lips between sunrise and sunset – this means no drinking, eating or smoking. Many Turks are not strict Muslims and in large cities or in resort areas it would not be expected that foreigners would observe this practice, so restaurants and bars will still be open as usual. In more rural and conservative areas however, especially as you head further east, you may find it more difficult to eat and drink in public during the day, and many restaurants and cafés will be closed until after dark. Much visiting of friends takes place during Şeker Bayramı to make up for the deprivation of the previous month.

Approximate dates (as they may vary by a day or so according to the lunar cycle) for Şeker Bayramı are:

- 30 August 2011 (Ramazan 1–29 August 2011)
- 19 August 2012 (Ramazan 20 July–18 August 2012)
- 8 August 2013 (Ramazan 9 July–8 August 2013)

The second festival is **Kurban Bayramı (Feast of the Sacrifice)**. This is a four-day national holiday. Traditionally a goat (or chicken or even camel, according to the family's means) is sacrificed at this festival, to mark Abraham's willingness to sacrifice his son Isaac. The meat is then distributed among family, friends, neighbours and the poor.

Approximate dates for Kurban Bayramı are:

- 6 November 2011
- 26 October 2012
- 15 October 2013

During both of these festivals, especially when they fall in summer, Turks pour out in a mass exodus from the cities, packing the resort towns along all the coasts to bursting. This is the only time you will experience difficulties in finding accommodation, and for this reason, if you are touring, it can be wiser to plan to be inland for the duration of one of these festivals.

In the eastern provinces religious adherence is more noticeable than in other parts of Turkey, and so in mosques and generally your dress should be more discreet. Fasting during Ramazan also badly affects the mood of the people, who become very grumpy and bad-tempered and do everything half-heartedly. If you complain, shoulders are shrugged helplessly and the word Ramazan is uttered as an excuse for everything that malfunctions or is not available. It also means that at sundown the restaurants are packed to bursting with men waiting for the Ramazan cannon to signify the end of the fasting each evening. After eating a mountainous plateful they lean back, burp and then smoke continuously to make up for the abstinence of the day.

On top of the religious holidays, there are the **secular public holidays**, decided by the government with fixed dates, when banks and government offices are closed:

1 January	New Year's Day
2 April	Van Festival, to celebrate the end of Russian occupation in World War I
23 April	National Sovereignty and Children's Day
19 May	Atatürk Commemoration and Youth Sports Day
5–10 July	Akşehir Nasreddin Hoca Festival in honour of the famous wit, consisting of plays of his anecdotes and folk dancing
30 August	Victory Day
28 October (half day) and 29 October	Republic Day

Some areas of eastern Turkey also celebrate **local festivals**, most of them in summer:

June	Rize Tea Festival
3–5 June	Aksaray Ihlara Folk Festival
25–27 June	International Kommagene Festival in and around Nemrut Dağı with folk dancing and extreme sports events
July	Black Sea Festival, Samsun
1–25 August	Samsun Fair and Folk Dance Festival
20–25 September	Çorum Hittite Festival held in Boğazkale, Alaca and Sungurlu, open-air festival with displays, music and folklore shows among the ruins
15 September– 5 October	Mersin Fashion and Textile Show, with music and folklore
21–25 September	Cappadocia Festival, grape harvest celebration and folkloric festival

9–17 December   Mevlâna Festival at Konya; hotels are packed at this time in Konya

OPENING HOURS Turkey shares the Saturday/Sunday weekend with Europe. Museums are open every day except Mondays, and the usual hours are 08.00–12.00 and 13.00–17.00. Tourist sites are usually open 08.00–17.00, sometimes just dawn to dusk, so the timings vary from summer to winter. Shops are open 09.00–13.00 and 14.00–19.00. Banks are open 08.30–12.00 and 13.30–17.00. In Ramazan opening hours can be curtailed, with everything closing at least an hour or two earlier.

 ## SHOPPING

Shopping for souvenirs is not as straightforward in the east as it is in other parts of the country, with the exception of Cappadocia, where there are many souvenir shops selling things from colourful knitted socks and gloves to embroidered headscarves, jewellery with semi-precious stones, carved wooden boxes, alabaster and pottery. In the east proper, however, souvenir shops are few and far between. Carpet shops can be found in most of the big cities, and the Kurdish areas like Diyarbakır and Hakkâri are good places to buy Turkish *kilims* (carpets) or saddlebags. Bargaining is essential for such items, and you should aim to knock about a third off the original price quoted. Feigning complete indifference is the key to getting a good price, both in your voice and your body language. (For bargaining tips, see page 66.)

In Erzurum you can buy the local black jet made into artefacts like worry beads and necklaces. Eros underpants, sold all over eastern Turkey, are another interesting possibility, and both men's and women's socks are surprisingly good buys.

ARTS AND ENTERTAINMENT

With the exception of Ankara, nightlife is virtually non-existent, as are organised events like concerts and plays. Some of the bigger cities like Trabzon and Erzurum have cinemas.

PHOTOGRAPHY

Make sure you never get your camera out around dams or airports, as these are considered sensitive military areas and possible targets for terrorist attack, so all photography is strictly forbidden.

Otherwise the usual advice applies: take photos early in the morning or late in the day for the best colours and results. Eastern Turkey has many highly photogenic places, so you will have fun with your camera trying to improve on the conventional shots. See pages 68–9 for photographic tips.

 ## MEDIA AND COMMUNICATIONS

Powerful businesses operate many of the press and broadcasting outlets, including the Doğan Group, the leading media conglomerate. The state broadcaster, TRT, based in Ankara, is kept company by over 300 private **TV** stations, more than a dozen of which enjoy national coverage, and over 1,000 private **radio** stations. TRT1 provides general radio entertainment, while TRT3 plays classical/jazz and pop music, with short news broadcasts in English, French and German. TRT4 plays Turkish classical and folk music. All these can be listened to online. Digiturk

Always look at both sides of a carpet to compare the colours and look at the closeness of the weave. The closer the weave and the smaller the knots, the better the quality and durability of the carpet. As older kilims are becoming rarer and fetch more money, dealers have not been slow to develop techniques for aging newly woven rugs. Fading in sunlight is the commonest method and can produce quite effective and pleasing results with mellower colours. Parting the surface and looking at the very bottom of the weave, make sure to check if the colour is the same as on the top surface. If it is different and has faded on top, it is a chemical dye. Comparing the colours on the top with those on the underside also gives an indication, as natural dyes will be the same on both sides. More harmful, however, is the practice of washing a kilim in bleach to produce the effect more quickly, as this reduces the life of the weaving, weakening the fibres of the wool. A quick sniff usually reveals this. As smaller kilims sell more quickly than larger ones, some dealers will cut up the larger ones into pieces and sell them as original. Watch out for the newer ends added to make them complete or an unnatural break in the pattern. If colours have been touched up to hide repairs or fading, the felt-tip colouring or shoe polish used may be disclosed by rubbing a wetted white cloth or handkerchief over the surface; these may even come off on your hand as you run it across the weave. Another common aging trick is dirt, along with deliberate scorch marks. A sign of authentic vegetable dye colours is when the colour changes mid weave, as it were, because a new batch has had to be mixed up which never totally matches. Pink and orange are colours which can never be produced from natural dyes so the presence of these colours and any other colours with a harsher brightness is always an indication that the weaver used chemical dyes and that the carpet is relatively recent. The quality of chemical dyes has now improved considerably and can sometimes be quite convincing.

Agreeing a price necessitates the usual bargaining (see page 85). If you want to pay by credit card you may do less well, as the dealer will be losing 6–8% to the credit-card company. Kilims are best used on top of another carpet or on an overlay to help them wear well. They should not really be used under a dining table or in a corridor where they would get heavy wear. Sharp pointed furniture legs or stiletto heels can also damage them. For cleaning, a cylinder vacuum cleaner is gentler than an upright one, especially on the fringes. By hanging a kilim on the wall you can prolong its life indefinitely and it will certainly outlive you if hung correctly with the fringes top and bottom. For cleaning you can use the hose-pipe method to simulate the river water, which is the traditional method or, far easier, use a good carpet cleaning powder and then just vacuum it and the dirt off. One age-old method used in eastern Turkey is to tread the carpet into the snow, and then to shake it out vigorously before it gets wet, which can be done throughout the winter months as snow is so abundant. In Europe this is likely to be an annual opportunity at best. Dry cleaning is not recommended, as it is far too harsh on the fibres. A simple outdoors shake-out of the dust is still the best method for more routine cleaning.

is the main Turkish satellite provider, with hundreds of Turkish and international TV channels including CNN and BBC World. There are two English-language daily papers, *Hürriyet* and *Today's Zaman*.

Whilst not strictly subject to censorship, there are still many highly sensitive topics, coverage of which can lead to arrest and prosecution. These are to do with the military, the Kurds and political Islam. It is not uncommon for journalists to be imprisoned, and radio and TV stations to be suspended for airing such topics. As part of the measures necessary to pave the way for EU entry, some of the most repressive sanctions have been lifted, but under Article 301 of the penal code it remains a crime to insult the Turkish nation. If you listen to the Turkish national anthem on YouTube, with its mix of totalitarian dominance and Italian operatic drama, you will get an inkling of the unshakeable rock of Turkish national pride that is definitely not to be messed with.

As part of the reforms intended to meet EU criteria on minorities, in 2004 the state broadcaster TRT introduced programmes in Kurdish, and in 2009 an official Kurdish-language TV station, TRT 6, was launched.

INTERNET ACCESS According to Internetworldstats, some 26.5 million Turks were online by 2008. As with other media, internet sites are blocked by the government if they are thought to be insulting to Turkish statehood. YouTube for example was banned for showing videos considered insulting to Atatürk. Most of the more expensive hotels have wi-fi access from your laptop – just make sure you have the correct adapter plug for the power supply. Some also have the clear RJ11 (American-style) plug which you can put direct into your laptop. Internet cafes are quite common in the cities (though trickier to find in the smaller towns). They are usually open 09.00-23.00 and cost around TL1-2 per hour. Watch out for the Turkish keyboard, which has the dotless 'i' where you would expect our normal dotted 'i'. Also, the '@' symbol has to be made by holding down the 'q' and the ALT keys simultaneously. If you have a Blackberry it will work fine throughout Turkey, just as in Europe.

TELEPHONES To make calls abroad from Turkey dial the international 00 followed by the country code, eg: 44 for the UK, 353 for Ireland, then the number, but removing the first 0 from the area code. To dial Turkey from anywhere abroad dial the international code 00 followed by the Turkey country code 90, then dial the area code, dropping off the first 0.

There are public phone booths which accept cards or *jeton* tokens which can be bought from PTT offices and local shops. Calling abroad from hotels is very expensive. Mobile phones work well in Turkey and even in the remotest corners

AREA CODES WITHIN EASTERN TURKEY

Adana	322	Erzurum	442	Niğde	388
Adıyaman	416	Gaziantep	342	Northern Cyprus	392
Ağri	472	Giresun	454	Ordu	452
Aksaray	382	Hakkâri	438	Rize	464
Amasya	358	Hatay (Antakya)	326	Safranbolu	370
Ankara	312	Iğdır	476	Samsun	362
Ardahan	478	Kahramanmaraş	344	Şanlıurfa	414
Artvin	466	Karaman	338	Siirt	484
Bartin	378	Kars	474	Silifke (or Tarsus)	324
Batman	488	Kastamonu	366	Sinop	368
Bayburt	459	Kayseri	352	Sivas	346
Bitlis	434	Konya	332	Tokat	356
Boğazkale	364	Malatya	422	Trabzon	462
Diyarbakır	412	Mardin	482	Tunceli	428
Elâzığ	424	Muş	436	Van	432
Erzincan	446	Nevşehir	384		

you will almost always find a good signal. Blackberries work well throughout the country too, off the back of the mobile GPRS network.

Useful numbers

Emergency	❭ 112	Police	❭ 155
International operator	❭ 115	Jandarma	❭ 156
Directory assistance	❭ 118	Fire	❭ 110
Reversed charges call	❭ 131		

POST OFFICE SERVICES Turkish post offices are easily recognisable by the yellow and black PTT signs. Major post offices are open 08.00–midnight Monday–Saturday, 09.00–19.00 Sunday. Smaller offices are open 08.30–12.30 and 13.30–17.30 Monday–Friday and may be closed at weekends.

As well as selling stamps and telephone tokens/cards, some post offices also exchange foreign cash and international postal orders.

Poste restante letters should be addressed *postrestant* to the central post office,

PHOTOGRAPHIC TIPS   *Ariadne Van Zandbergen*

EQUIPMENT Although with some thought and an eye for composition you can take reasonable photos with a 'point-and-shoot' camera, you need an SLR camera if you are at all serious about photography. Modern SLRs tend to be very clever, with automatic programmes for almost every possible situation, but remember that these programmes are limited in the sense that the camera cannot think, but only makes calculations. Every starting amateur photographer should read a photographic manual for beginners and get to grips with such basics as the relationship between aperture and shutter speed.

Always buy the best lens you can afford. The lens determines the quality of your photo more than the camera body. Fixed fast lenses are ideal, but very costly. A zoom lens makes it easier to change composition without changing lenses the whole time. If you carry only one lens, a 28–70mm (digital 17–55mm) or similar zoom should be ideal. For a second lens, a lightweight telephoto zoom will be excellent for candid shots and varying your composition. Wildlife photography will be very frustrating if you don't have at least a 300mm lens. For a small loss of quality, tele-converters are a cheap and compact way to increase magnification: a 300mm lens with a 1.4x converter becomes 420mm, and with a 2x it becomes 600mm. Note, however, that 1.4x and 2x tele-converters reduce the speed of your lens by 1.4 and 2 stops respectively.

For wildlife photography from a safari vehicle, a solid beanbag, which you can make yourself very cheaply, will be necessary to avoid blurred images, and is more useful than a tripod. A clamp with a tripod head screwed on to it can be attached to the vehicle as well. Modern dedicated flash units are easy to use; aside from the obvious need to flash when you photograph at night, you can improve a lot of photos in difficult 'high contrast' or very dull light with some fill-in flash. It pays to have a proper flash unit as opposed to a built-in camera flash.

DIGITAL/FILM Digital photography is now the preference of most amateur and professional photographers, with the resolution of digital cameras improving the whole time. For ordinary prints a 6 megapixel camera is fine. For better results and the possibility to enlarge images and for professional reproduction, higher resolution is available up to 24 megapixels.

Memory space is important. The number of pictures you can fit on a memory card depends on the quality you choose. Calculate in advance how many pictures you can

Merkez Postanesi, in the town where you want to collect your post. You will need to produce an ID card or passport when collecting your post.

Postcards and letters to the UK and Europe cost TL0.85, and TL0.90 to Australia, New Zealand and the USA. You should allow around 10 days for them to reach their destination.

LIVING AND WORKING IN TURKEY

If you want to stay in Turkey longer than the three-month period allowed on your tourist visa or to set up a business with or without a Turkish partner, you will need a residence visa. For that you need to have applied to your local Turkish consulate in your home country to get such a visa, submitting all documents relevant to your application at least eight weeks before your planned date of departure. Your application will be referred to the relevant Turkish authorities for their approval.

After obtaining the visa you must register with the local police within a month following your arrival in Turkey to obtain a residence permit. If you want to

fit on a card and either take enough cards to last for your trip, or take a storage drive or memory stick onto which you can download the content. A laptop gives the advantage that you can see your pictures properly at the end of each day and edit and delete rejects, but a storage device is lighter and less bulky.

Bear in mind that digital camera batteries, computers and other storage devices need charging, so make sure you have all the chargers, cables and converters with you. Most hotels have charging points, but do enquire about this in advance. When camping you might have to rely on charging from the car battery; a spare battery is invaluable.

DUST AND HEAT Dust and heat are often a problem. Keep your equipment in a sealed bag, stow films in an airtight container (eg: a small cooler bag) and avoid exposing equipment to the sun. Digital cameras are prone to collecting dust particles on the sensor which results in spots on the image. The dirt mostly enters the camera when changing lenses, so be careful when doing this. To some extent photos can be 'cleaned' up afterwards in Photoshop, but this is time-consuming. You can have your camera sensor professionally cleaned, or you can do this yourself with special brushes and swabs made for the purpose, but note that touching the sensor might cause damage and should only be done with the greatest care.

LIGHT The most striking outdoor photographs are often taken during the hour or two of 'golden light', after dawn and before sunset. Shooting in low light may enforce the use of very low shutter speeds, in which case a tripod will be required to avoid camera shake.

With careful handling, side lighting and back lighting can produce stunning effects, especially in soft light and at sunrise or sunset. Generally, however, it is best to shoot with the sun behind you. When photographing animals or people in the harsh midday sun, images taken in light but even shade are likely to be more effective than those taken in direct sunlight or patchy shade, since the latter conditions create too much contrast.

Ariadne Van Zandbergen is a professional travel and wildlife photographer specialised in Africa. She runs The Africa Image Library. For photo requests, visit the website www.africaimagelibrary.co.za or contact her direct ariadne@hixnet.co.za.

extend the permit for a further period you must apply to the same police headquarters before the permit expires. Household items may be taken into Turkey through a system called 'temporary import' provided that the validity of the residence permit is at least one year. Anyone wishing to apply for a work permit will need to supply various documents to the Turkish consulate including proof of job offer, normally in the form of a letter from the prospective employer.

GETTING MARRIED IN TURKEY Marriage in Turkey is a civil ceremony with no religious content. It can be held anywhere, subject to the discretion of the local registrar. It is legal for two British or Irish citizens to get married in Turkey as long as they follow the regulations. There are a number of tour operators and agencies who can make the necessary arrangements on your behalf. A list of these can be found on the website www.gototurkey.co.uk. In addition to your passport you will need a Certificate of No Impediment from your local Registrar of Marriages as well as a full birth certificate and, if previously married, a divorce or death certificate relating to the previous spouse. You will also need to contact the relevant British or Irish consulate in Turkey. Contact www.britishembassy.gov.uk for further details.

BUYING PROPERTY As stated in the constitution foreigners are able to acquire real estate in Turkey as long as there is a mutual agreement with their country of nationality, as indicated in Real Estate Law, Article 35. British and Irish citizens therefore do have the right to buy property in Turkey. There are some restrictions to this, which include the fact that foreign citizens are not allowed to buy property which is within the limits of a village, but only that which is within the limits of a municipality. The authority which is responsible for overseeing the purchase of property by foreigners is the General Directorate of Title Deeds and Cadastre, Ankara (✆ 90 312 4171260; e *webmaster@tapu.gov.tr; www.tapu.gov.tr*). For further information on buying property in Turkey visit www.turkisheconomy.org.uk/buyingproperty/property.html.

CULTURAL ETIQUETTE

Eastern Turkey is much more conservative and traditional than the rest of Turkey and your clothing and behaviour should reflect that, with bare arms and legs to be avoided. Ramazan is observed more strictly as well, and it may be harder to find places serving food and drink during the day especially in rural areas. The following general guidelines should also be followed:

- Always remove shoes before entering a mosque.
- Men and children are generally happy to be photographed, but women should be asked first.
- Outward displays of affection like kissing and petting are frowned on. A couple holding hands is acceptable but that is as far as it should go.
- Do not flatter or compliment people on their children. You will be suspected of putting the 'evil eye' on them.
- Do not eat with your left hand or take a present with your left hand.
- Set a good example by never junking your litter or leaving it behind after picnics
- Never go behind the iconostasis in Eastern Orthodox churches. The sanctuary is for priests only.
- Never take photos near bridges, dams or airports.
- As a man, never enquire after the health of women family members of another man's family.

- As a woman, only make the minimum eye contact necessary with Turkish men to avoid being misunderstood and hassled. Polite but unavailable is the message to send out with your body language.
- Do not make hand signals that involve your fingers – they mean different things in Turkey. For example making a circle with your thumb and index finger which means 'OK' or 'just perfect' in the West means 'homosexual' in Turkey.
- Avoid attempting to bribe an official of any sort. You could end up in prison.

CLOTHING The emphasis is definitely on casual and durable clothing for eastern Turkey. The dining rooms even in the best hotels are not formal and most people are dressed for comfort rather than style. Trousers or skirts and short sleeves are fine for most occasions, but shorts are generally to be avoided for both men and women except in the northern and southern coastal resorts. Low-cut tops or tight-fitting jeans are not a good idea, and will draw unwelcome attention. Loose clothes are a lot more comfortable for walking around in the heat of the day in any event. A thick pullover or jacket is essential for the evenings when the temperature drops sharply, and a thin waterproof plastic garment is advisable in the Black Sea areas where sudden rainstorms are common. Strong shoes are a must for the towns as well as the sites. Sandals are hardly ever suitable as there is too much dust, mud and dirt around. Women should be especially careful to cover bare arms, shoulders and heads for entering mosques. Bikinis are fine in the few hotels that have pools and on the Black Sea and Mediterranean coasts. Toplessness is not the practice and nudity is illegal.

TRAVELLING POSITIVELY

Eastern Turkey sees far fewer tourists than the western part of the country, and it is generally fair to say that it is less well developed, poorer and more backward than the western part. It has been likened to Turkey's Middle East. About 45% of Turkey's population lives here, yet it produces only some 8% of gross domestic product. Most seasoned observers of Turkey regard this discrepancy and the harsh reality it reflects for the largely Kurdish local inhabitants as the single most pressing issue that the government needs to address. Until it is, much of the Kurdish population will remain disaffected and potentially volatile, and the government will need to tie up large amounts of money and troops. Household monthly

STUFF YOUR RUCKSACK – AND MAKE A DIFFERENCE

www.stuffyourrucksack.com is a website set up by TV's Kate Humble which enables travellers to give direct help to small charities, schools or other organisations in the country they are visiting. The idea is to bring small items which will be of use and can be fitted in the rucksack. The charities get exactly what they need and travellers have the chance to meet local people and see how and where their gifts will be used.

The website describes organisations that need your help and lists the items they most need. Check what's needed in Turkey, contact the organisation to say you're coming and bring not only the much-needed goods but an extra dimension to your travels and the knowledge that in a small way you have made a difference.

www.stuffyourrucksack.com
Responsible tourism in action

expenditure in the southeast has been calculated as the lowest in the country – as low as US$150 a month – at least eight-times lower than in the western region of Marmara (which includes Istanbul). Yet the birth rate is the highest in the country, because it is also the region where fewest girls go to school, and poor education goes hand in hand with a higher birth rate. Studies have shown that women in eastern Turkey want on average three children, but end up having more like six. Handing out contraceptive devices is obviously not your role as a visitor, but if the subject arises, you can do your bit to help educate and encourage women to use contraception. With so many rivers and lakes, water scarcity is not a problem, neither is electricity shortage, so you need not be too worried about using the country's resources. An area where you can set a good example, however, is litter, especially in the countryside. Make certain you never leave any debris after picnics – there are plenty of bins in the towns where you can dispose of rubbish properly. Children often cluster round asking for money (*para* in Turkish), sweets (*bonbons*), or pens (*kalem*), but the problem will only get worse if you hand out goodies. Give generous donations in the churches and monastery offertory boxes, as these are communities that struggle to make ends meet.

The Anglo-Turkish Society based in London (*www.anglo-turkish-society.co.uk*) supports a variety of charities in eastern Turkey and is grateful for any donations.

VOLUNTEER WORK Having English as your mother tongue is a huge bonus when looking for work in Turkey, as there are so many paid opportunities for teaching English as a foreign language. If, however, you are over 18 and happy to volunteer your manual labour there is a growing range of organisations which will arrange work in Turkey, from archaeological digs to rural aid projects and conservation initiatives such as turtle protection and bird habitat surveys. The usual format is to live in villages, looked after by the villagers – a perfect way to get Turkish language 'immersion'.

Sift through websites like www.volunteerabroad.com/search/turkey and www.kwintessential.co.uk to get ideas. In Turkey the Istanbul-based Gençtur (*www.genctur.com*) runs programs from 3 to 24 months, and the ecologically-driven Ta Tu Ta (*www.bugday.org/tatuta*), also based in Istanbul, arranges volunteer work on organic farms all over the country, about ten of which are east of Ankara. Your stay is free except for a small contribution to cover your costs. Typical work includes berry-picking and molasses-making.

Part Two

THE GUIDE

3

Ankara

Telephone code: 312

Destiny caresses the few and molests the many.

As Turkey's modern capital, Ankara has many new roles, and it is the interplay and conflict of these roles that makes the city so intriguing today. When Atatürk moved his headquarters here in 1919 at the start of the War of Independence, it was a deliberate distancing from cosmopolitan Istanbul, a statement that Turkey was much more than its Ottoman past. Ankara then was a small town of only 30,000 inhabitants. Now official UN figures for 2009 estimate it is a metropolis of 4.8 million. It may be a modern city today, but its origins go back to the 2nd millennium BC when it was a Hittite settlement called Ankuwash. It is fitting therefore that the two major sights Ankara has to offer reflect both its ancient and its modern ties: the spectacular Museum of Anatolian Civilisations and the Cyclopean Anıt Kabir, Atatürk's mausoleum. One day should be sufficient to visit Ankara's attractions. In fact, in an energetic half day you can visit the museum (two hours), take a brief stroll around the medieval citadel (45 minutes), then visit Anıt Kabir (one hour), have lunch and set off for the Hittite heartlands, with the museum still fresh in your mind.

SETTING AND ORIENTATION

The first glimpse of the city for many will be the drive in from the international airport, Esenboğa, 28km to the north. The road leads through green, or in winter snow-covered, undulating hills and then suddenly drops down into a basin with colourful houses clinging to the steep hillsides. King Midas of Phrygia founded a settlement here called 'Ankyra', and the prefix *ank* is known to mean 'gorge' or 'ravine' in early Indo-European languages, an obvious reference to the setting. As the scenery unfolds you realise that the entire city is in fact built on a series of small steep hills within the basin. Wide main roads run in straight lines along the open valleys, with narrow side streets winding off uphill in zigzags. The main boulevard is called Atatürk Bulvarı, running for 5.5km from Ulus, the old part of town in the north, through the districts of Kızılay and Kavalıdere down to Çankaya in the south. A great Phrygian necropolis was found in 1925 to the south of the railway station.

The houses built on the steep slopes are highly distinctive, painted in blues, greens, mauves and yellows with red-tiled roofs. The whole effect is unlike anything European or Mediterranean, yet also unlike anything Middle Eastern or Arabic. Huddled together covering every inch of available ground, house-of-cards fashion, the impression is that if one collapsed it might bring down the entire hillside. These *gecekondular* (literally 'night-lodgings') are the houses built overnight by the exceptional numbers of Anatolian peasants migrating to the city in their ever hopeful search for work and a better standard of living. The rural influx that began in the 1960s has been almost entirely responsible for the surge in Ankara's population. Some still look like dreary shanty towns, but others have acquired a kind of permanence and become established neighbourhoods with their own schools and utilities. Half of Ankara's surface area consists of these *gecekondular*, and over half the population lives there.

The contrast between these gay crowded hillsides and the wide open boulevards of the new city adds to the oddness of Ankara and points towards the split identity of the city, which is more marked than that of any other in Turkey. While the main boulevards are lined with luxury high-rise hotels, European-style restaurants and cafés, impressive new embassies, ministries, government buildings and the fine Hacetepe University, in the older streets round the citadel and the Ulus Meydanı (The People's Square), the feel is more like a simple Anatolian town, sometimes even with traditionally dressed peasants going about their lives as they have always done.

This split symbolises in a very real way the curious dilemma of Turkey as a whole, trying on the one hand to project itself as a semi-European state with a face acceptable to doubting Western observers, and clinging on the other hand to customs and values nurtured and unchanged for centuries. In the Aegean and Mediterranean areas of Turkey this dilemma has now been largely resolved, with change and development welcomed by most, because of the attendant improvement in living and educational standards. East of Ankara the story is different. The sophisticated cosmopolitan Turk becomes harder to find, and the rougher side of the Turkish character comes to the fore. Ankara stands on the boundary of this divide, one foot in the 21st century, the other firmly planted in the lifestyle of centuries ago.

HISTORY

From its Phrygian origins in the 8th century BC, the city was ruled successively by the Lydians and the Persians. The name Ankyra appears in historical records for the first time in the Persian period (546–334BC), where it is mentioned as a stopping place on the Royal Road to Sardis. Ankara's next appearance in history was when Alexander the Great arrived here in 333BC after his famous cutting of the Gordion Knot some 100km to the west. Alexander went on to defeat the Persian king Darius III in a bloody battle and then a tribe of Galatians settled here from Europe, making Ankara their capital.

The Romans conquered the city in 25BC and under the emperor Augustus it became an important administrative and military centre sitting astride the Roman trade routes of Anatolia. When the Roman Empire was divided in half in AD395 Ankara maintained its importance under the reign of the Eastern Roman emperors. The Seljuks (see pages 112–13) conquered the city in 1073, finally bringing an end to the Byzantine Empire, and from that point on the city passed under the control of various Turkish *beyliks* (principalities), until political stability was established under the Ottomans.

By the end of World War I, which ended so disastrously for Turkey and brought about the disintegration of the Ottoman Empire, Ankara was no more than a small country town lost in the steppes. Then, when Mustafa Kemal (later Atatürk) chose it as the headquarters of the nationalists, Ankara became the symbol of the War of Independence, from where the war was planned and directed. In October 1923 it was officially named as the capital of the modern Turkish Republic and Atatürk himself did not set foot in Istanbul until 1927. The shift to Ankara was a deliberate break with the Ottoman past and an assertion that Turkey was not Istanbul as many Westerners believed, but Anatolia. One of the favourite nationalist epithets for Istanbul was *kozmopolit*, a word with disparaging overtones unlike the English 'cosmopolitan'. A recent Turkish dictionary defines it as: '[a person] having no national and local colour but assuming the outward form that suits his purpose'. For all the encouragement and positive discrimination given to Ankara to supplant Istanbul as Turkey's first city, it has not and is unlikely ever to do so. On holidays and at any other excuse, armies of civil servants rush lemming-like from their smart modern flats in Ankara to the charm of their decaying homes in overcrowded Istanbul.

CLIMATE AND WHEN TO VISIT

Raised up at 890m on the harsh Anatolian Plateau, the winters in Ankara are cold with much snow (30–60cm), which lasts from late November to the end of April. The skiing season at the nearby Elmadağ resort, 26km from Ankara, is between January and March. January is the coldest month with an average temperature of −0.2°C. Spring is very short and the hot weather begins at the end of May. July is the hottest month with an average temperature of 23.2°C. Nights are generally cool even in summer because of the altitude. The city is at its best in spring and especially autumn, when the warm sun and blue skies continue until early November. Air pollution is a problem from mid-October to mid-April, because the heating fuel, a soft brown lignite, produces a thick smoke, but from May to September the air is fine and there is less pollution than in most cities.

Republic Day on 29 October is Ankara's biggest festival celebration, marking the founding of modern Turkey, and there is pressure on accommodation then, as well as during the **International Ankara Music Festival** (*www.ankarafestival.com*), held annually in the last three weeks of April, when music lovers from all over the country descend on the capital.

GETTING THERE

For most people the reason for coming to Ankara is not so much to see the Turkish capital (with the possible exception of the museum), but rather because it is the most convenient starting point for any journey into the central and eastern parts of the country. It has many daily flight connections to Istanbul as well as many direct international scheduled flights from many European cities such as Amsterdam, Athens, Brussels, Cologne, Düsseldorf, Frankfurt, Munich, Paris, Rome, Stockholm, Stuttgart, Vienna and Zurich, as well as beyond Europe to places such as Baku, Damascus, Jeddah and Tehran. There are also excellent onward bus and train connections, as well as offices of international car-hire agencies like Avis, Hertz and Europcar.

BY AIR Ankara's international airport is called Esenboğa (flight code ESB) (*www.esenbogaairport.com*) and was voted the best airport in Europe in the 5–10 million passengers category in 2009. It lies 28km to the north of the city on the road to Çankırı. Lufthansa (*www.lufthansa.com*) seems to offer the cheapest flights from Europe, flying via Munich. Atlasjet (*www.atlasjet.com*), a Turkish airline based in Istanbul that flies to and from London (Stansted) and Manchester, and Pegasus (*www.pegasusairlines.com*) flying from London (Gatwick and Stansted), several German cities including Frankfurt, Cologne and Dusseldorf, Amsterdam, Athens, Bangkok, Barcelona, Beirut, Paris and Capetown) are the only two budget carriers serving Ankara. In 2008 Turkish Airlines founded Anadolu Jet (*www.anadolujet.com*) as a separate brand based in Ankara, a highly successful operation which has since more than trebled its fleet to 16 and flies to 12 international destinations and 29 domestic ones. Its fares are highly competitive. Air France (*www.airfrance.com*), British Airways (*www.ba.com*) and KLM (*www.klm.com*) also fly direct to Ankara and have offices in the city centre (see below).

There are 19 flights a day linking Ankara to Istanbul, running hourly from 06.00 to midnight. In addition there are domestic flights to all parts of Turkey from Ankara, namely to Antalya, Batman, Bodrum, Dalaman, Denizli, Diyarbakır, Elâzığ, Erzincan, Erzurum, Gaziantep, Hatay (Antakya), Kahramanmaraş, Kars, Malatya, Mardin, Muş, Samsun, Şanlıurfa, Trabzon and Van. All these flights are operated by Anadolu Jet (www.anadolujet.com) on behalf of the national carrier, Turkish Airlines. They fly once, sometimes twice a day and the maximum flight time is 95 minutes. For example the flight to Mardin leaves daily at 09.10 and arrives at 10.45, costing TL89 one way.

Airline offices in Ankara

✦ **Atlasjet** Cinnah Caddesi 43/1, Kızılay, Ankara; ✎ 4406070

✦ **British Airways** Atatürk Bulvarı 237/2, Kavalidere, Ankara; ✎ 4675557

✦ **Lufthansa** Cinnah Caddesi 102/5, Çankaya, Ankara; ✎ 4420580

✦ **Turkish Airlines** Esenboğa Airport; ✎ 3980100; Atatürk Bulvarı, Kavalidere, Ankara; ✎ 4280200

Airport transfer The drive into the centre by **taxi** takes about 30 minutes and costs about €35. Make sure the meter is started up. Taxis wait outside the main arrivals area at the taxi rank and you do not need to pre-arrange one. Airport **buses** shuttle daily every half hour from 04.30 to midnight between the airport and the Havaş Bus Terminal [82 A2] which is located 1km out from the city centre, taking 45 minutes and costing €10. The Havaş buses set off from outside the arrivals area and you pay on the bus. From the Havaş Bus Terminal (Gate B, 19 Mayis Stadium [82 A2]) you can take the metro from Maltepe station [82 A3] to Kızılay for the mid-range hotels or Ulus for the cheaper hotels.

BY TRAIN Ankara's train station (Ankara Gari) [82 A3] is centrally located a little to the west of the city centre. Depending on your luggage, it is a little far to walk, about 1km to Ulus or 2km to Kızılay. Take the metro from Maltepe station [82 A3], reached by a signposted underpass from the station, or pick up one of the waiting *dolmuş* taxis into the centre. Express trains are excellent and there are at least ten services a day to Istanbul taking about seven hours, costing around TL25 or TL80 for the sleeper. The train network links Ankara with most of the country and there are express services to Adana (daily, 12 hours, TL25), Diyarbakır (four a week, 35 hours, TL26), Erzurum (two a day, 24 hours, TL35), Izmir (three a day, 14 hours, TL26), Kars (two a day, 28 hours, TL35), Kayseri (two a day, seven hours, TL12), Malatya (six a week, 24 hours, TL20), Sivas (six a week, 22 hours, TL18), Tatvan (twice weekly, 41 hours, TL32) and Zonguldak (three a week, nine hours,

TL14). The station has places to eat, snack shops, ATMs and a left-luggage room (*emanet*). Even with the express trains, however, it can often be faster to go by long-distance coach.

BY COACH Ankara's huge coach station or *otogar* is called AŞTI and is about 5km out of town to the west. It has 80 ticket counters (*gişes*), and to help you find your way around there is a central information point where English is spoken. There are many different competing coach companies; the major ones with the best service and safety records are called Kamil Koç (*www.kamilkoc.com.tr*), Metro (*www.metroturizm.com.tr*), Ulusoy (*www.ulusoy.com.tr*) and Varan (*www.varan.com.tr*). In the vast building, departures are from the upper level and arrivals are on the lower level where there is also a left-luggage room. As at the train station, there are restaurants, ATMs, phones and kiosks selling snacks and newspapers.

Turkey's impressive long-distance coach network links pretty much everywhere, and on the whole there is no need to book ahead. Coaches for Istanbul leave every 15 minutes, take five to six hours to cover the 450km and cost about TL30. There are also frequent services to Adana (ten hours, 490km), Amasya (five hours, 335km), Antalya (eight hours, 550km), Bodrum (13 hours, 785km), Bursa (six hours, 400km), Denizli (for Pamukkale) (seven hours, 480km), Diyarbakır (13 hours, 945km), Erzurum (13 hours, 925km), Gaziantep (ten hours, 705km), Izmir (eight hours, 600km), Kayseri (four hours, 330km), Konya (three hours, 260km), Marmaris (ten hours, 780km), Nevşehir (for Cappadocia) (five hours, 285km), Samsun (seven hours, 420km), Sivas (six hours, 450km), Sungurlu (for Boğazkale/Hattuşaş) (three hours, 177km) and Trabzon (13 hours, 780km). Fares range from TL12 for Sungurlu to TL50 for Diyarbakır. The only time you need to book ahead is at public holidays (see page 57). The coaches themselves are comfortable and temperature-controlled, and on the longer journeys they make stops about every three hours at designated places where there are refreshments and toilet facilities. Soft drinks and sweets are often provided on board as well.

GETTING AROUND

ARRIVING IN ANKARA For details of airport transfers, see page 78. Having arrived at the AŞTI coach station (*otogar*), the cheapest way to get the 5km into the city centre is to get on the Ankaray metro, whose station is immediately next door. To reach the Ulus district where the cheaper hotels are, along with the citadel of Old Ankara and the museum, you will need to change at Kızılay [82 B5] onto the Metro line for Ulus. A slightly more expensive option is to catch a *dolmuş* (shared taxi) to Ulus-Balgat. A taxi from the *otogar* to Ulus costs about TL15, but has the advantage of taking you straight to your hotel of choice. The metro costs TL3 per token, which takes you on any journey lasting up to 45 minutes, and ten-token passes can be bought for TL12, which also work on the city buses and anywhere displaying an 'EGO Bilet' sign.

The train station [82 A3] is closer in, only about 1.5km southwest of Ulus Meydanı, so you can either walk, take a bus or *dolmuş* into the centre, or taxi for a little more. (For further information, see page 80.)

BY BUS Ankara's bus, minibus and *dolmuş* system runs very well and the destinations are written on the front of the vehicles. There is a pre-pay system where tickets in books of five can be bought from shops and kiosks displaying the 'EGO Bilet' sign for about TL10. The tickets are also valid on the metro (see also page 80).

BY METRO There are just two lines in Ankara's metro system, one running east–west called Ankaray, and one running north–west called Metro. The two lines cross at Kızılay station [82 B5]. The network runs efficiently between 06.15 and 23.45 every day and single journeys are subject to a flat fare of about TL3. It operates by a system of tokens which can be bought singly (TL3) or in ten-token passes for TL12 at all metro stations.

BY TAXI Taxis are plentiful and reasonably cheap. They are all metered with a TL1.70 fixed base rate and the average fare to cross the city is TL6. Rates go up by 50% at night. No tipping is required. They can be flagged down in the street, or else tend to wait in obvious places for fares such as at the airport, bus and train stations and the museum.

BY CAR Driving yourself round Ankara requires a bit of confidence as signposting is not good and driving practices can be chaotic. Many car-hire firms have offices at Esenboğa airport. The big international ones are Avis (*www.avis.co.uk*) and Europcar (*www.europcar.com*); Avis offers the added flexibility of different collection and pick-up points, which can end up saving you quite a lot of money. All of these can be booked in advance through their websites. (For further information, see page 59.)

TOURIST INFORMATION

There are two tourist information offices, one at the airport (*Esenboğa International Airport;* \ *3980345;* ⊕ *24 hours*) and one in the city centre, within a few minutes' walk of the train station, opposite Maltepe Ankaray metro station [82 A3] (*121 Gazi Mustafa Kemal Bulvarı, Tandoğan;* \ *2315572;* ⊕ *09.00–17.00 Mon–Fri, 10.00–17.00 Sat*). They can hand out free maps and the usual glossy brochures, which can be useful if you have not already picked these up at the Turkish Tourist Office in your own country before leaving.

Ankara also produces a monthly publication, *The Guide*, which you can pick up at bookshops and at the Rahmi M Koç Industrial Museum [82 D3] beside the citadel gate. This has comprehensive listings, like its equivalent publication in Istanbul.

TOUR OPERATORS

Unlike Istanbul, which is awash with local tour companies offering myriad tours all over the city, Ankara's much more limited attractions translate into far fewer such companies.

ANKARA ANIMALS

There are three animals associated with Ankara: the cat, the goat and the rabbit. The Ankara cat is a delicate fluffy white creature, not suited to hunting. Its large eyes can be green, yellow, copper or blue and the pure bred species originated from Ankara and is properly known as *Felis domesticus angoriensis*. The Angora goat is a much hardier creature, brought here by the Turks in the 13th century. Its shiny silver-white wool, called mohair, is widely used in the textile industry as it is easily dyed, heat-resistant, dirt-resistant and soft. The Angora rabbit is also white, but with red eyes, and its long shiny fur can grow up to 40cm. Much sought-after and hypoallergenic, the rabbits' wool is very light and highly heat-absorbent. The rabbits are shorn from the age of two to three months and each rabbit provides 1kg of wool a year.

Alabanda Tourism Cinnah Caddesi 67, Çankaya;
☎ 4405600; www.alabanda.com.tr
Ay-Fi Tourism Ali Suavi Sokak 23/54, Maltepe;
☎ 2324820; www.ay-fi.com

Raytur Gar Binası İçi, Ulus; ☎ 3114200;
www.raytur.com.tr
Saltur Atatürk Bulvarı 175/4, Kavalıdere;
☎ 4251333; www.saltur.com.tr
Tempotur Binnaz Sokak 1/4; ☎ 4282096

🏠 WHERE TO STAY

The more expensive modern hotels tend to be in the New City (Yenişehir) in the district of Kavalıdere, the mid-range ones tend to be grouped in the district of Kızılay, and the cheaper ones are in the Old Town area around Ulus Meydanı (Ulus Square). Before finalising any bookings, take the time to check websites like www.booking.com for Ankara, as good savings can be had sometimes on hotels that you might expect to be too expensive. This is particularly the case in the five- and four-star categories, where prices can sometimes drop by as much as 50%. The standard international hotels like the Hilton, Sheraton and Swissotel are all here, but are not included in the list below, which confines itself to smaller and more personal hotels. Distances are small, so if you choose to stay in the modern part of town in one of the more expensive hotels, it will still only take ten minutes or so by road to get into the old part of town to visit the citadel and museum

🏠 **Gordion Hotel** (42 rooms) Tunalı Hilmi Caddesi, Bülküm Sokak 59, Kavalıdere; ☎ 4278080; e efidan@gordionhotel.com; www.gordionhotel.com. Small luxury hotel in the heart of the business district close to embassies & ministries, excellent restaurants & fashionable shopping venues. Very unusual for Ankara, it is styled like a boutique business hotel, with luxurious Ottoman furnishings. The basement has an indoor pool & sauna with gym, while the roof has an excellent restaurant with good city views. $$$$$

🏠 **Mega Residence Hotel** (29 rooms) Tahran Caddesi, Kavalıdere; ☎ 4685400; www.megaresidence.com. Very exclusive small place aimed at the German market with beautiful pine façade & excellent Schnitzel restaurant & Italian snacks in the Gusto Bar. $$$$$

🏠 **Hotel Gold** [82 C6] (60 rooms) Güfte Sokak 4, Bakanlıklar; ☎ 4194868; www.ankaragoldhotel.com. Quietly located on a residential street south of Kızılay, this colourfully decorated hotel with its marble-floored terrace café offers a classy kind of luxury. $$$$

🏠 **Neva Palas** (60 rooms) Küçükesat Caddesi, Çankaya; ☎ 4195888; www.nevapalas.com. Modern hotel with central location in fashionable Çankaya, with elegant decorations throughout. 3 good restaurants with Turkish, international & vegetarian cuisine. $$$$

🏠 **And Butik Hotel** [82 D2] (6 rooms) Ickale Mahallesi, Istek Sokak no.2, Altindag; ☎ 3102304; www.andbutikhotel.com. Beautifully restored &

renovated Ottoman mansion open all year round. Courtyard garden. Excellent food. $$$

🏠 **Angora House Hotel** [82 D3] (6 rooms) Kalekapısı Sokak 16, Ulus, Kaleiçi; ☎ 3098380; e angorahouse@gmail.com. Set within Ankara's old citadel, this lovingly restored 19th-century Ottoman mansion was the first true boutique hotel, converted from what was once the owner's carpet shop. Walled courtyard. Rooms have Wi-Fi. Fabulous b/fast. ⏰ Mar–Oct. $$$

🏠 **Dedeman Hotel** [82 C6] (299 rooms) Akay Caddesi, Kızılay; ☎ 4176200; www.dedemanhotels.com. Part of the respected mid-range Turkish chain, the rooms are comfortable if a bit small & basic, but there are 3 restaurants, swimming pools, a sauna & fitness centre to make up for it. $$$

🏠 **Almer Hotel** [82 C2] (72 rooms) Çankırı Caddesi 17, Ulus; ☎ 3090435; www.almer.com.tr. Very good location close to the *otogar* & Ulus square. Clean pleasant rooms with b/fast buffet & evening restaurant. $$

🏠 **Atalay Hotel** [82 C2] (90 rooms) Cankırı Caddesi, Ulus; ☎ 3091515; www.atalay.com. Well located in the centre with good rooms, a restaurant offering international cuisine all day, & bar. Reliable babysitting service. Turkish b/fast buffet. $$

🏠 **Capital Hotel** [82 C2] (58 rooms) Çankırı Caddesi 21, Ulus; ☎ 3104575; www.hotelcapital.com.tr. Shares the good location of the Almer Hotel & offers good value food & accommodation with AC. $$

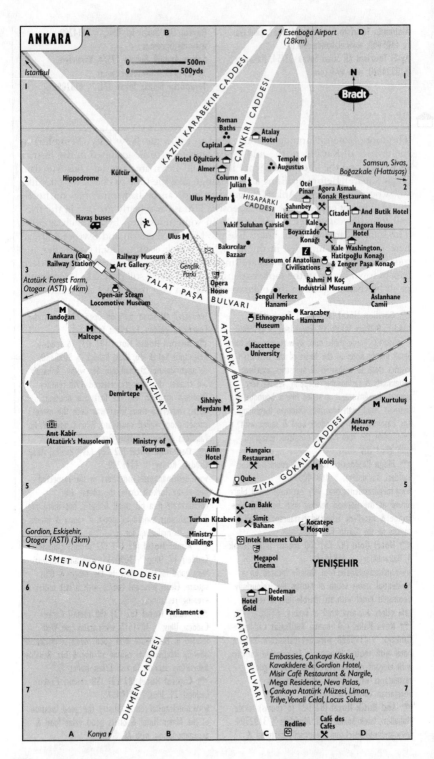

ANKARA

A · B · C · D

Esenboğa Airport (28km)

İstanbul

N

Bradt

0 — 500m
0 — 500yds

KAZIM KARABEKIR CADDESI

ÇANKIRI CADDESI

Roman Baths

Atalay Hotel

Capital

Hotel Öğültürk
Almer

Temple of Augustus

Samsun, Sivas, Boğazkale (Hattuşaş)

Hippodrome

Kültür M

Column of Julian

Otel Pınar

Ulus Meydanı

HISAPARKI CADDESI

Agora Asmalı Konak Restaurant

Şahınbey

Hitit

Kale

Citadel

And Butik Hotel

Havaş buses

Vakif Suluhan Çarşisi

Boyacızade Konağı

Angora House Hotel

Ulus M

Bakırcılar Bazaar

Kale Washington, Hatitpoğlu Konağı & Zenger Paşa Konağı

Ankara (Garı) Railway Station

Railway Museum & Art Gallery

Gençlik Parkı

Museum of Anatolian Civilisations

Atatürk Forest Farm, Otogar (ASTI) (4km)

TALAT PAŞA

Opera House

Rahmi M Koç Industrial Museum

Open-air Steam Locomotive Museum

BULVARI

Şengul Merkez Hanami

Aslanhane Camii

M Tandoğan

Ethnographic Museum

Karacabey Hamamı

M Maltepe

ATATÜRK

Hacettepe University

KIZILAY

Demirtepe

BULVARI

Sihhiye Meydanı M

M Kurtuluş

Ankaray Metro

Anıt Kabir (Atatürk's Mausoleum)

Ministry of Tourism

Aifin Hotel

Mangaıcı Restaurant

ZIYA GÖKALP CADDESI

Kolej

Qube

Kızılay M

Can Balık

Turhan Kitabevi

Simit Bahane

Kocatepe Mosque

Gordion, Eskişehir, Otogar (ASTI) (3km)

Ministry Buildings

Intek Internet Club

ISMET İNÖNÜ CADDESI

Megapol Cinema

YENİŞEHIR

Dedeman Hotel

Hotel Gold

Parliament

ATATÜRK BULVARI

DIKMEN CADDESI

Embassies, Çankaya Köskü, Kavaklıdere & Gordion Hotel, Misir Café Restaurant & Nargile, Mega Residence, Neva Palas, Çankaya Atatürk Müzesi, Liman, Trilye, Vonali Celal, Locus Solus

Konya

Redline

Café des Cafés

⌂ **Hitit Hotel** [82 C2] (50 rooms) Hisarparkı Caddesi 12, Ulus; ☎ 3108617. On the way up to the citadel, a simple budget hotel with friendly service. Well situated for the museum. $$
⌂ **Hotel Oğultürk** [82 C2] (68 rooms) Ruzgarlı Caddesi, Ulus; ☎ 3092900; www.ogulturk.com. Very close to the museum & citadel, this is a pleasant place with friendly staff & good management. Fine for solo women travellers. Very good restaurant. $$
⌂ **Şahınbey Hotel** [82 C2] (25 rooms) Hisarparkı Caddesi, Ulus; ☎ 3104955; www.sahinbeyhotel.com. Good location close to the museum & sights, 20 mins' drive from the airport.

Unexciting exterior but excellent value for money with an acceptable restaurant. Minibar in rooms. $$
⌂ **Alfin Hotel** [82 B5] (40 rooms) Menekse Sokak, Kızılay; ☎ 4178425; www.alfin.com. Good location close to Kızılay metro station, tucked up a side street off Gazi Mustafa Kemal Caddesi, friendly budget place, good for families. Reasonable restaurant. $
⌂ **Kale Otel** [82 C2] (25 rooms) Alataş Sokak 13; ☎ 3113393. Budget choice very close to the museum. B/fast extra. $
⌂ **Otel Pınar** [82 C2] (25 rooms) Hisarparkı Caddesi 14, Ulus; ☎ 3118951. In the same street

✖ WHERE TO EAT AND DRINK

As with the hotels, the expensive and classier places are to be found in the modern business and government ministry districts like Kavalıdere, while the more moderate places tend to be in the Kızılay district, and the cheaper places are grouped in the older Ulus part of town. The exceptions are the restaurants that have opened in recent years in converted Ottoman mansions within or close to the citadel and museum, which offer fine Ottoman cuisine and prices to match. For an amazing panoramic view of Ankara, the landmark 125m-tall Atakule tower in Çankaya has a scenic revolving restaurant-café-bar at the top, above its shopping centre, reached by a vertigo-inducing glass lift.

Ankara specialises in meat dishes, the most popular being forest kebab (*orman kebab*), cubes of meat simmered with carrots, onion and potato, flavoured with thyme. Traditional soups are called *toyga*, made from rice and yoghurt, *tarhana* made with dried yoghurt, tomato and pimento peppers and *keşkek* made with wheat and milk. The most common types of pastry are *ay böreği* (moon pastry) and *alt üst böreği* (topsy-turvy pastry). Sweet stuffings and desserts are also popular specialities of the region.

RESTAURANTS
✖ **Kale Washington** [82 D3] Doyran Sokak 5/7; ☎ 3114344; ⊕ from 09.30. Extremely fine restaurant formed by joining 2 17th-century houses. Hillary Clinton & other visiting dignitaries are said to have eaten here. The cuisine is Turkish international. $$$$$
✖ **Liman** Cinnah Caddesi, Çankaya; ☎ 4401547; ⊕ 12.00–02.00. Very plush place with cosy atmosphere, specialising in Ottoman & international dishes, especially seafood, such as bream in pomegranate sauce. Alfresco dining on the veranda in summer, good wine list with foreign & local wines. $$$$$
✖ **Hatitpoğlu Konağı** [82 B3] Sevinç Sokak 3; ☎ 3113696; ⊕ 19.00–01.00. Located in a converted Ottoman house just outside the citadel, this place offers good-value set menus if you have a hearty appetite. A bit touristy,

there is also live music daily except Sun. $$$$
✖ **Trilye** Hafta Sokak, Gaziosmanpaşa; ☎ 4471200; ⊕ 11.30–23.30. Upmarket fish restaurant in a small villa with its own garden, in Gaziosmanpaşa, the expensive suburb between Kavalıdere & Çankaya, a little to the east. Turkish & international cuisine, such as sea bass in a bamboo basket & inventive *mezze* variations. $$$$
✖ **Agora Asmali Konak Restaurant** [82 D2] Kale Kapısı; ☎ 3113511; ⊕ 11.00–22.30. Friendly place in a renovated house near the citadel gate, serving Turkish food under the shady vines of its garden in summer. Turkish music every evening. $$$
✖ **Boyacızâde Konağı** [82 D2] Berrak Sokak 7/9; ☎ 3102525; ⊕ 10.30–22.30. Another pair of converted Ottoman houses with traditional décor close to the museum, this place has very good fish

3

dishes along with Turkish classical music (*fasıl*). There are good views of the old citadel. $$$

✕ **Chez Le Belge** Sahil Caddesi, Gölbaşi; ✎ 4841478; ⏰ 10.30–22.00. A favourite place at w/ends to escape the city & eat French food on the shore of the Gölbaşi Lake (see page 96). $$$

✕ **Merkez Restaurant** Çiftlik Caddesi, Atatürk Farm; ✎ 2110250; ⏰ 10.00–22.00. Set in a huge garden on the western outskirts of Ankara within the Atatürk Forest Farm (see page 95), this place serves traditional Turkish cuisine. $$$

✕ **Vonali Celal** Çevre Sokak, Uskup Caddesi, Çankaya; ✎ 4282398; ⏰ 11.00–22.30. Specialising in Black Sea cuisine (also has a branch in Istanbul), with plenty of anchovies, meat cooked on hazelnut shells & sea bass casserole (*buglama*). $$$

✕ **And Butik** [82 D2] (see *Hotels* above) ✎ 3127978; ⏰ 10.00–22.00. In summer meals

can be served on the terrace with fine views. Turkish specialities include *saç kavurma*, a sizzling meat & vegetable mix. $$

✕ **Can Balık** [82 C5] Sakarya Caddesi 8/4, Kızılay; ⏰ 10.00–22.00. Very reasonably priced simple fish restaurant. $$

✕ **Mangalcı** [82 C5] Bayındır Sokak, Kızılay; ✎ 4355226; ⏰ 10.00–22.30. Friendly southeast Turkey flavour restaurant in the heart of Ankara where you can grill your meat of choice at your own charcoal fire at the table. Good *mezze*. $$

✕ **Zenger Paşa Konağı** [82 D3] Doyran Sokak 13; ✎ 3117070; www.zengerpasa.com; ⏰ 10.30–22.30. In the same street as the Kale Washington above, this place was the first of Ankara's restaurants to become established in a restored Ottoman house. Full of Ottoman memorabilia, there is also live music every evening, with meals authentically cooked in the original oven. $$

CAFÉS Kızılay is café-land in Ankara with loads of pavement cafés, especially along Ziya Gokalp Caddesi.

✕ **Café des Cafés** [82 D7] Tunalı Hilmi Caddesi 83, Kavalidere; ⏰ 08.30–midnight. Set in the New City, this place offers an unusual selection of Mediterranean bistro dishes, especially Spanish & Italian. $$

✕ **Misir Café Restaurant & Nargile** Bülten Sokak 4A, Kavalidere; ✎ 4683272 & Karanfil Sokak

34/A, Kızılay; ✎ 4193035; ⏰ 09.30–23.30. Both branches of this atmospheric Egyptian-style café are fun to take a break in. $$

✕ **Simit Bahane** [82 C5] Karanfil Sokak 36a, Kızılay; ⏰ 09.00–23.00. Atmospheric place with backgammon, newspapers & *nargiles* (water-pipes) $

BARS

♀ **Locus Solus** Bestekar Sokak 60, Kavalidere; ✎ 4686788; ⏰ 09.30–midnight. Terrace & beer garden with relaxed beanbag seating & comfy sofas. $$

♀ **Qube Bar** [82 C5] Bayındır Sokak 16b, Kızılay; ✎ 4323079; ⏰ 10.00–23.30. Provides food, & has a removable glass roof in summer. $

ENTERTAINMENT AND NIGHTLIFE

As the capital city Ankara has more nightlife than just about anywhere in eastern Turkey, though in practice few Western visitors will make this a priority. If wanted, the entire range is available, from cheap student bars to exclusive nightclubs (*gazinos*), many with live music. Alcohol is widely available, though excessive drinking is not by and large the Turkish scene. The liveliest area is in Kızılay between Sarkaya and Tuna Caddesi, packed with *gazinos* many offering live Turkish pop music. Young Western women should feel comfortable at most of them. Cinemas occasionally show Western films in the original language – the English-language paper *Hurriyet Daily News* gives listings. The modern cinemas like Megapol [82 C6] (*Konur Sokak 33, Kızılay;* ✎ 4194493) and Kavalıdere (*Tunalı Hilmi Caddesi, Kavalidere;* ✎ 4672971) are located south of Kızılay. The opera house in the Gençlik Parkı [82 B3] has a full season starting in the autumn. It doubles as a theatre and is known as Büyük Tiyatro (Big Theatre) (✎ 3242210).

New Ankara has the classy shopping malls you would expect to find in any capital city, but the more interesting shopping is to be found in the area around the citadel. Antique shops on Çıkrıkçılar Hill near Ulus are worth browsing through, as is the Bakırcılar Bazaar [82 C3] where a range of carpets, rugs, clothes, antiques, copperware, jewellery and ornaments can be found. On the walk up to the old citadel you will also find shops selling spices, dried fruits and other temptations. You could also stop off at the Vakıf Suluhan Çarşısı [82 C2] on Konya Caddesi behind the Ulus Hali food market, which is a restored caravanserai complete with mosque in its central courtyard and clothes shops, café and toilets. When bargaining, feigning total disinterest in the desired object is the key.

OTHER PRACTICALITIES

BOOKSHOPS **Turhan Kitabevi** [82 C5] (*Yüksel Caddesi 8/32, Kızılay;* \ *4188259*) has the best English-language selection, with coffee-table books, guidebooks, maps, fiction, magazines and newspapers.

HOSPITALS AND PHARMACIES
✚ **Bayındır Hospital** Atatürk Bulvarı 201, Kavalıdere; \ 4280808. The city's most modern private hospital.

✚ **City Hospital** Büklüm Sokak 53, Kavalıdere; \ 4663346. Has an up-to-date women's health centre.

There are many pharmacies all over the city, recognisable by their green cross outside.

INTERNET Wi-Fi is now available in many hotels, cafés and bars. The biggest concentration of internet cafés is in Kızılay around Konur Sokak. Some have over 100 terminals and are aimed at gamers.

🖳 **Intek Internet Club** [82 C6] Karanfil Sokak, Kızılay; ⊕ 07.00–midnight. Has a very reliable service, costing TL2 per hr.

🖳 **Redline** [82 C7] Tunali Hilmi Caddesi, Kavalıdere; ⊕ 10.00–23.00. Charges TL1.50 per hr.

MONEY AND EXCHANGE Almost all banks everywhere in town have ATMs, and there are also many exchange places such as Sakarya Döviz (*Sakarya Caddesi 6-A, Kızılay*).

POST The train station and bus station have PTT offices (⊕ *08.30–18.00*) with public phone booths. Ankara's main post office (*Merkez Postanesi, Esret Bitlis Caddesi, 8 Yenimahalle;* \ *3211715*) is in the same street as the bus station.

WHAT TO SEE AND DO

MUSEUM OF ANATOLIAN CIVILISATIONS [82 D3] (*Anadolu Medeniyetleri Müzesi, Ulus;* \ *3243160;* ⊕ *08.30–17.15 daily; attractive drinks & coffee area; adult TL20/student TL10/under 17s and over 65s free*)

Getting there From the Ulus Meydanı, the main square of the Old Town, recognisable by the inevitable equestrian statue of Atatürk in blackened bronze, you follow the road uphill till you reach a set of traffic lights on the brow. On foot you can fork diagonally right from here in the direction of the museum, but by road the one-way system dictates that you continue straight on towards the citadel in front of you, the road dropping to the very foot, before winding up to reach the front of the museum, recognisable at most times of the year by the large number of coaches parked outside.

Visiting the museum It is to visit this museum that most people will make the trip to Ankara, as it has achieved wide renown for the most spectacular and comprehensive display in the world of Hittite and Urartian finds. Small, but carefully and clearly laid out, the museum lives up to its reputation. The building itself is a renovated 15th-century *bedestan* (covered market) which lends itself very well for conversion into a museum because you can progress round the four galleries on all sides of the courtyard moving logically through time from the Neolithic to the Roman eras. In the centre, the big hall contains monumental Hittite stone carvings from sites like Carchemish (see page 212). The idea to begin such a collection was, like everything else in Ankara, Atatürk's, and it was originally called the 'Hittite Museum', to draw the world's attention to the newly discovered culture of Anatolia's forbears. It is set in well-kept and colourful gardens with various statues and rock-cut reliefs on display among the trees and shrubs, with benches where it is pleasant to sit and relax afterwards.

Stone Age exhibits On entering the museum and buying your ticket you turn right past the bookshop and postcard displays to come to the Neolithic (late Stone Age) displays. The first exhibit is a reconstruction of a cave sanctuary at Çatalhüyük (see page 179), 8,000 years old, which has the earliest murals ever discovered on a plaster coating of cave walls and showing paintings of bulls' heads, humans and leopards. These are the original reliefs, removed from the walls with great care, though they are heavily restored.

The exhibits here demonstrate that Neolithic Anatolian man in the 7th millennium BC developed earlier and more artistically than his neighbours. He was the first to apply his knowledge of plant and animal domestication, and so leave behind his hunting and gathering lifestyle and his caves as well, to live in settled villages instead. Older even than these paintings on manmade walls are the cave paintings found recently in the Van area, now on display in the Van Museum (see page 284). The paintings, in red or dark brown, show the images of dancing human figures, deer, mountain goats and scenes of hunting and trapping now extinct animals. The stylised animals are very similar to those still seen today in *kilim* and saddlebag designs, knitted socks, pottery and even gravestones. Also represented are gods and goddesses standing on deer and other animals, the goddesses with exaggerated genitals and motifs of the sun, all of which were important symbols passed down to the Hurrian and Hittite cultures.

Among the most intriguing exhibits in this section are what could pass for a Neolithic cocktail stick and an exquisite cup-shaped obsidian mirror, highly polished, perhaps the oldest mirror in the world. The earliest-known seals, symbols of private property, are also to be seen here.

In the next display cases are the earliest-known examples of the Anatolian earth mother, grotesquely fat by modern standards, with colossal arms, legs, breasts and belly. Female corpulence was much admired in Turkey until relatively recently. An Ottoman saying runs: 'She is so beautiful she has to go through the door sideways.'

In one of the displays the earth mother is sitting calmly resting her hands on two lions either side of her: this is one of the earliest representations of her in her dual role as fertility goddess and mistress of the animal kingdom. It is a concept that can be traced through the Phrygian Cybele, the Greek Artemis, the Roman Diana and ultimately the Christian Virgin Mary.

The Copper and Bronze ages The next period you come to is the Chacolithic (Copper Age). Hacılar (25km southwest of Burdur) is the main site excavated of this period and shows the first evidence of an enclosing city wall. The pottery is richer; it is shiny and painted; the geometric shapes used on it are again similar to patterns used in modern *kilims*.

An entrance to the vast central hall is marked by the colossal sideways-striding Hittite relief of the war god, muscle-calved and smiling very slightly. Wearing the typical Hittite short kilt and conical hat (signifying that he is a god) he stood originally outside the King's Gate at Hattuşaş. To preserve the chronology of your tour, however, you should not enter this hall of Hittite sculpture yet, but enter it later, from the second gallery where the other Hittite finds are displayed.

Instead, next are the exhibits of the 3rd millennium BC, the early Bronze Age, with a wealth of objects in copper, lead, tin, gold, silver, bronze, electrum (a mixture of gold and silver) and even iron, a metal many times more valuable than gold at that time. They reveal a high degree of metallurgical competence and an opulent lifestyle, with golden goblets, crowns and jewellery. There are some gold necklaces that are so finely worked in delicate filigree that you have to marvel at the precision tools they must have used, probably made from hard vitreous obsidian, found locally. This filigree technique of weaving fine gold or silver into jewellery and ornaments is still an important traditional handicraft of the Ankara region (still practised in the town of Beypazarı about 70km west of Ankara) and known as *telkari*.

Most of these exhibits are finds from the royal tombs of Alacahüyük and are among the most spectacular items in the museum. Thirteen of these tombs were excavated between 1935 and 1939. The women were found accompanied by their jewellery and toilet articles, the men by their personal ornaments and weapons. In each grave the body was surrounded by elaborately wrought bronze 'sun discs'. These distinctive discs, with their criss-cross patterns had some mystical property which scholars still argue about. They are generally agreed to be cosmological symbols of some sort, possibly representing the sun and its rays, sometimes with antlered stags in the centre. They are called 'standards' for want of a better word, as they appear to have been designed to be mounted at the head of a pole and used as a processional staff in rituals. These symbols continue to fascinate modern Turks and one was chosen as the emblem for the Ministry of Culture and

The pottery of Kültepe was very advanced and shows for the first time the painting in geometric shapes, often stripes and zigzags, which is now called Cappadocian ware, as it is thought to have been a development indigenous to that region. Some of the tall vases and jugs have shapes that are to our eye modern, not to say futuristic. Among these elegant vases and jars there are also large numbers of drinking vessels or *rhytons* (libation vases) in the shapes of animals and humans. Many of the animals are lions and large cats and have a comic and again almost modern appearance. It is uncertain which liquid they drank out of these vessels, but with Anatolia being the home of both the cultivated grape and barley, perhaps the Hittites asked their servants for 'a lion of wine' or 'a stag of beer'. As well as the drinking vessels there are many cylindrical seals and lead figurines of deities.

Tourism. The abundance of bronze bulls, stags and cows all points to the fact that central and eastern Anatolia were far more heavily forested than now. The prominence given to the stag suggests the mentality of a mountain people, and the deer and bulls which also figure frequently are un-Mesopotamian in style and subject. The culture of this indigenous Anatolian people, the Hatti, influenced that of their later conquerors, the Hittites.

The Assyrian colonies Having completed the first side of the courtyard you now turn left to enter the second side running across the back of the *bedestan*-cum-museum, with a wealth of objects on display from the Assyrian colonies (1950–1750BC). Assyrian merchants from northern Mesopotamia arrived in Anatolia attracted by the prosperity of the Hittite Empire. They established large trading colonies and introduced their long-developed cuneiform writing system. The main site for these discoveries was at Karum, the trading centre at Kültepe, near modern Kayseri. This writing looks dishearteningly difficult to decipher with endless repetitive symbols differing only slightly from each other. Maybe the Hittites found it difficult too, for they later changed to adopt a hieroglyphic script which was deciphered by a Czech linguist, Hrozny, in 1912.

Exhibits of the Old Hittite kingdom You come next, towards the far end of the second gallery, to the Old Hittite kingdom exhibits (c1700–1450BC). Many of the vases show reliefs of the sideways-on people similar to contemporaneous Egyptian and Minoan art. The Hittites were not, unlike the Hatti, indigenous, but came in a great wave from southern Russian and central Asia, making their appearance in Anatolia at the end of the early Bronze Age. Under the Hittite dynasty the ceramic industry declined and the first stone upright reliefs appeared. Turning back to retrace your steps to the middle of the second gallery, you enter the central hall which houses an astonishing display of monumental Hittite sculpture covering a span of eight centuries, from Hattuşaş (Boğazkale) and Alacahüyük to the Neo-Hittite sites at Carchemish and Aslantepe. Of particular note is the Chimaera from Carchemish, dated to the 8th century BC. This mythical creature had its home on Mount Olympos in Lycian Turkey and was passed to Greece through Homer's *Iliad* and Corinthian vase painting at the beginning of the 7th century BC. By the 6th century BC it was also found in Etruscan art.

From Phrygians and Urartians to Greeks and Romans You now arrive at the third side of the courtyard, turning left into the Phrygian exhibits, the Phrygians being the people who ruled central Anatolia after the collapse of the Hittite Empire (8th century BC). Most of these exhibits were found in the royal tombs at Gordion and are of special interest because of the extent to which they foreshadow the later artistic and cultural developments in classical Greece.

The next section displays the Urartian objects, the Urartians being contemporaneous with the Phrygians, but ruling in eastern Turkey over an empire that stretched from Lake Urmia near Tabriz in northwestern Iran to Sivas and Trabzon in the north and to Aleppo in the south.

The final part of the courtyard completing the three sides contains exhibits of the classical Greek and Roman periods. The most impressive exhibit here is an excellent coin collection, gold and silver, with all the city states in Anatolia represented, showing the heads of various kings and emperors. Here you can see the world's first ever coin, made from a mixture of gold and silver. It is from Sardis in Lydia and dates from 615BC.

CITADEL [82 D2] (*Kaleiçi, Ulus;* ☉ *always*) From the museum you can go on a short ten-minute walk up the road to the right towards the old citadel of Ankara, to get a glimpse of the contrast between Turkey old and new. The powerful walls still stand tall and on climbing up the steps through one of the gates you step back into medieval times. Cars can only penetrate to the outer edges. The once-crumbling houses here inside lining the narrow winding streets are beginning to be restored, some of them converted to restaurants and even the odd small hotel.

Walking uphill from behind the museum past the octagonal tower, you will come to the gate known as *Saatli Kapi* (Clock Gate), opposite which is an unusual museum housed inside a restored *han* called *Cengelhan*. This is the **Rahmi M Koç Industrial Museum** [82 D3] (✎ *3096800; www.rmk-museum.org.tr;* ☉ *10.00–17.00 Tue–Fri, 10.00–19.00 Sat/Sun; adult TL2*) with exhibits spread over three floors on diverse subjects like music, transport, computing, carpets and Atatürk.

The earliest citadel foundations belong to the Gauls, a wild and warlike race invited into Asia in 279BC from southern Europe as mercenaries by the King of Bithynia (on the southern shores of the Sea of Marmara). They made a nuisance of themselves all down the Aegean coast till the powerful King of Pergamum, Attalus, drove them inland. The Gauls settled in the Ankara region and even today there are a number of red-haired freckled Turks to be found here.

The main parts of the defence walls standing today are Byzantine with much subsequent Turkish construction. The geographical location of Ankara is on one of the great natural east–west highways of Asia Minor. Invading armies have marched to and fro throughout its history. After the Phrygians, Persians, Alexander and the Gauls came the Romans, Arabs, Turks, Crusaders and Mongols. The walls of the citadel and the houses within it reflect this variety with a hotchpotch of

3

FORGOTTEN CRAFTSMEN

Like their predecessors the Hittites, the Urartians were a people largely forgotten until rediscovered by archaeologists in the 20th century. Their characteristic sites were steep rock citadels on long thin spurs and their ruined fortresses can still be seen on mountaintops throughout the Van region. Urartian metal and ivory objects were highly prized and were exported to Phrygia, Greece and Italy. There are gold, silver and bronze objects with human and animal attachments. One of these, a huge bronze cauldron on a three-legged stand with cloven-hoof feet and bulls' head handles, is the earliest-known prototype of a style which found its way to Etruria and was passed from there to classical Greece. Especially lovely are the intricately worked wide gold belts and a superb ivory seated lion, reminiscent of the Chinese lion.

Ankara, though it has seen many armies march by, has been the setting for only one major battle: in 1402 the army of the Ottoman sultan Beyazıt was devastated by the Mongol hordes under the ferocious Tamerlane. The Ottoman Turks had been penetrating the shrinking borders of the Byzantine Empire, and until this battle it seemed certain that Constantinople would fall to Beyazıt. Instead Byzantium was reprieved for 50 years yet. The final assault came in 1453, when Beyazıt's great-grandson Mehmet II overwhelmed Constantinople's walls. There was also a more recent battle, in a valley near Ankara, where the climactic scenes of *The Charge of the Light Brigade* were filmed in 1936, starring Errol Flynn and Olivia de Havilland. The landscape was suitable for the Crimean War (1853–56) backdrop and the Turkish government made available free of charge 600 cavalry and 3,000 infantry for the 12 weeks of shooting, in the hope of obtaining good publicity.

stones from different eras, with fragments of ancient columns and capitals in modern use as doorsteps, windowsills, garden seats and lintels. If you approach the citadel from the west up Hisarparkı Caddesi, you can also spot the remains of the Roman theatre about halfway up on your left.

From the 11th century Ankara was in the hands of the Seljuk Turks and it was presumably Turcoman tribes who brought the long-haired goats from central Asia to Angora (as Ankara was known until Atatürk's time). The fine wool from these Angora goats (see page 5), known as mohair, was the foundation of the town's prosperity.

As you travel eastwards some understanding becomes essential of how modern Turkey came into being. Mustafa Kemal, later surnamed Atatürk (Father of the Turks), was born in Salonika, now Greece, then an Ottoman city, in 1880. He entered the army at the age of 12 and graduated from the War College in Istanbul in 1905. After serving with distinction in the Balkan Wars in 1911 and 1912, he led the Turkish forces in 1915 to defend the Gallipoli Peninsula and was largely responsible for repelling the British and forcing their subsequent evacuation. He also distinguished himself on the Russian front and in Palestine, emerging as the only real Turkish hero of the debacle of World War I.

The victorious Allies drew up their arrangements for the dissolution of the Ottoman Empire, 'the sick man of Europe', in the form of the Treaty of Sèvres in August 1920. The provisions of the treaty were very harsh, far harsher than those imposed on Germany. It has been described by historians as 'the signing of the death warrant of the Ottoman Empire'. The Arab provinces were to be placed under British and French mandates to prepare them for eventual independence. Anatolia's eastern provinces were to be divided between an autonomous Kurdistan and an independent Armenia. Greece was to have Izmir and its hinterland and Thrace, regions with a heavily Greek population going back to ancient times. Italy would get the southern half of western and central Anatolia, while France took the southeast. The straits were to be neutralised and administered by a permanent Allied Commission in Constantinople, and Constantinople itself would remain in Turkish hands as long as the rights of the minorities were upheld.

The treaty was never implemented, however, for while the Allies were imposing their terms on the sultan and his government in Istanbul, a new Turkish state was rising in the interior of Anatolia based on the total rejection of the treaty. Though the British and French were successful in establishing their mandates over the Arab lands, and the Italians were able to secure at least the Dodecanese for themselves, Kurdish and

MOSQUES Atatürk's patronage apart, Ankara has never been favoured by Turkey's rulers. It was too far from the major Seljuk cultural centres and the Ottomans largely ignored it. As a result the city is not well endowed with interesting mosques, and the only one to consider visiting is the **Aslanhane Camii** [82 D3], a 13th-century Seljuk mosque with a blue-tiled *mihrab* (prayer niche marking the direction of Mecca) and lovely carved woodwork on the ceiling and the 24 wooden columns that support it. A stone lion in the courtyard gives it its name of *aslan* (lion). The mosque is to be found below the citadel, to the northeast of the Museum of Anatolian Civilisations.

Completed in 1987, the gigantic **Kocatepe Mosque** [82 C5] is a curious hark-back to the imperial Ottoman mosques of Istanbul, precisely the heritage Atatürk was keen to distance himself from in Ankara. Its various dependent buildings also house the Ministry of Religious Affairs. Its imposing silhouette is today the main reference point of the modern city centre.

ANKARA'S ROMAN MONUMENTS The Province of Galatia was annexed to the Roman Empire by Augustus in 25BC, and the three Roman monuments that remain in the city can be visited on foot in an hour. About 400m north of Ulus Meydanı you can pay a brief visit to the **Temple of Augustus** [82 C2], the most prominent of Ankara's Roman remains. You will see the high wall of the temple next to a mosque. It began life as a temple to Cybele, the Anatolian fertility goddess and was then a Phrygian temple to the phallic god, Men, before becoming the Temple of Augustus and Rome. During his lifetime Augustus encouraged the deification of Rome and would only permit his own worship

Armenian hopes were suppressed, and the Greek army, after landing at Izmir in May 1919 and pushing deep into the interior, was routed by forces under the command of Atatürk. The Turkish nationalist movement, which had started among a small class of intellectuals, mushroomed during these struggles into a countrywide uprising bent on creating an Anatolian-based state for the Turks alone. The campaign against Greek forces, from 1919 to 1922, became known as the War of Independence. Atatürk's efforts were crowned by the Treaty of Versailles in 1923, which recognised Turkish sovereignty over approximately its present-day borders.

During the remaining 15 years of his life, Atatürk carried out a series of far-reaching reforms which were intended to westernise Turkey and integrate it into the modern world. His regime was effectively a dictatorship, and a single party, the Republican People's Party, enforced government policy. Atatürk terminated the caliphate, exiled the sultan, and in a series of edicts the Ministry of Religious Affairs was abolished, religious orders disbanded, religious property sequestrated and religious instruction forbidden. In 1928 Islam itself was disestablished and the constitution amended to make Turkey a secular state. Atatürk was not opposed to religion itself: his aim was to free the Turks from the clutches of the fanatics. Everyone could be a devout Muslim in his private life, but was not to mix religion with politics. The Arabic alphabet was abolished. Atatürk had asked the academics how long it would take to devise a new Latin alphabet for Turkish, and was told six years. He gave them six months. The fez, which he called a 'Greek headdress' was forbidden. He also introduced considerable reforms to bring the rights of women closer to those of men. He died in the Dolmabahçe Palace in Istanbul on 10 November 1938. The political parties today, ironically, usually ignore Atatürk's exhortation to keep religion and politics apart, and at every election still pander to religious traditionalism to get out the rural vote.

after his death, since his advisers assured him the people in the eastern provinces of Syria and Asia Minor expected it. At the beginning of the 6th century the temple was converted to a church, and following the Turkish conquest the church was converted to a *medrese* (theological college) attached to the adjacent mosque. When Lord Warkworth, an English MP, stayed in Ankara in the 1890s, he found the Turkish governor of Ankara 'an intelligent and liberal-minded soldier, cleaning and repairing the Temple of Augustus'. The setting, as so often in eastern Turkey, does much to detract from the attractiveness of the temple, and it can only be viewed from outside its tall green railings, usually kept locked. The adjacent Haci Beyram Mosque is dedicated to Ankara's favourite saint, the founder of the Beyrami order of dervishes, and his *türbe* (tomb) immediately in front of the mosque is a popular place of pilgrimage.

Column of Julian [82 C2] (*Jülyanus Sütunu, 250m north of Ulus Meydanı, just off Cankırı Caddesi*) This is the next Roman monument you pass, standing in the centre of the Hükümet Meydanı, moved from its original site. Built of brick rings, 15m high on a stone base, it is thought to have been erected in AD362 in honour of the Emperor Julian, but is known locally as Belkıs Minaret or the Queen of Sheba's Minaret for no reason anyone can establish. It usually has a large stork's nest on top. From here you can now walk out along the main road to see the Roman baths.

THE ORIGIN AND EVOLUTION OF THE TURKISH BATH

We do not know when the habit of indoor bathing first began, but a Hittite bathing area dated to 1200BC was discovered at a site near Gaziantep, and the world's earliest actual bath-house is thought to date to c850BC in the reign of the Assyrian king Salmanasar III, on the banks of the Tigris. Bathing areas within palaces were common in ancient Aegean and Greek settlements, but the first communal heated bath-houses with a continuous source of hot water began in Athens in the 5th century BC. The Romans developed this idea further, using air heated in a central furnace, and by 33BC there were 170 baths in Rome alone. All had large pools where bathers would wallow together, and though they initially had separate bathing areas for men and women, they began to have both sexes sharing the same area at the same time. This practice was banned at the start of the 2nd century AD when the bath-houses started to become centres for prostitution.

The tradition of the public bath passed into the eastern Roman Empire, where the Byzantines continued the practice of constructing bath-houses of architectural and social merit. In Europe, meanwhile, after the collapse of the Roman Empire, the grand pools of their fine bath-houses were replaced by the habit of bathing in a small tub. Once a month was considered quite sufficient and in 11th-century Spain baths were blamed for the spread of syphilis. When the Spanish king Alphonso VI's son was killed in battle, the king saw it as a sign from God that he was being punished for bathing too often, and ordered all public baths to be destroyed. In medieval times the Spanish religious authorities believed that Muslims took regular baths to wash away the sacred waters of Baptism, and in 1568 after all Muslims were expelled from Spain, the Church again ordered all baths to be destroyed. In the 16th century many of Europe's public baths were closed down, and in the 17th century the French king Louis XIV washed just once a year, in the spring.

Muslims on the other hand, ordered by their religion to be clean in body and soul, were quick to inherit the tradition of the Roman bath, and in the 8th century the Umayyads, the first Arab empire, built bath-houses in their desert palaces, now scattered across modern-day Israel, Jordan and Syria. The first baths to be built in Anatolia are believed to be the two Seljuk baths in Ani, dating to the late 11th century. Compared with the Roman baths the Seljuk baths were both small and plain.

Roman baths [82 C2] (*Roma Hamamları, 500m north of Ulus Meydanı;* ⊙ *08.30–12.30 & 13.30–17.30 Tue–Sun; adult TL5*) Discovered by chance in 1925 by architects making soundings for the construction of the nearby Ministry of Defence, the remains are not particularly impressive, but the foundations of ten rooms can be made out, with central-heating piping, fragments of marble paving and statues. They are thought to date from the time of the Roman emperor Caracalla (AD211–17) and were used well into the Byzantine period.

ATATÜRK'S MAUSOLEUM: ANİT KABIR [82 A4] (*Monumental Tomb, Anıttepe;* ⊙ *Apr–Sep 09.00–17.00 daily; Oct–Mar 09.00–16.00 daily; admission free*) The main interest in visiting this place is to see, in tangible form, the personality cult built around this remarkable man who died in 1938, a man whose picture still hangs in virtually every public place and building. The sheer scale of the building is the real shock. The sacred area occupies an entire hill over 1km² in the centre of Ankara, analogous say, to the whole of Hampstead Hill in London being a mausoleum precinct for Queen Victoria. There are two entrances at the foot of the hill which are guarded by neatly uniformed and armed soldiers. In summer a sound and light show is held here four evenings a week.

The entrance leads up through beautifully kept gardens to a parking area at the top. Guards in smart black and white uniforms stand at 10m intervals round the

Under the Ottomans baths gradually became more elaborate, more decorated and larger, and the first Ottoman bath built in Istanbul after the conquest in 1453 is described as accommodating 5,000 bathers. Istanbul alone had 237 public bath-houses and baths were also built across the sweep of their empire as part of the Islamic *waqf* (religious trust) system, where the income generated by the bath-house was channelled into supporting attached mosques, schools, hospitals and soup-kitchens for the poor. Private ownership of bath-houses was something that only began in the second half of the 19th century.

Excessive water and wood consumption was an inevitable consequence of the bath-houses' popularity and in the 18th century the Ottomans even had to introduce conservation measures, banning the construction of any further baths. Even so, the consumption of wood for heating water in the bath-houses reached such proportions that the entire Great Camlica Forest outside Istanbul was destroyed after being sold as fuel to the owner of the Grand Bath of Uskudar in the 19th century.

Islam stipulated that all Muslims had to perform 'minor' ablutions before prayers five times a day, and a 'full' ablution after sexual intercourse, masturbation, menstruation or childbirth. The Ottomans conformed to the Hanafi sect of Islam (see page 241) which said that women were free to go the bath-house as long as they did not expose their 'private parts', that is from their waists to their knees. Exposing this part of the body was considered sinful for both men and women, which is why the *pestemal* towel is issued to each bather to wrap round these parts. Massage or scrubbing by others of these areas is also prohibited.

Non-Muslims were permitted to use the bath-houses, in line with the Ottoman system of governing where all citizens of various religions and ethnic backgrounds were 'separate but equal'. However Muslims and non-Muslims were prohibited from using the same bath items, so they used separate pestemals that were easily distinguished from those used by Muslims, as well as separate *keses* (scrubbing gloves), dressing rooms and bathing cubicles. Jews even had separate small pools which, on their request, were blessed by a rabbi. All, irrespective of religion, paid the same small entrance fee.

edge. From here a colossal avenue 300m long flanked by lions of Hittite inspiration leads off in a dead straight line across the top of the hill to a vast open courtyard, and on the highest point, up a massive flight of steps, stands the monumental limestone mausoleum itself. The inspiration here is closer to the classical Greek temple. Inside the room is empty and stark, the walls and floor covered in marble and in the centre the gigantic stone of the sarcophagus itself, weighing 40,000kg. An atmosphere of reverence pervades and Turkish families walk around whispering. Nowhere outside are there any benches and no-one is allowed to sit on the steps or walls or to walk on the grass. The guards keep a sharp lookout for such irreverence and are not slow to tick you off should you transgress.

In the buildings surrounding the courtyard below the mausoleum are various pieces of Atatürk memorabilia, the most interesting of which is Atatürk's huge black car of 1932–34, looking as if it has been lifted straight out of an Al Capone movie. Among these buildings at the far end, opposite Atatürk's own, is the mausoleum of Ismet Inönü (1884–1973), Atatürk's first prime minister and his successor as president.

If you are still starved for Atatürk memorabilia and are in Ankara on a Sunday afternoon, you can visit the **Çankaya Atatürk Müzesi** (⊕ *13.00–17.00 Sun only; free but passport required*), the house where he lived during the War of Independence. The rather sombre ground floor is classic Ottoman style while upstairs gives a flavour of Atatürk's personal tastes. The 1920s villa lies in the Çankaya district on the 438-acre Presidential compound where the Pink Villa and Glass Villa, used for visiting heads of state and not open to the public, are also situated.

ETHNOGRAPHIC MUSEUM [82 C3] (*Talat Paşa Bulvarı;* ⊕ *08.30–12.30 & 13.30–17.30 Tue–Sun; adult TL3*) Housed in a magnificent white marble post-Ottoman building with an equestrian Atatürk statue outside, this museum has an excellent collection of old photos including Atatürk's funeral, along with mannequins acting out henna ceremonies, rug-making and circumcision ceremonies. There are also fine examples of Anatolian jewellery, Seljuk ceramics, Islamic manuscripts and calligraphy. Next door is the **Painting and Sculpture Museum** (⊕ *08.30–12.30 & 13.30–17.30 Tue–Sun; admission free*), with 19th- and 20th-century Turkish art. It is interesting to note the parallels with European art and how depictions of Atatürk become ever more abstract.

RAILWAY MUSEUMS If you have time to spare while waiting for a train at Ankara station you might consider looking in the two railway museums, both located very close by or even inside the station.

Open-air Steam Locomotive Museum [82 A3] (*Celal Bayar Bulvarı; admission free*) Steam-engine enthusiasts will love this collection of slowly rusting vintage locomotives, about 800m past the Tandoğan Kapalı Çarşı (covered market), southeast of the station.

Railway Museum and Art Gallery [82 A3] (*on Platform 1 of the railway station;* ⊕ *09.00–12.00 & 13.00–17.00 weekdays; admission free*) This small building served as Atatürk's residence for 18 months during the War of Independence, and beside it is his private railway carriage dating from the 1930s.

HAMMAMS Opposite the Ethnographic Museum is the square known as Opera Meydanı, and to the east of this are several *hammams* (Turkish baths). Many of the upper-range hotels have their own *hammams*, but if you want to try a more

It helps if you have an idea beforehand of what the ritual is. First of all, take with you a change of underwear as you should keep your genital area covered at all times, and your own soap and shampoo. Payment is always up front at the start, according to what level of bath you want, ie: just use of the bath facilities on your own or full wash and massage from an attendant as well. There is no time limit and the average period to allow is at least an hour, preferably two if you are having the massage and want a full relaxing experience. The bath attendant gives you a *pestemal* (thin cotton towel) and shows you to a changing cubicle in the *camekan* (changing room). Architecturally this is often the most beautiful part of the bath-house, with a domed ceiling. You emerge from the changing cubicle (having locked up your valuables) wearing only your pestemal and raised wooden clogs (*nalins*), clip-clopping on the marble floor to enter the *soğukluk* (cold room) where you adjust to the heat. After a few minutes you then pass through a wooden door into the *sıcaklık* (hot room), usually a square room with four arched side spaces and cubicles with marble basins at the corners. You are left here to adjust to the heat, pouring hot water over yourself, until the attendant calls you over to the central marble slab (*göbektaşı*) located directly above the wood or coal furnace, and begins to scrub you all over with the *kese*, a coarse mitten worn over the hand like a glove, made of plant or goat hair fibres. After this you are soaped and shampooed by the attendant till you are in a frothy lather all over, then rinsed off with more basins of hot water. Then the massage begins, starting at the neck and working all the way down the spine and to the feet, and you are asked to roll over from your front to your back for more of the same. The process finishes with another thorough soaping from head to toe, then a final rinse. You can stay as long as you like in the *sıcaklık*, and when you are ready, re-enter the *soğukluk* and the *camekan* where you are then given fresh towels, and can sit and rest, dry off, drink tea, coffee or refreshments and socialise with other bathers. When you finally get dressed and head back out into the outside world, your skin will feel glowing and wonderfully clean, having shed many layers of dead skin. A word of caution – avoid having a Turkish bath if you are a woman menstruating or if you have sunburn.

authentic one, seek out the 14th-century **Karacabey Hamamı** [82 C3] (*Talat Paşa Bulvarı;* ✆ *3102155;* ⊕ *daily: 06.30–23.00 (for men), 07.30–20.00 (for women); admission TL5*) built in 1444 in memory of Karacabey, commander to Sultan Murat II. It was restored between 1988 and 1990 but without altering the original architecture. Both the men's and women's sections have central pools with fountains in their changing/relaxing areas. No towels, shampoo or soap are provided, so bring your own. You can also try the 18th-century **Şengul Merkez Hamamı** [82 C3] (*Adçeşme Sokak;* ✆ *3110363;* ⊕ *daily: 05.30–22.00 (for men), 06.30–19.30 (for women)*), where a wash and massage costs TL10. It was restored in the 19th century and has a central dome over the cold-water area. Men and women have separate areas with opening hours set so they can come before and after work. Towels, soap and shampoo are provided here, but remember to bring along a spare set of underwear (or swimwear) to wear during the process. As you head further east the *hammam* experience becomes more and more authentic, so this may be the benchmark from which to begin your comparisons.

ENVIRONS OF ANKARA Various recreational areas have developed around Ankara for the use of residents who want to get out of the city, rather than for tourists,

HAMMAM TRADITIONS

In Ottoman times the hammam was pretty much the only place where women were allowed to go out of the home to socialise. Coffee shops were 'dense oceans of maleness', as were tea-gardens. Consequently, the weekly outing to the hammam was the great highlight of a woman's social calendar, where she would meet with friends and gossip about life, love and the future. Women of the household went in groups, mothers with daughters, sisters, aunts, while men tended to go singly. Men discussed politics and business with their fellow bathers, while women discussed marriage and men. Mothers used the occasion to eye up suitable brides for their sons, and much match-making took place here. Before an actual wedding night, it was customary for both bride and groom to come (separately of course) to the hammam with a group of friends and prepare for the great event. A woman visiting the hammam used to bring a bundle of up to 20 different items with her, including her own *pestemal* towel, wooden clogs inlaid with mother of pearl (*nalin*), *taş* (metal bowl for pouring water over the body made of silver, copper or brass), soap, shampoo, jewellery box, mirror, henna, kohl and rosewater for afterwards. She also brought three towels for drying – one to go round the hair, one round the shoulders and one round the waist – and a *yaygi*, a hammam carpet laid on the floor where she would sit to undress. All these personal items added pleasure to the hammam experience.

but just in case you find yourself in Ankara with a lot of time on your hands it is probably worth mentioning them.

The closest, originally a few kilometres west of Ankara but now swallowed up in the outskirts, is the **Atatürk Forest Farm** (*Atatürk Orman Çiftiği;* \ 2110170; *www.aoc.gov.tr;* ⊕ 09.00-17.00 *Tue–Thu & Sat–Sun*), which Atatürk set up in 1933 towards the end of his life as a model farm to introduce new agricultural methods to Turkey. While being an experimental farm, it is also a recreation area with restaurants, a zoo and a pool in the shape of the Black Sea.

Other recreational areas include the **Bayındır Dam** for good swimming 17km out of town on the Samsun road; **Gölbaşı Beach** 24km southwest of Ankara on Lake Moğan with attractive lakeside fish restaurants (see *Chez Le Belge*, page 84); and for skiing and climbing there is **Elmadağ** 18km east of Ankara, reached by following the same road as for Boğazkale and the Hittite heartlands.

4

Central Anatolia and the Hittite Heartlands

What does one mountain know about another mountain's anger?

After visiting the Museum of Anatolian Civilisations in Ankara, a day spent exploring the Hittite capital of Hattuşaş (Turkish *Boğazkale*) – a UNESCO World Heritage Site – and the nearby sites of Yazılıkaya and Alacahüyük will give you a fascinating insight into this mountain civilisation, a contemporary and rival to the river valley cultures of the Nile and Mesopotamia. A tough, practical people, the Hittites were the only ancient civilisation to exist and develop in inhospitable mountainous terrain. Simple accommodation is available in the nearby village and a visit involves several hours of walking, as the site covers a vast area.

This area will also give you a flavour of the character of central Anatolia, ranging from green fertile valleys to barren bleak hills with a succession of ascents and descents. In winter it is a snowy wilderness from late November to early March. Wide rivers cut through these rural landscapes, first the fine Kızılırmak ('Red River'), then the serene Yeşilırmak ('Green River') on whose banks the highly picturesque town of Amasya sits with its beautiful timbered Ottoman houses. Amasya, where there is good accommodation, deserves a day spent exploring its Seljuk and Ottoman mosques, along with its Palace of the Pontic Kings set on the ancient rocky citadel above, before then moving on to the cities of Tokat and Sivas, both noted for their fine 13th-century Seljuk monuments. A half day spent in each will cover the main sites.

GETTING TO THE REGION

The only airport in the region is Sivas, which you can fly to direct using Turkish Airlines or its subsidiary Anadolu Jet (see page 78), from Amsterdam, Baku, Brussels, Copenhagen, Dubai, Dusseldorf, Frankfurt, Hamburg, Istanbul, Izmir, Nicosia, London, Milan, Munich, Paris, Stuttgart, Vienna and Zurich, but not from Ankara as it is too close. From Ankara the choice is by train, by bus or by car, as all the main centres in this chapter lie on the railway line (see page 78) or the intercity bus route (see page 79). Travelling onwards to the east, the choices are again train, bus or car (see pages 58–9).

THE HITTITE HEARTLANDS

Clustered together here, just three hours' drive from Ankara, are the three major Hittite sites remaining in Turkey: the fine mountain capital Hattuşaş (modern Boğazkale), Yazılıkaya, the nearby religious sanctuary, and Alacahüyük, a very complete Hittite settlement, fortified and highly evolved. Being able to see all three in succession makes a very powerful impression, especially after visiting the Ankara museum where all the finds from the sites are on display.

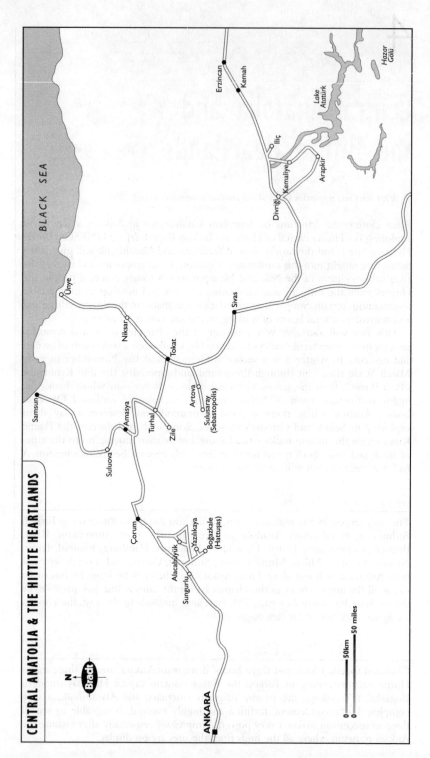

CENTRAL ANATOLIA & THE HITTITE HEARTLANDS

The modern name given to the small village closest to the Hittite capital, Hattuşaş, means 'Narrow Castle' in Turkish, and it is an odd juxtaposition of today's simple rural settlement with the colossal ruins of the highly complex Hittite capital – how are the mighty fallen.

🏠 WHERE TO STAY AND EAT All hotels are simple and are also the best places to eat.

🏠 **Aşıkoğlu Motel** (18 rooms) Boğazkale; ✆ 4522004; www.hattusas.com. Best location just outside the village, with a range of rooms from 3 star to 2 star. There are also basic camping areas. $$

🏠 **Hotel Başkent** (15 rooms) Boğazkale; ✆ 4522037; www.baskenthattusa.com; ⊕ Apr–Oct. A modern motel-style place up the hill *en route*

to Yazılıkaya, with simple rooms. Also has a large campsite for up to 50 campervans. $

🏠 **Hotel Baykal/Hattuşaş Pension** (8 rooms) Cumhuriyet Meydanı, Boğazkale; ✆ 4522013; www.hattusha.com. Right in the village square, a friendly, cheap & cheerful place with simple rooms & some shared bathrooms. $

OTHER PRACTICALITIES The village has a few shops selling food and groceries, a PTT office, a bank and even an ATM.

WHAT TO SEE
Hattuşaş, the Hittite capital (Boğazkale) *(Altitude: 1,025m)* (⊕ 08.00–17.00; *adult TL5, students free, ticket also valid for Yazılıkaya*)

Getting there The distance from Ankara is 206km but the roads are good so the drive by car or by coach takes under three hours. From the ASTİ terminal in Ankara take the Hattuşaş coach to Sungurlu, the closest point on the main road towards Çorum. They run hourly. From here it is a 30km detour off the main road to reach Boğazkale, which, if you do not have your own transport, can be done by *dolmuş* or by taxi.

Site visit If you have come from Ankara the same day the contrast between the city and village lifestyles will strike you forcibly. Geese wander across the street and circular dung cakes, later to be used as fuel, lie in heaps drying in the sun beside the simple houses. The site entrance lies just beyond the village of Boğazkale, a drive-in gateway to a huge fenced-in area. A tour of the site with a car takes about 90 minutes, or on foot more like three to four hours, as distances between the various parts of the settlement are long with steep climbs. In the village is the small **Boğazkale Museum** (⊕ 08.00–17.00; *closed Mon; adult TL3*), a disappointing collection of often fake artefacts, copies of what is now in the Museum of Anatolian Civilisations in Ankara, so do not bother with it if you have already seen that.

The site forms a three-cornered rocky plateau bordered by two valleys. It did not lend itself to building because of the uneven rocky surfaces. The modern name of Boğazkale means 'fortress of the narrow mountain pass', reflecting this topography, and to overcome these problems the planners often had to build up artificial terraces. The advantages of its location and the reason it was chosen by the militarily minded Hittites are twofold: firstly because the location between two valleys was well suited to building fortifications, since the natural slopes could be incorporated as part of the defence system, and secondly because compared with other areas of central Anatolia, it is blessed with an unusual number of brooks and springs. The land to the north of the settlement was also very fertile and well suited to agriculture.

Central Anatolia and the Hittite Heartlands **BOĞAZKALE**

4

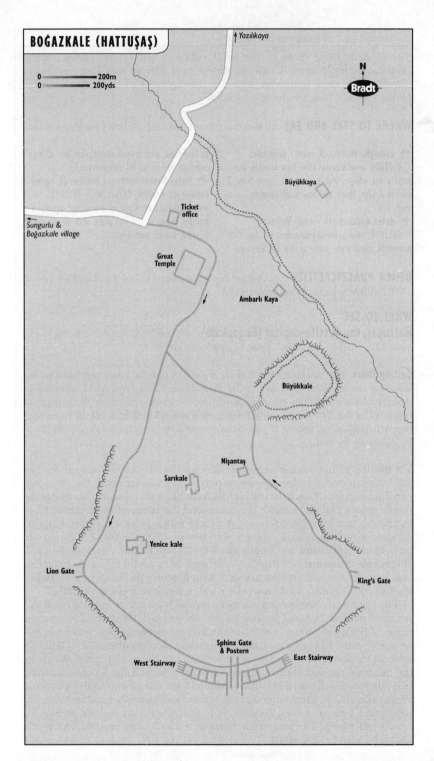

BOĞAZKALE (HATTUŞAŞ)

↑ Yazılıkaya

0 ——— 200m
0 ——— 200yds

N

Bradt

Büyükkaya

Ticket office

← Sungurlu &
Boğazkale village

Great Temple

Ambarlı Kaya

Büyükkale

Nişantaş

Sarıkale

Yenice kale

Lion Gate

King's Gate

Sphinx Gate & Postern

West Stairway

East Stairway

Hattuşaş became the Hittite capital in the 17th century BC and the first Hittite king called himself Hattusili, meaning 'the one from Hattusa', an identical linguistic usage to modern Turkish with '-li' stuck on as a suffix to the place name. It remained the Hittite capital, with kings with wonderful names like Suppiliuma and Muwatalli, until 1200BC when the city was invaded by hostile forces thought to be from the Black Sea area, burnt down and ransacked.

THE MYSTERY OF THE HITTITES

Three thousand years ago the Hittites rivalled the Egyptians as the greatest power on earth. Yet until a century ago the ancient Hittites were a mystery race, our only documentary evidence of their existence being in the Old Testament, where they were mentioned as a tribe living in Palestine: King David married Bathsheba, widow of Uriah the Hittite. When Egyptian hieroglyphs were later deciphered, an inscription on the wall of the Temple of Amun at Karnak was found to set out the terms of a mutual defence treaty between Ramses II and the king of the Hittites, Hattusili. Ramses II later married the Hittite king's daughter to cement the treaty.

No clue was found in the mystery of the lost Hittite Empire until 1834, when a Frenchman, Charles Texier, discovered at Boğazkale the ruins of extraordinary and puzzling rock palaces and monumental rock sculptures which he was unable to identify. German excavations in 1906 revealed thousands of cuneiform tablets which, once deciphered in the 1940s, uncovered the full history of the Hittite kingdom which ruled Anatolia from the 19th to the 13th century BC. The tablets show they were an advanced civilisation with a body of 200 laws covering every crime they could imagine. Intriguingly, the only capital offences were defiance of the state, rape and sexual intercourse with animals. Murder, black magic and theft could all be compounded by a money payment or by restitution of property. They were skilled in the making of bronze artefacts, jewellery and pottery in black or reddish brown. They used silver bars or rings for currency, with lead for smaller amounts. Much of their culture was taken over from the indigenous Hatti peoples, on whom the Hittites, when they arrived in Anatolia from the northeast, imposed themselves.

Their most memorable relics however are the simple but powerful sculptures cut into the rock at their settlements or their temples, often depicting their ceremonies and their weather god whose sacred animal was the bull. The figures are broad, squat and heavy, with none of the grace and subtlety associated with Egyptian or Babylonian art. They represent a tough mountain people, accustomed to a harsh climate and conditions, constantly prepared for war and attack, in contrast to the valley cultures of Mesopotamia and Egypt where man had peacefully pastured his flocks alongside great rivers with no need for defence fortifications.

The Hittites' military strength was awesome, necessary to their survival, but they were humane in the treatment of their conquered enemies (unlike the later Assyrians) and in peacetime they were governed by statesmen with sound and well-developed imperial policies. A practical and intellectually unpretentious people, they lacked the sophistication and finer graces of their Near Eastern neighbours. One touching account tells of a campaign by Mursilis I who penetrated into Mesopotamia as far as the walls of Babylon. Finding its defences unprepared, he entered the city and slew its king. Suddenly Mursilis and his simple highlanders were masters in this great world centre of civilisation amid its pomp and luxury. Feeling out of place and abashed, they soon withdrew to more familiar lands. Scholars have recently also found much to suggest a link between ancient Troy and the Hittite kingdom. The fall of Troy roughly coincides with the disintegration of the Hittite Empire.

None of the remains at Boğazkale today stand very high: you will not see here tall pillars, magnificent theatres and imposing façades. Most of what remains are foundations and low walls, but what cannot fail to impress is the size and scale of the conception. Hattuşaş covered an enormous area, at least 3km square, and the scale of all its buildings was vast. The defence walls were 6.5km long with nearly 200 towers, making it one of the earliest-surviving examples of a walled city. It is best to head first up to the highest point of the settlement, where you will find the three city gates – the Lion Gate, the Sphinx Gate, and the King's Gate – at each of the three corners of the top plateau set about 500m from each other. From here you gain a sense of scale: Hattuşaş at its apogee was three times the size of Themistocles's Athens.

Lion Gate You should begin your tour at the Lion Gate (Aslan Kapısı), clearly labelled. On the outer side of the gate the doorjambs carry two lions jutting out full-face to ward off evil spirits and defend the city. The left one is badly damaged but the one on the right is well preserved, with its mouth open in what was presumably meant to be a fierce growl. The deep eyes would originally have had inlaid white stone; the carved mane, whiskers and hair on the chest are all characteristically Hittite.

Sphinx Gate Next continue on to Yer Kapı, named after the two sphinxes which originally guarded the gate but are now in Berlin and Istanbul. Here you can climb to a perfectly preserved postern tunnel running for 70m through the hillside to the outer walls; you can still walk down this quite comfortably. On the far side, the doorjambs and lintel remain in place and there is a seat carved into the left doorjamb where the sentinel sat. From here you can turn left to see a section of the cyclopean wall angled to follow the contour of the hillside. Further along you come to a fine colossal stairway cut into the wall. Climbing it to the top you can then walk along the wall until you come to the corner edge from which you can descend by a second monumental stairway, labelled in German as *Westentreppe* (west staircase), before returning via the postern tunnel. In peacetime these two staircases were used to get into and out of the city, and in wartime they served to attack the enemy. The whole of Yer Kapı with its towers, gate, postern, cyclopean wall and two stairways is a remarkable example of the military architecture of the time and has a perfect symmetry.

Continuing on towards the third and final gate, you may notice on your left the scarcely recognisable remains of some temple foundations. On rocky outcrops the remains of well-built fortification walls are visible, known as Yenicekale and Sarıkale ('Newish Castle' and 'Yellow Castle'); both were small castles that were possibly also used as royal residences. These can be climbed up to if you are feeling energetic.

King's Gate This final gate is the least interesting of the three. On its outside doorjambs the smiling god relief now on display in the Ankara museum was discovered in 1907. It is called the King's Gate because the figure was at first thought to be a Hittite king and not, as subsequently agreed, a god of war. In 1968 a copy of the original was put here *in situ*. The original of this 14th-century BC relief is one of the best preserved and most outstanding examples of Hittite sculpture. The workmanship, as you can see even on this copy, is extremely fine: notice for example the cuticles of his nails and the hair around his nipples and on the upper chest. The shape of this gate, and of the Lion's Gate, which originally formed a parabolic arch, is distinctively Hittite and is also reminiscent of the Lycian tombs in southwestern Turkey.

Büyükkale You now continue on downhill past the poorly preserved Nişantaş, a 13th-century BC castle, with a long inscription in Hittite hieroglyphics cut into the rocky hill. A few metres further on you reach the clearly signposted Büyükkale ('Great Fortress') which was the residential palace of the Hittite kings in the 13th century BC. It was a fortified citadel within the outer fortification walls of the city and was protected by the steep drops on all sides. You reach it from the road now by a modern flight of steps which replace a lost Hittite ramp and lead to a poorly preserved citadel gate. Inside the once strong walls are the foundations of a series of large courtyards at different levels. In one of the rooms identified as an archive, 300 cuneiform tablets were found in 1906, including the famous treaty of 1279BC between King Hattusili III and Ramses II of Egypt. One of the other buildings was thought by the excavators to have been a great audience hall of the Hittite kings. The area on the highest terrace is believed to have accommodated the royal family, but only the magnificent setting can be appreciated today, so fragmentary are the remains. Two cylindrical rainwater cisterns can be seen carved in the rock.

Great Temple of the Weather God The road now winds down to this temple, clearly signposted. Built of limestone and some granite, it is the largest and best-preserved Hittite temple on the site. Its precincts are entered via the processional gate through which the Hittite Great King and his Great Queen would have passed as they went to worship as priest and priestess, accompanied by their entourage. Before the gate you pass a great water basin, now fractured, originally made from one colossal limestone block, with two lion heads and forepaws on one side. Once through the gateway a street leads straight ahead with its drainage system visible beneath the collapsed paving. The street turns right and in the corner is another large limestone water basin which was clearly connected to the drainage system. To the left of the basin, standing by itself in one of the temple rooms some 20m away, your eye will be caught by an enormous green marble stone, polished and smooth. This stone is a mystery; archaeologists who have devoted years of their life to excavations here choose never even to mention it, so its purpose remains unknown. It is tempting to think that, like the meteorite Black Stone of the Kaaba in Mecca, it may have had a religious significance, as it is so different from the limestone blocks all around.

Following the street to the right from the basin you come to the temple proper. Its outer courtyard walls would originally have been finished with plaster, possibly painted in several colours. The temple itself would have been covered by a flat roof. There is a lot for the imagination to supply here, but the first and abiding impression is of its great size. It was probably built in the 14th or 13th century BC and can be compared with the great sanctuaries of 19th-Dynasty Egypt. It was destroyed around 1200BC at the same time as the royal citadel.

Surrounding the temple are storerooms, 78 in all, in some of which more cuneiform tablets were found. The colossal storage jars are set into the ground and were not designed to be moved. The smaller ones had a capacity of up to 900 litres, while the largest held almost 3,000 litres. It is probable that they contained liquids, most likely wine and oil.

Yazılıkaya, the rock-cut sanctuary
Getting there From Boğazkale it is only a further 3km on to Yazılıkaya ('Carved Rock'), the 13th-century BC rock-cut sanctuary of the Hittite capital. Within 1km of Boğazkale the narrow tarmac road crosses a little bridge over a river from where you can have a very pleasant stroll along the riverbanks between the rocky hills rising either side. The path leads to the foot of Büyükkaya ('Big Rock'), a

rocky outcrop on the left of the river. At the point where this comes closest to the rock of Ambarlıkaya on the western side, the Hittites ingeniously built a bridge and walkway gallery over the gorge to make the city fortifications continuous. Under the bridge they built a portcullis which blocked access through the ravine in times of danger: the three pairs of perpendicular grooves down which it was lowered are still visible hewn into the canyon wall. The rest of the road to Yazılıkaya climbs quite steeply to reach a striking setting in a group of natural rock clefts set among pine trees.

Sanctuary area Formed of two natural rock galleries whose inner faces are carved with reliefs of the gods and goddesses of the Hittite pantheon, the Yazılıkaya temple was built between 1250 and 1220BC. In the first and main gallery of the temple, the left rock face shows the 42 warrior-like gods walking in sideways relief towards the right, while the right rock face shows 21 goddesses in a row walking towards the left to meet the gods in the middle. The gods are in their characteristically short kilts, conical helmets and Ali Baba–style shoes with curling toes, and are carrying either a mace or a scythe-shaped scimitar. Many wear earrings, though since the relief is sideways-on, it is not possible to say whether they are à la punk in one ear only. The rank of the gods is indicated by the number of horns decorating the conical helmet, from one for a junior god, up to five for a real superstar. The female deities are all wearing trailing gowns with tall cylindrical headdresses and long braids of hair down their backs. Most of the reliefs carry the names of the deities in hieroglyphs always written above the uplifted hand. The two most important are the two biggest, where the male queue meets the female queue. On the left we have Teshub, the weather god, standing on the shoulders of two mountain gods with heads bowed forward, and Hepatu, the sun goddess and wife of Teshub, standing on a panther, which is in turn standing with each foot on a mountain. It is interesting to note the extent to

RUINING THE RUINS

Apart from the Neo-Hittite site at Karatepe near Adana in southeast Turkey, Yazılıkaya is the only Hittite site to have its rock reliefs *in situ* and the only open-air temple to have survived to this day. All the more tragic then is the fate that befell it recently as a result of a French archaeologist's work. Over the years it has provided a wealth of information for archaeologists, the latest of whom, the Frenchwoman Smilia Masson, began her work here in 1976, publishing her findings in a book entitled *New Inscriptions at Yazılıkaya Temple* which was well received. After Madame Masson returned home it was discovered that some of the reliefs and inscriptions had been damaged and the watchmen employed to guard the temple were accused of negligence. The finger was first pointed at Madame Masson by a professor at Chicago University who produced a study casting doubt on the Frenchwoman's working techniques, with photographs to prove how her methods had damaged the rock carving. Similar accusations were subsequently levelled by Hittitology experts attached to London and Oxford universities. The damage was apparently caused by Madame Masson using latex on the rock surface to obtain an impression, which resulted in the removal of the centuries-old patina and so exposed the inscriptions to air and erosion. The use of latex for this purpose is common in archaeology, but for indoor areas only – it had never been used outdoors. Looking at photos taken before 1976 and comparing them with what you see today, there is unquestionably a deterioration, a fading of the relief contours. Each year the deterioration increases, and soon there may be little left to see at all.

which the Hittites depicted themselves as a mountain culture. Evidence is now mounting to indicate that this main gallery was used for the Spring Festival, an event which marked the beginning of the Hittite year and which lasted for many days with sumptuous feasts.

A cleft in the rock leads from this main gallery through into the long narrow smaller gallery. The door was originally paved in stone slabs which have long since disappeared. The four reliefs however are better preserved than those in the large gallery, maybe because they are more sheltered from the elements, but consist of isolated figures instead of a single unit. The 12 identikit warrior gods here, like the ones in the main gallery, were gods of the underworld. Nearby, the intriguing sword god is also thought to be a god of the underworld, though he is by no means fully understood by scholars. He has a man's head with conical helmet, denoting his godly status, but his torso is made up of a composite of four lions tapering down to a sword blade. On the opposite side is a large relief of the deity Sarumna, son of the sun goddess Hepatu and the weather god Teshub. His arm is protectively round a smaller figure known from the hieroglyph to be Tuthalia, a Hittite Great King. From the themes of these reliefs it has been speculated that this narrow chamber was used in funeral rites for the Hittite kings.

Alacahüyük (☉ daily 08.00–12.00 & 13.30–17.30; adult TL4)

Getting there There is no public transport between Boğazkale and Alacahüyük, so you will need your own car or a taxi. If you have spent the night at Sungurlu, you again take the right-hand fork towards Boğazkale, but after about 8km a yellow sign points off 22km to the left to Alacahüyük. About 12km after this turn-off there is a second turn-off suddenly to the left. A further 10km brings you to the pretty village of Alacahüyük, and the site itself lies on the near side of it. There is an attractive and well laid-out site museum where you buy your ticket.

Where to stay and eat There is a very simple hotel where a night could be spent if necessary, though most people will prefer to carry on to Amasya, an interesting town with Pontic rock tombs and Seljuk monuments which is one hour 45 minutes further on by road, and you can therefore reach it in time for lunch after visiting Alacahüyük in the morning from an overnight stop at Sungurlu.

Site visit Lying somewhat apart from the Boğazkale/Yazılıkaya cluster and difficult to reach without your own transport, the 14th-century BC Hittite site of Alacahüyük is often missed off the traveller's itinerary. This is a shame as it is in many ways the most attractive of the three and conveys most clearly the feel of a fortified Hittite city. The fact that the stupendous finds at the royal tombs here will still be fresh in your mind from the museum at Ankara (see page 88) also helps to lend the site a special significance.

Sphinx Gate The whole city at Alacahüyük was protected by an inner city wall, and you enter today through its monumental gateway. Called the Sphinx Gate after the massive female sphinxes facing outwards from the doorjambs, to the left of it are colossal stone slabs with a series of reliefs depicting scenes from the cult of Tarhunt, the thunder god. Particularly striking is the double eagle which has caught two hares in its talons, and there are also three priests in ritual gowns, a priest with four rams and worshipping a bull with the king carrying a long crook. The sculptor evidently started to work on the rock from both ends and had some difficulty in making them meet. The royal sun discs found in the royal tombs at Alacahüyük were carried on the top of such crooks. Also noteworthy are the attendant musicians, one playing a lute-like instrument, and on the next slab an

The emergence of the Hittites from almost total obscurity has been one of the great achievements of archaeology this century. In the English-speaking world the significance of the discovery of the lost Hittite Empire has arguably still not been fully recognised, probably because the bulk of the literature has been in German and the Hittite language was deciphered by Germans and a Czech. Yet this was one of the greatest Bronze-Age civilisations, speaking the earliest Indo-European language known.

entertainer either playing a wind instrument or doing a sword–swallowing act. On his right are two acrobats, one, his head shaven but for a lock, is climbing a free-standing ladder, while the other is ready to catch him. When compared to acrobats like the bull vaulters of Minoan Crete in the Palace of Knossos, these rather stumpy Hittite acrobats lack conviction.

Main Street From the gateway you enter the main street with the drainage system underneath still clearly visible. The street helps very much to give Alacahüyük the feel of a real town, a sense it is difficult to get at Hattuşaş. Those parts of the town that have been excavated are clearly labelled. In a hollow near the centre are the royal tombs where the treasure now displayed in the Ankara museum was found. The finds dated to the early Bronze Age, before the Hittite town you see today was built on top of the tombs.

Postern The postern is especially impressive but is difficult to find unless you know where to look. From the raised watchtower area to the left of the Sphinx Gate you must walk off to the west beyond the excavations for about 300m until you suddenly come on a signpost announcing it. Steps lead down and continue underground in a tunnel for 5m or so; then the tunnel turns sharply right and continues for a further 20m to come up outside the walls.

Museum The museum shows some impressive reconstructions of the city and some fine Hittite sun discs and pottery. Some of the pots are for all the world like modern teapots with lids. One particularly intriguing exhibit is the large free-standing Hittite clay bath, possibly the earliest manufactured bath in the world. Downstairs is a colourful ethnographic section with costumes, carpets and weapons.

AMASYA *Telephone code: 358*

Attractively located along the banks of the Yeşilırmak River, Amasya is often described as 'one of the loveliest of all Anatolian towns', and perhaps with such a build-up it is almost inevitable that your initial impression may be disappointment. The approach road leads through messy half-finished buildings with telegraph wires everywhere. Fortunately the town improves once you reach the centre and begin to explore the river frontage. At night the rock tombs and castle above are attractively illuminated. You will need the best part of a day to explore the town's many early Islamic monuments, Ottoman houses, rock tombs and the citadel. The Seljuks took Amasya in 1071 and it fell to the Ottomans under Beyazıt I in 1392. It is all quite compact, so you can walk everywhere.

GETTING THERE Amasya is 352km northeast of Ankara, 127km south of Samsun and 220km northwest of Sivas. Frequent intercity coaches link Amasya with all these cities. From Amasya there are two options for continuing your itinerary: either to head north to Samsun on the Black Sea, or to stay inland and continue visiting the Seljuk monuments of central Anatolia. This chapter continues with the latter option, but the former route is covered in *Chapter 12, The Black Sea Coast* (see page 366).

By train Amasya's train station is 2km out of town to the northwest, linked by taxi or *dolmuş* to the main square. Trains run twice a day to Samsun (three hours, TL7) or Sivas (five hours, TL12).

By bus The *otogar* is 2km northeast of the town centre on the road to Erzincan. The main bus companies have offices on the main square where you can check the timetable and buy tickets. They run a lot more frequently than the train, and to more destinations and are generally faster than the train. For example Samsun takes two hours, Ankara five hours. You can also head to Istanbul (ten hours, TL42), Kayseri (eight hours, TL37), Nevşehir, for Cappadocia (nine hours, TL52) and Tokat (two hours, TL11).

WHERE TO STAY

Apple Palace Hotel (35 rooms) Vermiş Sokak; 2190019; www.theapplepalace.com.tr. Set by itself 6km out of town on the hillside south of the river overlooking the Pontic tombs, this is Amasya's top hotel & even has a disco. Modern swish rooms. $$$$

Emin Efendi Konakları (20 rooms) Hazeranlar Sokak; 2120852; www.eminefendi.com.tr. Overhanging the river, there are in fact 2 pensions, I new, I old. The old one is pleasantly cluttered with a courtyard, while the new one has more modern comforts. The cellar has been converted to a living room with a fireplace & a piano. Meals provided. $$

Ezge Pansiyon Restaurant (2 rooms) Hatuniye Mh Yalı Boyu S; 2187300, 2130477; www.ezgipansiyon.com. Right on the waterfront with balcony overhanging the river, attractive walled garden. Traditionally furnished with dark

wood furniture & local kilims, the rooms are simple but have a rustic charm. The restaurant serves unusual regional dishes. $$

Grand Pasha Hotel (8 rooms, I suite) Hatuniye Mahallesi; 2124158; e grandpashsotel@kolayweb.com. Wonderful converted Ottoman mansion right on the riverbank. The 2 upstairs rooms are intricately painted & carved, while the lower ones are more modest. All rooms have en-suite bathrooms. Meals provided. $$

Ilk Pansiyon (6 rooms) Hitit Sokak; 2181689. Simple but authentic rooms in an Armenian mansion, with low beds & traditional furnishings. The owner is an architect whose ground-floor office doubles as the headquarters of an international programme of urban renewal sponsored by a Japanese university & supported by European funds. Meals provided. $$

WHERE TO EAT

Apart from the restaurants in the hotels mentioned above, there are a number of competing cafés for tea and snacks. You can also try:

Ali Kaya Restaurant Çakallar Mevkii; 2181505; ⏰ 11.00–22.00. Located close to the Apple Palace Hotel above, this is a simple restaurant with wonderful views over Amasya. Alcohol is served. $$

Yimpaş Supermarket Ziyapaşa Bulvarı. As well as being a supermarket where you can stock up with picnic food, this place also has a rooftop café with good views, where light meals are served. $

WHAT TO SEE

River houses The left bank which you walk along first is lined with a series of pretty cafés where it is pleasant to linger over tea or coffee while looking across the broad Yeşilırmak River to the rock tombs cut into the cliff face opposite. On the opposite bank a row of beautiful Ottoman timbered houses stand with

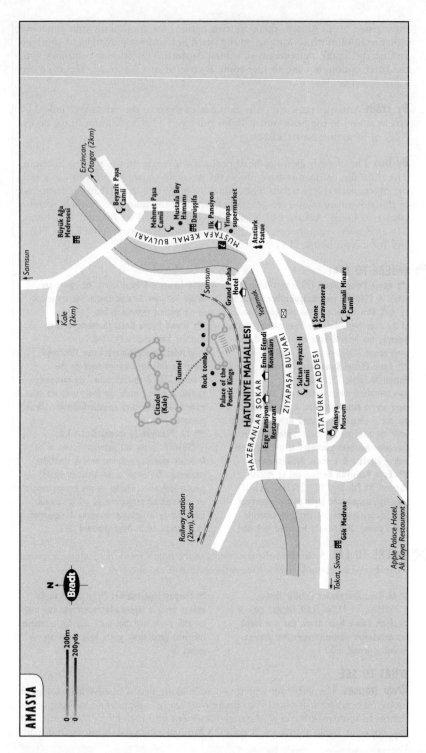

AMASYA

N Bradt

0 ___ 200m
0 ___ 200yds

Samsun →

Erzincan, Otogar (2km) →

Büyük Ağa Medresesi

Beyazıt Paşa Camii

Mehmet Paşa Camii

Mustafa Bey Hamamı

Darüşşifa

İlk Pansiyon

Yimpaş supermarket

Atatürk Statue

MUSTAFA KEMAL BULVARI

Kale (2km) →

Samsun →

Grand Pasha Hotel

Yeşilırmak

Citadel (Kale)

Tunnel

Rock tombs

Palace of the Pontic Kings

HATUNIYE MAHALLESI

HAZERANLAR SOKAR

Emin Efendi Konakları

Ezge Pansiyon Restaurant

ZIYAPAŞA BULVARI

Sultan Beyazıt II Camii

Stone Caravanserai

Burmalı Minare Camii

ATATÜRK CADDESI

Amasya Museum

Railway station (2km), Sivas →

Gök Medrese

Tokat, Sivas →

Apple Palace Hotel, Ali Kaya Restaurant →

The famous geographer of the ancient world, Strabo, was born in Amasya in 64BC when it was the capital of the Pontic Kingdom. He describes his birthplace in grand terms:

My native town is situated in a deep and large valley through which flows the river Iris. It has been provided in a surprising manner by art and nature for answering the purpose of a city and a fortress. For there is a lofty and perpendicular rock which overhangs the river, having on one side a wall erected close to the bank where the town has been built, while on the other it runs up on either hand to the summits of the hill. These two are connected to each other and well fortified with towers. Within this enclosure are the royal residence and the tombs of the kings.

balconies overhanging the river. Two disasters, the great fire of 1915 and the Erzincan earthquake of 1939, together with the periodic floods which sweep the valley, have reduced the number of these houses. Some have been restored but many remain dilapidated.

Palace of the Pontic kings (*Kizlar Sarayı;* ⊕ *daily Apr–Oct 08.00–20.00; Nov–Mar 08.30–17.30; admission TL5*) Crossing over the bridge you can walk up towards the rock tombs set in the cliff face overlooking the town. A yellow sign points over the bridge to the Kızlar Sarayı (Maiden's Palace) and the Hazaranlar Konağı (Museum House), a beautifully restored 19th-century Ottoman house in white and brown timber on the river converted into an **Ethnographic Museum** (✆ *2184018;* ⊕ *08.30–11.45 & 13.15–16.45 Tue–Sun*). The restoration of the 1865 house was completed in 1979. From here a sign points to *Kral Kaya* ('King's Rock') up some steps between the old houses. The ascent takes only ten minutes but is quite steep and can seem like a huge effort after a heavy lunch and wine. Strabo tells us that the town was founded by the Amazon queen Amasis, but however early the original settlement here, it was as the capital of the Pontic Kingdom that Amasya rose to prominence. This kingdom was founded in the 3rd century BC by an adventurer called Mithradates, whose uncle, one of the last of the Greek tyrants, had been executed. Mithradates escaped with a few followers into the Pontus Mountains and finally established himself at Amasya, where he built his palace and citadel. The kingdom survived for more than two centuries of turbulent history, finally being crushed by the Romans under Julius Caesar in 47BC.

Of the palace of the Pontic kings virtually nothing remains today but the terrace on which it stood. The modern name *Kızlar Sarayı* presumably refers to the Ottoman harem. The Seljuks and Ottomans rebuilt, but all that remains of their work is a little Turkish *hammam* over on the far right of the terrace.

Tombs of the Mithraditic kings (*Kral Kaya Mezarları*) Dating to the 4th century BC these tombs are above the terrace, carved out of hard basalt, and were used for cult worship of the deified kings. A remarkable tunnel with steps cut into the rock leads round to the two largest tombs. The left tomb was used as a chapel during Byzantine times. Near the tombs is the entrance to one of the three puzzling tunnels supposedly leading down to the river or to wells. Legends abound about star-crossed lovers whose tears created channels of water; another theory is that they were used in religious rituals; but the theory that they were sally ports for surprise attacks seems least likely, as no exit for them has ever been found. From here there is a pleasant view over the Turkish town and its monuments below.

Central Anatolia and the Hittite Heartlands AMASYA

4

A *medrese* (Arabic for 'school', literally 'place of study', Turkish *medrese*) was generally a charitable foundation, teaching – besides the Koran – Islamic jurisprudence, languages, mathematics, geometry, astronomy, medicine and music. Sports were also practised, and famous wrestlers often came from these schools. In many ways madrasas were the Islamic versions of the gymnasia of the ancient world, since gymnasia were as much for teaching as for sport, and frequently had schools and libraries attached. Their layouts too were similar, with buildings arranged round a courtyard. They were always on two floors, with the students' bedrooms upstairs and the classrooms, prayer room, professor's room, library and washrooms on the ground floor. The plan did not include a kitchen as meals were obtained from a public cookhouse. There was often also a small mosque for public use containing the tomb of the founder. The first known *medrese* was built in Nişapur, Iraq, in 1027 by Nizam Al-Mulk. Students in all these Seljuk institutions were provided with free board and lodging and given a monthly cash allowance.

Gök Medrese This Seljuk building of 1266 stands in the main street. You have to look hard at the exterior to see any of the turquoise tiles which give it its name, *gök*, 'sky blue'.

Burmalı Minare Camii Located behind the Stone Caravanserai is the Seljuk Twisted Minaret Mosque built in 1242, heavily restored in the 18th century after a fire. The spiral carving that gives the minaret its name is very unusual and reflects a high level of stonemason craftsmanship. Inside are three wooden galleries on the three sides facing the *mihrab* (prayer niche). Further uphill, away from the river, stands the Fethiye Camii, originally a 7th-century Byzantine church, now a functioning mosque.

Darüşşifa Meaning literally 'house of cure', this unusual building with its fine oriental-flavour portal was a lunatic asylum built in 1308 by the Mongols. In the 1980s it was still an abandoned ruin, but now it has been restored and is even used for concerts, exhibitions and other events. The musical element is apt, as music was commonly used in these early asylums in the treatment of the mentally ill, together with the sound of water in fountains.

Mehmet Paşa Camii Beyond the Mongol asylum there is a pleasant walk over a small footbridge to this early Ottoman mosque built in 1486, prettily set among tall trees along the river's edge. Inside is a beautiful carved marble *mimber* (pulpit).

Mustafa Bey Hamamı (⏲ *daily 06.00–10.00 & 16.00–23.00 (for men), 10.00–16.00 (for women)*) On the northern side of the Darüşşifa mental hospital you will find a working Ottoman bath-house dating to 1436. The hours are typical of Turkish baths, with the men having the slots before and after the working day, and the women allowed in the middle of the day while the men are out at work.

Amasya Museum (*Atatürk Caddesi;* ⏲ *08.00–11.45 & 13.00–16.45 Tue–Sun; adult TL3*) Set in attractive gardens strewn with sculptures from the town's past, Amasya's modern museum displays a range of Pontic, Roman, Byzantine, Seljuk and Ottoman artefacts found locally, including a bronze figure of the Hittite god Teshub known as the *Statuette of Amasya*, a fine bathtub and the finely carved wooden doors of the Gök Medrese Camii which illustrate the transition from Seljuk to Ottoman styles. The major attractions though are generally considered to be the gently decaying mummies of two Mongol governors and a Seljuk family displayed in glass cases inside the tile Seljuk *türbe* (tomb) of

MONGOL CONTRADICTIONS

It is one of the many curious contradictions in the culture of the Mongols that they often built extremely beautiful elegant buildings like the Darüşşifa, while at the same time laying waste to existing buildings and leaving swathes of destruction behind them. The mental institutions would have been much needed. The raids of these warrior horsemen throughout the 13th and 14th centuries spelt the end for many rulers in the Near and Middle East. The first wave of Mongols was led by Genghis Khan in 1243; he and his successors were responsible for the downfall of the Seljuk sultanate of Rum, the Crusader kingdoms in southeast Anatolia and, in 1258, the Abbasid caliphate in Baghdad. In its Arabic History course, Oxford University regarded this date as the end of Arab history – the destruction of Baghdad's irrigation system. Genghis Khan described himself as 'the scourge of god sent to men as a punishment for their sins'. Tamerlane, leader of the second wave, swept into eastern Anatolia in 1401, having already overrun central Asia, India, Persia, Iraq and Syria, leaving a second trail of destruction behind him. Exceptionally aggressive and warlike, the Mongols specialised in slaughtering wholesale anyone they came across, virtually wiping out the populations of the cities they took, and then building pyramids of the victims' heads. They destroyed the priceless palaces and libraries of the East, while the revered mosques of Bukhara served them as stables. Among their charming habits were drinking the blood of their horses by cutting a hole in the leg and having themselves buried surrounded by beautiful living maidens.

Tamerlane, an Anglicisation of *Timur Lenk*, meaning 'Timur the Lame' because of his lame leg (the result of an arrow wound to his thigh as a young man), claimed descent from and modelled himself on Genghis Khan, and crushed the chief early Ottoman cities of Ankara, Iznik, Bursa and Izmir. He then returned to his native steppelands without consolidating his victories, but leaving behind him a devastation from which it took the Ottomans 50 years to recover. In his avowed aim to conquer the world and establish an empire, Tamerlane failed, since, bringing with him no religion or culture, he could offer nothing on which to base his power except destruction. His reputation today therefore is not as a founder of a great dynasty, but as the most comprehensively destructive ruler in history. Yet any skilled craftsmen from the conquered cities were carried away to Tamerlane's capital in Samarkand, where, remarkably, they were ordered to build magnificent palaces and centres of learning. He could bear no rival centres, but wanted to create his own. Timur remains a popular boy's name in Turkey, maybe because of the associations with virility. Despite his lameness he lived to the age of 80, though could only walk short distances by himself, otherwise having to be carried. Contemporary sources are unanimous in agreeing that he loved learning and disputations, particularly about historical topics. He surrounded himself with scholars with whom he discussed learned historical and theological problems. He was described by Arab historians as being: 'tall in stature with a large brow and great head and very strong; his complexion was white mixed with red; he was broad-shouldered, had thick fingers, a flowing beard, and was paralysed in one hand and lame in his right leg; he had brilliant eyes and a loud voice and was fearless of death. He had reached the age of eighty in full enjoyment of his senses and his strength.

Sultan Mesut. They were found underneath the Spiral Minaret Mosque, mummified without removing the organs.

Beyazıt Paşa Camii Built in 1486 this mosque is on the riverbank set among trees and gardens at the Samsun end of town. Kept closed except at prayer times, the twin-domed floor plan was a precursor to the famous Yeşil Cami in Bursa. Further along the main street you come to the 17th-century **Taş Han (Stone Caravanserai)**, now used as metal workshops.

Büyük Ağa Medresesi Also at the Samsun end of town is this unusual eight-sided *medrese* (theological college) founded in 1488 by the Chief White Eunuch of Beyazıt II. It has a lovely interior arcade and courtyard.

Ascent to the citadel (*unfenced site, no specific opening hours or admission charge*) A little outside town on the Samsun road a yellow sign saying *Kale* (castle) points 2km up a small road. From where the road ends there is a ten-minute scramble up through the walls to the highest point for the best views, marked by a flagpole. The area of the castle is surprisingly large and the walls and towers are extensive but heavily ruined. Two of the towers are thought to be from Pontic days, but most of the walls are of Byzantine or Turkish reconstruction, repaired again in the 1980s. The grassy summit makes a lovely picnic spot, with superb views down to the river and the town. During Ramazan an old Russian cannon is still fired from here at sundown to announce the time when you are allowed to eat again after the day's fast.

SELJUK CIVILISATION

The Seljuks were originally nomads from the region of Samarkand and Bukhara descended from Selçuk bin Duqaq bin Temur Yaligh, sovereign of Central Asia, and ruler of the Tu-Kin people in the steppes of Mongolia. This Chinese name evolved to give us the modern name 'Turk' and the word *selçuk* means 'attack', 'charge' or 'violent agitation'. They worshipped their own weather gods and were renowned for their physical prowess. In the 11th century a wave of Seljuks surged out from their homeland, through Persia, Iraq, Syria and Palestine. Here they were converted to Islam and brought their new religion with them when, in 1067, under the leadership of Alp Arslan, they pushed up from Antioch (modern Antakya) into Anatolia and to Konya where they established their capital.

Although the Seljuks were effective fighters, once they had established themselves and the fighting was over, their greatest sultans, notably Alp Arslan, Malik Shah, Keykavus I and Keykubad I (Alaeddin), were enlightened rulers, laying down the foundations for commercial prosperity, education and the arts. Alp Arslan introduced the appointment of *vizirs* (ministers or advisors), and his first vizir, Nizam Al-Mulk, was responsible for founding universities, observatories, hospitals and mosques. Over the two centuries of their rule, the Seljuks evolved a remarkable **welfare state** where medical schools were linked with hospitals, orphanages, poor-houses, mental homes, baths and religious schools, all offering their services to the needy free of charge. Many of these institutions are still in existence.

The system of **caravanserais** they built facilitated trade and concentrated the trade routes; they were usually built a day's journey apart. The services they offered for the travelling merchants were for their time remarkable, with the central mosque and ablution fountain, the range of sleeping quarters, the baths to revive aching limbs, the cafés for refreshment, the blacksmith and leatherworker ready to do repairs, and musicians to relax and entertain. Stabling was offered for donkeys, horses and camels,

Laid out along one main street and dominated by rocky crags and a fortress, Tokat is visited today for its Seljuk monuments, a foretaste of what is to come in Sivas. The ground level in the 12th and 13th centuries appears to have been some 5m lower than today, as the monuments all sit this much lower than the current street level, thought to be the consequence of silt and earthquake debris being carried by floods down into the valley. Half a day is plenty to visit the town's sights.

GETTING THERE Tokat is 391km east of Ankara, 117km southeast of Amasya and 103km northwest of Sivas.

By bus Tokat's *otogar* is about 1.7km northeast of the town centre. Services are not as frequent as you might expect so it is worth checking ahead and reserving places through the various bus company ticket offices on the main street of Gazi Osman Paşa. Most companies provide you with a *dolmuş* taxi to the bus station from their offices in the town centre included in the price.

By road From Amasya to Tokat by road takes an hour and 15 minutes through pleasant landscapes of rural villages and fertile valleys. At Ezinepazar you pass the ruins of a Seljuk caravanserai, once the last stop on the road from Sivas to Amasya – today it is less than half an hour by car. A short detour 26km before Tokat to

with the doors varying in height to suit the height of each animal. Most remarkable of all however was that these services were offered free by the state, which funded the system through taxation.

In Seljuk architecture the elaborate tiles and carving distantly reflect Persian influence, and in the strength and power of their castles and minarets there are traces of Syrian Arab influence. But whereas the later Ottomans often converted churches to use as mosques, not a single Seljuk mosque was converted from a church or even raised on the ruins of a church. Without exception they built on new foundations. The Seljuks developed their own distinctive forms, such as the **cylindrical mausoleum (türbe)** on a square base with a conical roof, the most famous example being the Mevlâna Tomb in Konya. It has been suggested that this shape was meant to recall the pointed tents of the Seljuks' nomad origins, or that it was influenced by the similar shape of Armenian churches the Seljuks would have seen in eastern Anatolia. The double-headed eagle, symbol of the Seljuk state, can be seen on many of their buildings, which were usually constructed of red brick with plain high walls contrasting with the very elaborate decorations and carving in niches and doorways. The main entrance was always highly elaborate with honeycomb (or stalactite) carving known as *muqarnas*, as can be seen in the extant caravanserais and madrasas. The Seljuks were also prolific bridge-builders. Built solidly in stone with a single pointed arch, many remain in use today. The pointed arch, also used to great effect in windows and doorways, was possibly the inspiration for the later Gothic arch, taken back to Europe by the Crusaders.

The Seljuks' most important contribution to religion was the foundation of the **Mevlâna order of the Whirling Dervishes** at Konya, the Seljuk capital. This form of Islamic mysticism continues today despite Atatürk's dissolution of the order in 1925 in his attempts to secularise modern Turkey.

the village of Pazar will be rewarded with a particularly fine Seljuk caravanserai dating to 1238, called the Hatun Han.

GETTING AROUND
Distances are not great and walking is the best way to see the sights.

WHERE TO STAY

Büyük Tokat Oteli (59 rooms) Demirköprü Mevkii Karşıyaka; 2291700. Tokat's smartest place, complete with pool & expensive restaurant. Built in the 1980s. $$$$

Çavuşoğlu Plevne Otel (28 rooms) Gazi Osman Paşa Bulvarı; 2142207. Newly renovated & now with good b/fast buffet in a central location. $$

Otel Yeni Çınar (32 rooms) Gazi Osman Paşa Bulvarı; 2140066. Good comfortable rooms. First-floor restaurant offers the local Tokat kebab. $$

Yüçel Hotel (34 rooms) Meydan Caddesi; 2125235. Good value in a quiet location with its own hammam in the basement. $

WHERE TO EAT
Local specialities are the Tokat kebab, a sort of mutton stew with aubergines and potatoes, eaten mainly in summer with a slightly vinegary fromage frais called *çökelek*, and a sweet wine called *mahlep* made from small plums which is drunk as an aperitif.

Honça 'Tokat Evi' Restaurant Ali Paşa Hamam Sokak; 2133818; 12.00–20.00. Authentic Ottoman cuisine with many unusual dishes. Live music, outdoor seating but no alcohol. Credit cards accepted. $$$

Beykonağı Hotel Restaurant Ali Paşa Mah, Mithatpaşa Caddesi; 2143399;

07.00–midnight. Within the hotel, this fine restaurant serves traditional cuisine & alcohol. Credit cards accepted. $$

Sultan Restaurant Cumhuriyet Meydanı; 2148147; 07.00–23.00. Central location with outdoor seating & live music. No alcohol. Credit cards accepted. $$

WHAT TO SEE
Gök Medrese (*Gazi Osman Paşa Bulvarı*; 08.00–12.00 & 13.00–17.00 *Tue–Sun; adult TL3*) This is the main monument in Tokat, named for its turquoise tiles. Blue is a holy colour in Turkey and our word 'turquoise' is derived from Turkey. The *medrese* is indicated as *Müze* by a yellow sign pointing to the right at a roundabout on the edge of town, since it is now used as the museum for local archaeological finds. The road straight on continues to Sivas. Built in 1275 the *medrese* was closed for extensive repairs in the 1970s, reopening in 1982. So exhaustive has been the restoration that very few tiles remain. In the courtyard are

SELJUK TILES AND CARPETS

Tilework was something the Greeks and Romans never learnt, but the Seljuks brought this exquisite art with them from Persia. They evolved the Persian style into their own form of tile mosaics in plain colours and geometric designs, which so often embellish their mosques, tombs and madrasas. The distinctive turquoise blue of the Gök Medrese was one of their favourite colours, making their monuments instantly recognisable. The best examples of tilework are on display in the Karatay Medrese in Konya (see page 175).

Carpet weaving was the other great Seljuk art. Their colours are rich: blues, brick red and soft green, with sand and earth backgrounds. The motifs are geometric, often with stylised animal, bird or tree forms. Like the türbe's roof, this art recalled their nomadic background, for the carpet is the essential piece of tent furniture.

Seljuk tombstones, inscriptions, Roman column pedestals and capitals from Comana Pontica and from Sebastopolis. In an upstairs room are exhibits of the patterned cloth called *yamas*, made by using wooden stamping patterns on the cloth, a craft for which both Tokat and Sivas are famous. In a downstairs room are the 40 tombs of the founders, though tradition refers to them as the 40 maidens.

Voyvoda Han (⊕ *daily 08.00–19.00*) Next door to the Gök Medrese stands this large market building built in 1631 for the Armenian merchants who had traded here since the early days of the city. Tokat sheltered an important Christian community of Armenians and Greeks who made up a third of the town in 1455. Tokat, Sivas and Kayseri all had large Armenian communities up to the 1920s, but now very few remain. In the old market quarter of Tokat near the main square you can still buy the fine copperware for which Tokat has been famous for centuries.

Latifoğlu Konağı (*Gazi Osman Paşa Bulvarı;* ⊕ *08.30–12.00 & 13.30–17.30 Tue–Sun; adult TL2*) This superb 19th-century wooden house has been restored and transformed into a small museum, traditionally furnished to show the Ottoman lifestyle. Bedding was stored in cupboards during the day, leaving the low *sedirs* (bench-seating) to double as daytime seating. The upstairs is especially fine, with painted scenes of Istanbul and floral motifs on the walls, typical of Ottoman décor of the period.

Citadel Follow the yellow sign to *Kale* (castle) to reach the citadel that straddles the spectacular twin-peaked rock dominating the town. The remains are of Byzantine date, repaired by the Ottomans and still with a total of 28 towers. At the time of the Pontic kingdom where modern Tokat stands was ancient Damizon and its fortress guarded the approach to the temple-city of Comana Pontica 10km to the north. Nothing of this great sanctuary remains today, where the Anatolian earth mother was worshipped under the apt name of Ma. The high priests of the sanctuary ruled over a community of serfs with handmaidens of the goddess serving as temple prostitutes. Every two years a festival was held to worship the mother goddess, a very popular and well-attended kind of market-fair-cum-orgiastic feast in which a statue of the goddess, said to be the image of Artemis, was carried about in procession accompanied by frenzied worshippers practising flagellation.

Sebastopolis At Sulusaray, a village 48km from Tokat, a major archaeological discovery was made in summer 1988 of the Roman city of Sebastopolis, whose state of preservation promises to rival Ephesus, Turkey's greatest Roman city, on the Aegean coast. The first relics of the city, marble columns and inscriptions, were uncovered by a flood. The emperor Augustus is thought to have been the city's founder, in the 1st century BC.

Work at Sebastopolis (consult www.sebastopolis.net for progress on the excavations) is pressing ahead under both Turkish and European archaeologists and so far large sections of marble flooring and a gymnasium have been unearthed. A large Byzantine church, similar to that of St Nicholas in Demre/Myra, has also been unearthed, and a building with mosaic flooring has been illegally excavated. Some of the legal finds are on display in Tokat's Gök Medrese museum (see page 114).

Getting there From Tokat or Amasya an alternative route to the Black Sea can be followed via Niksar to Ünye. The route leads through pleasant mountain scenery and Niksar (ancient Roman Neocaesaria) is an old Pontic town with a Pontic fortress. St Gregory the Thaumaturge performed many miracles here. In the town there is also the fine Ulu Cami (Great Mosque) with a magnificent gateway. Most however will prefer to continue inland exploring the impressive Seljuk monuments at Sivas, and then the unique mosque–*medrese* complex at Divriği (see pages 126–7). You need your own transport to reach Sebastopolis.

Where to stay If you do decide to head along this route towards the Black Sea, the following place will be a welcome stop:

Ardıçlı Dağ Evi (8 rooms) Ardıçlı Koyu, Niksar; 5421242. Located 13km from Niksar on the Ünye road, in the village of Ardıçlı. Set in the little-known Kelkit Valley, Ardıçlı is a hill village high above Niksar. An elderly country doctor & his wife have set up this mountain lodge, 2 houses next to each other, each with 4 guestrooms sharing 1 bathroom & a living room. $

SİVAS *Telephone code: 346; altitude: 1,285m*

Sivas's population is three times the size of Tokat's, and the city is quite a thriving agricultural centre. In modern times it was proud to have served in 1919 as the location for the Sivas Congress where Atatürk first announced that Turkey would be independent and that a national assembly would be called. This was therefore the start of the War of Independence that would lead to the emergence of Turkey as we know it now. At the end of the 16th century a little more than half the population was Christian, mainly Armenian. Sivas also has the most important Alevi community in Turkey, estimated at 50% of the town's population.

In recent years Turkey has seen violent clashes between the Alevis and the Sunnis, the latter accusing the former of not respecting the commandments of Islam. These culminated in the arson attack on the Madımak Hotel in 1993 in which 36 Alevis were burnt to death. During the sultanate of Rum Sivas was one of the principal Seljuk cities and so was adorned with an abundance of beautiful Seljuk buildings, which is what visitors come to see today. Allow half a day to walk round.

GETTING THERE Sivas is 103km southeast of Tokat, 450km east of Ankara, 193km northeast of Kayseri, 246km southwest of Amasya and 252km west of Erzincan.

By air Sivas airport is 23km northwest from the city centre, with daily flights to Istanbul via Ankara.

By train The train station is 2km southwest of the city centre, and *dolmuş* taxis wait to take you into town for about TL1. From Sivas the train journey to Amasya takes four hours and costs TL6; Ankara (six hours, TL10); Divriği (four hours, TL6); Erzurum (six hours, TL11); Istanbul (11 hours, TL17); Kayseri (3.5 hours, TL6); Malatya, for Nemrut Dağı (five hours, TL10); Tokat (two hours, TL4) and Trabzon (15 hours, TL22). Sivas is also on the Istanbul–Lake Van line.

By bus The *otogar* is south of the city centre and there are services to most places, with similar timings to the trains, but more frequency. For example: Amasya (3.5 hours); Ankara (six hours); Istanbul (13 hours) and Tokat (1.5 hours). Prices are also similar to the trains.

By road From Tokat the road to Sivas climbs through low hills of about 700m to a plateau with snow-capped peaks in the distance. Some 10km before the village of Çamlıbel there is a ruined Seljuk caravanserai on the right-hand side of the

THE ALEVIS

Not to be confused with the Alawis of Syria, with whom they have little in common apart from a veneration of 'Ali, the Alevis are Turkey's second largest religious community, the first being the Sunni orthodoxy. They are mainly ethnically Turkmen of nomadic origin, with about 20% Kurds, and are closely connected to the Sufi Bektaşi sect in that they also venerate the 13th century saint Haçi Bektaş (see page 159). For centuries Alevis and Sunnis have viewed each other with mutual suspicion, and the Alevis have been persecuted for their traditions, beliefs and unusual rituals, which differ greatly from those of the Sunni orthodoxy. For example they do not pray five times a day, go on pilgrimage to Mecca or pay the *zakat* (alms) tax, on the basis that the Quran does not proscribe these things. Although they fall loosely under the banner of Shi'ism, they are very distinct in that they do not worship in mosques but in assembly rooms, and their prayer consists of music and dancing involving both men and women. Since the 1990s they have undergone something of a revival. Alevi women are never covered or in headscarves, as it is believed their internal not their external characteristics are what is important. They are encouraged to get the best education they can and are seen as capable of achieving the same level of spiritual enlightenment as men. Alevis share the Sufi concept of the perfect human being (*Insani Kamil*), in which they define this person as one who is 'in full moral control of his hands, tongue and loins, treats all equally and serves the interests of others'. Acts for which they can be expelled from Alevism are murder, adultery, divorce, marrying a divorced woman and stealing. During their prayer ceremony they sing in Turkish using mystical language, such as:

Learn from your mistakes and be knowledgable,
Don't look for faults in others.
Look at 73 different people the same way.
God loves and created them all, so don't say anything against them.

Estimates of their numbers range from 15% to 30% of the population, but are difficult to substantiate as they have no central authority and have at least four different groups. Today they see themselves as the counterforce to Sunni fundamentalism and are found in largest concentrations between Çorum and Muş, east of Lake Van. Tunceli province, a remote and heavily forested region north of Elâzığ is known to be predominantly Alevi, forested mountains being their preferred habitat, hence their other name as *Tahtacis*, People of the Woods.

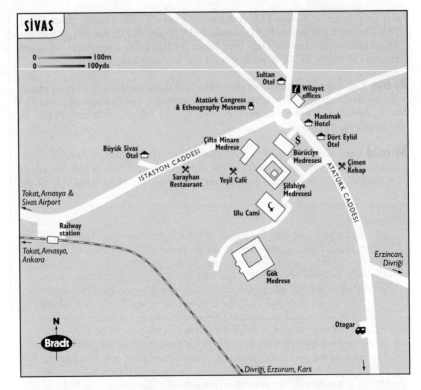

road, and just before the village is another, again on the right. These, like the ones at Pazar and Ezinepazar, were part of the series linking Amasya with Sivas. On arrival you follow the signs into the town centre, *Şehir Merkezi*, and there is no mistaking your arrival in the main square.

GETTING AROUND The main monuments are clustered close to the main square so everywhere is easily reachable on foot.

WHERE TO STAY

Büyük Sivas Otel (114 rooms) İstasyon Caddesi; ☏ 2254763; www.sivasbuyukotel.com. The city's main luxury hotel, a 7-storey block, rather impersonal, but at least with spacious rooms & plenty of marble & mosaic. $$$$

Dört Eylül Otel (35 rooms) Atatürk Caddesi; ☏ 2250074; www.dorteylulotel.com. Sivas's most modern hotel in a tall glass tower, furnished with dark traditional-style furniture. Good value. $$$

Sultan Otel (27 rooms) Eski Belediye Sokak; ☏ 2212986; www.sultanotel.com.tr. Sivas's best mid-range hotel with spacious rooms & bathrooms. In summer the roof bar has live music. $$

Otel Madımak (38 rooms) Eski Belediye Sokak; ☏ 2218027. Rebuilt on the same site as the earlier hotel which was burnt down in the 1993 anti-Alevi arson attack. Comfortable rooms on the first floor, with a kebab shop in the foyer. $

WHERE TO EAT

Sarayhan Restaurant Paşabey Mh, Tuzcular Çarsısı; ☏ 2243286; ⊕ 08.00—midnight. Traditional setting with local cuisine. Live music. Serves alcohol. Credit cards accepted. $$$

Çimen Kebap Atatürk Caddesi, Hayrat Sokak; ☏ 2248128; ⊕ 08.00—midnight. Traditional Sivas cuisine in the town centre with live music & alcohol. Accepts credit cards. $$

✗ Yeşil Café Belçuklu Sokak; ✆ 2222638; ☉ 09.00–20.00. With green décor as its name suggests (*yesil* is Turkish for 'green'), this unlikely place has an international menu with pasta & Schnitzel in case you have overdosed on local cuisine. The balcony has good views over the town's Seljuk minarets. $

WHAT TO SEE

Çifte Minare Medrese (☉ *always; admission free*) To the right of the main square in a large open grassy area the famous Çifte Minare Medrese rises above the trees. Dating from 1271, it is the most attractive of Sivas's Seljuk monuments, set among the pretty gardens of the small municipal park. The notion of twin minarets flanking the entrance as found here and at Erzurum was brought by the Seljuks from Persia. The ruins lie among the flowers and grassy banks with birds singing in the trees and local people lingering on the benches in the pleasant atmosphere. The curious thing is that on walking up to the façade expecting to enter, you discover that this is in fact all that remains of it. Like some film set, it is very convincing seen head-on, but the illusion crumbles when seen from any other angle.

Şifahiye Medresesi (☉ *always; admission free*) Also called the Darüşşifa of Keykavus I, and built earlier than the other monuments in 1217, this *medrese* lies immediately across the alley from the Çifte Minare Medrese. Carefully restored in the 1980s, it is the largest and most elaborate medical institution ever built by the Seljuks, with four *iwans* (three-sided roofed recesses open to the courtyard), a combined hospital and medical school, also looking after mental patients. Music and hypnosis were the favoured methods of treatment for these. On the türbe of Keykavus inside, the decorative motifs of the glazed tilework include the age-old swastika motif, eight-pointed stars and Kufic inscriptions. Of the various styles of Arabic writing, the square Kufic script, being particularly well adapted for mosaic, was found to be the most appropriate for Seljuk faïence. There are also Hittite throwbacks in the tilework, with marching lions in relief. The courtyard today has a lovely rose garden, with cafés and craft shops in the *iwans*.

Bürüciye Medresesi (☉ *08.00–20.00 daily; admission free*) To the left of the Şifahiye Medresesi, beyond the foundations of a *hammam*, this Seljuk *medrese* also dates from 1271 and like the Şifahiye Medresesi also has cafés and craft shops in its courtyard. Its portal boasts all the stylistic elements of the Seljuk monuments of Anatolia, including the vegetal sculptured motifs which are reminiscent of the Great Mosque of Divriği.

Gök Medrese (☉ *always; admission free*) From the back of the parkland behind the Çifte Minare Medrese you can walk for five minutes following the signs to reach this *medrese*, often considered the masterpiece of Sivas's monuments and formerly the town's museum. Also built in 1271 by the famous architect and *vizir* Sahip Ata whose work is also prominent in Konya and Kayseri, this is reckoned to be the most beautiful *medrese* built by the Seljuks by virtue of its design, the delicate stonework on the porch and façade, and the lovely mosaics of brick and tile in the *mescit* (prayer room) and the two *iwans*. After years of being closed for restoration, it is finally open to the public. As with the Gök Medrese in Amasya, it looks incongruous today among the modern buildings with washing hanging from the balconies, almost as if it is an oversight which someone forgot to knock down.

Ulu Cami (Great Mosque) Still a working mosque, but visitable outside prayer times, this thoroughly inconspicuous building is the oldest Turkish building in Sivas, dating to 1197. With its leaning austere brick minaret and its corrugated iron roof it looks from the outside more like a factory than a mosque. Inside it has a forest of 50 pillars and retains a certain atmosphere of Anatolian charm.

Atatürk Congress and Ethnography Museum (*Inonü Bulvarı;* ⊕ *08.30–12.00 & 13.30–17.30 Tue–Sun; adult TL3*) With its entrance at the back opposite an army barracks, this is the imposing Ottoman school building where the Sivas Congress was held in 1919. The ground floor is the ethnography section which has some early carpets and kilims as well as some fine embroidery. The earliest item is the 12th-century wooden carved *mimber* (pulpit) taken from the Kale Camii in Divriği. There is also a pair of carved wooden ceiling roses and other fragments taken from dervish monasteries closed down on Atatürk's orders in 1925. The upstairs is conserved as it was for the Sivas Congress, complete with old photos and Atatürk's bedroom.

5

Central Eastern Turkey and the Euphrates Headwaters

Man is a river, woman is a lake.

You might imagine eastern Turkey to be a vast dry steppe land, but you would be wrong. The eastern part of Turkey holds colossal quantities of water, with many huge rivers, and the central eastern region covered in this chapter is utterly dominated by the mighty Euphrates River and by the Southeast Anatolia Project (GAP – Güney-Doğu Anadolu Projesi). Consisting of a series of dams on the upper Euphrates, and culminating in the massive Atatürk Dam 60km north of Urfa, this project is the most ambitious ever undertaken by Turkey or by any other Middle Eastern country (see page 23). Its aim is to transform the lives of the semi-nomadic people, often sheep-raisers, many of them Kurds, from the flatter regions further south through enabling huge irrigation schemes to become a reality. In the more mountainous upper reaches of the Euphrates covered here, however, the landscape has been transformed, not into gigantic agricultural areas where crops can be cultivated, but into a series of huge lakes. Nowhere is this more striking than from the summit of Nemrut Dağı, where the view over the vast newly created Lake Atatürk is awesome.

As a visitor the highlights of this region are the rarely visited upper gorges of the Euphrates south of Erzincan, the Seljuk masterpieces at Divriği, Harput Castle and the now-flooded Pertek Castle, and of course the ascent to Nemrut Dağı itself at 2,150m, famous and much-photographed site of the colossal statues built by the power-crazed ruler of a local dynasty to guard his burial mound.

GETTING THERE AND AROUND

This is a region which is perhaps more difficult to reach and get around than any other in all of eastern Turkey. There are airports at Erzincan, Elâzığ, Adıyaman and Malatya which link with Ankara and Istanbul, but once you have arrived in the area, neither trains nor buses will be much help, as the sights themselves all lie off the main roads. This is a case therefore where you either need your own transport, or else resign yourself to taking a long time to travel around using a mixture of local buses and hitchhiking.

WHERE TO STAY AND EAT

There is decent to simple accommodation in Erzincan, Elâzığ, Malatya and Adıyaman (for Nemrut Dağı), but very little in the smaller towns like Iliç, Harput and Keban. See individual towns for listings.

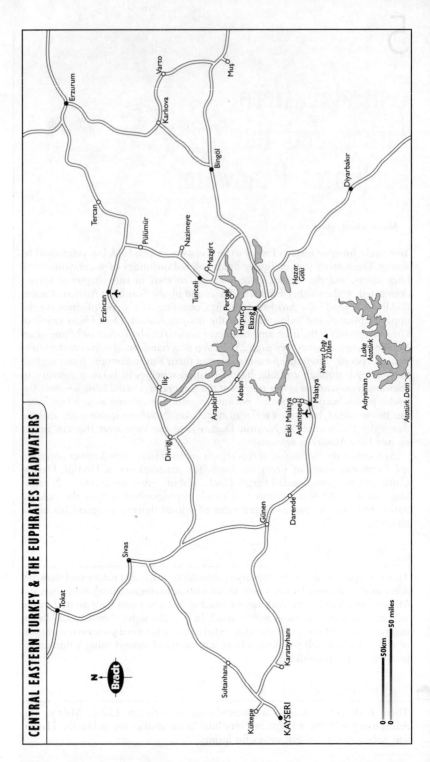

CENTRAL EASTERN TURKEY & THE EUPHRATES HEADWATERS

The main towns listed above have a few restaurants, but it is best in this part of Turkey to be as self-sufficient as possible, as there will rarely be anywhere to eat when you are travelling in the remoter parts. Stock up therefore with picnic supplies and plenty to drink before venturing off into the Euphrates gorges.

ERZİNCAN   *Telephone code: 446*

Flattened by earthquakes in 1939, 1983 and 1992, Erzincan today is a modern city with no antiquities of any sort. The 1939 quake registered 7.8 on the Richter scale and killed 32,700 people, while the 1992 quake had 498 fatalies yet registered 6.8 in magnitude, a reflection partly of where it struck and partly of better-built housing. Its name is even said to mean 'life-crusher', a graphic reference to the havoc wrought by earthquakes here. It lies on the North

---

THE EUPHRATES RIVER

Almost mythical in its associations, the Euphrates is historically always associated with ancient Mesopotamia, along with the Tigris. Geographically, however, 94% of its water comes from the Turkish highlands, and it begins under the name of the Euphrates at the point where two streams, the Murat Su and the Kara Su, converge near the town of Keban. The Murat Su rises 70km northeast of Lake Van, midway between Lake Van and Mount Ararat, while the Kara Su rises some 30km northeast of Erzurum. From their confluence to the point where the Euphrates discharges into the Persian/Arabian Gulf in Iraq is estimated to be 2,289km, making it the longest river in southwest Asia. Its first 526km flow through Turkey, then 604km in Syria and the final 1,159km in Iraq. It enters Syria at the ancient site of Carchemish (see page 212), now on the Turkish–Syrian border.

Etymologically the name derives from the Greek form of the original name *Phrat*, which means 'fertilising' or 'fruitful', in turn based on the Sumerian and Akkadian names, and many ancient cities evolved on its banks, such as Mari, Sippar, Nippur, Shuruppak, Uruk, Ur and Eridu. In the Old Testament a river named Perath (Hebrew for Euphrates) is named as one of the four rivers that flow from the Garden of Eden (Genesis 2:14). In the Hebrew Bible it is often simply referred to as 'the river', *ha-nahar*, and marks the northeastern border of the land God promises to Abraham and his descendants: 'To your descendants I give this land from the wadi of Egypt to the Great River, the river Euphrates' (Genesis 15:18).

In Islam the river is not mentioned in the Koran, but does figure in the Hadith or sayings of the Prophet Muhammad a number of times, prophesying that it will dry up and reveal gold and treasure which will cause war and strife:

Muhammad said: 'The hour will not come to pass before the river Euphrates dries up to unveil the mountain of gold, for which people will fight. Ninety-nine out of a hundred will die in the fighting, and every man among them will say: "Perhaps I may be the only one to remain alive"' (*Sahih of Al-Bukhari*).

Inevitably there is much controversy over water rights and use of the river, with both Syria and Iraq fearing Turkey will take too much as a result of the GAP Project with its 22 dams and 19 power plants on the river (see page 23). Turkey insists it will honour its international obligations in the water use, but downstream, Syria and Iraq remain worried. Whenever a water or electricity shortage occurs in Syria, the Syrians accuse the Turks of turning off the tap upstream. The flow of the river varies seasonally, much of its power locked up in winter in the heavy snow, released in spring as the waters melt. The heavier the snowfall in winter, the more water in spring and summer.

Anatolian Fault line at an altitude of 1,185m, close to the Euphrates Valley, ringed by mountains of over 3,000m which are snow-covered for much of the year. In summer it is crushingly hot and dusty. Strung out essentially along one main street, it has the feel of being at the ends of the earth. Its population today is back at 87,000, having recovered from the earthquakes.

In the 3rd and 4th centuries it was the capital of Armenia before Erzurum, and the Armenian Saint Gregory the Illuminator lived here. Up to the end of the 19th century Armenians accounted for around one-sixth of the population. In 1243 the Mongol hordes overran it, displacing the Seljuks. The destruction wrought on Erzincan by earthquakes and Mongols has been especially sad, as in the 19th century it was considered one of the most beautiful cities of Asia, with over 79 mosques. During World War I the Russians occupied the city for 18 months.

GETTING THERE AND AWAY There is one daily flight to and from Istanbul and three flights a week to and from Ankara. Consult www.anadolujet.com (Turkish Airlines' subsidiary for internal flights) for exact timings and prices, which vary according to season. The airport is a few kilometres south of the town. There is a train station which, if you do not have your own transport, is the best bet, as the *Doğu Ekspresi* stops here, having come from Erzurum, and follows the course of the upper Euphrates through highly scenic gorges to Divriği (see page 125). There is just one train a day, taking three hours, and continuing on to Sivas, having started in Kars and travelling via Erzurum. Consult www.tcdd.gov.tr, the website of Turkish Railways for exact timings, prices and types of seat available. By road the most attractive approach is from Sivas to the west, with a vertiginous descent in hairpin bends to the town.

 WHERE TO STAY AND EAT Very few western tourists come this way, and there is no need to book ahead. The town's best hotel is the **Büyük Erzincan Otel** (*88 rooms; Erzurum Karayolu;* \ *2260910; www.buyukerzincanoteli.com.tr; $$$*), at the edge of town. It even has an outdoor pool, tennis courts, a market, a hairdresser, disabled and child facilities and a doctor on site, but you will have to ask directions as it does not announce itself. Otherwise, take your pick from any of the simple places ($) along the main street, but ask for a room at the back, as the main street is very noisy at night. You can stroll around to find a restaurant, but none serve alcohol. To get a beer you will have to seek out one of the slightly seedy bars, only open evenings and tending only to get going after 22.00. Solitary women would not be advised to try them.

THE EUPHRATES GORGES

This next section assumes you have your own transport, and also includes a diversion to Divriği, site of the UNESCO World Heritage mosque/*medrese* complex. The total distance from Erzincan to Elâzığ is 344km, for which a full six hours' driving should be allowed. Public transport is not really feasible. If you make the additional detour to Divriği, allow a further three to four hours, so if you plan to do the whole trip in a day, be sure to have an early start.

WHAT TO SEE Setting off fully equipped with a full tank of petrol and plenty of food and drink, you follow signs for Kemah, the first town on the route. The road follows the course of the Euphrates as it starts to gather pace, flowing at this point fairly gently through scenic gorges with plenty of trees and greenery. The railway track follows the same course and you may well see one of the old trains, both passenger and freight, pass by. The road at one point crosses a dramatic bridge across the river in a gorge, and a monument marks the spot where 14 soldiers were killed in the construction of the bridge. An hour's drive will bring you to Kemah, a simple town of 2,500 people, and beside the gorge is an attractive tea garden enclosed in whose grounds are a trio of türbes (see page 113), 12th-century conical tombs belonging to local saints, still with traces of blue tilework on their exteriors.

The drive onwards to Iliç is another 60km along roads that are almost totally empty. There are no petrol stations between here and Elâzığ and nowhere to stay, but the landscape is beautiful, with endless camping and picnic spots beside the river. The soil on the hillsides is red, making the river itself reddish brown at this point as it gathers momentum and starts to develop some rapids, making it suitable for white-water rafting in inflatable dinghies. There are a few simple settlements, clusters of three or four huts built of the red stone. The narrow tarmac road winds on out of the river gorge, climbing to a pass at 1,630m, from where it is a further 25km to Iliç. Ignore the turning marked 78km to Divriği here, as there is a much closer road further ahead, some 12km after Iliç, from where the turn-off to the right is only about 43km, though the road is poor and only partially tarmac. Better still, do it from Arapgir as described later in this itinerary.

DETOUR TO DİVRİĞİ *Telephone code: 346; altitude: 1,250m*

Those with an interest in Islamic architecture usually feel it is imperative to make the difficult journey to Divriği, 174km east of Sivas in its own remote valley beside a tributary of the Euphrates River. The reason is the 13th-century Baroque mosque-*medrese* which is certainly unique in Turkey, so unique that UNESCO has now put it on their list of World Heritage Sites.

GETTING THERE AND AWAY: THE ROUTE OPTIONS

By car The problem with a visit to Divriği is where to go next. It takes two and a quarter hours to drive there from Sivas and the scenery is not exactly great *en route*. The hillsides and landscape are barren, crossing a pass whose summit reaches 1,950m, with snow-topped mountains for most of the year, and requiring snow-chains in winter. Accommodation is poor, so most people tend to drive all the way again to spend the night: a lot of driving to see one building.

There are three alternatives: first, not to bother, but to go from Sivas south to Kayseri and Cappadocia, or north to Tokat and Amasya; second, to take the road to Erzincan and fork south at Zara for 90km to reach Divriği along a difficult and high-altitude road; third, to take the infinitely more scenic route to approach Divriği from the Elâzığ direction, either having driven south from Erzincan through the Euphrates gorges, or having driven north from Elâzığ. Either way, the starting point is Arapgir, from where it is 77km to reach Divriği, through remote landscapes of heavily forested hillsides. At times the road, often in poor condition, crosses small streams and hump-backed bridges. In winter heavy snow from November to March makes this route impracticable.

By train There is a train station at Divriği, and devotees can leave Haydarpaşa Station in Istanbul at 08.30 and arrive the next morning at 09.30 for about TL32. Trains to and from Sivas take three hours and cost TL6, and services to and from Erzurum take seven and a half hours and cost TL12.

By minibus Hourly minibuses go from Sivas to Divriği, taking three hours each way, costing TL12.

Apart from the dilemma of how best to reach Divriği and how to continue your itinerary afterwards, the building you have come to see also poses its own imponderables. The mosque-*medrese* was commissioned in 1228 by a local emir and the daughter of another local emir, and maybe it is in this that the answer to the dilemma lies.

After the Battle of Manzikert, the victorious Alp Arslan sent his commanders to found various *beyliks*, small Turkish emirates, under the rule of a local *bey* or chieftain. Divriği, along with Erzincan, Kemah and Şebinkarahisar, came under the control of a commander called Mengücek, who founded a local dynasty named after himself. We know that the mosque was commissioned by a Mengücek emir called Ahmad Shah, and that the adjoining *medrese*/hospital complex was commissioned simultaneously by Turan Malik Sultan, daughter of the Mengücek *bey* of Erzincan. This pair must have been linked in some way, not only because of the simultaneous commissioning, but because the two buildings share the *qibla* wall (that facing Mecca), making the whole appear like one large building from the outside.

A tradition of wealthy women commissioning public buildings existed throughout Ottoman times, notably the case of Süleyman The Magnificent and his wife Roxelana who commissioned the Şehzade Mosque in Istanbul in 1544, with its pair of unique ornately decorated minarets, to commemorate their eldest son who died tragically young. In 1561 Princess Mihrimah, daughter of Süleyman the Magnificent and Roxelana, commissioned the highly unusual Rüstem Pasha Mosque in Istanbul, to commemorate the death of her husband, its interior and exterior walls covered in flowery, highly feminine tiles. The architect of both these mosques was the great Sinan, but these buildings were most untypical of his minimalist style. These unusual touches, it seems reasonable to speculate, might be the input of the female founder into the architect's work, more delicate flowery elements which she found more expressive of her emotions and which better represented what she wanted created in the permanence of the building. Maybe here at Divriği this unique twin building represents a commemoration of a loved one in the same way, or even a celebration of a union.

 WHERE TO STAY The **Divriği Belediyesi Oteli** (\ *4181825;* $) is run by the town council, offering clean rooms with en-suite bathrooms but no breakfast.

WHAT TO SEE The town itself is unremarkable, with a fair degree of building work going on. As the road drops down into the mountain-ringed bowl where the town sits, you must look out for the pointed conical dome and the minaret of the mosque in sand-coloured stone, raised up on a small terrace. Originally a Byzantine stronghold, Divriği was taken by the Seljuks after the Turkish victory at Manzikert in 1071 and held until 1251. During this time it was beautified with what many art historians regard as the loveliest and most unusual of Seljuk buildings which, uncharacteristically, the Mongols spared when they took the town later in the 13th century, even though they dismantled the citadel. The inscriptions on the building praise the Seljuk sultan Alaeddin Keykubad I.

The lavishness and intricacy of the stone-carved portals certainly have a delicate quality not generally found in these parts of Anatolia. The architect, called Hürremshah, was from Ahlat on the northern shore of Lake Van. Craftsmen from Tiflis in Georgia and Armenian craftsmen from the Van area are known to have worked on the carving. Prior to the Mengücek emirs, Divriği had been an important stronghold for the Paulician Armenians, a sect of iconoclast Christians founded in the 7th century, ancestors of the later 12th- and 13th-century Cathars in the French Pyrenees. Heavily persecuted by the Byzantines, they were given refuge in Divriği by the Emir of Malatya in the 9th century for their semi-independent state. The architect and craftsmen would therefore have been familiar with Armenian church architecture, like the church on Akdamar for example, where human and animal figures abound. Here at Divriği the occasional bird or animal is hidden away in the garlanded fronds. The central Asiatic Turks had always used animal figures, scrolls and fronds in their decoration. After the conversion of the Seljuks to Islam, abstract geometric patterns were incorporated as well. The carved animal and human figures on the Şifahiye Medrese and Gök Medrese at Sivas, the türbes of Niğde and Kayseri, the walls of Diyarbakır and these portals of Divriği are all a continuation of the animal style employed by the old Turkish tribes of central Asia.

The *medrese*, originally a hospital, now derelict, may be locked but a guardian usually appears to open it for you and may even proudly produce his visitors' book for you to sign. The second portal leads into the mosque, in which some of the carpets are virtually museum pieces and the *mimber* (raised pulpit) is one of the most beautiful in Turkey. In the middle of the mosque is a rectangular water basin above which is a dome to the sky. The most elaborate of the three portals is around the corner on the far side of the mosque. This is the one most reminiscent of Moghul art; you almost expect to see elephants emerging from the elaborate carving.

ONWARDS TO ELÂZIĞ

Continuing from the Divriği turn-off for the remaining 28km to Kemaliye, the road climbs out of the gorge with hairpin bends and on through gorges where it has been repaired after landslips. At the bridge over the Kemaliye Karanlık Kanyon (Kemaliye Dark Canyon) is a memorial with a long list of the people killed in making the road and bridge.

Kemaliye is a small town with a population of 2,250, and all the houses have roofs of silver corrugated iron, best suited to the snow which covers them for a large chunk of the year. The town is clean and attractively laid out, and a new well-designed place is now open called Café Canyon, with excellent views down into the gorge.

Right at the edge of town watch out for the lone wooden house perched up on an outcrop by itself, reached by steps only, with sweeping views down onto the dammed Euphrates. There are many fountains/springs at the roadside where water can be picked up, and many camping possibilities. At Beşpınar there is no longer a ferry but a bridge across the water. The road winds above the lake and there are a couple of places where small tracks lead down to the shore for a refreshing swim in the beautiful green cool water of the Euphrates. Even in mid-July the temperature of the water is wonderfully invigorating and slightly takes your breath away. It is a long thin lake at this point rather than a river.

Elâzığ is a further 120km from this point. The road climbs up to another pass at 1,200m and leaves the river for a patch, arriving at Arapgir. After Arapgir the road improves a lot, and there is another fork right to Divriği and Sivas, and left to Keban. The flat road crosses a high plateau and climbs to another pass at 1,475m. Shortly before Keban at a bridge just before crossing the lake, is a very attractively situated restaurant/café set on the grassy bank with shady outdoor tables under the trees, called the Keban Alıbalık Tesisleri. It specialises in trout from the lake and is very popular with local people at weekends. One curious side effect of the dam has been on the fish which used to breed in the upper stretches of the Euphrates. They now collect in confusion before the dam, creating a

The Keban Dam was the first of the series of dams on the Euphrates as part of the GAP scheme designed to bring electricity and irrigation to underprivileged parts of the country, a series that culminated in the even more colossal Atatürk Dam near Urfa completed in 1990. Over 50 known archaeological sites were flooded as a result of the construction of the dam and while it was being built between 1968 and 1974 a frenzy of archaeological salvage work was undertaken. Five foreign archaeological teams, two British, two American and one German, all self-financed, set to work to excavate as many sites as possible before the flooding in 1974. What they salvaged is on display in the museum at Elâzığ University (see page 129). Most of the sites were early Bronze Age settlements, important for contributing evidence to man's first settled existence in Anatolia after he had stopped his nomadic wandering and hunting.

fisherman's paradise. Once over the bridge you have a good view towards the huge Keban Dam to the left, and the new town of Keban is just round the corner, its houses with conspicuous solar panels and even wind turbines. Be aware that photography is not permitted in areas around dams in Turkey, so make sure you do not fall foul of this rule.

ELÂZIĞ *Telephone code: 424; altitude: 1,067m*

With a population of 320,000, Elâzığ is an unremarkable place, approached by wide, endless straight boulevards. It was only founded in 1862 by Sultan Abdul Aziz, and the only reason to stay here is to see the museum and the nearby Ottoman town and castle of Harput, and because it is the best base. Even so, there are not many hotels, and what there is tends to be overpriced.

 WHERE TO STAY

🏠 **Marathon Hotel** (54 rooms) Bosna Hersek Bulvarı; ↘ 2388686; www.themarathonhotel.com.tr. Plush place with 8 storeys, & the higher, the quieter, the better. Its clientele is almost exclusively local businessmen. Unusually there is no smoking in the b/fast area, & this is observed. $$$
🏠 **Elâzığ Mavigol Hotel** (34 rooms) Diyarbakır Yolu, Hazar Gölü Sivrice; ↘ 4251020;

The town's other distinction is its grapes, the long white *kecik memesi* (goat's teat) and the *okugözü* (ox-eye), a full midnight-blue grape from which the famous full-bodied red wine Buzbağ ('ice vineyard', not 'bagpipe'!) is made. The reference to ice refers to the peculiar technique used here at 1,250m, where the grapes were allowed to hang till the first frost, then crushed while still frozen. The wine has high tannic levels. The state-run vineyards belonging to Tekel can still be seen on the hills around Harput to the north of the city, and if this area is in fact where Anatolian man had his first settlements, it could well have been here too that he first cultivated the grape, an accomplishment thought by some to have originated in eastern Turkey. Anecdotally it was here on the banks of the upper Euphrates that Noah planted his vineyards (Genesis 9). Turkey's first commercial winery was established by Atatürk in 1925, and today Turkey is the world's fourth-largest producer of grapes, with over 60 grape varieties grown commercially.

www.mavigol.com. 30km from Elâzığ on Lake Hazar to the south. AC, restaurant, outdoor & indoor pool. $$

⌂ **Turistik Otel** (20 rooms) Hurriyet Caddesi; ☏ 2181772. Central, but noisy, with modern clean rooms. $

✖ **WHERE TO EAT** Eateries are also expensive for what they are, and there is nowhere in particular to recommend. There are many fast-food kebab and *köfte* places along Hurriyet Caddesi, the main street, and tucked up the side streets, and also *pastahanes* where you can sit at tables eating sticky pastries and tea, coffee or hot chocolate.

WHAT TO SEE

Elâzığ Museum Closed since 2006 and planning to reopen in 2011 after renovation, this museum is on the university campus. It will still house the items salvaged from the Keban excavations before the flooding, and its collection of Urartian objects – gold belts, ivories and jewellery – is even more magnificent than that at the Ankara museum. Upstairs there will be an ethnographic section with costumes and carpets.

HARPUT

A signposted road leads 5km from the northeast corner of Elâzığ to what was once the Urartian citadel of Harput. Now almost derelict its population moved down to Elâzığ when the new town was built in the 19th century. The road up to it leads through a heavily militarised area, with many soldiers presumably stationed here to protect the dam. Kurdish insurgents have succeeded in delaying the GAP Project through various terrorist attacks over the years, so the Turkish government is taking no chances. It is a dead-end road leading to Harput only, a town with various 12th- and 13th-century buildings remaining. Only 100 years ago Harput had 800 shops, ten mosques, ten religious schools, eight churches, eight libraries, 12 caravanserais and 90 *hammams*. Earthquakes helped with the destruction and precipitated the move to Elâzığ. Follow the sign to the *Kale* (castle) and you will pass the 12th-century **Ulu Cami**, with its severely leaning brick minaret. Having been in ruins for some 60–70 years, it was restored and reopened in 1994, and now has a very attractive interior with elegant arcades. It is simple but well looked after with a wooden roof over the courtyard. Close by is the **13th-century tomb of Arap Baba**, much revered locally. After removing your shoes and entering through a low door, a plain wooden coffin lies before you. The guardian may raise the lid and pull aside the clean grave clothes to reveal the embalmed naked and hairless body, brown like leather, with the back of its head bashed in – not for the squeamish.

The road leads on past various shops selling souvenirs to the impressive **castle** itself, located on a rocky outcrop, its Urartian origins overlaid with Roman, then Byzantine, then Ottoman defences. From its 1,400m summit you can at least see Lake Elâzığ, formed by the damming of the Euphrates. There is no entry fee or gate to close the site, and a 13th-century Artukid mosque and palace are being excavated on the top. The defences look at their most impressive from below. Despite its impregnable appearance it was taken by Tamerlane, by a Persian shah and finally in 1515 by the Ottoman Selim the Grim. A large church, Meryemana Kilise, is built into the cliff below, and there are also the remains of a ruined han, Dabakhane, and a crumbling hammam. Close to the castle entrance is an attractive tea garden, shaded by trees.

PERTEK

Crossing the vineyards on a small track to join the only tarmac road that heads north you can take a small diversion to reach the edge of the lake, and be confronted after some 20km with the road heading straight into the water, where it once ran, now flooded. Before the creation of the Keban Reservoir this was the main Erzurum road. A couple of small car-ferries now shuttle to and fro every ten minutes or so, breaching the gap in the road, carrying some 20 vehicles each across to the other side where the road emerges from the lake again. Some pleasant cafés have grown up on the lakeshore to refresh those waiting for the ferry. Various hilltops now protrude as islands from the lake, on one of which stands the superb medieval castle of Pertek. Dating from 1367 this magnificent castle once stood proudly guarding the river valley of the Euphrates, but is now stuck indignantly on its rocky island outcrop, cut off in the middle of the lake. Previously accessible simply by scaling the hill from the roadside, the well-preserved castle is now impossible to reach except by swimming (a feat not to be undertaken lightly) or by hiring a boat privately from Pertek (not straightforward either, as boats have some difficulty in mooring on the steep rocky slopes).

ROUTES FROM ELÂZIĞ

Elâzığ is a natural crossroads and from here you have to decide which direction to continue your itinerary: north, south, east or west. This chapter continues westwards in a loop towards Malatya and Nemrut Dağı, thereby linking in to *Chapter 6, Cappadocia*, which covers the regions to the west. If however you choose to head south towards Diyarbakır, this will link in to *Chapter 8, Southeastern Turkey, the Tûr Abdin and the Kurdish Heartlands*; if you head east this will link in to *Chapter 9, Lake Van Region*; and if you head north to Erzurum you will link in to *Chapter 11, Northeastern Turkey and the Georgian Heartlands*. The alternative routes south, east and north are described briefly here before focusing on the route west.

THE WAY SOUTH If you have already seen Malatya and/or Nemrut Dağı you can head south to Diyarbakır on a pleasant route that takes you past Hazar Gölü, the lake source of the Tigris. Buses run several times a day along this route, taking 90 minutes and costing TL3.

THE SWIFT TIGRIS

Although shorter than the Euphrates, whose headwaters begin just 30km northwest of Lake Hazar, the Tigris is faster flowing and carries more water. This difference is reflected in its etymology, as the original name in Sumerian was *Idigna* or in Akkadian *Idiqlat* meaning 'running water' or 'swift river'. In Sumerian mythology it was created by the god Enku who ejaculated and filled the river with flowing water. The gentler-paced Euphrates carries more silt.

Mentioned in the Old Testament as the third of the four rivers flowing out of the Garden of Eden (Genesis 2:10), it is 1,862km long: the first 400km flows through Turkey, then just 44km through Syria and the remaining 1,418km through Iraq where it joins with the Euphrates for the last 100km before flowing out into the Persian/Arabian Gulf at the Shatt Al-Arab. Baghdad stands on the banks of the Tigris.

The altitude of Hazar Gölü, the lake source of the river, is 1,223m and it is 90m deep in the middle. Even the hardy locals do not consider it swimmable before mid-June. The road skirts the attractive northern lakeshore and there are simple restaurants serving the lake fish, large and white, like a kind of freshwater mackerel. Lake eels are also sometimes on offer.

THE WAY EAST Heading east from the Tunceli fork you can pass through Bingöl and Muş, eventually reaching Bitlis and Lake Van, a distance of 325km, possible in one longish day. Buses ply this route between Elâzığ and Tatvan, taking eight hours and costing TL15. Bingöl (Turkish for 'a thousand lakes'), a Kurdish town set in the mountains, was destroyed by earthquakes in 1949, 1966 and 2003. An earthquake belt runs northeast from here to Varto and southwest to Malatya, where there was also a minor earthquake in 1986. The region is rich in lakes and streams and is an area for pasturing sheep, goats and cattle. Much of the population is semi-nomadic and Alevi (see box page 117).

Just after Bingöl a spectacular road forks off left and runs north through the mountains to Karlıova and then to Erzurum. It is motorable but difficult and should be driven with care.

The road on eastwards crosses a pass at 1,640m before dropping to Muş. A town with little to offer the tourist today, until the end of the 19th century Muş was inhabited by poverty-stricken Armenians, with Kurds in the mountains and on the plain. The Armenian castle above the plain is a sorry ruin. In the hills around, reachable with difficulty and a guide, are several ruined Armenian monasteries, notably Surp Karapet, known locally as Çanlı Kilise, with fine stone carvings. To reach Surp Karapet you fork left towards Varto 45km to the north. *En route*, near the village of Tepeköy on the steep bank of the Murat River, are the ruins of the Urartian castle Kayalıdere Kalesi, excavated under British archaeologist Seton Lloyd (1902–96), where many rich individual finds were made in an Urartian temple. Near the village of Yaygın a track leads off right 4km to the village of Ziyaret. Here you must take a guide and walk two hours in a north-northeast direction to reach Surp Karapet, also known as the Church of John the Baptist. Taxis which know the route will also drive there. Little remains of the once large monastery, as the stones are being systematically carried off by the local Kurds for their own building purposes.

THE WAY NORTH One unusual route rarely tried by travellers is via Tunceli and Erzincan to Erzurum. A lot of the route, though highly picturesque, is difficult and there is one 25km stretch of bad unsurfaced road. Accommodation is scarce, especially in Tunceli, and the trip requires your own transport. The town is surrounded by a high wall of mountains and the region is one of wild charm and great natural beauty with many mountain lakes and excellent hunting in the hills.

Some of the prettiest places to visit are the waterfalls at Karapğlan and Nazimiye, the Bağın hot springs on the banks of the Peri creek at Mazgirt and the mineral water springs at Pülümür. The mountainous landscape is also ideally suited to guerrilla warfare, and has been the setting for several clashes between Kurdish dissidents and the Turkish army.

Turning left at the T-junction towards Erzincan you come after about 20km to a road leading right to **Altıntepe (Hill of Gold)**, an important Urartian site, set on top of a 60m high volcanic mound. Working here between 1959 and 1968 Turkish archaeologists have uncovered a wealth of objects, many of them now in the Ankara museum. Tombs are built into the hillside in typical Urartian fashion, as at Van Kalesi, and in one of them, a man and a woman were found completely undisturbed in stone sarcophagi, the woman in all her best clothes and jewellery, her household objects in bronze, pottery and wood laid around her. The man was buried with many weapons and a beautiful gold belt. The famous bronze cauldron on three legs with bulls' heads handles on display in the Ankara museum was found here. On the hilltop above, a temple, palace and great hall have been found in very good condition, better than that at Çavuştepe (see page 288), one wall even having coloured murals. On terraces below are the foundations of spacious houses with three to six rooms. Other finds include the world's oldest stone toilet, bath and sink, and some fine later Roman floor mosaics. The richness of the finds here when compared with those at Van Kalesi, Çavuştepe and other Urartian sites indicates just how much must have been stolen and illegally exported from these other sites before proper precautions were taken by the government to clamp down on such activities.

A further 16km brings you to Erzincan (see page 123). About 90km along the route from Erzincan to Erzurum you pass the village of Tercan, near which stands the distinctive conical *türbe* of Mama Hatun built in the 13th century. This magnificent tomb stands in the middle of a circular walled courtyard entered through a large stalactite portal. Close by is a caravanserai, in which the tallest stable was for camels, the middle one for horses and the smallest for donkeys and mules. This and the *türbe* were built by the local Saltuklu emir of Erzurum in 1192 and are more restrained than Seljuk architecture. The nearby Mama Hatun Bridge is also from the late 12th century.

The road leads on through attractive mountain scenery to Aşkale (see page 342), where it joins with the route from Trabzon to Erzurum described later in *Chapter 11*.

THE WAY WEST TOWARDS CAPPADOCIA If, from Elâzığ, you want to go to Cappadocia, the region of weird lunar landscapes and rock-cut churches, the only way is to go by road (coach, minibus, *dolmuş* or private car) in one long and boring day via Malatya to Kayseri. The route to Malatya takes one-and-a-half hours through featureless dull landscapes of barren hills. The only highlight comes shortly after halfway there, where the road begins a steep descent off the central Anatolian Plateau, often leaving the cloud and rain behind as you drop down into the plain of the Euphrates. If this is your first sight of the great river (see box, page 123), you cannot fail to be impressed. Even diminished by the Keban Dam upstream, it still has a power and majesty unlike other large rivers. Much of this is obviously association, as you can readily imagine life and early civilisation growing up on its banks. The water is a deep green as it flows through the serene and fertile valley. The road used to cross it high above on the old bridge, but now crosses it even higher, on a modern suspension bridge built in the 1980s. Far below on the bank is a heavily ruined Ottoman caravanserai built on the instructions of Sultan Murat.

The road is now flat all the way to Malatya, still at an altitude of 915m. Traffic is light so speeds can be high. Some 10km before reaching the city, a newly surfaced road is marked off to the left to Nemrut Dağı Milli Parkı, 84km. This is an attractive alternative route to reach the summit of the famous isolated Nemrut Dağı sanctuary set up at 2,150m with commanding views over the entire region.

The crowds take the route up from Adıyaman, from where all the organised tours run, but if you want to escape the crowds and have your own transport, this route is preferable and extremely attractive. It is narrow but tarmac all the way with quite a few potholes, but still fine for a saloon car. Where the road divides, take the right fork to Tepehan. There are also two places to stay on the way up, listed below, and you can return by a different route that takes you over wild terrain to Eski Kahta Castle, from where you will link up with the conventional approach from Adıyaman (see pages 215–22).

Where to stay (Malatya side)

Güneş Otel (15 rooms) ☏ 3239378; e nemruttourmalatya@yahoo.com. Set just before the entrance to the Milli Park (*adult TL6*), 5 mins below the summit. Of the hotels in Malatya, this is the smarter if slightly more institutional option, a little more expensive & with better plumbing. It is run by a local teacher & only open May–Oct, as the snow makes it inaccessible in winter. He runs tours up from Malatya that involve seeing the ruins at sunset, & again at sunrise, so the clientele is mainly groups. Dinner & b/fast inc. $$

Nemrut Daği Eviniz Karapınar Aile Tesisleri ve Otel (6 rooms) Located on the road

half an hour below the summit, this charming place is a bit basic, but the setting compensates. Sitting above waterfalls with trout pools, you cross a bridge to reach the simple house, with several different outdoor & indoor sitting areas. Dinner is trout from the pools & b/fast is bread & homemade jam & cheese. The rooms are adequate & the plumbing & wiring a touch Heath Robinson, but the constant soothing sound of rushing water & the clarity of the mountain air more than make up for it. There is even a tiny mosque at the end of the drive. Aimed at Turkish families with their own transport. Dinner & b/fast inc. $

What to see

Nemrut Daği (⊕ *daily dawn to dusk; adult TL6; barrier closed out of hours*) If you choose to approach this colossal mountain from the Malatya side, the road to the top takes a good two hours to drive the 84km. The tarmac road ends within sight of the hilltop sanctuary, leaving just a path to climb the final ten minutes' walk, and brings you direct to the East Terrace with the sacrificial altar. The amount of climbing on foot is a little less than from the conventional side, where the car park leaves you with a walk of more like 15–20 minutes. Also, instead of being one of the crowds coming from the car park, where you often have to walk in single file behind large tours, your route is pleasantly crowd-free. The only downside – if you consider it such – is that there are no facilities such as shops, restaurants, toilets, etc, apart from what is on offer at the Güneş Motel.

See *Chapter 8* for a full description of the ascent from Adıyaman and the site itself.

MALATYA *Telephone code: 422*

Malatya is situated 247km northeast of Gaziantep, 242km east of Sivas and 254km west of Diyarbakır. Like Elâzığ, Malatya is a new town of the 19th century that grew up when the old town of Eski Malatya declined. A large, sprawling and ugly city, it is a centre of commerce for the area, with a fast-growing population (currently 411,000), quite sophisticated shopping and surprisingly good food. Capital of the province of the same name, Malatya has its own airport with daily flights to Ankara and Istanbul. Fruit has long been one of its specialities, and today dried apricots are its main export. In the past it was famous too for the quality of its apples, but today it is impossible to buy a true Malatya apple because the only trees remaining are in the garden of a local family which keeps them all for private consumption, a sure sign that they must be good. It will take no more than half a day to visit the local sights of Aslantepe and Eski Malatya, so the only reason to stay here is if you want to approach Nemrut Dağı from this side and want to stay in a bit more luxury than the simple places on the mountain can offer.

GETTING THERE AND AWAY

By air Atlasjet (*www.atlasjet.com*) flies daily to and from Istanbul, as does Onur Air (*www.onurair.com.tr*). Turkish Airlines (*wwwanadolujet.com*) flies daily to and from Ankara and twice daily to and from Istanbul. The airport is 35km northwest from the city and an airport bus costing TL7 runs you into the centre.

By train The train station lies 1km out of the city centre to the west, and trains run to Adana (TL16), Ankara (TL25), Diyarbakır (TL13), Istanbul, Kayseri and Sivas. Services are a lot less regular than coach services, with usually just one or two departures a day. Prices are also a little more expensive than the coach.

By coach Malatya has a huge *otogar* 4km to the west of the city centre with frequent services to all neighbouring cities such as Adana (eight hours, TL25), Adıyaman (2.5 hours, TL15), Ankara (11 hours, TL45), Diyarbakır (four hours, TL20), Gaziantep (four hours, TL20), Istanbul (18 hours, TL50), Kayseri (four hours, TL25) and Sivas (five hours, TL20). Most bus companies have shuttle minibuses to take passengers out there from their offices in the city centre. Varan and Ulusoy are probably the best.

WHERE TO STAY

Bezginler Hotel (56 rooms) ☎ 3241252. Outside the centre to the north by the ring road, this is Malatya's most modern & smartest hotel with a marble foyer & modern amenities like satellite TV. It has its own bar & licensed restaurant. $$$

Grand Akkoza Hotel (45 rooms) ☎ 3262727; www.grandakkozahotel.com. Out on the ring road, this is a good-value modern glass-fronted place with spacious rooms, complete with hammam, sauna & gym. $$

Malatya Büyük Otel (25 rooms) Halep Caddesi; ☎ 3252828. Opposite the Yeni Cami, so the call to prayer may intrude, but very good value, with spacious clean rooms & a good b/fast. $

WHERE TO EAT

There are many inexpensive places to eat along the main street of Atatürk Caddesi, but the one worth singling out is **Nostalji** (*Müçelli Caddesi*; ☎ *3234208;* ⊕ *08.00–23.00;* $), located in an old Malatya mansion crammed with Ottoman memorabilia. This place is an oasis of calm offering snacks and simple dishes and is popular with students.

WHAT TO SEE

Aslantepe (⊕ *08.00–17.00 Tue–Sun; TL3*)
Getting there On the eastern outskirts of Malatya a yellow sign points off right to Aslantepe Höyüğü and a blue sign to Eski Malatya. The colours are significant because Aslantepe, a Neo-Hittite site, is a ruin, whereas Eski Malatya despite its name ('Old Malatya') is now an inhabited village again, new life on the site of the old Seljuk town. At 3km after this turn-off the road splits with no signposts. Veer right for Aslantepe which you then reach after about 5km near the village of Ordusu.

History and site visit Italian archaeologists from La Sapienza University in Rome, currently under Professor Marcella Frangipane, have been working at the site for many years, tending to come in the winter with their students. The first excavations however took place in 1932 under the French, who had to laboriously remove a ruined 16th-century Turkish palace standing on top of the tumulus before they could begin. The French handed over to the Italians in 1961.

The most significant find is that of 'the world's first palace', dated to 3350BC, currently being prepared to open, thanks to a joint Turkish–Japanese project, as an open-air museum, but roofed for shade and protection. The palace is a huge complex of religious, economic and administrative buildings, the first example of its kind. Access is through a 20m-long corridor, decorated with paintings and motifs that are surprisingly well preserved with red coloured paint. Later layers overlay the site, with Byzantine graves and skeletons.

The late Hittite site was occupied from 5000BC to 712BC until the Assyrian invasion, after which it was abandoned for a long time. It then grew up again as a Roman village between AD500 and AD600, later becoming a Byzantine necropolis. The name Aslantepe means 'Lion Hill', and is so called because of the stone lions found here guarding the north gate to the Hittite city. This gate, reconstructed with the lions, is now in the vast central hall of sculptures at the Ankara museum. The Hittite name of this site is Kammamu, later Milid (the original name of Malatya), and was the capital of a new Hittite kingdom after the fall of Hattuşaş. The lions, with beautifully stylised manes, are thought to date back to the 11th century BC. The figure of a king cut from a vast limestone block over 3m high was found near the gate, and is now also in the museum. The colossal handsome figure with a curly beard is thought to be 8th century BC and shows much Assyrian influence in his hairstyle and dress. Also found on the site and likewise removed to the Ankara museum were a series of five reliefs depicting a king pouring a libation of wine to the weather god, the weather god attacking a flaming dragon, and scenes from lion and stag hunting. These hunting scenes again show Assyrian influence with the hunters riding in chariots.

For the non-specialist and the uninitiated, the site itself can be a bit underwhelming and confusing. You climb from the entrance beside the tree-shaded guardian's house, where his hospitable family may invite you to tea and feed you apricots and white mulberries, up onto the large shadeless mound where the excavations are taking place. The setting however, overlooking the green valley of a Euphrates tributary, is attractive. It was not, like Hattuşaş, a natural fortress, but the Neo-Hittites brought with them from their ancestors their superb wall-building techniques and so the place was adequately fortified against the Urartians and Assyrians, serving for some while as the regional capital until it finally disappeared from history.

Eski Malatya (Battalgazi)
Getting there To reach Eski Malatya you continue straight on for about 7km after the fork to Aslantepe. On arrival the walls are visible to the right of the road and you continue till you reach a main fork which leads to the main square inside the old Seljuk town, now the beneficiary of much municipal spending.

History and site visit A newish village of several thousand people has grown up scattered within the walls, with people encouraged to move back in. A huge 17th-century Ottoman caravanserai has been restored by the main square, with many souvenir shops growing up, and some of the Seljuk monuments, especially the Ulu Cami, have been excellently restored. Inside the caravanserai there are fireplaces with their tapering stone canopies, one for each of the parties staying the night. It does not have the beauty and ornamentation of the earlier Seljuk caravanserais to be seen in central Anatolia, but its size and preservation nevertheless make it impressive, and it is interesting to imagine Ottoman travellers warming themselves in front of their fires in the cold nights of the plateau. There are also some fine examples of Ottoman houses, traditionally built with pounded earth walls, overhanging first floors and closed courtyards. Originally a Roman

5

and then a Byzantine town with 53 churches and numerous monasteries, Eski Malatya has suffered from systematic re-use of its masonry, clearly visible in many fragments now re-employed in the houses. Add to that sacking by Byzantine emperors, Arab armies and a visit from the ubiquitous Mongol Tamerlane, and you begin to understand why so little was left above ground.

The walls, built under Justinian on a Roman camp, cover an extensive area and you can walk or drive round large sections of it. Once you have spotted the distinctive red brick of the Ulu Cami's minaret, head across to it, the ground level set down a good couple of metres below today's level. Now totally restored and still a working mosque, it is always open. The brick-built dome should be studied closely from the inside, to admire the Iranian technique built on an octagonal base. It also has a deep *iwan* (recessed chamber) opening onto the prayer room, and the arch of the iwan still has some of its abstract blue tile decoration and graceful lettering on the tiles.

ON THE WAY TO CAPPADOCIA

The road on towards Kayseri and Cappadocia climbs over many ranges, reaching 2,000m at its highest point. It is a five-hour drive to cover the 351km distance with no stops. Petrol stations are few and far between, so fill up in Malatya if you are in your own car. The trip can be done by bus, but not direct. On the way you may like to stop over at **Darende**, 110km west of Malatya, where you can enjoy freshly cooked trout from the river in one of the restaurants in the dramatic canyon close to the town, very popular with local families at the weekend. The town itself is also interesting with an early mosque/*medrese* complex, now a museum, a castle on a rocky outcrop and a fine rock pool where you can enjoy the water.

 WHERE TO STAY The **Tiryandafil Otel** (*15 rooms;* \ *422 6153095;* $$) is a surprisingly good hotel with spacious rooms and a very good restaurant (no alcohol) on the outskirts of town about 1km from the centre.

WHAT TO SEE

Karatay Hanı Some 60km before Kayseri a yellow sign points left 12km to this fine and well-preserved caravanserai, in many ways the most rewarding one to visit in central Anatolia. (The other two very fine caravanserais are both called Sultanhanı: one near Aksaray, the other near Kayseri.) The detour also takes you through some interesting Turkish villages. Karatay Hanı was built by the great Seljuk *vizir* Celalettin Karatay in 1240. The quality of the stonework throughout is very high and it was restored carefully in 1964. On the impressive outside walls are water spouts in the shape of humans and animals. To the right of the entrance is the *hazine* or treasury (corresponding to a modern reception desk and safe area) with a small door leading to the inner treasury for the valuables. To the left of the entrance were the kitchen and dining room. On the right side of the open courtyard were the series of bedrooms for the guests, with the three rooms nearest the entrance forming the hammam with openings in the vaulted roof. The vaulted arcade on the left of the courtyard was used as a depot, a bazaar and as stabling for the animals. Steps near the kitchen lead up onto the roof where you can see deep water tanks above the hazine and the kitchen for use in the kitchen and the hammam. There are also two mosques. The high main hall at the end of the courtyard was used as the winter quarters and has a fine conical dome.

Kültepe Karum At 20km before Kayseri, after the road from Sivas joins in from the right, a yellow sign points right to the site of the Assyrian trading colony

Kültepe Karum, whose name will be familiar from the many Assyrian finds unearthed here now on display at the Ankara museum (see page 88). Like so many very ancient sites it is interesting for its history rather than its visible remains today, and a visit here does more for the expert than the interested amateur. Excavated since 1984 by a Turkish professor, it was here that he found the earliest Anatolian written documents in cuneiform script. In the megaron-style buildings found here, archaeologists have also noticed a striking resemblance to the Mycenaean palaces of 1,000 years later. Long before they built an empire of their own, the Assyrians of northern Mesopotamia established great trading colonies in Anatolia to reap the rewards of the prosperity of the times (2nd millennium BC), and they called these trading colonies 'karums'. This one at Kültepe (Kanesh to the Assyrians) was the foremost of these, and all the others were subordinate to it. They imported tin, garments and cloth using caravans of 200 to 250 donkeys (the black donkeys of Cappadocia), in exchange for gold and silver.

Access to this centre at Kültepe was by way of Carchemish or Harran to Birecik, Maraş and Elbistan: it became a great corridor for cultural as well as commercial exchange. It is perhaps the most ancient and important route of cultural exchange in the world, following either the Euphrates up into the heart of eastern Anatolia, or westwards along tributaries through the Taurus mountains to central Anatolia and the west.

The Assyrians had no desire to exercise political power in Anatolia but confined themselves to purely commercial affairs. Their cuneiform tablets did not therefore concern themselves with weighty political treaties, but with dull records of their business transactions. They also introduced the habit of using cylindrical seals, already widespread in Mesopotamia; just as had happened in Mesopotamia, their manufacture and use developed into an art in its own right. The appeal of marking something with your own stamp has always been universal: today's equivalent can be seen in the designs of company logos, seeking to project a particular image.

On reaching the junction with the main Sivas road from the right, a detour can also be made towards Sivas to see the great caravanserai called **Sultanhanı**, 45km north of Kayseri, built in 1236. It is on a slightly smaller scale than that of its namesake near Aksaray, but it is otherwise very similar in design and appearance. It too has been carefully restored. It does not warrant a special detour unless you have not been able to see the other Sultanhanı or the Karatay Hanı.

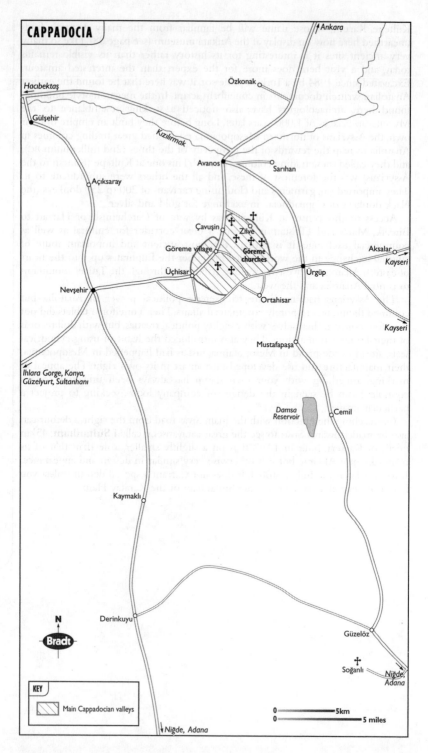

CAPPADOCIA

Ankara

Özkonak

Hacıbektaş

Gülşehir

Kızılırmak

Avanos

Sarıhan

Açıksaray

Çavuşin

Zilve

Göreme village

Göreme churches

Aksalar

Kayseri

Üçhisar

Ürgüp

Nevşehir

Ortahisar

Kayseri

Mustafapaşa

Ihlara Gorge, Konya,
Güzelyurt, Sultanhanı

Damsa
Reservoir

Cemil

Kaymaklı

Derinkuyu

Güzelöz

Soğanlı

Niğde,
Adana

N

Bradt

KEY

Main Cappadocian valleys

0   5km
0   5 miles

Niğde, Adana

6

Cappadocia

Telephone code: 384

Grieve for the living, not for the dead.

Cappadocia, this region of weird volcanic landscapes and rock-carved churches, was largely forgotten by the western world until 1907, when a visiting French priest, Guillaume de Jerphanion, decided to devote the rest of his life to the study of its churches, publishing his vast research in the 1930s and 1940s. Since then the renown of the area has spread worldwide and Cappadocia has become one of the most visited and photographed areas of Turkey. In 1985 it was awarded UNESCO World Heritage Site status. Many of the valleys link up with each other, making excellent walking or riding territory, and even with a whole week at your disposal, you will not see everything Cappadocia has to offer. A three-day visit should be your minimum. The chapter begins with a description of Kayseri, the city on the eastern fringes of Cappadocia, to link in with where *Chapter 5* ends, assuming an approach from Malatya (see page 136).

WHEN TO VISIT

Be warned that the invasion of tourists may mar your enjoyment of the region if you visit at high season, in July and August, when school holidays mean most people, foreign and local, come. Daylight hours are long, though it can be a bit dusty and dry, hot during the day with warm evenings. May, June, September and October are the optimum months for the best weather; it is not too hot, but you also have the spring blossoms or the autumn colours. September also has the advantage of being when the local grapes, apples, pears, plums, apricots and walnuts ripen. The Wine Festival begins in Ürgüp (see page 158) in early September each year, and the apricot and poplar trees turn to lovely yellows, reds, and greens under clear blue skies. It will still be busy, but not as bad as high summer, especially if you also avoid weekends. Outdoor pools only function from mid-June to the end of September. March and April are cold and unpredictable, so you may get rain or it may be sunny, but the greenery at least is lovely as the snows melt. During winter, from November to March, the snows come in earnest and it is very cold, so many hotels close for this entire period. The snow can lend magic to the landscapes though, and you will certainly have the place much more to yourself: no queuing to get into the churches, for example. February is the lowest season of all, when snow-chains may be necessary if you are renting a car.

HISTORY

It is probable that even in pre-Christian times the rural population of Cappadocia made use of natural caves. They were easily extended, with the soft rock so readily carved out that early Christians would have found them ideal for hiding from pagan persecution. The area became an important frontier province during the 7th century when the Arab raids on the Byzantine Empire began. By now the soft tufa had been tunnelled and chambered to provide underground cities where a settled if cautious life could continue during difficult times. When the Byzantines re-established secure control between the 7th and 11th centuries, the troglodyte population surfaced, now carving their churches into rock faces and cliffs in the Göreme and Soğanlı areas, giving Cappadocia its fame today. Their churches and monasteries were many and small: the landscape was suitable for recluses in search of the spiritual life, and the region was distant from the contending doctrines of orthodox Constantinople and Monophysite Syria. St Basil, a 4th-century Father of the Church from Caesarea (Kayseri), opined that small and disciplined communities were most conducive to religious feeling. At any rate here they flourished, their churches remarkable for being cut into the rock, but interesting especially for their paintings, relatively well preserved, rich in colouring, and with an emotional intensity lacking in the formalism of Constantinople; this is one of the few places where paintings from the pre-Iconoclastic period have survived. Icons continued to be painted after the Seljuk conquest of the area in the 11th century, and the Ottoman conquest did not interfere with Christian practices in Cappadocia, where the countryside remained largely Greek, with some Armenians. But decline set in and Göreme, Ihlara and Soğanlı lost their early importance. The Greeks finally ended their long history here with the mass exchange of populations between Greece and Turkey in 1923.

GETTING THERE AND AWAY

BY AIR The two airports that serve Cappadocia are Nevşehir (see page 159) and Kayseri (see page 145), both linking with Istanbul (three flights a day) and Izmir (four flights a day).

BY TRAIN The closest train stations to Cappadocia are at Kayseri and at Niğde (see page 145). Niğde is on the line that runs between Ankara and Adana and a daily service leaves for Ankara at 23.30 (taking just over nine hours, TL27) and for Adana taking four hours, TL17. Kayseri is on a line that runs east to Tatvan (twice a week, 24 hours, TL22), north to Ankara (four times a day, eight hours, TL15), and west to Istanbul (twice a day, 22 hours, TL22).

BY BUS Buses run to Cappadocia from Istanbul (travelling overnight) or from Ankara. Most arrive in Nevşehir or Kayseri, from where you can pick up a *servis* taxi to take you on to Göreme, Avanos, Ürgüp or Uçhisar. They run hourly from Ankara, taking five hours and costing about TL26. From Istanbul they travel daily taking 11 hours and costing about TL42.

BY ROAD From Kayseri the road onwards to Niğde passes through what must be one of the bleakest landscapes in Turkey, a flat, featureless, treeless waste, with no hills or contours at all. A yellow sign points off to the right, indicating 41km to Göreme, opposite a flat lake just by a petrol station; this is the most direct approach to the fairy chimney landscape most people visualise as Cappadocia proper. If you reckon you will continue south and turn instead up the road through Derinkuyu and Kaymaklı (the underground cities), be warned that you are sentencing yourself to a further 120km of bleak landscapes.

The first route is the best one to approach the Göreme region, soon becoming pleasantly hilly as it winds over the beginnings of the Cappadocian landscape.

Following the eruption of three volcanoes – the 3,916m Mount Erciyes near Kayseri, the 3,268m Hasan Dağı near Aksaray, and the 2,963m Melendiz Dağı near Niğde – over 30 million years ago, the volcanic ash consolidated into a soft porous rock called tufa, which covered an area of about 4,000km . The soft tufa eroded during millennia of wind, snow and rain, but where it was protected by a harder block of stone above, the result was the curiously shaped fairy chimneys or cones you see today, some standing as much as 50m high and often still capped by the protecting fragment of hard stone. They are called 'fairy' partly because of their unreal appearance, but also because local folklore talks of men being carried off by *peris* or fairies after venturing into old churches in the rocks. The greatest concentration of chimneys is in the Zilve Valley and the Peribacalar Valley between Avanos and Ürgüp. Unlike the usual harsh greys and blacks of most volcanic landscapes, the rocks here are soft shades of pale grey, yellow, mauve, pink and umber. This variation in colour is due to the variety of metals and minerals spewed out during different eruptions. Where, in the cones, you appear to be looking into open caves or terraces, these were originally rooms, now exposed, as the façades have eroded away. Some were also dovecotes, and the fallen façades expose the nests, rows of little holes in the rock face. A constant battle is waged between the tourist authorities and the local farmers, who like to block up the cave entrances and use the churches as pigeon-cotes. The pigeons are highly prized for their droppings which are used as fertiliser, perhaps accounting for the distinctive taste and bouquet of the local wine.

A third route has now also been built for the approach from the east, shortening the distance from the present 88km to 50km from Kayseri, leading through Aksalar. All these roads approaching from the east bring you into Ürgüp over a small bridge. Most buses and coaches follow the dull route from Kayseri towards Ankara, then turning south to Avanos to approach Ürgüp.

GETTING AROUND

Distances are small and all the towns centred on Göreme are connected with frequent local shuttle buses. For example, the 5km journey between Ortahisar and Ürgüp costs TL1.50 and runs every half hour. Many places also rent out mountain bikes (TL15 a day), scooters (TL30 a day), or cars (TL90 a day). There are also plentiful taxi services.

SUGGESTED EXCURSIONS Cappadocia covers a large area and the sheer number and variety of places to visit can be a little bewildering on first arrival. To help plan your stay the following is a table of day excursions which can all be done from a base of Ürgüp, Göreme or Avanos.

1 Ortahisar, Uçhisar (lunch), Göreme
2 Çavuşin, Zilve (lunch), Avanos, Sarıhan, Özkonak, Peribacalar Valley
3 Ürgüp, Mustafapaşa, Soğanlı (lunch), Derinkuyu, Kaymaklı, Nevşehir
4 Ürgüp, Avanos (lunch), Hacıbektaş, Gülşehir, Nevşehir
5 Nevşehir, Ihlara (lunch), Güzelyurt, Sultanhanı (if you are going on to Konya)
6 Ürgüp, Mustafapaşa, Soğanlı (lunch), Eski Gümüş, Niğde (if you are going on to Adana the same day)

TOURIST INFORMATION

There are tourist information offices (⊕ *daily 08.30–17.00*) in Avanos, Nevşehir and Ürgüp, all located in the main streets and clearly signposted (see maps). They hand out useful walking maps and have lists of local hotels.

LOCAL TOUR OPERATORS

Cappadocia is awash with tour operators. Most agree a set price for their main tours at the start of each season, but standards still vary. Among the more reputable ones are:

Argeus Tours Ürgüp; ☎ 3414688; www.argeus.com.tr. Arranges packages of 3–9 days, & an 8-day mountain-biking tour.
Heritage Travel Göreme; ☎ 2712687; www.turkishheritagetravel.com. This company is based at the Kelebek Hotel & Cave Pension & the minimum price for a day's tour is TL60 for 4 people.
Kirkit Voyage Avanos; ☎ 5113148; www.kirkit.com. Organises treks in the area from 2 hours to a full day. Based at the Kirkit Pension.
Mephisto Travel Çavuşin; ☎ 5327070; www.mephistovoyage.com. Based at the İn Pension,

offering trekking & camping packages from 2 days to a full 14-day exploration round Cappadocia & the Taurus Mountains. It also runs bicycle tours, horse-cart tours & rents out bicycles. It can also arrange Cappadocia tours for disabled travellers.
Middle Earth Travel Göreme; ☎ 2712559; www.middleearthtravel.com. Specialising in adventure tours & treks, from local 1-day outings to treks in the Kaçkar Mountains, the Lycian Way or even Mount Ararat.
Nomad Travel Göreme; ☎ 2712767; www.nomadtravel.com.tr. Offering local tours into all the outlying valleys.

⌂ WHERE TO STAY

There is so much accommodation of all ranges in Cappadocia it is difficult for any visitor to know where to start. So that it is easier to make a decision, all the listings are given here for the central cluster of Ürgüp, Uçhisar, Göreme, Mustafapaşa and Avanos, as any one of these can be used as your base. Listings are given separately for Kayseri (see page 147) and for the Ihlara Gorge (see page 162), as they are set somewhat apart.

ÜRGÜP

⌂ **Sacred House** (12 rooms) Dutlu Cami Mh B; ☎ 3417102; ⊕ all year. The most aesthetically perfect of the cave hotels in the area, with prices to match. Authentic antiques. Champagne & caviar are served by the owner dressed in a white knight outfit. Suitable for children & pet-friendly. Restaurant & Wi-Fi available. $$$$$
⌂ **4 Oda** (5 rooms) Esbelli Mah; ☎ 3416080; www.4oda.com; sometimes closed in winter. One of the first troglodyte hotels to be established, with many personal touches like wine presses & a well-tuned piano. Huge b/fast. $$$$
⌂ **Esbelli Evi** (10 rooms) Esbelli Sokak; ☎ 3413395; sometimes closed in winter. 65km to Kayseri airport. Described as 'the world's classiest cave', Esbelli has the façade of a fine stone

mansion with a labyrinth of hidden courtyards with its rooms carved into the soft volcanic rock. The owner is a lawyer & fastidious bachelor, & the house is very popular with the Ankara diplomatic community. Pretty garden, pets not allowed, AC in rooms & Wi-Fi. $$$$
⌂ **Kayadam** (7 rooms) Esbelli Mah; ☎ 3416623; www.kayadam.com; sometimes closed in winter. A small hotel of great charm with modest but comfortable rooms re-carved to fit bathrooms. Suitable for children & pets. Attractive garden. Excellent b/fast & views. $$$$
⌂ **Serinn House** (5 rooms) Esbelli Sokak; ☎ 3416076; www.serinnhouse.com; closed in winter. Ultra-modern chic in old caves. Minimalist décor with black four-poster beds, a 'New York

loft' style as opposed to 'Anatolian authenticity'. No children, no pets. Attractive garden. Designer b/fast too. $$$$

🏠 **Yunak Evleri** (30 rooms) Yunak Mh; ☏ 3416929; ⊕ all year. Very unusual in that the owner decided not to alter the external appearance of the cave rooms at all. As a result an entire network of caves is transformed internally into the height of luxury, yet looking from the outside the same as they have done for the last 1,000 years. Some are set in hidden courtyards, full of secret passageways & hidden areas. Own restaurant. Excellent staff & service. $$$$

🏠 **Ürgüp Evi** (10 rooms) Esbelli Mah; ☏ 3413173; f www.urgupevi.com.tr; ⊕ all year. At least half-a-dozen cave hotels have now been carved into the Esbelli Hill in Ürgüp. This one is

very fine, & even rents out a cave-house called the Mary Hall which is attached. Attractive garden. Meals on demand. Suitable for children. No pets. Wi-Fi. $$$

🏠 **Cappadocia Palace** (13 rooms) Duayeri Mahallesi Mektep Sok; ☏ 3412510; www.hotel-cappadocia.com. Good-value hotel with spacious comfortable rooms in a converted Greek house with an attractive restaurant. $$

🏠 **Razziya Evi** (7 rooms) Cingilli Sokak; ☏ 3415089; www.razziaevi.com. Excellent mid-range place in a restored house with its own *hammam* & attractive courtyard. $$

🏠 **Hotel Elvan** (8 rooms) Barbaros Hayrettin Sok; ☏ 3414191; www.hotelelvan.com. Very good-value place with rooms round a courtyard, good dining room & tiny roof terrace. Clean & homely. $

UÇHİSAR

🏠 **Les Maisons de Cappadoce** (32 suites, 16 apts) Semiramis AŞ, Belediye Meydanı; ☏ 2192813; www.cappadoce.com; ⊕ all year. Here you can enjoy the cave home of your dreams designed by a French architect, where b/fast is delivered in a basket. Uçhisar is an amazing Cappadocian village cut into the region's tallest fairy chimney. The hotel has a pool & restaurant, & is suitable for children & pets, with attractive garden. $$$$

🏠 **Lale Saray** (12 rooms) Göreme Caddesi; ☏ 2192333; www.lalesaray.com. Comfortable, tastefully decorated place with good restaurant & terraces. The rooms have minibars & massage showers. $$

🏠 **Les Terrasses d'Uçhisar** (18 rooms) Eski Göreme Yolu; ☏ 2192792; www.terrassespension.com. Excellent value with

great views from the upstairs rooms. The stylish rooms show the owner's French chic. Superb location & terrace, & fine restaurant. $$

🏠 **Kilim Pension** (9 rooms) Tekelli Mahallesi; ☏ 2192774; www.sisik.com. Set around a shaded courtyard, the rooms are nicely decorated. There is also a rooftop terrace & attractive restaurant. $

🏠 **La Maison du Rêve** (30 rooms) Tekelli Mahallesi; ☏ 2192199; www.lamaisondureve.com. Spread over 3 floors & built into the edge of a cliff, this place has a spacious terrace with stunning views, a basic restaurant & scooters for rent. $

🏠 **Uçhisar Pension** (8 rooms) Kale Yani; ☏ 2192662; www.uchisarpension.com. Simple place with clean rooms & en suites. Lovely views. $

GÖREME

🏠 **Fairy Chimney Inn** (8 rooms) Güvercinlik Sokak; ☏ 2712655; www.fairychimney.com; closed Nov–mid-Mar. A perfectly conceived conversion of a true Cappadocian house to a comfortable inn, executed by a German doctor of anthropology. Design without apparent effort makes it a rarity in these cave conversions. $$$

🏠 **Göreme House** (11 rooms) Eselli Mah; ☏ 27112060; www.goremehouse.com; ⊕ all year. Converted into a small hotel in 1997, this triple-storeyed complex has a communal courtyard with a colonnaded portico. The owner is a ballooning expert who offers his guests special deals. No children, no pets. Restaurant. $$$

🏠 **Kelebek Hotel** (11 rooms, 11 suites) Yavuz Sokak; ☏ 2712531; www.kelebekhotel.com. This place is in 2 parts: the old pension with 2 8m-tall fairy chimneys in its courtyard, & a new part in a splendid mansion in a spacious garden. It has its own small pool, *hammam* & fabulous views. $$

🏠 **Arch Palace** (10 rooms) Unlu Sokak; ☏ 2712575; www.archpalace.com. Clean simple place with rooftop restaurant & lovely views. $

🏠 **Paradise Caves Hotel** (12 rooms) Muze Caddesi; ☏ 2712248; www.paradisecaveshotel.com. With fairy chimney rooms & a charming multi-tiered terrace this hotel has plenty of authentic atmosphere. $

🏠 **Shoestring Cave Pension** (14 rooms) Aydinli Mahallesi; ✆ 2712450; www.shoestringcave.com. One of the original Göreme pensions, this place now has a swimming pool on its terrace. Some

rooms have marble bathrooms en suite, others are rock-cut dorms. Good b/fasts are served in the courtyard. $

MUSTAFAPAŞA
🏠 **Old Greek House** (10 rooms) Şahın Caddesi; ✆ 3535306; www.oldgreekhouse.com. Wonderfully genuine place with large rooms & comfortable beds run by the same family who have lived in the Ottoman Greek house since 1938. Its restaurant also serves excellent Ottoman cuisine prepared by local women. $$$

🏠 **Hotel Pacha** (12 rooms) Sinasos Meydanı; ✆ 3535331; www.pachahotel.com. Lovely relaxed atmosphere in a family-run restored Greek/Ottoman house, with excellent food served on the upstairs terrace overlooking the courtyard. $$

AVANOS
🏠 **Kirkit Pension** (11 rooms) Atatürk Caddesi; ✆ 5113148; www.kirkit.com. Relaxed & simple place set in converted stone houses, with good home cooking eaten in the courtyard or indoors in a vaulted dining area. $$

⛺ **Ada Camping** Jan Zakari Caddesi; ✆ 5112429; www.adacampingavanos.com. Good river setting for this family-run campsite, complete with pool, lots of shade & a restaurant. $

✖ WHERE TO EAT

ÜRGÜP Ürgüp's restaurants are of a higher standard than those at Göreme, although the choice is more limited.

✖ **Ziggy's** Yunak Mahallesi; ✆ 3417107; 🕐 11.00–23.00. Fun place with Tintin's Snowy dog as its logo & named after the David Bowie song. The atmosphere has a touch of Istanbul sophistication & the 12-course set menu offers an amazing selection of *mezze*. $$$
✖ **Dimrit** Yunak Mahallesi; ✆ 3418585; 🕐 10.00–20.00. Lovely hillside terraces offer fine

views, especially at sunset. The large menu has everything from salads, fish & grills to house specials. $$
✖ **Somine Café & Restaurant** Cumhuriyet Meydanı; ✆ 4318442; 🕐 10.00–22.00. Roof terrace for outdoor eating & large indoor dining room. Good range of salads & *mezze*. $

UÇHISAR
✖ **Elai** Eski Göreme Yolu; ✆ 2193181; 🕐 10.30–14.30 & 18.30–23.00. Offering both international & Turkish cuisine, this establishment has a fine terrace with stunning views for pre-dinner drinks. Inside, the dining room has velvet curtains & ceiling beams. $$$

✖ **Le Mouton Rouge** Belediye Meydanı; ✆ 2193000. Decorated like a French bistro, this place offers simple meat & salad dishes. $$
✖ **Kandil House** Göreme Caddesi; ✆ 2193191; 🕐 10.00–22.00. Simple café for snacks & light meals, with lovely views over Rose Valley. $

GÖREME
✖ **A'laturca** Müze Caddesi; ✆ 2712882; 🕐 11.00–23.00. Elegant & stylish place offering typical Anatolian cuisine. It has lots of seating areas, inside & out. Try the local Erciyes kebab. $$$
✖ **Dibek** Hakki Paşa Meydanı; ✆ 2712209; 🕐 09.00–23.00. Excellent & traditional restaurant in a 500-year-old building with low seating round circular tables in alcoves. They offer their own wine

& the well-known Cappadocian dish *testi kepap* (pottery kebab) where the meat is slow-cooked in a pottery dish & then broken at the table. $$
✖ **Nazar Borek** Müze Caddesi; ✆ 2712441; 🕐 10.00–22.00. Producing cheap filling meals like *gozleme* (stuffed savoury pancake) & *borek* (filled deep-fried pastries), this is a good venue for vegetarians. There is often a special dish of the day. $

There are many ATMs throughout the area, especially at Göreme. There is also a good number of internet cafés, specifically at Göreme and Ürgüp. 1001 Books (*Müze Caddesi, Göreme;* ⊕ *08.00–20.00*) is an excellent bookshop selling English books, guidebooks and free magazines.

KAYSERİ *Telephone code: 352; altitude: 1,055m*

Kayseri lies on the eastern fringes of Cappadocia, but there is no sign here of the famous Cappadocian landscapes. One of their creators *is* here, however, in the form of the now extinct volcano Mount Erciyes, rising up behind the town, though visible only in fine weather. Its eruptions aeons ago spewed out the volcanic tufa which was to be moulded by wind, rain and man into fantastical shapes. At 3,916m it is snow-capped all year round, and a minor ski resort in winter. A road leads quite a long way up it, and you can go for summer walks here in the cooler mountain air.

HISTORY The modern name Kayseri is an adaptation of the name Caesarea given to the town in honour of Caesar Augustus when this was the capital of the Roman province of Cappadocia Prima. As the main town of Cappadocia, Kayseri owes its importance to the fact that it stands astride the major trade routes east from the Aegean and north and south between the Mediterranean and the Black Sea. But its exposed position on the high plateau made it easy prey for all the invading armies which poured to and fro across Anatolia in medieval times, including Arabs, Turcomans, Seljuks, Mongols, Mamelukes and finally Ottomans in 1515. Today the monuments which have survived and which are the town's tourist attractions are the 13th- and 14th-century Islamic buildings, built either by the Seljuks or by the later Turcoman emirs, first the Danishmends, then the Karamanids, who ruled the area after the collapse of Seljuk power. Their settings are uninspiring, on flat ground surrounded by ugly modern buildings which always manage to look half-finished. Even more unfortunate is the black basalt used in the older constructions, a colour so dingy and depressing, especially when wet, that it is hard to find the architecture beautiful.

GETTING THERE AND AWAY The approach to Kayseri from Malatya is, as so often with the towns and cities of eastern Turkey, somewhat insalubrious. A wide road leads through scruffy suburbs and eventually brings you to the main central square with the inevitable equestrian statue of Atatürk, and the black walls of the citadel looming off to the left.

By air There are three daily flights to Istanbul taking 90 minutes, and the same to Izmir. The flights are run by Turkish Airlines (*www.anadolujet.com*) and Onur Air (*www.onurair.com*) and cost around TL75 one way. Consult their websites for up-to-date timings which vary between summer and winter schedules. The airport lies about 10km to the north and a taxi costs roughly TL15 to the centre, or TL2 for a *dolmuş*. Many of the hotels in Cappadocia also run shuttle buses to and from the airport. There are no flights from Ankara to Kayseri (too short a distance) and to reach the other main cities you need to take an intercity train or coach.

By train Trains run to a similar number of destinations as the bus, but take a bit longer and cost a bit less. For example the train to and from Ankara leaves five times a day, takes eight hours, and costs TL13, while the bus costs TL25 and takes

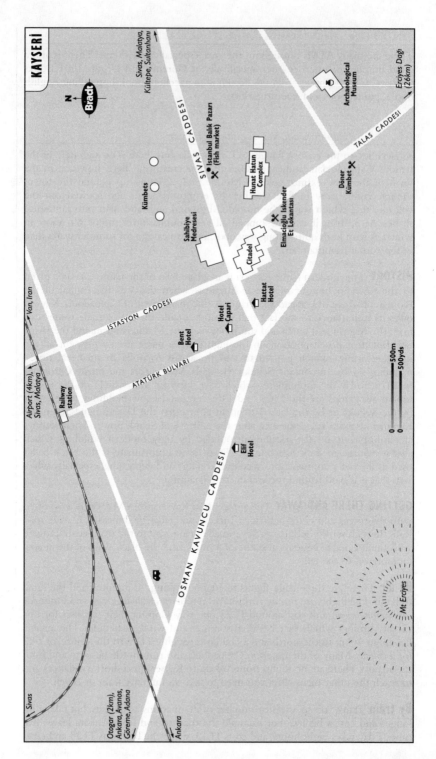

KAYSERİ

Sivas, Malatya,
Kültepe, Sultanhanı

SİVAS CADDESİ

Istanbul Balık Pazarı
(Fish market)

Kümbets

Sahibiye
Medresesi

Hunat Hatun
Complex

Citadel

Elmacıoğlu İskender
Et Lokantası

Döner
Kümbet

TALAS CADDESİ

Archaeological
Museum

Erciyes Dağı
(26km)

Hattat
Hotel

Hotel
Çapari

İSTASYON CADDESİ

Bent
Hotel

Van, Iran

ATATÜRK BULVARI

Airport (4km),
Sivas, Malatya

Railway
station

Elif
Hotel

OSMAN KAVUNCU CADDESİ

Sivas

Otogar (2km),
Ankara, Avanos,
Göreme, Adana

Ankara

Mt Erciyes

0   500m
0   500yds

Bradt

N

146

only five hours. Trains from Kayseri also run to and from Adana (six hours, TL15), Istanbul (18 hours, TL23), Kars (20 hours, TL27), Malatya (nine hours, TL16) and Tatvan (24 hours, TL23). The train station is on Çevre Yol, just 500m from the central square, so is within walking distance of the centre. A taxi costs TL2.

By coach There is a big *otogar* just west of the city centre complete with luggage storage, car rental, café, barber and internet café. Being on a north–south, east–west crossroads, there are buses in all directions. For example there are hourly services to and from Göreme (90 minutes, TL10), and Ankara (hourly, five hours, TL22). Other destinations include Adana (five hours, TL23), Erzurum (10 hours, TL42), Gaziantep (six hours, TL26), Malatya (five hours, TL26), Sivas (three hours, TL18) and Van (13 hours, TL52).

🏠 WHERE TO STAY

🏠 **Bent Hotel** (24 rooms) Atatürk Bulvarı 🔌 2212400; www.benthotel.com. Small but comfortable rooms overlooking the Mimar Sinan Parki. Good mid-range choice. $$
🏠 **Hotel Çapari** (26 rooms) 🔌 2225278; www.hotelcapari.com. In a quiet street off Atatürk Bulvarı. Very good value. Comfortable rooms with satellite TV & big minibars. $$

🏠 **Elif Hotel** (18 rooms) Osman Kavuncu Caddesi; 🔌 3361826; www.elifotelkayseri.com. Rooms at the back are quieter. All have basic bathrooms with minibar & TV. No alcohol is allowed & the management is quite conservative. $

✖ WHAT AND WHERE TO EAT
In the food shops you can try the local speciality *bastırma*, thin-sliced beef dried in the sun and rolled in garlic and herbs, with a slightly aniseed flavour. It is a sort of Turkish version of Parma ham with none of the subtlety but you may well find yourself addicted. It is also found in many other parts of eastern Turkey and is good for picnics as it lasts well.

✖ **Elmacıoğlu Iskender Et Lokantası** Millet Caddesi; 🔌 2226965; ⏰ 09.00–22.30. This is Kayseri's best restaurant on the 1st & 2nd floors with picture windows overlooking the citadel. Smart waiters in bow ties serve the house special, *iskender kepap* (sliced meat with tomato sauce & yogurt), or *bastırma* (highly seasoned cured beef) in *pide* (flat pitta bread). $$
✖ **Istanbul Balık Pazarı** Sivas Caddesi; 🔌 2318973; ⏰ 08.00–23.00. A very reasonably priced fish restaurant complete with nautical decorations. $

WHAT TO SEE
Sahibiye Medresesi Built by the Seljuks in 1268 and located just off the main square, this is now a parade of shops selling plastic knick-knacks and newspapers. Sahip Ata was the famous architect who designed it, and there are plans to convert it into a medical clinic or student residence in line with its original function.

Citadel Built between 1210 and 1226 the citadel has been renovated and turned into a shopping precinct with jewellery shops. From the outside it is well preserved with all its 19 black basalt towers standing, and it is considered one of the finest extant examples of Seljuk military architecture. This is difficult to appreciate today because the walls scarcely rise above the encroaching modern buildings.

Bazaar Behind the citadel the bazaar area of town has also been restored.

Hunat Hatun Complex (⏰ 08.00–17.00 Tue–Sun; adult TL3) Opposite the citadel just off a small open area stands this building which is the first mosque complex to be built by the Seljuks in Anatolia. Now an ethnographic museum of local crafts, it has a fine Turcoman tent decked out with all the nomadic paraphernalia. The complex consists of the mosque itself, a *medrese*, a *türbe*, a *hammam* and a *çeşme* (fountain). Founded in 1238 the name comes from the founder, a Greek woman, Mahperi Hunat Hatun, wife of Alaeddin Keykubad I. The large building with the huge outer façade is the mosque, and the smaller building to the left is the *medrese*.

Kümbets Dotted about the town are a number of Seljuk tombs with a high drum and conical dome, called *kümbet* in Turkish. These were a distinctively Seljuk innovation introduced into Turkey from Persia, and with their conical shape they are thought to hark back to tents. Their style was later copied by the Danishmends and the Karamanids. Mummified bodies were put in the crypt and above this on the main floor was a cenotaph and prayer room reached by an external flight of steps.

The most beautiful of all the *kümbets* is probably the Hudabend Hatun at Niğde (1312) built by the Mongols, which has reliefs of birds, stags and animals with human heads, as well as the usual floral and geometric ornamentation. In the later Ottoman *türbes* the sarcophagus and prayer room were located on the same level and the decoration was on the inside rather than out, and usually restricted to coloured glazed tile facings. Ottoman *türbes* are not found in the east, but are concentrated around Bursa, Iznik and Istanbul. The most famous *kümbet* in Kayseri, the **Döner Kümbet**, is on the way to the museum. Its name, Revolving Kümbet (like the *döner* or revolving kebab) is so called because its 12 sides suggest revolving. It is thought to date from 1276 and is the tomb of a Seljuk princess. The outer walls are decorated with tree of life symbols, a pair of winged leopards, a griffin and a two-headed eagle, the Seljuk symbol of royalty. It stands now, neglected and with grass growing out of its roof, looking faintly lost, as if it has been dumped in someone's back yard. There are more *kümbets* in Kayseri than in any other Turkish town.

Archaeological Museum (*800m southeast of the citadel;* ☉ *08.00–17.00 Tue–Sun; adult TL3*) This small modern museum houses many finds from the site of Kültepe 47km to the north (see page 137), including pottery and cylinder seals and the famous alabaster idols with two or three heads, used in the cult of the earth mother, along with many of the so-called Cappadocian tablets in Assyrian cuneiform.

ÜRGÜP *Telephone code: 384*

Ürgüp is an attractive rural town situated in the heart of the main Cappadocian valleys, unlike Nevşehir 22km to the west which is on the edge. A hilly place, the winding cobbled streets are lined with many grand Greek houses with fine loggias and carved decoration round the doors and windows. Many of the houses are set partly into the cave-riddled cliff faces, and the local people still use these caves where their ancestors lived as garages, storage and stabling. The town's atmosphere is pleasant and calm. One curiosity which has sadly now died out is the travelling library on the back of a donkey, the brainchild of the local librarian, voted Librarian of the Year in 1969.

SHOPPING The main street offers some very good souvenir shops, with a vast selection of silver jewellery with a range of semi-precious stones like amethyst, lapis lazuli, jade, amber, ivory and garnet. There is also elaborate woodwork, boxes and metalwork and good carpets, as well as the locally knitted colourful woollen socks and gloves. The covered bazaar (*kapalı çarşı*) was one of the largest built by the Ottomans and is a good place to wander round and the adjoining 15th century *bedesten* (covered market) specialises in carpets and *kilims*. Normal grocers' shops for stocking up are all over the central part of town.

ORTAHİSAR *Telephone code: 384*

Ortahisar is a small village that sits 2km up a dead-end valley off the main road, 5km west of Ürgüp. Its chief attraction is a huge honeycombed cone fortress, but it also now has its **Culture Folk Museum** (⊕ *09.00–19.00 Tue–Sun; adult TL5*) on the main square where mannequins in local costume act out the chores of daily life from bread making to *kilim* weaving. In the village are the **Harın Church** with huge columns and the **Sarıca Church**, ruined but with a good fresco of the Annunciation. A brief look round Ortahisar need detain you no longer than half an hour or so, but if you want to explore fully and do some walking, you can visit the 13th-century **Halaşdere Church** (meaning 'hospital', because it was used as such in the past), 1.5km away, a vast monastic ensemble on several floors thought to have been carved by Armenian stonemasons; the **Tavşanlı (Rabbit) Church**, 3km away, with fine frescoes and a lot of unusual green painting; the **Balkan churches**, 2km away, a monastic ensemble with a few frescoes; the **Kepez churches**, 3km away; the **Uzum (Grape) Church**; and finally the **Pancarlı (Beet) Church**, still in use in 1923 and with 11th-century frescoes. You will need a guide (ask at the small tourist office on the main square; ⊕ *08.00–17.00*) to find these churches, unless you want to spend the entire day wandering about the valleys in the hope that you will stumble upon them.

UÇHİSAR *Telephone code: 384*

Once a scruffy village, now dominated by rather exclusive cave hotels carved into its tall fortress cone, similar to that at Ortahisar, Uçhisar ('Three Fortresses') lies 6km further on from Ortahisar, up a fork to the left. A path signposted *Kale* (castle) leads through the houses and climbs right to the top of the citadel cone, from where there is an impressive view of the whole Göreme Valley. At night it is illuminated, looking like some colossal hollowed-out gourd for Halloween.

GÖREME *Telephone code: 384*

Göreme is situated 8km west of Ürgüp, 8km south of Avanos, 3km north of Uçhisar, 9km east of Nevşehir and 94km west of Kayseri.

One of the great centres of Christianity from the 6th to the 10th centuries, the Göreme Valley, now an open-air museum, is the most visited place in all Cappadocia, and the undisputed highpoint, thanks to the quality of its churches and their internal frescoes. Allow a good two hours to walk round its nine

The frescoes in Cappadocia were executed largely by local monks, and the majority of the Cappadocian frescoes reflect the relatively primitive provincial style when compared to the contemporary frescoes at Constantinople, where the great artists of the time were at work. The flowering of Byzantine art here was brought to an abrupt end by the Mongol invasions of the 14th century, but though they normally left a trail of destruction behind them, it is not the Mongols who are to blame for the defacement of the Göreme frescoes. Much of the damage was in fact carried out by the Greeks themselves: they apparently believed in the miraculous medicinal powers of a brew made by adding broken fragments of the frescoes to water. The custom was then for the Christian to carve his name and the date beside the chunk he had chiselled out, just to make sure God had registered who he was. The Turkish graffiti on the frescoes are mainly post-1923. The defacement, literally, of Christ, Mary and the saints was carried out by local Muslim villagers for whom the representation of the human form was impious, as it means creating man, which only God is permitted to do. Having scratched off their faces, they were considered dead. With so much lost in previous generations, the authorities realise it is essential that no more damage is done to the frescoes in our time, so it is forbidden to use flash photography or to touch the paintings.

churches, designated a UNESCO World Heritage Site. The surrounding valleys of Zilve, Mustafapaşa, Uçhisar, Ortahisar and Çavuşin contain over 400 churches, and the entire area is a network of valleys close together, all of which collectively are considered to form the core of Cappadocia.

GÖREME OPEN AIR MUSEUM (⏲ 08.00–17.00 daily; adult TL15; parking charge; no flash photography) The museum is 1.5km from Göreme village on the road which climbs towards Ürgüp. Come early or late, preferably on weekdays, to avoid the crowds; there are shops, post, ATMs and cafés by the entrance.

Göreme's churches From the car park it is about a 200m walk to the ticket office, and then a further 100m or so along the cobbled path to reach the first church, **St Basil**. The paintings inside are rather mediocre and represent Basil, George and Theodore on horseback and St Catherine, and the grate-covered holes in the ground were tombs. From here another 100m brings you to the much more interesting Apple Church.

The graffiti of centuries are cut deeply in the **Elmalı Kilise (Apple Church)**, the second painted church on the Göreme circuit. All churches are carefully arrowed and labelled. The original entrance to the Apple Church is through a narrow arcade tunnel suitable for one-way entry and exit only, then opening up into a dome over four pillars. Recently however an easier access has been devised via the adjoining **St Barbara Church**, cut into the back of the same rock. The sanctuary of the Elmalı Church is in the shape of a Greek cross. If you get a chance to look at the frescoes through the crowds, you can make out the four Evangelists on the pendentives. On the vaulted roofs are scenes from the life of Christ starting from the Nativity, the journey to Bethlehem, the Adoration of the Magi, the Raising of Lazarus, the Last Supper, the Betrayal by Judas, the Road to Golgotha and a very fine Crucifixion with angels in the sky above, the placing in the tomb and finally the Resurrection, all dating from the 11th century. The colours are shades of grey, dark green, red and ochre. Christ Pantokrator is

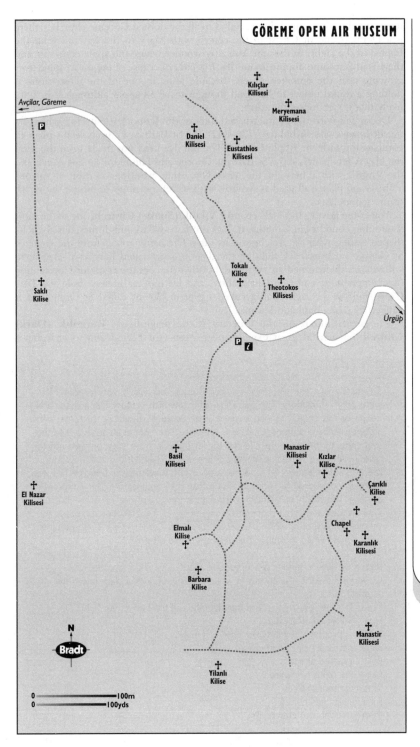

GÖREME OPEN AIR MUSEUM

Avçilar, Göreme

Kılıçlar
Kilisesi

Meryemana
Kilisesi

Daniel
Kilisesi

Eustathios
Kilisesi

Saklı
Kilise

Tokalı
Kilise

Theotokos
Kilisesi

Ürgüp

Basil
Kilisesi

Manastir
Kilisesi

Kızlar
Kilise

Çarıklı
Kilise

El Nazar
Kilisesi

Elmalı
Kilise

Chapel

Karanlık
Kilisesi

Barbara
Kilise

N

Bradt

Manastir
Kilisesi

Yilanlı
Kilise

0 — 100m
0 — 100yds

Cappadocia GÖREME

6

represented in the central dome, and as in all the domed Göreme churches, there is a Deisis (scene of Christ in the centre, with Mary to the left and John the Baptist to the right) in the apse. You may wonder where the apple comes in, and there is in fact some dispute about this. It is either because of the dwarf apple trees growing near the entrance, or else because Jesus, in one of the illustrations, is holding a round object in his hand thought to be an apple, although it is more likely that it symbolises the earth.

Decorated with the geometric red lines of the Iconoclastic period when the use of images was forbidden (726–842), the St Barbara Church seems plain in comparison with the Apple Church. The red dye used was made from the local red clay. A few panels show St Barbara, George and Theodore on horseback and the Virgin, with Christ in the apse. The other paintings consist of various animals and plants, all used as symbols with secret meanings to escape the wrath of the iconoclasts.

You come next to the 11th-century **Yılanlı (Snake) Church**, one of the most interesting churches in Göreme. It does not have pillars and domes, but an arch-shaped ceiling with the frescoes on its sides. The name comes from the scene of St George on horseback fighting the dragon, represented here as a serpent, in whose coils the damned are wrapped. In other frescoes the emperor Constantine (first emperor to embrace Christianity) and his mother Helena hold the True Cross, and on the right wall a naked Egyptian hermit called St Onuphrius is flanked by saints Basil and Thomas.

The next church on the itinerary is the magnificent **Karanlık (Dark) Church**, restored at great expense over a ten-year period and so charging a

CHURCH DATING AND SYMBOLISM

The dating of these churches and monasteries was usually very difficult. Most were pre-11th century with just a few after the 13th century. The architectural design of the church tended to follow the accepted Byzantine patterns, with arches, pillars and a dome. Of course, the pillars were not at all necessary to the soundness of the structure, and sometimes the pillars can even be seen not to quite reach the arch, the pendentive or the dome. Their curious smallness was in line with St Basil's views on small monastic units. The paintings of the churches are generally considered far more significant than their architecture. The iconoclastic paintings are much duller in their geometric designs of red or ochre, but the symbols used are slightly more interesting, mostly of the cross, but also of fish and various animals, all of which had secret meanings. The following is interesting to bear in mind when looking at the churches of the region:

Pigeon or dove = fertility, peace, goodwill, purity, love and innocence
Cockerel = alertness, prophecy (a white one is good luck, a black one is the devil)
Peacock = the resurrection and transfiguration of the body after death
Lion = victory and salvation
Rabbit = prophecy, sexuality, the devil and magic
Deer = eternal being and healing
Bull = a sacred animal
Fish = the pious followers
Vine = symbol of Jesus
Fir = fertility and healing
Palm = heaven and eternal life

separate additional entrance fee (*adult TL8*). The name comes from the fact that the church originally only had one window, making it very gloomy inside, a blessing as it helped preserve the exceptional colours from the damage of sunlight. The church was part of a monastery, very carefully carved into the rock, recreating the architecture of a constructed church rather than a cave-church, complete with engaged columns and capitals. The paintings too are executed with a greater degree of refinement and skill than the other two columned churches in Göreme. Lapis lazuli powder was used to colour the strong deep blue of the background. The care taken in the execution of the paintings, particularly the remarkable scene of Judas's Betrayal, suggests that the church must have had an important patron. The scenes of the life of Christ are the same as those in the Elmalı Church, but in a different order, and arranged in borders in a more regular and symmetrical fashion. Beside the church is a rock-cut refectory, its table and benches cut from the tufa, the place of honour at the head of the table reserved for the head of the community. Some 15 monks are thought to have lived here, and the smoke-blacked kitchen and little larder complete the monastic ensemble.

Just after the Karanlık Church you come to a little chapel, thought to be dedicated to **St Catherine**, represented to the right of the sanctuary, heavily engraved with graffiti by the faithful, determined to gain her favour.

Next comes the **Çarıklı Kilise (Church with the Sandals)** reached by an iron staircase and built above a refectory. The name comes from the shoe-prints visible at the bottom of one of the pictures of Christ – the word *carik* means a kind of moccasin. With a similar range of colours as those used in the Elmalı Kilise, the iconography here is a little less rich and the execution more awkward and naïve. Judas's Betrayal is one of the best scenes.

Near the exit of the open-air museum the last area on your right is the **Kızlar Kilise (Girls' Church)** or convent, with steps leading up to it. It is on three levels with a refectory and kitchen, and some 300 nuns are thought to have lived here. On the other side of the site entrance, opposite the convent, is the monastery, similar in concept.

There are various other interesting churches in the Göreme area, many of them closed for restoration, such as the Meryemana Kilisesi (Virgin Mary Church) and the Kılıçlar Kilisesi (Church of Swords).

Tokalı Kilise The loveliest of all the Göreme churches is not even inside the open-air museum. It lies apart, on the opposite side of the road from the car park, back down the hill about 75m, but is covered by the same ticket. If you can only visit one church in all Cappadocia, you should make it this one. The biggest and most interesting of the Göreme churches, the name Tokalı means 'Buckle', from a buckle which once adorned the ceiling, now vanished. Inside it is magnificent. It is a complex of two churches, built 100 years apart. The first church, Tokalı I, was built at the beginning of the 10th century, and its frescoes, painted in what is known as the 'archaic' style, show some 30 scenes from the life of Christ. Passing on into the second church, Tokalı II, the frescoes are of similar scenes to those in Tokalı I, but the artistic style employed here and the care of execution makes this the most sophisticated of any of the Cappadocian churches. The style is known as 'classical' and dates to the 11th century, when the churches adopted the ground plan of a Greek cross, covered with a dome resting on pendentives and columns. The exquisite deep-blue background made from lapis lazuli powder covers all the surfaces, including the pillars, and the scenes themselves depict miracles including the Marriage at Cana, where water was changed into wine, the Feeding of the Five Thousand and the Raising of Lazarus. Other scenes are the Annunciation, the Journey to Bethlehem, the Nativity, the Flight into Egypt, the Entry into Jerusalem and the Last Supper.

Göreme village In the centre of the village is the so-called Roman Castle, a fairy chimney with a rock-cut Roman tomb, complete with temple façade and column tops. If you want to spend a few days' walking, Göreme is the ideal base, as it lies in the centre of the Göreme National Park and all the valleys link up. You need plenty of time to explore these valleys, each one taking between one and three hours. The following is a list of interesting ones which can be linked together to make longer walks, but make sure you have plenty of time and daylight, as signposts are few and far between:

- Zemi Vadısı (Love Valley) – west of the Göreme Open Air Museum, with some amazing rock formations
- Ballidere Vadısı (Honey Valley) – behind Göreme village
- Güllüdere Vadısı (Rose Valley) – connects Göreme and Çavuşin
- Kılıçlar Vadısı (Swords Valley) – 300m from Tokalı Kilise off the road to Göreme village
- Güvercinlik Vadısı (Pigeon Valley) – connects Göreme and Uçhisar

ÇAVUŞİN   *Telephone code: 384*

(☺ *daily 08.30–17.00; admission charge*) Returning to Göreme village and forking along the valley along the flat towards Avanos, the landscape soon opens out and you reach the Çavuşin Church, slightly set back to the right of the road. After paying your entrance fee you have to climb up the iron steps on the right to reach the church, its front section worn away by erosion, exposing frescoes of the archangels Gabriel and Michael guarding the entrance to the church. Inside, the frescoes are rather different from those at Göreme, in unattractive orange and yellow colours. Some experts believe they are the work of Armenian craftsmen. The left-hand steps lead up into the monastery next door with four carved graves inside. This church was used as a pigeon-cote until quite recently, which helped preserve it from the attentions of irreverent visitors. In the village of Çavuşin itself, some 400m before this church but also on the right, is the church that is generally regarded as one of the oldest in the region, that of St John the Baptist, with parts of it dating from as early as the 8th century. Its façade has recently collapsed and it is now heavily ruined, but the interior still has fine paintings. The whole village is subject to frequent landslips.

ZİLVE

Soon beyond Çavuşin there is a fork off to the right, reaching Zilve after 3km, a pretty series of three valleys dug out with troglodyte dwellings. There is no village here any more, as the local Turks who moved in after the Greeks left in 1923 also had to leave in 1950–55 because of the danger of landslips and the effects of erosion. Just a simple restaurant now stands here at the head of the triple valley, where, when the weather is warm enough, the tables are all spread out among the trees. Even in May it is usually still too cold to sit out.

The Zilve Valley is one of the most enjoyable areas of Cappadocia to walk round and also boasts the most interesting and numerous fairy chimneys. Although much frequented by tours, these generally only take 20 minutes to go to the main part and then return, leaving the best parts of the valley untouched;

it takes at least an hour for even an energetic individual to do the circuit of the three valleys.

Set off first of all into the right-hand valley, the main one, where after a little while the path leads past a charming little rock-cut mosque, the only one of its kind. The most spectacular part, however, is the monastery complex, cut into the right-hand cliff face, a huge bowl cut out from the rock with a gallery running round halfway up, from which a tunnel leads off up steep steps to the very ceiling of the dome. You begin by clambering up the rickety metal steps and then up steep earth steps with hand-holes in the walls to reach the gallery, about 15m above the ground. To clamber on up one of the tunnels you really need a torch as it is pitch black and in the darkness it is impossible to find the hand-holes to pull yourself up. On the opposite side of the valley a flight of metal steps leads up to a rock-cut complex from which a tunnel links up with the second valley. With a torch, this is fun to do, and there are steps to get you down the far side.

Scattered around in the second and third valleys are more churches and even a rock-cut mill with a grinding stone. The whole area is overrun with myriad little footpaths dashing up and down the hillsides which you can skip along, mountain-goat style. About 1km from the valley entrance on the road back to rejoin the main Avanos road you will often find local youths selling a good selection of colourful wares including woollen socks and gloves.

SARIHAN *7km from Zilve*

On the outskirts of Avanos, just before crossing the river, a yellow sign points off 5km to Sarıhan, the **Yellow Caravanserai** (⊕ *08.00–midnight; adult TL3*). The road leads straight to it. The *han* itself is remarkable for the soft colour of the stone which coated its exterior, and for its very small proportions: it cannot have held many travellers. Its state of preservation used to be rather poor, as local people had run off with the large exterior facing stones, but it has now been restored. The setting is pleasant, in a slight dip and with no village nearby, a most unusual phenomenon. It also stages a Whirling Dervish performance (see box, page 175) at 21.30 April–October and 21.00 November–March (✆ *5113795; adult TL25*) which needs to be booked in advance but most hotels will do it for you.

AVANOS *Telephone code: 384*

Avanos is a pretty town on the banks of the Red River, the Kızılırmak, the longest river in Anatolia. The distinctive deep-red soil which colours the water is much in evidence all around and on a rainy day you and your mode of transport are soon covered in it. The famous pottery is made from this local clay, exported from earliest times to Greece and Rome.

ÖZKONAK *15km north of Avanos*

(⊕ *daily Jun–Sep 08.30–19.00; Oct–May 08.30–17.30; adult TL8; dolmuş taxis run here from Avanos, taking 30 minutes, cost TL2*) From Avanos you can drive the main road 11km north towards Kayseri and fork off left 9km on a small road to Özkonak, the most recently opened and largest of the Cappadocian underground cities, once housing 60,000 people. Lying off the beaten track, it is less crowded than the better-known Derinkuyu and Kaymaklı, though not as impressive. Returning from Avanos back towards Ürgüp, you will pass along a crest from which you can look down into the much-vaunted Peribacalar Valley (Valley of the Fairies) with its forest of red earth cones.

(☉ *daily 08.00–20.30; adult TL2*)

GETTING THERE To escape the crowds of downtown Cappadocia a pleasant excursion is to the Soğanlı Valley. In a half day it can also be combined with a round trip to Derinkuyu and Kaymaklı, the other two underground cities, besides Özkonak, that are open to the public. From Ürgüp you follow the road south marked with a yellow sign to Mustafapaşa. The drive for this stretch is more picturesque than usual, through forested valleys and colourful villages, and passing by the lovely blue-green reservoir of Damsa. Mustafapaşa is an attractive village with houses richly decorated round the doors and windows. It was Greek until the 1920s, since when the Turks have whitewashed over the paintings in its churches. One two-storey monastery however still preserves its frescoes and now serves as a hotel.

At Güzelöz you follow the turn-off left to Yeşilhisar and continue a further 9km until you see the yellow sign pointing off right 5km for Soğanlı.

WHAT TO SEE

Valley churches The overall setting of Soğanlı is far more attractive both as a village and as a valley than the more famous Göreme. It is closer to the original setting and is still unspoilt by the mushrooming hotels and billboards that mar the landscapes of the Cappadocian heartlands. The frescoes are generally less impressive and more fragmentary, so that in the **Geyikli Kilise (Church with the Deer)** for example, the deer are difficult, not to say impossible, to spot. There are some 60 churches in all in the Soğanlı Valley, but many are filled up with earth or have been turned into pigeon-cotes by the villagers.

An attractive road winds through the valley passing signs to the **Tokalı Kilise (Church with Buckle)** and the **Gök Kilise (Church with Sky)**, up paths to the right of the road. Some 3km further on you arrive at the pretty village of Soğanlı itself, set into a huge tabletop mountain, with the road forking to either side of it. A map at the fork on a large metal sign marks all the churches. In the cones above the village the white squares mark the pigeon-cotes, painted to attract the birds' attention. The villagers keep them to produce droppings which are used as fertiliser for their fields.

Take the left fork first, past prettily laid-out restaurants with tables on outside terraces, to the end of the road. A sign points off to the Church with the Deer, which you can scramble up to on the left, and various other churches lie on the right-hand side of the road. A guardian will probably offer to take you on a guided tour, but you can find them yourself if you prefer. The most interesting ones are along the right-hand side of the valley, and particularly noteworthy are Yilanli Kilise (Church with a Snake), Saklı Kilise (Hidden Church), Meryemana Kilise (Church of the Virgin Mary), Karanlık Kilise (Dark Church) and the extraordinary three-storeyed Kubbeli Kilise (Domed Church or Church with a Beret) in its own curious rock formation just to the right of the road.

(☉ *daily Nov–Apr 08.00–17.00; May–Oct 08.30–18.30; adult TL15*) One of Turkey's most memorable events is a visit to Derinkuyu, the biggest and deepest of Cappadocia's underground cities. Prepare yourself for a remarkable experience.

GETTING THERE A bus runs every half-hour between Nevşehir and Niğde, stopping at Derinkuyu and costing TL3. Returning to Güzelöz and turning left, the road brings you after 21km to the dirty little village of Derinkuyu. A yellow sign announces the underground city and there is a huge car park beside it. Needless to say, the city itself is nowhere to be seen.

SITE VISIT The name Derinkuyu means 'Deep Well', and this is the deepest of the four underground cities currently open to the public (the others being Kaymaklı, Özkonak and Özlüce). If you only want to visit one, the one you choose will depend on your priorities: if you are inclined towards claustrophobia, then Kaymaklı (see page 159) is the one to go for, as it only has four underground levels as opposed to Derinkuyu's eight, and yet it is in some ways more interestingly arranged; if you are short of money, Özlüce, 7km northwest of Kaymaklı, has no admission charge, being more modest and less developed; Özkonak (see page 155) is the least visited and the least crowded. But Derinkuyu is the ultimate underground experience, so if you can cope with the depths and like caving, go for it.

The entrance could hardly be less prepossessing, a little hut like a public convenience from which steps lead down, with no clue from the outside as to its extent underground. There is no compulsory guided tour; you can hire a guide, but the way is marked by arrows and signs, and after buying your ticket you can simply descend into the city, which is fully illuminated by electric lights.

The underground city at Derinkuyu came to light by accident only in 1963. There is controversy over who were its original builders, but it is thought likely by Turkish experts that the first level was built by the Hittites and used as a store

THE UNDERGROUND CITIES – CLAUSTROPHOBES BEWARE

Throughout history the local people used the underground cities as retreats to escape the invading hordes of armies which poured across the Anatolian Plain. They were certainly inhabited in the 7th century BC, and Xenophon, the ancient Greek historian, mentions them in his work *Anabasis*. Around 40 have now been identified in the area of Cappadocia. They were used as a place of retreat as recently as 1839 to hide from the invading Egyptian army under Ibrahim Paşa. Today unfortunately they are no longer a retreat from the armies of tourists pouring over Cappadocia, who now pour right underground by the coachload. Tours wreak havoc in these cities: Derinkuyu has eight visitable storeys (Turkish *kat*) and there is only one single-file stairway to the bottom. If you encounter a tour on Kat 2 you have no hope of reaching Kat 8 for hours, and if two tours encounter each other on the narrow stairs then you have a total blockage. A one-way system has had to be enforced. The full number of storeys at Derinkuyu is still not known, but it is thought to be as many as 18 or 20, only the top eight of which are open. At least 20,000 people are thought to have lived down here, sometimes for six months at a stretch, enough to make a sensitive mortal shudder.

The cities are an elaborate network of tunnels, stairways and chambers hollowed out of the rock, never so low that you cannot stand up, but rarely spacious. The inhabitants must have had an excellent sense of direction to find their way around inside the maze of tunnels. In the lower levels several of the tunnels could be sealed off from the inside by large circular cartwheel-shaped stones, sometimes with holes in the centre for attacking the enemy or as spyholes. Some of the tunnels even link up with other underground cities in the area, to serve as escape routes, and one of them is known to link up Derinkuyu with Kaymaklı, 9km away. This astonishing tunnel, provided with ventilation ducts, is broad enough for three or four people to walk abreast.

area: Hittite seals have been found by local inhabitants digging new foundations for their houses, and certainly the Hittites built a surface city at Göllü Daği, 20km southwest of Derinkuyu.

It is thought the first step would have been to dig the air chimneys, 70–80m deep, until water was reached and then to cut sideways until reaching the next air chimney. The volcanic tufa was very soft to cut out, only hardening on contact with the air, which is why its surface feels hard to the touch. It is still used today for building, cut into regular-shaped blocks. One theory is that rubble from the digging was emptied into streams and carried away by the current. Both above and below ground, the tufa chambers make very agreeable living areas, with good circulation, constant temperatures, year-round humidity and above all, no insects.

Scholars have concluded that at Derinkuyu the first two storeys contained kitchens (clearly communal, as relatively few exist), storage chambers, bedrooms, dining halls, wine cellars, stables and toilets, whereas the lower levels were hiding places with wells, churches, armouries, dungeons, graves and a meeting hall. Illumination was by oil lamps. It would help today's visitor to have a few of the rooms furnished with carpets, furs and pottery, to encourage the imagination to visualise what it was like to live here. There are no carved benches or bed platforms and therefore very little to help you identify the rooms.

On the first level there is a large open area which was used as a missionary school with two long tables cut out of the earth and a baptism basin at the end. On the lowest level, a church is carved out in the form of a cross and opposite it is a hall with three central columns hewn out of the rock, thought to be a meeting hall. Under the modern village are many further underground chambers, some of which open up into the houses still inhabited and used by the occupants as storage space, like an elaborate basement. The villagers of Derinkuyu still depend on the wells on the bottom level for their water but have now installed motor pumps to replace the old hand-turned wheels they were still using in the 1960s.

THE CAPPADOCIAN WINE TRADITION

The famous Cappadocian wine was also made underground, and you can still see the wine presses. The grapes were dropped from the surface down the appropriate ventilation shaft into the wine-press area. The volcanic soil lends itself well to viticulture, and wine fermented well in the dark cellar-like caves. Cappadocia's climate in terms of sunshine hours and humidity has been established to be the same as Bordeaux. Wine production gave the Cappadocians their main source of income in times of recession. Gregory of Nyssa boasted in a letter written in the 4th century to his friend Adelphios about the quality of the region's wine. Some may find it surprising that this winemaking tradition continues now in a predominantly Muslim country, but the Turks of Cappadocia (and of Izmir) have perpetuated the traditions of those who inhabited these regions before them and have learnt their winemaking secrets. A Wine Festival is still held every year at Ürgüp each June, which wine producers from the whole world attend, and the jury awards medals to the best wines. Local wine producers are Turasan, Kavalidere and Kocabag, the last being undoubtedly the best Turkish wine producer, regularly awarded Gold Medals for its excellent dry whites. The reds can be a little bitter. They do not keep, so drink them young.

The websites www.travelatelier.com and www.vinotolia.com offer excellent wine-tasting tours of the area, combined with walking in the valleys and exploring churches, especially those with grape frescoes.

(☉ *daily 2 Oct–16 Apr 08.00–17.00; 17 Apr–1 Oct 08.30–19.00; adult TL15*) This is the most visited of the underground cities mainly for reasons of convenience, as it fits most easily into an itinerary. Discovered in 1964, the village of Kaymaklı above ground is as unprepossessing as Derinkuyu, but the entrance to the underground city is far prettier with steps leading up to a honeycombed mound.

Souvenir stalls have sprung up all around. On top of the hillock long narrow graves have been carved out of the rock. Underneath it is far less extensive than Derinkuyu, with only four storeys open, but it is still interesting to explore the bedrooms, warehouses, wine cellars, ventilation chimneys, water depots and a church with double apse and stone doors which could be rolled open or shut from the inside.

NEVŞEHİR *Telephone code: 384*

This is the main town of Cappadocia and therefore the commonest transport hub, but as a town it is an unexciting place with little to detain you. It was settled by the Hittites between 2000BC and 1200BC, and after the Hittite collapse at that time it came under the protection of the Assyrians and the Phrygians. Nevşehir means 'new town', and it has a range of modern functional hotels. Unless it is unavoidable, you are better advised to stay in Ürgüp, Göreme or Uçhisar, or even in Avanos, all of which give you a much better flavour of the special Cappadocian atmosphere, and are in any event closer to the main valleys and sights.

North of Nevşehir on the road to Gülşehir, a sign marks the so-called Açıksaray (Open-air Palace), where there is an interesting church with an elaborate façade cut out of the rock. There are no frescoes inside, but the walls, ceilings and niches are carved with cross motifs.

HACIBEKTAŞ

This is the monastery of the 14th-century dervish called Hacı Bektaş, who founded the Bektaşi order which was closely connected to the Janissaries. The prefix 'Hacı' means 'pilgrim', from the Arabic *hajj* for the pilgrimage to Mecca, and denotes that he would have made this, a duty prescribed to all Muslims at least once in their lifetime. The order survived the extermination of the Janissaries in 1826 and was dissolved only in 1926 along with the Mevlevis of Konya (see page 172) and all the other dervish orders. The Bektaşis were much concerned with the villages and rural poor. They had a reputation for free-thinking and loose ways and also retained the old Turkish tradition of allowing women to participate unveiled in their ceremonies. See also *The Alevis* on page 117.

GETTING THERE If you have several days in the Göreme region, another half-day excursion can be made to the north, to the Hacıbektaş Monastery. From Ürgüp you follow the road to Avanos and then a pleasant narrowish tarmac road leads north along the riverbanks for 20km or so with attractive rural views until it joins up with the main road from Nevşehir at Gülşehir. From here a yellow sign points to the right to Hacıbektaş, 25km.

SITE VISIT The monastery is prettily set among gardens and was opened as a museum in 1964. It is visited more by Turks as a holy shrine and by schoolchildren on educational outings than by coach tours. In the main courtyard there is the soothing sound of constantly running water, and around it are living rooms and a kitchen. Beyond the courtyard you come to the mosque and the two *türbe* shrines. The smaller one, with rags tied in the trees outside representing the supplications of pious visitors, is that of Sultan Belim, the secondary founder, while the large contains Hacı Bektaş himself. The domed ceilings are lavishly painted and in the larger *türbe* there are also displays of clothing, purses, belts and earrings worn by the dervishes. Shoes are taken off during the visit and the most interesting thing is watching the Turks and the children peering reverently at the displays with awed whispers and kissing every tomb in sight. The stairs in the main courtyard lead up to a library which is still used as a children's classroom.

IHLARA GORGE *45km southeast of Aksaray*

(🕐 *daily Apr–Oct 08.00–19.00; Nov–Mar 08.30–17.00; adult TL5; parking fee TL2*)
If you are tired of crowds and find yourself unable to enjoy the main Cappadocian sights for the sheer number of visitors, then one trip you should make as an independent traveller is to the splendid Ihlara Gorge, formerly called the Peristrema Valley by the Greeks. There are four entrances to the gorge: the main one down the 360 steps from the resthouse, Ihlara Vadısı Turistik Tesisleri; a path behind the derelict **Star Otel** in Ihlara village; at Belisırma and at Selime at the head of the gorge.

The trip can take a full afternoon, or an entire day if you want to do some extra walking. It takes about two and a half hours to walk from the resthouse to Belisırma, and a further three hours to walk from Belisırma to Selime. To walk all the way from the Ihlara resthouse to Selime at the head of the gorge, stopping for lunch at Belisırma where several restaurants have opened along the riverbank, will take seven or eight hours.

GETTING THERE AND AWAY

By road The drive is scenic and takes one-and-a-half hours from Nevşehir. About 14km before Aksaray and 4km before reaching the turn-off to Ihlara and Güzelyurt, the road passes through Ağzıkarahan village, named after the caravanserai immediately to the left of the road. It is built on huge proportions, its main gate facing west and the whole building is in a lovely soft reddish-coloured stone. The façade is elaborately worked. Inside the open courtyard is a mosque, its colossal interior section like a cathedral with high vaulted ceilings. The fork off to Ihlara and Güzelyurt, 10km before Aksaray, follows a narrow tarmac road for the first 19km across flattish landscapes dominated by the snow-covered Hasan Dağı Volcano, 3,268m high. For the final 12km the road becomes more winding, passing through several half-troglodyte villages partly built into the rock face and partly in primitive houses with flat-topped roofs. The last of these is Selime, at the entrance to the gorge, recognisable by the fine conical *türbe* which you pass here on the bank of the Melendiz River. From here the road crosses the river and continues on the main road for the final 6km to Ihlara. On arrival at the edge of the village itself, turn left at the junction, following a tarmac road for another 1km, and you will suddenly come upon a fine modern resthouse with superb terraces laid out with wooden tables and benches overlooking the canyon below. This marks the starting point for the descent into the gorge, and in summer (from mid-May to mid-November), there is simple accommodation here for keen walkers.

By public transport Ten buses a day travel from Aksaray, or else you will have to take a taxi.

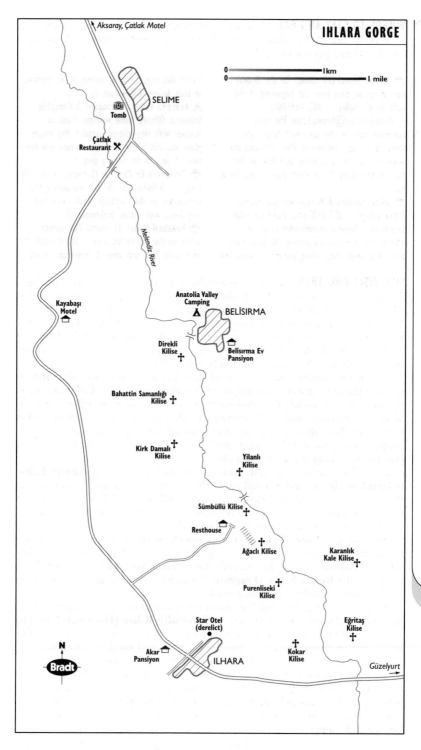

Aksaray, Çatlak Motel

0 ———————————— 1km
0 ———————————— 1 mile

SELIME

Tomb

Çatlak
Restaurant ✗

Melendiz River

Kayabaşı
Motel

Anatolia Valley
Camping
▲   BELİSIRMA

Direkli
Kilise ✝   Belisırma Ev
                 Pansiyon

Bahattin Samanlığı
Kilise ✝

Kirk Damalı ✝
Kilise

Yilanlı
Kilise
✝

Sümbüllü Kilise ✝

Resthouse

Ağaclı Kilise ✝   Karanlık
                        Kale Kilise ✝

Purenliseki ✝
Kilise

Star Otel   Eğritaş
(derelict)   Kilise
                                        ✝

N

Akar
Pansiyon   ILHARA   Kokar
                              Kilise ✝   Güzelyurt →

Bradt

WHERE TO STAY AND EAT There are simple pensions at Ihlara village and Selime, ie: at both ends of the valley, and at Belisırma there are camping facilities and a couple of basic pensions too.

Çatlak Motel (20 rooms) On the Aksaray side of Selime, 3km from the beginning of the walk up the valley; ☎ 382 4545006; e catlakpansion@hotmail.com. The most upmarket place in the area, with large light rooms & en-suite bathrooms. They also own the restaurant of the same name at Selime at the start of the valley, & can drive guests there for a fee. $$

Akar Pansion & Restaurant (18 rooms) Ihlara village; ☎ 382 4537018; closed Dec–Mar. Simple but adequate accommodation in the village, with a restaurant serving the local river trout, & a small shop selling picnic provisions. The owner also runs a shuttle service in his minibus to both Selime & Belisırma. $

Å **Anatolia Valley Restaurant & Camping** Belisırma. Offering some welcome shade in summer with vine-covered pergolas, this simple place also has a few 'treehouses' where you can sleep if you do not have a tent. $

Belisırma Ev Pansion (5 rooms) In the old village of Belisırma on the hill overlooking the restaurants on the riverbank. Good views, but very basic with shared bathrooms. $

Kayabaşi Motel (15 rooms) 2km outside Selime on the way to Belisırma; ☎ 382 4545565. A newly built place with clean & comfortable rooms. $

SITE VISIT AND TREK Suitably refreshed from the resthouse you can now begin the descent into the Ihlara Gorge down the specially built wide concrete steps. The 150m-deep canyon was formed thousands of years ago by erosion from the Melendiz River, flowing north into the Tuz Gölü (the Great Salt Lake). The river is the product of melting snow from the Hasan Daği Volcano and the Melendiz Mountains. While the steep descent down the concrete steps takes only a little over five minutes, the ascent is obviously at least double that.

The major churches are indicated by signs, but it is fun to go a little further afield to the more distant churches, as walking along the canyon bed is extremely pleasant with the sound of the rushing river and the wind in the tall poplar trees. Wildlife is abundant, with birds, frogs and lizards, and there are far more butterflies to be seen here than almost anywhere east of Ankara, including blues, large coppers and painted ladies. After the bleak and featureless wastelands of the plateau this is indeed a sight to behold.

Just before the bottom you come to the first church, the **Ağaçli Kilise (Church under a Tree)**. Carved out of the cliff, it is cross-shaped and older than the other churches, but its frescoes have been well preserved. On the wall facing the door is a fresco of Daniel between two lions and on the ceiling is a dragon.

Turning right at the bottom and following the path along you come after a few minutes to the **Purenliseki Kilise (Church with a Terrace)** which has fragmentary frescoes. Continuing along the path round the jutting-out cliff, where a colossal landslip has recently taken place, you come, just round the corner, to the **Kokar Kilise (Fragrant Church)** with some attractive paintings on the outside windows, but none inside.

Retracing your path to the bottom of the concrete steps, you continue along the valley and soon come to the lovely **Sümbüllü Kilise (Hyacinth Church)** which lies directly below the restaurant terrace 150m above. It has attractive arches and an elaborate façade carved in the rock, making it the loveliest of the churches from the outside. It has two storeys, and its fragmentary frescoes date to the 14th century. Just a few metres after the Sümbüllü Church you come to a pretty wooden bridge over the river, the only place where you can cross before Belisırma. Though the river is not particularly deep, often less than 1m, wading across is not recommended as the current is very fast and the bed is uneven and slippery.

Crossing the bridge and turning to the left you soon come to a path leading up to the right to the base of the cliff, where **Yılanlı Kilise (Church with a Snake)** is tucked. Shaped like a long cross, the church has frescoes showing the Archangel Michael judging people according to their sins and good deeds. The sinners are in the coils of the snakes, coming to a grisly end. In the dome is the Christ Pantokrator (Christ Ruler of All, in eastern iconography always carrying the New Testament in his left hand and raising his right hand in blessing) and the angels.

From here it is a two-hour walk on a narrow, brambly path to the end of the gorge, and the signposts to the churches are less frequent. If you want to walk on to Belisırma, the village at the end of the gorge towards Selime, the best thing to do is to cross to the other bank, as all the remaining churches are on that side. These are the **Kırk Damalı Kilise (Church with 40 Roofs)** which has a fresco of St George between a Greek and his Armenian wife. Next there is the **Bahattin Samanliği Kilise (Church with a Granary)** which is very small, and finally the **Direkli Kilise (Columned Church)**, a monastic church with three aisles and good paintings. You then reach a bridge at Belisırma and can walk back on the other riverbank for variation.

Returning to the wooden bridge by the Sümbüllü Church but continuing on the same bank and walking further upstream, you can do a very pleasant walk which rewards you ultimately with the discovery of two further rock churches, both unmarked and not that easy to find. The first, the **Karanlık Kale Kilise (Dark Castle Church)** is identifiable by its two decorated arched entrances, set high up from the river level but still at the base of the cliff, directly next to a high waterfall which gushes over the top of the cliff. The traces of painting inside are fragmentary. Climbing back down to the river level you now walk on across an open field-like part of the river bank to reach the **Eğritaş Kilise (Church with a Crooked Stone)**, consisting of large interlinked chambers, again set above the river, but where the cliff juts out into the gorge. The frescoes here are extensive, but because of erosion they are very exposed to the wind and sun now and so are gradually deteriorating.

FRESCO ART: SIMPLE OR COMPLEX?

Scholars have detected a great diversity in the frescoes throughout the canyon, reflecting the variety of origins in the monastic way of life here. Some show oriental influence from Syria and Egypt, with styles, symbols and legends never encountered in Byzantine art. The façades with round vaults lined side by side, like the Sümbüllü (see page 162) are Syrian in style.

In the full 16km of the gorge there are over 100 rock-cut churches and many monasteries, as the valley was a favoured retreat for Byzantine monks. St Gregory (330–90) was born in nearby Güzelyurt (see page 164), an attractive troglodyte village, and went on to become a theologian and is considered one of the Fathers of the Greek Church. He wrote a memorable passage about the difference between life in Constantinople, where everything is full of complexity and contradiction, and life in rural Cappadocia where matters are simple and straightforward:

> When I ask how many coppers I must pay, they reply with minute distinctions on the born and the unborn. If I ask the price of bread, I am told the Father is greater than the Son. I call to ask the servant if my bath is ready, and he replies that the Son was created from nothing.

Less visited than most parts of Cappadocia, Güzelyurt ('Beautiful Place' in Turkish) can be an interesting add-on to a half day spent at Ihlara, and is in some ways like a mini Ihlara, with its own valley to walk through, and even its own underground city, signposted as 'Antique City' (⊕ 08.00–18.30; adult TL5). The Ihlara ticket is meant to cover entry. Much smaller than Derinkuyu or Kaymaklı, it still gives you a feel for the realities of living underground, and at one stage you have to plunge through a hole in the ground to reach the next level down. The next thing to visit is the **Byzantine Church of St Gregory**, built in AD385, restored in 1835, and then converted into a mosque when the Greeks left in the exchange of populations in the 1920s (see page 18). Known today as Büyük Kilise

FROM CARAVANSERAIS TO HOTELS

In the 13th century the Seljuks built a chain of *hans* (Arabic *khans*, caravanserais) across Anatolia at roughly a day's journey apart along the Uzun Yol ('Long Road'), ie: Silk Road, linking Konya to Persia via Kayseri and Sivas, to provide merchants and their camel caravans with the facilities they needed on their journey. The sultan paid for the construction and maintenance of the *hans* out of taxes levied on the goods being traded, so that merchants using them were not charged directly for staying there. In the cities, on the other hand, there was a charge for the use of *hans* and also for entering and leaving the cities. Had there been 'room rates' for these rural *hans*, some might have been tempted to camp rough to save money, thereby exposing themselves to theft and attack in the night. It was in the sultan's interest therefore to subsidise these lodgings, to ensure the safe continuity of trade. This particular one was built between 1232 and 1236 by the great Seljuk sultan Alaeddin Keykubad I, and along with the other Sultanhanı, 45km northeast of Kayseri on the Sivas road, is the largest and most luxurious in Turkey. In the *hans* the travelling merchant would attend to the safety of his goods and wares, to the repair of his carts and the needs of his animals, do his buying and selling, perform his ablutions and devotions, and then pursue his journey a day or so later. In time of war the buildings also served as storage for food and munitions.

These were the requirements which the building had to meet, and its ground plan and architecture reflected those requirements. A strong gateway was built, the only external architectural feature, in which all the decorative effort was concentrated. The elaborate portal here at Sultanhanı is a fine example, its richly sculptured gateway contrasting sharply with the solid plainness of the powerful exterior walls. This use of contrast, especially effective when seen from a distance, is one of the most striking features of Seljuk architecture and is used frequently to great effect. Around the open courtyard are arched and vaulted storerooms for baggage, hay and oats, separate private rooms with hearths, dormitories for the servants, washrooms, gateway rooms for the innkeeper and janitor, a coffee room, repair shops for the carts, a blacksmith and stable for the animals. A stairway leads up from one side of the courtyard to the flat roof for the evening assembly, where the evening breezes were welcome in summer. Within, the huge cathedral-like covered hall served as winter quarters, and in the middle is a dome with an opening for light and ventilation. The hubbub in here during the long cold winters must have been quite something.

Subsequently, Ottoman *hans* were usually built in cities and acquired a more commercial character, serving as markets as well as lodgings, until they lost their lodging function altogether, this being fulfilled by hotels.

Camii (Big Church Mosque), the whitewash on the walls is being removed to reveal the original frescoes. A little further into the valley look out for the **Sivisli Kilise (Anargyros Church)** with square pillars and a dome with fine frescoes, then the **Koç (Ram) Church** and the **Cafarlar (Rivulets) Church**. Monastery Valley, as it is known, continues for 4.5km with fine scenery and panoramas and yet more rock-cut churches, some with interesting architectural features. The Güzelyurt area is also famous for its pottery made from fire-resistant soil, different in form from Avanos pottery. Beyond Güzelyurt, 4km on the road towards Niğde, you pass through the picturesque troglodyte village of **Sivrihisar** at the foot of a rocky outcrop with the ruins of a Byzantine fortress on top. Beyond Sivrihisar to the left of the road after 2km is the charming little **Kızıl Kilise (Red Church)**, dating to the 5th century and almost intact.

SULTANHANI

Having come this far, those with an interest in caravanserais could make the 40-minute detour east of Aksaray on the Konya road to visit the famous **Sultanhanı**, the largest and best-preserved caravanserai in Turkey. It is a tedious journey 39km beyond Aksaray through a bleak and featureless landscape and must have been deadly dull for travellers who moved as walking pace through it, and a real relief to arrive eventually at the *han*.

The small town of Sultanhanı has now grown up around the *han*, which stands in a clearing among the houses, about 500m off the main road. The guardian will sell you a ticket (⊕ *07.00–19.00; adult TL5*) and local sellers will try to interest you in their wares.

From Sultanhanı a further 100km across the Anatolian steppe brings you to Konya, Turkey's most religious city.

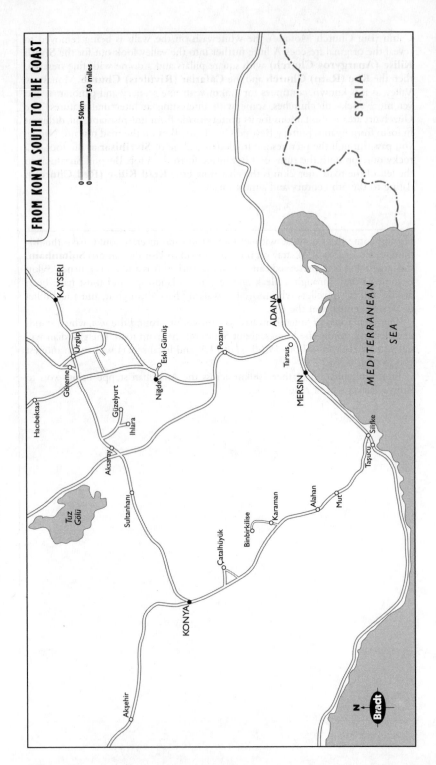

FROM KONYA SOUTH TO THE COAST

0   50km
0   50 miles

KAYSERI

Ürgüp
Göreme
Eski Gümüş
Hacıbektaş
Güzelyurt
Niğde
Ihlara
Pozantı
Tarsus
Aksaray
ADANA
MERSIN
Sultanhanı
Tuz
Gölü
Silifke
Binbirkilise
Karaman
Taşucu
Çatalhüyük
Alahan
Mut
KONYA
Akşehir

SYRIA

MEDITERRANEAN SEA

N

Bradt

7

Konya and South to the Coast

The greatest luxury is simplicity.

For those who know something of Islamic history, the name 'Konya' conjures up a certain magic and mystery, for this was the home of Sufism, Islamic mysticism, with its famous Whirling Dervishes. Their centre was the Mevlâna Tekke in the heart of Konya, and with its unforgettable blue-green dome, it remains the highlight of any visit. The city also still boasts a number of exceptionally beautiful Seljuk buildings, more or less well preserved, all dating from the 12th and 13th centuries when Konya was chosen as capital for the most powerful Turkish state of the Middle Ages in Anatolia, the Seljuk sultanate of Rum.

A full day should be allowed to visit the Seljuk monuments, starting with the famous Mevlâna Tekke, now a museum, followed by a walk round the mosques and madrasas clustered on the hill which was the original citadel. If you are very pushed for time, it could be compressed into half a day at a pinch. Avoid Mondays, as some of the monuments close on that day. After your stay in Konya, you can head south to the coast by either of the routes described later in this chapter, making a dramatic descent from the Anatolian Plateau, and arriving in the more familiar Mediterranean world where beach hotels await.

KONYA, THE SELJUK HAVEN

The 12th and 13th centuries were a period of great political upheaval, when the Arab 'Abbasid caliphate in Baghdad was crumbling and the Mongol armies were ravaging the eastern Islamic world. The population lived in fear, and Konya was one of the few places that was considered safe from the Mongol onslaught. Scholars, theologians, artists and intellectuals from all over the region fled their native lands to seek refuge and shelter at the Seljuk court. Among them was a Sufi master called **Bahaeddin Veled**, originally from Balkh (now in Afghanistan). He and his family, including his son Celaleddin, also born in Balkh in 1207, had been wandering through Iran fleeing the advancing Mongol hordes of Genghis Khan. After long migrations the family finally reached Anatolia via Damascus, and Bahaeddin joined the court at Konya, where he taught for a few years before his death, to be succeeded by his son, Celaleddin, later known as **Rumi**, 'the one from Rum', a reference to the Seljuk sultanate of Rum, whose capital was at Konya. Persian was the language of court, used in literature and poetry, and Rumi wrote in this, his mother tongue. The population of Konya spoke partly Greek, as there had been a strong Christian community here before, and partly Turkish, and Rumi occasionally used both these languages in his verses, as well as his native Persian. His work was never as popular with Arabic-speaking Sufis however, as it translated less well into Arabic and they found the imagery too alien.

Apart from the cluster of Seljuk buildings in the centre, the modern city of Konya today is rather unprepossessing. It is essentially a city of the steppe, a small oasis of relative greenery surrounded on all sides by vast, bleak horizons. Like all cities of the plateau at altitudes over 1,000m, its climate is one of extremes: very hot and dusty in the summer months, bitterly cold and snowy in winter. As Turkey's most religious city, dress is noticeably conservative, so you should make an effort to cover up bare arms and legs here, especially if you have arrived from the coast and are therefore more used to the Mediterranean ways. In Ramazan too, Konya is one of the few places where restaurants and cafés close during the day, which can make life difficult when you have been walking in the heat and are desperate for a cold beer. Konya is also the centre of Turkey's carpet trade, something you will not be allowed to overlook by the local traders.

HISTORY According to Phrygian tradition Konya was the first city to emerge after the Flood: excavations have uncovered prehistoric, Hittite and later Roman settlements here. None of these remain today, but the excavated evidence can be seen in the local archaeological museum. Konya owes its importance throughout history to its location on the junction of major trade and communication routes. The Romans built ancient roads which were followed by the Seljuks and then by the Ottomans, and today's main roads follow the same course, as can be seen from the number of Seljuk caravanserais still standing at the roadsides. The name 'Konya' comes from the Greek *eikon* (image), which in Latin became Iconium, a reference to the image on the town's main gateway of Perseus brandishing the head of the Gorgon (Medusa). According to Greek mythology Konya was the place where he struck off her snaky-haired head and fastened it to a column, before founding the city. Iconium was subsequently embellished by the Roman emperors Claudius and Hadrian, Saints Paul and Barnabas stayed here in AD47, AD50 and AD53 in the course of their apostolic journeys in Asia Minor. In AD395 it became a Byzantine city and the seat of a bishop, and in the 7th, 8th and 9th centuries it was exposed along with the other cities of southeastern Turkey to successive raids from the growing Muslim armies of Syria. Sacked by the Seljuk Turks in 1069, Konya became their capital in 1097, and remained an extremely prosperous city until the mid 13th century. Its principal monuments date from that period, especially from the reign of Sultan Alaeddin Keykubad I (1219–36).

KONYA CARPETS

Konya carpets, known as *Ladikgülü,* from the name of a nearby village called Ladik, are still made in the traditional way today, although at the end of the 19th century their makers succumbed to the use of chemical dyes. The styles and motifs used are, however, largely unchanged, and are still inspired by the nomadic world and classical Ottoman style. The carpet typically has a central triple arch, and sometimes a *mihrab* or prayer niche. The borders have stylised motifs of flowers such as tulips and carnations, hence the suffix *gül*, meaning 'rose'. The carpet is usually quite small, always with a red weft forming the background, and the other typical colours used are terracotta, coffee brown, soft yellow, blue, dark blue, green and white. Konya rugs are prized for their luxurious wool, among the richest in the world, which comes from the rural areas around the city.

GETTING THERE AND AWAY

By air The airport lies 18km northeast of the city centre, and costs about TL30 by taxi. There are flights to and from Istanbul three times a day. Turkish Airlines do the route and they run a Havaş shuttle bus into town. Consult www.anadolujet.com for up-to-date schedules. Other airlines flying to and from Konya are Amsterdam Airlines (*www.amsterdamairlines.nl*), a Dutch charter flying to Amsterdam, Atlasjet (*www.atlasjet.com*) flying to Istanbul (Atatürk) and Teheran, Corendon Airlines (*www.corendon-airlines.com*), a Turkish airline based in Antalya flying to and from Amsterdam and Copenhagen, and Pegasus Airlines (*www.pegasusairlines.com*) flying to and from Copenhagen and Istanbul Sabiha Gökçen. The airport is also used by NATO.

By train The station lies 3km southwest of the centre. The daily train to and from Istanbul takes 14 hours (TL26), but the journey to and from Ankara on the new high-speed link takes just 75 minutes (TL25).

By bus Regular bus services run to and from Ankara (four hours, TL20), Istanbul (12 hours, TL45), Kayseri (four hours, TL25) and Sivas (seven hours, TL30). The *otogar* is 7km out of town to the north.

GETTING AROUND Everywhere is reachable on foot, and to reach the *otogar* or the train station, there are regular trams running 24 hours a day. There are also plentiful minibuses and taxis. You can rent a car from Decar based at the Dedeman Hotel (see below).

TOURIST INFORMATION There is a tourist office on Mevlâna Caddesi (⏀ *08.30–17.30 Mon–Sat*) that gives out city maps and leaflets on the Mevlâna Museum.

LOCAL TOUR OPERATORS

Selene Tourism Ayanbey Sokak; ☏ 3536745; www.selene.com.tr. Organises Konya tours & dervish performances.

WHERE TO STAY Konya's hotels are surprisingly unexciting and often a bit overpriced, thanks to the large throughput of tourists and pilgrims coming to watch Whirling Dervishes in action in Mevlâna's home town, in the hope this will be the real thing. If you have your own transport, you might consider staying out of town at Sille (see page 178) where the accommodation has a bit more character. Bear in mind that due to Konya's conservative mindset alcohol is less freely available and minibars full of spirits will not be found.

⌂ **Dedeman Konya** (125 rooms) Özalan Mahallesi; ☏ 2216600; www.dedeman.com. The Turkish chain of Dedeman offers a consistently high level of service & accommodation, & this 18-floor modern place opposite the Kipa Mall on the outskirts of town is no exception. It boasts a health club & live music in its rooftop restaurant/bar. $$$$$

⌂ **Hotel Balıkcılar** (51 rooms) Mevlâna Karşişi; ☏ 3509470; www.balikcilar.com. A 5-storey block in the town centre, this place has 2 restaurants,

sauna & *hammam*, & its own *sema* (Whirling Dervish dance) performances. $$$$

⌂ **Kaya'nin Evi** (3 rooms, sleeping 5) Sille, 7km west of Konya centre, off the Beyşehir–Sille highway, Sille junction; ☏ 2570920; e naringokce@yahoo.com. Restored by a local couple, this old house is rented out in its entirety, with modern bathrooms & satellite TV. $$$

⌂ **Mevlâna Sema Otel** (35 rooms) Mevlâna Caddesi; ☏ 3504623; www.semaotel.com. Very good

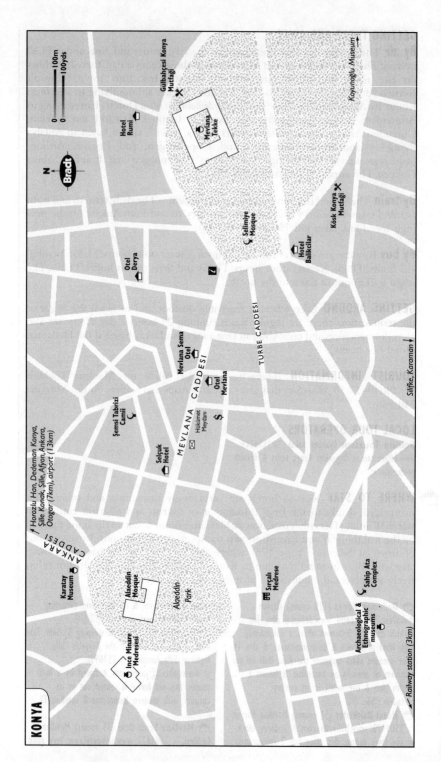

KONYA

Horozlu Han, Dedeman Konya,
Şille Konak, Afyon, Ankara,
Ötogar (7km), airport (13km)

ANKARA CADDESI

Karatay
Museum

Alaeddin
Mosque

Alaeddin
Park

İnce Minare
Medresesi

Sırçalı
Medrese

Archaeological &
Ethnographic
museums

Sahip Ata
Complex

Railway station (3km)

Şemsi Tabrizi
Camii

Selçuk
Hotel

MEVLANA CADDESI

Hükümet
Meydanı

Otel
Mevlana

Mevlana Sema
Otel

TÜRBE CADDESI

Silifke, Karaman

Selimiye
Mosque

Otel
Derya

Hotel
Balıkcılar

Köşk Konya
Mutfağı

Mevlana
Tekke

Hotel
Rumi

Gülbahçesi Konya
Mutfağı

Koyunoğlu Museum

N

Bradt

0   100m
0   100yds

central location though street rooms can be noisy. Comfortable rooms. $$$

🏠 **Hotel Rumi** (45 rooms) Durakfakih Sokak; ☎ 3531121; www.rumihotel.com. Excellent location beside the Mevlâna Museum. The rooms are elegantly furnished, & the b/fast room has lovely views over the museum. AC & *hammam*. $$$

🏠 **Selçuk Otel** (78 rooms) Babalık Sokak; ☎ 3532525; www.otelselcuk.com.tr. Good location in the city centre with fish tanks in the lobby. Indoor pool & sauna. $$$

🏠 **Otel Mevlâna** (22 rooms) Cengaver Sokak; ☎ 3520029. Simple option for backpackers, with fridges & bathrooms. Good value. $$

✖ **WHERE TO EAT** The many tea gardens in the Alaeddin Park are recommended for snacks and relaxed refreshments. Konya is also famous for its *lahmacun*, meat-topped pizza, which is good as a light snack.

✖ **Köşk Konya Mutfağı** Menguc Caddesi; ☎ 3528547; ⏰ 11.00–22.00. Excellent value restaurant serving Turkish classic dishes, run by a well-known Turkish food writer. Outside seating in a pretty rose garden. $$$

✖ **Gülbahçesi Konya Mutfağı** Gulbahce Sokak; ☎ 3510768; ⏰ 08.00–22.00. Good-value restaurant with upstairs terrace overlooking the turquoise Mevlâna Tekke. Occasional *sema* performances. $$

✖ **Horozlu Han** 5km northeast of Konya on the Ankara road, on the left. This small Seljuk caravanserai built 1246–49 has been converted to a restaurant, & has a lovely 2-storey lantern tower topped with an octagonal pyramid. $$

✖ **Sille Konak** Sille, 7km west of Konya; ☎ 2449260. Home-cooked food in a beautifully restored Greek house, the women of the family who own it do the cooking, while the menfolk wait on the customers. Various local specialities are on offer. $$

ENTERTAINMENT AND NIGHTLIFE The **Mevlâna Festival** (☎ *3534020*) runs for two weeks in December every year, ending with the climax of the anniversary of Mevlâna's death on 17 December, or his 'wedding night' with Allah, as Mevlevis think of it. Devotees flood in from all over the country and beyond, so tickets and accommodation need to be organised well in advance.

Whirling Dervish dances (*semas*) take place throughout the year weekly at 20.00 on Saturdays behind the Mevlâna Museum. The performance lasts about an hour, is free, and tickets need to be booked through the local hotels, tourist office or tour operators, as they tend to fill up quickly.

SHOPPING Konya has a bazaar that stretches from Türbe Caddesi for over 600m, about 100m south of Mevlâna Caddesi. It sells a complete range of items, from religious knick-knacks to carpets. There are also food shops where you can stock up with provisions.

OTHER PRACTICALITIES The main post office and banks with ATMs are based round Hükümet Meydanı at the eastern end of Mevlâna Caddesi.

WHAT TO SEE

Mevlâna Tekke (Museum) (☎ *3511215*; ⏰ *09.00–18.30 Tue–Sun, 10.00–18.00 Mon; headscarves required for women, no shorts for men; adult TL5*) The heart of the holy Seljuk city, this famous and striking monument is the highlight of any trip to Konya. Former *tekke* (lodge/monastery) of the Whirling Dervishes, Celaleddin Rumi, aka Mevlâna, meaning 'Our Master', is buried here (see box, page 173). A sacred Islamic shrine and object of pilgrimage from all over Turkey, the *tekke* was the centre of mystic Sufi culture for more than six centuries until the dervish sects were banned and dissolved by Atatürk in 1925 because he saw them as impediments to progress, pulling people backwards into superstition and ritual, and the following year it was opened as a museum. It is crammed full of precious works of art and

SELJUK AND TURKISH CARPETS

Most Turkish carpets are of the *kilim* variety, *kilim* being a Turkish word from the Persian *gelim* meaning 'to spread roughly', thought to be of Mongolian origin. They are characterised by their rug-like size and flat weave, giving them almost no pile. *Kilims* were traditionally made by women for use in their own homes and not for sale.

Marco Polo and Ibn Battuta, both travelling through Anatolia in the late 13th century, commented on the beauty and artistry of the Turkish carpets. Some of the earliest examples still surviving today were found at the beginning of the 20th century in Konya in the Alaeddin Mosque under layers of other later carpets, and these are now displayed in Konya's Mevlâna Museum and its Ethnography Museum, and in Istanbul's Museum of Turkish and Islamic Arts. Often carried by the camel caravans and exported, Turkish carpets were highly prized in Europe, especially by the Venetians and Florentines, and feature from time to time in the European religious paintings of the Renaissance, the earliest being dated to 1420. In the works of Lotto for example, a 15th-century Italian painter, and the Flemish painter Hans Holbein the Younger, Turkish carpets are shown under the feet of the Virgin Mary, or on the tables of wealthy Europeans: they were perceived as too special and expensive to be put on the floor.

For the early Turks the carpet was the only piece of furniture, ideally suited to the nomadic lifestyle, easily packed up and bundled onto the back of a camel or horse to move to the next area of good grazing. Carpets were used not only as floor coverings in the goat-hair tent that was the portable home, but also as wall hangings, tent dividers and prayer rugs, as well as being made into large bags for cushions or saddlebags or smaller bags for salt, bread, grain or clothes.

Traditionally natural dyes were used for colours from roots, bark, berries, vegetables and minerals. In the second half of the 19th century aniline chemical dyes became available and their use has gradually replaced most of the old vegetable dyes. Obtaining natural dyes often involved a lengthy and laborious process and also had the problem that no two colours ever came up quite the same. Today's weavers are often all in favour of the new chemical dyes for the sake of convenience. They have also been freed from the constraints of the availability of plants in their particular region, a factor which traditionally dominated the choice of colours, such as the Turcoman red, the blue of southeast Turkey and the blue and red of the Baliksehir region in northwest Turkey.

The designs and patterns on a *kilim* also give clues to its provenance, though you would have to be quite an expert before you could identify these differences. Some designs however are common to all rugs, the best-known pattern being the prayer rug with its solid block-shaped arch of colour representing the *mihrab* or prayer niche which faces Mecca in a prayer wall. Such rugs were used exclusively for prayer and the range of symbols frequently to be seen on them are the hands of prayer, the mosque lamp, the Tree of Life, the water jug, the jewel of Muhammad or the star of Abraham. Many carpets can also be seen as representations of gardens, with stylised flowers, notably the omnipresent *gül* or rose, conscious or unconscious reflections of Paradise. (See also box, page 177.)

opulent furnishings, even housing what purports to be a remnant of the Prophet Muhammad's beard. Awed visitors creep respectfully from one exhibit to the next, and the air of profound reverence is almost overwhelming. Over 1.5 million visitors come to pay their respects every year, mainly Turks, and to ask for help and support from Rumi. It is at its quietest on weekdays and early in the morning.

The entrance leads into a small pretty courtyard with an ablution fountain or *sadirvan*. It was around this fountain that the dervishes used to perform their whirling *sema* dance in remembrance of Mevlâna. Removing your shoes, you then enter the room where calligraphic displays are on show, then pass on to the mausoleum whose Ottoman silver doors bear the inscription:

Those who enter here incomplete will come out perfect.

The heavily decorated tombs of Mevlâna, his father, his son and other distinguished dervishes, lie in the main building draped in richly embroidered velvet cloths and with the distinctive turban on top. Mevlâna's own is an exquisitely carved sarcophagus covered in his poetry. The turquoise tiled conical fluted dome, patterned on the outside with a band of his calligraphic verses and on the inside with stars, rises directly over his tomb. The bulging treasures, carpets, gold and silver ornaments and such like were all gifts from sultans and princes, many of whom were members of the order themselves. Note the large 13th-century bronze bowl labelled *Nisan taşi* (April bowl), used to collect spring

THE WHIRLING DERVISHES

Rumi/Mevlâna was said to dictate most of his verses in a state of rapture or even trance, induced by the turning and whirling movement which he developed. Spinning round and round, the boundaries of selfhood were felt to dissolve, enabling more and more closeness to God, aiming to reach the ultimate state of *fana'* (oblivion/annihilation). Contemporary sources said that the hammering of the goldsmiths in the bazaar of Konya inspired these repetitive movements, as did the watermills in the gardens of the nearby village of Meram. The rhythmical pattern of the lyrics often seems to mimic music and dance and he uses the imagery of song and dance to express the inner song of his soul and its longing for union with God. The ceremonial dance, known as the *sema*, usually held on Friday after the noonday prayer, is always conducted by the dervishes wearing their special dress: a white (white symbolises mourning) sleeveless tunic called a *tennure*, a jacket with long sleeves called the *destegul*, and a black (black symbolises the tomb) overcoat called a *khirqa* cast off before the dance begins as a symbol of spiritual resurrection. The special tall felt hat, symbol of the Mevlevis, is called a *sikke*, and represents the tombstone. The ceremony begins with a slow, solemn chant, then the flute, followed by the drums, begins the plaintive lament of the separation of the soul. The dance itself is governed by very strict rules, codified by Mevlâna's son Sultan Veled, with the sheikh, distinguished by the black scarf on his turban, standing in the most honoured corner of the dancing place, and the spinning performed on the right foot. Representing a prayer addressed to the Universe, the dance offers a cosmic vision of the world. The Mevlevis believe that man is separated from the Absolute Being by 18 worlds, and the number 18 takes on great significance in the repetitions of the dance. The right hand is held open towards the sky to receive divine grace, and the left hand is held downwards to pass the grace down to earth. The sheikh is the pole, the point of convergence of the temporal and the non-temporal, who spins in the centre, while the other dancers gyrate around the room, forming, in the course of their movement, two arcs, one representing the assimilation of souls into matter, the other symbolising the ascension of souls towards God. The dance ends when the sheikh is back in the centre, symbolising the unity with God, and the flute begins again in improvised celebration. The ceremony ends with chantings from the Koran.

Rumi's most famous work is a great mystic poem of 25,000 verses written in Persian. It is known as the *Mesnevi*, the name used to describe this poetic form based on verses in rhyming couplets, and has acquired a mystical status sometimes referred to as 'the Koran in Pahlavi' (ie: Persian) or 'the Sufi Bible'. His mysticism shared many similar ideas with Ibn 'Arabi, his contemporary from Damascus, but his work was more accessible and had a more popular appeal. The notion of the 'perfect man' was developed by Ibn 'Arabi and expanded by Rumi, seen as the embodiment of the mystery of God, a symbol of the divine who inspired ordinary mortals to seek God. In 1244 Rumi fell under the spell of a wandering dervish called Shamseddin (Shams) Tabrizi who believed himself to be a reincarnation of the Prophet Muhammad, and who even insisted on being addressed as Muhammad. Rumi saw him as the perfect man of his generation. They met in a Konya street and Rumi was immediately consumed by an intense mystical love, a love so all-consuming it caused him to neglect his family and disciples. They rebelled and demanded that Shams leave. Shams went to Syria, but Rumi found separation from him so intolerable that Sultan Veled, Rumi's son, had him brought back. Their meeting is described by early sources as being so intense, with each falling at the other's feet, 'that one did not know who was lover and who was beloved.' Once again their relationship grew so all-consuming that this time his disciples had Shams killed, stabbing him and throwing his body into a well. The distraught Rumi sought Shams everywhere, but in vain, and through his experience of the intense grief and sorrow at the separation and loss devoted even more effort into mystical music and dancing, eventually transforming his feelings into a symbol for the love of God, God's yearning for humanity and humanity's yearning for God. He decided that, whether they knew it or not, everyone was searching for the absent God, aware that at some deep level he or she was separated from the source of being:

rainwater. The water was considered holy and its blessing was distributed to those seeking cures by dipping the tip of Mevlâna's turban in it, then touching their skin.

In the adjoining mosque, added in Ottoman times by Süleyman the Magnificent, the *mihrab* is quite exquisite, with elegant calligraphy and turquoise tiles. Next door to the tombs is the *semahane*, also added by Süleyman, an opulent vaulted ceremonial hall with fine carpets, including Mevlâna's prayer rug, where the *sema* used to be performed. Today it is used to exhibit the reed flutes (*ney*), tambourines and cymbals, all musical instruments used in the dervish ceremonies, along with dervish clothing.

The formal establishment of the Mevlevi Order (popularly known as the Whirling Dervishes) with a true hierarchy and organisation of the dancing ritual was left to Rumi's son, Sultan Veled (died 1312). The centre of the order was always Konya, but the dance spread Rumi's poetry and music throughout the newly emerging Ottoman Empire, and many smaller *tekkes* (Sufi monasteries) were founded all over the Ottoman Empire, as far away as Syria and Egypt, though the Arabic-speaking lands of the empire were never as captivated by the lyrics, since the original Persian imagery did not translate very well into Arabic.

Next to the Mevlâna Tekke Museum is the huge **Selimiye Mosque**, severe in its early Ottoman style. It was built between 1566 and 1574 and named after Sultan Selim II who was governor of Konya at that time.

ELSEWHERE IN KONYA The other monuments in Konya are mainly grouped around the Alaeddin Park, in the centre of which rises the Alaeddin Tepesi (Aladdin's Hill), the former acropolis of Roman Iconium. In Seljuk times this hill was the site

Listen to the reed, how it tells a tale, complaining of separateness. Ever since I was parted from the reed-bed, my lament has caused men and women to moan. I want a bosom torn by severance, that I may unfold [to such a person] the power of love-desire: everyone who is left far from his source wished back the time when he was united to it.

This experience of union and identification with the beloved is what he describes in the following famous passage:

'A certain man knocked at his friend's door: his friend
    Asked: "Who is there?"
He answered: "I". "Be gone," said his friend, "'tis too soon!
    At my table there is no place for the raw.
How shall the raw be cooked but in the fire of absence?
    What else shall deliver him from hypocrisy?"
He turned sadly away, and for a whole year the flames
    Of separation consumed him:
Then he came back and again paced to and fro beside the
    House of his friend.
He knocked at the door with a hundred fears and reverence
    Lest any disrespectful word might escape from his lips.
"Who is there?" cried the friend. He answered: "Thou,
    O charmer of all hearts."
"Now," said the friend, "since thou art I, come in, there
    Is no room for two I's in this house."

(Mesnevi 1:3056-64)

of the Sultan of Rum's palace and gardens, and one small fragment of the palace still stands. Powerful walls, now disappeared, used to enclose the whole citadel.

Alaeddin Mosque (🕐 08.30–17.30) The major monument is the Alaeddin Mosque, the largest Seljuk mosque in Konya. It took 70 years to build; the sequence of construction is uncertain and the plan is irregular, but the 13th-century part built for Alaeddin Keykubad I, Sultan of Rum from 1219 to 1231, is known to have been designed by a Damascene architect, hence the more exotic Arab style. Eight Seljuk sultans are buried here. Suitably dressed and headscarved, you can probably come in outside the strict visiting times, as long as you do not coincide with prayer time. The entrance today is on the east, but the original entrance on the north has a magnificent portal that re-uses some earlier Byzantine and Roman decorative elements. In the courtyard are two enormous Seljuk *türbes*, one of which is entered from the prayer hall, but the other, built by Kilic Arslan II (1155–92), on an octagonal ground plan with a pyramid roof, has a fine blue-tiled interior with eight cenotaphs. The prayer hall boasts 42 columns recycled from antiquity, topped with Roman and Byzantine capitals, and the *mihrab* is adorned with lovely blue and black Seljuk tilework.

Karatay Museum (*Alaeddin Meydanı*; ☎ 3511914; 🕐 09.00–12.00 & 13.30–17.30 Tue–Sun; adult TL5) Standing opposite the Alaeddin Mosque and now a museum of exquisite tiles, this former theological college, the Karatay Medrese, was built in 1251 by a Seljuk emir and *vizir* named Karatay. Its elaborately carved entrance portal is considered to be one of the finest examples

The extensive use of tiles in religious buildings and in tombs is no accident. Ever since the magnificent mosaic garden depicted on the walls of the Great Umayyad Mosque in Damascus, widely held to be a vision of Paradise, attempts have been made to bring such visions into holy buildings. In Islam, the significance of such visions is more profoundly moving, as both the Arabs and the Turks came originally from regions where either desert or bleak treeless steppeland was the dominant feature, with severe shortage of water. It is hardly surprising, therefore, that the dominant colours of their tiles were green and blue, symbolising fertility and water, the two things most lacking in their own world and which they most longed for in the next. The superb flower tiles from Iznik turn the interiors of the grander Ottoman mosques and tombs into gardens, attempts to recreate the Garden of Paradise. Even calligraphy has been compared to flowers with waving stems, and women's headstones are often extensively carved with blooms.

of Seljuk stonework anywhere. Recently refurbished, the interior displays tiles from both the Seljuk and the Ottoman periods, the most beautiful of which were rescued from the now-disappeared Seljuk palace on the Alaeddin Hill/citadel, and from the Seljuk summer palace on Lake Beyşehir.

They include representations of humans, lions, leopards and birds, as well as the Seljuk two-headed eagle. Nowhere in the Koran is there any mention for or against the representation of living things, and the prohibition that is generally taken as read in Islamic art stems from an account in the Hadith (Sayings of the Prophet), where Muhammad is recorded as saying: 'Whoever makes a picture, Allah will torture him with it on the Day of Judgement until he breathes life into it, which he will never be able to do'. Shi'a and mystical orders of Islam were much less stringent about adhering to such Hadith, which is why we see many more representations of living things in their art.

Surpassing even the tiles in beauty is the magnificent domed ceiling covered in 24-pointed stars in yellow against a deep-blue background. The colours are superb and the stars appear to shine with an extraordinary brightness.

İnce Minare Medresesi – Museum of Wooden Artefacts and Stone Carving

(*Adliye Bulvarı;* \ *3513204;* ⏰ *09.00–12.00 & 13.30–17.30 Tue–Sun; adult TL5*) On the far side of the Alaeddin Park stands what was once the İnce Minare Medresesi, Medrese of the Slender Minaret, though its minaret is more stubby than slender these days, having been truncated by a lightning bolt in 1901. The building itself is a small but fine *medrese* with an elaborate, almost Baroque portal, built between 1265 and 1267. On either side of the entrance to the main room, notice the winged angels, symbol of kindness, carved out of marble. These 13th-century bas-reliefs used to adorn the entrance to the Seljuk citadel of Konya. In the *iwan* there is a collection of Seljuk wooden carved items, including mosque doors and Koran reading stands. On the right-hand side wall is a 12th-century Seljuk bas-relief depicting a dragon and an elephant, further evidence of how the Seljuks did not feel constrained by the Arab Islamic tradition of forbidding images of living things. The Koran itself does not proclaim a specific ban on such things, but simply warns against the worshipping of idols. The Seljuks, converts to Islam in the 10th century, had, thanks to their Persian and Turkic heritage, a freer interpretation of such matters.

Sırçalı Medrese – Tombstone Museum

(*Sırçali Caddesi;* \ *3534031;* ⏰ *08.30–17.30 Tue–Sun; admission free*) This former theological college was built

DECODING A TURKISH CARPET

The motifs used in Turkish carpets are a kind of language that can be decoded, though this ability is increasingly being lost as commercialism is taking over, and as most new carpets and *kilims* are produced in factories following motifs and colours laid down by the factory owners and distributors. To succeed in the market place, many carpets are having their individuality taken away and forced to conform to patterns and designs seen as suiting more Western and European requirements. Originally, however, the patterns and colours were never dictated by commercial motives but reflected the identity of the weaver, their family and their tribe. Each carpet was a work of art, a statement or message, using symbols to represent sorrow or happiness, regrets or aspirations. Working on the carpet was a therapeutic process, a way of escaping into another world, a way for the nomadic woman to express herself. Some symbols express the yearning of a young girl to get married, others express grief at the loss of a child. Birds, animals and flowers were commonly used, each with a particular meaning:

- Eagle = power and strength
- Parrot = protection, escaping from danger
- Peacock = immortality
- Paradise bird = Paradise
- Dog = protection, trust, defence
- Lotus = rebirth, immortality
- Iris = religious liberty
- Blossom = youth, spring, newly wed
- Pomegranate = fertility
- Hyacinth = regeneration
- Tree of life = direct path from earth to heaven
- Lily = purity, spirituality
- Peony = power
- Tulip = prosperity
- *Herati* = water garden
- Amulet = thwarts evil eye

Other symbols include:

- Cross = faith
- Star = spirituality, good luck
- *Mihrab* = gateway to Paradise
- Hand = prayer rug
- Diamond = women; two diamonds attached together = man and woman
- Comb = cleanliness
- Jug, ewer = purification

Colours also have meanings and associations and are not just chosen at random. The commonest colours are red, signifying beauty, wealth, courage, luck, joy and faith, and blue, symbolising power or force, solitude, an allusion to the after-life. Other colours are used more sparingly, such as green, the holy colour of the Prophet Muhammad, meaning hope, renewal, life or spring; orange meaning humility and piety; yellow meaning the sun, joy of life; white meaning purity and cleanliness; black for mourning and destruction; gold for power and wealth; and brown for fertility.

in 1242 by a Seljuk *vizir* called Bedreddin Muslih and now houses a small collection of 14th- and 15th-century Seljuk tombstones, along with some later Ottoman ones. Its name means 'Glazed', so called from the glazed tiles used in its decoration, and the *iwan* still has some blue tiles with fine calligraphy on its arch.

Sahip Ata Kulliyesi (⊕ *09.00–12.00 & 13.00–17.00 Tue–Sun*) Destroyed by fire in 1871, this mosque complex was rebuilt in 13th-century style. Of the original Seljuk mosque complex built in 1269–83 by the Seljuk *vizir* Sahip Ata, only the fine brick and stone portal remains. It used to lead into an oratory, a *hammam* and a *türbe*. You can still see the fine blue Seljuk tiled *mihrab* that survived the fire.

Archaeological and Ethnographic museums (*Larende Caddesi;* \ *3513207; ⊕ 09.00–12.30 & 13.30–17.00 Tue–Sun; adult TL3*) Beside the Sahip Ata complex is this pair of modern museums, both with the same hours and entry fee, where the only evidence of Konya's pre-Seljuk history is to be found. The most notable exhibit is a Roman sarcophagus with a bas-relief showing the 12 Labours of Hercules, dating from the 3rd century, of the type known as Sidymara. Hercules's exploits also figure large in the other exhibits. Besides Roman objects, there are also Neolithic finds including the touching skeleton of a young girl clutching her jewellery and an Assyrian oil lamp imaginatively fashioned to resemble a bunch of grapes. The Ethnographic Museum has an interesting assortment of Ottoman craftwork, with some gigantic keys forming the most surprising exhibits.

Şemsi Tabrizi Camii Standing in a park some 250m northwest of the Alaeddin citadel is this mosque which still contains the fine 14th-century tomb of Shamseddin Tabrizi, Rumi's Perfect Man and inspiration of much of his mystic work (see pages 174–5). Rumi even used Shams's name as his pen name, so keen was he to merge with spiritual muse. The original tomb where Shams's body, retrieved from the well, had been dumped and hurriedly plastered over, was found in the 1970s underneath this memorial by the then director of the Mevlâna Museum (see box, pages 174–5).

Koyunoğlu Museum (*Kerimler Caddesi 25; ⊕ 08.30–17.30 Tue–Sun; admission free*) About 1km from the centre of town, this rarely visited museum is the Ottoman house of a well-to-do Konya railway inspector named Izzet Koyunoğlu, who travelled the country collecting all sorts of bits and pieces, now on display here. They range from a stuffed pelican to valuable old clocks, and there are also some fascinating old photos of Konya and Whirling Dervishes taken around 1900.

ENVIRONS OF KONYA

Meram An attractive escape from the city is the small holiday resort of Meram, 8km west of Konya's city centre, where in summer the banks of the river Meram are lined with restaurants and tea houses designed to catch the cooling breezes from the water. The town also boasts a charming 15th-century *hammam* called Ibrahim Bey, still functioning and fed by hard limewater springs.

Getting there and away *Dolmuş* taxis run to Meram from the centre of Konya.

Sille In this valley 7km northwest of Konya there is an interesting series of hermit caves in the cliffs and some Byzantine rock-church ruins, some with fragmentary frescoes. The most noteworthy is St Helen's Church (Aya Elena Kilisesi) just before the village, a domed Byzantine church whose vandalised frescoes date from 1880, when the original ones were restored. In World War I it was used as a military depot and a field hospital.

Getting there and away A bus (no. 64) to Sille runs about every minutes from Mevlâna Caddesi in Konya, near the post office. It takes 25 minutes and costs TL1.5.

Zazadin Hanı At 24km northeast of Konya, take the Aksaray road and after 19km turn left towards the village of Tomek. The striking thing about this caravanserai is its entry portal in alternating black basalt and white marble (a style known in Syria as *ablaq*), very sober and refined, with no stalactite *muqarnas* (stalactite decoration). Built in 1236 by Sultan Keykubat I it stands in the middle of nowhere in the immense steppe. Its thick walls with round and square towers testify to its defensive character, a haven for its travelling merchants. The façade has a series of Romano-Byzantine elements recycled, such as a Roman *stela* and Byzantine coffin.

Getting there and away Unfortunately Zazadin Han can be reached only with your own transport.

SOUTH TO THE COAST AT SİLİFKE

From Konya you can head south away from religious conservatism to the beaches at Silifke, along an interesting and spectacularly scenic route that can be done in a day if you have your own transport and incorporating a number of unusual excursions on the way. By public transport things will be much slower, and you should reckon on a full day's outing just to visit Çatalhüyük, and maybe consider spending a night at Karaman.

ÇATALHÜYÜK (⏰ *daily 08.00–17.00; adult TL3*) The most ancient and important Neolithic and Bronze-Age site in Turkey, and thought to be the oldest known city in the world (see page 87), the mound of Çatalhüyük rises 20m above the featureless plain. Discovered in 1958 by British archaeologist James Mellaart, the finds date back as early as 6800BC and reveal a remarkably advanced Anatolian culture with sophisticated tools, jewellery, sculpture and above all, extraordinary wall paintings which decorated their shrines. Like most Neolithic and Bronze-Age sites, it is not that inspiring for the amateur to look at today, although digs are still ongoing from June to September involving archaeologists from all over the world. The on-site museum helps put everything in context and also has a good eight-minute film explaining the significance of the settlement. The exhibits are reproductions of the pottery items found here, as the originals are all under far greater security in the Ankara Museum of Anatolian Civilisations (see page 86). At its peak around 8,000 people were estimated to have lived here in this streetless settlement in tightly packed dwellings entered through holes in the roof and connected by ladders. There are over 13 levels of housing, built over the 1,400-year lifespan of the settlement, as when one level began to wear out after about a century, it was filled in and another built on top. The dead were buried under the floor, as testified by the many skeletons found, and the houses seem to have doubled as shrines in a kind of ancestor worship. No evidence has been found of any central organisation or of any weapons, leading archaeologists to believe that this egalitarian society somehow never needed to fight an enemy.

Getting there and away
By road The route starts off uneventfully with more bleak landscapes until after one-and-a-half hours you reach the town of Karaman, a surprisingly green oasis in the barren colourlessness of the plateau. *En route*, some 50km from Konya, you will have noticed a road off to the left leading after 26km to Çatalhüyük. A taxi from Konya to Çatalhüyük there and back will cost around TL70.

7

By minibus You need to take the Karkin minibus from Konya's Eski Garaj that leaves at 09.00 and get off at Kük Köy, from where it is a 1km walk to the site.

KARAMAN (*Telephone code: 338*) The Karaman region was for a long time inhabited by Turkish-speaking Orthodox Greeks who wrote Turkish in Greek script. When the Seljuk sultanate of Rum fell, central Anatolia split into many provinces with local governors and the Karamanid emirs used the town as their capital. In the town centre you can still visit the Ak Tekke (White Monastery) dating from 1371, a former monastery of the Mevlevi dervishes, and the Yunus Emre Mosque dated to 1349 beside the tomb of Yunus Emre, the great Turkish poet of the time, whose verses are carved into the wall of a poetry garden at the back of the mosque. Mevlâna's mother is also buried here in the Mader-i-Mevlâna (Aktepe) Mosque, dating to 1370 and with the distinctive dervish tall felt hat carved above the entrance.

Getting there and away Buses run regularly between Karaman and Konya (two hours, TL20). The train also stops here on its way between Konya and Adana, taking three hours to reach Karaman from Konya and costing TL7.

Where to stay, eat and what to see The **Nas Hotel** (*10 rooms; Ismetpasa Caddesi; 2144848; $$*) is in the centre of town, offering comfortable, adequate rooms.

Karaman's **Hatuniye Medresesi**, a 14th-century fine Karamanid theological college with an elaborately carved portal, now houses a restaurant. It is next door to the small **Karaman Museum** (⊕ *08.00–12.00 & 13.00–17.00 Tue–Sun; adult TL3*) on Turgut Özal Bulvarı.

BINBIRKILISE (*42km northwest of Karaman*) An excursion which requires more time, and which can use Karaman as a base, is to the region called Binbirkilise ('A Thousand and One Churches'), an important monastic centre from the 9th to the 11th centuries. The route is fine until the nearest village of Maden Şehir, then the rough dirt track continues for the last 8km to reach the most impressive group of ruined churches and monasteries near the hamlet of Degler. Some of them are still lived in by local families or used as barns. Sir William Ramsey and Gertrude Bell made a study of these Byzantine buildings in 1905. The trip requires a taxi or your own transport, but it gives an interesting flavour to the ex-Christian life in these areas, and the scenery is lovely.

ALAHAN MONASTERY (*92km northwest of Silifke, 22km north of Mut, signposted 2km up a dirt track off the main road to Konya; always open; admission free*) After leaving Karaman the road south crosses a pass at 1,610m and you suddenly enter a heavily forested belt of mountains, a very welcome change after the bleak plateau. Shortly after, in a valley just opposite a little café, a sign points left off to Alahan, a further 2km up a reasonable track.

This is a detour not to be missed, as Alahan is the site of a remote ruined Byzantine monastery complex, the like of which is rarely to be seen. The setting is magnificent, on a terrace overlooking the lovely Göksu Gorge with the wild mountains of the Taurus all around. The only other form of life you may encounter here is goats, although a site guardian is sometimes in evidence.

At the beginning of the complex you will notice a series of caves cut into the cliff. These were the cells for the early monks, with little nooks carved out for cupboards. You arrive first at the more ruined of the two churches, the great western basilica, known as the Church of the Evangelists, built at the end of the 5th century, with elaborate relief sculptures of the four Evangelists on its beautiful doorway. On the insides of the pillars of the main door are reliefs of the archangels Gabriel and Michael, trampling underfoot a pair of female figures wearing Phrygian headdress (representing Cybele, the Anatolian fertility/mother goddess), along with a bull representing the sacred animal of the cult of Mithras, and a male torso representing a priest of the cult of Isis. This scene depicts the triumph of early Christianity over paganism. From here you next pass the stark baptistery to the Church of the East, built some 50 years later in the early 6th century, with a simple but beautiful façade, remarkably well preserved. Inside, the arches and slender columns give a marvellous impression of grace. The buildings backing into the cliff, some of them cut into the rock, are the refectory, kitchen, bakery and guest quarters. Many carvings of animals and abstract motifs are to be seen in the complex on blocks of the softly coloured stone.

Getting there Without your own transport you will have to be dropped at the Alahan turn-off from a bus travelling between Karaman and Mut, and walk the rest of the way.

DESCENT TO THE COAST Some 20km after Alahan you reach Mut, down in a valley surrounded by mountains. A brief stop can be made here to see the sturdy 14th-century Turkish fortress built on the edge of town. The local children are very friendly and charming. From Mut the final 77km passes through some of the most spectacularly beautiful mountain scenery in Turkey, following the gorge of the Göksu River through the Taurus Mountains. At one point, just 7km short of Silifke, there is a magnificent viewing area to the left of the road, with stunning views down into the Göksu Gorge. A nearby plaque erected in 1971 commemorates the drowning of the German emperor Frederick Barbarossa in the river below here on 10 June 1190, on his way to Palestine for the Third Crusade.

SİLİFKE *Telephone code: 324*

Ancient Seleucia, first founded in the 3rd century BC by Seleucus I, general to Alexander the Great, the town has a pleasant open feel, on the banks of the wide Göksu River, overlooked by the Crusader castle on the acropolis summit.

Of the ancient town nothing remains except the Roman bridge over the river and the scant remains of a Roman temple, the Temple of Jupiter, later turned into a Christian basilica, which sits incongruously in the middle of town. The best thing is to head straight up to the castle where there are several restaurants offering wonderful panoramas. Vast, overgrown and crumbling in places, the castle is not well maintained and there is no ticket office or official entrance. Entry is therefore by a narrow path around the east side of the castle where a breach in the walls can be crossed. Once inside you can clamber all round the edge of the fortress, taking care to avoid the crumbling sections. Originally Byzantine and built in the 7th century as a defence against the Arab raids, it was rebuilt by the Crusader knights of Rhodes into this colossal structure with 23 towers and bastions. In the cellars is a cistern whose waters are reputed never to dry up. The Ottoman sultan Beyazıt I later built a mosque inside the castle.

GETTING THERE AND AWAY There are buses from Silifke's *otogar* 800m out of town near the junction of the main roads north to and from Konya, west to and from Antalya and east to and from Mersin (two hours, TL6). The bus to Adana takes two hours (TL15), and to Antalya nine hours (TL35).

WHERE TO STAY AND EAT

⌂ **Göksu Otel** (25 rooms) Atatürk Bulvarı; ☎ 7121021. A pleasant place in town on the north bank of the river, aimed at businessmen but with a very good restaurant on the ground floor. $$

✕ **Baboğlu Restaurant** On the roundabout opposite the *otogar*; ☎ 714204; ⏰ 10.00–22.00. This is Silifke's best, with very good fish, lamb & chicken dishes. $$

WHAT TO SEE

Diocaesarea (*38km north of Silifke;* ⏰ *08.00–12.00 & 13.00–17.00 Mon–Fri; adult TL2*) Although a visit to this site involves a considerable detour along a signposted but winding road, it is well worth it if you have the time, as the scenery is attractive and the site is one of the most impressive on the Cilician coast. Without your own car, you will need to take a minibus to Uzancaburc from near Silifke's tourist office, which runs every couple of hours.

From about 8km outside Silifke, the road through the mountains and pine forests is dotted with Roman tombs often in the form of temples, some of which are remarkably well preserved and even with bones still inside. On the right at the entrance to the village of Uzancaburc, a road leads to Ura, a village identified with the ancient city of Olba. Here are the remains of a nymphaeum, an aqueduct and several Byzantine churches.

Uzancaburc itself is a pretty village, isolated in the mountains. From the village square and car park, notice to the left the half-sunken Roman theatre dating from the 2nd century. Then, passing through a monumental Roman arch which spans a colonnaded street, you come to the Temple of Zeus Olbius, built at the beginning of the 3rd century BC by Seleucus I. It is the oldest-known temple in the Corinthian order in all of Asia Minor, and was later transformed into a Christian church at the start of the Byzantine era. Most of its columns are still standing.

Beyond the wall of the temple enclosure you can see on the right another colonnaded street leading to a Roman gate, and beyond this the remains of the Temple of Tyche dating to the 1st century BC, a vast foundation with five Corinthian columns on high bases. Returning to the arch near the village square, turn left, and after passing the school and a small restaurant, follow the path that leads to a powerfully built five-storey Hellenistic tower still standing nearly 25m high, and which has given the village its name, as Uzancaburc means 'tallish tower'. A stone has slipped, blocking the entrance, so only a slight person can enter now.

Continuing northwards you will find a path that winds down for 500m to reach the Greek and Byzantine necropolis with sarcophagi, some of which still have bas-reliefs.

Narlıkuyu, the Baths of the Maidens (*20km east of Silifke on the Adana road;* ⏰ *08.00–17.00 Tue–Sun; adult TL3*) Crossing the marshy delta of the Göksu River east of Silifke, a renowned wetland with over 330 species of bird (see page 9), you soon come to the attractive little village of Narlıkuyu ('Pomegranate Well'), where there is a series of very good if pricey fish restaurants suspended on stilts overlooking the sea. On the village square before the restaurants is a tiny museum, once a 4th-century Roman bath, whose floor depicts a very fine mosaic of the three graces. The fountain of the baths was reputed to endow its bathers with beauty, intelligence and long life.

Getting there and away *Dolmuşes* run frequently between Narlıkuyu and Silifke and Kızkalesi (TL1).

Heaven and Hell (Cennet ve Cehennem) (⏰ *daily 08.00–17.00; adult TL3*) From the village of Narlıkuyu a signposted small road winds off the main road

for 3km to reach the legendary if disappointing Heaven and Hell, two caves so different from each other that they earned these epithets. The Vale of Heaven (Cennet Deresi) is a huge 250m-wide natural chasm at the edge of a field of the scattered Roman and Byzantine ruins of ancient Paperon. The ruins are scant, the only striking building being right on the edge of the 70m-deep chasm, a high-walled basilica. The descent is by easy steps to the bottom of the chasm, and from here less easy steps, sometimes slippery, continue down 200m to the cave mouth where you will see a pretty little early Christian church, dedicated to the Virgin Mary in the 5th century, recently restored. Bathed in a strange bluish light when seen from below deep inside the cave, the church appears to have been built of older stones from the 2nd and 3rd century BC. In the apse are traces of murals. Inside the cave you will hear the roar of an underground river which according to tradition is the Stream of Paradise, which flows out at the Fountain of Knowledge at the Roman baths of Narlıkuyu below. The ascent is less easy, and about an hour should be allowed for the total visit. The general atmosphere of the place, with rags tied in bushes representing the supplications of visitors, and the rubbish of picnics littering the area, is far removed from heaven.

From the parking place a second path leads off to the right to the Vale of Hell (Cehennem Deresi), a frightening 120m-deep narrow pit, accessible only with a guide for those with experience of pot-holing. These days it is merely viewed from a platform above. According to both Christian and Muslim traditions, this was one of the entrances to Hell. The ancient Greeks of Asia Minor believed that this was where Zeus incarcerated the 100-headed monster Typhon, and that the underground river was Styx, the mythological boundary between the Underworld and the world of the living. Rags of clothing and pennants are tied in the trees and bushes around it by superstitious locals to ward off evil spirits who might escape from below.

Kızkalesi (Castle of the Maiden) (27km east of Silifke; 5km east of Narlıkuyu; boat trip to the island TL5; ⊕ daily 08.00–18.00; adult TL3) Twenty years ago there was nothing on this beach except a BP Mocamp and camping area, but in recent years a string of good hotels have grown up along the fine sandy beach, making this an excellent stopping place on your tour eastwards.

Long famous for the highly photogenic Castle of the Maiden which sits on its own island 200m offshore and which graces many a Turkish tourism poster, there are in fact two castles here, the other being readily accessible on the shore (adult TL3), and called Korykos Castle. Both were built in the 12th century by Leon II, King of Little Armenia when this region of Cilicia fell under their rule and served as commercial stopovers for the Genoese and the Venetians in their sea trade further east. The Armenian kingdom disappeared in 1375, but many of their castles fell into the hands of the Turcoman Karamanid rulers, who ruled from their capital at Karaman (see page 180). Peter I, King of Cyprus, seized it from them in 1360, and the Lusignan knights held it until 1448, which is why it is sometimes mistaken for a Crusader castle.

Kızkalesi itself was originally linked by a causeway to Korykos, long since washed away, which is why it appears to be floating in the sea 200m offshore. Strong swimmers can reach it but the more conventional approach is by boat, set up courtesy of entrepreneurial locals, and taking 15 minutes to reach the island. Its name derives from the local legend that the king built the castle to protect his beautiful daughter after it was predicted that she would die of snakebite. One of her admirers unwittingly sent her a basket of fruit in which a snake had hidden, and on reaching in, she was bitten and died. The boat-taxi is a recent enterprise, as most local people believed the fatal snake lived on in the castle, so left the island well alone. The castle was restored by the Karamanid rulers, and the ramparts have been recently renovated so that you can now walk round them, admiring the towers and the little chapel in the centre of the enclosure, and of course, the view.

The land castle is approached from the beach itself, through a breach in the walls, then through a gate into the second enclosure. You can still walk along the ramparts in places, and look out for recycled stones in the walls taken from the ancient city of Korykos whose remains are scattered nearby. It was a pirate refuge before Pompey's campaign of elimination in 67BC, and Cicero lived here when he was Governor of Cilicia from 51BC to 50BC.

Getting there Buses run frequently between Silifke and Mersin, stopping at Kızkalesi.

Where to stay There are now many relaxed beach hotels here, some with pools as well as the beach. Among the best value are:

Yaka Hotel (27 rooms) \ 324 5232444; www.yakahotel.com. Popular with local archaeologists. Spotless rooms, lovely outdoor garden eating area. $$$

Baytan Hotel (24 rooms) \ 324 5232024; www.baytanotel.com. Perfect location right on the beach with some greenery. The spacious rooms are a bit worn, but the rooftop terrace is a fine place for a beer. $$

EAST TO MERSIN

Continuing east between Korykos and Mersin, the remains of many ancient cities can be seen, indicating how much more populous this part of Cilicia was in antiquity than it is now. None of the ruins are particularly spectacular or impressive and are difficult to explore without your own transport, so most people will content themselves with peering at what they can see as they pass. As so often, it is the tombs which have survived the best, and along several stretches of the road, rock tombs and sarcophagi can be seen lining the sides.

The first of these is beside the village of Ayas, only 3km beyond Kızkalesi, noteworthy for a fine house tomb which has survived well. On the coast side of the road is the ancient site of Sebastea of Cilicia (also known as Elaioussa), currently under excavations financed by Rome University. Below the village is a ruined theatre, and below that, a baths, an aqueduct and a city gate. A Byzantine church stands almost on the beach. Further on, about 7km east of Kızkalesi, a road leads 3km off inland to the village of Kanlıdıvane (meaning 'Bloodstained Place'), the site of ancient Kanytelis (⊕ 08.00–18.00; adult TL3), where you can see a 17m-tall Hellenistic tower and vast Roman necropolis. The origin of the gory name is a vast chasm, 90m long by 70m wide by 60m deep, which lies at the heart of the ancient city and which local people believe was where criminals were tossed and then eaten by wild animals. At about 10km before Mersin a road leads off 1km to the sea at Viransehir, site of ancient Soli, occupied since the end of the 3rd century BC, later destroyed by the Armenians and rebuilt in the 1st century BC by Pompey, and thereafter named Pompeopolis in his honour. The people of Soli spoke such poor Greek that the term 'solecism' was coined, meaning 'a grammatical offence'. The principal remains of the city are the splendid columns of the street nearly 500m long running down to the ancient harbour. Only about 20 of the original 200 columns, with Corinthian capitals, are still standing, leading to the sandy beach. Inhabitants of Mersin come out to swim here.

Once east of Pompeopolis you have left behind the rocky coastline and mountains of rugged Cilicia and have entered its flat and fertile plain. Most of the plain today is covered in rice fields and cotton plantations, with all signs of antiquity long since buried. The scenery is monotonous, as the area from Mersin to Adana is a huge alluvium created by three large rivers. After the Arab invasion the population decreased markedly and the plain became a winter home for the Turcoman nomad tribes who spent the summer up on the Anatolian Plateau. In the 7th and 8th centuries it was therefore largely devoid of permanent settlers, and there was still buffalo hunting in the marshes of the delta. The cultivation of cotton dates back to the 1840s when both the crop and the peasants to grow it were imported from Egypt. It is now one of Turkey's chief export earners. Approaching from the west, Mersin, now renamed İçel after the name of its province, is the first city on the plain. In the late 1980s the Turkish government initiated a housing scheme to encourage nomads who had been displaced by Kurdish guerrilla activity in the eastern provinces to settle here. It has met with mixed success; many of them are still unemployed and finding it hard to adjust to city life.

MERSİN (İÇEL)

A highly industrialised modern port, Turkey's largest on the Mediterranean, Mersin is not somewhere most visitors will choose to stop unless they are catching the car ferry to Famagusta in Northern Cyprus. If you are obliged to stay here while waiting for the ferry, the only distractions are a small museum (⊕ 08.00–12.00 & 13.00–17.00; adult TL3) set in a pretty garden, housing a range of archaeological items found locally from Neolithic to Byzantine times, and, beside the museum, a Greek Orthodox church which has some interesting icons, which you can see if the caretaker lets you in – a tip or church donation will be expected.

GETTING THERE AND AWAY

By ferry Turkish Maritime Lines (\ 324 2312536) has its office at the dock from where the car ferries depart to Gazimağusa (Famagusta) on Mondays, Wednesdays and Fridays at 20.00, returning from Gazimağusa on Tuesdays, Thursdays and Sundays also at 20.00. The journey takes ten hours and tickets must be bought a day in advance. The passenger fare is TL60 one-way, TL115 return, and the car fare is TL140 single, TL280 return.

By bus Mersin's *otogar* is on the eastern outskirts of town, reachable by bus from opposite the Mersin Oteli. Buses run regularly to and from Adana (one hour, TL4), Silifke (two hours, TL8), and Alanya (eight hours, TL23).

WHERE TO STAY Mersin's hotels are aimed at the business market, so they are more functional than exciting.

If you need to stay overnight in order to catch the ferry to Northern Cyprus, the **Lades Motel** (*22 rooms; Inonu Caddesi, Tasucu; \ 324 74140741; www.ladesmotel.com; $$*) is a good-value place with private beach, two restaurants and an outdoor pool.

SOUTH TO THE COAST AT TARSUS

If, after visiting Cappadocia, you are heading south towards Adana, there is one jewel on the edge of the Cappadocian boundary that should not be missed: this is Eski Gümüş, the 10th-century rock-cut monastery, only rediscovered in 1963 by an English professor. Before that it was used as stabling by the villagers for their animals, and as a result the condition of the frescoes here is almost perfect, far better than those in the churches at Göreme, which the guardian disparagingly refers to as *bozuk*, an onomatopoeic Turkish word equating to the German *kaputt*.

If your departure point is Ürgüp, you can also incorporate the Soğanlı Valley (see page 156), before heading on to break your journey at Adana or even Antakya.

WHAT TO SEE

Eski Gümüşler Monastery
(*9km east of Niğde;* ⊕ *daily 08.30–12.00 & 13.00–17.00; adult TL3*) The whole complex is set behind tall trees and cut into the promontory behind, so on arrival you cannot see the entrance properly. Once through the gate, however, you will pass through the arched carved entrance into a rock-cut passageway leading out into a square courtyard open to the sky, with all the rooms cut into the rock on four sides. This style of rock-cut monastery is unique in Cappadocia.

The main church is quite lovely with four tall fine pillars supporting the dome, all carved from the rock. The frescoes are in exquisite colours with deep blues often used as the background. Even the pillars are beautifully covered in painted decoration. On the left wall as you enter are an Annunciation scene and a Nativity. In the central apse Christ Pantokrator reigns in the centre, flanked by the Virgin, Archangel Michael, the symbols of Matthew and Luke, and John the Baptist, along with the Apostles and the Evangelists, the Virgin praying and the priests. The left-side apse has a remarkable fresco of the Virgin and Child, where the Virgin is smiling serenely. All the frescoes are thought to date from the 11th century. The area above the main dome by the altar was damaged by damp, and this is the only damaged patch in the church, the result of natural rather than manmade causes for a change. The pillars have cuts near the bottom where wax was collected from candles and then re-used. A shaft with hand-holes in the walls leads up to the higher storey which was bedrooms and a library for the monks. A metal staircase has been built up from the outside to help you reach it more easily. On the walls of the bedroom above the church are extraordinary wall paintings of animals showing deer, lions, ostriches or storks, and men hunting them with bows and arrows, thought to illustrate Aesop's Fables.

There is a large refectory which would probably have accommodated 50–60 monks, with a rock table and benches either side still visible but set down at floor level, as the ground level has since risen. The other curious complex of rooms is the bathroom which even has a huge wheel-shaped stone for rolling across as a privacy door. Inside this complex there is also the entrance to an underground city with two levels of subterranean rooms. Notice too a wine-press area, and above the main entrance a slit for pouring hot oil on enemies' heads.

Getting there and away Just 1–2km before Niğde a yellow sign points off left 4km to Gümüşler. It then forks and you follow the one marked Eski Gümüşler Manastırı. The narrow road gradually climbs to the village, at the far end of which you will spot a yellow sign announcing it. Minibuses run from Niğde's *otogar* every hour to Gümüşler.

NİĞDE *Telephone code: 388*

The modern road now bypasses the town but if you are interested in Seljuk and Mongol architecture you may like to make a short detour here to see some very fine monuments. As you approach the town you will notice the 11th-century citadel rising up above it. Near this is the striking Alaeddin Mosque (1223), looking like a caravanserai with a minaret, together with the Mongolian conical *türbe* of Hudabend Hatun (1312). This superb 16-sided *türbe* is more beautiful in many ways than the more famous Döner Kümbet of Kayseri, boasting superb carvings and on a much larger scale than most *türbes*. Other buildings worth taking a look at are the

Mongolian Sungur Bey Mosque and Tomb (1335) with beautiful portals, the Ak Medrese (1409), now a museum containing relics of the area from Hittite times through to Ottoman times, the Eskiciler Çeşme (Fountain) built in 1421 and the Şah Mesciti, a little 15th-century oratory with recycled Byzantine capitals.

GETTING THERE Buses run from Niğde's *otogar* to and from Konya (four hours, TL20), Adana (four hours, TL15), and Ankara (five hours, TL25). Niğde is also on the Ankara–Adana train line but there is only one service a day, either early morning (06.00) to Adana or late at night (23.30) to Ankara.

DRAMATIC DESCENT TO THE MEDITERRANEAN

South of Niğde and heading for the coast at Tarsus the scenery is very dramatic and alpine-looking. Snow-covered peaks rise up to 3,585m and the lower slopes are covered in pine trees. On joining the main highway from Ankara the sudden increase in the volume of traffic comes as something of a shock. There has been so little traffic on the roads generally that the numbers of trucks transiting here seems grossly excessive. There are also many holidaying Germans towing caravans.

From Pozantı southwards a toll motorway takes you down the final 75km to the coast at Tarsus. The road makes a spectacular descent through the Cilician Gates towards the coast, passing many places to stop and eat, ranging from very simple truck stops to prettily laid-out restaurants. It is worth avoiding this route in reverse, heading inland from the coast, as the heavily laden trucks crawl up the painful climb in first gear, and you have an endless series of them to overtake around the hairpin bends.

TARSUS *Telephone code: 324; 30km east of Mersin (Icel)*

Famous as the birthplace of St Paul and as the place where Cleopatra landed from Egypt to meet Mark Antony, Tarsus today cannot fail to disappoint. Very little of its illustrious past remains and only the ancient centre of town, where a portion of black basalt-paved Roman street has been exposed to a depth of 2–3m below today's street level, complete with *stoas* or covered walkways, gives some help to the imagination for conjuring up the scene so vividly described by Plutarch and Shakespeare.

ROMANCE AT TARSUS

Antony summoned Cleopatra here in 41 BC from Egypt to discuss his strategy for the East and, as he discovered, to embark upon one of the great love affairs of history. Plutarch sets the scene: 'She came sailing up the Cydnus on a galley whose stern was golden; the sails were purple, and the oars were silver. These, in their motion, kept tune to the music of flutes and pipes and harps. The Queen, in the dress and character of Aphrodite, lay on a couch of gold brocade, as though in a picture, while about her were pretty boys, bedight like cupids, who fanned her, and maidens habited as nereids and graces, and some made as though they were rowing, while others busied themselves about with the sails. All manner of sweet perfumes were wafted ashore from the ship, and on the shore thousands were gathered to behold her.'

Cleopatra was able to sail right up to the city of Tarsus as there was a large lake between it and the sea that has since silted up. Nor have the sweet perfumes of history lingered: today there is only an old Roman gate at the entrance to the town from Mersin, variously called St Paul's Gate, Cleopatra's Gate or the Gate of the Bitch.

ST PAUL OF TARSUS (c5BC–AD67)

After his conversion to Christianity on the road to Damascus (cAD33–36) Saul (his original Hebrew name) changed his name to Paul, the Greek version of the name. Fleeing persecution in Palestine, he returned to Tarsus and from there began his missionary journeys around Roman Asia Minor, preaching the Gospel, converting many Jews and pagans to Christianity, and writing his famous letters, collected in Acts at the end of the New Testament. He called himself Apostle to the Gentiles and is the undisputed author of at least seven of the epistles in Acts, which contain accounts of his travels and deeds. He seems to have had an unusually egalitarian attitude towards women for his time, and is considered one of the most influential New Testament authors. He died in Rome, although the exact details of how are not known. Many of his words are so familiar to us they have almost entered our subconscious, such as:

> Render therefore to all their dues: tribute to whom tribute is due; custom to whom custom; fear to whom fear; honour to whom honour.

> God hath chosen the foolish things of the world to confound the wise.

> When I was a child, I spake as a child, I understood as a child, I thought as a child: but when I became a man, I put away childish things. For now we see through a glass darkly; but then face to face.

> O death where is thy sting? O grave, where is thy victory?

Paul was born as Saul in Tarsus about 46 years after Cleopatra's meeting with Mark Antony, and was evidently proud of his birthplace, declaring to the Roman commander of Jerusalem: 'I am a Jew, a Tarsian from Cilicia, a citizen of no mean city.' In the backstreets of the old quarter of town, signposted *Antik Şehir*, an old stone well with metal lid calls itself *Sen Pol Kuyusu* (St Paul's Well), a draw for pious and curious visitors who come and pay TL2 for a sip of its water, in the hope of gaining some *baraka*, blessing from the saint. The well is said to be on the site of St Paul's house.

The river Tarsus, the ancient Cydnus, is particularly cold and turbulent, and even Alexander the Great, bathing in the Cydnus in 333BC, caught a severe chill. Today you can still visit the spectacular waterfall, *şelale*, on the river in Tarsus, lined with shaded tea-gardens and restaurants. In Hellenistic times Tarsus became a great and prosperous city, rivalling Pergamum and Alexandria both commercially and culturally, controlling the Cilician Gates, the strategic pass through the Taurus Mountains into the Anatolian heartland. Capital of the Roman province of Cilicia, Cicero was sent off to be governor here from 51–50BC, to get him out of Rome.

Among his most famous sayings was: '*O tempora, O mores!*' 'What times! What habits!' (In *Catilinam, I i*)

GETTING THERE AND AWAY Minibuses run regularly to and from Mersin (TL2) and Adana (TL3).

WHERE TO STAY Just above the waterfall, the **Tarsus Mersin Oteli** (*35 rooms; Şelale Mevkii;* \ *324 6140600; $$$*) has a lovely location, though the rooms are a bit worn.

188

8

Southeastern Turkey, the Tûr Abdin and the Kurdish Heartlands

When a great man becomes a bridge, take the long way round (Kurdish)

This part of Turkey is in the process of being gradually transformed thanks to the GAP Project (see page 23) which is bringing water and irrigation to the region. As a result, from having been one of the poorest areas of the country, it is now seeing something of a boom, with plenty of government investment in industry, agriculture and tourism. Gaziantep is the outstanding example of what money can do, and its sensitively renovated old monuments and superb modern museum, exhibiting some of the most stunning mosaics in the world, is a definite highpoint. Antakya, ancient Antioch, also has good mosaics, though they look a little tired in comparison to Gaziantep's. Northeast of Gaziantep almost everyone finds time to visit the famous and highly photogenic mountain sanctuary of Nemrut Dağı, even though it is so remote, and further east the Kurdish capital of Diyarbakır stands menacingly with its black walls and unusual collection of churches. South from Diyarbakır a definite excursion should be made to Mardin and the Tûr Abdin monasteries, still functioning remnants of Eastern Christianity. Finally, on the way to Lake Van, Hasankeyf in its gorge on the river Tigris is a highly recommended lunch stop. Seven nights is the minimum time you will need to explore this rewarding area, full of contrasts, where Turkey meets Syria and the Mesopotamian Plain.

If you are heading for the coast imagining you will have a spell of rest and swimming on sandy beaches, your experience here will not be a particularly salubrious one, as the stretch from Mersin eastwards is a huge flat alluvial plain created by the three large local rivers, the Tarsus, the Seyhan and the Ceyhan. Lining the highway that runs between Mersin and Adana is an endless sprawling ribbon of industrial development with factories belching out smoke, and beyond, rice fields and cotton plantations reach as far as the eye can see. In the summer months it is particularly hot and sticky, far hotter than the Aegean coast to the west. To reach a coastline that is pleasant for a few days' relaxation you must either head west to Silifke and Taşucu where there are a few good beaches with hotels, or continue east and fork south towards Antakya to reach the coast at Arsuz (Uluçinar) or Samandağ. Inland from Adana is the Ceyhan Dam and reservoir, a popular spot with local residents for boating and picnics.

ADANA *Telephone code: 322*

As the centre of a rich agricultural region and the prosperous cotton industry, Adana has grown rapidly and continues to do so, becoming Turkey's fourth most populous city after Istanbul, Ankara and Izmir. As such it is a major transport hub

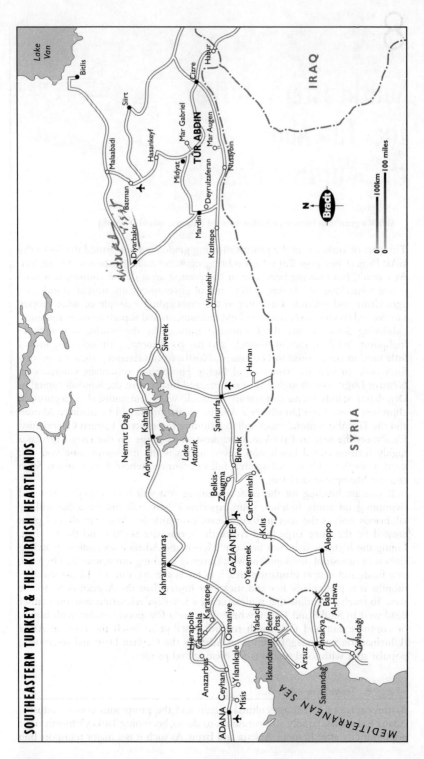

SOUTHEASTERN TURKEY & THE KURDISH HEARTLANDS

Lake Van

Bitlis

Siirt

Malabadi

Hasankeyf

Midyat · Mar Gabriel

Batman

Diyarbakır

TUR ABDIN

Mar Augen

Nusaybin

Deyrulzaferan

Mardin

Kızıltepe

Viranşehir

Cizre

Habur

IRAQ

Harran

Siverek

Şanlıurfa

Nemrut Dağı

Kahta

Adıyaman

Lake Atatürk

Belkis-
Zeugma

Birecik

Carchemish

SYRIA

Kahramanmaraş

Kilis

Aleppo

GAZIANTEP

Yesemek

Hierapolis

Castabala

Karatepe

Osmaniye

Yakacık

Belen
Pass

Bab
Al-Hawa

Anazarbus

Yılankale

Ceyhan

Misis

ADANA

İskenderun

Antakya

Arsuz

Samandağ

Yayladağı

MEDITERRANEAN SEA

N

Bradt

0 — 100km
0 — 100 miles

in the region, its airport having many daily flights to Istanbul and Ankara. It also has a big American military base.

GETTING THERE AND AWAY

By air The airport is 4km to the west of the city centre. (See www.adanahavaalani.com; ☏ 4350308.) Both Turkish Airlines (*www.anadolujet.com*) and Onur Air (*www.onurair.com.tr*) operate regular daily flights from Adana to Ankara (one hour), Istanbul (90 minutes) and Izmir (90 minutes). There are plenty of taxis available to take you into the centre (TL10).

By train The station is just 1.5km north of the main street where most of the hotels are to be found (İnönü Caddesi). Its façade is decorated with fine tiles. The *Toros Ekspres* runs to Gaziantep at 05.05 three times a week (six hours, TL9), while the *İcanadolu Mavi* train runs to Istanbul's Haydarpaşa Station (19 hours, TL32), travelling via Konya. It leaves daily at 14.10. Check with www.seat61.com for the up-to-date situation of these services as they can sometimes be suspended. A new overnight sleeper service from Adana to Aleppo began in June 2010 running weekly on Fridays leaving Adana at 00.05, arriving Aleppo 08.20. From there several services a day run to and from Damascus.

By bus The *otogar* is 6km west of the centre, 2km beyond the airport. *Dolmuşes* also run from here to pretty much anywhere, costing a little more than the buses but with quicker journey times. For example, the bus to Adıyaman (for Nemrut Dağı) runs seven times a day, takes six hours and costs TL35. The bus from Adana to Antakya costs TL15 and takes about four hours.

GETTING AROUND Taxis are readily available to take you from the airport to the city centre (TL10) or from the *otogar* (TL15).

TOURIST INFORMATION Adana's tourist office is on the main street of Atatürk Caddesi, with a smaller one at the airport. It has a few maps and leaflets to hand out. Opening hours are: 08.00–12.00 & 13.00–17.00 daily.

WHERE TO STAY As you would expect from Turkey's fourth largest city, the full range is here, from the Hilton to the backpacker's delight.

⌂ **Adana Hiltonsa** (308 rooms) Sinanpasa Mahallesi; ☏ 3555000; www.adana.hilton.com. Fabulous location on the river with amazing views over the Sabanci Mosque. Outdoor & indoor pools, sauna & 2 restaurants. $$$$
⌂ **Bosnalı Hotel** (11 rooms) Şeyhan Caddesi; ☏ 3598000; www.hotelbosnali.com. One of the few remaining mansions along the bank of the Seyhan River near the old stone bridge, now painstakingly restored to be Adana's first boutique hotel. At 110 years old, it used to be owned by a Bosnian. AC & Wi-Fi. $$$$
⌂ **Mavi Surmeli** (117 rooms) Inonu Caddesi; ☏ 3633437; www.mavisurmeli.com. Swish &

luxurious central modern block with spacious rooms. Sauna & 2 restaurants. $$$$
⌂ **Butik Hotel Princess Maya** (32 rooms) Turhan Cemal Beriker Bulvarı; ☏ 4590966; e princessmaya@ttnet.net.tr. One of Adana's few boutique hotels in an older 4-storey building in the city centre has its own restaurant. $$$
⌂ **Mercan Hotel** (32 rooms) Ocak Meydanı; ☏ 3512603. Much more characterful place with good stylish rooms & b/fast area. $$
⌂ **Selibra Otel** (26 rooms) Inonu Caddesi; ☏ 3633676. Spacious basic rooms with en-suite facilities. Very good value. $

WHERE TO EAT The famous hot **Adana kebab** is the obvious speciality here, minced lamb spiced up with hot red pepper, then charcoal-grilled like *köfte*. The standard accompaniment is flat Arab-style bread, chopped red onions and parsley. The famous Adana drink is *salgam*, made from boiled turnips, carrots and vinegar, and is unmistakeable in its colour, bright red, as well as its taste. Local people swear it helps an upset stomach by killing off bacteria, and enjoy it as an accompaniment to kebabs and *rakı*.

✗ **Halikarnas** Güzelyalı Mahallesi, Uğur Mumcu Bulvarı 54/B; ✎ 2345783. Excellent fish restaurant with good meze. Friendly service. Try the sea bass in apple vinegar. Licensed. $$$

✗ **Öz Asmaaltı** Pazarlar Caddesi; ✎ 3514028; ⊕ 11.00–23.00. Adana's finest restaurant outside the hotels, close to the Mercan, the décor is plain but the *mezze* & kebabs are memorable. Licensed. $$$

✗ **Guest** Cemal Paşa Mahallesi, Etem Ekin Sokak, Arsava Apt; ✎ 4592028. An elegant yet homely place serving an international menu. Guest chicken with tropical fruit is the house speciality. In summer you can dine outside in the garden & at w/ends there is live jazz. Licensed. $$

✗ **Café Keyif** Ziyapaşa Bulvarı; ✎ 4577820; ⊕ 08.30–22.00. Convincing imitation of a British pub, serving salads & Efes beer, with fun outside seating in booths. $$

✗ **Kebap 52** Kurtuluş Mahallesi, Sinasi Efendi Caddesi; licensed kebab place serving an excellent Adana kebab. Outdoor terrace. $

✗ **Unal Et Lokantasi** Dörtyol Ağzi, Teknosa arkası, Cınarlı ishanı; ✎ 3631585. Simple kebab restaurant famed for its Konya *tandir* kebab, slow baked lamb shank served with rice, onion & tomato. Unlicensed. $

ENTERTAINMENT AND NIGHTLIFE Cazara (*Ziyapaşa Caddesi;* ✎ *4593305;* ⊕ *11.00–03.00 Mon–Sat*) offers live music with heavy metal and guitar bands.

SHOPPING AND OTHER PRACTICALITIES The high-rise Cetinkaya shopping centre standing on Kuruköprü Meydanı (at the western end of İnönü Caddesi) will provide you with pretty much anything you may be looking for.

There are plenty of internet cafés along İnönü Caddesi. Car hire is available from Avis (✎ *4355975; www.avis.com*) and Hertz (✎ *4533045; www.hertz.com*), both with offices on Ziyapaşa Bulvarı. Avis also has an office at Adana airport.

WHAT TO SEE As with Mersin and Tarsus, Adana's history stretches back to the 1st millennium BC, but very little remains to be seen today. The city's only ancient monument of note is the fine 319m-long bridge, **Taş Köprü (Stone Bridge)**, built under Hadrian and restored under Justinian, which spans the Seyhan River in the centre of the city. Of the bridge's original 21 arches only 14 have survived. It was repaired on several occasions under the Ottomans, and still carries much traffic. It was built here as the lowest possible ford over the wide river, when it was a vital part of the Silk Road linking the heartland of Anatolia to the coast through the mountain pass known as the Cilician Gates.

On the main street that leads up to the Taş Köprü, just 200m before reaching the river, stands Adana's **Ulu Cami (Great Mosque)**, a distinctive building immediately recognisable by its alternating black and white stonework, an architectural feature known as *ablaq*, commonly used in neighbouring Syria and associated with Mameluke times (1315–1516). This mosque was late Mameluke, built in 1507 by Halil Bey, emir of the Ramazanoğlu Turks who ruled Cilicia before the Ottoman conquest in 1516. Inside, the Iznik and Kütahya tiles used to adorn the walls of his tomb and the prayer niche are among the finest in Turkey. It can be visited except during prayer times. Close by in Adana's old quarter is the **Çarşi Hamamı**, a lovely domed Turkish bath with marble interior, still functioning and open to all. Just opposite it is the late Ottoman clock tower built in 1881, a city landmark, beside which you will find the **Kapali Çarşi (Covered Bazaar)**.

The fairy chimneys of Cappadocia were
formed over millennia as the soft, porous
tufa rock was eroded by wind, snow and rain,
leaving only the stacks protected by a
fragment of hard stone (SS) page 141

above   *Gecekondular*, little houses of every hue built by the many Anatolian peasants who have flocked to Ankara, cling to the steep hillsides around the Turkish capital (KD/DT) page 75

below   Covering over 1km² in the centre of Ankara, the sheer size of Atatürk's Mausoleum is testament to the personality cult that still surrounds the founder of the Republic of Turkey (TI/DT) page 93

bottom   The natural fortress of Uçhisar, now the highest village in Cappadocia, is riddled with manmade dwellings and dovecotes, some of which now serve as high-end hotels (E/DT) page 149

right **Diyarbakır is considered to be the unofficial capital of Kurdistan, and the black basalt walls enclosing its Old City give it a unique feel within Turkey** (RL/A) page 231

below left **With a mountain setting and chalets, the little resort of Uzungöl has an almost alpine feel** (M/DT) page 351

below right **Mardin's Old Town is full of beautifully carved, Arab-style buildings, many of them recently restored** (SI/DT) page 245

bottom **Amasra, a small port on the Black Sea coast, is prized for its pretty beaches and natural setting** (KD/DT) page 369

above left Many of Safranbolu's traditional Ottoman houses have been restored; their beautifully carved ceilings and plasterwork corresponded to the wealth of the owner (BC/DT) page 370

above right Işak Paşa Sarayı contains a maze-like series of rooms with intricately carved portals (SS) page 300

left The name of Sirçali Medrese in Konya means 'glazed madrasa', after the exquisite glazed mosaic tiles used in its decoration, painted with Koranic inscriptions (IS/A) page 176

below Şeytan Kalesi, or Devil's Castle, is one of the most dramatically sited castles in the country, perched above a 300m-high gorge (DD) page 325

above left   The area around Yusufeli is dotted with medieval ruins and Georgian churches, including the remains of Işhan Monastery, dating from the 7th century (IS/A) page 331

above right   The ribbed dome of Mardin's Sultan Isa Medresesi, built in 1385, overlooks the Mesopotamian Plain (NG) page 248

right & below   Sumela Monastery clings Tibetan-like to a high cliff-face above deep evergreen forests. Its impressive wall frescoes are only reachable on foot up a steep path (AY/DT) (SH/DT) page 359

above   A nomadic tribe caravan in the Taurus Mountains (IS/A) page 233

below   Whirling dervish dances (*semas*) are the centre of attention during the Mevlâna Festival in Konya, celebrating the anniversary of the death of the Sufi mystic Celaleddin Rumi, aka Mevlâna (MI/A) page 171

above left   Kurdish nomad children living on the lower slopes of Mount Ararat (DD) page 304

above right   Terraced tea plantations cover the slopes of the Pontic range all along the Black Sea coast (EP/A) page 343

right   Market stalls selling spices, dried fruits and other wares line the paths up to Ankara's old citadel (SS) page 85

below   Tea is an integral part of any business transaction; here customers have tea in a harness maker's shop, Ankara (IS/A) page 350

Vast, eerily blue lake Van's tiny islands are graced with
Armenian churches, including the 10th-century
Akdamar Church, a masterpiece of early art
(IS/A) page 273

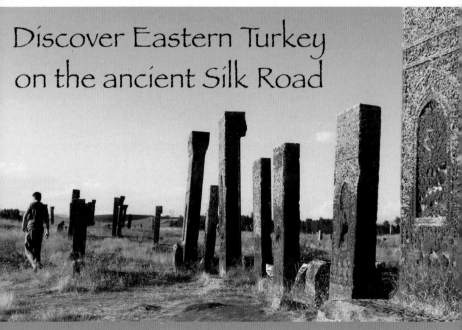

Discover Eastern Turkey
on the ancient Silk Road

Back at the river fronting the modern bridge is the gigantic **Sabanci Central Mosque**, completed in 1998, the largest mosque in Turkey, modelled on Istanbul's Blue Mosque and Edirne's **Selimiye Mosque**, the masterpiece of the great Ottoman architect Sinan. It is the only other mosque in the whole country to have six minarets like the Blue Mosque. It is named after Sakip Sabanci, the richest man in Turkey, an incredibly successful businessman who had his own bank, Sabanci Bank. He died in 2004 but was a generous philanthropist and a pious man. The mosque accommodates 20,000 worshippers and one of the minarets has a lift to the top.

Archaeological Museum (*Behind the Sabanci Central Mosque;* \ *4543855;* ⊕ *08.30–12.00 & 13.30–17.00 Tue–Sun; adult TL5*) This modern building is where you must come to get a feel for Adana's rich past, as all the local finds are on display here, from Hittite times through to the Hellenistic and Roman eras. Look out for the figure in crystal of a Hittite god and some exquisite Urartian gold belts dating from c600BC. The finest Roman exhibit is a marble sarcophagus with battle scenes featuring Achilles, and the Roman mosaic with animals listening to music is also interesting.

Ethnography Museum (*Inönü Caddesi;* \ *3633717;* ⊕ *08.30–12.00 & 13.30–17.00 Tue–Sun; adult TL3*) Set away from the other sites to the west of the old quarter, this museum is housed in an old church. As well as weaponry, copper kitchenware, carpets and textiles, it includes a reconstruction of a traditional Adana Ottoman house.

FROM ADANA TO ANTAKYA

Eastwards from Adana there are a number of excursions which, with your own transport, you can make *en route* to Antakya or to Adıyaman (Nemrut Dağı), some more interesting than others.

The first and least interesting comes 28km after Adana, where a sign points right to Yakapınar, the name of the modern village where the **mosaic of Misis**, such as remains of it, is to be found. This mosaic, originally the floor of a basilica, represents Noah's Ark and the animals, but is very fragmented and difficult to make out. It dates from the 4th century, as does the bridge which crosses the Seyhan River 200m further on. This and a few scattered remains of column drums and capitals are all that remains of the ancient Roman city of Mopseustia, named after its founder Mopsus. The mosaic is housed in a simple museum (⊕ *09.00–17.00 Tue–Sun; adult TL2*).

Some 14km east from the Yakapınar turn-off you should start looking out for the magnificent **12th-century Armenian castle of Yılanlıkale** (⊕ *always open; adult TL1*) on a hill about 1km to the right of the road. You will notice a small tarmac road heading the 2km across to it, and this takes you to within ten minutes' walk of the summit. The hill is not high but the castle dominates the flat river plain with ease, and from the top you can see the river snaking over the plain. It did not, however, earn its name 'Castle of the Snake' from this, but from the Armenian king who built it, who was known as the King of the Snakes. Snakes still abound in the region and are eaten with relish by the local pigs whose flabby snouts protect them from bites. As you walk closer you see the elaborate lines of the castle's defence unfold. You enter through the first gateway in the walls and proceed up through the second to the magnificent main gate between two powerfully built towers. A recent landslip near the entrance now means that a bit of clambering is necessary to pass through this gateway. Its ceiling has simple vaulting as well as a slit for pouring oil on the enemy. Once inside, the castle opens before you. Stairs can still be climbed up to the main watch tower by the gate, remarkably preserved and offering an excellent panorama. The keep is difficult to climb into as the entrance is now too high to reach without steps or a ladder. Inside are huge vaulted rooms of the royal family; in some of the lower rooms little frogs hop around in the dark. Steps lead onto the walls which can be followed for a while.

A pleasant detour can be made from Ceyhan, 6km beyond the Yılanlıkale turn-off, to the **ruins of Anazarbus**, a Roman–Byzantine city 30km to the north. The site is in a lovely setting on the very edge of the Cilician Plain at the foot of a mountain. From Ceyhan you pass through Ayşehoca, from which a road to the right takes you to the little village of Anavarza 4km away. Founded after the 1st century BC, Anazarbus flourished during the Roman period. It was destroyed and rebuilt twice at the beginning of the Byzantine era. In the 7th and 8th centuries it was pillaged several times by the Arabs, eventually becoming the Arab town of 'Ain Zarba. From the 10th to the 12th centuries it was governed by Cilician Armenians who made it their capital. Ravaged frequently by the Mamelukes, it was finally abandoned. The 3rd-century triumphal arch, Corinthian in style, is the most interesting monument left standing. From the theatre a stairway cut into the rock leads up to the upper town, passing a small Byzantine oratory with fragmentary paintings. The fortress at the top is well preserved and encloses the funerary church of the Cilician Armenian kings, which still has some frescoes inside. From the summit you can spot a few arches that remain from the ancient city's aqueduct. The village of Anavarza has a handful of tea-houses and a simple shop, but it is probably best to have some refreshment supplies of your own.

Modern highways, some of them toll-motorways, have transformed journey times in this part of Turkey, but whichever type of road you are on, you come on some point to a major fork; right to İskenderun and Antakya, left to Osmaniye and Kahramanmaraş. In the arc of that fork on a low hill at the outlet of the narrow valley which commands the Plain of Issus, stands another 12th-century Armenian fortress, Toprakkale, built of lowering black basalt. Much fought over by the Armenians and the Crusaders in medieval times, it was abandoned around 1337. It is difficult to reach as there is no proper road to it, and inside it is not as well preserved as Yılanlıkale. The walls are quite crumbling and care needs to be taken not to fall down any cisterns overgrown with scrub and brambles.

By heading left at the fork to Osmaniye, you lose a lot of the heavy lorry traffic which is pushing on into Syria and Iraq. These busy patches make driving far more of a strain than on the normally empty roads of the Anatolian interior, and if you are self-driving, your itinerary would do well to avoid these main transit routes wherever possible.

SOUTH TO ANTAKYA

South of Toprakkale, at the point where the road turns south towards İskenderun, you leave the Cilician Plain behind and enter a region now called Hatay, formerly known by the French ruling powers as the Sanjak of Alexandretta.

ISSUS You come first to the Plain of Issus, the scene of Alexander the Great's famous defeat of the Persians under Darius III in 333BC, after which he was able to penetrate southwards to Syria. A little further on at the sign to Yeşilkent are the remains of a fine Roman aqueduct beside the road, which used to bring water from the Amanos Mountains to the city of Issus. Other remnants of Issus are a harbour, water reservoirs, a chapel and a temple. Dörtyol, near the coast, is the terminal of the oil pipeline from the Kirkuk oilfields in Iraq.

THE HATAY

The name 'Hatay' is thought to come from Hatina, the name of a political union established on the Amik Plain by Hittite principalities in 1190BC. Atatürk gave the province this name as a reference to the unity of the areas around Iskenderun and Antakya into one political entity. It is a region with a very mixed population, as one might expect from its geographical location, with large communities of Arabs, Muslims and Christians mixed in together. With the collapse of the Ottoman Empire after World War I it was incorporated into Syria under the French Mandate in 1918, but the French gave it to Turkey in 1939 to buy Turkish support in anticipation of a new war against Germany. The Syrians have never accepted the transfer and most Syrian maps still show it as part of Syria. At a stroke, Aleppo was effectively severed from its port of İskenderun (Alexandretta), its natural outlet to the Mediterranean. Pleasantly hilly, it is a welcome contrast with the flat Plain of Cilicia.

YAKACIK About 20km before İskenderun is a short detour to Yakacık, the former Payas, where you will see a huge **16th-century Ottoman caravanserai complex** named after Sokullu Mehmet Paşa, *vizir* to three different sultans between 1564 and 1579. It is the largest complex in the region (⊕ *08.00–17.00; adult TL3*), and includes a mosque, a Koranic school (*medrese*), a double baths and a covered bazaar with 45 shops, a soup kitchen and spacious courtyards, leading to a bridge over a moat to a fortress on the sea, known as the Tower of the Jinns. The complex was built at the order of Selim II with the advice of the great architect Sinan, famous for his many mosques, including the Süleymaniye in Istanbul, and the Sokullu Mehmet Paşa Mosque, where the great *vizir* is buried. Close by is **Payas Fortress**, built by the Crusaders, then demolished and rebuilt by the Ottomans in the 16th century. Surrounded by a moat, it has seven bastions and eight towers. It was used as a prison in the last century.

İSKENDERUN You next reach İskenderun, the former Alexandretta, founded by Alexander the Great after his defeat of the Persians. The modern highway today bypasses the city, a busy port and commercial centre, which has an attractive seafront lined with good hotels and restaurants, and an atmosphere that is an attractive combination of Mediterranean, Anatolian and Syrian. Nothing remains to be seen of its past monuments. From Iskenderun a small road leads 30km south along the coast to Arsuz (Uluçınar), a beach resort much favoured by Arabs crossing from Syria, with restaurants and disco-bars.

BELEN PASS Whether on the old road or the new highway, the road to Antakya now heads inland winding its way steeply up through the mountains to the Belen Pass. Sometimes regarded as the Gates to Syria, Belen has been the transit point of all armies throughout history. When Süleyman the Magnificent returned through here from his military campaign in Iran in 1548, he commissioned a fine caravanserai, bath and mosque here, built according to a design by Sinan, his great court architect. The caravanserai has now been restored as a culture centre and the baths are still in use today. Belen is an attractive place, becoming increasingly popular as a summer resort and famous for its spa waters used in the bath which are meant to aid stomach and digestive problems.

ORONTES RIVER The views from the top and during the descent are spectacular over the Orontes Valley and Lake Amik, an artificial lake created by blocking the

Southeastern Turkey, the Tür Abdin and the Kurdish Heartlands **SOUTH TO ANTAKYA**

8

The name 'Hatay' is thought to come from Hatina, the name of a political union established on the Amik Plain by Hittite principalities in 1190BC. Atatürk gave the province this name as a reference to the unity of the areas around Iskenderun and Antakya into one political entity. It is a region with a very mixed population, as one might expect from its geographical location, with large communities of Arabs, Muslims and Christians mixed in together. With the collapse of the Ottoman Empire after World War I it was incorporated into Syria under the French Mandate in 1918, but the French gave it to Turkey in 1939 to buy Turkish support in anticipation of a new war against Germany. The Syrians have never accepted the transfer and most Syrian maps still show it as part of Syria. At a stroke, Aleppo was effectively severed from its port of İskenderun (Alexandretta), its natural outlet to the Mediterranean. Pleasantly hilly, it is a welcome contrast with the flat Plain of Cilicia.

195

Orontes River lower down. The Orontes originates in Lebanon's Bekaa Valley and flows into the Mediterranean at Samandağ. It is 380km long, and only the final quarter of it flows through Turkey. The name Orontes means 'coming from the east'. It flows in reverse direction to normal, from south to north, hence its local name 'Asi, meaning 'rebel' in Turkish and in Arabic. The hillsides all around are covered in pine forests, very impressive and extensive, reminiscent of Syria's Ansariye Mountains. On the descent a short detour of 4km can be made to see the castle at **Bakras**, one of the main strongholds of the Mamelukes in the defence of northern Syria. Set up on a peak it was built to control the route to the Arabian Peninsula by the Byzantines and Mamelukes rather than Crusaders, who captured it in 1097 during their siege of Antioch. It was abandoned after the Ottoman conquest in the 16th century.

ANTAKYA *Telephone code: 326*

Antakya is 198km from Adana, 254km from Gaziantep and 309km from Kahramanmaraş.

Although modern suburbs now sprawl untidily round the edges of the city, the old centre of Antakya, the site of ancient Antioch, pleasantly situated on the banks of the Orontes River, still has a certain charm if you go in search of it. Your best chance of finding it is to spend a night or two in the guesthouse of either the Catholic or the Protestant church, both of which are close to the old quarter. The city's reputation is for tolerance and multiculturalism. At one time Greek, Hebrew, Persian and Latin were all spoken in its streets. Libanius, Roman philosopher and historian, described it thus: 'If your aim in travelling is to get acquainted with different cultures and lifestyles, it is enough to visit Antioch. There is no other place in the world that has so many cultures in one place.'

HISTORY In the scramble for power that followed Alexander's death at the age of 33 from fever, four states emerged under four of Alexander's generals. Seleucus got Syria, a large portion of Asia Minor and eastward to India; Ptolemy got Egypt; the rest of Asia Minor went to Antigonus; and Antipater acquired Macedonia. Throughout the Hellenistic and Roman periods it was Antioch in Syria and Alexandria in Egypt that stood out as the most influential and enduring. In its Roman heyday Antioch's population was estimated at half a million, a heterogeneous and excitable collection of Cretans, Macedonians, native Syrians and expatriate Jews. Specialising in sumptuous games and entertainments, it became a byword for luxury and depravity, without neglecting literature, scholarship and the arts. The Old City was destroyed by a series of earthquakes in the 6th century, but its location ensured its commercial prosperity throughout invasion by Armenians, Persians, Byzantines, Seljuks and Crusaders. It was held as the capital of a Frankish principality for most of the 12th and 13th centuries. The town never recovered from its capture and destruction by Sultan Baibars of Egypt and his Mamelukes, and from its long occupation by Arabs until taken by Selim the Grim in 1516.

GETTING THERE AND AWAY

By air Hatay airport (*Turkish Airlines office;* \ *4440849*) has recently opened and offers twice-daily scheduled flights to and from Istanbul and Izmir, and once a day to and from Ankara. These flights are operated by Turkish Airlines (*www.anadolujet.com*), who also fly from here to Ercan in Northern Cyprus. Germania Airlines (*www.flygermania.de*), a low cost German airline, also flies between Hatay and Berlin-Tegel and Hanover, while Hamburg International Airlines (*www.hamburg-international.de*) flies between here and Cologne/Bonn and

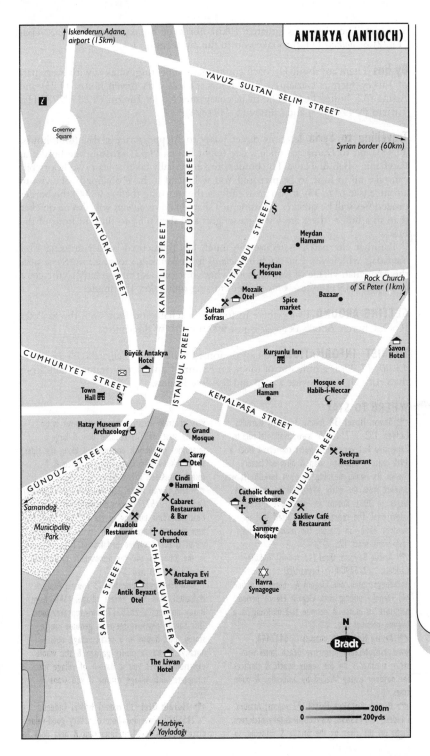

ANTAKYA (ANTIOCH)

Iskenderun, Adana, airport (15km)

YAVUZ SULTAN SELIM STREET

Syrian border (60km)

Governor Square

IZZET GÜÇLÜ STREET

KANATLI STREET

ISTANBUL STREET

ATATÜRK STREET

Meydan Hamamı

Meydan Mosque

Mozaik Otel

Sultan Sofrası

Spice market

Bazaar

Rock Church of St Peter (1km)

CUMHURIYET STREET

Büyük Antakya Hotel

Kurşunlu Inn

Savon Hotel

ISTANBUL STREET

Town Hall

Yeni Hamam

Mosque of Habib-i-Neccar

KEMALPAŞA STREET

Hatay Museum of Archaeology

Grand Mosque

Saray Otel

İNÖNÜ STREET

Cindi Hamami

Catholic church & guesthouse

Svekya Restaurant

KURTULUŞ STREET

GÜNDÜZ STREET

Cabaret Restaurant & Bar

Sakliev Café & Restaurant

Samandağ

Municipality Park

Anadolu Restaurant

Orthodox church

Sarımeye Mosque

SARAY STREET

SIHALI KUVVETLER ST

Antakya Evi Restaurant

Havra Synagogue

Antik Beyazıt Otel

N

Bradt

The Liwan Hotel

0 ——— 200m
0 ——— 200yds

Harbiye, Yayladağı

Southeastern Turkey, the Tûr Abdin and the Kurdish Heartlands ANTAKYA

8

197

Stuttgart. The airport is situated 19km north of Antakya and there are taxis (TL22) or *dolmuş* (TL2) to take you to the city centre.

By bus There are about 11 coach companies connecting Antakya with every part of Turkey, such as Gaziantep (four hours, TL18), Urfa (seven hours, TL25) and Adana (3.5 hours, TL15). The main companies are Jet Turizm (\ *2272797*), Has Turizm (\ *4440031*) and Ulusoy (\ *4441888*).

Travelling to Syria Jet runs direct buses to Aleppo twice a day (four hours, TL18), and to Damascus once a day (eight hours, TL32), crossing the border at Reyhanlı – Bab Al-Hawa. The border crossing usually takes at least two hours, but can take up to four, so be prepared. You will need to have obtained your visa in advance (see page 45). If you cross early in the morning (before 08.00) the border procedures will be quicker. Crossing in a shared taxi or *dolmuş* will also be quicker than in a bus, as there are fewer passengers and they tend to push in front of the buses.

Another alternative is to use the much less frequented border crossing after Yayladağ, which you can reach by *dolmuş* from Antakya, crossing into Syria near the Armenian village of Kassab, from where microbuses run regularly to the coast at Lattakia (45 minutes). This border crossing only takes 15 minutes.

GETTING AROUND Everywhere in town is reachable on foot, even the St Peter Rock Church. Antakya's *otogar* is just 500m north of the centre.

TOURIST INFORMATION Antakya's tourist office (⊕ *daily 08.30–12.00 & 13.00–17.00*) is a little out of town, on Atatürk Caddesi, ten minutes' walk from the centre. It can provide a map and few free leaflets.

WHERE TO STAY

⌂ **Savon Hotel** (38 rooms, 3 suites) Kurtuluş Caddesi 192; \ 2146355; www.savonhotel.com.tr. Expensive but very plush hotel converted from a 19th-century Ottoman soap & olive-oil factory (hence its name, meaning 'soap' in Turkish). It was derelict from the early 1960s till its conversion began in 2001. Rooms are plush but a little impersonal. The courtyard lends itself well to outdoor eating in season. The refined & pricey restaurant seats 125. $$$$

⌂ **Antik Beyazıt Otel** (43 rooms) Hükümet Caddesi; \ 2162900; e beyazıt@ antakbeyazitoteli.com. Elegant AC hotel in a fine old French building with elegant French period furniture to match. A definite feel of living in a bygone colonial age. $$$

⌂ **Arsuz Hotel** (45 rooms) \ 6432444; www.arsuzotel.com. Attractive beach hotel with straw sunshades on the sandy beach, & terraces for outdoor eating shaded by umbrellas & palm trees. $$$

⌂ **Büyük Antakya Hotel** (72 rooms) Atatürk Caddesi; \ 2135858; www.buyukantakyaoteli.com. Right on the river by the bridge & museum, so

very centrally located, though the river is no beauty spot with its reduced flow & large quantities of rubbish accumulated along the sides, so there's no river-facing terrace. Disco & 1 restaurant. Good b/fast buffet. $$$

⌂ **The Liwan Hotel** (24 rooms) Silahi Kuvvetler Caddesi; \ 2157777; www.theliwanhotel.com. Beautiful stone building in the old part of town, now elegantly furnished with crystal chandeliers, velvet chairs & carved bed frames. A piano stands in the lobby to add the atmosphere of Antakya from 100 years ago. $$$

⌂ **Beytuturab-Toprakev** (3 rooms) Atatürk Mahallesi, 2km from Ekinci village, 15km from Hatay airport; \ 2638217; www.toprakev.com. This simple place is set in a genuine single-storey mud house in a small village outside Antakya. It has a pretty garden & the whole experience gives you a flavour of village life, complete with village cuisine if you want it. $$

⌂ **Mozaik Otel** (30 rooms) Istiklal Caddesi; \ 2155020; www.mosaikotel.com. Very good-value place with an excellent restaurant & next door to

Sultan Sofrası. Mosaics figure in the décor, & the Orontes is close by. $$

🏠 **Catholic Church Guesthouse** (8 rooms) Kurtuluş Caddesi, Kutlu Sokak; ✆ 2149001; e domenicobertogli@hotmail.com. It is usually necessary to make reservations in advance, but you may be lucky & take a chance. There is a nominal fee & the rooms are spotlessly clean, but no AC, which can be a problem in high summer. There is a communal kitchen where you can prepare meals & keep your provisions in a communal fridge. Everything is very clean & you are expected to keep it that way & do your own washing up. When the priest is here you are expected to attend mass. During my stay the other guests were a pair of holidaying Polish priests, a Swedish apprentice priest & his psychology-student girlfriend. $

🏠 **Saray Otel** (35 rooms) Hürriyet Caddesi; ✆ 2149001. Beside Ulu Cami, good value with spotlessly clean AC rooms. $

✖ **WHERE TO EAT** Antakya's specialities include pomegranate syrup, orange blossom water, salty yoghurt and aged goat cheese (*çokelek*). The local extra virgin olive oil is also very good. The influence of Syrian and Lebanese dishes can easily be recognised in the rich variety of appetisers (*mezze*), and the altar meal of the Hittites (*ashir*) is still being served. Ottoman and French influence can also be detected, and together all these cultures have produced an incredibly opulent cuisine. Wine is freely available in Antakya, and most restaurants serve it. Shops also sell beer and wine freely in a way that is noticeably more liberal than many other cities in eastern Turkey.

✖ **Svekya Restaurant** Kurtuluş Caddesi 58; ✆ 2133947. A very fine restaurant elegantly laid out in the small rooms of an old house, with linen tablecloths & fresh flowers. $$$$

✖ **Anadolu Restaurant** Hurriyet Caddesi; ✆ 2153335; www.anadolurestaurant-haysim.com; ⏰ 10.00–23.30. An excellent restaurant offering all the local specialities. $$$

✖ **Antakya Evi Restaurant** Silahi Kuvvetler Caddesi; ✆ 2141350; ⏰ 10.00–22.00, closed Sun. One of the very few licensed places outside a hotel, set in a restored 19th-century mansion, with traditional Arabic-style food. A treat. $$$

✖ **Sakliev Café & Restaurant** Kurtuluş Caddesi, Doner Sokak 7; ✆ 2153132. ⏰ 10.00–23.00. An attractive place in a restored house with a courtyard for outdoor eating. $$

✖ **Cabaret Restaurant & Bar** ⏰ 10.30–midnight. In the old quarter, a delightful place in an old house with a tiny courtyard. The bar is upstairs, a pull for Antakya's youth, with a lively atmosphere & music. $

✖ **Sultan Sofrasi** Istiklal Caddesi; ✆ 2138759; ⏰ 09.30–22.30. Excellent range of local cuisine, very good value in a restored elegant stone mansion, next door to Mosaik Otel. $

SHOPPING AND OTHER PRACTICALITIES Antakya has its own Carrefour supermarket at the entrance to the city. A whole cluster of ATMs can be found around the roundabout by the museum.

There is also a post office on Cumhuriyet Alanı close to the museum roundabout (⏰ 08.30–12.00 & 13.30–17.00 Mon–Fri).

Turkish baths The oldest bath-house in Antakya is called **Yeni Hamam** (meaning 'New Bath'), but other functioning baths are the **Saka**, **Cindi** and **Meydan**. They were constructed during the Mamluke and Ottoman eras and are still used today for circumcision ceremonies, bachelor or bride parties before a wedding and other fun social events.

WHAT TO SEE The city today is only a shadow of its former self but is still very picturesque in places with its narrow lanes leading down to the Orontes and its segregated districts where the various religious communities held themselves apart in Ottoman times. Church bells ring out and mingle with the call to prayer here in a way that is reminiscent of the Old City of Damascus. The old stone paved streets have a central channel for rainwater drainage, and the houses appear modest from the outside, just presenting simple doors with no windows on the ground floor. Inside they often turn out to be elegant stone and wooden residences with fruit trees and central fountains in their courtyards, as in Syria. The main street which runs from one end of the city to the other and is now called Kurtuluş (Salvation) Caddesi after the liberation from the French Mandate, follows the line of the original Roman street, the magnificently colonnaded Cardo Maximus, 2.5km long and 10m wide with more than 3,200 columns, now buried some 10m below the current street level. Covered with marble and adorned with bronze statues, early sources say it was lit at night with torches, making it the world's first illuminated street. It was opened to traffic in 1935. The outline of the ancient city walls, 12km long in total, gives an indication of the extent of the city in its heyday. Mostly destroyed by earthquakes today, they were said to have 360 towers. There were once five city gates, of which only the Iron Gate, still standing to 18m high, remains, straddling a deep valley. As a centre for licentious living, Antioch was chosen by Peter for his first mission to the gentiles, and here his converts were the first to be called Christians. St Barnabas and St Paul later stayed here.

Thanks to earthquakes and the ravages of earlier conquering armies, remnants of Antioch's colourful history are few. The latest relic of the past to disappear was the Roman bridge across the Orontes, demolished in 1970 by the State Water Authority in order to widen the river bed. Today's bridge replaces it. What does remain, however, is a picturesque bazaar quarter and the **Mosque of Habib-i-Neccar**, originally a Byzantine church, converted in turn from a classical temple. Habib-i-Neccar is mentioned in the Yasin Sura of the Koran and was living in Antioch during the formative years of Christianity, working as a carpenter, carving wooden idols to the pagans. When the first disciples arrived, he heard their message about their belief in one supreme God and became their first convert, stopping his carving of idols. He was beheaded by the local pagan community for trying to save the disciples from death by stoning, and the mosque was built where his head is said to have fallen to the ground. Considered sacred by Muslims and Christians alike, its minaret was added later, and is not a church tower as some have thought. In the old bazaar area on Uzun Carsi (Long Market) is a fine 17th-century inn, Antakya's oldest, called **Kurşunlu Hani**. It was used as a stopping place on the annual pilgrimage to Mecca (the *Hajj*) that set out as a massive camel caravan from Istanbul. The two things most people come to see though are the St Peter Rock Church (Sen Piyer Kilesesi), said to be where Peter preached for the first time and founded the first Christian community, and the Archaeological Museum, famous for its collection of Roman mosaics. Some 4,000 Christians still live in the Hatay region and are not in any way persecuted or excluded by their Muslim co-residents. Antakya is still the centre of the patriarchates of Syrian Orthodox, Greek Orthodox, Greek Catholic, Maronites and Syrian Jacobites. The Antakya Patriarchate is currently situated in Damascus.

St Pierre Kilesesi (Rock Church of St Peter) (⊕ *08.30–12.00 & 13.30–16.30 Tue–Sun; adult TL8*) This landmark church receives a phenomenal number of visitors, Christian and Muslim alike, and is well signposted about 2km out of the centre on the Aleppo road, followed by a 500m climb up hill to where it is cut into the cliff of Mount Staurin, the Mountain of the Cross. There is also a large car park. The wall across the front of the cave was built by the Crusader knights in 1098, on their way through to Jerusalem. The cave measures 13m long by 9.5m wide and 7m high. On the floor there are still traces of mosaic, and there are fragmented patched of red on the walls. To the right of the altar is a tiny rock pool which was used for

baptisms, thought to cure sickness. The church was repaired in the 19th century by the Capuchin monks, and they remain its custodians today. There is a festival held here every year on 29 June, attended by a representative of the Vatican, and the cave-church was declared a pilgrimage site in 1963 by Pope Paul IV. These days it is used with special permission for special ceremonies like weddings. According to legend the cave-church was founded in AD47 by Peter, Paul and Barnabas as the first church after the main church in Jerusalem. Matthew is said to have written his Gospel here in Antakya. There used to be underground catacombs where early Christians could hide from the authorities to avoid being punished for illegal religious activity, but this escape tunnel was blocked off by a landslide in later years. It can still be seen in the far left corner of the cave, at about shoulder height. About 100m to the left above the cave look out for the very worn relief cut into the cliff of a bust flanked by someone on foot. It is thought to represent Antigonus, companion to Alexander the Great and his heir in Asia Minor.

Other places of worship The majority of Antakya's 1,500 Christians remaining here today are Greek Orthodox and their church is a large 19th-century building on Hükümet Caddesi that is decorated with some very fine Russian, Byzantine and Syrian icons. Said to be one of the most magnificent of the Eastern Orthodox churches, it is built of stone with four gates. It also houses a school, a library, a shelter for the poor and a graveyard. The **Catholic church** is a haven of serenity away from the bustling streets, just behind the Sarimiye Mosque, approached from a small side street. It has been here since 1977 and has a very pretty courtyard with orange trees, stone benches and an old well, and an attached school. The chapel itself is small with some late icons, and the priest is Italian, who goes back to Italy every summer for his holidays to visit his mother. Antakya's **Protestant church** is now in the rather grand former French consulate having been purchased by the Korean Protestant Church in 2000. This goes back to the 1950s, when Turkish troops fought as part of NATO against the Koreans. There is also a small **synagogue** on Kurtuluş Caddesi not far from the Catholic church, usually locked, but recognisable by the Star of David above its discreet doorway.

Archaeology Museum (*Gunduz Caddesi;* ❧ *2146168;* ⊕ *08.00–18.00 Tue–Sun; adult TL8*) The mosaic exhibits in this museum, built by the French when Hatay was part of the French protectorate of Syria, on the main square just by the bridge, used to be considered the finest in Turkey, and second in the world only to the Bardo Museum in Tunisia. These days, however, they look distinctly second rate compared with the extraordinary collection of mosaics from Zeugma, now beautifully displayed in the modern museum at Gaziantep. All discovered in the region of Antakya, these mosaics formed the floors of private houses in Roman Antioch and in nearby Daphne, the finest ones dating from the 2nd and 3rd centuries. They are ample testimony to the luxurious lifestyle enjoyed by its citizens, many showing scenes of banqueting and dancing, as well as mythological subjects. Dionysus, Orpheus, Thetys and Hercules figure large, and it was against this supposedly licentious lifestyle that the early Christians here preached.

Apart from the mosaics the museum also has a magnificent Sidymara-style white marble sarcophagus dated to the mid 3rd century. It was unearthed when digging the foundations for an apartment block in 1993. Inside there were gold coins and beautiful gold jewellery, and the skeletons inside were fully dressed: two adults and a child. There are also some fine Hittite stone carvings, notably the double lion table. Most of the artefacts on display here were discovered in excavations conducted by the Chicago Oriental Institute, The British Museum and Princeton University.

8

The mosaics of Antioch are famous as much for their subject matter as their abundance and good state of preservation. These were people who knew how to enjoy themselves and many of the scenes have a certain exuberance and *joie de vivre* sometimes verging on the decadent. There are many remarkable mosaics, including *Narcissus and Echo*, the *Four Seasons*, the *Drunken Dionysus*, propped upright by a small concerned companion and a dog tugging at his wine flask, and the *Rape of Ganymede* abducted by Zeus in the shape of an eagle, followed by a sumptuous banquet of fish, ham, eggs and artichokes. Look out too for the dramatic Evil Eye mosaic (dated 2nd century AD), where the eye is being attacked by a raven, a dog, a snake, a scorpion, a centipede, a panther, a sword and a trident, while a horned goblin turns the other way. All classes of society believed in magic during antiquity, and even though witchcraft was forbidden and could be punished by death, most people still consulted soothsayers for personal protection. Evil Eye mosaics like this one were generally hung at the entrance to homes. The inscription 'KAICY' is Greek for 'the same to you too' – in other words it is wishing good luck to those who look with good eyes and bad luck upon those who look with bad eyes. For those whose intent is evil or who intend to cast evil spells, it wishes their eyes will be ripped out by daggers, spears or wild animals. In another mosaic also dated to the 2nd century AD a hunchback is blessed with a huge erect penis. Many of the mosaics also have water themes, Antioch being blessed with abundant water. The fine *Boat of the Psyches* was unearthed in Daphne in the 3rd century, and notice too *Oceanus and Thetys*, and Thalassa emerging from the waves, a paddle in one hand, and his wet wavy hair held back by lobster claw ties. The boy riding a black dolphin is also very famous. Fishing mosaics were considered to bring good luck during the Roman era, and fish were a symbol of wealth and status. Most of the mosaics date from the 3rd and 4th centuries AD, a time when the empire was starting to fall apart.

In his *Decline and Fall of the Roman Empire* Edward Gibbon wrote:

> Fashion was the only law, pleasure the only pursuit, and the splendour of dress and furniture was the only distinction of the citizens of Antioch. The arts of luxury were honoured, the serious and manly virtues were the subject of ridicule, and the contempt for female modesty and reverent age announced the universal corruption of the capital of the East.

SOUTH OF ANTAKYA

As you head south towards Syria on the old road that leads out past the Rock Church of St Peter, look out for a sign up to Antakya Kalesi forking up to the right to climb up to the crumbling fortress of Antioch which stands on top of Mount Staurin. From the fork it is a further 10km of winding road bringing you up eventually to drive in through fragmentary Roman walls and a few crumbling buildings, till the road ends at a simple café with stupendous views. Local people like to come up here in summer to catch the cooler breezes, and the pine trees offer some shade, but there is a lot of vandalism too.

HARBİYE Also south of Antakya lies Harbiye, ancient Daphne, the pleasure suburb where most of the lavish villas used to be situated. Apollo's pursuit of the nymph Daphne is reputed to have taken place here and the laurel (*daphne* in Greek) into which she was turned still grows all around. Apollo called out to her: 'Daphne!

From now on you shall be the holy tree of Apollo. Your leaves that do not turn yellow and do not fall to the ground will make up the wreath on my head. Esteemed heroes and those who achieve victory in war will always wear your leaves on their foreheads. In song, in prose, our names will be uttered as one.' A sanctuary and oracle of Apollo was established here which became celebrated throughout the ancient world. It was in Daphne that Mark Antony married Cleopatra in 40BC, and that the Olympic Games of Antioch, successor to the games of ancient Olympia, were held. Nothing remains of the buildings, but the gardens with their cypress and laurel trees and little waterfalls produced by the abundant springs are the favourite picnic and strolling place of the residents of modern Antakya. Restaurants serve the local trout and craft stalls sell the local laurel soap along with stone and marble pieces carved into turtles, fish, cats or other traditional motifs. The soap is made from laurel oil and has various antiseptic properties, protecting against fungal growths, acne and dandruff. It is also said to be effective against hair loss. The 9km trip is easy to do with frequent *dolmuş* taxis running from Kurtuluş Caddesi in upper Antakya, but don't expect too much as it can be a bit scruffy and litter-strewn.

With your own transport you can fork off the main Antakya–Samandağ road at Uzunbağ, just after Karacay, to see the utterly abandoned ruin of St Simeon's monastery. The site of the 6th-century monastery, with its three heavily ruined basilicas, is reached after 7km of bad road, and is situated on the summit of Saman Daği, with commanding views over the mountains and the sea. It took ten years to build. Traces of mosaic can still be seen and the base of the pillar, once much taller, from which St Simeon (see box below) preached against the temporary pleasures of the flesh (as in the much more famous St Simeon Stylites' Basilica near Aleppo). The complex octagonal monastery grew up around this pillar.

SELEUCIA AD PIERIA If you continue on to the coast south of Antakya, the road brings you to the sandy fishing beach at Samandağ. A little to the north is the village of Cevlik near which are the ruins of Seleucia ad Pieria, the ancient port of Antioch and once one of the greatest ports on the Mediterranean. Little remains now except for some ruined gates and walls, with a fine water tunnel cut into the rock for 1,300m, devised as a flood defence. It is 7m high and 6m wide and is known as the Titus ve Vespasian-yus Tuneli, as it was begun under Vespasian and completed by his son, Titus. In summer a fee of TL3 is charged for entry. Nearby is a rock-cut necropolis, also thought to be Roman, but with crosses carved inside they are likely to have been used by early Christians later. The 14km-long coastline is a public beach, and the natural gulf is an important bird migration route, as well as a spawning area for green turtles and *Caretta caretta* (loggerhead) turtles, both of which are on the Endangered Species List and protected by a conservation programme in Turkey. Cevlik has a few pensions and a campsite.

VAKIFLI Near Samandağ the village of Vakıflı is the only Armenian village in Turkey. The Church of the Virgin Mary at the entrance to the village was built in 1895 and is still open for services. Several of the old Armenian houses here have been restored and are now in use as pensions. The village is tiny, with a population of only 32 families, about 150 people, and is kept impeccably clean and tidy. In summer the population expands with all the family and friends who visit from the Armenian community in Istanbul. During the deportations of Armenians in 1915 the villagers of Vakıflı were evacuated to Port Said by French and British warships, but most of them returned in 1919 when Hatay became part of French-mandated Syria. When in 1939 Hatay was passed over to the Turkish Republic, most of the local Armenians decided to leave, many of them moving to Lebanon's Bekaa Valley where they found themselves caught up in more civil strife. Since 2004 the villagers have turned to organic farming to earn their living, and also sell their handicrafts like embroidery.

CROSSING INTO SYRIA Returning to Antakya and forking east, the main Syrian border post, used by buses and trucks, is reached after about 50km, from where it is a further 50km to Aleppo (Arabic *Halab*). Shortly after Reyhanli, just 1–2km before the border crossing at Cilvegözü, look out for a sign to the left to the Kızlar Sarayı (Palace of the Maidens), a ruined Byzantine nunnery that belongs unmistakably to the Forgotten Cities of Syria, one of many such remnants of beautiful stone-built churches or monasteries that litter the countryside to the north and west of Aleppo. Kızlar Sarayı still has a fine tall tower and many outbuildings. The closest village is Guverada.

The **border crossing** itself, at the Bab Al-Hawa frontier post, is always busy and can take anything from two to four hours. Make sure you have obtained your **Syrian visa** in advance, either in your home country before departure, or from the Syrian embassy in Ankara, where a single-entry visa costs €20 (see *Chapter 2*, page 45). If you want to minimise the time taken, either arrive before 08.00 or after 20.00, or make the crossing in a private or shared taxi (*dolmuş*). Also make sure, before even attempting to cross, that you do not have any Israeli stamp in your passport, otherwise you will be refused entry even with a visa.

Alternatively you can cross from the much less busy Yayladaği due south of Antakya, which enters Syria very close to the Armenian mountain village of Kasab. Here it is unlikely to take more than half an hour, but buses do not run this way, so you will need your own car or to take a taxi.

MOUNT CASSIUS (KELDAĞ) Hill walking is a rewarding experience in this part of Turkey and one of the most rewarding is the two-and-a-half-hour climb up to the summit of the ancient Mount Cassius (*Jebel Akra* in Arabic, *Keldağ* in Turkish). The starting point is the village of Yayladaği, 6km from the Turko-Syrian border, and a guide is advised. Your goal on the summit is the Barlaam Monastery, built by St Barlaam, who arrived here in the 5th century. In the Middle Ages the mountain was known as Mount Parlier, a corruption of the saint's name. The summit was originally crowned by a sanctuary to Zeus built during the Seleucid era, and even before that it was venerated by the Hittites who made sacrifices to their gods here. Throughout antiquity sailors arriving safely at Seleucia ad Pieria would give thanks to Mount Cassius and pray to it for a safe voyage before departure. The Roman emperor Hadrian, wanting to test a local legend that from the summit of the mountain one could see both the sunset and the sunrise at the same time, was struck here by a thunderbolt whilst making a sacrifice to Zeus at sunrise. Excavations have shown that the monastery was built on the much more ancient foundations of the Zeus/Jupiter Cassius temple, and today the blocks have been scattered by the many earthquakes of the last 2,000 years. It was completely abandoned in 1268.

From Antakya you can head east within Turkey by retracing your steps on the main highway then forking east via Osmaniye to Gaziantep. Alternatively you can use the yellow road via Kırıkhan and Islahiye, which shortens the distance to 167km and is a perfectly good road, also saving the motorway toll if you are in your own transport. The route leads you through fertile valleys with fields of wheat and vineyards, all irrigated by the water from the GAP Project, and grapes and figs are sold from stalls along the roadside. From Gaziantep or from Urfa further east you can head north for Adıyaman and Nemrut Dağı.

GAZİANTEP *Telephone code: 342*

Gaziantep is 128km from Adıyaman and 132km from Şanlıurfa.

Long hailed as the capital of the pistachio nut, Gaziantep now has a further claim to fame – its extraordinary collection of mosaics, rescued from the nearby site of Zeugma before it was flooded by the Birecik Dam on the Euphrates, which now eclipse those of Antakya. It is well worth making sure your itinerary includes a stop in Gaziantep to see them in the Archaeology Museum, as they are one of eastern Turkey's major highlights. As well as the museum, Gaziantep's old quarter all round the Seljuk citadel in the centre of town has been the focus of extensive restoration work in recent years, transforming what was once a collection of semi-derelict medieval and Ottoman buildings into a vibrant series of museums, markets and hotels. The funds to achieve all this have come from the GAP Project (see page 23), of which Gaziantep has been a major beneficiary. It has the confident feel of a city that is going places and is deeply proud of its heritage and identity. As a result Gaziantep now makes an excellent base from which to explore this part of Turkey, with good interesting accommodation and fine restaurants, and with Antakya, Urfa, Harran and Nemrut Dağı all within striking distance as day trips. As well as the restoration of public buildings, Gaziantep has also embarked on the restoration of many of its beautiful Ottoman houses, some with fine wall and ceiling paintings. This too has been funded by EU grants, and is known as the Hidden Arts at Ayintap Houses Project (*www.ayintaphiddenarts.org*).

HISTORY Occupied for over 8,000 years, the name 'Ayntap' is a corruption of the Arabic *ayn tayyib*, meaning 'good spring'. It passed from Hittite to Persian to Greek to Roman rule, then the Byzantines were displaced by the Seljuk Turks in 1070. In Ottoman times there was a fair-sized Christian community, mainly Armenians, and there are still Armenian churches and mansions scattered about the old quarter.

GETTING THERE AND AWAY
By air Gaziantep's airport (called Oğuzeli) is 20km to the southeast of the centre and is served by Turkish Airlines (*www.anadolujet.com*) to Ankara and Istanbul, Cyprus Turkish Airlines (*www.kthy.net*) to Ercan, Northern Cyprus and London Stansted, Onur Air (*www.onurair.com.tr*) to Istanbul, Pegasus (*www.flypgs.com*) to Istanbul and Sun Express (*www.sunexpress.com.tr*) to Izmir. Germania Airlines (*www.flygermania.de*) flies to and from Gaziantep to Berlin-Tegel and Hanover, and

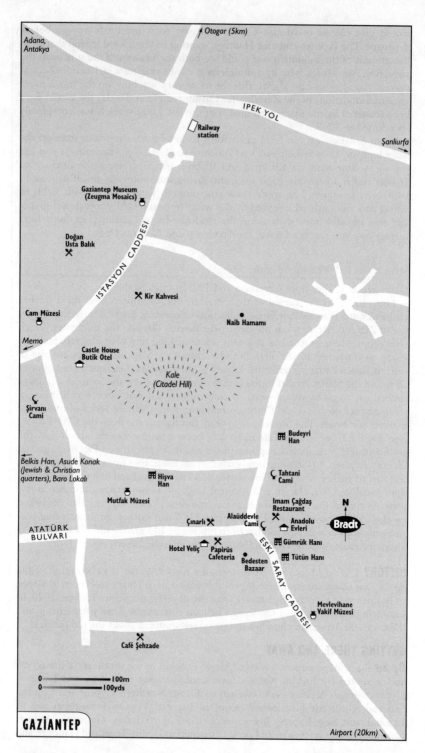

Otogar (5km)

Adana,
Antakya

IPEK YOL

Şanliurfa

Railway
station

Gaziantep Museum
(Zeugma Mosaics)

Doğan
Usta Balık

Kir Kahvesi

Cam Müzesi

Naib Hamamı

Memo

Castle House
Butik Otel

Kale
(Citadel Hill)

Şirvanı
Cami

Budeyri
Han

Belkis Han, Asude Konak
(Jewish & Christian
quarters), Baro Lokalı

Hişva
Han

Tahtani
Cami

Mutfak Müzesi

Imam Çağdaş
Restaurant

N

Çınarlı

Alaüddevle
Cami

Anadolu
Evleri

Bradt

ATATÜRK
BULVARI

Hotel Veliç

Papirüs
Cafeteria

Gümrük Hanı

Tütün Hanı

Bedesten
Bazaar

ESKİ SARAY CADDESİ

Mevlevihane
Vakif Müzesi

Café Şehzade

0 ────── 100m
0 ────── 100yds

GAZİANTEP

Airport (20km)

ISTASYON CADDESİ

Hamburg International Airlines (*www.hamburg-international.de*) flies to and from Stuttgart. Each of these companies runs an airport shuttle bus to and from their respective town centre offices. There are also taxis (TL25) and *dolmuş* services (TL2.50) into the centre.

By train The *Toros Ekspresi* runs to Istanbul via Adana and Konya but with only one departure three days a week. The station is 500m north of the citadel. At the time of writing all trains into and out of Gaziantep were suspended due to long-term engineering work. Check with www.tcdd.gov.tr and www.seat61.com for the current situation.

By bus The *otogar* is 6km to the north of the city centre, linked by buses or minibuses. Services run to all main destinations, such as Adıyaman (for Nemrut Dağı) (three hours, TL12), Diyarbakır (five hours, TL20), Van (12 hours, TL30) and Antakya (four hours, TL12), but there is no direct bus to Syria – you will have to get a bus to Kilis at the border, then get a separate bus to Aleppo.

GETTING AROUND Everything in Gaziantep is walkable, and there are abundant taxis if your limbs fail you. For touring in the area you can arrange car hire through the tour operator Arsan (see below).

TOURIST INFORMATION Gaziantep's tourist office (⊕ *08.00–12.00 & 13.00–17.00 Mon–Fri*) is to be found in the city's Atatürk Kultur Parkı, and has some maps and brochures to hand out.

TOUR OPERATOR Arsan (*Nolu Sokak;* ℡ *2206464; www.arsan.com.tr;* ⊕ *08.00–19.00*) is an English-speaking tour company which can arrange local tours, even down into Syria.

🏠 WHERE TO STAY

🏠 **Anadolu Evleri** (10 rooms) Koroğlu Sokak, Şahinbey; ℡ 2209525; www.anadoluevleri.com. Close to the bustling bazaar, this beautiful series of 3 Ottoman mansions has been converted tastefully by the owner, Timur, part Turkish, part American, who used to work in the music industry before going on a motorcycle tour of the world & deciding Gaziantep was the place to settle. The relaxed ambiance pervades the whole place, with its lovely courtyard, painted ceilings & antique furniture. $$$$

🏠 **Castle House Butik Hotel** (8 rooms) Şeferpaşa Mh; ℡ 2314142; www.kaleevi.com. Opened in 2007 this attractive small hotel is built into the walls of the *kale*. The rooms are beautifully furnished in traditional style, keeping many original features but with no comforts spared. A traditional stone building, it was a mill & a coffee shop in its previous incarnations. It has a lovely terrace just below the citadel walls, with seating for 120

people, & where it serves everything from tea & coffee to full meals with alcohol. $$$

🏠 **Asude Konak** (5 rooms) Şekeroğlu Mahallesi; ℡ 2312044; www.asudekonak.com. The local owner has spent 10 years restoring this place to its current condition, even to the level of delicate lace in the bedrooms, which are decorated in traditional style. Small but welcoming, home-cooked meals are also on offer. $$

🏠 **Belkıs Han** (5 rooms) Kayacık Ara Sokak; ℡ 2311084; www.belkishan.com. Closed in winter, no credit cards. Lovely old stone house converted & restored by its owner, a painter & businesswoman with great charm & full of personal touches. Some rooms have shared bathrooms. $$

🏠 **Hotel Veliç** (18 rooms) Atatürk Bulvarı; ℡ 2212212; www.velicotel.com. Dull modern concrete block on the main road with small rooms, but pleasant top-floor b/fast area with good views over the city. $

✗ WHERE TO EAT
Famous for its pastry shops (all 180 of them), Gaziantep produces the best baklava in Turkey, filled with its renowned local pistachio nuts. All in all

Gaziantep is something of a gastronomic centre, with its heavy Syrian influence and lively café culture. It is starting to call itself the Paris of the East.

✕ **Baro Lokalı** 100 Yil Atatürk Kultur Parkı; ☎ 3394140; ☉ 09.00–22.00. This place in the park has a lovely shaded terrace & serves wine & *rakı* with its excellent main courses & *mezze*. $$

✕ **Çinarlı** Çinarlı Sokak; ☎ 2212155; ☉ 09.00–22.30. Spread over 3 small dining rooms with Turkish carpets & weapons for décor, this place sometimes has live music in its upstairs larger dining area. The food has a good range of more unusual but traditional dishes beyond the ubiquitous kebabs. $$

✕ **Doğan Usta Balık Restaurant** ☎ 3395656; ☉ 09.30–23.00. Unusual in that it specialises in fish, though also serves meat & chicken. The ambiance is quiet & homely. Licensed. $$

✕ **Imam Çağdaş** Kale Civari Uzun Çarşi; ☎ 2312678; ☉ 08.30–22.30. A very special pastry shop as well as a restaurant serving local kebabs, this is one of Gaziantep's famous institutions, with a deserved reputation. Friendly atmosphere. Unlicensed. $$

✕ **Memo** 23 Nisan Mahallesi, Universite Bulvarı 249/1; ☎ 3601313; ☉ 10.00–midnight. Excellent meat dishes & kebabs spiced in an Arab style, with *meze* & salads. Licensed. A guitarist & singer perform live most evenings. $$

✕ **Kir Kahvesi** Köprübaşi Sokak; ☎ 2301982; ☉ 10.00–22.30. A café set at the foot of the *kale*/citadel, this attractive place was restored in an old house in 2007. Traditionally furnished, it can seat 34 people inside & 136 outside on its attractive terrace from where there are fine views up to the citadel. $

✕ **Papirus Cafeteria** Noter Sokak; ☎ 2303279; ☉ 08.30–23.00. This highly atmospheric place is in a historic old house off Atatürk Caddesi, with a shady courtyard & upstairs rooms with frescoes. $

✕ **Café Şehzade** Gaziler Caddesi; ☎ 2310350; ☉ 08.30–20.00. Housed in an 800-year-old *hammam* (bath-house) this place is wonderful to linger in having a drink or light meal. $

✕ **Tutun Hanı** ☎ 2317689; ☉ 09.30–17.00. A coffee house in a restored caravanserai in the heart of the bazaar, as is the atmospheric **Tahmis**. You can smoke a *nargile* (water-pipe – see page 31) here. $

SHOPPING AND OTHER PRACTICALITIES Gaziantep has its own Carrefour supermarket on the western outskirts of town, and its petrol stations have their own eateries and snack shops selling things like Red Bull and accepting credit cards, just like any European petrol station. Further east, this sort of thing becomes very rare. The post office, ATMs, banks, internet cafes and exchange offices can all be found round the main square.

WHAT TO SEE Allow at least a full day to enjoy all the city's sights listed here.

Gaziantep Museum (İstasyon Caddesi; ☎ 3248809; www.gaziantepmuzesi.gov.tr; ☉ 08.30–18.00 Tue–Sun; adult TL3; excellent shop with gifts & cafeteria; small garden round the edge with stone benches among more statues & reliefs) The mosaics are displayed on the ground floor and basement, while upstairs has a fine bust of Dionysus and the lesser exhibits. As well as the mosaics the museum has some fine Hittite reliefs from Yesemek and Carchemish, notably the 9th-century BC storm god Teshub, and some Roman sculptures reminiscent of the art of Palmyra in Syria. The basement also has the magnificent statue in bronze of Mars, which was discovered in a broken amphora. He was the god of war, and also fertility, a very important god for Zeugma, base of the Fourth Legion, always ready for war, and near the Euphrates River and its fertility, and this duality is symbolised by the flower and the spear. Over 60,000 seals were also found, together with 3,750 silver coins. Mosaic art began in the 3rd millennium BC when the Sumerians used it on their walls, as in the Varuk temple, with simple black/white and red terracottas. In Gordion in the 8th and 7th centuries BC black and white pebble mosaics were used, then in Greece from the 5th century BC colour began to be used. Most of the tesserae for the Zeugma mosaics were produced from the coloured stone collected from the banks of the Euphrates, supplemented by glass tesserae for any missing colours such as orange, light blue or dark green. Such damage as exists was due to the fire of the Sassanian sack of AD256, which melted the glass tesserae, but the condition of most of them is extraordinarily complete. See pages 210–11 for more information on the Zeugma Mosaics.

Gaziantep Kalesi (⏰ *08.30–16.00 Tue–Sun; admission free*) Originally the Seljuk citadel, now home to a Panorama Museum telling the story of how Gaziantep acquired its epithet 'Gazi', meaning 'warrior', as an honour from Atatürk in recognition of the fight its inhabitants put up in a ten-month siege by invading French armies in 1920–21. It is called Panorama because you walk round in a huge circular stone tunnel inside the citadel, with the pictures and explanations on the walls.

All around the *kale*/citadel many mosques, *hans* and old buildings have been restored with money from the GAP scheme, the EU and the local *belediye* (municipality). The Antique Glass Museum at the foot of the *kale* opposite the Castle House Butik Hotel is set in a renovated old house and apart from displaying glass, sells handmade olive oil and its own wine, and has an attractive courtyard where refreshments are served.

Walking uphill above the *kale* you pass the **Emine Goğuş Mutfak Müzesi**, a kitchen museum in an old house with displays of traditional cooking utensils and mannequins in old costumes and fezzes showing how meals used to be taken round a large communal copper dish. The shops in this area, selling local white cheeses and fruit, are reminiscent of those in Damascus's Straight Street. The **Hişva Hanı** (Cotton Ball Caravanserai) close by here above the *kale* is currently being restored, dating to 1577, and is Gaziantep's oldest, with a black and white-striped entrance and single-storey interior.

Gaziantep also has what it calls its Culture Street, the Eski Saray (Old Palace) Caddesi, which starts some 300m southeast of the citadel, and which boasts 18 *hans*, nine mosques, four *hammams*, the **Mevlevihane Wakif Müzesi** (⏰ *09.00–17.00 Tue–Sun; admission free*). The **Bedesten Bazaar**, approached down a flight of steps, is very reminiscent of Aleppo's Khan Shouneh near the Aleppo Citadel. The early Ottoman **Tahtalı Cami** or Wooden Mosque dates to 1557 and as its name suggests was originally made of wood. Its *mihrab* is made of red marble with trefoil arched niches. Its *mimber* is beautifully decorated with marble stars, rosettes and geometric patterns, very Mamluk in style. It was renovated in 1804. The **Gümrük (Customs) Hanı** dates to 1873–78 and has been heavily restored, while the **Inceoglu Hani** dates to 1890, a two-storey soap factory and inn, one of the few that has survived to the present day.

Some 300m southwest of the citadel in the Christian and Jewish quarters, look out for the **Hasan Suzer Ethnography Museum** (⏰ *08.00–12.00 & 13.00–17.00; adult TL2*) set in one of the traditional houses with their black and white arched doorways, entering into the private courtyard complete with well, cellar and stabling. Mannequins act out scenes from daily life. Nearby what is now the **Kurtuluş Cami** (Salvation Mosque) was originally an Armenian cathedral built in 1892. In the War of Independence and for a while after in the 1920s it was used as a prison. Now its pleasant courtyard is graced with plum, fig, mulberry and walnut trees, and recycled Corinthian columns used in the church support the porch inside.

ENVIRONS OF GAZIANTEP
Yesemek Open-Air Museum (*113km southwest from Gaziantep*; ⏰ *daily dawn–dusk; adult TL2*) If you have your own transport this rarely visited site makes a very rewarding day excursion from Gaziantep. It was the Hittite quarry and

Scores of mosaics, more than 800m in total, were rescued from the site of Zeugma, a Roman garrison town housing 5,000 soldiers and their commercial potential in cash, dating from the 2nd and 3rd centuries. Founded originally in the 4th century BC by Seleucus I Nicator as a bridgehead for his armies, the word Zeugma means 'bridge' or 'span' in Greek. One of the most major archaeological finds of the last 50 years, the site is also known as the Ruins of Belkıs, like the Queen of Sheba, a reference to the extreme prosperity and richness of the region. A whole series of 12 houses belonging to the upper-class Zeugma residents had remarkable mosaics on the floor of their dining rooms which would have been flooded under the Euphrates in 1996–2000 as part of the GAP scheme. In their natural setting many of them would also have been water-covered, as shallow pools in the centre of courtyards.

MOTHER EARTH GE *2nd century AD, the bottom of a shallow pool in the House of Euphrates.* The borders are incredibly elaborate with frames within frames, each decorated differently. The innermost one is an octagon of red wave crests, and in the centre is Gaia (Ge), holding a cornucopia from which fruit spills, and crowned with a wreath of pomegranate flowers and leaves. Her chin and neck show an early restoration attempt, where the colour is different.

EUPHRATES *2nd to mid 3rd century AD, saved in 2000 by experts from the University of Nantes, also the bottom of a shallow pool in the House of Euphrates.* Almost entirely complete, it depicts three personifications of the river god Euphrates, the main male god in the centre, river weeds and twigs in his hair, flanked by two female figures who may represent its branches. The building behind the female to the left may be the temple of a spring. The three panels are separated by an enormous guilloche (plait) border between two smaller borders of red stepped pyramids.

EROS AND PSYCHE *2nd to mid 3rd century AD, House of Poseidon.* In a remarkable border with a rich acanthus scroll decorated with yellow cornucopia curving round to encircle large stylised flowers or fruits – grapes, apples, pears, plums, pomegranates, figs and pine cones, Eros and Psyche (Soul) are seated, their legs and feet pointing away from each other and their heads turned slightly towards each other. Eros's left arm is round Psyche's shoulder.

CROWNING OF APHRODITE *2nd to mid 3rd century AD.* Hunting scenes with lions, bears, stags, boars, tigers and panthers form the border. Aphrodite is shown born naked from the sea, seated on a scallop shell held by two male sea centaurs, one older and one younger, with lobster claws adorning their heads. A dolphin swims in the sea in front of her.

MARRIAGE OF DIONYSUS AND ARIADNE *Late 2nd century AD.* A feast scene depicting half-naked gods and goddesses drinking to musical accompaniment. The faces were exceptionally detailed, using 400 tesserae for each of the ten figures, while the clothes used only 225 and the background 144. It was rescued from flooding in 1992 but left locked *in situ*, and sadly then fell victim to theft in 1998 when six of the ten figures were stolen. They have never been found.

ACHILLES REVEALED *2nd to mid 3rd century AD, House of Poseidon.* One of the popular episodes of the Trojan War, where Achilles has been hidden, disguised as a girl, by his mother Thetis, to prevent him being sent off to join the Trojan expedition. Odysseus (far right in cross-laced hunter's boots) hears of the deception and goes to the court of King Lycomedes, King of Scyros (far left), to find him, where Achilles is disguised as one of the king's daughters. Odysseus lays out gifts for the women and then has a horn blown as if for battle. Achilles forgets his disguise and thinking from the battle horn that they are being attacked, picks up the shield and spear which were among the gifts, exposing his identity as his woman's tunic falls to expose his right breast. One of the real daughters to his left, reaches out her arm to him as if to prevent him leaving on the expedition.

TRIUMPH OF POSEIDON *2nd to mid 3rd century AD, House of Poseidon, on the floor of a shallow pool.* At the centre Poseidon rides his golden chariot drawn by a team of two grey hippocampi or sea-horses with the forepart of a horse, the hindpart of a marine animal. Oceanus and Tethys are shown below him, their busts rising from the surface of the sea with serpents coiled round their shoulders. Lobster claws rise from Oceanus's temples and Tethys's head is adorned with a pair of wings. Various sea creatures decorate the rest of the background, such as octopuses, eels, dolphins and shrimps.

TRIUMPH OF DIONYSUS *2nd century AD, forming the vertical part of the T-bar in the composition with Pasiphae and Daedalus in the House of Poseidon.* The thick swastika-meander band in perspective at the top was the partition between the two mosaics. There are many Dionysian scenes among the Zeugma mosaics. Legend has it that Dionysus was the first to build a bridge (made of ivy and vine) across the Euphrates, and the place where the river was spanned was called the span (Greek *zeugma*). The figures are identified by Greek inscriptions and show Dionysus standing in a chariot, his wreathed head nimbused (ringed with a cloud denoting his status as a god on earth, like a saint's halo), dressed in the triumphal style in a long tunic with gold band above the waist, above the visible arm and wrist. The chariot is drawn by panthers and Nike or Winged Victory holds the reins of the panthers. On the right a whirling female (labelled *bacchante* meaning the same thing as maenad, ie: mad or frenzied follower of Bacchus/Dionysus in his orgiastic rituals) dances while clashing her cymbals.

PERSEUS AND ANDROMEDA *2nd to mid 3rd century AD, House of Poseidon.* Saved in March 2000, another pavement from the House of Poseidon. It depicts the rescue by Perseus, totally naked bar a cloak over his shoulder, of the maiden Andromeda, daughter of the Ethiopian king of Hoppa. In one hand Perseus carries the head of the Medusa whom he has just slain and in the same hand he holds the weapon (*harpe*) given to him by Hermes to kill her. He wears a Phrygian cap on his head and the winged sandals on his feet also given to him by Hermes. With his other arm he reaches out to help Andromeda down from the rock where she has been chained as an offering to the sea monster, an attempt to appease the anger of Poseidon. Her mantle is gold and she wears a headdress and her naked arm bears two bracelets. The sea monster lies in coils at Perseus's feet. In between the two human figures is the round mirror with handle that Athene gave to Perseus so that he would not look at the head of the Medusa while slaying her and be turned to stone. Both figures are labelled in Greek and Andromeda's head is flanked by the broken chain. The sea monster is labelled *ketos*. Perseus later takes Andromeda to Greece and marries her. His facial expression is curious. Whereas she looks at him with gratitude, he is avoiding her eye and appears to be looking down at the water jar. The facial expressions in all the mosaics are strangely deadpan, no matter how dramatic the event in which they are taking part. No mouth is ever open; no-one even smiles.

continued overleaf

GYPSY GIRL OR MAENAD *End 2nd century AD.* Discovered in 1998, this face, all that remains of a once much larger mosaic, has become the iconic image of Zeugma. Always referred to as the Gypsy Girl probably because of the gypsy gold earring, she is in fact variously thought to be a Maenad (mad frenzied woman) who takes part in the Dionysian orgiastic festivals, the Earth Mother Gee or even Alexander the Great – the face could be male or female, as could the hair, jewellery and headgear. The rest of the mosaic is thought to have been stolen and partly destroyed by robbers in the mid 19th century.

PASIPHAE AND DAEDALUS *2nd century AD.* This is the largest mosaic in the museum and shows Pasiphae, wife of King Minos, labelled above on the left, beside one of her daughters (unlabelled but possibly Ariadne), then an old servant in the centre giving instructions to Daedalus with his son Icarus. They are using the tools shown at their feet to make the wooden cow in which Pasiphae will hide herself. The bull's head with the cupid at her feet symbolises Pasiphae's passion for the white bull with whom she has become infatuated thanks to a spell cast on her by Poseidon, as a punishment on King Minos. In the legend, Daedalus shows her how to climb into the wooden cow and conceal herself in its hindquarters, so that the bull can mate with her. The resultant offspring was the fabled Minotaur. In the upper right corner of the mosaic is a pair of identical buildings with gabled roofs and small windows. This may represent the Labyrinth, which King Minos asked Daedalus to build, and where he spent the rest of his days in shame concealed with Pasiphae and the Minotaur. Daedalus and Icarus were also imprisoned there by the king, till they escaped by building wings for themselves. This mosaic formed the horizontal bar of the T-form design of the dining room mosaic in the House of Poseidon, facing the guests as they entered.

sculpture workshop from which gigantic basalt blocks were cut out and carved into the lions, sphinxes and other reliefs that now adorn their cities. Many pieces can be seen scattered over a large area, left *in situ*, some half-completed, making a fascinating open-air museum to explore. It was in use from 1375BC until the collapse of the Hittite Empire. Drive first to Kilis, then take the road west towards Hassa along the Syrian border, before forking off to the right on a gravel road signposted for Yesemek.

TOWARDS URFA

From Gaziantep you can head due east 140km to Urfa, passing through an almost treeless landscape of rolling hillsides of wheat.

CARCHEMISH At 48km there is a turn-off south to the small frontier town of Barak near Carchemish (Turkish *Kargemiş*), the site of the capital of the most powerful of the Neo-Hittite kingdoms which prospered after the collapse of the Hittite Empire at Hattuşaş (Boğazkale). The city had to repel many attacks from the Assyrians before eventually being annexed in 717BC to the Assyrian Empire by Sargon II. Because of its closeness to the Syrian border the site itself is difficult to visit, subject to military restrictions and the local Karkamiş Dam construction. Dams are considered military installations and all photography is strictly forbidden, so be careful in this area. It used to be possible to be accompanied by a military escort from the *jandarma*. There is in fact little to see on the site today, as during the excavations just before World War I the colossal bas-reliefs which were found here decorating the city gates were moved to Ankara and are now on display in the Ankara Museum of Anatolian Civilisations. They represent mythological scenes with processions of warriors and courtiers and are reminiscent of Assyrian art. It was this dig that contributed some of the first clues to the identity of the Hittites. Among the archaeologists involved were such luminaries as T E Lawrence, Sir Leonard Woolley and D G Hogarth, and Gertrude Bell was a visitor to the excavations. The citadel itself is on a 40m-high hill overlooking the Euphrates, and the palace originally stood at the centre of it approached by a wide monumental way.

BELKIS-ZEUGMA Shortly after the Carchemish turn-off to the south, there is a turn-off to the north to Belkıs-Zeugma, original site of the extraordinary mosaics now in Gaziantep Museum. Since the mosaics were relocated, there is no longer much reason to visit, but the acropolis hill still rises beside the waters of the Birecik Dam, with various piles of stones and some pillars. Plans are afoot to do a bit more with the site, and put in some labelling at least.

BİRECİK The only town of interest *en route* to Urfa is Birecik, on the banks of the wide green Euphrates overlooked by the ruins of a fortress perched on a rock, probably built by the Crusaders in the 12th century. Birecik's other distinction is as one of the world's two remaining nesting places for the bald ibis, a hideously ugly and nearly extinct bird. It leaves Birecik in July to fly to its winter home in Morocco and returns in mid-February. For as long as anyone can remember its return has heralded the end of winter and the coming of spring and is celebrated by the villagers in a remarkable festival each year. Some of the oldest villagers believe spring will not come if the bald ibis does not return; the World Wildlife Fund has a project here to protect the species. From here Urfa is another 81km east.

THE ROUTE TO MARAŞ

If from Gaziantep you are not heading south to Antakya and Hatay the best route east is to fork left at Toprakkale towards Maraş. This route takes you via Karatepe to Adıyaman (for the ascent of Nemrut Dağı), a journey that can be done in a day.

KARATEPE From Osmaniye a yellow sign points off left 34km to Karatepe, Aslantaş and Hierapolis. Although this is a detour of some three hours in all, it is well worth it if you have the time and your own transport (hiring a taxi from Osmaniye for the day will cost about TL75), as the scenery *en route* is very attractive and the site of Karatepe is remote and unusually beautiful. Here you can see Neo-Hittite stone reliefs *in situ* in a quantity and state of preservation unique in Turkey or for that matter in the world. It is also an excellent picnic spot in the lovely wooded setting overlooking the Ceyhan Lake. The name Karatepe (Black Hill), describes the pine-covered hills on which the site, once the summer palace of the Neo-Hittite king Asitawanda, stands dominating the valley and the lake below. Karatepe was only discovered in 1945, having lain on the hillside covered in brambles and scrub for 27 centuries. It was under these brambles that the final key was found to the puzzle of Hittite hieroglyphs. Philologists had struggled for 50 years to master the main elements of the language's structure, but now, from a bilingual text in Phoenician and Hittite hieroglyphs they could understand the meaning of the individual words for the first time.

The route is well signposted all the way. About 12km from Osmaniye the road runs through pleasant open fields. From a fine castle on a hillock, columns march across the fields towards the road. This is the site of **Hierapolis Castabala**, capital from 52BC of an independent kingdom under a ruler called Tarcondimotus. He took the part of Pompey against Caesar, providing him with vessels, and in 31BC he was killed at the Battle of Actium where the fleet of Cleopatra and Mark Antony was defeated. The dynasty was short-lived, coming to an end in AD17. The last 9km to Karatepe passes through pretty wooded hillsides and several hamlets to the area that is now designated the **Karatepe National Park (Milli Park)**. Neatly laid out with wooden tables and benches set among the trees, refreshments are now served here. The Turkish Archaeological Institute was responsible for the excavations here: increasingly it is the case in Turkey that excavations of genuine Anatolian civilisations like the Hittites, Urartians and Seljuks are conducted by Turks, whereas the Greek and Roman sites tend to be funded by foreign institutions.

Nothing of the site is visible from the car park, but is approached along a forest path for 300m till you reach a double gate into the old Hittite city. On the summit of the hill is a Hittite palace inside defence fortifications laid out on a polygonal plan with 28 towers. Intriguingly, nothing remains of the city itself, except two sets of gates, these first ones and another set on the other side of the hill. Why the gates have remained so well preserved with such detail left on the carvings while nothing remains of the city itself is a puzzle. The same is largely true of Hattuşaş (Boğazkale), where it is the gates of the outer fortifications which have survived, leaving very little inside. It certainly shows where the Hittite builders concentrated their efforts. Only at Alacahüyük does the town remain with buildings still recognisable inside the walls and streets leading off.

The gates at Karatepe are guarded by colossal sphinxes and lions. Huge basalt blocks along the inside of the first gate are cut with astonishingly well-preserved reliefs. The scenes show hunting and fishing, a bull being killed for the king, the king seated at his meal reaching out for one of the flat loaves in a large bowl and holding a meat patty in his left hand. Two servants wave fans to keep away insects and create a breeze. There are also people riding in chariots, dancing bears and a series of particularly fine gods, notably the monkey god (with enormous erect penis), the snake god and a sun god very like the Egyptian Horus with a falcon's (or perhaps here an eagle's) head.

The reliefs on the further gate are if anything better preserved than the first one, with one of the lions still having his ivory eyes intact. The mother suckling her child by the palm tree shows strong Egyptian influence. Though not beautifully executed or particularly naturalistic, it is nevertheless a very expressive scene.

ONWARDS TO ADIYAMAN (BASE FOR NEMRUT DAĞI) VIA KAHRAMANMARAŞ

Returning to Osmaniye the highway continues eastwards for some 50km until the turn-off to Kahramanmaraş. Most of the heavy truck traffic continues towards Gaziantep for Syria and Iraq, while on the Maraş fork the road almost empties.

A further 50km brings you to **Maraş**, a city which few foreign visitors will stop off at from choice, for it has nothing to see except a small museum set in the Ottoman citadel displaying Hittite sculptures. It has been described by those with over-active imaginations as marking the entrance to another world, that of oriental Turkey, where the people and landscapes become rougher and where any maritime influence has worn away. It was held by the French until 1920, and three years later its large Armenian population was expelled. Because of the resistance offered to the French by the local population in the War of Independence, Atatürk added the epithet 'Kahraman' (hero) to its name and on maps you will see it marked as Kahramanmaraş.

The road heads northeast towards Malatya and at Gölbaşi forks due east towards Adıyaman, passing through attractive hilly scenery, sometimes following

THE NEO-HITTITES AND THEIR ART

The reliefs here at Karatepe are all thought to show Assyro-Aramean influence in such things as the defined tresses of the hair, the hair styles, the style of dress with the long Assyrian tunic and tasselled sash replacing the characteristic short Hittite tunic, and the appearance of chariots. A lot of the subject matter for the reliefs is light-hearted as befits a provincial summer palace. The ordinary mortals shown here in these reliefs are, as Seton Lloyd observed: 'a graceless folk with sloping foreheads and receding chins, such as are known to have inhabited large areas of Anatolia at that time.'

The Karatepe remains have been dated to c800BC, long after the fall of the Hittite Empire at Hattuşaş. These were the so-called Neo-Hittites, the people whom the Israelites knew and who are mentioned in the Old Testament. It seems doubtful that the Israelites knew of the mountain Hittites of Anatolia, for when King David married Bathsheba, the widow of Uriah the Hittite in about 1000BC, the Hittites had long been driven out of their mountain homeland. Forced southwards from the cities and pastures of the plateau towards the plains of northern Syria, they founded a series of small and disunited city-states striving to retain their independence on the fringes of the Assyrian Empire. The artistic style and quality of these cities of the Hittite diaspora, like Karatepe, Carchemish and Ugarit, are generally inferior to that of the earlier Hittite kingdom. The somewhat crude and hybrid style of art seen here is thought to have been executed by craftsmen from many different nations. Part of the difficulty may also lie in the hard black basalt so plentiful in the northern Syrian Plain, but coarse and much more difficult to carve than the fine white limestone used for the reliefs of the old kingdom.

the course of rivers, sometimes climbing up and down hills, making the gradual ascent onto the Anatolian Plateau. It is possible, having set out with your own transport from Adana (or even Antakya) in the morning, to visit Yılanlıkale and Karatepe, and then drive on via Maraş to reach Adıyaman that evening. The distance from Adana to Adıyaman is 362km. A scenic alternative approach to Nemrut Dağı is from Malatya (98km), described in *Chapter 5*, pages 132–3.

Adıyaman is an undistinguished sprawling town at an altitude of 700m. For travellers it serves purely as a base from which to make the ascent to Nemrut Dağı, as it has the biggest range of accommodation.

NEMRUT DAĞI

Along with Cappadocia and the Sumela Monastery, Nemrut Dağı is one of the best known sites east of Ankara, and most people will have seen photos of the large stone heads on the top of the mountain. Virtually unknown until after World War II and not even mentioned in the 1960 edition of the *Guide Bleu*, the site was first excavated by the American School of Oriental Research in Connecticut in 1953. The first outsider to come upon it, however, was a German engineer called Karl Puchstein, who in 1881 stumbled upon the statues whilst conducting transport route surveys for the Ottomans. Since the building of an approach road in the 1960s the site has been regularly visited and now, with the upsurge in visitors to Turkey, the droves of people heading up the mountain in organised minibus tours have reached the proportions of a pilgrimage.

Nemrut Dağı has almost no significance historically, being no more than a vast funeral monument to the ruler of a small local dynasty with delusions of grandeur, but for all that – or because of that – it is astonishing, unlike anything else in the world. This kingdom, extending from Adıyaman to Gaziantep, was called Commagene, and was established in the 1st century BC by a local ruler called Mithradates. The Seleucid dynasty in Syria to the south was disintegrating and the Commagene rulers managed to rule independently until AD72 when the Emperor Vespasian incorporated it into the Roman province of Syria. Cicero, Governor of the Province of Cilicia to the south, referred to the Commagenes scathingly in his letters as this 'petty kingdom' with its 'petty princelings'.

GETTING THERE AND TIMINGS You should think of the ascent of Nemrut Dağı as a day trip from either Adıyaman or Malatya (see page 133). Heading east from Adıyaman you reach Kahta after 35km, and at the beginning of town a sign points left to Nemrut Dağı. Local pension owners lie in wait at this point to convince hesitant travellers that the road is *bozuk* ('broken') and that they need to be taken up in one of their minibuses at exorbitant cost. With your own transport you can rest assured the road is perfectly good tarmac all the way, and that even coaches now manage to get to the car park at the top. The distance to the top is 52km of winding road and takes about two hours to the top and two hours back down again. The route from Malatya is 98km, taking two-and-a-half hours to the top, and means you can stay in the Güneş Hotel some 500m below the summit (see page 133). Less able-bodied people might prefer the Malatya approach as the walk up from where the track above the Güneş Motel ends is only some 100m (five minutes), whereas on the other side the walk up from the car park is 750m (20 minutes) long. Before the building of the road in the 1960s the summit was accessible only by donkey and on foot and took two days. The mountain is snow-covered mid-October–end April, so the route to the top cannot be counted on to be passable during the intervening winter months, and most of the local

A POWER-CRAZED KING

Antiochus (62–32BC), son of Mithradates, imagined for himself great ancestors, claiming descent on his father's side from Alexander the Great. This Persian and Macedonian ancestry is reflected in the statues and reliefs surrounding the tumulus where Antiochus depicts himself as at home with and as an equal among the great kings and gods. The strangeness of this subject matter would be interesting but not exceptional were it not for the setting Antiochus chose for his mausoleum: Nemrut Dağı, at 2,206m, the highest mountain in his kingdom (not to be confused with the volcano of the same name on the western shore of Lake Van). The site is extremely remote and inaccessible and it is this bizarre setting which gives the whole monument, in its isolation and unexpectedness, a surreal feel. This essentially oriental concept of gods enthroned on a mountain has its antecedents in the Hittite reliefs where the most important gods always stood on top of mountains, or even as early as the Babylonian Ziggurat of Ur, a manmade symbol of a mountain.

The name 'Nemrut Dağı', Mountain of Nemrut (rather than Mountain of Antiochus which would be more accurate), dates from the 8th century when many ruins in the region of Mesopotamia were named after Nemrut, the biblical Nimrod, grandson of Ham, son of Noah (The Throne of Nimrod on Urfa citadel for example). Always emblematic of an archetypal evil person or tyrannical king in Jewish and Islamic tradition, some sources describe Nimrod as building the Tower of Babel to defy God, aiming to make it so high that any future flood God might send would not engulf it. Pieter Bruegel's famous painting *Tower of Babel* shows a typical Nimrod inspecting the stonemasons. The root of the word Nemrut – m r d – means 'rebel' in Hebrew and Old Babylonian, and even in modern Arabic.

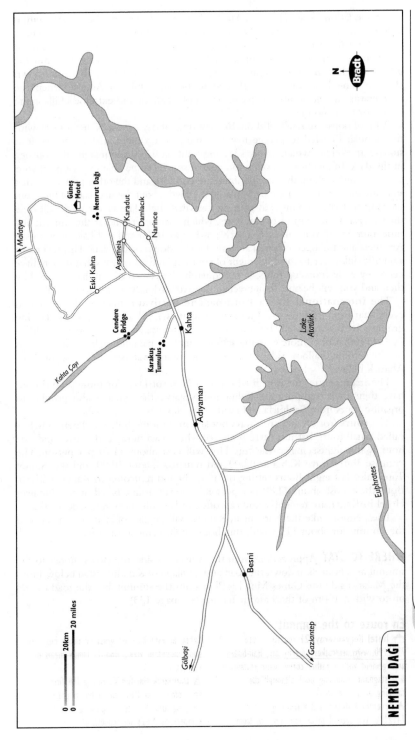

NEMRUT DAĞI

accommodation closes. There used to be up to 5m of snow on the summit within living memory of the older villagers, but now it is more like 1.5m, or 50cm at Arsameia. Of course, this dramatic reduction in the winter snowfall has major consequences in the amount of water that subsequently finds its way into the great rivers like the nearby Euphrates, resulting in less water for all further down the line. The best season is reckoned to be June, July or August, when the temperature at the summit is pleasantly cool, without the extreme chill or the earlier or later months.

A lot of nonsense is talked about the best time of day to visit Nemrut Dağı, with the popular line fed to people that you must be up there at dawn to see it at sunrise, an exercise which involves leaving Kahta at 02.00 and making the journey in the dark. In practice it is often too cold at sunrise to be able to get out of your transport and walk up the last 20 minutes in comfort, and the other problem is that so many tour operators have perpetuated the myth about the necessity of the dawn viewing that the summit is at its most crowded then. The clever ones will time their arrival to miss most of the tours, which means arriving at the summit any time after 13.00. You can in fact arrive as late as 16.00 and still have time to see Arsameia and the queen's burial area on the way down before dark. This will make a terrific difference to the enjoyment of your trip, and also means that if there have been any early-morning mists, as is frequently the case, they will have cleared by then and you will be able to appreciate the extraordinary setting to the full.

The **International Kahta Kommagene Festival** is held on the mountain every year from 25 June to 27 June, with symposia, exhibitions and folk dancing groups. It is organised by the Kahta Municipality and Tourism Office (\ *4311100*). Other more extreme activities include paragliding from the tumulus on the summit, balloon rides over the tumulus and watersport contests on Lake Atatürk below.

The main centres for organised tours to Nemrut Dağı for those who do not have their own transport, are Kahta and Malatya, though it is also possible to organise tours from Şanlıurfa and even Cappadocia (see page 142).

The **tours** from Kahta are always hooked in with the hotels and pensions. So-called 'small tours' last just three hours, of which two hours is the drive and one hour is the sightseeing at the top. This will cost about TL70 per person. The 'Sunrise Tours' leave Kahta at 02.00 and return at about 10.00, and the 'Sunset Tours' also last eight hours setting off at 13.30 and returning to Kahta at 21.30. Both these cost about TL80 per person. Nemrut Tours, based at the Nemrut Hotel in Kahta, are reputable and can offer an English-speaking guide as well.

The pensions like the Karadut in Karadut village also offer transport tours to the summit for about TL75 with one hour's sightseeing at the top.

 WHERE TO STAY Approaching from the Adıyaman side, the closest hotels to the summit are about 8km down the road at the village of Karadut, listed below. From the Malatya side the Güneş Motel is 2km from the summit, but the road carries on to within 100m of the Eastern Terrace (see page 133).

En route to the summit

🏠 **Hotel Kervansaray** (21 rooms) \ 416 7372190; www.nemrutkervanseray.com. Half-board arrangement with a rather corny rustic restaurant & a stagnant swimming pool, although the camping area is good. $$

🛖 **Arsemia Kafeterya & Kamping** \ 416 7412118. The second place you come to from Kahta, at Eski Kale; no grass or shade but very good mountain views. Homely family meals on request. $

🛖 **Damlacık Garden Camping** The first place you come to at Damlacık, it has a grassed camping area & a secure parking area for campervans. Meals on request. $

☖ **Karadut Pension** (11 rooms) Karadut village; ✆ 416 7372169; www.karadutpansiyon.net.

Simple but clean small rooms, with camping facilities at the back. Meals on request. $

Kahta
☖ **Zeus Hotel** (25 rooms) ✆ 416 7255694; www.zeushotel.com. The most luxurious place around, with a fully functioning pool & cared-for garden. AC & good bathrooms with flat-screen TVs. Campers are also allowed in a special plot. $$$

☖ **Pension Kommagene** (18 rooms) Mustafa Kemal Caddesi; ✆ 416 7259726. Clean simple rooms, with camping at the back. Dinner & b/fast on offer for extra. $

✖ **WHERE TO EAT** The café in the car park below the summit serves simple meals and there are several places offering simple accommodation on the way up from Kahta, so it is not essential to take a picnic, though it does give you more freedom. Apart from the food on offer in the hotels and pensions, the other option if you have your own transport is these licensed restaurants on the gigantic Atatürk Lake, 4km east of Kahta.

✖ **Akropolian** Baraj Yolu; ✆ 416 7255132. On a hill 1km set back from the lake but with a lovely garden overlooking it. Fresh lake fish is the speciality. $$

✖ **Nesetin Yeri** Baraj Yolu; ✆ 416 7257675. Right on the lakeshore, with a lovely shady garden. Serving the local lake trout (*alabalık*) but not the highly vocal frogs. $

WHAT TO SEE
Mount Nemrut National Park (UNESCO World Heritage Site) (*Nemrut Dağı Milli Parki*; ⊕ *May–Oct 08.00–20.00 daily; closed Nov–Apr; adult TL6 including Arsameia, price the same from the Malatya side*)

The Route up from Kahta You can stop off at the various sites of interest either on the way up or the way down, whatever suits your timing and itinerary best.

Karakuş tumulus Within 10km of setting off from Kahta you will pass a huge artificial mound to the left of the road, marking the burial place of Antiochus's wife. It is called Karakuş (Black Bird) which may be a local interpretation of the clumsy eagle on top of one of the pillars. The mound was originally ringed with columns of which only three now remain, topped with an eagle, a lion and an inscription naming the queen of Commagene who is buried inside. In a clear hierarchy, from here the tumulus of her husband on the summit of Nemrut Dağı is visible as the highest point to the northeast.

A simple refreshment place has set itself up beside the burial mound.

Cendere Roman bridge Round the next corner the road takes you on a new bridge over the Cendere River, tributary to the Euphrates. Stop for a moment to walk across the fine 2nd-century Roman bridge here, with an inscription on the centre of the arch. Dedicated to the Roman emperor Septimius Severus it is still in superb condition (the road used to cross over it till a few years ago) with excellent workmanship in the stone blocks and three of the original four columns still standing. The river and dramatic gorge here are favoured places for local people to come on Fridays, often arriving by tractor, and swim in the shady gorge. A simple tea place has set itself up beside the bridge. The road all the way up is clearly marked with yellow signs so there is little danger of taking a wrong turning. In the area of the bridge the scenery is made very lovely by the wide shingled river and the surrounding fertile slopes covered with vines and wheat. The gradient is never very steep and the road is fine even for motorbikes. The worst patches tend to be in the villages where the local tractors and pick-up trucks can churn up the surface and create ruts. Children from the villages are now very used to the seasonal steady stream of tourists weaving their way up the mountain from May onwards and try to sell their local wares and crafts.

Eski Kahta (Kocahisar Köyü) and Yeni Kale About 5km onwards from the Roman bridge you can take a signposted detour to Eski Kahta, also known as Kocahisar, well worth it for the sight of the dramatic castle known as Yeni Kale (New Fortress) perched on a vertiginous crag. The descent from the Malatya side joins up from here, entering the village from the other side (see page 133). Called 'New', this fine castle is a 13th-century Mamluk fortification which you can walk up to from the village. Since 2005 it has been closed for restoration, and is likely to remain closed for a while longer, as the leader of the works died when he fell off the edge after missing his footing. There are some Arabic inscriptions above the main gateway detailing the time and originator of the construction. The Café Roma is a simple but pleasant tea/coffee place under shady vines below.

Arsameia (Eski Kale) Some 2km back along the main road to the summit a fork to the left leads you to Eski Kale (Old Fortress), site of the ancient Commagene capital. Here at the park entrance you will be asked to pay the TL8 admission fee that covers the whole of the Nemrut Daği site, so keep your ticket to show again at the summit. From the car park you walk up the path to arrive at a damaged relief of the Persian sun god Mithra, then past a second and clearer relief of Mithradates with Helios-Apollo wearing a cap with sun-rays radiating from it, and on to a large cave cut into the rock of the hillside, thought to have been used as a storage area and cistern. From here the path climbs up the hill to the main area of the ruins where there is a superb relief of a naked larger-than-life Hercules shaking hands with Mithradates, the founder of the Commagene dynasty. The cult of Hercules was widespread under the Syrian Seleucids, and this relief, like the statues of the Nemrut Daği summit, combines Hellenistic portraiture with stocky, heavy forms. (An 1880s cast of this relief can now be seen in the antiquities gallery of the newly redesigned Ashmolean Museum in Oxford, having emerged from the vaults now that there is room to display it. The iconography of shaking hands with the gods is taken from the Babylonian New Year festival.) Cut into the enormous rock wall below the relief is an inscription, and below that is a tunnel; its steps can still be walked down quite a long way, but the tunnel is now blocked at the bottom with debris and fallen rock. Its purpose is not known for sure but it is thought to have been used to fetch water from the river below.

From the tunnel the path climbs a little further to the highest point of the hilltop, through a heavily ruined gateway and various wall foundations. This was the town of Arsameia; the ruins are scant with nothing recognisable except a cistern and a few column bases. But the setting at the summit is lovely and makes a marvellous picnic spot among the long grass and spring flowers. There is a superb view down into the valley and across to the Mamluk castle known as **Yeni Kale** on a lower cliff outcrop.

From Arsameia there is a short cut that leads to the summit in about 16km, but it is a smaller road with precipitous hairpin bends, joining the main route about 6km before the summit car park. Most organised tours do both routes in a loop, one up the other down. Either way, the final 10km of the climb is far steeper, especially the final 3km, and has been laid with basalt block cobbles. As a result it is rather bone-rattling compared with the earlier stretches. In the final village below the summit there are a number of pensions and camping places. Look out too for the mud-brick houses with grass growing on their flat roofs. These have the advantage of providing good insulation against summer heat and winter cold, while chickens and livestock can fatten themselves on the lush summer grass.

Nemrut Dağı summit (altitude 2,206m) Beside the car park there is a modern building that doubles as a café and shop selling all sorts of souvenirs from local carpets to woollen socks and gloves. It is always quite chilly at the summit because of the altitude and you will need to be walking about for at least an hour to explore it properly, so warm clothing will definitely be required. Follow the path that leads up about 600m to arrive after a climb of some 15–20 minutes to reach the **Eastern Terrace** with a large rectangular sacrificial altar on its edge, which doubles as a helicopter landing pad for VIP visitors. The aerial views from here over the colossal jagged shape of Lake Atatürk created by the Atatürk Dam on the Euphrates in 1992 are totally breathtaking. The scale of the GAP Project really hits home from here (see page 23). In Antiochus's day of course, the view would have been simply over the Euphrates River, snaking its way across the plain far below.

Sitting majestically with their backs to the tumulus, facing the dawn, are what you have come all this way to see: the **five figures**, from left to right, of Apollo representing a synthesis of Mithra, Helius and Hermes; the only female anywhere on the mountaintop sanctuary, the Commagene fertility goddess representing Tyche, Fortuna and elements of local goddesses; Zeus (also Ahura and Mazda) in pride of place in the centre; Antiochus himself, recognisable from his moustache and beard and open mouth; and finally Hercules (also Artagnes and Ares). On the backs of the statues long Greek inscriptions detail the descent of the Commagenes and the rites to be used in their worship, with dawn sacrifices on the altar. Each Commagene god incorporates several similar deities, following the principle known as syncretism which the Greeks used after Alexander's death to try to unite Greek, Persian and other Near Eastern peoples. Their heads, tossed to the ground by earthquakes and by extremes of heat and cold over the centuries, were rearranged in order in the late 1990s to help visitors understand who they actually were. As a result they now stand to their full 10m height. They were always flanked by a lion and an eagle, the animals of the gods. The fine lion here is reminiscent of the Neo-Hittite lions at Karatepe. Like them he does not seem fierce but appears rather to smile benignly at the world below. In an attempt to protect the statues from the attentions of visitors a metal chain has been up in front of them to urge people not to climb on or touch them, and not to picnic or litter the area. All in vain, however, as in practice most people still pose endlessly for photos with their arms round the gods, 'me and my mate Zeus'-style, simply dismantling the chain, then putting it back again afterwards. As to the tumulus itself, signs now forbid people from climbing up it. It has yet to be excavated properly and the tomb of the king himself found, despite numerous tunnelling attempts by the American excavators since 1953.

There is certainly something rather absurd about the whole place, something ludicrous about the ego-inflated king's choice of final resting place. Seen from below on a clear day from the queen's burial mound, this **tumulus of the king** perched on the mountain top looks for all the world like a giant anthill, and certainly given the smallness of the kingdom and the shortness of its duration, its subjects must have spent most of their lives carrying rocks up the remote mountainside. Whether it was done with slave labour or how long it took is not known. No other Commagene buildings have survived besides the capital of Arsameia where the kings had their palace, so maybe there was no time left for the Commagene citizens to build anything else after they had seen to their king's needs.

From the Eastern Terrace a path to the side leads down to the Güneş Hotel and another leads round the far side of the tumulus past the heavily ruined Northern

Terrace and on to the Western Terrace, which is smaller overall, but has some of the finest pieces of carving. The five seated statues are as on the Eastern Terrace, backs to the tumulus, here facing the sunset rather than the dawn. They are less imposing and in poorer condition except for the heads, which for some reason better preserved. The head of the goddess Fortuna with garlands of vines, grapes and other fruits in her hair is especially lovely and is bigger than that of the clean-shaven Apollo who looks rather insipid and effeminate. Some visitors have seen in this head the spitting image of Elvis Presley. These statues again show the stylistic mix of Greek and oriental: the seated deities, 8–10m tall, have heavy static bodies, while the heads show the idealised Hellenistic features, often with Persian headdress.

Returning to Adıyaman you can now skirt the western edge of Lake Atatürk to reach Şanlıurfa (ancient Edessa) after 90 minutes of passing through fertile landscapes, making a gradual descent from the plateau at 800m onto the plain where it crosses the Euphrates. You could make a short detour here to see the **Atatürk Dam**, centrepiece of the mighty GAP Project. Fourth-largest dam in the world at 200m high, it is an impressive sight. Producing 900 billion kWh of electricity annually, it provides the whole of southeast Turkey with water and electricity, irrigates three million hectares of dry land and encourages the rural population to stay put rather than migrate to the cities. It aims to create 1.8 million new jobs.

After passing the lake you reach a T-junction at which left leads northeast to Diyarbakır and right leads south to Urfa. By this time you are down on the flat northern Mesopotamian Plain, even though the altitude is still over 500m, and the scenery is frankly dull. About 40km from Adıyaman, 1km to the west of the Adıyaman–Urfa motorway, are a group of 60 rock tombs known today as **Turuç (Kuyulu)**, or Tharse in ancient times. Difficult to spot from a distance, the tombs

THE LION HOROSCOPE – THE WORLD'S EARLIEST?

Around the statues here several superb reliefs have survived, unlike on the Eastern Terrace. Three of them show Antiochus shaking hands with Apollo, Zeus and Hercules. The finest, though, is the lion relief with a crescent moon, the planets and stars, in fact an astronomical chart which, from the conjunction of Mars, Mercury and Jupiter, was originally thought by scholars to suggest the date of 7 July 62BC: about the time Antiochus was set on his throne by the Roman general Pompey. This lion relief is thought to be the earliest horoscope in existence. It depicts 19 stars and three planets on the body of the lion and a crescent on the neck of it. Each star is shown as having eight rays emanating from it, while the three planets have 16 rays and are lined up along the lion's back. Their names, Mars, Jupiter and Mercury, are written beside them in Greek. Scholars studying the horoscope have concluded that Antiochus had this lion horoscope built to show all future comers how he was singled out by the gods, after an astrological event took place that only occurs every 25,000 years. This event, now thought to have taken place on 14 July 109BC, was that Mars (representing Hercules), Mercury (representing Apollo) and Jupiter (representing Zeus) all passed one after the other by Regulus, the star of the Commagene people, represented by the star above the crescent round the lion's neck. The crescent itself is thought to represent the kingdom of Commagene. The ancient Greeks believed that the most perfect humans were chosen by the gods to live among them and to shed light over them as constellations, hence Antiochus's belief that he had been thus chosen, and could sit among the gods as an equal. Over on the far side of the terrace are reliefs of Antiochus standing with his Persian ancestors, recognisable by their long gowns.

are reached by about 12 steps carved into the rock, leading down into the burial chambers, some of which have reliefs with various figures on the walls. Take a torch.

ŞANLIURFA (URFA) Telephone code: 414; altitude 518m

Do not expect too much of Urfa (as Şanlıurfa is called in common speech). In fact, if you are short of time you could miss Urfa and Harran altogether without shedding too many tears, and go straight on to Diyarbakır and Mardin. With the exception of the Halil Ar-Rahman Mosque and its Pool of Abraham, there is little of any great excitement here. It is a town of historical associations rather than tangible reminders of the past. As the *Guide Bleu* somewhat scathingly puts it (translated from the French): 'Urfa requires of its visitors a sort of almost mystic or purely intellectual sympathy for the history of civilisations, for religions and for the lands of Genesis, as nothing spectacular awaits you here; everything will be in your powers of imagination, your ability to feel and understand.' Be that as it may, thanks to a great improvement in its accommodation facilities, it is now firmly on most organised tour itineraries of all nationalities, especially pilgrimage tours, because of its biblical links. If you want to get a feel of the Middle East through the Arab cultures of Turkey, then a visit to Mardin via Diyarbakır gives you this far better than Urfa or Harran, and the scenery en route is also far more interesting. At least the roads have improved hugely in the last 20 years, thanks to the money from the GAP Project. In eastern Turkey conversation among strangers used to be not about the weather, that topic of such endless fascination to the English, but about the state of the roads.

HISTORY Urfa is a town of no great beauty, dusty and oppressively hot in summer, muddy in winter. Many of the Arab-style houses of the 15th century with gracefully carved windows and doors have been demolished to make way for new roads and buildings, with little attempt at restoration. On road signs you will see it called Şanlıurfa (Glorious Urfa) which is the epithet awarded to it after the independent Turkish Republic was declared. Kahramanmaraş (Hero Maraş) and Gaziantep (Warrior Antep) were the other two towns so honoured by Atatürk for the fight all three put up against the invading French armies in 1920.

When Alexander the Great passed this way after his victory of the Plain of Issus he named this town Edessa after the Macedonian city. In the 2nd century Edessa became the earliest Christian centre in Mesopotamia, and a school of religion and philosophy flourished here until the Arab conquest in the late 7th century. Edessa remained in Muslim hands until the 11th century when Count Baldwin detached himself from the First Crusade's march on Jerusalem and established a small Christian state here. When Saladin retook Edessa 50 years later the pope in Rome responded by calling for a Second Crusade. Edessa's history has therefore not been without incident, but like so many other once important cities in the region it never recovered from the Mongol invasion led by Hulagu in 1260, and which had destroyed Baghdad two years earlier.

GETTING THERE AND AWAY

By air Urfa now has its own new airport called GAP, 15km south of the city, in the middle of nowhere, heavily militarised and guarded with towers and fences. Flights from here are run by Turkish Airlines (*www.anadolujet.com*) to and from Ankara every day and by Turkish Airlines to Istanbul (Atatürk and Sabiha Gökçen).

By bus Urfa's *otogar* is on the western edge of town on the main road to Gaziantep. Connecting services link in all directions, such as south to Harran (30 minutes, TL5) and north to Adıyaman, for Nemrut Dağı (two hours, TL10).

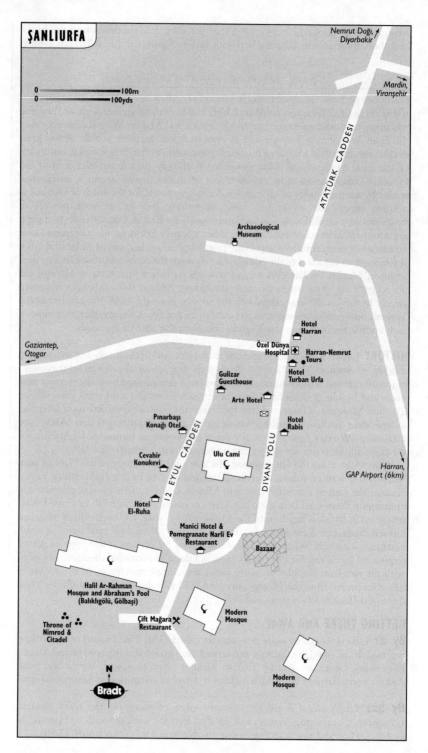

ŞANLIURFA

0 _____ 100m
0 _____ 100yds

Nemrut Dağı,
Diyarbakir

Mardin,
Viranşehir

ATATÜRK CADDESI

Archaeological
Museum

Gaziantep,
Otogar

Hotel
Harran

Özel Dünya
Hospital

Harran-Nemrut
Tours

Hotel
Turban Urfa

Gulizar
Guesthouse

Arte Hotel

Hotel
Rabis

Pınarbaşı
Konağı Otel

12 EYUL CADDESI

DIVAN YOLU

Ulu Cami

Cevahir
Konukevi

Harran,
GAP Airport (6km)

Hotel
El-Ruha

Manici Hotel &
Pomegranate Narli Ev
Restaurant

Bazaar

Halil Ar-Rahman
Mosque and Abraham's Pool
(Balıklıgölü, Gölbaşı)

Modern
Mosque

Throne of
Nimrod &
Citadel

Çift Mağara
Restaurant

N

Bradt

Modern
Mosque

TOURIST INFORMATION There is no tourist office but a good local travel agency is **Harran–Nemrut Tours** (*Köprübaşi Caddesi, behind the Özel Dunya Hospital;* ✎ *2151575;* ☉ *daily 08.30–18.00*). Run by a local English teacher, he can organise tours to Nemrut, Harran and Mardin, as well as organise flight and bus tickets with no surcharge. He can also sort out car hire.

⌂ WHERE TO STAY

⌂ **Hotel El-Ruha** (16 rooms) Balıklı Gol; ✎ 2154411; www.hotelelruha.com. Fabulous location close to the Sacred Lake, complete with pool, sauna, *hammam* & 2 enormous caves for the 'traditional nights' live music evenings. No alcohol allowed, but very luxurious rooms with thick-pile carpets. $$$$

⌂ **Manıcı Hotel** (12 rooms) ✎ 2159911; www.maniciurfa.com. Newly opened in 2009 in an amazing location at the foot of the citadel & close to Abraham's Pool. In an old building so over-restored it might as well be new. The colour scheme is ultra garish & over the top, real *Arabian Nights* fantasy style, with exotic orange & purple cushions etc. $$$$

⌂ **Cevahir Konukevi** (6 rooms, 1 suite) Valı Fuat Caddesi; ✎ 2159377; www.cevahirkonukevi. Formerly the governor's guesthouse, it was sold off in 2005 & converted to this fine boutique hotel by an energetic young woman. Her excellent cuisine can be sampled in the courtyard seating area, or else in a private upstairs room reclining on low couches à l'Arabe or like the ancient Greeks. The roof terrace has lovely views over the citadel & Abraham's Sacred Pool. AC. $$$

⌂ **Hotel Edessa** (64 rooms) Balıkgöl Mev. 63200; ✎ 2159911; www.hoteledessa.com. Situated in the old town centre in front of the Halil Ar-Rahman mosque & Fish Lake, this used to be the best in town before the El-Ruha & the Manıcı opened. The old period building still has charm but is a bit run-down. Unlicensed restaurant. $$$

⌂ **Hotel Harran** (118 rooms) Atatürk Bulvarı; ✎ 3132860; www.hotelharran.com. Modern hotel much used by businessmen. Swimming pool & summer terrace dining with Turkish musicians. Licensed restaurant with traditional local specialities, plush & a touch formal. $$$

⌂ **Pinarbaşi Konağı Otel/Restaurant** (8 rooms) 12 Eylül Caddesi; ✎ 2153919. Eat in one of the private upstairs rooms or on the roof terrace, & then the low couches convert to beds for the night. Simple en-suite bathrooms. Live music in the courtyard below. $$

⌂ **Hotel Rabis** (18 rooms) Sarayonu Caddesi; ✎ 2169595; www.hotelrabis.com. Urfa's most modern place with comfortable rooms & a good roof terrace. Good value. AC. $$

⌂ **Gülizar Guesthouse** (8 rooms) Irfaniye Sokak; ✎ 2150505; www.gulizarkonukevi.com. Between Water Sq & Earth Sq, 10km from Urfa airport. An exquisite stone-carved old Syrian-style mansion with courtyard. Dinner is served in the private rooms on the low benches that then convert into beds, with the genuine wool bedding emerging from the cupboards. Old-fashioned & very courteous service. No alcohol & only 1 bathroom, downstairs. $

✗ WHERE TO EAT

Urfa is famous for its kebabs; its *çig köfte* and *içli köfte* (deep-fried meatballs covered in bulgur (cracked wheat); and on the sweet side *sillik*, a pancake filled with walnuts. There are also many *pastahanes* serving pistachio baklavas and other sticky pastries all along the main street. To sit with tea or a fizzy drink, the many *çay bahçesi* (tea gardens) around the Sacred Lake under the shady trees are a wonderful place to linger and drink in the ambiance.

✗ **Pomegranate Narlı Ev Restaurant** Attached to the Manıcı Hotel; magnificent terrace overlooking the citadel. $$$$

✗ **Çift Mağara** Directly above the Sacred Pool, the name means 'Double Cave' because the inside dining area is cut into the rock facing the citadel, but the outdoor terrace has much better views. No alcohol but very good *köfte*. $$

ENTERTAINMENT AND NIGHTLIFE In the old quarter around the Ulu Cami and the Sacred Lake there are several Konak Evleri, lovely stone 19th-century mansions set round courtyards. Most are restaurants though some also offer basic accommodation in the rooms off the courtyard, where you can eat or sleep on the Ottoman-style cushions. These are lacking in privacy but quite atmospheric and fun, and they are ideal for large parties like weddings and other celebrations. Most nights in season and especially at weekends they have live traditional music in the courtyard, and enthusiastic souls may feel tempted to get up and dance along. Alcohol is never present at these occasions but the atmosphere is lively enough without it.

OTHER PRACTICALITIES There is a huge fee-paying underground **car park** just off the busy road at the foot of the citadel which is the best place to park, as Urfa's one-way system and busy streets do not lend themselves to easy parking elsewhere.

The **post office**, **ATMs** and **internet cafés** are on the main street, as is the well-equipped private **hospital** called Özel Dunya (Private World) (\ 2162772).

WHAT TO SEE
Balıklıgölü Area, Gölbaşi (Lakeside, with Abraham's Sacred Pool) (*At the foot of the citadel set in a landscaped complex of mosques & madrasas*) This is undoubtedly the highlight of Urfa and you will enjoy the atmosphere most if you sit and join the local people at one of the tables under the trees around the pools for a tea or cold drink – alcohol is not on offer. Try the bitter local coffee, *murra-mirr*, drunk without sugar and made from local berries. During Ramazan the restaurants round the pools contrive to function by putting up cloth fences like windbreaks so that people can eat inside without offending the public outside. Avoid the *faux pas* of asking for fish. There are in fact two pools: the larger one below the citadel with a fountain and rowing boats, and the original Balıklıgölü (Lake with Fish) which is the sacred Abraham's Pool.

To reach the pools you stroll past the bazaar to reach at the foot of the citadel a complex of several mosques set in landscaped rose gardens. Some of the mosques are 17th-century Ottoman, some older, like the famous Halil Ar-Rahman Mosque at the western end of Abraham's Pool.

Citadel (⊕ 08.00–20.00; adult TL2) From the fish lakes a wide path with steps leads up to the top of the citadel, restored by the Crusaders and Turks, but with traces from Hellenistic, Roman and Byzantine times. A pair of Corinthian columns crowning the top are known as the **Throne of Nimrod** and Abraham was supposed to have been tossed from up here onto the funeral pyre below, now the lake. Another version is that they are the remains of a temple of Baal. One of them bears an inscription in Syriac. From this vantage point there is an excellent view over the town. At night it is beautifully floodlit, and you can descend through a fine long tunnel cut into the rock, to emerge at the bottom on the western side of the citadel.

Bazaar (⊕ 07.30–18.30 Mon–Sat) The covered part of the market is the oldest and most interesting, and you will hear Turkish, Arabic and Kurdish being spoken by the merchants and artisans. Built by Süleyman the Magnificent in the 16th century, look out for the *bedestens* (covered halls) where goods were stored, each with their own product such as silk, leather, etc. In the Gümrük Hanı, a 16th-century *bedesten*, you can sip tea and coffee with the local shoppers and vendors.

Ulu Cami Distinguished by its fine tall octagonal minaret with a clock on top, originally the belfry of an earlier Byzantine church on the same site, Urfa's Ulu Cami (Great Mosque) is based on a design similar to the Great Mosque at

Legend has it that when Abraham passed this way, he was thrown on a funeral pyre by an angry Nimrod, the Assyrian king, for destroying the pagan idols in the temple. To save him, God created a lake which put out the fire and the burning coals became fish. Abraham of course, whose name means 'Father of a great multitude', is revered not only by Jews and Christians but by Muslims too, and this event is always portrayed as a clash between good (Abraham) and evil (Nimrod). And so this spot attracts Muslim pilgrims, who come to enjoy the pool and linger, watching the sacred carp. The spot itself encourages a certain amount of lingering as it is charming and peaceful, with attractive landscaped gardens intersected by canals leading to the pool. The water comes from the Spring of Callirrhoë. There are several restaurants and cafés round the pools where families sit and relax, and it is not unusual to see head-scarved older women sitting with their husband and children, smoking just like the men. Even rowing boats are now for rent on the larger lake, filled to bursting with family members old and young, large and small, all enjoying the occasion. The Muslim tradition with sacred places has always been to enjoy them, viz picnicking on the graves of departed family members in Cairo's City of the Dead and taking thermos flasks of tea into Damascus's Great Umayyad Mosque. Children in particular are encouraged to enjoy themselves, so they grow up feeling religion is part of normal everyday life, not just confined to the hush and whispers of church on Sundays. There is also a large new fountain in the centre of this pool.

Abraham's Pool is immediately behind the larger pool, a long thin rectangle, the water a beautiful green colour surrounded by graceful arches. The sacred carp, grey, and ranging from colossal salmon-sized monsters to tiny ones the size of goldfish, are severely overcrowded and are beginning to show signs of cannibalism. This is evidently their answer to the population problem: their sacred status forbids killing them and anyone eating them will go blind according to local superstition. At the side of the pool cooked chickpeas are for sale to feed the fish, who appear in fact very bored by this fare. On occasion however you can also buy sprigs of a green herb which drive them beserk. Wherever the sprig lands immediately becomes a seething wriggling mass of carp. Either the fish are very keen on their greens or else the herb has some drug-like property and they are all frantic for their 'fix'.

Aleppo and was founded in the 12th century by Nureddin. Completely walled and enclosed in its own courtyard, it is entered by a beautiful carved gateway. The tall cypress trees and fine tall gravestones arranged in a small graveyard in one corner give the place an atmosphere of calm and serenity. You can visit as a non-Muslim as long as you are respectfully dressed, with bare skin and hair covered if you are female.

The streets all round the Ulu Cami form Urfa's old quarter and you can take a few minutes to stroll round, getting a feel for the old-style houses, all built round private courtyards, showing nothing to the street beyond their front doors.

Archaeological Museum (⏰ *08.00–17.00 Tue–Sun; adult TL3*) Out of town on a road to the northwest, this museum's main exhibit is a fine mosaic found in a rock chamber in a valley near the citadel, representing seven people whose names are inscribed above them in Syriac. Other exhibits are from the Great Mosque at Harran, and some Assyrian and Hittite reliefs taken from the Hittite site at Sultantepe 15km south of Urfa.

SOUTH TO HARRAN

The terrain south of Urfa has been transformed from dry dusty plains into lush cultivated crops, thanks to the irrigation of the GAP Project, and it is now a dual carriageway instead of a pot-holed track as it was in the 1980s. At 15km south of Urfa on the road to Harran a small road forks off left and leads to a mound in the middle of the plain known locally as Sultantepe, the Hill of the Sultan.

Some 28km eastwards on a bad track you can reach Eski Soğmatar, the sanctuary of the heathen Sabians who as late as the 14th century were still making human sacrifices. There is little to see here; it is of interest above all for its associations.

HARRAN (ALTINBAŞAK) *Telephone code: 414*

Most people make the journey to Harran because of its biblical associations. It was 18 centuries before Christ that Abraham was called from Ur of the Chaldees to go to Canaan according to the Old Testament. He stopped at Harran for several years until God told him to move on:

> So Abram departed, as the Lord had spoken unto him: and Abram was seventy and five years old when he departed out of Haran. And Abram took Sarai his wife, and Lot his brother's son, and all their substance that they had gathered, and the souls that they had gotten in Haran; and they went forth to go into the land of Canaan
>
> *Genesis 12:4-5*

Harran lies 35 minutes' drive south of Urfa across a totally flat and featureless plain towards the Syrian border. Reconciling this wasteland with the image conjured up of Mesopotamia where civilisation grew up on the banks of fertile rivers is no easy matter, as Robert Byron mused in his *Road to Oxiana* (see page 248). The Southeast Anatolia Project is slowly but surely in the process of transforming this landscape back to fertility. Nearly all of the 22 dams have now been completed, but with the massive change in climate and environment have come some less desirable changes: reported cases of malaria have doubled according to the Turkish Health Ministry, and of course Syria and Iraq, the two countries downstream of the project, complain bitterly of reduced waterflow.

THE FIRST WORK OF LITERATURE – *THE EPIC OF GILGAMESH*

It was here that the British archaeologist Seton Lloyd found tablets of the Babylonian *Epic of Gilgamesh*, dated to c2000BC and other tablets written in Assyrian and Sumerian hieroglyphs. Sumerian hero and King of Uruk, Gilgamesh, two-thirds god, one-third man, together with his friend Enkidu, fought the giant Humbaba, and his exploits seduced the goddess Ishtar. When he spurned her advances, she made Enkidu die. Mad with grief Gilgamesh abandoned his kingdom and set off on a series of peripatetic wanderings in search of immortality. He ends by resigning himself to his mortality and returns to his kingdom. The moral is summed up by the famous words spoken to Gilgamesh: 'You will never find that life for which you are looking. When the gods created man they allotted to him death, but life they retained in their own keeping.' With its flood story and its hero's wanderings, the *Epic of Gilgamesh* is widely regarded as the earliest work of literature, foreshadowing the biblical flood story and the wanderings of Homer's *Odyssey*.

THE SIN-WORSHIPPING SABIANS

The mystical Sabian sect was, because of its belief in one God, recognised by Islam as on a par with Christianity and Judaism. The Sabian religion united Neo-Platonic philosophy with Babylonian astrology, considering the planets as embodying spiritual beings created by God as part of the universe, especially the moon, whose god they called Sin. The Sabians had a holy script, the believers sacrificed to the sun and the moon, and they had an initiation ceremony and a kind of communion. Facing always to the north, they prayed at dawn, midday and sunset. The principal deity was worshipped in the form of a pillar or holy stone, and under him were the sun god (Shamash), the moon god (Sin), Saturn (Kronos), Jupiter (Bel), Mars (Ares), Venus (Balti) and Mercury (Nabuq). Every day of the week was dedicated to one of these deities. The main moon god sanctuary was at Harran where the cult was practised into the 12th century. In 830 the caliph Al-Mamun was filled with indignation at the dress, long hair, and scandalous behaviour of the Sabians and gave them the choice of converting to Islam or to Christianity or face exile or hanging. One medieval Arab chronicler wrote of their wild practices: 'There was no hill that was not moist with the blood of sacrifices, and no high place that was empty of libations. Youths in multitudes were given as sacrifices, and maidens slaughtered to female idols and to the sun and the moon and Venus and other luminaries.'

GETTING THERE AND AWAY

By minibus There are hourly departures to Harran from Urfa's *otogar* that will drop you in New Harran, a ten-minute walk from the old part.

WHERE TO STAY

Bozdan Motel (8 rooms) ⟍ 4413590; e bazdal@ttnet. At the entrance to town when you arrive from Urfa, attractively designed to mimic beehive house architecture, built round a central courtyard & set back in its own grassy garden. Sadly the interior does not live up to the promise of the outside, & the rooms, although spacious, are poorly cleaned & the bathrooms badly finished & with defective plumbing. In summer it is also severely mosquito-infested, so make sure you are prepared. The staff's attitude is summed up by the slogan on the T-shirt of one of the waiters: 'I'm here to hurt your feelings'. $$

Harran Evi ⟍ 4412020 **& Kultur Evi** ⟍ 4412477. Both these places offer simple accommodation, in high communal beds raised up on stilts (*tahts*) to be safe from scorpions & non-flying insects, out of doors in summer (the coolest place to be), & inside the beehive huts in winter, sleeping on mattresses on the floor. This is the way the local people themselves live. Washing facilities are communal & basic. $

WHERE TO EAT

Nowhere serves alcohol, so any notions you may have of enjoying the sunset over a relaxing beer will be dashed. Harran Evi has a pleasant garden with rustic seating for simple refreshments.

WHAT TO SEE

Beehive houses Visitors come mainly to see the mud-brick beehive houses clustered together like a termite colony, more typical of northern Syria, and to imagine Abraham and his family living in just such a house, unchanged for centuries. These windowless cones are built as the only way to achieve a roof without timber, and so the shape is dictated by the only material to hand in abundance – mud. They are thought to have kept exactly the same design since Abraham's time, except that modern ones now have electricity wires and TV

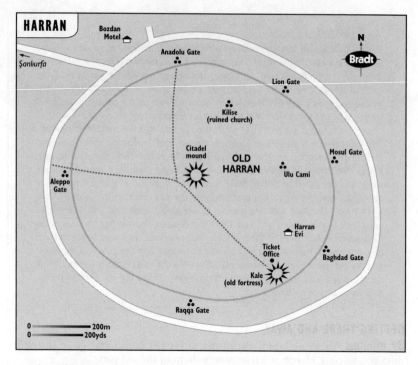

aerials sticking out. The high dome collects the hotter air and the temperature inside is said to remain within liveable ranges in the extremes of both summer and winter. The mud withstands minor earthquakes and wind pressure and sudden rainfall runs off the steep roof before the mud brick can absorb it. Be warned that tourism is a newly discovered source of wealth and the local youths and children are very persistent in offering their services as guides. *Para* (money) and *kalem* (pen) are words you will hear a lot of from here eastwards.

Jacob's Well Another biblical association attaches to a well about 1km northwest of Harran, called Bir Yakub, Jacob's Well. Was it here that Jacob kissed Rachel and that Rebecca, later to marry Isaac, drew water for Abraham's servant? Local youths will offer to take you there on their motorbikes for a fee so you can judge for yourself.

Ulu Cami and Old City The original settlement at Harran is indicated by a mound at the centre of the stone-walled city and you can make a complete circuit of the walls (4km in total, so preferably with your own transport or even on the back of a local guide's moped). The site is extensive and shadeless. First built by the Roman emperor Justinian, the walls are heavily ruined for the most part, but they can be traced by ramparts and ditches where the stones have vanished. You enter the city at the western side (where the main road from Urfa first arrives at it) at the Aleppo Gate, restored by Saladin in 1192 but now much ruined. There were six gates, the others being the Raqqa Gate (towards Syria), the Baghdad Gate, the Mosul Gate, the Anadolu Gate and the Lion Gate, all except the last named after the destination that the road led to from that gate. At the centre of the city and to the northeast of the mound is the other monument of note, the vast and ruinous Ulu Cami. T E Lawrence, who travelled past Harran *en route* from Aleppo to Urfa in 1909 when he was still an Oxford student, mistook from a distance the 33.3m-tall square brick minaret of this mosque for a campanile. He wrote in his diary: 'The tower of Harran cathedral was in sight for four hours'. The mosque was founded in the 8th century by the Umayyads and rebuilt in the 12th century by Saladin. Within its courtyard is a pretty marble fountain, and scattered all around are carved capitals and fragments of rose-coloured column. The mosque was part of the earliest Islamic university complex, a kind of forerunner of the *medrese* system which the Seljuks and Ottomans expanded.

Kale (Old Harran Fortress) (⊕ *daily 08.00–18.00; adult TL2*) Walking through the city and over the mound, coming down the other side, you come to a cluster of beehive houses, some of them now acting as tourist centres and offering simple accommodation and food. Beyond them at the southeast corner of the walls is the most prominent monument of Harran, a large crumbling 11th-century fortress built on the site of a moon temple, and surrounded by a moat-like ditch. The site ticket office is set up beside it and also charges for car parking. It is better preserved inside, the vaulting still intact in many rooms. One of the towers has an impressive ten-sided shape. Watch your step as there are many unguarded holes in the floor where you could fall through the ceiling to the level below.

EAST TO DİYARBAKIR

The drive northeast to Diyarbakır takes just two hours across what used to be bleak wasteland. No more speculation about whether to blame climatic change, too many goats, Mongolian destruction of irrigation works or too many centuries of armies fighting each other and foraging – the GAP Project has transformed it into fertile fields of wheat. The road east to Mardin via Viransehir should be avoided as you will share the 162km of road with the oil tankers for whom it is the main transit route to Mosul in Iraq. At Viransehir (City of Ruins), the Roman city of Constantina, the basalt defence walls and towers run for over 2km, repaired in the 6th century by Justinian.

DİYARBAKIR   *Telephone code: 412; altitude 670m*

Diyarbakır, 177km from Urfa and capital of the Kurdish heartlands and sometimes referred to as the unofficial capital of Kurdistan, has boomed in recent years with a huge suburban sprawl and blocks of flats, testimony to the money that has poured in thanks to the GAP Project, and to the need for extra housing for local Kurds who have chosen to settle here to take up the new jobs that have come with the boom. Towns in southeast Turkey like Diyarbakır used to be populated with Ottoman officials, Arabic-speaking townspeople and Turkish-speaking Armenians, along with Kurdish chieftains who had their mansions in the towns. The mass settlement of Kurds here began with the expulsion of the Armenians during and immediately after World War I, when they moved into Armenian houses and even took over some of the trades that had always been an Armenian preserve. Diyarbakır always had the confidence of a place that has been important for centuries, and has always been the key city of Turkey's southeast, so now that confidence has redoubled. Most people enjoy their stay here more than in other eastern cities. It has a special identity, special in the same way that Avila in Spain, Aleppo and Damascus in Syria and Fez in Morocco are special, all cities that have until recently been bounded within their walls. Inside it has grown up with distinctive quarters, Armenian, Christian, Kurdish and Arab, each with its own community buildings, churches and mosques, and in the narrow winding streets there is the feel of hidden courtyards behind large carved wooden doors, inward-looking, Arab-style.

The approach from the north, west or east sadly gives you no feel for the setting of the city and its walls, and it is really only from the air that you can appreciate the great Old City enclosed in its black basalt walls. In its position at the limit of navigability on the Tigris and at a convenient crossing point, Diyarbakır, backed by the eastern Taurus Mountains, dominates the expanse of the northern Mesopotamian Plain. Once inside the walls you are not aware of the Tigris, but perhaps because the city is concentrated within the walls, you can feel the vitality humming in the streets which are busy with confident colourful people. The produce in the shops, especially the fruit, vegetables and local Kurdish cheese, is better quality than anything you will find further east. There is even a cheese market just devoted to the Kurdish white cheeses, just off the main street Gazi Pasa, close to the Büyük Kervanseray Otel.

Because of its strategically important position on the Tigris, commanding the southeastern lowlands, the city is an important base for the Turkish military and used to have an American airbase until it was closed down in 1997 as part of the general closing down of American airbases in Europe. The headquarters of the Turkish Seventh Army, which is responsible for security throughout southeastern Turkey in addition to its NATO duties, was recently moved out of the ancient citadel to a modern building several kilometres outside town, and the tactical

THE PATH TO ENLIGHTENMENT

Diyarbakır has a predominantly Kurdish population and until recently was a natural centre of Kurdish dissident groups. In the Kurdish revolt of the 1920s Diyarbakır played a major role and in 1925 a special tribunal at Diyarbakır tried the leaders and closed the *tekkes* (dervish monasteries) of the Nakşibendi dervish order, which had been implicated. After Turkey's 1980 military coup, thousands of suspected dissidents were locked up in the prison, Turkey's most notorious. Today though there is no real evidence of tension or hostility, and you can walk and talk freely in all areas of the city. No incidents have occurred here for years, and the flat terrain of the region does not lend itself to guerrilla activity. In the neighbouring mountainous Province of Siirt however, there are still occasional Kurdish guerrilla attacks on the Turkish army.

Back in the 1980s peasants armed with agricultural tools could be seen lining up in the morning by the walls, hoping to be chosen to pile into trucks and go off to work in the fields for the day. The squalid streets were full of children and flies, each family with an average of eight offspring. In those days the city's young and forward-looking mayor saw the cycle thus: 'Overpopulation fosters a lack of development, which fosters ignorance, which fosters dependency on religion, which fosters overpopulation by discouraging birth control, which results in further retarded development.' Now his prayers have been answered as the Southeast Anatolia Project has enabled the conversion of an area of bleak wasteland nearly the size of England into irrigated fields. And another unexpected twist is that Sufism, mystical Islam, has come back into vogue with Diyarbakır's young, and with tacit official approval. Strictly speaking Sufism is illegal under the constitution introduced by Atatürk, but evidently the authorities are relieved that the young Kurds, formerly unemployed and living in the slums, have found a new channel for their energies. One Kurdish student admitted: 'We were all pretty wild once. I was arrested for stabbing a man a few years ago, but religion set us straight. Who needs the Kurdish Workers' Party when you've got God?'

Ancient and traditional enemies of the Armenians, the Kurds are a distinct racial group indigenous to the region known as Kurdistan, which today straddles the modern borders of Turkey, Syria, Iran and Iraq, encroaching also on small areas of Armenia and Azerbaijan. There are 25 million Kurds in total, a very large number indeed for a 'minority': only a handful of Arab states have entire populations larger than this. By far the greatest number are in Turkey, estimated at 12 million, making up 15% of the population, 10% of the population in Iran and 23% of the population in Iraq. The Kurdish language, Indo-European like Persian, Armenian and most European languages, has several dialects, all of which are mutually unintelligible, a fact which has not helped the Kurds in their attempts to unite: there are currently seven separate Kurdish national movements. Kermanji is the purest dialect, spoken in the Hakkâri, in northern Iraq, and in the Kurdish province of Iran. Like Persian, it uses the Arabic alphabet. Within Turkey the Kurdish language was until recently banned from schools, universities, the radio and television. In late 2009, however, a more enlightened government has realised the futility of such bans and the resentment it stores up, and has relaxed the rules, so that Kurdish TV and radio channels are now allowed, Kurdish schools have been set up, and it is even possible to study Kurdish at university. Most Kurdish children are bilingual, speaking Kurdish at home and Turkish at work and at school. When Prime Minister Recep Tayyip Erdoğan unveiled his radical plan for a democratic initiative to include rather than exclude the Kurds of eastern Turkey, he said: 'Our nation wants solidarity and unity. It wants to stop the crying of mothers. It does not want blood and death', a reference to the 40,000 lives lost since the PKK launched its armed struggle in 1984.

The majority of Kurds, having originally been Zoroastrians like the Persians, gradually accepted Islam after the Arab conquest of the 7th century and are now Sunni Muslims, like the Turks, but unlike the Persians who are now Shi'a. Even today, however, some 50,000 Kurds are still said to be *Yazidi* or peacock-god worshippers, often unfairly referred to in the West as devil-worshippers. They call themselves Zoroastrians. These are the ones whom the Turks and Armenians have most feared in the past. They worship the sun and water is sacred to them. For fear of the power of evil (for them the universe is a struggle between light and dark, good and bad), and they never refer to Satan by name. Children are dedicated to both God and Satan. James Morier in his 19th-century novel *Ayesha* says of them: 'Their name is synonymous with blasphemers, barbarians and men of blood. They never eat cabbage because the Devil inhabits the leaves and they abominate the colour blue.'

wing of the Turkish air force attached to the joint US–Turkish base has been donated 44 F-104 Starfighter planes by Canada.

HISTORY The city takes its present name from the Arab tribe, the Beni Bakr, who took the city in AD639, Diyarbakır meaning 'Place of the Bakr'. Enclosed within its 5km-long walls built by the Byzantines and subsequently added to and decorated by various Arab, Kurdish and Turkish dynasties, Diyarbakır has more historical mosques, churches and other notable buildings than any other Turkish city except Istanbul.

The Kurds have always been a **nomadic mountain people** and in Turkey they used to be officially known as 'mountain Turks', the existence of a separate Kurdish race being studiously ignored by the authorities. Erdoğan's government has recently realised the futility of such a policy, and now Kurds are far more integrated at all levels of society. By and large, throughout their history, they did not resist invaders, but were content to pack their tents and drive their animals to still higher mountains away from the main passes. Owing to these evasive tactics of non-resistance they have been nominally ruled by Arabs, Mongols, Seljuks, Ilhans and other Persian rulers, Black Sheep and White Sheep Turcoman chieftains and Ottomans, up to the time of their division between three main countries after World War I. Under the 1920 Treaty of Sèvres drawn up by the Allies, Kurdistan was to have become an autonomous state, and had it not been for Atatürk's War of Independence, this Kurdish state would now exist. Ironically however the Kurds joined Atatürk in warding off the Greek Christians and the Persians on both fronts, and then, not surprisingly, felt cheated when Atatürk declared the Turkish Republic and abandoned the caliphate for a secular state. In the **Kurdish revolts** that followed in the 1920s and 1930s, hundreds of thousands of Kurds were killed or deported by the Turks. In the 1980s and 1990s there were many clashes between Kurdish guerrillas and Turkish armed forces, but since 2000 such attacks have reduced dramatically, though they are not entirely a thing of the past, especially further east in the Hakkâri and Doğubeyazıt areas.

Though they practised a policy of evasion in the face of conquerors marching through, the Kurds have been far from unwarlike themselves and have been ready to fight in other people's wars away from their home ground. The Hasanwaghs and the Marwanids in the 19th century both established dynasties, and because they adopted Arabic as their language are often wrongly referred to as Arabs. The great Saladin, hero of the Crusades, was a Kurd, and the Kurds are naturally proud to have produced one of the greatest heroes of Islam and the Muslim leader most respected in the West.

The Turks have always had great difficulty collecting taxes from the nomadic Kurds. Whenever they expected a visit from the tax-collector, they packed up their chattels and migrated to the mountains, only returning to the plains when their spies told them the coast was clear. The authorities have long had a resettlement programme for the Kurds, trying to persuade them to depend less on their pastoral ways and do some farming to become food suppliers for the big cities. This is a key part of the rationale behind the GAP Project, with incentives for Kurdish nomads to abandon their age-old practice of growing only what they need to survive themselves, and selling their livestock from time to time to purchase their other needs.

GETTING THERE AND AWAY

By air The airport is just 5km to the southwest of the city centre. Flights are operated by Turkish Airlines (www.thy.com) to Istanbul (two hours) and Ankara; Onur Air (www.onurair.com) to Istanbul; Pegasus Airlines (www.flypgs.com) to Izmir (two hours), Ankara (one hour) and Istanbul and Sun Express (www.sunexpress.com.tr) to Izmir, Antalya, Bursa and Istanbul. Taxis run to the city centre for TL15, and the airlines run shuttle buses from the airport to their city centre offices.

By train The station is also to the southwest, on İstasyon Caddesi, 1.5km from the centre, and the *Güney Ekspresi* (South Express) sets off to and from Istanbul four days a week, calling at Malatya, Sivas and Kayseri. Consult the Turkish Railways website www.tcdd.gov for exact timetables and fares, which vary according to season.

By bus Diyarbakır's *otogar* is 14km from the centre on the road to Urfa. All the bus company offices are in town on İnönü Caddesi or Gazi Caddesi, and services run

THE NOMADIC WAY OF LIFE

Freya Stark in her book *Riding to the Tigris* (1959) reflects romantically on the nomad way of life:

> It is easy for the peasant, and for all of us who live in civilisation and think to make the world more habitable, to point out that the nomad does very little. He leaves things as he finds them, destroying them in a small way if it suits him. He does not spend his life as we do in altering the accidents that happen to us so as to make them more bearable – but he accepts them with gaiety and endures them with fortitude, and this is his triumph and his charm. We may think reasonably enough that we dominate circumstances more than he does, since we adapt them to our needs: but he has discovered that the meaning of life is more important than its circumstance – and this freedom of the soul, in which all things that happen come and go, makes him splendid – him and his gaunt women and dogs and horses, on the edge of starvation in the rain and the sun. His life does not allow him to forget the greater size of the world; and no amount of civilisation is worth the loss of this fundamental sense of proportion between the universe and man.

Looking at Diyarbakır's faceless residential tower blocks on the outskirts of town, you cannot help wondering whether they are happier with what they have now.

everywhere you would expect, such as to and from Şanlıurfa (three hours, TL15), Van (seven hours, TL30) and Mardin (90 minutes, TL7). A taxi out there costs TL20.

There is also a separate minibus terminal (called *Ilce Garaji*) located 1.5km southwest of the city walls, on the same road that also leads to the train station and the *otogar*, from which regular services run to more local places like Batman (90 minutes, TL7), Malatya (five hours, TL15) and Mardin (again 90 minutes, TL7). Buses run from Kibris Caddesi out to this *Ilce Garaji* for TL1 or you can take a taxi (TL20).

By car There is now a new dual carriageway leading most of the way from Urfa to Diyarbakır. Both sides of the road are flat treeless plateau, now covered in cornfields, green, yellow or brown, depending on the time of year you pass by. On the way you pass through Siverek, a small town from which a drive of 30km northwest takes you to a *feribot* (car ferry) crossing over Lake Atatürk towards Nemrut Dağı and Adıyaman, an interesting alternative approach to the mountain sanctuary if you have your own transport.

GETTING AROUND The one-way system as you arrive from the north at Harput Kapısı does not allow you to drive down the main north–south street (Gazi Caddesi). To reach the southern part of the walled city, follow signs for Mardin Kapi which will loop you round the circle of the walls to get there. Once inside the walls everything is easily walkable on foot. Taxis are also plentiful to run you to the *otogar* (TL20), airport (TL15) or train station (TL4).

TOURIST INFORMATION There are two tourist offices (⊕ *09.00–12.00 & 13.00–18.00 Tue–Sat*): one just beside Harput Gate, the other less than 300m away, also close to the northern walls, just outside the next ex-gate. Both have maps and leaflets to hand out but as ever look blank if you ask anything out of the ordinary.

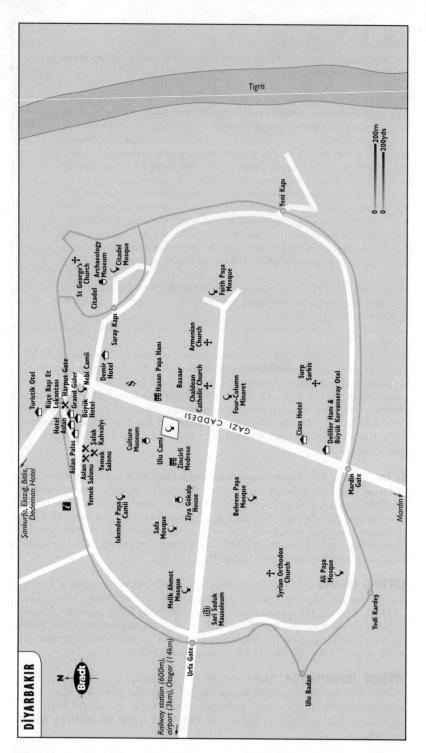

DİYARBAKIR

N

Bradt

Tigris

0 ————— 200m
0 ————— 200yds

St George's Church
Citadel
Archaeology Museum
Citadel Mosque

Saray Kapı

Yeni Kapı

Faith Paşa Mosque

Turistik Otel
Küçe Başı Et Lokantasi
Harput Gate
Grand Güler
Nebi Camii

Hotel Aslan
Aslan Palas
Büyük Hotel
Şafak
Yemek Kahvalyı

Demir Hotel

Hasan Paşa Hani

Armenian Church

Bazaar
Chaldean Catholic Church

Surp Sarkis

Şanlıurfa, Elazıg, Bitlis, Dedeman Hotel

Yemek Salonu
Yemek Salonu

Culture Museum

Ulu Cami
Zincirli Medrese

Four-Column Minaret

Class Hotel

Deliller Hani & Büyük Kervanseray Otel

GAZI CADDESI

İskender Paşa Camii

Safa Mosque

Ziya Gökalp House

Behrem Paşa Mosque

Mardin Gate

Mardin

Melik Ahmet Mosque

Sari Saduk Mausoleum

Syrian Orthodox Church

Ali Paşa Mosque

Yedi Kardeş

Railway station (600m), airport (3km), Otogar (14km)

Urfa Gate

Ulu Badan

236

WHERE TO STAY

🏠 **Class Hotel** (120 rooms) Gazi Caddesi, very close to the Büyük Kervanseray but a little closer to the centre; ☎ 2295000; www.diyarbakirclasshotel.com. Diyarbakır's fanciest & most expensive place, very plush, with outdoor pool, gym, sauna & *hammam*. The street exterior presents a modern glass-fronted building, but inside it conceals the *Cizmeci Köşkü*, a traditional Ottoman house that has been converted to provide elegant lounges for hotel guests. $$$$$

🏠 **Dedeman Otel** (98 rooms) Elâzığ Caddesi, on the Elâzığ road in the New City; ☎ 2290000; www.dedeman.com. The businessman's choice on the outskirts of town, 5km from the airport, offering excellent facilities with outdoor pool to match. $$$$

🏠 **Turistik Otel** (45 rooms) ☎ 2112295. The city's newest addition, just outside the walls near Harput Gate. $$$$

🏠 **Büyük Kervanseray** (45 rooms) Gazi Caddesi beside the Mardin Gate; ☎ 2289606; e hotelkervanseray@superonline.com; ⏱ May–Oct. If you can afford it, this should be your base of choice, a large Ottoman caravanserai formerly called Delliler Hani (Caravanserai of the Guides, who showed pilgrims around) built in 1521–27. Originally it had 72 rooms, 17 shops & stabling for over 800 camels & was a stopover on the Silk Road *en route* to Syria. The spacious courtyard with its mature trees & colourful flowers offers a wonderful retreat from the city bustle, & all meals are taken here. The rooms, all set on the upper floor as they would originally have been for the merchants, are dark & not very spacious, but have AC, a fridge & good en-suite bathrooms. In the second courtyard at the back away from the street there is a very fine swimming pool. $$$

🏠 **Büyük Hotel** (35 rooms) İnönü Caddesi; ☎ 2281295. Reliable choice, if rather dull, but good for solo women travellers. AC. $$

🏠 **Grand Güler** (50 rooms) Kıbrıs Caddesi; ☎ 2281735; e grandgulerhotel@hotmail.com. Rendered distinctive only by its blue mosaic façade onto the street, this place is favoured by low-budget tour groups. Restaurant, AC. $$

🏠 **Aslan Palas** (14 rooms) Kıbrıs Caddesi; ☎ 2289224. The most basic option to consider, rooms have AC but no b/fast. $

🏠 **Hotel Aslan** (22 rooms) Kıbrıs Caddesi; ☎ 2247096. Clean & bright, the best of the budget options. $

✗ WHERE TO EAT

Many of the cheaper places to eat are along Kibris Caddesi close to the hotels. **Aslan Yemek Salonu**, **Kuce Basi Et Lokantasi**, **Safak Kahvalyi** and **Yemek Salonu** are all good choices for simple kebabs, *pide* and sometimes a sticky dessert, though you may have to go direct to the *pastahanes* to make sure these are really fresh. There is nowhere that serves particularly special food, so your choice will be made on the basis of ambience or price. Alcohol is only available in the hotels.

✗ **Büyük Kervanseray** ☎ 2289606; ⏱ 08.00–22.30. In the courtyard of the converted caravanserai hotel, this is a very relaxing ambiance, spacious & open with trees & flowers. It is also fully licensed. $$$

✗ **Hasan Paşa Hanı** ⏱ 09.00–22.30. Although there are no actual restaurants in this attractively restored 16th-century caravanserai there are a number of tea-houses scattered among the shops for a quiet break in your sightseeing. $

SHOPPING

The main handicrafts of Diyarbakır to look out for in the shops are gold- and silverwork, copper and silk. Silk clothes, handkerchiefs and scarves are famous. Weaving is also renowned, so *kilims*, saddlebags and prayer rugs are good buys, along with embroidered towels. Almost opposite the Büyük Kervanseray Hotel is an impressive cheese market (*Peynir Çarşişi*) selling all the different types of local Kurdish white cheese, perfect for picnics. Fruit and groceries can also be bought along the main street.

OTHER PRACTICALITIES

There is a huge hospital on the outskirts of town as you approach from Urfa, with a massive modern A&E department. The post office (⏱ 08.30–12.00 & 13.00–17.00 Mon–Fri), ATMs and internet cafés are all clustered along Gazi Caddesi, the main street within the walls of old Diyarbakır, so there is no reason to set foot in new Diyabakir unless you are unfortunate enough to need the hospital.

WHAT TO SEE It takes several hours to walk around the various quarters of old Diyarbakır within the walls, looking in the mosques and churches and the citadel, will take several hours and should not be rushed. There will be plenty to keep you occupied if you spend a whole day and a couple of nights here. Almost everything is on the flat and distances are not long – the length of the main street north to south is less than 1km – but the narrow winding streets mean that you easily lose all sense of direction and seem to have walked miles between mosques which are only 200m apart as the crow flies. Sometimes you will spot a minaret rising up between a gap in the buildings only 50m away, but arriving at the mosque in question takes you a further ten minutes while you weave round and round the narrow lanes. Although you will inevitably get lost, the distances are too small to make this a real problem as you soon stumble upon a major monument, and all the mosques have their names up on plaques outside to help you. Signposts have also recently been erected courtesy of funds from the EU and GAP, pointing to the main sights, which helps enormously.

The teenagers of Diyarbakır, often students at the university or local technical colleges, are unusually charming and quite sophisticated. If they offer to escort you round the town and along the walls you will spend a very informative and enjoyable couple of hours during which the teenagers are courtesy itself. They will also keep at a healthy distance any impish younger children, who tend to yell 'turist, turist!' to alert the neighbourhood of your approach.

The walls Your first priority should be to see the walls, originally Roman. They stand more or less intact for their 5.5km length, except for two stretches which were demolished in the 1930s to make way for modern roads, at the Mardin Gate and the Harput Gate. Of the original 82 towers, some round, some square, some polygonal, all but five are still standing. Most are built with two storeys and are 10–12m high, but some have three or even four. The average thickness of the walls is 3–5m. The lower levels were used as storerooms, while the upper levels were kept for military purposes. By far the best way to get a feel for the extent and power of the defences is to walk along the top of them. Walking around at ground level, inside or outside the walls, is actually very difficult as there is no one circuit road, so you constantly have to skirt obstacles and end up walking twice the distance. The best stretch for a walk is from the **Urfa Gate** to the **Mardin Gate**: a wide grassy path allows two or three abreast; in just a couple of places it narrows to less than 1m and the drop on either side may cause a few anxious moments for those not happy with heights. At sunset this is an especially enjoyable stroll, with fine views from the **Yedi Kardeş (Seven Brothers) Tower** south across the walls to the Tigris Valley. The sound of the dusk call to prayer from the many mosques also lends atmosphere, mingling with the breezes wafting over the city. A complex of modern low buildings on the summit of a hill due south is the Shell headquarters for the region, as Turkey's oil reserves are all in the southeast, mostly near the dynamically named town of Batman. To the east, opposite the citadel and reached by a new bridge across the Tigris, is the Diyarbakır University Area.

The original walls of Diyarbakır date back to AD297 when the city, then known as Amida the Black, was taken from the Persian Sassanids and annexed to the Roman Empire. Successive Byzantine rulers rebuilt and strengthened them. In their present form, however, they are the work of the Seljuk Malik Shah who rebuilt them completely when he took the city in 1088. The outsides of the walls are also rich in inscriptions and reliefs, and the Ulu Badan (Great Wall) and the Yedi Kardeş Tower are two of the most interesting for the elaborate decoration outside. The lions and eagles are Seljuk. A path leads round to these from the Urfa Gate so you can view them well.

Descending the walls at the Mardin Gate, or slightly before, is possible on slightly crumbling steps, or else you can just retrace your steps and make your descent at the Urfa Gate again. Inside the Urfa Gate and a little to the right as you face in towards the city centre is the fine **mausoleum of Sarı Saduk** with Kufic inscriptions. You can then set off to the Melik Ahmet Paşa Mosque which you will have noticed from the walls with its distinctive conical pointed dome and tall minaret. Built in 1591 it has a lovely *mihrab* covered in glazed tiles, the same as those on the base of its minaret.

Around the Harput Gate and the citadel (İç Kale)
The Harput Gate on the north side of the walls is the best preserved and the first gate you will see on arrival from Urfa or from Van. In its slightly squat and thick-set power it can remind you of Hittite fortifications. It was known to the Arabs as Bab Al-Armen, the Gate of the Armenians, either because it led to the Armenian quarter of the town or because it led to Armenia. It is enclosed by railings which mean you have to admire its reliefs and inscriptions from afar. On the corner of the main street and the street at right angles to it where a cluster of hotels are, you will notice a pretty little domed mosque, the **Nebi Camii** or Mosque of the Prophet, built in 1524 by the White Sheep clan. Its tall minaret is striped with alternate basalt and pale limestone, stones common to the region, the local architects perfecting the technique of using the contrasting stones in many buildings of the city to great effect. It has even been speculated that the striping may represent the white and black totem sheep respectively of the two Turcoman tribes, the Akkoyunlu and the Karakoyunlu (*ak* 'white', *koyun* 'sheep', and *kara* 'black') who both set up important states in this part of Turkey. Stone versions of the black and white sheep they used in their burials can be seen in the Erzurum and Van museums. Their first capital was at Erciş on the northern edge of Lake Van.

The **Saray Kapı (Palace Gate)**, the main entrance to the citadel, is generally considered the most beautiful of the gates. It is just outside it that moth-eaten horses stand attached to carriages to take people on a circuit of the town. A pointed Artukid arch dated by its inscription to 1206–07 leads into what was once a military closed-off zone but is now open to the public and being redeveloped into the new showcase museum for the area. Just below the pointed arch a broad flight of steps leads past the impressive black citadel mosque, the **Prophet Süleyman-Nasiriye Mosque**, looking almost fortified itself, and with the prophet's *türbe* in its courtyard. Its interior decoration is sombre and simple. It was built by the Artukids in 1160. The palace referred to in the gate's name is the palace of the Artukids, Turcomans who governed the Diyarbakır region from the 11th to the 15th century. They encouraged the arts and were keen builders. They were also keen on the un-Islamic use of animals on coins and buildings, and their animal embellishments can be seen here on the walls of Diyarbakır. Their most beautiful work however is at Mardin, especially in the Sultan Isa Medresesi. Above the pointed arch here in the citadel the Artukid symbol of a lion attacking a bull can still be seen carved into the stone. The bull symbolised worldly goods and the lion was the warrior strong enough to seize them, a graphic way of stating 'Unto him who hath shall be given'.

Inside the citadel are two former churches, **St George's Church** and **Küçük (Small) Church**. St George's used to be a prison but has now been restored with imaginative use of glass to replace or protect the missing sections, such as the fine glass door. It was built around the 4th–5th century in black basalt with a fine view over the Tigris. Sometimes the building is also called the Kızlar Manastırı (Women's Monastery). It has a domed roof over the centre, opening out into four *iwans* from each side to form the shape of the Byzantine cross.

For each successive ruler the citadel was always the centre of administration for the city, starting from when the Roman first built the walls. Süleyman the Magnificent built 16 bastions and two new gates. Today, apart from the two churches, the citadel also contains the Artukid Palace, the Hazreti Süleyman Mosque, the Lion Fountain and the tumulus of Virantepe, thought to date back to the Hurri-Mitani (4000–3000BC), as well as various Ottoman administrative buildings, used by Mustafa Kemal (Atatürk) in 1917 as his headquarters when he was the Commander of the 2nd Army, now open to the public as an Atatürk Museum and Library. The military moved out of the citadel in 2007 and work is in hand to convert the whole of it to a tourist centre, with plans to move the Archaeological Museum (see page 244) here as well.

Diyarbakır's mosques Just like the churches of the walled Old City, the mosques too are scattered about in an apparently random manner, apart, that is, from the main mosque, formerly the cathedral, the Ulu Cami, which has pride of place right in the heart of the city, as befits its role since pre-Christian times as a sacred site of worship. It is the only mosque in the city which has been converted from a church – the others were all built from scratch in the 15th and 16th centuries.

Ulu Cami (Great Mosque) From the Harput Gate the long main (originally Roman) street cuts the city in half, leading to the Mardin Gate at the other end. As it must have been in Roman times, it is full of the hubbub of markets and voices and gives you the feel of being in a great provincial capital. Some of the shops along the early section are now very modern and swish, especially the clothes shops. Walking south along it, after 350m you come to the main square. On the left is the 16th-century striped **Hasan Paşa Hanı**, the biggest and most beautiful *han* in the city with a little fountain in the central courtyard. It is still in use and the whole **bazaar** area is behind it.

On the right a large arch leads into the open **courtyard** of the Ulu Cami. This remarkable structure, originally the Cathedral of St Thomas, the largest church in Diyarbakır, was subsequently adapted to become the main mosque of the city, and was extensively renovated by Malik Shah in 1091–92 to become the first of the great Seljuk mosques of Anatolia, just three years after he conquered Diyarbakır. It is considered the fifth Harem-i-Şerifi (Sacred Enclosure) of Islam and the courtyard is constantly milling with people, old and young, almost all men. Women, especially foreign ones, are a rarity here but you should not feel intimidated by the stares. As long as you cover your head and limbs and take off your shoes you can enter the prayer hall without any qualms. Inside, the high central bay is reminiscent of a Gothic cathedral and the effect is very grand if somewhat austere. It is clearly modelled on the Great Umayyad Mosque in Damascus, and like that extraordinary building, it was used as a pagan temple in pre-Christian times. Both within the mosque and the courtyard the columns and capitals have clearly been re-used from Byzantine buildings, with Greek inscriptions peeping out sideways and incongruously from the courtyard walls next to Arabic Kufic. Earthquakes and fires over the centuries have befallen the mosque, but each time, it has been restored and new elements added, resulting in today's amazing blend. The separate minaret is tall and square, a style typical of Diyarbakır, often with a short conical top added by the Ottomans later. In the interior courtyard there is a sundial dating back to Roman times.

The east and west sides of the courtyard (the side you enter through is east) consist of elegant two-storeyed **arcades**: with their blend of classical columns, Seljuk arches and Greek and Kufic inscriptions they are strangely beautiful. In the centre of the courtyard are two free-standing conical **ablution fountains**, called *sadirvans*, with taps all around and stone slabs and hooks provided. Among the Turks in particular water is important, not only for religious and ablution purposes, but also in city and social life, in art and architecture, and many houses have central pools and fountains and even water running through in an open channel like a private river. This is because they belong to the Hanafi School of Islamic Law (*hanafi* means 'tap' in Arabic) which stipulates that all ablutions must take place under running water, not from a stagnant basin. Originally the four sides of the courtyard represented the four schools of Islamic Law, the Hanafi, the Shafa'i, the Malaki and the Hanbali. Today only the Hanafi and Shafa'i schools, the two schools found in this region, use the mosques for their slightly different prayer rituals. In the far right-hand (northern) corner of the courtyard an arcade of columns leads into the small dark **Mesudiye Medrese** with a *mihrab* of black basalt. Built in 1198–99, its architect was from Aleppo, and the building is architecturally similar to the **Zinciriye Medrese** in the southwest corner of the Ulu Cami.

On the main street almost opposite the Ulu Cami is the very fine black and white-striped Hasan Paşa Hanı, a huge caravanserai built in 1572–75, very solidly constructed with a two-storey arcade facing onto the courtyard, and a central fountain of six columns. The stables could accommodate 500 horses. Today it is still in use, restored in 2006, and is a good place to buy jewellery, carpets and antiques.

Safa Mosque Built in 1532, This is one of the loveliest of the mosques, with its elegant and gracefully decorated white minaret, Persian in feel, with traces of blue geometric tilework near the bottom, still in a near perfect state. The entrance leads into an open courtyard with five graceful arches in the characteristic black and white-striped stonework. Inside is an ornamented painted ceiling with blue and green tile beading. It is attributed to Uzun Hasan, the great leader of the White Sheep clan.

Nebi Camii (Prophet's Mosque) (1530) Built by the White Sheep, this mosque is considered architecturally important for providing the link between the Akkoyunlu and the Ottoman styles.

Iskender Paşa Mosque (1551) Set in a restful garden with two patches of plain green tiles, this mosque is listed as having been built according to a design by Sinan, the great Ottoman court architect to Süleyman the Magnificent, in an inverse T-shape. Iskender Paşa was the 12th Governor of Diyarbakır and is buried here.

Fatih Paşa Mosque (1522) Tastelessly colourful with mother of pearl in the *mihrab* and crassly painted domes in the gallery outside, this is also known as the Kurşunlu Mosque. It was the first Ottoman building to be erected in the city, after the conquest in 1516, by the first Ottoman governor.

Behrem Paşa Mosque (1572) The largest mosque in Diyarbakır after the Ulu Cami, the mosque has a very pleasant interior and tiling all around the walls. The *mimber* is in white and pink marble with an attractive green and beige conical pointed hat on top. The *mihrab* is attractive too, and unusually there is stained glass in the windows. This Ottoman decoration is colourful but restrained. There is a splendour in the decoration, as in the mosque's proportions, within the limits of the severe local style.

Shaikh Mutahhar Camii (Four-Column Minaret) (1512) The local name is Dört Ayakli Minare because of the four pillars supporting the tall square free-standing minaret, the only such construction in all Anatolia. The four basalt pillars are about 2m high, so people can walk right under it, though the local people believe that walking around the pillars seven times will make a wish come true. They are thought to represent the four schools of Islamic Law, with the minaret shaft itself being the body of Islam. A beautiful White Sheep construction, the minaret has alternate black basalt and white limestone courses.

Melek Ahmet Paşa Mosque (1587–91) Another Sinan mosque, this Ottoman structure has attractive tiles inside and a decorated minaret base. Its plan with a store and warehouse on the ground floor and the mosque itself on the upper floor was common in faraway Istanbul, but is unusual here.

Ali Paşa Mosque (1534–37) Like Behrem Paşa, also attributed to a design by Sinan and built by a governor of Diyarbakır, this is a complex of religious buildings near the Yedi Kardeş Tower that has evolved over time. It includes a mosque, *medrese, zikr* hall in a single rectangular room with a gable vault, and a bath. The mosque still has some wall tiles which have motifs not characteristic of Iznik or any other classical Ottoman tile centres, so it is assumed they were the product of local tile workshops.

Diyarbakır's churches Before the advent of Islam the inhabitants of Diyarbakır practised three religions: sun worship (*Shemsis*), Judaism and Christianity. The Christians were divided into five denominations: Gregorian (Armenian), Yakubi (Suryani-Kadim), Orthodox (Greek), Assyrian (Nestorian) and Keldani (Chaldean). Each had their own church and attached school and most date back to the 3rd century. Over the centuries many fell into disrepair as the communities dwindled, but about seven are still standing, though some are heavily ruined such as Surp Gregos, the huge Armenian church. From the street the only thing that gives them away is the carving of animals, usually lions, at either side of the top of their doorways.

Meryem Ana Kilise (Syrian Orthodox Virgin Mary Church) (*Alipaşa neighbourhood; ⊕ 09.00–12.00 & 14.00–17.00; admission free, but donation appreciated*) A glimpse inside the world of these churches and their tiny communities (this one has just 30 in its congregation) is a fascinating step back into life much as it was lived in earlier centuries. Stepping into a large open courtyard, beautifully paved with fine stones, a grandma sits knitting in the shade, her black skirt getting splashed periodically by the enthusiastic jumping of the children playing in the central courtyard fountain. Behind the courtyard is a complex of buildings, once a large monastery founded here in the 7th century, now a school. The deacon shows you round proudly, unlocking the immaculately kept church, recently renovated thanks to donations from the Syrian Orthodox faithful living in America and Istanbul. The donations also enabled the restoration and conservation of 15 early paintings now on display in the church, notably Abraham's sacrifice of his son Isaac, the Assumption of the Virgin Mary, and various early saints such as Saint Ephrem (303–73). First founded in the 3rd century, Saint Ephrem was baptised here, and other early saints spent time here. From 1034 till 1933 the church served as the centre of a Syrian bishopric and was recognised as the patriarchate when Jabob II, the patriarch who came here from Deyrulzaferan Monastery near Mardin (see page 250) lived here until his death in 1871. On the same site where the church now stands, there was a Temple to the Sun 6,000 years ago, and there are various fragments of older buildings still in the current structure, such as the four pinkish marble pillars supporting the dome and a few old Roman capitals. The altar is also very old. Services are held in Aramaic or Syriac, the language of Christ. In the street opposite is the Protestant Diyarbakır Kilise, only installed in this building since the early 2000s. It can be visited between 09.00 and 18.00.

Marpetyun Keldani Katolik Kilisesi (St Antoine Chaldean Catholic Church) (*Şeftalı Sokak 2;* \ *2246505;* ⊕ *09.00–18.00; admission free, but donation appreciated*) Still used by the few remaining families of the Chaldean Catholic faith, the church is signposted just after the Four-Columned Minaret. From the outside it is just a door onto the narrow street, but inside it is quite a large complex, with an attractive well-tended courtyard and lots of derelict buildings, perhaps originally a monastery or school. The church itself is built of the local black basalt and has four naves connected by arches. The floor in front of the apse is paved in fine old black and white stone in a diamond shape. The church was restored in the 17th century.

An old records book shows how the congregation numbers used to be much larger. The church has some interesting oil paintings of saints and religious scenes decorating its walls, and still retains a very serene atmosphere in spite of a certain amount of kitschy clutter.

Surp Giragos (Armenian Church) (*Balıkçıbaşı, Yeni Kapi St; not signposted; no specific opening hours*) Less than 50m from the St Antoine Chaldean Catholic Church, the entrance to this extraordinary Armenian cathedral and its outbuildings is not announced from the outside because its site is now entered via a very simple house, still lived in at subsistence level by a local Kurdish woman and her children. She is indifferent to the gigantic ruin in her back garden, as her immediate needs are far more pressing, namely how to feed her children. She does not mind you poking about as long as you like however, although a contribution to her finances would be much appreciated. Its roof long since fallen in, the enormous building still retains many of its architectural details, rich carving and even some paintwork. The date 1883 is carved onto the back wall. Some characteristic Armenian animal carving also appears on some basalt blocks. There is still a well/fountain in the courtyard in front of the church.

Surp Sarkis (Armenian Catholic Church) (*No specific opening hours*) Situated near the Mardin Gate this church is thought to have been built in the 16th century. Today it is a roofless ruin, built of black basalt, but the main architecture of five naves linked by four arches and with two storeys of columns. You will need to ask for help in finding it.

Diyarbakır's museums
Culture Museum (Cahit Sitki Taranci House) (⊕ *08.00–17.00 Tue–Sun; admission free*) Home to the poet Cahit Sitki Taranci (1910–56), a contemporary of Ziya Gökalp, this is an attractive traditional Diyarbakır house built in 1820, bought by the Ministry of Culture in 1973 and now displaying the poet's personal possessions and a display of local crafts.

Ziya Gökalp (House) Museum (⊕ *08.00–17.00 Tue–Sun; adult TL2*) This is a typical Diyarbakır house and Ziya Gökalp, the turn-of-the-century philosopher said to have been the first person to develop the idea of Turkish nationalism, was born and raised here. The house was bought in 1956 and converted into a museum, displaying his personal possessions, old photos and various memorabilia, including the books in his library. None of it is desperately interesting, but the guardian will show you round enthusiastically.

Archaeology Museum (*Elâzığ Caddesi;* ☉ *08.00–17.00 Tue–Sun; adult TL2*)
Originally housed in the Zinciriye Medrese beside the Ulu Cami when it first
opened in 1934, this moved in 1985 to its new building opposite the Dedeman
Hotel on Elâzığ Street. Its collection ranges from Neolithic and Urartian to White
Sheep and Black Sheep dynasties of the 14th and 15th centuries before the
Ottomans took the city. At the time of writing, it was set to move to the citadel.

Hammams Scattered about the Old City you will notice some circular buildings
with single flattish domes. One of them is on the main Gazi Caddesi close to the
cheese market. They are the old Ottoman bath-houses of the city, lit by small
circles of glass set into their domes. Most are no longer in use. (See pages 92–3.)

AROUND DİYARBAKIR

Gazi Paşa Kösk (*2km south of Diyarbakır;* ☉ *daily 08.00–dusk; adult TL1*) Less than
2km along this road, tucked into the foot of a cliff overlooking the Tigris, a sign
points off to this building, originally a White Sheep 15th-century villa in striped
stone, which is another of the houses where Atatürk stayed, and exhibiting some of
the great man's belongings. Standing now in a park with a playground and very
popular with picnicking families at the weekend, it is a typical example of the sort
of two-storey villa where the wealthy of Diyarbakır would go to for their weekends
in the summer. It lies set back from the road and there is a fine view from the terrace.

On Gözlü Köprüsü (Ten-Eyed Bridge) (*3km south of Diyarbakır*) A few moments

later you pass an elegant bridge over the Tigris with ten arches of carefully
worked basalt, 178m long and 5.6m wide. It bears an inscription announcing it
was built in 1065. At the Feast of the Sacrifice local people throw slips of paper
with their wishes into the river under the bridge. The road leads on through poor
rural villages which look increasingly Middle Eastern, through a landscape that is
quite hilly and fertile, with many flowers in spring. There are vines being
cultivated on the hillsides and olive trees growing wild. In summer makeshift stalls
at the roadside sell figs, apples and peaches. A pass on the way is 890m at its
summit, followed by another one at 1,070m.

ONWARDS TO MARDİN

Leaving Diyarbakır by the Mardin Gate the road seems quite narrow and minor
compared with the main busy roads from the west. There is very little traffic and
the road follows the Tigris south for the first 2km, during which you can look
back onto a wonderful view of the black walls of Diyarbakır rising above the river
plain, a view you can never get from the city itself.

From Diyarbakır you can drive straight on east through Silvan and Bitlis to
Lake Van. This route is 402km and can be done in a day, but it is monotonous,
passing through bare and colourless uplands, and there is also heavy lorry traffic
from the oilfields around Batman and Siirt. At Silvan there is a modest Ulu Cami
built by the Artukids in 1228, all that remains, apart from a few fragments of
defensive wall, of the city that was once called Miyafarikin.

The longer but much better way to Van is to make the interesting trip south
to Mardin, an important Syrian Christian centre with lovely Syrian-influenced
architecture, and from where you can visit a number of monasteries on the Tûr
Abdin Plateau. Then you can make the spectacular journey to the impressive ruins
of Hasankeyf on a cliff overlooking the Tigris, finally passing through
mountainous scenery to Bitlis and Lake Van. This route will add a minimum of
two nights to your itinerary, but it is well worth it.

Mardin is 96km south of Diyarbakır. As you approach from the north, the modern town now sprawls unattractively over the hill before you can see why you have come here, but be patient. You must continue right up onto the rocky crag where old Mardin sits, perched, facing south over the Syrian Desert. Only then do you begin to catch glimpses of the beautifully decorated buildings, Arab-style, which are Mardin's real attraction. Some are almost like palaces, hinting at the past splendour of the town. Back in the 1980s many were decaying, but now a significant number have been restored and put to use either as museums or as plush hotels or restaurants. Mardin generally has cleaned up its act, and the squalor of the back streets 20 or 30 years ago is a thing of the past. Allow at least a half day here to appreciate it properly, either overnighting here or at Deyrulzaferan, the nearby Syrian Orthodox monastery, if you have set it up in advance.

GETTING THERE AND AWAY

By air There are flights from Mardin airport (\ *3125151*) (20km to the south) five days a week to and from Ankara and Istanbul, run by Turkish Airlines (*www.thy.com*) and Pegasus Airlines (*www.izair.com.tr*) to and from Izmir. Minibuses run there from town (TL2) but there is no specific shuttle bus laid on. Taxis into the town centre cost TL25.

By rail A new train line running once a week between Gaziantep and Mosul in Iraq follows the Syrian border, stopping at Nizip, Karkamiş (Carchemish), Akçakale, Ceylanpınar, Şenyurt and Nusaybin, but is currently suspended (as of February 2010) at the request of Iraqi Railways. The total journey usually took 17 hours. When operating, this line connects to Mardin by a 30km branch line from Şenyurt, 25km to the south, taking 40 minutes, but running very infrequently. Mardin station itself is 5km south of the town. At the time of writing the nearest functioning train station is therefore Diyarbakır (see page 234). Check the current situation on www.tcdd.gov, the Turkish State Railways website or on www.seat61.com.

By bus The local minibus terminal (*Ilce Otogar*) is in the southeastern part of town near the exit road to Nusaybin and Deyrulzaferan. There are regular (almost hourly) departures to Diyarbakır, Midyat (90 minutes, TL6) and Nusaybin on the Syrian border (one hour, TL6), and a little less often to Savur (one hour, TL5). Services also run to Urfa and Cizre.

By road It takes just over an hour to drive to Mardin from Diyarbakır, 96km away. Urfa is 188km away.

GETTING AROUND Walking is the only sensible way to get round Mardin. There is only really one long main street, which does rise and fall a bit as it runs along the cliff, and the climb up to the citadel is quite steep, but there is no other way. If you are in your own car, park in the main square by the museum, as the roads are narrow and there is a one-way system. May and September are the best times to visit, when walking around is not too punishing in the summer heat.

TOURIST INFORMATION The tourist office (☉ *daily 08.30–17.30*) is in the main square beside the museum and has internet facilities (free for tourists), spotless loos that charge a fee, and some maps and brochures to hand out.

WHERE TO STAY

WHERE TO STAY Mardin and Midyat are the two bases for exploring the area, though if you set it up in advance, you can sometimes stay the night at Deyrulzaferan Monastery or at Mar Gabriel. The fanciest places are definitely at Mardin, four-star (their own categorisation) expensive boutique hotels in converted renovated old houses, and at Midyat there are also a couple of good but less expensive options.

🏠 **Artuklu Kervansarayı (Boutique Hotel)** (43 rooms) Cumhuriyet Caddesi; ✆ 2137353, 2137354; www.artuklu.com. Unusual conversion of a series of old Mardin mansions that manages to achieve a medieval castle feel. 2 restaurants. $$$

🏠 **Erdoba Evleri (Boutique Hotel) Mardin** (39 rooms) ✆ 2127677; www.erdoba.com.tr. Built over several periods between 1300 & 1946, this hotel is called Erdoba Houses because it is in fact a group of old mansion houses, restored into 4 separate parts or wings, called the Assyrian, Babylonian (the most modern), Seljuk & Ottoman. From the street it is not at all apparent how extensive the place is, with stairs & terraces running off in all directions. There is also an excellent if pricey restaurant & several communal meeting areas, with stunning views from the terraces. $$$

🏠 **Zinciriye Butik Otel** (15 rooms) Medrese Mah (to the right of the steps as you climb up to the Sultan Isa Medresesi) ✆ 2124866; www.zinciriye.com. Beautifully converted old Mardin house, offering traditional stone walls in the rooms, a *majlis*-style lounge where you sit on cushions on the floor, & a café/restaurant with a fine terrace & superb views. $$$

🏠 **Basak Hotel** Cumhuriyet Caddesi, Kisla Sokak 2; ✆ 2126246. One of Mardin's cheapest places to stay with basic rooms & shared bathrooms. About 5mins' walk from the main square. Even cheaper are beds on the roof in summer. No food provided. $

There are more budget places tucked along and just off the main street, Cumhuriyet Caddesi. They change regularly, so you had best explore the options yourself.

WHERE TO EAT

✗ **Cercis Murat Konağı** Cumhuriyet Caddesi; ✆ 2136841; ⏰ 12.00–22.00. This place will be one of the culinary highlights of your time in eastern Turkey, a place not noted for its cuisine, so make the most of this opportunity. Set on the main street quite near the beginning of the Old Town, & entered through an unprepossessing doorway from the street, you climb up steps & enter suddenly onto a stunning terrace sheltered & secluded between 2 traditional stone-carved Mardin houses, beautifully decorated & with breathtaking views over the Plain of Mesopotamia. Not only are the views & décor stunning, but the food & wine are also on an entirely different level of gourmet cuisine, & beautifully presented. It is an all-woman enterprise, run by a woman & with local women in the kitchen. Be sure to try their own wine, reasonably priced at TL30 a bottle. $$$

✗ **Turistik Et Lokantası** Cumhuriyet Meydanı 49; ✆ 2121647. This unlicensed place on the main square has excellent unusually spiced local meat dishes as well as a selection of vegetables & salads. $

There are several attractive tea houses and simple non-licensed restaurants clustered about in the main square in front of the museum and tourist office.

WHAT TO SEE In contrast to black Diyarbakır, Mardin is sometimes called 'the White City' because of the distinctive pale limestone used here. Famous for the beautiful ornate carving on the outsides of its buildings, British historian Arnold Toynbee, no mean traveller, called Mardin 'the most beautiful town in the world'. The commonest motifs used are vines hung with grapes, doves, water drops (symbolising lifewater) and even naked human figures. Wood is almost never used here in house construction, owing to its shortage. Begin by walking east from the main square along the main street, examining the architecture of some of the fine

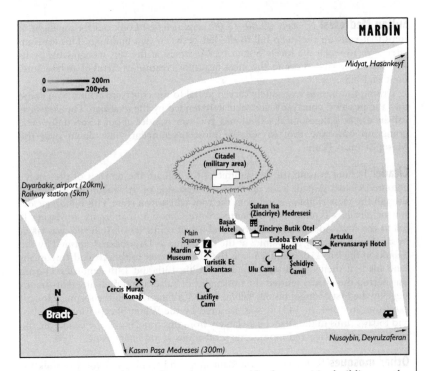

Midyat, Hasankeyf

0 ———— 200m
0 ———— 200yds

Citadel
(military area)

Diyarbakır, airport (20km),
Railway station (5km)

Sultan Isa
(Zinciriye) Medresesi
Başak
Hotel   Zincirye Butik Otel
Main   Erdoba Evleri
Square   Hotel   Artuklu
Mardin   Kervansarayi Hotel
Museum
          Turistik Et   Şehidiye
          Lokantası   Ulu Cami Camii

N   Cercis Murat
          Konağı   Latifiye
                        Cami

Bradt

Nusaybin, Deyrulzaferan

Kasım Paşa Medresesi (300m)

stone-carved private houses along the way, notably the exquisite building on the left with three stone arches, just a private house. The shops along the main road have become quite trendy, with organic soap and other natural products, as well as many jewellery shops.

Mardin is famous for its delicate filigree silverwork, known as *telkari*. The quality of the fresh produce in the shops here is excellent, with wonderful fruit and vegetables, far better than you will find as you head further east and north. The covered bazaars around the Ulu Cami and the Rehaniye Mosque have some *bedestens* and are good places to stroll and buy spices, myrrh, soaps, local almond sweets, textiles, jewellery and all kinds of local crafts. Many of the shopkeepers are Arabs and Arabic can be heard spoken here more than in any other Turkish town. Local people use their flat roofs to dry red chilli peppers, liberally used to flavour the meat and often put out on the table along with the salt.

Mardin Museum (*Cumhuriyet Meydanı;* ✆ 2127797; ⏰ 08.00–17.00 Tue–Sun; adult TL3) Mardin's museum used to be located inside the Sultan Isa Medresesi but in 1995 it moved to the main square into the fine three-storey building that was originally the Church of the Virgin Mary and the Syriac Catholic Patriarchate building dating to 1895. The museum is very tastefully arranged, with modern lighting showing off the collections to best possible effect. The pieces range from early Bronze Age through Assyrian, Urartian, Persian, Roman, Byzantine, Seljuk, Artukid and Ottoman periods, illustrating the historical richness of the area. Some of the silver jewellery is especially fine, including pieces worn on the forehead or round the ankle. Notice the elaborate and very unusual Christian stone carvings from Midyat and Hasankeyf where large communities of Christians once lived. The building itself is also very fine, with lovely delicately carved columns, capitals and arcades in its courtyard.

Sultan Medresesi (🕘 *daily 09.00–18.00; admission free*) Look out for the flight of steps that runs up the steep hill to the left between two buildings. This leads up after 50m to reach the lovely Sultan Isa Medresesi at the top, recognisable by its striking white ribbed dome, the most beautiful creation of Artukid architecture, built in 1385.

Passing through its exquisitely carved portal to the courtyard within, you come into the peaceful courtyards, immaculately tended by the guardian. The *medrese* is still in use as a theological school and you can wander about respectfully, even going up onto the roof to see the most magnificent view down over the Mesopotamian Plain.

Citadel Behind you up on the summit of the hill are the remains of the sandy-coloured citadel. A path leads up from the west side of the Sultan Isa Medresesi, though the view is just as good from the roof where you were. This hilltop citadel was originally a Roman and Byzantine fortress known in antiquity as Marida. It fell to the Arabs in 640 and after two-and-a-half centuries of Arab rule was taken by the Sunni Kurdish Marwanids at the same time as Diyarbakır. Captured by the Seljuks in the late 11th century it was then handed over to the Artukid Turcomans who made it their capital throughout the 12th, 13th and 14th centuries. During this period the citadel resisted the onslaughts of Saladin and then an eight-month siege by the first Mongol hordes, falling finally to Tamerlane in the second Mongol campaign in 1394. In 1431 it was captured by the White Sheep Turcoman clan, and today's ruins in the citadel date largely from this time. Inside the citadel are the ruins of a vast palace and mosque, now off-limits as a military zone.

Other mosques Returning to the main street and turning left you can walk for another 100m or so to reach a tall white minaret with an attractive restaurant and tea area on a terrace looking on to it. Retracing your steps and then forking sharp left down the hill will bring you to the 11th-century **Ulu Cami**, the oldest mosque in Mardin. Originally Seljuk but much restored after the various struggles to take the town, the cylindrical minaret had to be rebuilt when a mine exploded here during the Kurdish revolt of 1832. The fluted dome, like that of the Sultan Isa Medresesi, is typical of Mardin's architecture.

Nearby in the back streets at a similar height to the Ulu Cami is the 14th-century **Latifiye Cami** which you should visit for its exquisitely carved entrance

THE MUD OF MESOPOTAMIA

Reconciling this flat parched plain with the image of fertility conjured up by the river cultures of Mesopotamia, the Fertile Crescent, requires a major feat of the imagination. Robert Byron in his *Road to Oxiana* (1937) described the contrast:

It is little solace to recall that Mesopotamia was once so rich, so fertile of art and invention, so hospitable to the Sumerians, the Seleucids, and the Sasanids. The prime fact of Mesopotamian history is that in the thirteenth century Hulagu destroyed the irrigation system; and that from that day to this Mesopotamia has remained a land of mud deprived of mud's only possible advantage, vegetable fertility. It is a mud plain, so flat that a single heron, reposing on one leg beside some rare trickle of water in a ditch, looks as tall as a wireless aerial. From this plain rise villages of mud and cities of mud. The rivers flow with liquid mud. The air is composed of mud refined into a gas. The people are mud-coloured; they wear mud-coloured clothes, and their national hat is nothing more than a formalised mud-pie.

THE POWERS OF SOAP

There are five types of Mardin soap, each with its own particular properties:

ALMOND SOAP Moisturises and softens the skin through the almond oil, preventing cracks in hard skin

PISTACHIO SOAP Maintains the hair and skin in good condition because of its high Vitamin E content

DAPHNE (LAUREL) SOAP Prevents dandruff, fungal infections and eczema thanks to its disinfectant properties and is said to prevent the occurrence of varicose veins. Putting a bar of this soap in wardrobes and cupboards also keeps moth and insects away. This is the same as the famous soap of Antakya and Aleppo, pale green in colour.

BITTIM SOAP Effective against hair loss and brittle hair. It is also said to prevent dandruff and obesity.

OLIVE OIL SOAP Increases blood circulation around the hair follicles, prevents hair loss and static hair, and contains Vitamins E, A and D.

They are all handmade and hand-cut, hence their slightly rustic appearance, and are then laid out to dry on shelves for two or three weeks before being put on sale.

---

façade on its eastern side and for the view, from the windows inside the mosque, over the town and valley below.

There is one final building worth visiting but it is a long 500m walk down to the bottom of the town and back up again. This is the **Kasim Paşa Medresesi** built in the 15th century by the White Sheep clan. It is similar in arrangement to the Sultan Isa Medresesi, with a beautiful rectangular pool in its courtyard. If you have time you can also ask for directions to the **Şehidiye Mosque**, built in the 13th century by the Artukids with very beautifully carved windows and portals, in the eastern part of the town.

THE TÛR ABDIN

The Tûr Abdin translates literally as 'the Servants' Plateau', but the French phrase it more elegantly: 'Montagne des Serviteurs de Dieu'. This highland region between Mardin and Cizre with Midyat at the centre is to the Syrian Orthodox Church what Mount Athos is to the Greek Orthodox Church. The history of Syrian Orthodoxy has been less happy in its outcome than that of Greek Orthodoxy, however.

Sometimes known as Jacobites, they owe their founding to Jacob Baradai who in the 5th century was sent to Antioch by the Monophysite-leaning Empress Theordora, wife of Justinian. From there he roamed for 35 years, dressed only in a horse-hair blanket, preaching and converting across Syria and the Tûr Abdin.

Among the legends associated with the region is the one that Noah's Ark came to rest on Mount Kadur east of Cizre (rather than on Mount Ararat, the more popular story). At any rate, Noah's grave in Cizre is a point of pilgrimage for Christians and Muslims alike.

GETTING THERE AND AWAY You can walk to Deyrulzaferan in an hour and a half from Mardin. Otherwise you can take a taxi (TL25 for the return while they wait for you to look round).

✕ WHERE TO EAT

Deyrulzaferan Light meals and snacks are served during the daytime from 08.30 up until 18.00 when the monastery closes to visitors in the café at the foot of the monastery. There is also a good selection of ice cream and an excellent souvenir shop.

WHAT TO SEE Allow at least a night in the area to visit the main monasteries, or at least three if you want to explore properly. From a base of Mardin, the excursion to Deyrulzaferan takes a half day.

Deyrulzaferan Monastery (*4km east from Mardin;* ⊕ *daily 08.30–12.00 & 13.00–17.00; adult TL3*) From 1160 until the 1920s this was the most important of the monasteries and seat of the Syrian Orthodox Patriarchate. Before that the seat had been Antioch, from which the patriarch was driven out, and since the 1920s he has been resident in Damascus. The easiest of the monasteries to visit and the one that is most geared up to visitors, Deyrulzaferun (literally 'Monastery of Saffron', a reference maybe to the soft yellow colour of its stone) even has opening hours and an entry charge. So alive is it to making money out of visitors that it has also built a cafeteria/restaurant and shop complex at its foot with a large car park, a system reminiscent of the Islamic *waqf* where shops, markets and coffee houses support the adjacent mosque through their income. Visitors are taken round in groups by one of the monastery's young trainees, someone who, even if they are not planning to become a monk, is at least a member of the Syrian Orthodox congregation. This is all thanks to the new *mutran* or bishop, a remarkably erudite man with a theology degree from Oxford, who keeps however to the tradition of leaving his long white beard untrimmed and wearing his long black robes and distinctive black cap embroidered with white crosses. He has invigorated this once-thriving community, and though there are only a handful of fully trained monks, fewer than five, the monastery still functions as a boarding school for children of Syrian Orthodox families, and about 30 young boys are taught here at any one time. There is in addition a community of helpful adherents, including gardeners and cooks. If you stay the night here, the first mass of the day, conducted like all services here, in Aramaic, is at 07.00, a confusing experience in which priests and young boys helping to give parts of the service appear to come and go randomly, until the *mutran* himself appears for the final part. The service is highly ritualised, with much tuneless chanting. The young boys seem to act out many roles, disappearing behind the altar screen and reappearing again in a different set of robes and a different-coloured sash for different parts of the service. There is no participation by the congregation, which consisted of one old man, two young women and four children at the time of my visit. Breakfast is then not until 09.15, served in the communal refectory, with the *mutran* sitting by himself at the head of the room. The evening service is at 18.00, after visiting hours, with the evening meal served around 19.45. The food is simple fare, grisly mutton, rice and cucumber with lots of flat Arab bread. These meals are regarded as eating occasions, not chatting occasions, so much of the meal takes place in silence. Any chatting usually takes place later, sitting on the benches and chairs in the courtyard. It is a big help to be able to speak some Turkish or Arabic.

The monastery lies at the end of its own road that forks off the main road south to Nusaybin about 1km after leaving Mardin. Winding along the final 3km small

In the early centuries of Christianity there was debate over the human and divine natures of Christ. Eastern theologians had decided that though born of Mary, the man in Christ had been entirely absorbed into the divine. Christ had one nature, the divine, and the adherents of this view were Monophysites. However at the Council of Chalcedon, across the Bosphorus from Constantinople, it was decided by the assembled church that Christ had two natures, unmixed and unchangeable but at the same time indistinguishable and inseparable, and this is the view of the Greek Orthodox and Roman churches to this day. The issue may not seem terribly important, or even comprehensible, and really it was more of a slogan by which the cultures of East and West denounced each other. But after the Council of Chalcedon, Monophysism became a heresy as far as Constantinople and Rome were concerned, and the churches of Egypt, Syria and Armenia, denied and denying both spiritual communion with the West and military aid, were ultimately swamped by the Islamic tide.

Even so, in the highlands of the Tûr Abdin the Syrian Orthodox Church flourished. During the Middle Ages there were four bishoprics and 80 monasteries here, and the population was prosperous through trade and farming. Persecution came from fellow Christians, Crusaders from Edessa (Urfa) and Antioch; later the Mongols left their mark; and the last great period of suffering came in World War I and after, when Turkey's Christian minorities became involved in the Allies' intention to carve up the old Ottoman Empire. Now only 23,000 Syrian Orthodox Christians remain in Turkey, survivors of the massacres and deportations shared also by the Greeks and Armenians.

The Tûr Abdin is now classed by the Turkish government as a distressed area, to be aided by a succession of one-year plans. The dearth of hotels in the area makes it quite difficult to visit, and in any case only four monasteries remain active. The rest are ruins, sometimes by themselves in the middle of nowhere, sometimes incorporated into villages.

villages can be seen along the way, originally all Syrian Orthodox, now with many houses abandoned and new ones built, lived in mainly by Kurds who have moved into the area. In the sandy-coloured cliffs behind are caves, at one time inhabited by monks, and above the monastery itself, even the remains of a castle can be seen.

Site visit After being led up the tree-lined path by your escort you enter the fine gateway of the monastery that faces out across the plain with commanding views. The cliff rises up behind, sheltering the building. On climbing the steps and entering the courtyard the first stop is usually the old church, built at the time of the Byzantine emperor Anastasius (491–518) above the grave, it is said, of 12,000 martyrs, buried under the earth floor. The most remarkable thing about this partially underground chapel is the ceiling, made with beautifully crafted stone blocks fitted together without mortar but held up by the design itself. It was said to have been the site of a very early temple used by sun-worshippers as early as 2000BC. The window from which they used to watch the sun rise on the east was blocked up when it became a church. The room above is entered by a pair of enormous 300-year-old walnut doors and contains the grave niches of earlier patriarchs and bishops.

The tour then moves back into the courtyard and into what is now used as the monastery's church where all services are held. Its benches have the capacity to seat about 50 and the simple 18th-century building is decorated with arches and various paintings and coloured drapes around the carved stone altar. The original wooden one was burnt in a fire some 50 years ago. To the left of the altar is the patriarch's throne carved with all the names of previous patriarchs going back to 792, and to the right of the altar is the *mutran's* throne. You may also be shown into a small side room where there is a carved walnut altar made entirely without nails, and a floor mosaic said to be over 1,500 years old, taken from the St Pierre Kilesesi rock church in Antakya, ancient Antioch (see page 200).

The courtyard itself has a wonderfully peaceful quality with mature trees. Round the edge are the bedrooms and offices of the *mutran* and his helpers, while upstairs leads to the simpler rooms of the students and guests, with separate areas for male and female. Facilities are basic but clean. From the upper terrace there are fine views out over the Syrian Plain.

Mar Augen Before heading east to Midyat one very rewarding excursion if you have the time (three hours' minimum from Mardin) and your own transport, is to the abandoned monastery of Mar Augen, beyond Nusaybin. You should not attempt it unless you are prepared for some rough driving through fields, followed by a stiffish 30-minute climb. The effort for those who do will be rewarded, for apart from its own interest, it is the most spectacularly sited of all of the Tûr Abdin monasteries. The dead-flat transit route to Nusaybin and Iraq passes through bleak featureless plains following the edge of the Syrian border, marked by barbed-wire fencing and guard posts. No birdwatching with binoculars or photography should be indulged in here.

At Nusaybin to the right of the road, all that remains of the Roman city of Nisibis is a triumphal arch. There is also an ancient church, Mar Yakoub, still in use, with the bones of the saint in its crypt. The town today is a mere shadow of its former self, and the most impressive monument is the ornate railway station, built by the Germans just before World War I, the furthest Turkish station on the Berlin–Baghdad railway. No international services run to here, just one daily slow train to Gaziantep. The town became the capital of the Roman province of Mesopotamia at the beginning of the 3rd century.

About 25km after Nusaybin on the road east towards the Iraqi border, and just 1km after the unlikely motel called Nezirhan, you turn off left to Girmeli. Take the track that leads about 1km to the village, and on the far side of the village the road crosses a small bridge and you come immediately afterwards to a junction of three roads. Take the one on the far right and follow it for about 3km towards the hills in front of you. Although it is a little tricky in places and heavily overgrown it can be driven slowly and with care in a normal saloon car. It ends directly at the foot of the cliff beneath the monastery which perches about halfway up. The ascent up the rocky path is quite steep and can be taxing on a hot day; it takes around 30 minutes. As you approach you can see the lower outer walls of the monastery and remains of its former terracing where the monks once grew their produce. Several hundred monks once lived here. The Muslim family living here now have a separate house they have built at the back, under the cliff face, and only use the monastery to grow a few vegetables in its courtyard.

The monastery church has a large vaulted nave, now totally bare, with no frescoes or decoration left. The church is thought to date from CAD400. Outside in the cloister a bucket can be lowered into the deep well to pull up water which is quite drinkable. Out on the terrace the view is superb down over the plain and to your tiny speck of a car below. The family will probably welcome you and offer you tea. They seem to live quite happily alone here, the children playing with each other and the father making occasional trips down to the village of Girmeli with his donkey to get supplies.

EAST TO MİDYAT

Between Mardin and Midyat the scenery is quite biblical-looking, with olive trees and rolling hills and a sense of being up high. There is even a pass whose summit is 1,115m en route.

MİDYAT *Telephone code: 482*

Midyat itself is a small town of some 56,000 inhabitants with a certain amount of faceless modern sprawl around the edges the same as all the towns of eastern Turkey. A curious place in two halves, you turn right to reach the modern Muslim half, and left to reach the old Christian centre, raised up on a mound. The older buildings are recognisable by the colour of their soft yellowish stone and the church bell towers rising up above the houses. Most of the inhabitants in the Christian section today are Arabs ethnically, with very few Kurds – the Kurds are grouped in the modern half of town. In the 1980s about 5,000 people here were thought to still be Syrian Orthodox Christians, but that number has since dwindled.

GETTING THERE AND AROUND Regular minibuses leave to and from Hasankeyf (45 minutes, TL5) from the *otogar* in old Midyat 200m south of the roundabout on the Cizre road. You could base yourself in old Midyat and make day trips to Hasankeyf and Mardin using these local buses. (For further information, see *Mardin*, page 245.)

WHERE TO STAY

Midyat

Hotel Matiat (85 rooms) ☎ 4626881; www.matiat.com.tr. A plush modern 8-storey pink block on the edge of the Kurdish half of town, complete with large swimming pool, children's water slides, licensed restaurant, bar & internet facilities. $$$$

Midyat Kultur Evi (6 rooms) 47500 Midyat; ☎ 4621354. Right in the centre of the old Christian town, this fine old stone building with magnificent stone carving round its doors & windows doubles as the local Ethnographic Museum, some rooms furnished in the traditional style which can be rented out as required. The best room of all is right at the top, on its own special floor, though the rooms immediately below it are also very special & spacious, with en-suite bathrooms. Because it gets a steady stream of visitors, all paying the TL1 entry fee, the rooms are quite noisy until the museum closes at 18.00. There is no b/fast, but the guardian will let you have hot water to make your own tea & coffee & lend you plates & a knife to make your own. For the evening meal he will even send out to the local *lokanta* if you want, & you can then eat your take-away perched on the roof terrace feeling for all the world like lord of the manor, watching the sunset, listening to the call to prayer, the sheep baaing, the cocks crowing & the horses clattering. Once total darkness descends a bat comes out to eat the mosquitoes. $$

Nusaybin

Nezirhan Motel (74 rooms) 24km east of Nusaybin on the main road to Cizre; ☎ 4463416; www.nezirhan.com. Unlikely place designed like a huge concrete caravanserai. Ask for a room at the back away from the main road & the generator. There is an unexpected Olympic-sized pool at the back, as well as a basketball court. Rooms have AC but are a bit run-down. $$$

WHERE TO EAT
In Midyat, the best restaurant in town apart from in the Matiat Hotel is **Citan Lokantası** (⏱ 09.00–22.00; $$), on the Mar Gabriel road out of town just south of the junction roundabout.

WHAT TO SEE
There are five churches in Midyat and five priests to look after them. The churches are generally kept locked, though if you ring the bell the priest

or some helper will generally come to let you in. Mar Stephanos is worth looking inside, with an east–west nave and a classical elegance in its design. Izozoel Church, on the highest point of the town to the north, has a very lovely bell tower, one of Midyat's finest examples of stonework. The best-known church is Mar Philoxenos, formerly in ruins, but recently restored and now called Mar Aznoyo.

From the Christian half you now take the turn marked Cizre and Habur to make a visit to Mar Gabriel, the real heart of the Syrian Orthodox community in Turkey today. The scenery around is of gentle hills and valleys and the monastery's setting is far less attractive than that of Deyrulzaferan.

Mar Gabriel (*18km east of Midyat;* ✎ *4621425;* ⊕ *daily 09.00–11.30 &* *13.00–16.30; admission free, but donation expected*) The largest and oldest of the monasteries of the Tûr Abdin with a community of around 20 monks and nuns and a bishop who is head of the Syrian Orthodox Church in Turkey, Mar Gabriel (also known as Deyrulumur) has been the beneficiary of large donations made by émigré members of its community now living mainly in America or Istanbul. Its purpose is to keep the Syrian Orthodox Church alive and to that end it teaches the Syriac language and runs a school for students sent by the émigrés, wanting to keep their links with their old roots and culture. The total community numbers about 80. Approached up its own tarmac dead-end road 2.5km to the left off the road to Cizre, it is clearly signposted. Unlike Deyrulzaferan there is no café for refreshments, no shop, nothing at all outside the walls apart from a large car park. All around are well-cultivated gardens and terraces with pistachio trees and olive trees. The stream of visitors is fairly constant, most of them Turkish, many of them Muslim.

You will be shown around by a member of the community, always male. It was founded in the early 5th century by Simeon, who came from an aristocratic family in Mardin and was the real originator of monastic life on the plateau. Under Simeon in its heyday the monastery boasted 400 monks, some coming from as far afield as Egypt. The courtyard has none of the rustic charm of Deyrulzaferan, and the atmosphere is much more bustling and efficient. The tour takes you round the church, the original dining room and kitchen and into a chamber with a row of tombs called the Church of 40 Martyrs where St Simeon and St Gabriel are buried. From here a vaulted arcade leads through to the lovely dark old St Mary Church, no longer used, with a fine ancient brick dome modelled on Aya Sofya, built by Theodora, wife of Justinian. In the dome behind the altar are lovely glass mosaics in gold, blue and green. Upstairs is the bishop's reception room with whitewashed walls and red chairs lined up around three sides, with pictures of the bishop and the patriarch in Damascus. Visiting VIPs are offered tea here.

The number of visitors is such today that the monastery no longer offers hospitality, but back in the 1980s it was a different story. Then, if you happened to arrive around a mealtime you would be automatically invited to join the bishop and monks in the refectory. Clad in scarlet robes, the bishop sat in the centre of the head table, with three monks either side of him, a curious collection of faces of all types and ages, each with a beard of a different length, possibly suggestive of a kind of hierarchy among them. Running at right angles from either end of his table, two further long refectory tables ran down the sides of the room, one for the monastery laity, the other for any guests who might arrive. The bishop spoke good English and was quite a roguish conversationalist. He would tell of his many important visitors, the British and German ambassadors for example, various government officials, religious dignitaries, all of whom would contact him by phone or letter in advance to give him warning of their arrival, so that they could be accommodated in the new and comfortable extension.

Churches along the way to Hasankeyf Returning to Midyat and heading north towards Hasankeyf, on the way to Lake Van, look out for the fork off after 4km to the right towards Dargecit, also marked with a brown sign to Mar Yakoub. Originally part of a monastery probably founded in the 4th century and one of the most important in the Tûr Abdin, all that remains now is the 4th-century church in the village of Salah, recently restored. It lies 10km along the road towards Dargecit, then 3km left along a difficult track. On the lintel, arches above the doors and on the door jambs inside there is some fine carved decoration and the entrance to the central choir is also finely carved. The pillars which support the arches are decorated with birds and garlands. Outside, the southern façade has beautiful moulding with carefully worked stone. It was built on the ruins of a Zoroastrian temple and was lived in by priests until the 19th century. The local population here is now entirely Kurdish.

Some 5km further on up a dirt track to the right is Mar Kyriakos at the entrance to the village of Arnas, now called Bağlarbasi. This too used to be part of a monastery, facing a galleried courtyard. The cloister of the choir is 8th century and the church itself is probably 6th century.

At 7km east of Arnas is the church of Mar Azaziel at the edge of the village of Kefr Zeh, now called Altintaş, built on the same plan as Mar Kyriakos, on the summit of a hill.

South of Kerburan at the end of the track the village of Khakh, now called Anıtlı, has two churches, the 6th-century Mar Sovo, destroyed by Tamerlane and still in ruins, and the lovely El Hadra (The Virgin), also called Meryemana, at the entry to the village on the right. This graceful 7th-century church with a decorated pyramid dome and two storeys of elegant blind arches, supported by columns with Corinthian capitals, is the most beautiful of all the Tûr Abdin churches and has recently been restored. Around the doorjambs and lintels are palm-tree decorations, garlands, pearls and acanthus leaves. Some have unkindly likened it to a fancy wedding cake. In the middle of the village itself on a slight hill is a group of fortified houses where 5,000 Christians were besieged by Ottoman troops in 1915 for months, but won. Even so, today there are fewer than 20 Christian families remaining here.

ONWARDS VIA HASANKEYF TO LAKE VAN

The road from Midyat north to Hasankeyf is very interesting as you begin to make an impressive descent off the plateau, eventually catching your first glimpse of the wide Tigris as the road winds down into the valley and Hasankeyf which marks the northern border of the Tûr Abdin. The visit to Hasankeyf, a spectacularly sited ruined town on a cliff overlooking the Tigris, is the main reason to drive this route from Diyarbakır via Mardin to Lake Van, rather than heading straight to the lake.

HASANKEYF *Telephone code: 488*

HISTORY Founded by the Romans as a frontier outpost, Hasankeyf later became the Byzantine bishopric of Cephe. When the Arabs took the town in 640, they called it Husn Kayfa (Fortress Cephe), from which its present name has derived. It served for half a century as an Artukid capital in the 12th century, and it was the skilled Artukids who built the bridge across the Tigris here, whose crumbling supports can still be seen rising above the water. The bridge was described by early travellers as being the grandest in all Anatolia. From 1232 the town served as the capital of the Kurdish Ayyubid kings before falling to the Ottomans in 1416.

GETTING THERE AND AWAY Minibuses run frequently between Hasankeyf and Midyat to the south (TL5) and Batman to the northwest. There are also two daily services to and from Van (six hours, TL30). Both leave Midyat at around 10.30.

WHERE TO STAY Only very basic accommodation exists in Hasankeyf. For anything above $ you will have to head to Batman some 40km northwest. The **Hasankeyf Motel** (*7 rooms; Dicle Sokak;* \ *3812005;* $) is in an excellent location right on the Tigris by the bridge, but offers only very basic rooms, no breakfast or meals.

WHERE TO EAT Try to make your itinerary coincide with a lunch or dinner stop here at Hasankeyf, for there are now at least 12 restaurants lining the riverbank below the cliff, all specialising in the river trout. Apart from the dramatic setting what makes them really memorable is that they are set partly in the water on stilts, so you take off your shoes and climb up into your own private platform ringed with a low rail and padded out with carpets and cushions on which to sprawl. It feels like a giant cot and you can revert totally to childhood by dangling your feet over the edge to bathe them in the cooling Tigris while you wait for your food and drink to arrive. These raised-up beds are called *Çardak* and can also be seen everywhere in this part of Turkey on the roofs of houses, where the whole family sleeps on hot summer nights.

You will have to decide between the pull of alcohol or the river, as there is now a place called **Yolgecen Hanı** (\ *3812287;* ⊕ *09.00–22.00;* $), which has its dining rooms cut into the cliff overlooking the river and serves *rakı*.

WHAT TO SEE

Site visit (*always open; picnicking forbidden in the site; adult TL3*) Allow a good two hours for a proper visit to the site, so with your lunch stop on the river, a half day should be allocated in your itinerary. As you approach you notice in the cliffs rising up from both sides of the river numerous hollowed-out caves, some inhabited by animals, some used for storage. On the left of the road you can see behind the modern ribbon development an extensive area of ruined houses, among which are three ruined mosques. If you have the energy and inclination you can spend a fruitful hour exploring this area, as many of the houses date from pre-1260, the date of the Mongol sacking of the town, and still have decorations inside with fragments of tiles. From the outside they do not appear to hold much promise, but inside you can stumble upon some very attractive patterned ceilings. In the midst of the modern town, a tall distinctive minaret of a red-brick mosque is built of very finely carved stone and with a stork's nest on top. Below it to the right are the remains of the once-sturdy Artukid Bridge, now reduced to four thick-set arches drowning in the strong river current. Just to the right of the bridge, opposite the town on a little mound, are the ruins of what was once a convent, for Hasankeyf was an important Syrian Christian centre before the Mongol invasion.

On the cliff top above the town you can see the ruins of the Artukid city, which you approach by climbing up through the narrow gully between towering cliffs. Here is where you must buy your ticket and where a whole collection of makeshift souvenir stalls have grown up, selling everything from locally made musical instruments to stuffed animals and goatskin rugs. From this point you walk up to the colossal sandy-coloured stone gateway on the right, the original entrance to the Artukid city. Passing through this magnificent gateway, recently restored, you now begin to climb up the broad stone-laid path that zigzags up the side of the cliff. It is not particularly steep and only takes ten minutes or so, much less than you might think on looking up from below. On the way up you pass more caves in the cliff face, many with doors and interconnecting chambers inside, used as houses until recently. Indeed, some caves are still inhabited by troglodyte families. Most local people are Kurdish here, with very few Arabs. Your chances of avoiding being spotted by the local children are minimal, and you will probably by now find yourself surrounded by a small retinue determined to offer their services as guides. They can however have their uses, such as warding off ferocious dogs by throwing stones at them.

At the top of the path you come first to a fine ruined hall with carvings on the walls, part of the 12th-century palace of the Artukid kings. Its outer wall is perched right on the cliff edge and from the window you have a sheer drop down into the Tigris with a fabulous and vertiginous view over the bridge and town below.

After climbing a little higher you begin to see the sheer extent of the ruined city on the vast cliff top. The houses extend for at least 2km over the undulating slopes of the summit, and on the most prominent mounds stand the major buildings, notably a mosque and two saints' tombs with their domed roofs. The mosque is especially fine with gates leading into its grassy courtyard and the steps up its minaret still climbable. The buildings are all of a sandy mud colour, and considering they do not appear very sturdily built, it is surprising that they have survived so well over more than eight centuries. You could spend hours up here exploring properly but none of the houses seem to have any special features or decoration and so the whole is more exciting for its setting and size.

Ayyubid türbe As you leave Hasankeyf, crossing the Tigris and continuing west along the far bank, look out for one final monument. Standing by itself some 500m past the bridge in the fields close to the river is an unusual little red-brick building with an onion-topped dome. Covered on the outside in exquisite turquoise glazed tiles, this is the best-preserved and finest example of Ayyubid architecture in Turkey, showing much Persian influence. It is the *türbe* of the Ayyubid king, Zein El-Abdin, a Kurdish descendant of Saladin, and though it appears quite small from a distance, you will be surprised how huge it is when you stand below it. Formerly reachable only by tramping across muddy ploughed fields, it now has a small track leading off to it, and even a simple tea-house not far away on the riverbank.

SAVED FROM FLOODING

Hasankeyf has been the centre of an international crisis in recent years, as it was to have been totally flooded as part of the GAP Project. The Ilisu Dam on the Tigris was projected to create a lake from Batman to Midyat, displacing 37 villages and many other archaeological sites apart from this one. Obviously the Artukid village on the cliff would not be affected, but everything else on the banks of the river would be lost underwater forever. Much controversy was sparked by the project and there was massive local resistance, with the Mayor of Hasankeyf setting out to mobilise international agencies to get involved in fighting the project. In 2002 some of the foreign investors withdrew from the project as a result of the bad publicity, and now the scheme has finally been shelved, probably forever. It had been planned not for irrigation but for energy generation, but happened to coincide with an economic crisis in Turkey which reduced demand for energy.

FROM BATMAN TO SIIRT

From Hasankeyf the road begins by following the north bank of the Tigris Gorge for a while before heading north to reach Batman (altitude 560m) with a growing population of around 300,000. The superbly named Batman lies at the heart of Turkey's oilfields and you will notice nodding donkeys at the sides of the road, testing for new supplies. Batman is booming, with many five-storey residential blocks going up to accommodate new workers, many of them Kurds who are being encouraged to settle in this area, to stem rural migration to Ankara or Istanbul. As long as there is employment for them here, they are likely to stay.

Turkey is not self-sufficient in oil and has to buy additional crude from Saudi Arabia, Iraq, Iran, Algeria and Russia. The Iraqi pipeline used to produce good transit revenues and there is now also an Iranian pipeline, as well as the Blue Stream natural-gas pipeline built under the Black Sea to transport Russian gas. The asphalt by-produced at Batman used only to be sent west to resurface the roads around Ankara and Istanbul, but now it is also used in the east, as in the new dual carriageway that heads north from Batman to join the main east–west road.

The road to the right before Batman leads off along 91km of empty roads to Siirt, a wild town in the Kurdish heartlands, rarely visited because it is not on a through route to anywhere, or at least only with great contrivance. The area east from here towards the Iraqi border has in recent years been a hotbed of Kurdish dissidents, but things are slowly improving with the government's new policy of inclusion. Siirt itself was first settled by Babylonians and Assyrians, and later flourished particularly under the Abbasid caliphate of Baghdad. Set in pastureland, the mountains which surround the town are snow-capped most of the year, though the summers are very hot. The whole region is full of tributaries of the Tigris, formed by snowmelt from the mountains.

Of the town's monuments the Seljuk Ulu Cami built in 1129 is the most interesting, with its tall brick minaret decorated with turquoise tiling in geometric patterns, disused until recently, but now emerged from prolonged restoration. Its carved walnut *mimber* has been removed to the Ankara Ethnographical Museum. Also worth seeing are the 13th-century Cumhuriyet Cami, founded in the 8th century under the Abbasid caliphate, and the Kavvan Hammam, an 11th-century Seljuk bath.

Siirt is famous for its especially warm, soft blankets made from a kind of mohair goat raised on local pastureland. Freya Stark, on her travels in these Kurdish lands, bought some of the goatswool material and had it made into a suit in Paris by Chanel 'where the material was wondered at and admired'. Kurdish rugs and saddlebags can be bought cheaply here.

In some parts of the Old Town there are some remarkable Arab-style mud-brick houses, like those found in Yemen, very tall, several storeys high, with decoration round the windows and receding plastered walls. The New Town is developing at the foot of the hillside, but these tall old buildings, windowless until their upper storeys, are to be found through arches and up narrow streets. There is still much fellow feeling in this part of Turkey with the Arab world, and until recently you sometimes see photos of King Hussein of Jordan where you would normally expect to see the omnipresent Atatürk. Kurdish guerrillas used to thrive in the difficult mountainous terrain around Siirt and even now there are occasional clashes with the Turkish military.

FROM BATMAN TO BITLIS

From Batman north to the Diyarbakır–Bitlis road you run alongside a large tributary of the Tigris and its broad flood plain for a while. The scenery is very attractive with unusual hill formations and the snow-covered mountains of the Van region in the background. Flocks of sheep can sometimes still be seen here accompanied by shepherds looking like giant yetis in ankle-length shaggy coats of thick felt hanging in a dead-straight line from very broad shoulders. It is a curious fact that many eastern Turks are impervious to rain. In the towns and villages the men walk about in shirtsleeves, usually hatless, as if they are not even aware it is raining. The women, wrapped up in their garb with only their faces peeping out, are much better protected.

On reaching the Diyarbakır–Bitlis junction you could make a short detour of 4km back towards Diyarbakır to take a quick look at the superb bridge at Malaabadi which runs just next to the modern road bridge. Built in 1146 by the Artukids, it has one of the largest spans of any single-arched bridge. Near Malaabadi a road forks off north to the remote mountain village of Sason. In the 19th century a tribe of people were found living here who were neither Christians nor Muslims, speaking a mixture of Arabic, Kurdish and Armenian. They had no churches or mosques and no institution of marriage. Women went free and unveiled but could be bought and sold.

You now return to the junction and continue eastwards through Baykan to Bitlis, a highly picturesque road leading through gorges with rushing rivers and many unusual rock formations in the surrounding mountains, with various minerals making the rocks look sometimes green, sometimes red. The scenery is semi-Alpine, sometimes with pine trees, sometimes with poplar trees along the river valleys rustling in the stiff breeze and the white water rushing down from the distant snow-peaked mountains. Cows and the occasional flock of sheep graze peacefully near the roadsides. The road itself is slowly being improved, and the aim is to make it into dual carriageway eventually.

At the end of this road, always climbing gradually through the valleys and mountains, you reach Bitlis, the town which is the real gateway to Turkey's eastern extremities. From here you are on the edge of the Lake Van region, the highpoint of any journey to eastern Turkey.

BITLIS *Telephone code: 434; altitude: 1,500m*

Formerly on the outer fringes of the Byzantine Empire and the kingdom of Armenia, Bitlis is the gateway to a different world. You are here coming to the edge of an unknown, a blank in most people's minds, and as you approach past the factories outlying the town and enter the steep black gorge with its curious houses set up on the cliffsides, you have a strange sensation of entering an alien environment. The houses have whitewash painted round their windows, contrasting sharply with the very dark chocolate-coloured stone used in all the buildings. This stone has the characteristic colour found all over the Van region. Many houses also have layers of thick wooden beams between the stonework as protective shock absorbers against earthquakes. Some of these solid old houses still have Armenian inscriptions in a band at first or second-floor level, for the town was Armenian until the Seljuk conquest. The other thing that strikes you is how separate each house is, each in its own green garden. Walnuts are a particular speciality. Today the population is 45,000 and it has its own university on the eastern side of town.

GETTING THERE AND AWAY Minibuses run regularly to and from Tatvan (30 minutes, TL3). The minibus stop is 100m from the Dideban Hotel. Buses also run from there to and from Batman (TL7, 90 minutes), from where you can get connecting buses to and from Diyarbakır.

WHERE TO STAY AND EAT

🏠 **Sark Memer Otel** (50 rooms) Harmantepe Mevki Best Sigara Fabrıkası, 58400 Bitlis; ╲ 2281166; www.trtrail.com/sark-mermer-otel.html. On the right as you enter town from the west, a short walk from the centre. Some deluxe rooms. $$$

🏠 **Dideban Otel** (30 rooms) Nur Caddesi; ╲ 2262820. In town on the right as you enter from the west, with a very good restaurant. $$

WHAT TO SEE As you come into the town proper you can glimpse some intriguing ruins down in the gorge near the river, looking like a gateway. This river, the Bitlis Suyu, is another tributary of the Tigris. Continuing along the main street you glimpse to your left the fine Şerefiye Mosque with *türbe* attached. Within its courtyard you get a good impression of its powerful arches and minaret, all built in perfectly masoned blocks. It was built surprisingly late, in 1528, by a local Kurdish emir. The town remained the capital of a Kurdish *beylicate* until the mid 19th century. A little further up the main street is the Ulu Cami, a curiously malformed mosque built in 1126 by the Artukids. Its interior is exceptionally garish with a bright green carpet and crass modern blue and white kitchen tiles, and odd pieces of Koranic inscription set in the walls. The minaret stands separately with blind arcading and an odd domed roof. Also in the town is the Ihlasiye Medrese, the 16th-century PaOa baths and several *türbes* of the 17th century. Inside the Ihlasiye Medrese is **Il Kultur Merkez** (⊕ 08.00–17.00 Mon–Fri), a cultural centre sponsored by the EU, an attempt to put underrated Bitlis on the tourist map. It hands out useful city maps and brochures on the region.

Bitlis today is famous for its Virginia-type tobacco and for a light-coloured honey with a lovely flavour. There used to be a very important trade route from Mesopotamia up through Siirt and Bitlis to Van, as the Bitlis Valley is the only approach possible to Lake Van from the south and west, through a small break in the mountains that cut off this part of Turkey from the rest of the country. In the 19th century there was even a British consulate here. The population today is largely Kurdish, but up to the 1920s nearly half the inhabitants were Armenian.

As you leave and the road climbs up out of the gorge you can see on your left the impressive walls of the citadel lowering ominously above. Said to have been built originally in Alexander the Great's time (by one of Alexander's generals called Budles, from whom the town is thought to take its name), the walls today are largely Ottoman.

You are now within 150m of the altitude of Lake Van, and as you journey along the last 25km from Bitlis you enter the snowline even as late as May. The road is raised up above the level of the ground either side to keep it clear of the heavy waterlogging which occurs each year when the snows melt. Set down just to the right of the road is a heavily ruined caravanserai, a relic of the once-important trade route from the south, and the last caravanserai you will see on your journey from here east and north.

A major road joins from Muş to the left and the final approach to the lake is a massively wide dead-straight road like an airport runway. Over to the left you will see the massive hulk of Nemrut Dağı, the extinct volcano that created Lake Van, and the road that snakes up and over the crater rim and down to the two lakes inside. Ahead you will soon set eyes for the first time on the startlingly blue water of Lake Van.

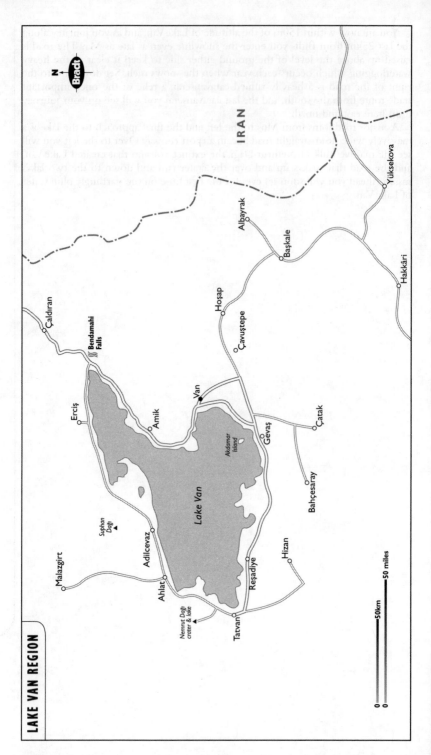

LAKE VAN REGION

9

Lake Van Region

When the times don't suit you, make sure you suit the times.

No-one forgets Lake Van. Make sure you spend at least three days around the shores of this, Turkey's biggest lake, seven times bigger than Lake Geneva, enjoying the water and the scenery and visiting the castles, churches, mosques and tombs left round its shores by earlier civilisations. May and September are the best times to come. In winter from mid-October to mid-April it is too snowbound to be able to enjoy it properly. The high summer months of June, July and August are the best for climbing in the area however, so if you want to scale the two huge volcanoes that stand on the northern and western shores, Nemrut Dağı (not the same as the more famous mountain sanctuary of Antiochus further west, though sharing the same name) and Süphan Dağı, come then. These require camping on the mountain, so at least three further nights are necessary. The area has almost

THE STRANGE BUT BEAUTIFUL LAKE VAN

Lake Van has a quality that verges on the eerie, a quality born partly of its vivid and piercing blueness and partly of its magnificent setting 1,750m above sea level and encircled with peaks rising to 3,000m and even 4,000m, snow-covered for most of the year. It is a lake you will never tire of, its aspect always changing with the different seasons and from different parts of the shoreline. Some views of it are reminiscent of the mountain lakes of the old Yugoslavia, with somewhat gaunt and treeless shores, while at other points where there are trees and flowers in the foreground it can take on an alpine look. Strangely, all views share the pale and timeless light which is reflected from the water to the sky, and by and large you have to concede it is unlike any other lake in the world. Its breathtaking beauty and serenity will haunt you in many a quiet moment.

It was the eruption of Nemrut Dağı aeons ago that formed Lake Van by creating a huge dam of lava thereby blocking the flow of water out to the west. Today the lake is curious in that it still has no outflow. Several small rivers of snowmelt flow into it, but its level remains constant through evaporation during the hot summer months. This peculiarity has resulted in the waters being highly alkaline with natural sodas. Fishermen simply trail their dirty clothes behind their boats to get a whiter-than-white wash, and the local people also insist it removes dandruff. Swimming in the lake water is like gliding through silk and it leaves a lovely smooth feeling on the skin. But immersing yourself only becomes a pleasure from late May onwards, and even then it is pretty bracing, though by late July it is just refreshing. Six times saltier than the sea, it is very buoyant and even the most leaden of people can float. Pollution is almost non-existent and the water is beautifully clear. Its great depth is not certain, but readings of 250m have been recorded.

unlimited hill walking opportunities, where the goal can be a remote mountaintop Urartian citadel or a ruined Armenian monastery long abandoned in the wilderness. Until the mid 1960s this whole region was a restricted zone which no-one could enter without special permission. The roads were unspeakable then, and terrible in the 1980s, but they are very good now, so moving about has been transformed. If you can spend a week based at Lake Van, following the itineraries described in this chapter, you will not regret it; in fact it is likely to be one of the most memorable experiences of your holiday, maybe even of your life.

HISTORY

The serenity of the lake hides its troubled history well. The Hurrian ancestors of the Hittites were the first rulers here in the 2nd millennium BC. It was the Urartians however, coming from the south and the southeast around the great Zab Valley in the Hakkâri region, who created the greatest empire and period of stability, ruling from 900BC to 500BC. Their civilisation only began to be truly appreciated in the 20th century with the excavation of their hilltop citadels and palaces and the discovery of their beautiful gold artefacts.

The dearth of wildlife along Lake Van's shores is striking. The only birds to be seen are gulls, and, more rarely, cormorants and pelicans, mainly on the northern shore near Adilcevaz. The Van fish do not live in the lake but are washed down from freshwater rivers when the snows melt and are then caught near the estuaries from April to June in nets and baskets. There are only two varieties: a kind of carp (called *gögört*) which can be up to 50cm long like a large salmon in shape, and a type of grey mullet (called *ince kefal*). The local people often do not even bother to discriminate, simply calling them all *balık*, fish. The excess catch is pickled for eating later in the year.

The curiosity of Lake Van's wildlife, however, is its so-called Van cats. These fluffy white creatures, seen in kitsch postcards everywhere around Van, have one blue eye and one green eye. Their other peculiarity is that they are said to like swimming and will gaily dive into the water for the sheer pleasure of it. Some say they even dive in to catch fish if they are feeling hungry, so this must be a springtime sport only. They are also meant to be very affectionate. Today they are dying out, mainly because there is no systematic or careful breeding, so as time goes by their peculiar characteristics are being diluted by cross-breeding. The Agricultural Directorate of the Van Province has now begun to breed cats of the true strain, so gradually its numbers may build up again.

A century ago the shoreline was much more wooded and green, but man has left his mark and only very few wooded stretches now remain. Cuneiform documents dating back to the Assyrian invasion here in the 8th century BC talk about cutting down forests as dense as rushes. 'Van in this world, Paradise in the next' is the old Armenian proverb that summed up the once-legendary fertility of this region. In some of the villages however, like Adilcevaz, there are still excellent fruit trees, especially apricots. Van was also where the cantaloupe melon originated. The pope in Rome once had a farm of his own called Cantalupo and he imported Van melons to grow on it. From there they spread all over the world as cantaloupes.

GETTING THERE AND AWAY

BY AIR Arrival by plane in Van is an experience to be relished. Sit on the left side of the plane (on the right side on departure from Van) and you will be rewarded with a superb view in clear weather right down inside the crater lakes of Nemrut Dağı, and of the snow-covered volcanic cone of Süphan Dağı on the northern lakeshore. The plane then crosses the lake and lands close by Van Kalesi, whose curious appearance is enhanced from the air. Turkish Airlines (*www.thy.com*) flies daily to and from Istanbul (two hours) and to and from Ankara (one hour); Pegasus Airlines (*www.flypgs.com*) flies six times a week to and from Ankara and Sun Express (*www.sunexpress.com.tr*) flies six times a week to and from Izmir and three times a week to and from Antalya. The airport is 4km southwest from the city centre, on the lakeshore, and is called Ferit Melen, the name of a native of Van who after a lifetime in the civil service became prime minister in the 1970s. Taxis from the airport into town cost TL20 or there is a *dolmuş* service for TL2.

BY TRAIN AND BOAT Trains, the *Van Gölü Ekspresi*, run direct from Van to Istanbul, via Muş, Elâzığ, Malatya, Sivas, Kayseri, Ankara and Eskişehir, twice a week, and on to Tabriz and Teheran via Özalp and Kapıköy once a week. It leaves Istanbul's Haydarpaşa station on Wednesdays at 23.55 and arrives in Van on Fridays at 21.30. A one-way ticket costs c€22 and the cost of the ferry crossing is included. These services used to be much more frequent, but the demand has dwindled with improvements in the road network. The large ferry steamers run straight across the lake from Tatvan to Van, carrying the railway coaches (not cars) to connect the railways, but timings are erratic and there are often unexplained lengthy delays. In theory the '*Ekspres*' service takes three-and-three-quarter hours to cross the lake. Only choose this route if you have plenty of time and a day or two more does not affect your itinerary. In addition smaller ferry boats link the other points of the shore with Van and Tatvan and there are landing stages at Ahlat, Adilcevaz and Erciş on the northern side, and Edremit, Gevaş and Reşadiye on the south side. The trip along the northern shore takes one-and-a-half days, and along the southern shore eight hours. Van's docks are west of the centre on the lakeshore. The railway station (*İstasyon*) is in the docks and you can get there by minibus for TL1 from the main square called Ferit Melen Meydanı or Beş Yol.

BY BUS Van's *otogar* lies 3km out of town on the Doğubeyazıt road and services run frequently from here to Doğubeyazıt (three hours, TL10), Erzurum (six hours, TL25), Tatvan (2.5 hours, TL10) and even Trabzon (12 hours, TL40). For journeys to the south towards Çavuştepe, Hoşap and Hakkâri, you need a different bus terminal, called the *Yüksekova Garaji* or the *Başkale Garaji*, both on Cumhuriyet Caddesi. Minibuses run roughly every hour in daytime. For Akdamar and Gevaş minibuses run hourly from another small bus stand near the Otel Aslan off Zubeydehanim Caddesi.

GETTING AROUND

The climate plays a vital role in this (see *Other practicalities*, page 266). Nemrut Dağı crater is closed by snow for all but July and August. An ordinary saloon car will get you to the top in the summer. Car hire can be arranged through Avis-Urartu Turizm next door to the Büyük Asur Oteli on Cumhuriyet Caddesi in Van (\ *432 2142020*) for about TL90 per day. Getting around Van town itself can be done on foot, though you may want to use the minibus for the 3km to Van Kalesi, the same one as for the railway station and docks as above.

TOURIST INFORMATION

The Van tourist office (⊕ *08.30–12.00 & 13.00–17.30 Mon–Fri*) is on the main street of Cumhuriyet Caddesi and gives out free maps and leaflets of the area. Guides often lurk round the hotels touting their services.

⌂ WHERE TO STAY

Accommodation in the Van area is generally unexciting and to date there are no boutique hotels, partly perhaps because there are no old buildings in Van itself to restore to their former grandeur. There are a few slightly run-down places with lakeshore beaches, and these are listed separately under each town below.

✗ WHERE TO EAT

The standard of food even in the supposedly good hotels in this part of Turkey falls far short of the level you would expect from this class. The famous Van fish is very rarely available in restaurants (supposedly in abundance from April to June), and when you ask why, the usual answer is that it is eaten in people's homes, not in restaurants. The other local speciality which is readily available is the *otlu peynir* (herb cheese), a Kurdish delicacy often eaten at breakfast, always served at Van's famous breakfast salons on Kahvaltı Sokak (Breakfast Alley) (see map page 280). White and creamy yet quite hard and crumbly, it has two types of herb liberally sticking out of it. These herbs, grown in the mountains, are said to have certain curative properties for the kidneys and urinary channels. Individual listings are again given under each town.

ENTERTAINMENT AND NIGHTLIFE

A festival is held in Van on 2 April when the end of Russia's World War I occupation is celebrated.

SHOPPING

In Ottoman times Van was famous for its finely worked silver, in the form of belts, necklaces, cigarette cases and holders, pipe mouthpieces and the like. As the local tourist leaflet euphemistically puts it: 'Today this craftsmanship has almost disappeared.' The silversmiths were all Armenians.

Handicrafts which are still going strong are the weaving of Van *kilims* or rugs. The predominant colours in these are red, white and dark blue. The designs are usually geometric, with occasional stylised motifs of animals or plants. They are all handmade and natural dyes from local plants and roots are still sometimes used.

OTHER PRACTICALITIES

The winter is very long, from September to May, and the summer season is really only the three months of June, July and August, when it gets very hot during the day, but cools off very quickly at night. The air and water here are both very refreshing. Swimming begins from mid to late May at the earliest, unless you are a masochist. The water then heats very quickly throughout June, July and August, cooling down again very quickly at the end of September. (For further information on the range of temperatures throughout the year, see *Chapter 1*, pages 6–7.)

Van's ATMs and internet cafés can all be found along the main street of Cumhuriyet Caddesi. Tatvan also has one or two along its main street, but that is it, so make sure you have enough cash to last.

WHAT TO SEE

The order followed in this chapter assumes your approach is from west to east, so begins with Tatvan, then follows the northern shore from Nemrut Dağı, to Ahlat and Adilcevaz, then Süphan Dag. It then follows the southern shore from Reşadiye via Akdamar Island to Van city itself, and ends by following the road deep into the wild remoteness of Turkey's southeast corner with the town of Hakkâri, via the Urartian palace at Çavuştepe and the fairy-tale Kurdish fortress at Hoşap.

TATVAN *Telephone code: 434*

Arriving from the west at Tatvan you will come to a large T-junction and ahead of you is the small harbour with the large ships of the Denizcelik Bankası (Turkish Maritime Lines). These ships form the link from the terminus of the railway line here across the lake to Van where the railway resumes, leading eventually to Iran. The trains literally drive onto the ships, locomotive, carriages and all, to be ferried across. Whether or not you are using the train, Tatvan is not a place to linger in, as it consists of just one 3km-long street lined with the usual shops, banks, coffee houses and offices. Its main virtue is as a place to stock up with supplies from the food and grocery shops for your camping trip up Nemrut Dağı, where you will need to be self-sufficient for two to three days. Although no great beauty spot, the town has cleaned itself up a lot in recent years. Back in the 1980s the main street was riddled with potholes and very muddy, yet, as so often throughout eastern Turkey, the inhabitants seemed curiously unperturbed by the filth of their streets. Young girls in school uniforms of white dresses, white shoes and socks would skip across the muddy streets on their way to school with little attempt at avoiding the puddles. Frederick Burnaby, travelling the region over 100 years earlier, was struck by the same attitude:

'Why do you not clean the street?' he enquired of an old Turk, who had just waded across the mud to visit his friend's house.

'The mud will dry up in the summer months,' he replied, 'why trouble our heads about it now?'

The town was under Russian occupation for several years until 1917, and still feels a bit like a distant outpost of Siberia, except that now it has a Carrefour supermarket, a bowling alley and a CineMed.

🏠 WHERE TO STAY

🏠 **Otel Dilek** (17 rooms) Yeni Çarşi; ℡ 8271516. Tatvan lakeside, looking basic & rather run-down though with en-suite bathrooms. $$

🏠 **Tatvan Kardelen** (25 rooms) Belediye Yanı; ℡ 8259500. A modern high-rise block with reasonably spacious rooms but low on atmosphere. $$

Rough camping inside the Nemrut Dağı crater beside the lakes is good if you can be self-sufficient for water and catering.

NEMRUT DAĞI CRATER (3,050M)

From Tatvan a road runs north round the shore of the lake and 4km after the big T-junction an unmade road marked Nemrut forks left. From this point the road on up to the crater is the best part of 25km and in the summer months of June, July and August is perfectly feasible in a saloon car. The rest of the year it is snowbound, as the summit is after all over 3,000m high, nearly 1,000m higher than the other more famous statued Nemrut Dağı further west.

The remarkable thing about this crater is that the road crosses over the rim and disappears 700m down inside it, running right up to two huge lakes, one hot, one cold. The crater, 7km in diameter, is one of the largest complete craters in the world. The hot lake is the smaller of the two, and is only 'hot' in places where some volcanic bubbles come up from its floor. The volcano was last active in 1441 but a few places still have small amounts of steam and heat escaping from fissures. The cold lake is very cold, too cold for most people to swim in, but the hot lake makes for excellent swimming in the summer months, and camping by its shore while you explore the crater and climb to its rim is an unforgettable experience. No-one lives inside the crater, though *yürük* nomad camps can occasionally be seen here grazing their cattle on the rich summer pasture. There is a makeshift seasonal refreshment hut that has set itself up on the shore of the cold lake, where tea and simple food is available, but that is it, and there are no camping facilities as such, ie: no wash-blocks. The contrast between the bleak outside of the cone and the lusher vegetation on the inside is striking, as though another world lies sheltering inside. The spot is very peaceful, and even has some areas of woods. It never has more than a handful of visitors, so it is easy to be very secluded by choosing a camping spot a little set apart. The climb of some 700m up to the rim is very steep and takes about two–three hours, but the views, gazing out over the deep-blue lakes from above while enjoying your well-earned picnic, are truly stunning.

AHLAT

Returning from Nemrut to the shore road continue on to Ahlat, once an important Armenian town on the lakeshore, now a sprawl of modern houses. The Arabs took the town in the 9th century and it remained in Muslim hands when it was ruled by the Seljuks and the Kurdish Ayyubids. In 1245 the Mongols took the town and then White Sheep Turcomans held it for a while before it was nominally incorporated into the Ottoman Empire in 1533. In practice Ottoman power did not extend into these remote regions and real power was exercised by the Kurdish emirs of Bitlis.

Often referred to as a ghost town in recent accounts, Ahlat today is no such thing, and its famous extensive **cemetery** and distinctive **kümbets** rise incongruously out of cultivated fields or from among clusters of modern houses, so that they are no longer straightforward to find. In all these *kümbets* (literally 'dome', but also Turkish slang for the human posterior) the body was buried in the crypt underneath, while outside steps lead up to the upper chamber, a prayer room with its own *mihrab*, symbol of the Gate of Heaven through which the deceased would hope to pass. Most tombs in Islam did not have *mihrabs* as it is not permitted to pray to the dead in Islam in the way it is permissible in Christianity to pray to saints. The tall conical shape is unmistakably Armenian-influenced, and Ahlat's Armenian stonemasons were in fact famous for their work. The traditional grave tent of the central Asiatic nomad, with its circular body and pointed conical roof, is almost certainly the inspiration for the characteristic shape of Armenian, Seljuk and Georgian buildings. Only Kayseri has tombs in numbers and variety to rival Ahlat.

The **Ulu Kümbet (Great Kümbet)** is the first one you will see and the largest – it is to the right of the road and set about 300m away in a field with a few simple houses nearby. On the left of the road is the scruffy neglected graveyard extending beside the little museum where you can park and walk back to the *kümbet*. The museum is a rather feeble affair on the main road, opened in 1971 (⊕ *08.00–17.00 Tue–Sun; adult TL2*), with two rooms containing Urartian pottery, jewellery and bronze weapons, some Roman glassware, Ottoman costume embroidery, highly fragmentary Seljuk pottery and a few Seljuk and Byzantine coins. The museum attendant watches you, slightly incredulous that you can show interest in these old relics, and once you have gone, goes out to sit in the sun again. Such an attitude is no recent development, and Burnaby remarked in the 19th century how the locals in a village where he stayed could not understand his getting up so early and riding through deep snow simply to explore an old cave nearby. 'Curiosity about antiquities,' he comments, 'does not enter a Turk's composition. He lives for the present. What has happened is finished and done with'.

Another 1km or so further east you will spot on your left two more *kumbets* about 400m from the road and known as the **Çifte (Twin) *kümbets***. Both date from the late 13th century. Taking the dirt track that leads off to the left here, you come to a T-junction at which you can turn right to reach them. From the outside these two are the least exciting of the *kümbets*, but inside the larger of the two has the remains of some coloured plaster decoration. Returning now to the T-junction and following the road straight on, parallel to the main road, you pass after 200m or so another *kümbet* to the right in someone's front garden and then a much prettier little *kümbet* just to the right of the road, calling itself **Emir Ali Kümbet**, of a different style with no steps leading up, but just an open section below.

Continuing along the earth road and passing a cluster of rural village houses behind walls until after 150m or so the road opens up into a grassy space to reveal the best-preserved and prettiest of the *kümbets*, standing next to an oratory (*mescit*) which is usually kept locked. This is the *kümbet* and *mescit* of Bayındır, unknown in history but described as a great king and propagator of the faith in the inscription which also gives the date of 1481. This *kümbet*, instead of being closed in at its upper storey, has an open colonnaded arcade supporting its conical roof, so that you can look out from inside. It has been speculated that this served as a minaret for the oratory and was used for calling the faithful to prayer. All the *kümbets* for some reason have their entrance on the north. In the burial chambers underneath anything from one to four people were buried.

From here the earth road leads back towards the lake past the extensive **Seljuk cemetery** to the left, described in earlier accounts as the *pièce de résistance* of Ahlat, mournful and atmospheric, covering about 2km. Today its once-striking setting overlooking the lake has been spoilt by the encroachment of modern houses, telegraph wires and TV aerials which simply serve to make the huge tombstones look like neglected anachronisms. Covered in lichen and leaning at drunken angles, many are 2m tall, carved with elaborate designs showing Armenian influence. One of these, a circular design with swirls within it, represents eternal life. The inscriptions on the tombstones are generally in verse, extolling symbolic virtues.

As you leave the town heading eastwards if you look to your right you will see the dark chocolate-brown walls of the old fortress of Ahlat about 200m away by the lakeshore, built in the 16th century by the Ottoman Sultan Süleyman. A track leads down to the main gateway and you can walk through into the open courtyard enclosed within the walls. Walking towards the far corner of the enclosure down towards the lake, you pass through what is almost a landscaped garden with tall poplar trees and small running streams which have been channelled off to make a water system. The ruins are all covered in grass and you can walk high up along the battlements. A ruined mosque almost obscured by tall poplars tempts you with a climb up the steps to the top of its minaret, though the view is not as good as you might expect because you arrive at the top facing north towards the town rather than towards the lake. Like many minarets it has 99 steps, one for each of the names of Allah. The mosque itself is now used as a potting shed, housing various gardening oddments like wheelbarrows.

🏠 **WHERE TO STAY** On the lakeshore here a new hotel and marina has just been built, **Büyük Selçuklu Otel** (*43 rooms; Sahil Yolu, Ahlat;* 4125695; $$$) which promises to be the best accommodation along the northern shore of Lake Van.

DETOUR TO MALAZGİRT

From Ahlat a rough road heads north 58km to Malazgirt, site of the momentous Battle of Manzikert in 1071 when the Seljuk sultan defeated and captured the Byzantine emperor, thereby establishing the Turks for the first time in Anatolia. The town today has little of note to offer the visitor other than the remains of the black basalt walls of its fortress, and many Armenian spoils reused in the construction of the new houses. An easier approach is from Patros via Erciş, but it is a much longer way round.

ON TO ADİLCEVAZ

The shoreline between Ahlat and Adilcevaz has some good stretches of beach where you can find deserted areas to swim and picnic. Some parts are almost like sandy beach, others are pebbly. The dearth of wildlife contributes to the air of stillness that always seems to surround Lake Van. The occasional cow or donkey grazes on the lush meadows by the shore, and the villagers sometimes keep geese and ducks. As far as wild animals are concerned however, there is just the occasional gull, the very occasional bird of prey and the even more occasional (harmless) snake. When the weather is good there is nothing more restful than lying on the grass by the silent shores of Lake Van with a picnic or paddling in the icy clear water.

ADİLCEVAZ *Telephone code: 434*

At Adilcevaz, 25km from Ahlat, you come to the small but perfectly formed chocolate-coloured mosque on the lakeshore, built by Sinan in 1557–58. Set by itself with its tall minaret and nine cupolas it almost looks like a toy beside the vastness of the lake. The ablutions area is separate to the side, and the entrance is down the steps and round to the back. Inside, its proportions are very lovely and there are none of the garish trimmings so often found in city mosques. Above it rises a Seljuk castle on a steep outcrop overlooking the lake. If you fancy the exercise you can climb up to it in about 30 minutes. There is not a great deal left on top beyond the walls and towers, but the views are breathtaking over the lake towards the snow-covered mountains. This was the site of the discovery of the Urartian relief in polished basalt of the king standing on a bull, now erected in the garden of the Van Museum and considered by some to be the finest ever piece of Urartian stone carving. The relief was originally from Kefkalesi, the Urartian citadel towering over the valley to the west of the village, but it evidently tumbled down and was reused in constructing the walls of this Seljuk castle.

Beside the lakeside mosque a road leads off into the village of Adilcevaz proper, a very attractive village built on the slopes of a well-watered valley, with water running down in channels beside the road and very green tall poplar trees separating the prosperous-looking houses.

GETTING THERE AND AWAY Without your own transport the only possibility is by bus to and from Van. These run daily but only until 14.00.

WHERE TO STAY If you get stuck in Adilcevaz the **Hotel Kent** (*8 rooms;* \3113231; $) is the only option, in the centre of town with squat toilets and basic rooms.

WHAT TO SEE
Kefkalesi If you can devote half a day to the excursion, you could head further inland away from the village northwards to Kefkalesi itself, with a ruined

Armenian monastery at its foot. Heading north for about 6km on the track that leaves the back of the village you will come to a huge rock spur with precipitous cliffs and a valley leading up either side of it. Head up the left side of the left valley and after about 30 minutes' walk you will reach the Monastery of the Miracles of Ardzgue, abandoned in 1915 by its Armenian monks. Its monks had unearthed part of a large gold basin which they claimed was the basin in which Jesus was first washed after birth, and this relic was regarded as having the power to perform miracles, hence the monastery's name. In practice the relic was almost certainly part of an Urartian gold basin. The roof partially collapsed in the 1980s but enough remains for you to notice its octagonal drum base for its dome, and the unusual short pillar supports, free-standing columns on the western side. This design is unique in Armenian architecture. One section of it had to be rebuilt after the 1648 earthquake. From the church the track continues up the left side until eventually entering the Kefkalesi site from the north. The more direct route to Kefkalesi runs from the right-hand side of the valley. It sits on the summit of the outcrop at 2,200m and Turkish archaeologists have uncovered a temple built with massive blocks and the foundations of an Urartian palace with 30 recognisable rooms, some with huge storage jars and various inscribed blocks.

SÜPHAN DAĞI (4,058M)

Adilcevaz is also the starting point for the climb up the massive hulk of Süphan Dağı, the highest mountain in the Van region at 4,058m and the third highest in Turkey after Ararat and Cilo Dağı in the Hakkâri. Its height was originally recorded as 4,434m, making it easily the second highest in the country, but revised military mapping in the 1980s reduced the figure. Be that as it may, this huge volcanic peak dominates the northern shore of the lake and is covered in snow all the year round, though in high summer there are only patches left high on the cone. The *jandarma* at Adilcevaz like to be informed that you are on the mountain, so it is wise to stop off there to let them know. Their building is clearly identifiable at the back of the village by its red flag.

The usual approach involves one or sometimes two nights' camping on the mountain, and with a 4x4 you can drive up a track on the southwest slopes to a point above a communications mast at about 2,500m, where there is a fine flat area with plenty of space for tents and a vehicle. You are well above the tree line here, so be prepared for there to be no shade at all. No actual mountaineering skills are required, just sure-footedness and a certain level of fitness, especially for the final scramble up massive boulders. The standard ascent involves arriving and setting up camp around 16.00, resting, eating and trying to get some sleep before making a start around midnight or 02.00, the idea being that you can make most of the ascent of the lower slopes while it is still dark and therefore cooler, so by the time the sun comes up you are already above the 3,000m mark where it is naturally cooler. You reach the summit around 10.00–12.00 and then descend much more quickly in three or four hours back to your base camp. There is a path that can be followed at the beginning, but after that it is just a question of continuing up the cone. Having a guide along is helpful though not essential.

If you are a keen birdwatcher you may enjoy going east beyond Adilcevaz 20km or so to Arin Gölü near Göldüzü, a freshwater lake where lots of birds come to fish. The northeast corner of the lake from here on to Erciş and around Lake Van is scenically the least impressive section of shoreline.

Unless you coincide with a local Turkish climbing party, the chances are you will have the mountain to yourself. The higher sections of the cone are very steep and the terrain crumbly, so you need to be sure-footed and careful. At this height as you start to enter the snowline there are, even in high summer, a surprising number of alpine-like tiny colourful flowers in yellows, blues and whites. The other deceptive aspect of the volcano is that all along, what you think is the top as you climb from below, turns out to be a false summit. Reaching what you imagine to be the rim of the crater, you in fact descend slightly into a massive and beautiful grassy bowl, in the centre of which is a huge volcanic plug of massive boulders. These form a 400m rock wall which you have to scramble up to reach the actual summit, which even then, turns out to be huge, covering an area of at least 1km, with various hillocks on top, so it is difficult to be sure which is the highest point. If you are equipped for it, one very good option is to camp here in this grassy bowl, with its flowers and chunks of snow nestling in the crevasses. You are totally away from the cares of the world, in another entirely separate world, and the only other life you may encounter is a shepherd with his flock of sheep grazing on the rich high pasture, guarded from wolves or bears by his sheepdogs. The views over the lake are superb, but Nemrut Dağı, though lower, is the more exciting of the two volcanoes because of its fine crater lakes and lusher vegetation. The beauty of climbing in these remote mountains is summed up well by Sidney Nowill, the experienced English climber of these parts, as that sensation of living, 'for a time completely free of every worldly link, self-reliant and untrammelled by any human agency or service, something which is healthful and cleansing to achieve, if only once in a lifetime.'

WHERE TO STAY

 Club Natura Van (9 rooms) Off Muradiye road on the northeast tip of Lake Van, 65km from Van airport; ☏ 2672108; www.clubnatura.com. Set on a lonely headland in the middle of nowhere & beside a large fruit orchard, this row of simple bungalows faces out over the lake & Süphan Dağı.

The rooms are simple but with en-suite bathrooms & small private terraces in front of each room with its own steps up. A little to the south lies the isle of Adir with its 13th-century church of St George, very rarely visited. Bring a canoe. $$

REMOTE MONASTERIES SOUTH OF LAKE VAN

From Tatvan as you head along the main road towards Van city, the road leaves the lakeshore almost immediately and heads off inland, climbing through scenic mountain stretches with abundant water flowing in bubbling streams down the hillsides, and through attractively rural green valleys whose lush yellow flowering meadows have many beehives producing the famous Van honey. After 8km a road forks right to Hizan and Bahçesaray, and for the adventurous this can be the first stage of a journey to visit some extremely remote Armenian monasteries. You really need your own transport here, unless you are prepared to spend at least a couple of days waiting for infrequent buses and staying in extremely basic places. They cannot be reached without a guide and require several hours' journey from Hizan on horseback or on foot. In order of distance from Eski Hizan they are: the 11th-century Gökçimen Kilise; the Convent of the Mother of God of Hzar with a well-preserved 11th-century church; and the 11th-century Convent of the Holy Cross of Hisan founded by Gregory the Illuminator, the first Armenian patriarch. From Bahçesaray, 106km southwest of Van, deep in the mountains, you can also walk with a guide in several hours to Aparank Monastery (founded in 358–59, but consisting now of a cluster of five Armenian churches ranging from the 10th to the 17th centuries), the remotest of all, high in the mountains. If you approach Bahçesaray from Van, you have to cross the Karabel Pass, at 2,985m the highest road pass (unsurfaced) in Turkey, and always the last to open after the winter snows in May/June. Bahçesaray used to have a population of 12,000 a century ago, while today it is about 4,000, and inhabited solely by Kurds. Many of the churches were used as places of refuge when the island of Akdamar was seized, and are currently in use as barns. The local honey is especially delicious.

Back on the road along the southern shore of Lake Van, after 30km a fork leads off to the left to Reşadiye, a town on a lovely little peninsula. On one side is a beach and on the other is a natural terrace with shady trees ending at the cliffs high above the lake. The road then climbs to a scenic pass at 2,234m, entering the Province of Van, before dropping back down to the lake level. Look out for a sign to the left towards the lake marked Altınsaç, about 12km before reaching Akdamar. This is a worthwhile excursion if you have at least two hours to spare and your own transport, to visit the Church of St Thomas, a well-preserved church whose Armenian name is Kamrak Vank, much less well known than Akdamar and therefore much less visited. The tarmac ends after 3km and the gravel track then skirts the lake to reach Altınsaç (Golden Hair) village after 14km. The church stands by itself about 3km further on, clearly visible on a mound overlooking the lake, and can only be reached on foot. It still has its roof, as well as a large covered courtyard added in the 17th century.

AKDAMAR ISLAND

When the road finally rejoins the lake after 100km from Tatvan, you will spot for the first time the little island of Akdamar in the lake, a distinctive shape with a large outcrop of rock on its further side, then flattening out to a small terrace on the lakeshore side. It is on this terrace that the famous Armenian Church of the Holy Cross of Akdamar stands, a masterpiece of early Armenian art and the cathedral church of the independent Armenian kingdom of Vaspurakan.

In 2007 the government completed an 18-month restoration of the 1,100-year-old church, costing US$1.5m. In a symbolic gesture of huge significance, in September 2010 the Turkish government permitted an Armenian church service to take place here for the first time in nearly 100 years. The world's press crowded onto the normally quiet island for the event.

HISTORY In 313 the Edict of Milan announced the toleration of Christianity throughout the Roman Empire, Gregory was ordained at Caesarea (Kayseri) in Cappadocia, and the Armenian Church was for a time subservient to Rome. Gregory however preached the new faith in the Armenian language and soon the national church developed characteristics of its own. He was given the title of Catholikos of the Armenian Church, a title which was to be inherited by the members of his family. With encouragement from the Persians, ever keen to create a rift with the West, an Armenian alphabet was developed by the monk **Mesrop Mashtots** in 404, and a school of translators into Armenian was set up in the early 5th century. Beautiful **illuminated manuscripts** were produced in a style which blended what had been inherited from Urartu with Persian and Syrian influences.

In 451 the Armenian Church refused to accept the verdict of the Council of Chalcedon and continued to hold its **Monophysite doctrine**. Like the Syrian Jacobites and the Egyptian Copts, this meant they believed that the human nature of Christ was absorbed in the divine, a view which alienated them from other

The origins of the Armenians are not known for certain and ancient classical historians were no less confused. Herodotus calls them Phrygian colonists, while Strabo, an Anatolian, thought they were related to the Babylonians or the Syrians. Today the most probable theories are either that they came into Anatolia from the direction of the Caucasus, the same route as the Hurrians and the Hittites, or they are an original Anatolian people. Like the Hittites, their language is Indo-European.

The Armenians make their first appearance in recorded history in the annals of the Persians, c500BC, as the people who had taken over the land of Urartu following the collapse of the Urartian state. Set free from Persian domination, like the rest of Asia Minor, by Alexander the Great in 331BC, Armenia chose to retain its Persian-style administration, with regional *satraps* who were virtually independent kings running their own armies. The process of Hellenisation never reached Armenia, though Alexander's opening up of the Eastern world gave them the opportunity to extend the boundaries of their legendary commercial skills beyond Mesopotamia to Egypt, India and central Asia. Under Tigranes the Great (94–54BC) Armenia was a prosperous and extensive empire, but when the Romans under Lucullus invaded the country to put an end to the troublesome Pontic kingdom, Armenia was also taken. From this time on it was to remain a client state to Rome and later to Byzantium, a useful bulwark against Persia.

In 280 Armenia became the first country to adopt Christianity as the state religion, when the Armenian king Tiridates, who had worshipped the Persian gods until then, was finally converted by his minister Gregory, later the St Gregory the Illuminator. Together they set about the destruction of the pagan temples at Ani and Tercan and broke to pieces the golden goddess of Anahid at Erzurum. The result was war with Persia and massacres of Christians in Persia.

Christians including their neighbours the Nestorians and the Georgians, and above all the Greeks. Their links with Syria and the Jacobite Church soon became stronger than with Byzantium, and it was the mutual antipathy of the Greeks and the Armenians that finally exposed Asia Minor to the Muslim takeover. Once more, a religious division was used as an excuse for a political and racial one.

The Arab outsurge in the 7th century flowed over Armenia too, and it remained for centuries under **Islamic control**. There is no evidence of persecution by the Arabs, but at this time many Armenian families left, usually the wealthier ones. It was in fact the Byzantines who were the first to forcibly send the Armenians away, when in 578, 10,000 Armenians were taken from their homes to be settled in Cyprus to till the soil and provide soldiers. Others were settled in Crete, Thrace and Calabria. Though many Armenian soldiers became prominent in the Byzantine army, they retained, even in their exile, their nationality and insisted on their descent.

Armenia asserted itself again in the late 9th century under the Bagratid family. A branch of this family continued to rule Georgia until the 18th century. Claims from rival families however helped to weaken the country, and it was one of these rivals, King Gagik I of the Artsuni family, who retired from war and administration to the serenity of Akdamar Island on Lake Van. Here in the 10th century Gagik built his golden-domed palace and his cathedral church with a monastery beside it. As late as the 1890s some of the monastery buildings were still being used by a handful of monks, scarcely literate, living at subsistence level. Of the palace no trace remains today and of the monastery only a few walls are left. The church however, built between 915 and 921, is in astonishingly good condition, all the more remarkable as it receives no maintenance from the authorities and has never been restored. All its exterior walls are covered with Bruegel-like reliefs cut into the stone of various Old Testament scenes as well as some Armenian fantasy tales. The shape of the church is typically Armenian, small in plan, only 15m by 12m, but very tall, with the dome reaching a height of over 20m. It must be one of the smallest cathedrals in the world.

Throughout the 11th, 12th and 13th centuries Armenian towns, notably Kars, Muş and Malatya, were sporadically attacked by Turcoman hordes and in 1239, Ani itself, their capital, was sacked by Genghis Khan and his Tartar Mongols. From this point on, the Armenians were ruled by Arabs, Kurds, Persians, Seljuks and eventually by the Ottoman sultans who took over their land in the 16th century. Throughout this troubled history, Armenians continued to emigrate, some to Russia and Poland, some to the Near East and, most recently, to North America. During World War I the Turks caused the deaths, either by slaughter or deportation, of at least one million Armenians.

GETTING THERE AND AWAY A pair of **ferries** shuttle to and fro between a small landing stage on the lakeshore and the island, taking about 15 minutes to make the 2km trip. You pay for your ticket (TL5) on boarding and the boats carry up to 50 people. At weekends it is a very popular outing with local families, often taking their barbecues and picnic stuff with them to make a day of it on one of the island's beaches. Many organised tours now follow this example and get taken a simple barbecue lunch across. The boats run daily from about 08.00 until dusk. Without your own transport you will have to get a **minibus** from Van to Gevaş, the nearby village, a distance of 44km, costing TL3. Services run regularly but the returns stop after 16.00, so be careful not to get stuck, as you will end up paying an exorbitant taxi fare.

WHERE TO STAY AND EAT Close to the Akdamar jetty there are now several basic hotels, many offering lakeside camping. If you don't take your own food there are now a couple of good places on the lakeshore close to the landing stage serving food and refreshments. There is even a simple place on the island itself for basic refreshments.

WHAT TO SEE On the island the ferries moor at a stone quayside from which a stepped path leads up to the church through terraces which were once the gardens of the monastery. On a little rock, separated from the island as you approach, stand the remains of a tiny chapel, maybe the private chapel of King Gagik.

In May the island is ablaze with flowers and shrubs, growing where once were gardens and orchards. The side of the Church of the Holy Cross of Akdamar you see first from the path is best viewed by climbing up onto the grassy roof of the forechurch building. From here you have a superb close-up view not only of the side immediately facing you, but also of the side facing the lakeshore up as far as the porch, itself a later 18th-century addition.

Climbing back down now to the ground level and looking at the carvings on the far side of the porch, you will spot a fine **relief of David and Goliath**. David has the cheeky grin of a real young upstart. On the rear façade of the church is an Adam and Eve relief, heavily defaced with graffiti and much of their faces missing.

Despite a programme of restoration in 2007, the inside of the church today is a total wreck, heavily defaced with graffiti and fire smoke. The 10th-century murals which once adorned the walls have the appearance now of unfinished drawings. The golden bell that once hung here and the illuminated Armenian Bible are today in museums in Moscow.

The **relief of Jonah and the Whale** is one of the most impressive, a highly ludicrous series of three in which it looks as if Jonah is being fed to the whale by men in a boat; the whale resembles an elongated pig with ears and teeth; and Jonah spewed out onto the land looks like a man reclining on the treetops. The Armenian use of perspective lends an unintentionally comic air to all the scenes.

The **Abraham and Isaac reliefs** just before the porch can also be seen well from this vantage point. Abraham has hold of Isaac, about half his size, by the hair as though he is about to thrash him. To the left of them, halfway up a vine, is a happy-looking goat, evidently thinking, 'There but for the grace of God go I.' On the west wall a faintly cross-eyed Gagik offers a model of the church looking like a birdcage to the clergy, and there are also many Armenian crosses (*khatchkars*) looking a bit like detailed Celtic crosses. All over the walls are reliefs of vines and bunches of grapes, often intertwined with curious bear-like creatures. The Armenians had a particular weakness for fanciful animals, preferably fighting or devouring one another, and griffins, lions and dragons can be seen all over the church.

The island is a very charming spot to linger and enjoy a picnic. There are numerous shady spots to sit under the trees, many of them almond, where you can catch the breeze and enjoy a lovely view down over the church, with colourful flowers in the grassy foreground, the shimmering lake and the snow-topped mountains behind. Spring comes earlier to Akdamar than to other parts of the Van region, so at mid-May it is already at its most colourful. By late June and July it is already quite yellow and dry-looking. Stone tables are laid out in some areas, but despite the large numbers of people pouring across the island, they all seem to disperse surprisingly quickly and you can always find a secluded spot. The Turks picnicking *en famille* devote all their concentration to the preparation of their barbecues and scarcely give the church a second glance as they stagger past laden with pots and pans. Scattered round the church are gravestones of Armenian Christians who wished to attain saintliness. Their rich floral designs contrast with the abstract Seljuk tombstones in the cemetery at Ahlat. One tradition claims that the grave of Simon, one of the Disciples of Christ, is on the island somewhere.

In the hottest months of July and August you can find spots to swim on the pebbly beaches and linger as long as you like, as you are not tied to any particular ferry for the return. When you want to leave you simply stroll down to the quayside and sit on one of the waiting boats until it fills up sufficiently for the owner to feel it is worth a trip back. No-one wants to see your ticket.

A trite story about how the island got its name has been handed down through generations. One of the priests on the island had a daughter called Tamara who fell in love with a Turkish shepherd on the shore. They could not meet openly so the shepherd had to swim across to the island at night, directed by a light Tamara held out for him. The priest however smelt a rat and locking Tamara in her room went out himself the next night with the light. The shepherd swam across towards it, but it then moved to a different place, so he changed course. Again and again the light moved until the shepherd was exhausted with following it. Finally managing to swim to the place where the light was, he emerged to find a group of priests waiting for him, brandishing sticks. He was too tired to struggle and as he sank beneath the waves his final words were 'Ah…Tamara'.

The final stretch eastwards from Gevaş near the Akdamar landing stage and Van keeps close to the lakeshore and there are now even lakeside holiday villas for sale and quite a lot of camping sites. Gevaş itself, like Ahlat on the northern shore, has a cemetery with gravestones, dominated by the large pyramid-roofed *türbe* (dated by inscription to 1358) close to the main road, of Halime Hatun, a female member of the Karakoyunlu dynasty. Just 10km before Van, Edremit has grown up to become a kind of lakeside resort, with lots of tea-gardens and restaurants for the inhabitants of Van to escape the city in high summer.

VAN *Telephone code: 432; altitude 1,727m*

The whole Van area was closed to visitors until 1960, though looking at it now it is hard to believe it has only so recently opened its doors to the outside world. Approached from Akdamar, Van is unprepossessing, with a sprawl of modern building heralding the outskirts and the university on the right. Atatürk had wanted to establish the main university of eastern Turkey here, but after his death Erzurum was substituted; wrongly, people now agree. Van today is the most forward-looking city of eastern Turkey with a range of schools including a large mixed grammar school, a Girls' Teachers' Training School and a Boys' Commercial Training School. Competition for places in the secondary schools and institutes is intense and the desire to be educated is strong.

The highpoint of any visit is the exploration of Van Kalesi, the enormous freakish Urartian citadel 3km from the centre of town on the lakeshore, and the annihilated Eski Van (Old Van), the former Armenian town below it. Van's small museum is also worth a look. Allow a half-day minimum for Van's sights, so it is best to stay a night here, maybe in one of the lakeside hotels.

HISTORY As so often throughout eastern Turkey, waves of conquerors passed this way. In the 7th century BC the Persian Medes, having overthrown the Assyrian Empire with the fall of Nineveh in 612BC, spread into the Van region and displaced the Urartian culture which had been weakened through years of rivalry with the Assyrians. In the 5th century BC the area was the scene of several great battles during the **retreat of the ten thousand** led by the Greek general Xenophon. Greek resistance to Persian power was to continue, culminating in the victories of Alexander the Great. In 331BC on his way to Persia, Alexander took the Van region, and after his death it became part of the Seleucid Empire. When the Romans overthrew the Seleucids, the region passed for a time into Roman hands.

In the 1st century BC, claiming he was heir to the Romans, the Armenian king Tigranes the Great, of the family of Artaksias of the Huns, captured Van from the Romans and founded the **first Armenian kingdom** here, called Vaspurakan. Later, in 66BC, the Romans under Pompey recaptured Van once more, but in the 3rd century AD the Sassanians of Iran scattered the Romans from Van, killing the Armenian king Khosrow Parhis and forcing the Armenians to adopt their religion. So unhappy were the Armenians about this state of affairs that they joined forces with the Romans to oust the Sassanians, and from then on for some time, Van was ruled by Armenians under Roman domination.

The Roman Empire's control here ended with the outsurge of the Arabs in the 640s, who captured Van and converted it to Islam. Then in 1054 the first Turkish raids on the Vaspurakan kingdom began at the time of the Seljuks under Tugrul Bey. A few years later in 1071, the famous Seljuk warrior Alp Arslan won his great victory over the Byzantines at Manzikert, which opened the way for the Turks to move westwards into the whole of Anatolia. But then followed in the 13th, 14th and 15th centuries a series of attacks, first by the Mongols, then by the Black Sheep Turcomans, and again by the Mongols under Tamerlane, who, needless to say, destroyed Van Kalesi.

From 1503 the region was held by the Iranian Safavids for a time, until in 1514 at Çaldıran the Ottoman sultan Selim the Grim defeated the Iranian shah and incorporated the region into the Ottoman Empire with a local governor at Van. All of these successive rulers used the rebuilt Van Kalesi as their stronghold.

German scholars of the 19th century were the first to write about and begin excavations at Tilkitepe (near Van airport) and at Van Kalesi from 1937 to 1939.

The Armenians: a troubled history The Kurds have long been enemies of the Armenians, a conflict born not only of religion, but also of lifestyle, with the contempt of a nomadic people for settled townsfolk dealing in commerce. The Armenians also had the gift of irritating the Muslims by their often arrogant manner. When the Young Turk dictatorship ordered the removal of the two million or so Armenians, many were only too happy to oblige. The feeling was, however, mutual, and the Armenian volunteers on the Russian side, when Turkey collapsed, also took their revenge. More than 600,000 Kurds are said to have been killed in eastern Anatolia between 1915 and 1918. The 'Genocide Section' of the Van Museum focuses on these. The Turkish view on the matter is that the Armenians were a disloyal minority who connived with the Russians to partition Turkey and set up an Armenian state. As traitors to the country at a time of national crisis, they deserved their fate, however extreme.

The Armenians of course see things differently and cite the words of the British prime minister David Lloyd George, spoken in 1922: 'Since 1914 the Turks, according to testimony – official testimony – we have received, have slaughtered in cold blood one million and a half Armenians, men, women and children, and five hundred thousand Greeks without any provocation at all.'

During the period 1908–18 Turkey was dominated by the Young Turks. They came to power by a revolution proclaiming liberty, equality and fraternity. But far from establishing a democracy, by 1914 the Young Turks had established, under a triumvirate, an **absolute dictatorship**, silencing all opposition, including liberal and westernised Turks.

Already in 1911 at a Congress of Young Turks the following secret resolution had been carried: 'Sooner or later the complete Ottomanisation of all Turkish subjects must be realised. It must, however, be clear that this objective can never be attained by persuasion. On the contrary, it must be achieved by force of arms.'

Even before the rise of the Young Turks the Armenians had suffered: in 1895 and 1896, tens of thousands of Armenians perished in officially instigated massacres; at Urfa over 2,000 people including women and children were burnt alive in their cathedral. Another massacre in 1909, said to have claimed 30,000 Armenian lives in the Province of Adana, was deliberately prepared by the government, as a local Young Turk member later admitted.

Nevertheless, far from being disloyal, at the outbreak of World War I, over 250,000 Armenians were serving in the Turkish army, and they only established an independent state in 1918 with the collapse of the Ottoman Empire and in response to the gross violence they had suffered.

The holocaust reached its peak from 1915 to 1918. In 1915 the Minister of the Interior, Talaat Bey, a member of the Young Turks triumvirate, ordered: 'All rights of the Armenians to live and work on Turkish soil have been completely cancelled, and with regard to this the Government takes all responsibility on itself , and has commanded that even babies in their cradle are not to be spared.' A German journalist and eye witness of the events which followed wrote: 'This diabolical crime was committed solely because of the Turkish feeling of economic and intellectual inferiority to that non-Turkish element, for the set purpose of obtaining handsome compensation for themselves.' That compensation, apart from laying waste to Armenian civilisation in Turkey, amounted to seizing material wealth valued at US$ 14 billion in gold. Henry Morgenthau, the American ambassador to Turkey at the time, wrote: 'If this plan of murdering a race is to succeed it would be necessary to render all Armenian soldiers powerless and to deprive of their arms the Armenians in every city and town. Before Armenia could be slaughtered, Armenia must be made defenceless.' In 1918 the Minister of War, Enver Pasha, another of the triumvirate, announced 'an order for the whole Armenian race'. All Armenian civilians from the age of five 'to be taken out of the towns and slaughtered', and Armenian soldiers 'to be taken into solitary places away from the public eye and shot'.

Viscount James Bryce said in 1920: 'About the middle of 1915, as soon as the fear that Constantinople might be captured by the British Fleet had vanished, Talaat and Enver issued orders for the slaughter of all the adult males among the Armenian Christians in the Asiatic parts of the Empire, and for the expulsion from their homes and enslavement or transportation into the deserts of northern Arabia and Mesopotamia, of the women and children. These orders were carried out. Nearly a million persons were killed, many of them with horrible tortures, some, including bishops and other ecclesiastics, roasted to death.' The English historian Arnold Toynbee wrote of the deportations and slaughters: 'They fell behind and were bayoneted and thrown into the river, and their bodies floated down to the sea, or lodged in the shallow river on rocks where they remained for ten or twelve days and putrified. All this horror, both the concerted crime and its local embellishments, was inflicted upon the Armenians without a shadow of provocation.'

Of the Turkish and Armenian arguments you can take your pick.

Anyone personally involved in the massacres would have to be extremely old today, and the Turks do not feel guilt for the deeds of their fathers or grandfathers. But the fathers or grandfathers felt no guilt either, and this character trait seems to be reflected in two Turkish proverbs:

The cat which eats her kittens swears they look like mice.

Even if guilt were made of sable, no one would choose to wear it.

Before World War I the population of Van was 80,000 (315,000 in the whole province). When the first census of the new Turkish Republic was taken in 1927, Van's population was 6,931 (75,437 in the province). By 1986 Van's population was 92,000 (570,000 in the province). At present it is close to 400,000, almost entirely Kurdish. Some 70,000 Armenians still live in Turkey today.

WHERE TO STAY

🏠 **Büyük Urartu Otel** (75 rooms) Cumhuriyet Caddesi; ☎ 2120660; www.buyukurartuotel.com. Van's fanciest hotel, complete with central heating, indoor pool, sauna & disco. A modern 5-storey block in the centre of town. $$$$

🏠 **Akdamar Otel** (72 rooms) Kazım Karabekir Caddesi; ☎ 2149923; www.hotelakdamar.com. In the town centre, this was for a long time Van's best hotel before the Büyük Urartu came along. A little worn these days. Central heating, 3 restaurants. $$$

🏠 **Buyuk Asur Oteli** (45 rooms) Cumhuriyet Caddesi; ☎ 2168792; e asur_asur2008@

hotmail.com. The best mid-range option, with spacious rooms & a pleasant downstairs lounge with terrace. $$

🏠 **Tuşpa Hotel** (63 rooms) 11km from Van on the Edremit road; ☎ 3122966; www.tusbaotel.com. A 4-storey building, rather ugly & utilitarian in design, but in an excellent position on the lakeshore, & with a lovely terrace restaurant. The food is nothing special but the location makes up for everything. No credit cards. Taxi from here to the airport TL30; a crazy price but you are a captive market. $$

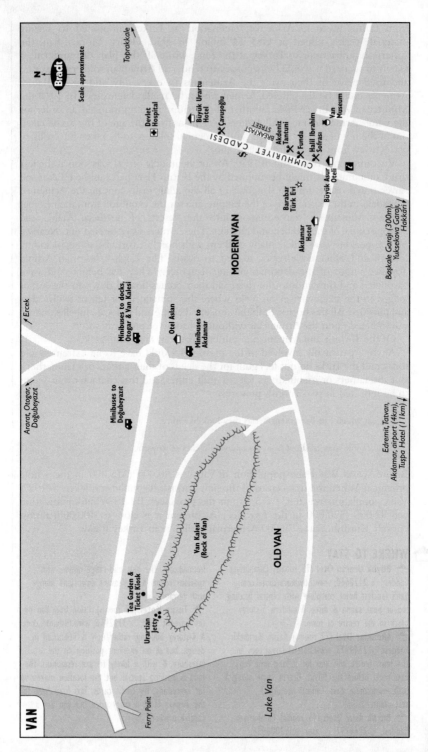

VAN

Lake Van

Ferry Point

OLD VAN

Van Kalesi
(Rock of Van)

Tea Garden &
Ticket Kiosk

Urartian
Jetty

Ararat, Otogar,
Doğubeyazit

Minibuses to
Doğubeyazit

Minibuses to docks,
Otogar & Van Kalesi

Otel Aslan

Minibuses to
Akdamar

Ercek

MODERN VAN

Devlet
Hospital

Büyük Urartu
Hotel

Çavuşoğlu

CUMHURIYET CADDESI

BREAKFAST
STREET

Akdeniz
Tantuni

Funda

Halil Ibrahim
Sofrasi

Van
Museum

Büyük Asur
Oteli

Barabar
Türk Evi

Akdamar
Hotel

Başkale Garaji (300m),
Yuksekova Garaji,
Hakkâri

Edremit, Tatvan,
Akdamar, airport (4km),
Tuşpa Hotel (11km)

Toprakkale

N

Bradt

Scale approximate

☐ **Otel Aslan** (17 rooms) Özel İdare İş Merkezi Karçışı; ✆ 2162469. Tiny rooms, some with shared bathrooms, but very cheap & central. No b/fast, but you can eat this at Van's famous Breakfast St (Kahvaltı Sokak) close by. $

✗ WHERE TO EAT

Van has a number of specialities, notably its breakfast, always eaten in Breakfast St (Kahvaltı Sokak), a string of places in a pedestrianised side street that runs parallel to the main street of Cumhuriyet Caddesi. They are all open from 07.00 until 12.00. Full breakfast will cost about TL8.

Just stroll along the main street, Cumhuriyet Caddesi, to find many good but unlicensed restaurants such as **Halil İbrahim Şofrası** ($$), **Akdeniz Tantuni** ($), and *pastahanes* like **Funda** ($) and **Çavuşoğlu** ($).

ENTERTAINMENT AND NIGHTLIFE

Van's most popular bar, **Barabar Türk Evi** (*Sanat Sokak;* ✆ *2149866*), is on the first floor of a dull-looking building, but plenty of beer is available and it is full of students from the university. At weekends there is live Kurdish music.

SHOPPING

Urartu Carpet Market

On the road out towards the airport, this place has been built by the government in the style of a castle/caravanserai with carpet workshops round a central courtyard. Here you can watch young girls who are being trained up in carpet weaving from the age of 16, to keep the skill alive, and you can also buy from a large selection of carpets, saddlebags and dowry bags. Silk work is the most skilful and the most expensive and can have up to one million knots per square metre. You will be offered some apple tea and it is a pleasant place to while away some time. Sometimes there is even a Van cat wandering about.

OTHER PRACTICALITIES

Everything like the PTT office, banks with ATMs, bus company offices and internet cafés are to be found on the main street of Cumhuriyet Caddesi.

WHAT TO SEE

Modern Van, dating totally post-1918, as a town is rather a disappointment generally. The surprise is that, contrary to expectations, it is not built on the lakeshore but is set back about 3km from the lake on flat ground with no views of the lake at all. The second surprise is its smallness. As the main town on the shores of a lake seven times the size of Lake Geneva, it is natural to expect something, however remotely, approximating to Geneva. Yet it has less than half the population of Urfa, none of the sophistication and hum of Diyarbakır, none of the beautiful architecture of Mardin and none of the setting and atmosphere of Bitlis. Having thus reduced your expectations, you can enjoy Van for what it is – a comfortable base from which to explore the surrounding area and a lively modern commercial centre. It will grow on you. The population today is 70% Kurdish.

Van Kalesi

(*3km north of Van;* ⊕ *daily 09.00–dusk; adult TL2*) A visit to Van Kalesi is best done towards the end of the day so that you can get the benefit of the sunset over the lake and mountains. It takes three to four hours to make a thorough exploration.

Getting there There are two ways of visiting Van Kalesi and Eski Van (Old Van). Your first option is to follow the sign for the 3km straight to Van Kalesi along the road that leads along the right (northern) and less precipitous side of the citadel to reach an attractive **tea-garden/restaurant**. The ticket kiosk is also here. Behind it, a little obscured by a copse of willow trees, you will notice some gigantic stone blocks,

In the period 1900–1260BC, contemporary with the Hittites, a warlike and aggressive people, the **Hurrians**, established a kingdom stretching as far south as Nusaybin with Van as its capital. The Hurrians struggled with their Hittite neighbours to the west, and in 1400BC they suffered a humiliating defeat at the hands of the famous Hittite king Shuppiliuma. Dispersed in small tribes after their defeat, they gradually grew strong again, and, reunited, called their empire Urartu, a name taken from the mountain of Ararat. They retained Van as their capital, calling it Tushpa (from the storm god Teshub), and in the 300 years that their empire flourished, they extended east to Lake Urmia in Iran, west to Malatya, north to Kars and Erzurum and south to Diyarbakır, Mardin and Hakkâri, and even to Aleppo in northern Syria and to Mosul in Iraq. The map in the museum shows all 32 sites.

The first scientific excavation of an Urartian fortress city was undertaken from 1936 by Russian archaeologists at a site called Karmir Blur, overlooking the river Zanga near Yerevan, now the capital of Armenia. No reports of the results were available in English until 1953, but the findings formed the basis of knowledge of Urartian civilisation, subsequently added to by work which Turkish archaeologists have undertaken at Altıntepe near Erzincan, at Patnos and at Çavuştepe.

In the Assyrian reliefs found at Van, the Urartians are shown as similar in appearance to the Hurrians and the Hittites, with a short stocky build, belted waists with daggers and wearing earrings and bracelets. Like the Hittites, their symbol was a lion. Their **cuneiform script**, taken from the Assyrians, found carved in their fortresses and temples, has been deciphered and tells us much about their kings and their achievements. Grammatically the Urartian language is close to the Hurrian and the Hittite. Like the Assyrian kings, the Urartian monarchs took on grandiose titles and prided themselves on their battle tactics, usually demolishing a fort when they captured it and sending all the booty back to the palace of Van.

all that remains of the **Urartian jetty** which the lake once came up to. One of the blocks carries an inscription of Sarduri I. This road links up to that which runs on to the current landing stage for the train ferries and other boats, now some 500m away. From the tea-house you can climb up a steepish but short path to explore the hilltop fortress, then make a separate approach round the lakeside of the outcrop to where the ruins of Old Van lie. The second option is to head straight to Old Van, then walk across the flattened city, then climb up the sheer side of the citadel to explore it, descending at the tea-garden on the other side. The first way involves less energy and is shorter and quicker, but the second is more satisfying because you discover the magnificence of the setting gradually and see all the sections of the long thin citadel which you might otherwise miss.

What to see Looking at the sheer face of the citadel it does not look as if it can easily be climbed. Legend says that there are 1,000 steps cut into the rock, and though as you approach, short runs of steps can be seen, none of them link up so it is not, alas, possible just to climb an enormous flight of steps to the top. If however you head for the lowest end of the outcrop, to your right, you will notice one short flight of steps quite close to the ground. It is a very easy five-minute scramble from here up to the lowest walls. At the walls you follow the path to the right, where you can clamber through a breach, and a path then leads over the crest of the citadel.

Had you approached the citadel as described in the first option (straight from Van rather than via Old Van), you could climb up from the tea-garden to a small cemetery where there is an oratory and a tomb. Above this shrine (but below if you are already atop the citadel) is a platform of limestone rock, site of an Urartian temple, with a curved-back bench cut out of the rock wall. Two huge arched niches are carved here which locals say once held two gold statues of ancient goddesses. The Americans, they say, took them away after their excavations in 1935–37. The western or lakeside niche has a black basalt statue base with a cuneiform inscription recording the work of the great warrior and builder King Menua.

If heights do not bother you, an alternative route along the citadel follows the narrow path along the top of the battlements. At one point a path forks down left and leads round to an impressive flight of wide rock-cut steps down to a wide terrace on the cliff edge which appears manmade.

From the platform a further five steps lead down to a huge tomb entrance hollowed out of the sheer rock face, a cave-like opening readily visible from Old Van below. Inside is a large square cut chamber with smaller rooms leading off from each of the three side walls. It must have taken years to hollow out this vast area, for the ceilings are very high. This is the tomb of Sardur II (c765–733BC), a warrior Urartian king, and the chambers were probably used for various rituals and sacrifices. In the 19th century they were also used as quarters for troops or dungeons for prisoners.

A multi-age castle sits within the citadel walls and from here the path to it is quite tricky to find. If you continue along the battlement walkway, you come soon to a huge cleft in the rock, which divides the lower citadel from the upper citadel. Only experienced rock climbers would be advised to attempt bridging this gap. Retracing your steps a short way, you discover a path forking down towards the oratory below, and then running along the side of the citadel for 200m or so until it leads up to a slope of earth or mud, depending on the season, which you have to clamber up to get to the castle on the higher level of the citadel. A telegraph pole marks this point and is a useful landmark to remember for your return route.

You can now climb up to the highest point of the castle, a large open grassy area on which stands the inevitable representation of the great Atatürk. Lower down, near the cleft between the two halves of the citadel, another path leads down to the Old Van side of the outcrop and round to another flattened terrace, this time with two large rock-cut tombs in the cliff face. Each one has the same three chambers leading off the main one as before. These are the tombs of King Ispuini (815–807BC) and Menua (804–790BC).

By the other route, you follow the path along the crest of the citadel passing several crumbling Ottoman buildings, including barracks, a *medrese* and a mosque which still has its minaret with steps inside, until you come to the castle. In Ottoman times Van was an important military base, and the 17th-century Turkish traveller Evliya Celebi said that up to 3,000 Janissaries and artillery men lived in it. The castle construction clearly shows the large blocks of the original Urartian fortress at the bottom level of stonework, then the smaller blocks of the Armenian castle, then topped with the mortar and clays of later Turkish periods. An inscription in one corner of the cyclopean walls boasts: 'I, Sardur, the illustrious king, the mighty king, the king of the universe, the king of all lands, a king without equal, I erected these walls.'

Following the wide ramp-like path slightly downhill and through an arch, you now reach the open flattened-out part of the mountain top with white limestone sides and floor. (It is this flattened area you reach first if you have climbed up from the tea-house on the modern Van side.) Over on the far side of this, overlooking Old Van, iron railings and a gate now block off access to the rock-cut steps which lead down the cliff face to the tomb of King Argistis (790–765BC), son of Menua.

The vertical rock face around this tomb is covered in Urartian cuneiform inscriptions, heavily defaced, dating from 765BC. The local tourist office says it was tourists who came and hacked off pieces of the inscription to take away as souvenirs, so it had to be sealed off for protection. If you do not mind heights, you can in fact climb down a second outer staircase just below the railings, which, though much more damaged, is still manageable. If you want to go into the tomb, a torch is necessary as there is a large hole inside which you cannot see by natural light. One tourist recently fell into this hole and hit his head badly, so care is called for. In front of the cave a large footprint in the rock is claimed by some locals as the devil's, while others say it is that of Ali, the Prophet Muhammad's son-in-law.

Wandering around Van Kalesi up and down the little paths and gullies is a very enjoyable experience, rather like exploring an adventure playground, and is especially lovely at sunset. As you make your way back towards the lower citadel for the climb down to Lake Van, the view over towards the mountains growing pink across the lake is an unforgettable sight.

Eski Van (⊕ *daily; no fee, unfenced*) Also called the Rock of Van, the citadel is a narrow outcrop nearly 2km long, rising 100m, with sheer sides to the south. The flatness of the surrounding land makes it look particularly striking, a strange aberration. One Turkish traveller of the last century described it as a kneeling camel in profile. At its foot, where now little remains beyond rubble-like mounds, nestled one of the largest populations of Anatolia, surrounded by its 16th-century Ottoman walls, and with its bustling streets so attractive the saying ran: 'Van in this world, Paradise in the next.' Today it must be one of the most vivid examples anywhere in the world of a town which has been quite literally razed to the ground, and nothing you will have read can prepare you for the total devastation here.

What to see Beyond the southern walls to the left of the earth mound, two conical *türbes* with columned supports for the domes stand like a memorial to the dead city. Within the walls, mud mounds are all that remain where the walls of houses once stood, and grass grows inside. Sometimes cattle can even be seen grazing here, or local families come to picnic on the grass on holidays and weekends. There is a nearby stream which becomes marshy towards the lake, and Kurdish women often wash their *kilims* and carpets here. Apart from the two mosques near the road, the only other buildings left standing are a ruined *hammam* near the foot of the citadel, and another two older mosques with minarets. The first of the mosques near the road is 16th century, the Kaya Celebi Camii, now just a shell, totally ruined and covered in grafitti inside, but still with a surprisingly lovely lace-like lattice work *mihrab* in white stone. The second Ottoman mosque, closer to the lake, has now been restored. It is called the Hüsrev Paşa Camii (1567) and has the tomb of Hüsrev Paşa attached to its eastern side. The two colours of stone used in its construction give it the distinctive striped look seen so often in Diyarbakır's mosques and in Syria. The mosque directly under the cliff to the left (lakeside) was the 13th-century Ulu Cami and the steps of its broken minaret can still be climbed. On its walls was once rich turquoise tile decoration of geometric forms and flowers, looking Persian in influence, of which slight traces remain. Set halfway up the cliff face above this minaret is a huge flattened piece of rock like a colossal plaque with a cuneiform inscription in Babylonian, Persian and Median, of the 5th century BC. The man who carved this must have hung over the rock edge on ropes for many weeks.

Van Museum (*Kişla Caddesi*; ⊕ *08.00–12.00 & 13.00–17.00 Tue–Sun; adult TL3*) This small unassuming modern building tucked up a side street is well worth a visit for its Urartian Archaeology Hall. Pretty much everything in it is worthy of scrutiny. The most remarkable exhibits are of the Urartian gold jewellery with beads, fibulas (decorative safety pins) and bracelets worn by the upper classes, and

MASSACRE OF THE ARMENIANS

Throughout the vicissitudes of Van's history the Armenians remained in the majority until the early 20th century. An English visitor to the town in the 1890s found two-thirds of the population to be Armenian. The town beneath the citadel was at that time totally walled with four gates built by the Ottomans, narrow streets, wooden balconied houses and crowded bazaars, and was inhabited by Muslims and Christians. There were government offices and even several foreign consulates. On the site of today's modern Van was the so-called 'garden suburb' where many of the wealthier Armenian Christians lived separately, going into the walled medieval city to conduct their business. They also had six churches in the Old Town, all made of wood, so they burnt easily. A bad earthquake in the 1950s destroyed what was left of the fine Armenian houses in the garden suburb.

The Van version of events told today is that the town was burnt down by the Armenians when the Turks were away fighting the Russians in 1914, and it was in revenge for this that the Turks later drove the Armenians from Van. The Russians had provoked the Armenians in Van to side with them and the Allies against the Turks in the war. Then in 1915 the Russians occupied Van for nearly three years, during which time the Armenians tried to oust the Turks, killing many who refused to leave. When the Russians withdrew, unable to sustain the war effort because of the revolution at home, the Turks recaptured the city and punished the Armenians for their treachery by burning it and killing many of their inhabitants. The Turks say that the Armenians realised their hopes of setting up their own independent state were ruined, so they left Van and the surrounding towns of their own accord. They do, however, admit that the town was destroyed so utterly that it was uninhabitable, so they had to rebuild a new city from scratch. They deny it was a genocide and say that the nmumber of people who died was less than a million,

Up to the late 19th century the official Turkish attitude to the Armenians was one of careless tolerance. Under the Ottomans the Armenians, led by the Patriarch of the Armenian Church, had their own General Assembly and their own councils to control education, law and property.

Much of the blame for why this tolerant relationship went wrong is laid at the door of Russia, who, disguised as the protector of the Christian communities in Turkey, set Armenians and Turks against one another with a view to ultimately controlling the Bosphorus. The Crimean War (1856) too was a struggle for influence in Turkey and for the control of the military and trade routes. The victory of the British and the French inclined some Armenians to turn to the West for support in a bid for independence. The Governor of Sivas told Frederick Burnaby, travelling here in 1876: '25 years ago the Turks and the Christians got on very well together, but ever since the Crimean War the Russian government has been actively engaged in tampering with the Armenian subjects of the Porte and has been doing its best to sow the seeds of dissension amongst the younger Armenians, by promising to make them counts and dukes in the event of their rising in arms against the Porte.'

The Pasha of Erzincan, whom Burnaby spoke to in 1877, ominously predicted: 'If there be a war in Asia Minor, the Russians will do their best to excite our Kurds to massacre the Armenians in the neighbourhood of Van, and will then throw all the blame upon our shoulders.'

URARTIAN BUILDERS AND FARMERS

The skill of the Urartians as builders was noteworthy. They favoured long thin spurs as sites for their fortress cities, and scattered all over their empire are over 30 such fortresses, large and small. The largest are Van Kalesi, Toprakkale and Çavuştepe, built with colossal blocks of carefully dressed stone, each block often weighing up to 27,000kg. They also built elaborate water systems of canals and dams, the most impressive being the Menua Canal (today called Semiran Canal) which brought water from 65km away to the foot of Van Kalesi, a remarkable feat of engineering.

As a result of their constant battles with the Assyrians and the Cimmerians (barbarous Europeans who had come in by a land route north of the Black Sea), Urartu suffered a loss of manpower, and so the necessary population to remedy the situation was secured from neighbouring lands, with 'men from the Halitu region and women from Manna' brought in to be resettled in Urartian domains.

Using their advanced irrigation channels they became expert at growing crops and some historians claim to have evidence that the cultivation of wheat first began here, then spreading to other parts of the world. They also developed animal husbandry, breeding horses around Lake Urmia in Iran which became famous throughout Asia Minor.

decorated with lions, bulls, eagles, goats, horses, mythological creatures, plants like opium poppies, pomegranates and even human faces. There are pin heads with snakes, ducks, chickens or cockerels, a style that is unique to the Urartians and which have been found nowhere else in the ancient Near East. They were worn by men and boys as well as women. The chief Urartian god was Haldi, with the lion as his sacred animal, representing power. The beads themselves came from Caucasia, Iran, Afghanistan and India, and agate and opal were among the exotic raw materials.

The other interesting exhibit is the rock carvings found on the Trishin Plateau 120km south of Van at an altitude of 2,200m. There are literally thousands of carvings dating from 9000BC to 8000BC (Mesolithic) up to 3200–2000BC (early Bronze Age), showing hunting scenes of bison and reindeer which are now

METALWORKING GENIUS

The field in which the Urartians were most accomplished was their metalwork, and they were more advanced than the Assyrians or any other people of their time. Urartian metalwork in gold, silver and bronze was highly prized and exported to Greece and Italy. Evidence is mounting for the fact that the ancient Greeks and Etruscans copied heavily from Urartian objects in their own work. Many objects found at Crete, Delphi and Olympia, and the Etruscan tomb finds, show close resemblance to Urartian originals. An Assyrian relief in the Yüksekova district shows an Urartian temple inside and out full of valuable metalwork objects. The style of this building, with its gabled roof and pillared façade, has close affinities with the architectural orders we now think of as Greek Doric and Ionian. Like the Hittites, the Urartians believed in a variety of gods, the chief ones being the storm (or weather) god and the sun god. In their inscriptions the kings recorded that all their deeds in peace and war were done in the name of the gods, and they performed sacrifices of animals to their deities at propitious times of year. As potters they were competent but not exceptional, making the standard glazed red earthenware vessels.

extinct, very similar to the animals used today in *kilims* and saddlebag designs and on knitted socks, pottery and even gravestones.

Upstairs is the Ethnography Hall with coins and jewellery up to Roman and Mamluk times, and the Genocide Section drawing attention to the thousands of Muslims murdered at the hands of the Armenians in the area (see page 279). On the stairs themselves is a very interesting detailed map of the area round Van, showing all the monasteries and churches (16 in total) and all the Urartian sites (32 in total).

Toprakkale The large outcrop of mountain rising above the city of modern Van with a radio mast on top and white slogans carved into it alongside the star and crescent is Toprakkale (Earth Castle), site of another 8th-century BC Urartian palace citadel, the second largest after Van. Some talk of an underground palace here, a huge room 25m by 50m cut into the rock reached by a flight of rock-cut steps; it is in fact no more than a cistern. The site lies within a military area and is only visitable by obtaining a permit from the local *wali* (governor). The remains on the hilltop are no longer considered worth visiting any more anyway, and certainly a perhaps premature state of ruination often seems to accompany historic sites which find themselves within military zones.

Other monasteries around Van The Armenian **Yedi Kilise Monastery (Seven Churches Monastery)**, known to Armenians as Warak Vank, was out of bounds to visitors in the 1980s, but now the modern village, also called Yedi Kilise, where it stands behind the new village mosque, can be reached by taxi from Van (cTL30). It lies some 9km southeast of Van city, on the slopes of the Warak Mountain under Susan Daği (2,750m). The once-famous monastery, founded in the 8th century, housed 300 monks in its heyday. King Gagik's daughter and her husband are buried here. The local people claim that earthquakes over the centuries have taken their toll on it, which is why the remains are so fragmentary. In the 19th century rich Armenians used to come here on summer outings, but now Kurdish peasants live in the ruins. The largest of the seven churches that remain, dedicated to Mary, was whitewashed and in use as a grain store in the 1980s but has now been restored. Its main entrance portal has intricately carved stonework and the interior has remnants of 17th-century frescoes and crosses carved into the walls. It is often kept locked but the guardian will generally appear with the key and unlock it for a fee. The women of the village are also keen to sell you their colourful knitted socks and gloves.

Other monasteries exist, extremely remote, in the region but are not visitable without a guide and long journeys. For the totally undauntable there is the excursion to the convents of **Aparank**, southwest of Van, a three-day trip involving 216km in a 4x4, then 20 hours on horseback. The **monastery church of St John** is another tricky one to visit, set on its own long narrow island, Carpanak, some 25km northwest of Van and about 1.5km from the long thin promontory on the lakeshore. Unless you have your own inflatable or canoe, you have to persuade a boatman from the Van Iskelesi (docks) to take you on the 90-minute journey, then wait for you, something for which he will expect at least TL150. The island is uninhabited except for a large gull colony, and you could even consider camping here if you are well prepared. The church itself is well preserved, originally dating from the 12th century originally, but heavily restored in the 1700s, and still complete with its dome and pyramid roof. There is talk of it being converted into a museum.

On the lakeside north of Çarpanak Island a recently excavated hilltop Urartian citadel, known as Ayanis, stands overlooking the lake, still with a fine central temple compound, and well-preserved cuneiform inscription on its doorway. The only way to reach it is by car, turning left to the village of Alaköy, 20km north of Van on the main road. From Alaköy the road is not tarmac for the last 8km or so, passing through a village called Mollakasim until you see the obvious hilltop site overlooking the lake. You have to do the final section on foot.

Another remote spot to visit to escape the crowds is Çatak, an attractive mountain town 86km south from Van, reached by forking off south a few kilometres before Gevaş. Excellent trout can be caught in its streams, and there is hunting for partridges, ducks, hares, mountain goats and foxes in its forests. About 60km along this road is a lovely waterfall called Ganiyisippi, Persian for 'White Spring', gushing over a cliff. The trout is never available in restaurants in Van and is not sold commercially. Bears, wild boars, wolves, beavers and stone martens can be hunted at the right season in the Zilvan Valley near Erciş. In Çatak itself are the remains of the Armenian church of St John the Baptist, whose roofless walls now provide an enclosed garden which is used by the villagers.

TOWARDS HAKKÂRI

Leaving Van on the road south, signposted to Hakkâri 204km away, you will be heading into Turkey's remotest region, the extreme southeast, bordering on Iraq. The dauntless Freya Stark recalls this wild mountainous corner of Turkey in the 1950s as 'one of those dwindling regions where a four-footed animal is still the only help to locomotion'. Today there is a good tarmac road all the way and the bus or *dolmuş* journey takes between three and four hours. However as so often in eastern Turkey, there are interesting things on the way, which are difficult to see without either taking a tour or having your own transport, and as always, it comes down to time. On a tour or driving your own car you can visit the Urartian palace at Çavuştepe in the morning, have a picnic lunch at the fairy-tale castle of Hoşap, then continue to Hakkâri and back again to Van before dark if you wish. Using public transport, you will have to allow at least two days for the same thing. Buses run regularly from Cumhuriyet Caddesi in Van to Başkale, Hakkâri or Yüksekova taking about four hours and costing TL17, but you will have to ask to be dropped off at the Çavuştepe turn-off and walk the 2km up to the site and back, then flag down the next passing bus on to Hoşap and do the same again.

ÇAVUŞTEPE   22km south of Van

(⊕ *daily; 08.00–dusk; adult TL3*) As soon as you are clear of the outskirts of Van the road begins to climb and soon reaches a low pass at 2,225m before dropping quickly down to a major fork in the road, right to Elâzığ and Gurpinar, left to Hakkâri. The hills are more barren along this initial stretch than on the southern shore of Lake Van. The road arrives at Çavuştepe after some 10km of flat road from the junction, and only 22km from Van. Passing through the village you will notice to your right the characteristic long thin hill, the shape favoured by the Urartians for their palaces, and on this is the royal citadel of Çavuştepe, built between 764BC and 735BC by King Sardur II, son of Argishti, the best preserved of any of the 32 Urartian citadels. The buildings on the summit were for the king and his family only, while the Urartian laypeople lived down on the flat, roughly where the present village now lies. The fact that ordinary people never appear at all in Urartian art – the players are all kings, priests and gods – has led some scholars to speculate that the Urartians might have been a slave society.

The road to the site is signposted and leads up to the lowest collar on the citadel crest. From here a courteous guardian is usually waiting for you and will show you photos of the Turkish excavations which took place here in the 1970s, before accompanying you round the palace. On a hot day the bare hilltop can be punishing with no shade at all, so make sure you have your own supply of water, as there are not always drinks available on site, although he does sell a few souvenirs. The tour begins by following a path along the so-called lower temple area, then up steps and along a broad corridor, almost like a sacred way, which runs along the crest and links the temple area to the palace. A stone basin near the path was used for holy water. The temple has a superb series of highly polished black basalt stone blocks, so smooth that it feels like the highest-quality marble to the touch, beautifully carved in Urartian cuneiform. Nearby is a sacrificial altar where the Urartians honoured or appeased their gods. An extraordinarily advanced water system with a series of large cisterns hollowed out of the rock to collect the rain or snow is evident. Below the citadel there are still traces of a huge water channel system that brought water from the mountains.

The palace, at the far end of the hill crest, would originally have been a three-storeyed building; archaeologists have drawn impressive reconstructions of what it would have looked like. It has a recognisable *harem* area where the women and children would have lived, and in the corner, just on the edge of the hill, is a little water closet with a drainage tunnel leading hygienically off down the hill.

Returning now to the car park and climbing up to the upper section of the citadel, you come to a flattened area of limestone with an upper temple. The standard of preservation and the masonry is not, however, of the same quality as that of the lower temple.

HOŞAP *58km southeast of Van*

(⊕ *daily 08.30–12.00 & 13.30–17.00; adult TL3*) At 35km beyond Çavuştepe, having skirted a lake and climbed a small pass, suddenly, on crossing the brow of a hill, the unmistakeable castle of Hoşap appears before you, standing on a hill above a small village. As you descend gradually into the valley, the magnificent castle seems unreal, like a hallucination from a fairy tale, with its crenellated battlements and turrets, the whole perched precariously on its hill. Built by Sarı Süleyman, a local Kurdish despot of the Mahmudi tribe, in 1643 when Ottoman power was slipping, it is the best example of a Kurdish castle to be seen in Turkey today. Its appearance is such that you might be inclined to believe the local tradition that the Kurdish *bey* had the hands of the architect cut off after it was finished, to ensure no similar castle could be built elsewhere.

In the village just below the castle a fine bridge of light and dark stone, bearing an inscription dating it to 1671, crosses the little stream which gives the village its name of Güzelsu, 'Beautiful Water' (Hoşap means the same in Kurdish). A modern road bridge 100m further on crosses the stream and winds up a track that leads round the back of the hill to the castle's main entrance. The entrance gate is very impressive indeed, set in a powerful and colossal round tower. Carved above it are inscriptions in Farsi script and a medallion in the shape of a teardrop with a stylised lion on either side. The initial entrance way appears to lead into the hillside itself with a fine vaulted ceiling carved from the rock. A dark tunnel-like passage leads up into the interior of the castle, which suddenly becomes very open and grassy. Parts of it are like a meadow, and you almost expect to see cows and sheep grazing inside. There is in fact considerably less left inside than you would expect from the strength of the outside walls.

You come first to a large circular area of wall which you look down into from above. This is said to have been the conference hall, a sort of Knights of the Round Table room, and beam holes in the wall show that it originally had two storeys. The path then leads on up to an edge of the castle with a heavily ruined

bath, mosque and *medrese*, so heavily ruined in fact that you simply have to take
the guardian's word for it. Tiny traces of blue decoration are left round the inside
of some of the windows. The castle is known to have had 360 rooms, two
mosques, three baths, dungeons, fountains, storerooms and a well.

Looking over to the east, away from the road, you can follow the line of mud
defence walls running over the nearby hills, once encircling the town below. Freya
Stark graphically describes their crumbling aspect: 'The flesh of their battlements
[had been] sucked by weather to look like the skeletons of caterpillars creeping
about the lower hillocks.' A higher path climbs higher still up to the keep which
is the best-preserved part of the fortress.

HAKKÂRİ *Telephone code: 438; altitude: 1,720m*

Lured on by mountains you can now continue south following the river valley
until the road begins a steep climb over a pass of 2,790m where snow lies until late
May. The landscapes up to this point, though mountainous, are not particularly
striking, mainly owing to the absence of any greenery, even in springtime. In the
distance the mountain massif of the Cilo Daği and Sat Daği, the main peaks of the
Hakkâri region, rise before you, beckoning you ever deeper into the remote
valleys. Freya Stark commented that in her opinion international congresses should
be held in quiet places like this, instead of in busy capital cities, 'places where the
grassy skyline is a lifting of earth untroubled with houses, and cattle grazing along
the coolness of buried waters bring the smoothness of their own lives into the
mind of the gazer – if an international congress ever has the time to gaze'.

From here on there are no particular monuments to visit, and the journey to
Hakkâri is really for the magnificent scenery which begins at the Zab Valley. In
the past the main reason for foreigners to come here was for the mountaineering
in the peaks east of Hakkâri and south of Yuksekova, and pack animals and guides
could always be found at both these towns. But with the problem of Kurdish
insurgents, climbing in the Hakkâri region has been totally forbidden since
1985. Until the political situation is totally settled you would be well advised to
stick to the main routes in this area and not head up small tracks into the villages.
The main road however remains perfectly safe. Exactly 100km from Van and
12km from Başkale, the highest town in Turkey, there is an army checkpoint, the
only one until near Hakkâri. It stops all traffic, checks papers and passports and
searches all vehicles. The soldiers are very good-natured on the whole and
inspect your luggage quite carefully and gently, doing their best to restrain their
curiosity. They have obviously been instructed not to hassle people who are
clearly tourists. It continues to function after dark, and there is no question of
the road being closed at night.

An excursion can be made from near the checkpoint left, up a narrow stabilised
road 12km to the town of **Albayrak**. This town consists largely of the buildings
of the former Armenian monastery of Surp Bartolomeos, St Bartholomew. The
monks did not live in one large central building but in separate houses like a
village. A military station is housed here today and it helps if you are a competent
Turkish-speaker so you can explain you have come to look at the monastery
buildings. The church looks like a Greek temple, but its roof collapsed in a recent
earthquake. It has features reminiscent of the Persian Sassanid style with many fine
relief carvings. This road continues along the valley of the Greater Zab and after
20km in superb landscapes you reach the village of **Soradır** (2,400m), only 15km
from the Iranian border. The large numbers of trucks plying this road are
smuggling cheap petrol in from Iran, an activity which the authorities turn a blind
eye to as long as a maximum of 500 litres is smuggled per trip. Soradır has a yellow

Armenian church dating to CAD600 standing alone on a hillock, and is seen as the forerunner in style to Akdamar, resembling the style of church still found in the Republic of Armenia. It is used today as a grain store.

From the main road checkpoint the road now climbs gradually up to **Başkale**, Turkey's highest town at 2,500m, huddled up against the slope of a mountain. It looks like a godforsaken place on a bleak treeless plateau and must be truly grim in winter. Today's inhabitants are totally Kurdish, and the houses are either old mud hovels or new ugly concrete blocks – there is nothing in between. The road continues along the plateau, then begins a slow descent into the Zab Valley, leading eventually to Hakkâri town. The Zab River flows through Hakkâri to join the Tigris below Mosul in Iraq. From this point on the scenery becomes more grand as the road winds round the valley with very lush fields and brilliant green grass, so bright it is almost dazzling higher up the mountain slopes. There are no villages here at all, and all you pass are flocks of sheep and goats and small herds of cows.

The road now reaches a fork, left to Yüksekova across the river. The crossing into Iran here is quicker than via Doğubeyazıt to the north. The town used to be the base for mountaineers to make their departures to the Çilo and Sat peaks, though its own appearance, set on a high open plateau, is not remotely mountainous.

The road to Hakkâri stays on the right-hand side of the river, and the ever-beckoning snow-covered mountains in the distance get closer and closer as you wind on through the valley. Spanning the river along the way are several precarious-looking bridges used by the nomads and their livestock. There is also a chairlift-style bridge, worked on a winch. The Greater Zab countrymen, and women too for that matter, must suspend themselves by a pulley, and then heave their way across the turbulent river. Landslides and flash floods after summer thunderstorms cut the roads off here quite frequently.

A deserted village on the left bank could, with its mud-brick houses and grassy roofs, be mistaken for any field, and can easily be missed altogether. This might be the abandoned Nestorian village which early accounts have seen in this valley. Isolated and rugged, the history of the region is one of villages not empires. The armies of conquerors bypassed it, preferring to stay on the flatter ground, and

NOMAD CONTENTMENT

On the lush grassy riverbanks the occasional black nomad tent can be seen in idyllic settings. The colourfully dressed children playing on the riverbanks, their clothes glinting in the sun, look as if they could not have a more perfect place to grow up. As Freya Stark writes: 'The life of insecurity is the nomad's achievement. He does not try, like our building world, to believe in a stability which is non-existent; and in his constant movement with the seasons, in the lightness of his hold, puts something right, about which we are constantly wrong. His is in fact the reality, to which the most solid of our structures are illusion; and the ramshackle tents in their crooked gaiety, with cooking pots propped up before them and animals about, show what a current flows round all the stone erections of the ages. The finest ruin need only be lamented with moderation, since its living essence long ago entered the common stream. No thought of this kind is likely to come into the head of the Turkish Yürük (though it could be familiar to the imagination of the Arab); they are happy to shelter their goats in the warmth or the shade that they find, whether the ruins be of Nineveh or Rome. Their women were cheerful and fierce, unlike the peasant, and dressed in brighter colours – equals of their men or of anyone, as one may be if one lives under the hardness of necessity and makes insecurity one's refuge.'

though the Urartians and Akkadians came here, they moved north when the time was ripe, to found their empires elsewhere.

In the final 10km before Hakkâri the road makes a spectacularly steep climb out of the Zab Valley to higher mountain slopes of poplar trees and green grass. Here finally stands the town of Hakkâri, directly facing the 4,135m massif of Cilo Daği. From a distance it has almost the look of an Alpine ski resort in summer; it is certainly unlike any other town you will have visited in Turkey. Although you feel it must be higher, at 1,700m it is in fact marginally lower than Van. With a population of 20,000, almost entirely Kurdish, it is a small place but very spread

THE PERSECUTED NESTORIANS

Until World War I there were many Nestorian Christians living in the villages here. The doctrine of Nestorius, Bishop of Constantinople from 428–31, was rejected as a heresy in 431 at the Council of Ephesus, but welcomed in Syria and Persia. Nestorius's works were burnt by papal order, and he was carried off and mutilated by Nubians, dying finally in the Egyptian Desert in 451. Their centre grew up first in Edessa (Urfa), but when in 489 the Edessa school was closed, the students and teachers moved to Nisibis (Nusaybin) and then on to Persia, where their school flourished under the protection of the Sassanids. The Mongols and Tamerlane later destroyed their centres in Persia and in Baghdad, and in the 15th century many Nestorians fled north to these mountain valleys where they lived alongside the Kurds. They were good and industrious farmers, carefully building terraced fields and irrigation systems which are still in use today. Their houses and churches were simply and neatly built of stone, and they were wholly opposed to the use of images in their churches. Their patriarchal church, Mar Shalita, lies on a high platform some 20km northeast of Hakkâri, reachable today only on foot and with a guide. It is used now by shepherds as a dung cake store. A Nestorian church was described in early accounts as being in this stretch of the Zab Valley, but it must now be so heavily disguised as a cow shed that it is invisible to all but the well-trained eye. Scattered in the mountains are said to be around 20 more Nestorian churches: the simplicity of their architecture is disappointing but the landscape compensates.

Centuries of isolation in Hakkâri surrounded by Muslims made the Nestorians a distinct people, but originally they were Syrians from northern Mesopotamia, and they still spoke a form of Syriac. They believed in the predominantly human nature of Christ, and that Mary was Mother of Christ, not Mother of God. The Syrian Orthodox Church holds the opposite doctrine, that Christ's human nature was absorbed in the divine, while the Greek Orthodox and Roman churches hold the more subtle view of two natures, unmixed, unchangeable, indistinguishable and inseparable.

The relationship of the Nestorians with the Kurds deteriorated in the 19th century, and in 1852 the British embassy in Constantinople heard reports of massacres of Nestorians by Kurds and the selling of women and children as slaves into the Arab parts of the Ottoman Empire. The ambassador of the time, Sir Stratford Canning, actually rescued some of the slaves, buying them back with money raised by public subscription. In 1915 the Nestorian patriarch lent his support to the Allies against the Turks, but the Russians failed them, and they were forced to leave their small farms and escape east to Iran and Iraq, where a few still live today. The Kurds moved into their abandoned houses, still called *nesturi*, and all that remains in Turkey to remember them by is the coloured cross knitted on the toe of the woollen socks by the local Kurdish women.

out. The road winds up and through it for at least 3km, passing first the petrol station, then other newish buildings until it reaches the centre of town, recognisable by the bust of Atatürk. The modest hotels are grouped here.

GETTING THERE AND AWAY Buses to Hakkâri from Van take four hours (TL15) and run regularly. Buses also run often to Yüksekova (TL7) from where you can continue to the Iranian border crossing at Esendere-Sero. You can also take the daily number 6 bus that runs to Sirnak (six hours, TL20) through impressive mountain scenery.

WHERE TO STAY AND EAT

🏠 **Hotel Senler** (27 rooms) Bulvar Caddesi; ✆ 2115512. Centrally located & good value, with good-sized rooms & clean bathrooms. $$

🏠 **Hacibaba Kebap Salonu** Cumhuriyet Caddesi; ✆ 2113003. Just off the main square this is a good safe bet, with the usual range of kebabs, salad & bread. $$

OTHER PRACTICALITIES In winter the main road through from Van to the Iranian border is kept open by snowploughs and is only shut for a day or so if there have been large avalanches. The remoter side valleys however are cut off for nearly half the year by heavy snow, although by way of compensation it is not as cold as it is on the bitter and windswept hills further north. May is really too early to visit Hakkâri as the temperature is too cold to sit outside. June, July and August are the best times to visit. The Kurdish tribes who live here are semi-nomadic, living in the villages in the winter, and moving up to the high pastures for the summer, often no more than half a day's walk away. Always keep your passport on you in case you should need to show it at a checkpoint.

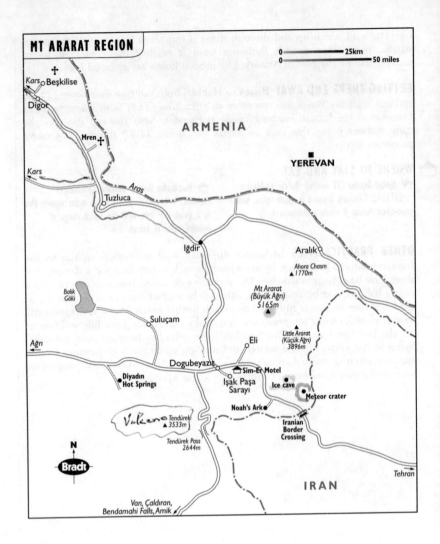

MT ARARAT REGION

0 ——— 25km
0 ——— 50 miles

Kars ⊕ Beşkilise

Digor

Mren ✝

Kars

ARMENIA

YEREVAN

Aras

Tuzluca

Iğdir

Aralık

Balık Gölü

Ahora Chasm
▲ 1770m

Mt Ararat
(Büyük Ağrı)
5165m
▲

Suluçam

Eli

Little Ararat
(Küçük Ağrı)
3896m
▲

Dogubeyazıt

Sim-Er Motel

Ishak Paşa Sarayı

Ice cave

Meteor crater

Diyadın Hot Springs

Noah's Ark ●

Iranian Border Crossing

Volcano ▲ Tendürek 3533m

Ağrı

Tendürek Pass 2644m

N

Bradt

Tehran

IRAN

Van, Çaldıran, Bendamahi Falls, Amik

10

Mount Ararat Region

Big head, big headache

This chapter begins by covering the journey from Van to Doğubeyazıt (the base town for Mount Ararat), followed by the sights to see in the area of Doğubeyazıt and ends with an account of the ascent of Ararat itself. With the exception of the famous and much-photographed palace of Işhak Paşa Sarayı just outside Doğubeyazıt, the sights in this part of Turkey are all natural rather than manmade, and range from things like ice caves to waterfalls, and the extraordinary erosion feature claimed to be Noah's Ark.

Towering above at all times and dominating all views is the massive presence of Mount Ararat itself, a mountain with an almost tangible aura. If you are not planning an ascent of Ararat, two nights spent at Doğubeyazıt will be sufficient, but if you are, add on at least a further five nights (for full details, see pages 304–11).

FROM VAN TO MOUNT ARARAT (DOĞUBEYAZIT)

GETTING THERE AND AWAY Buses run regularly in the mornings from Van to Doğubeyazıt via Çaldıran (three hours, TL10). Without your own transport you will not be able to stop at the places described en route below.

WHAT TO SEE As you leave Van heading north towards Mount Ararat, the mountain itself is not visible. For that pleasure you have to wait until you cross

---

MOUNT ARARAT – 'BIG PAIN'

Mount Ararat is the stuff of dreams – and nightmares. Rarely has a mountain so steeped in myth and tradition looked the part. Often wreathed in cloud with its upper slopes tantalisingly out of view, treacherously changeable weather is the mountain's speciality. At 5,165m it is the highest peak in Turkey (for comparison Mont Blanc is the highest in the European Alps at 4,810m and Mt Elbrus is the highest in Russia's Caucasus at 5,642m). It sits in the furthest reaches of eastern Turkey, within a few miles of both the Armenian and the Iranian borders. A dormant volcano that last erupted in 1840, its summit permanently covered in snow, its sheer vastness makes the rugged Anatolian Plateau all around seem flat and the town of Doğubeyazıt (1,528m) at its foot totally dwarfed and subservient. Its colossal cone dominates the landscape for over 50km in every direction, with Little Ararat at 3,896m to its right, like a child beside its parent. In Turkish the mountain is called Büyük Ağri (Big Pain) and Little Ararat is called Küçük Ağri (Little Pain). In summer the snow retreats up the mountain to cover the top third only, while in winter it comes right down to the base.

the pass at Tendurek (2,644m) some 100km further on. Still in the outskirts of Van, a turn-off to the right to Özalp leads, after about 10km, to the castle of Anzaf, a minor Urartian fortress built to guard the trade routes from Iran to the capital at Van, and overlooking Ercek Gölü, a lake at 1,803m. Like Çavuştepe it has an upper and a lower section, with colossal blocks of stone surviving to two or three layers.

Amik Once out of Van the main road remains dead flat and straight, and after about 20km there are various roads leading off towards the lakeshore. This stretch of shoreline is known as Amik, famous for its orchards and natural beaches, and widely used by picnicking families in the summer months. *Dolmuş* taxis and minibuses ferry the holidaymakers to and fro. The beaches here are long, a mixture of sand and pebbles, and the spot, with its plentiful trees and rich green grass facing the volcanic cone of Süphan Dağı on the opposite shoreline, is thought of as the most beautiful stretch of the lake.

Bendamahi Falls About 10km after leaving the northeast corner of the lake a sign points left to Şeytan Köprüsü (Devil's Bridge), an attractive single-arched Seljuk bridge over the Bendamahi River. Just 1km further north another sign points left to the Muradiye Şelalesi, waterfalls also known as the Bendamahi Falls. Not visible from the road, they lie just a short distance along a track that ends at a car park with a few refreshment stalls and basic shops selling snacks, ice cream and soft drinks. From here a marvellously mobile suspension bridge made of wooden slats and thick metal wire handrails bounces atmospherically as you cross the gorge for the best views of the waterfalls or to sit on the terrace of the simple café on the other side. Whole families cross together, on the safety in numbers principle, bent grandmas and agile young girls clutching the arms of their male escorts in terror. The falls themselves are only about 10m tall, but are still attractive and impressive in spring and early summer when they carry the maximum snowmelt. Van fish are found in the greatest abundance at the point where this river runs into the lake.

Çaldıran The virtually empty road continues to Çaldıran, a bustling place with a large military base set in the flat open plain. From here on to the pass at Tendürek the road passes very close to the Iranian border, which is why there is a stronger military presence with police patrols and various checkpoints. In the 1980s the section of road from Çaldıran to just before Doğubeyazıt was not surfaced and was quite rough in places. Before May it was not passable at all as the melting snows created a river which was too deep to be forded at one point, so it used to be necessary to drive the long way round via Erciş, Patnos and Ağrı, a dull drive that added 150km to the route. Now the tarmac highway from Çaldıran to Doğubeyazıt is excellent all the way, transforming timings. The worst section of road used to be the final 15km before Doğubeyazıt, where it skirted an old lava field.

Tendürek Volcano As the wide tarmac road snakes up to the Tendürek Pass, look across to the west to see the huge hulk of the Tendürek Volcano that gives the pass its name. The whole area between the road and the volcano is a massive jagged lava field, awe-inspiring in its scale. At 3,301m it is not one of eastern Turkey's highest peaks, but the vast low-relief mound, nearly 40km in diameter at its base, has twin summits called East and Central which are 6km apart. In summer the saddle area inside the crater between the two summits is home to several-dozen Kurdish nomad families, camped here with their black goat-hair tents and animals, guarded as ever by ferocious dogs. With a local guide engaged at Doğubeyazıt you can reach

Armenian tradition has Ararat as the centre of the universe, with a belief that the Armenians themselves came down from the slopes of the mountain. Ararat is also cited in Genesis as the final resting place of Noah's Ark after the Flood:

> And after the end of the hundred and fifty days the waters were abated. And the Ark rested on the seventh month, on the seventeenth day of the month, upon the mountains of Ararat.

In the 1970s and 1980s the search for the Ark gained momentum, with many climbers claiming to return with pieces of it. The American astronaut and born-again Christian James Irwin was the most zealous of the climbers, making several attempts from 1982 onwards, before falling and having a near-death experience on the mountain. He never returned to Ararat, but the extraordinary manner of his rescue convinced him that God had been watching over him. Today's visitors are taken to a different site, opposite Ararat, where the remains of what appears to be a huge boat rest on the hillside. Given that the volcano has erupted many times since the Flood, a sceptic is inclined to view the Ark's chances of escape from total burial under tons of lava as decidedly slim.

Ararat was long considered by the Arabs to be the roof of the world. Here, it was believed, the two great rivers, the Tigris and the Euphrates, had their source, bringing life and civilisation to the open plains of Mesopotamia. The British climber-scholar Viscount James Bryce, who scaled Ararat in 1876, wrote these moving words from the summit:

> Below and around, included in this single view, seemed to lie the whole cradle of the human race, from Mesopotamia in the south to the great wall of the Caucasus that covered the northern horizon, the boundary for some many ages of the civilised world. If it was indeed here that man first set foot on the unpeopled earth, one could imagine how the great dispersal went as the races spread themselves down from these sacred heights along the course of the great rivers down to the Black and Caspian Seas, and over the Assyrian Plain to the shores of the Southern Ocean, whence they were wafted away to the other continents and isles. No more imposing centre of the world could be imagined.'
>
> *Transcaucasia and Ararat 1877*

the saddle in a 4x4 vehicle. Beside the East summit is a crater 500m across filled with water in summer, and a nearby vent hole still gives off warm vapours. The main Central summit looks down over a crater on its west side that is about 150m deep and 1km in diameter, still giving off sulphurous fumes in places.

As the road drops down the other side of the Tendürek Pass you will have, weather permitting, your first view of Mount Ararat, unmistakeably looming up to your right.

DOĞUBEYAZIT *Telephone code: 472; altitude: 1,950m*

The small town of Doğubeyazıt is well known for two things: its location at the foot of Mount Ararat which makes it the starting point for all ascents of the mountain, and the photogenic Işak Paşa Sarayı, ruins of a 19th-century local chieftain's palace just outside town. As a town it is much improved in recent years and now even has the distinction of a pedestrianised main drag with proper paving and even a bit of landscaping, where before there were just muddy or dusty earth streets. The mayor, a Kurdish lady, has evidently been given a budget to help beautify the streets and has done her best. The population today is 100% Kurdish, though in the past there were also many Armenians living here. Most people stay at least a night here to admire Ararat and to visit Işak Paşa Sarayı 6km out of town.

GETTING THERE AND AWAY Doğubeyazıt has no airport. The closest is Ağri, two hours away, which in theory has flights run by Turkish Airlines (*www.thy.com*) to and from Istanbul, Ankara and Izmir, though in practice these are frequently cancelled for lack of demand, so you are safer to rely on Van airport. Doğubeyazıt also has no train links, so bus and minibus are your only public transport options.

By bus For destinations further afield you have to use the main *otogar* in town by the Belediye building, at the start of the road up to Işak Paşa Sarayı, a short walk from all the main hotels. Services often run via Erzurum (four hours, TL20), and the bus journey to and from Istanbul takes 18 hours and costs TL50. The first one sets off at 09.00 and others run at two- to three-hourly intervals. Ankara takes 15 hours and costs TL50, while Izmir takes 25–26 hours and costs TL75. Seats should be booked the day before from the offices inside the *otogar* itself, and you are allocated a specific seat number.

By minibus Minibuses link Doğubeyazıt to Van (three hours, TL10) four times a day up until 14.00 and to Kars via Iğdır where you have to change. Minibuses run from the main road just past the Petrol Ofisi station, and also run in the other direction to the Iranian border (TL4).

GETTING AROUND Everywhere in town is easily reachable on foot. For Işak Paşa Sarayı there are regular minibuses from the main *otogar* or you can take a taxi to cover the 6km distance from the town centre (TL20 return, waiting included).

TOURIST INFORMATION AND TOUR OPERATORS There is no tourist office but guides for Ararat lurk round the *otogar* and all the hotels offer tours to the surrounding sights.

WHERE TO STAY

Golden Hill (35 rooms) Cevreyolu Uzeri; 3128717. The newest in town, 2km from the centre. It has a sauna, *hammam*, bar & restaurant, but no AC. $$$

Sim-Er Motel (125 rooms) Iran Yolu; 3124842; e dbeyazit@simerhotel.com; www.simerhotel.com. Since 1977 when it first opened this low-rise place has been the hotel of choice for climbers, thanks to its position by itself out of town directly opposite Mount Ararat. It is getting a bit run-down now, & has no pool, just a pleasant setting in its own slightly scruffy gardens. The restaurant serves local & international food, from a buffet when there are enough guests. The rooms have digital TV, central heating & minibar & are functional & comfortable. $$$

Hotel Ararat (60 rooms) Belediye Caddesi; 3124987. Opposite the town hall above Büyük Pasajı Market, the hotel begins from the first floor where there is a big lobby area. It has heating & AC, satellite TV & minibar & even claims a swimming pool. Rooms have views of Ararat one way or Işak Paşa Sarayı the other. $$

Grand Derya (70 rooms) Dr Ismail Besikci Caddesi; 3127531. Doğubeyazıt's fanciest offering in town, the only place with AC, which in high summer is something you may long for. Its 7-storey building is ugly & functional, but it has its own restaurant, a relative rarity in town, providing, according to its own brochure (sic) 'the pearless taste of Turkish kitchen'. Proximity to the mosque can be an issue at the dawn call to prayer. $$

Isfehan Hotel (85 rooms) Emniyet Caddesi; 3124363; e isfehanhotel@yahoo.com. Spacious rooms, some with balconies having sideways views

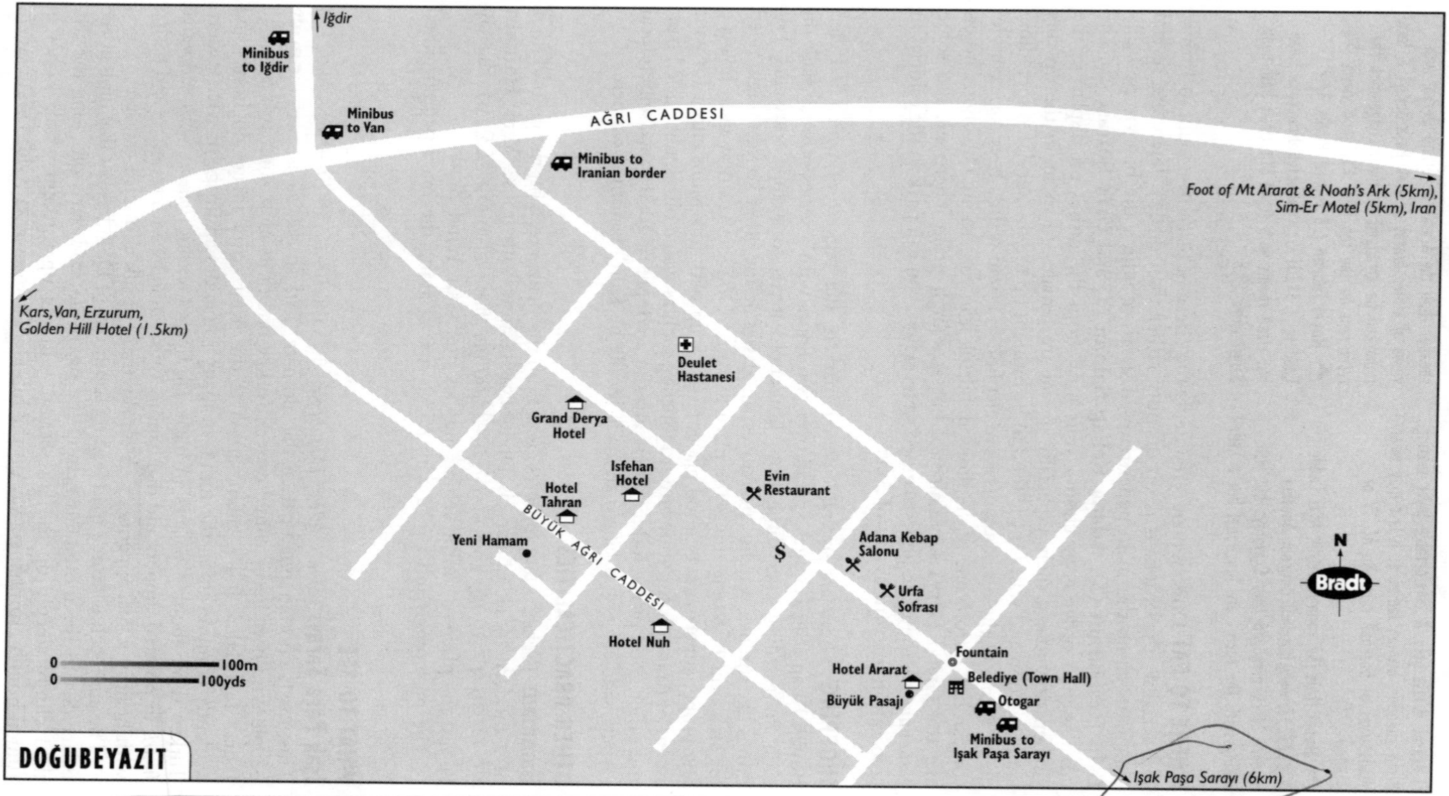

DOĞUBEYAZIT

Foot of Mt Ararat & Noah's Ark (5km),
Sim-Er Motel (5km), Iran

İşak Paşa Sarayı (6km)

Minibus to Iranian border

AĞRI CADDESI

İğdir

Minibus to Van

Minibus to İğdir

Kars, Van, Erzurum,
Golden Hill Hotel (1.5km)

Deulet
Hastanesi

Evin
Restaurant

Adana Kebap
Salonu

Urfa
Sofrası

Hotel Ararat

Büyük Pasajı

Fountain

Belediye (Town Hall)

Otogar

Minibus to
İşak Paşa Sarayı

Grand Derya
Hotel

Isfehan
Hotel

Hotel
Tahran

BÜYÜK AĞRI CADDESI

Hotel Nuh

Yeni Hamam

N

Bradt

100m
100yds

299

of Ararat. B/fast only, & comfortable foyer seating. Mixed clientele; Iranian ladies at b/fast may wear headscarves or baseball caps. No AC, TV or minibar. $$

🏠 **Hotel Nuh** (57 rooms) Büyük Ağri Caddesi; ☎ 3127232; www.hotelnuh.8m.com. Another modern block arranged over 5 storeys but with willing staff. The rooms are functional but a little

cheaper than the Ararat or Grand Derya, with views of either Ararat or Işak Paşa Sarayı, & local tours can be arranged by the management. The restaurant on the top floor has good views. $$

🏠 **Hotel Tahran** (28 rooms) Büyük Ağri Caddesi; ☎ 3120195; www.hoteltahran.com. Small but clean rooms with small but clean bathrooms. B/fast extra. $

✗ **WHERE TO EAT** Doğubeyazıt is reputedly the cheapest place to eat out in Turkey, and certainly the emphasis is on quantity rather than quality. There are several restaurants along the main pedestrianised street, of which the best are probably **Evin Restaurant** ($), **Adana Kebap Salonu** ($) and **Urfa Sofrası** ($). The usual way to order is to choose your meal from the dishes on display in the kitchen downstairs, then, especially if you are female, go to sit in the upstairs family section and wait for the food to be brought up to you. Service is incredibly quick. None of these restaurants serve alcohol, so if you want a beer for example, you can buy it from one of the shops and drink it in your room. The bigger hotels like the Grand Derya serve alcohol but at a high price. There are also some *pastahanes* on the main pedestrianised street where you can pack in the calories in preparation for your ascent of Ararat.

SHOPPING There are several covered markets, the biggest of which is called Büyük Pasajı (Big Passage), spread over two floors with a series of small stalls on each floor selling everything from household items to strange souvenirs. For things like torches, watches, penknives, sunglasses or any other kit you might need for an ascent of Ararat, this is the place to come. Doğubeyazıt now even boasts a few proper supermarkets, good places to stock up with provisions either for your ascent of Ararat or for your onward journey, such as water, olives, nuts, dried fruit and other good picnic fodder. There are also a couple of good shops selling local carpets, saddlebags and *kilims*, all made locally by Kurdish nomad women.

OTHER PRACTICALITIES

Hammam Tucked a few minutes away from the main street, on the ground floor of a modern block of flats, is Doğubeyazıt's new bath-house, **Yeni Hamam** (🕓 *07.30–17.30 (for women), 07.30–22.00 (for men); all-in-cost TL5*), which may be just the place to soothe aching muscles after your Ararat climb.

The post office and banks with ATMs are all along the main pedestrianised street.

WHAT TO SEE

Işak Paşa Sarayı (*6km south of Doğubeyazıt;* 🕓 *08.30–17.30 Tue–Sun; adult TL3*) This much-photographed palace, the ultimate 'Turkish *château*' is, even for many people who have never visited eastern Turkey, one of its most familiar scenes, like India's Taj Mahal. It has often served as the front cover image on books and evidently conjures up in the minds of many romantics an image of what eastern Turkey is all about – palaces in bleak landscapes, exotic *harems* with seductive *houris* in pointed slippers and diaphanous veils, eunuchs with scimitars and pashas with healthy sexual appetites, rich on the trade of silk and spice caravans.

The approach is from a road leading south out of Doğubeyazıt that ends at the palace. Set in the mountains behind the town the road starts off along the flat, then climbs steeply up the last section, winding up through whole slopes of ruined houses crumbling away on the hillside. This was Eski (Old) Doğubeyazıt, originally a Seljuk town, which at its peak had 120,000 houses and a population of 250,000. The town was totally abandoned in 1930 when, according to the local version of events, the people left to go to the cities and find more lucrative work than farming. This defensive explanation neatly sidesteps the fact that the Turks destroyed the town and dispersed its population after its involvement in a Kurdish revolt against the authorities. A photograph taken in 1897 shows it as a thriving town of stone-built flat-roofed houses, but from its appearance today you could be forgiven for mistaking it for a medieval ruin. This is largely because all the woodwork and some of the stone blocks have been removed to build the modern town of Doğubeyazıt.

As you approach the palace, raised up dramatically on a terrace like a stage set in front of you, look out for the dark wooden-arched door set low down in the walls which leads out onto the grassy terrace at the foot of the palace. This was the *harem* garden, a secluded spot not visible from any part of the palace except the *harem*. Coach tours tend to visit in the late afternoon or early morning, so if you avoid those times you have a good chance of having the place to yourself. You enter through a huge wide gateway into the vast courtyard where the ticket office is tucked to the left. A huge restoration/renovation programme has left the place looking unnaturally modern.

The palace has a sybaritic feel to it and was definitely conceived more as a pleasure dome than as a defensive castle. Yet the Russians also occupied it on other occasions and they are blamed by the Turks for the blackened cooking residues that coat the walls of rooms designed for more elegant purposes. They also ran off with the gold-plated doors of the entrance during the 1917 invasion, and these are now in a museum in Moscow. A fair degree of restoration was carried out in 1956. For all its hotchpotch elements it is hard to dislike anything in it.

From the outer courtyard you pass through an elaborately carved portal into the slightly smaller inner courtyard. Directly ahead lies the entrance to the *harem*

İŞAK PAŞA'S PLEASURE PALACE

The remarkable building was only built around 1800 on the orders of İşak Paşa, the feudal overlord of this area, which was nominally under Ottoman control. He is thought variously to have been a Kurd, a Georgian, an Armenian or a Jew, and made his money by dominating the lucrative silk caravan routes from his palace vantage point. In its architecture the palace is equally mixed, with elements of Seljuk, Persian, Georgian, Armenian and Baroque Ottoman style. Frederick Burnaby, travelling here about 80 years after it was built, says it belonged to a Kurdish chieftain: 'who expressed the wish to have the most beautiful residence in the world, and, after conversing with numerous architects upon this subject, had accepted the service of an Armenian.' The Armenian proceeded to design a magnificent palace with large stained-glass windows and every possible comfort. The pasha was pleased and to ensure that the Armenian could not construct a similar one for a rival chieftain, ordered his hands to be cut off. The poor man died shortly afterwards as a beggar. The pasha met with his just deserts, dying of a snake bite, 'after committing all sorts of excesses'. At the time of Burnaby's visit, the palace was being used as a barracks in the run-up to the preparations for war against Russia in 1877. The large stained-glass windows which had been bought at great expense had all disappeared and their place was filled with sheets of Turkish newspaper. The marble pillars and alabaster carving over the portico were chipped and hacked at, and in the *harem* 400 soldiers slept in the rooms the pasha had intended for his concubines.

or women's quarters, and to the right is the entrance to the mosque and the *selamlik* or men's quarters with a reception area and audience hall. Over on the left are the remains of store houses. In the right-hand corner of the courtyard are the free-standing tombs of the pasha and his favourite wife, with steps leading down to the grave chambers.

The entrance to the *harem* is the most richly ornate of the three portals. It leads into a maze-like series of rooms, with a large blackened kitchen and dining area, still with its roof intact. Next to it are two charming circular bathrooms, one hot, the other cold. On the cliff edge all around the palace are the long thin *harem* bedrooms, 14 in all, each with its fireplace at the end and its window overlooking the valley. Near the bathrooms, on the outer edge of the palace, is an equally charming water closet with a large window. In the centre of the *harem* is the superbly colonnaded feast room, with mirrors in the blind arches so that the *harem* women could partake of the feast but not be seen by the guests of the pasha. To get an overview of the *harem* it is fun to climb up some steps to the roof level and walk along the tops of the walls looking down into all the rooms.

Entering the *selamlik* and mosque area you pass through an open-roofed courtroom where the pasha also gave audience. On the outer edge are a few more long thin bedrooms, used by male guests, some of them still with the remains of their carved wooden balcony supports overlooking the side valley below. The mosque is especially fine, divided into two parts with marble pillars in one half. It still has much of its original decoration and stone carving on the ceiling and columns, with the original lamp chains. A gallery runs along beneath the dome, but access to this and the minaret is now locked. The stone-carved pulpit is also charming and you can still climb the steps and deliver orations to the imagined masses. The mosque is no longer in use so there is no need for you to feel particularly reverent; in its time as a barracks the mosque has doubtless witnessed much irreverence.

Over on the far side of a cleft in the valley the road leads on beyond the palace to a large mosque with a new concrete dome and an Urartian castle lowering over it. This can be approached from the side on a path from the collection of tea-gardens and souvenir stalls that has grown up in the cleft. From the path you can clamber inside through a breach in the walls and explore the full extent of the castle, fully walled even right to its highest point. This is the only point at which a view of Ararat can be had, as it is blocked from the palace of Ishak Pasha by this large rock outcrop. Clambering down onto the lower part of the castle and looking back up onto the cliff walls that face out over the valley towards the palace, is a relief showing a man with his arms outstretched to sacrifice a goat to a woman, thought to be a goddess, holding out her arms to receive the sacrifice. The style of the figures and their dress is Assyrian, and they are thought to date from as early as the 9th century BC.

Welcome refreshments after your clambering can be had either in the popular tea-gardens used by local people, or in the smarter and more expensive place set by itself above the palace, with stunning terrace views.

Ice cave An excursion to this together with Noah's Ark form an interesting half-day outing to the east of Doğubeyazıt on the road towards the Iranian border. You pass along the foot of Ararat and see where the track leads off towards the mountain, the approach all climbers use, close to the Sim-Er Motel. You will need to be shown the ice cave's exact location by a guide, but it lies to the south of Mount Ararat, to the left of the main road to Iran, about 25km east of Doğubeyazıt. It is totally concealed about 4km off the road, reachable on a difficult dirt track that takes you to within 200m of the cave entrance, down on the flat, with wonderful views to Little Ararat and Big Ararat behind. The cave is 100m long and 50m wide, and descends 8–10m underground. When you first enter the cave it feels very hot and humid, then quite suddenly when you cross an invisible threshold, the temperature plummets to very cold, so cold that ice forms on the floor of the cave where drops of moisture from the roof falls onto the frozen ground. This forms ice stalactites and stalagmites of varying sizes, some very big indeed, which can be seen all over the cave floor as you descend deeper inside, and which have an eerie glow. The natural phenomenon that causes this acute temperature change is not really understood, but it makes for a memorable outing.

Noah's Ark (Nuh Gemisi) (⏱ *daily dawn–dusk; adult TL3*) Returning to the main road and continuing a little further towards Iran, a signposted road soon forks right to Noah's Ark. Without your own transport you will have to take a local tour organised through one of the hotels. About 30km east of Doğubeyazıt it lies at the end of the specially built tarmac road, where a museum and adjacent house have been built by the local Kurd who was in attendance throughout the studies made on this amazing structure. The museum explains in great detail and with many copies of excerpts from press articles, how the structure has been tested and fits exactly with the dimensions of the Ark as given in the Bible and how even the original anchors have been found.

The structure itself lies on the ridge of the hill behind the museum, and is reached by a path that sets off to descend gradually towards it. From above it certainly does look very boat-like in shape and it is so tempting to believe everything in the museum. Once you are down beside it, and find a place to climb inside, it becomes much more difficult to visualise what is what, but you can climb right to the top of the structure and look back onto it, with extraordinary views of Ararat bearing down. As the crow flies the spot must be about 15km from the

THE FLOOD TABLET IN THE BRITISH MUSEUM

Recently covered in the BBC's *History of the World in 100 Objects*, Neil MacGregor, Director of the British Museum, talks about the decipherment in 1872 of what has come to be known as the 'Flood Tablet'. Dated to the 7th century BC the clay tablet, written in Akkadian cuneiform, the language of Babylonia and Assyria, was found in the palace of the Assyrian king Ashurbanipal (reigned 664–631BC), part of the king's library. Now the most famous cuneiform tablet from Mesopotamia, it is the 11th tablet of the *Epic of Gilgamesh*, the longest piece of literature in Akkadian, and describes how Gilgamesh meets Utnapishtim, who, like Noah in the Hebrew Bible, is warned by God about an impending great flood, and told to build a boat for himself, his family, his most precious possessions, wild and domesticated animals and skilled craftsmen. God then sends the flood, which Utnapishtim survives, first sending out a dove which returns, then later sending out a raven which does not, proving that dry land has reappeared from the flood waters. Versions of this flood story have now been found at Hattuşaş, the Hittite capital, Emar in Syria and Megiddo in the Levant, showing that it was part of a common pool of legend shared throughout the Middle East, and whose impact, as Neil MacGregor points out, has had reverberations throughout world literature reaching into Homer and *A Thousand and One Nights*. The reading of this tablet in 1872 by George Smith, an assistant in the British Museum who taught himself Akkadian, came just 12 years after Darwin published his revolutionary *On the origin of species* and added to the religious debate of the time about the theory of evolution and the sacredness of the Bible. (See also page 228, on the *Epic of Gilgamesh*.)

summit of Ararat, but with the tumultuous volcanic activity and earthquakes of this area, who knows how much the terrain must have moved and changed since biblical times. Other theories are that it is simply an elaborate soil erosion.

Closer still to the Iranian border (just 6km) before it and 35km east of Doğubeyazıt) is a meteorite crater created in 1913 that can sometimes be visited above the tiny village of Hallaç, if the political situation is sufficiently stable. It is 35m in diameter and 60m deep, the second largest in the world after the one in Alaska.

Fish Lake (Balık Gölü) and Diyadın Hot Springs (52km northwest of Doğubeyazıt and 51km west of Doğubeyazıt respectively)

A fun day tour (or longer if you are equipped for camping) from Doğubeyazıt can be done in a 4x4 or rugged saloon car by heading initially west on the main road to Ağri and Kars, then forking right to Sulucam after 14km. After Sulucam the road is unsurfaced and continues for a further 16km to reach the wild and remote lake. Lying at 2,250m and encircled by bare and rounded hills that rise to 2,800m, the 11km-long lake offers chilly swimming in summer. It is estimated to be 150–200m deep and is frozen from the beginning of January until the end of April. The whole area is wonderfully peaceful, cool and calm, and utterly uninhabited but for some Kurdish nomad encampments. In fact the headman here owns most of the horses used in the Ararat ascents, and can also arrange for you to horse ride in the hills round the lake if you wish. There used to be a simple lakeside hotel here but it has fallen into disrepair, probably a casualty of when tourism plummeted after the Kurdish guerrilla activity in the area. The lake is about 95km and, as its name suggests, is famous for its fish, the most popular being carp and speckled trout. The local people keep fishing boats and sell their catch at local markets. As a spot to camp and get away from civilisation, this is one of the best, though there is a complete lack of shade on the treeless shore. Birdlife here is interesting during the spring and autumn migrations, with ducks, gulls, swans and cormorants. Close to the shore on the northern part of the lake is a small island, just 50m long and 30m wide, which carries the remains of an Urartian fortress and graves dating back to 2000BC, together with an irrigation channel and dam, suggesting that the Urartians used the lake for irrigation.

THE ASCENT OF ARARAT

From afar the slopes of Mount Ararat look deceptively easy to climb, but in practice the jagged lava fields are very tricky to negotiate, and significant numbers have been killed in the ascent. Long considered impossible to climb by local

PRIVATE HOT SPRINGS

The hot springs can be visited on the return to Doğubeyazıt. They are reached by initially heading west further along the Ağri–Kars road and over the Ipek Pass at 2,040m. Soon after the pass a road forks left towards Diyadın, which you follow and about 5km beyond Diyadın at the village of Ilica, the hot springs can be found on the edge of the village beside a dramatic gorge. They are signposted and have been walled off to create a few private bathing areas around small pools where women can bathe discreetly away from prying eyes. These walled enclosures can be rented from an attendant by the hour, and even have basic changing areas. The rectangular pools made to look like swimming pools contain the hot spring water, the last thing you want on a hot summer's day, but very pleasant in the cooler temperatures at the end of the day. Before or after bathing, you can walk through the nearby gorge to admire the scenery.

people, it was first climbed in 1829 by a German, Professor Parrot, on his third attempt, and then by a steady trickle of German, Russian and British and most recently Turkish mountaineers. All ascents were still discounted by both local Kurds and Turkish officials until the 1950s, and even today some villagers do not believe it is possible to ascend the mountain. Political problems dogged the area for most of the 20th century, and before 1982 there were no more than a handful of successful ascents, many of them illicit. The base of its cone covers an area in excess of 2,500km, a fact which helps us to understand why, in summer 2008 when the PKK kidnapped three Germans from Camp 1 at 3,200m and hid with them on the mountain for ten days, the Turkish military had no chance of finding them, or indeed of sealing off the mountain. The risk of kidnap by Kurdish separatists is small, but when times are tense, the Turkish authorities close the mountain to climbers. It was closed for several years in the 1990s, but reopened in 2000. It was closed again for six weeks after the recent kidnap of the Germans, thereby thwarting my own honeymoon ascent, and making us divert instead to climbs of Nemrut Dağı and Süphan Dağı, two volcanoes on the northern shore of Lake Van. Whole communities of Kurdish nomads live on the lower slopes of Ararat in the summer months, below 3,200m, either in villages or in tented encampments with their livestock of sheep, cattle, horses and chickens to enjoy the rich pastures.

PRACTICALITIES A climb up Mount Ararat is not something to be undertaken lightly. First of all, because of its sensitive location so close to the Armenian and Iranian borders, a military permit is required, something which has to be applied for by the guide organising your climb at least two months in advance. It costs €50 and the money goes towards the rescue fund should you need to be medivacked off the mountain. Two days before my own climb in summer 2009, an Iranian woman climbing without a permit slipped and fell on the ice, crashing into rocks, breaking both legs and all her ribs. The Turkish authorities refused to send a helicopter up to fetch her as she did not have a permit. One person on average dies on Ararat every year and it is not worth the risk of not having a permit.

Local guides On arrival in Doğubeyazıt, especially if you arrive at the bus station, you will almost certainly be approached by local guides offering climbs up Ararat. All of them are doing this illegally, without permits, which is why they offer prices of only €300, about half what the *bona-fide* tour operators charge. They also tell you that it can be done with just two nights' camping on the mountain, something which carries with it a high risk of altitude sickness. Most of the people who take up these offers are Iranians who have come over the border and who are already acclimatised from living in Tehran (1,200–1,700m) and climbing Mount Demavend (5,610m). Some of them even climb the whole thing in a day, but this should not even be contemplated unless you are fully acclimatised and extremely experienced.

Professional tour operators and guides There are only a handful of truly experienced tour operators through whom you can reliably book online from overseas for the full Ararat experience. They will organise the military permit for you, provide you with tents, foam mats, sleeping bags, trekking poles and crampons, arrange the horses/mules for carrying the kit and cook your food for the full three-night/four-day adventure. For a group of climbers, usually up to a maximum of ten, there should be two guides, a cook and the muleteers who will come up to the 4,200m camp. Beyond that point only the guides come with you, and it is important to have more than one, so that if anyone runs into difficulties and has to turn back, one guide can accompany them while the other carries on. They generally collect you from Van airport and include in their price some local

10

sightseeing, such as Işak Paşa Sarayı, and two or three nights' hotel accommodation in Doğubeyazıt and one night in Van. Prices range from €400 to €750 for seven-day treks, depending exactly what is involved. Recommended companies are:

Anatolian Adventures Kadıköy, Istanbul; ↘ (216) 41852222; www.anatolianadventures.com. Experienced tour operator based in Istanbul so they escort you from there to Van if required. They offer 7-day Ararat climbs from €690, the 3 volcanoes (Ararat, Süphan, Nemrut) in a 10-day tour & Ararat with Taurus mountains for acclimatisation in a 14-day trip.
Ararat Summit Adventure www.araratsummit.com. Specialises in outdoor adventure treks & climbs & white water rafting in the Kaçkar region. Organises 4-day & 7-day climbs of Ararat, treks with Ararat & the Kaçkar, Mt Demavend in Iran & ski-tours of Ararat in winter for highly experienced skiers.
Ararat Sunrises www.araratsunrises.com. Organises a range of trips including 4-day & 7-day ascents of Ararat, trekking in the Kaçkar & even a special over 55s Mt Ararat climb for

€400 pp, maximum group size 8.
Mount Ararat Trek Doğubeyazıt; ↘ 6961965; www.mountararattrek.com. Offers a range of 4-day, 7-day & 14-day treks up Mt Ararat (including Mt Süphan) with full support of mules & guides. Tents provided.
Mount Ararat Expedition www.araratexpedition.com. Offers 4-day, 5-day, 6-day & 7-day ascents of Ararat, fully supported with guides & horses, as well as 9-day & 12-day treks to include additional sightseeing & Mt Süphan.
Sobek Travel Niğde; ↘ (388) 2321507; www.trekkinginturkeys.com. A long-established company based in Cappadocia & specialising in Cappadocian treks as well as climbs of 8 days up Ararat, the Kaçkar & Ararat (15 days) & Ararat with the Taurus & Cappadocia (15 days) as preliminaries for fitness & acclimatisation.

Equipment You should have all your own clothing and footwear, including enough warm clothing for the final assault on the summit, where temperatures are often −20°C. You will need long-johns under warm trousers, then waterproof or ski-trousers on top, together with at least three layers on your top half. A head torch is also essential for the final summit climb in the dark. The more technical kit like crampons, trekking poles and camping gear can be supplied by your tour operator by prior arrangement. Suncream, sunglasses/ski-goggles and lip-block are also essential.

All food and soft drinks are provided by the tour organiser, although you can obviously supplement with any of your own special climbing favourites.

ARARAT ASCENT

Day 1 The drive in a 4x4 or truck from Doğubeyazıt up to Eli village at 2,200m where the mules/horses are waiting takes about an hour. It is generally done in the morning, setting off around 08.00 or 09.00. The walk from here to Camp 1 at 3,200m is very pleasant trekking up through the grassy lower slopes of the vast mountain. The gradient is rarely steep and the terrain underfoot is mainly earthy paths, rocky in places. The path leads through a couple of black-tented Kurdish nomad encampments where it is customary to stop and drink *ayran* (sour yoghurt) or sweet black tea, for which a small payment is expected. At a normal relaxed pace, incorporating a picnic lunch stop, the trek up to Camp 1 takes about four hours to climb the 1,000m in altitude.

Camp 1 is a grassy slope (also called *Yeşil Yayla*, 'green meadow') with space for about 30 tents and on any night in the summer climbing season it is normal to have around 10–15 tents pitched there. It is a pleasant spot with an icy rushing stream of meltwater running down the side of it and ringed with large boulders which can give privacy for bodily functions. The hardy can even perform thorough dawn or dusk ablutions in the freezing water. From Camp 1 in clear conditions the snow-capped summit is visible far above, and guides will also point

A SUMMER-ONLY CLIMB

Although Mount Ararat is 730m lower than Mount Kilimanjaro (5,895m), in difficulty it rates as a harder climb because of the snowy/icy conditions for the final 500–600m and the dangerously changeable weather conditions. The terrain above 3,200m is also trickier, especially the boulder field above the 4,200m camp. As the season is so limited, with climbing only possible from mid-June to mid-September, this is the time when most people will be on the mountain. That said, unlike Kilimanjaro (or even Everest) which has become a commercial trek and is climbed by thousands every year, Ararat is climbed by only a relatively small number each year, and of those who attempt it, only about 30% succeed in reaching the summit. Its Turkish name of Büyük Ağri (Big Pain) is well deserved. That said, the walk from 2,200m up the lower slopes to Camp 1 at 3,500m, is no more than a pleasant uphill trek with beautiful landscapes, and if you have doubts about your fitness or are worried about altitude sickness, you can still enjoy the mountain and its ambience hugely from Camp 1, and leave Camp 2 and the summit assault to the enthusiasts. Your joints may thank you. For the real masochists it is now also possible to organise winter climbs (see the list of tour operators on page 306), where you carry your skis up (mules/horses cannot be used) and wear them on the way down, but these people obviously never reach the summit.

out where Camp 2 can be spotted high above on a stony ridge. Most people aim to strike camp by 15.00 so that they have shelter by the time the usual rain or hail storm comes down the mountain anytime between 16.00 and 18.00.

There is always a good sense of camaraderie on the mountain at Camp 1, and the nationalities blend and chat as much as language differences permit, all united in the sense of impending adventure. Kit is compared and previous climbing experience is discussed. Numerically more Iranians come to climb Ararat than any other nationality and many of them speak very little English. Since permits were finally granted to Armenians in 2007, more and more of them also now come, totally determined to climb what for them is 'their' mountain. Otherwise there are handfuls of Germans, a few French and smatterings of other European nationalities. Americans are very rare.

Day 2 Now you are on the edge of the uninhabited part of the mountain. From Camp 1 upwards you quickly leave behind any nomad encampments and grassy slopes and progress within an hour into the snowline, though the path itself stays on increasingly steep rocky gradients.

Day 2 is treated by the proper guides as the acclimatisation day, on which you trek at a leisurely pace up the path towards Camp 2, reaching altitudes of 3,900–4,000m, then returning to Camp 1 to spend the second night. For people who are already acclimatised it is possible to press on straight up to Camp 2 for the second night. For those taking the acclimatisation day, this can be a bit frustrating, watching the others break camp and leave, while knowing that they themselves will be setting off only to come back again for a second night. It is however a wise precaution if you have not acclimatised in advance and have never experienced high altitude before and therefore do not know if you will be affected.

Day 3 This is the day where you will feel like a dog who has been straining at the leash, suddenly let loose. From here on you know that everything is for real and upwards all the way. You will have walked the majority of the route the day before so you know exactly what to expect. The terrain underfoot quickly becomes loose and stony after leaving the grassy slopes behind, and from the point where the path crosses the river of meltwater, the gradient increases as the track zigzags up the rocky boulder field. In places the lower grassy parts that are still well watered have stunning flowers in blues, yellows and whites lining the path, but soon after crossing the stream, all vegetation ceases and the terrain is either rock or snow.

The altitude of Camp 2 is 4,100m or 4,200m, depending on which of the two flattened terraces of rock you choose. The upper area is a little larger and flatter, so if there is space, that should be your preferred choice. To reach it from Camp 1 takes about four hours and most people set off from Camp 1 at 08.00 or 09.00 and aim to arrive up there for a late lunch around 13.00. Very often this is the crossover point where you will meet those climbers who set off the day before and who are now returning from the summit, so much excited chatter and quizzing goes on by those still heading up of those now on their way down.

By mid afternoon tents will be pitched and a meal eaten so that everyone can then retreat into shelter in time for the customary afternoon storms and rockfalls. Also, since most climbers set off for the summit anytime between midnight and 02.00, it is important to get as much sleep and rest as possible beforehand. Now that

THE SUMMIT – A PERSONAL ACCOUNT

I well recall the sense of elation when Ahmet turned to me and said it was only 50m to the summit. It was probably the worst thing he could have said, as at that point I assumed I had already made it, and started to quicken my pace. The Armenian party who started up the mountain from Camp 2 ahead of us and whom we had overtaken, then been overtaken by several times in sequence, had been climbing just behind us at that point, and I wanted to go all out for the summit. Suddenly the fog came down and we could barely see a few metres ahead. Confusion reigned and the Armenian party shouted to us to stop. Their guide said it was too dangerous to carry on and that we should all be roped up to each other so that no-one got lost. This took an age in the wind and fog, and meanwhile I was still itching to get ahead.

Now, all roped together, we inched our way upwards in zigzags for what seemed like hours. The gradient had become a lot steeper, but I wanted to walk straight up, not in senseless zigzags that would take longer. I felt we must be within sight of the summit at least, but still looking up I could see nothing. Our pace was dictated by the slowest and, because of the ropes, was painfully slow. Mentally this was the most difficult part of the climb to deal with. I had felt so close, and now it seemed I would never get there.

Suddenly the fog was blown away in a huge gust of wind, and looking up, I saw the summit for the first time, still distressingly far away. How could those final 50m take so long? By now the air was getting very thin and for the first time I was aware of how exhausted I was and how much I was panting. Actually seeing the summit was a spur, and I knew I was going to do my utmost to get there. All thoughts of safety and not taking risks disappeared from my mind, and I let go of the rope and forced myself upwards. A couple of the Armenians had the same urge and we almost raced for the summit, no doubt an absurd spectacle to those lower down.

The summit was so windy and such a small spot that my main emotion was fear of being blown over the edge. How ridiculous it would be to die because of the vanity of wanting to stand up tall. So I planted my rear firmly beside the summit pole and dug my crampons in to be certain I would not fall or slip while beginning the process of getting my camera out of my daypack. It required taking gloves off, a process made very tricky by the high winds and icy temperatures, but the Armenians had started on it, so I did too. All of us were covered in freezing snow, hair, eyebrows and eyelashes thick with ice. The sense of camaraderie and achievement was immense. We had shared in an the summit is within striking distance – on average a five- to six-hour climb – you will also have the sense of everything switching to a different gear. This is what you have come for, and everything becomes deadly serious. The reason for an ascent so early and in the dark, is to ensure enough time to reach the summit and return to Camp 2 before noon, because in the afternoon rockfalls and avalanches precipitated by the melting snow begin to become a real danger and are to be avoided at all costs. Early morning is also the best chance of good weather and therefore good visibility. The guides will check that you are adequately kitted out, that you have enough warm garments for both the top half and the bottom half of yourself (a minimum of two but preferably three warm layers), waterproof ski-gloves, head torch and of course crampons, which will be fitted for size to your walking boots. You will then be expected to carry these in your daypack, along with water and food. It is also advisable to take some basic medicines like paracetamol, ibuprofen and pastilles to suck. Most people spend the next few hours in their tent with the wind howling round, wondering what on earth they have let themselves in for and whether to abort now, before it is too late. 'Do you think this is wise?' we asked ourselves; 'Do you think we may be throwing our lives away?'

experience none of us were ever likely to have again. From the summit the winds were so strong we could only see below in brief snatches when the wind blew the fog away. It would come and go in a very disorientating way, making it difficult to get our bearings and focus downwards long enough to see where Camp 2 might be far below us.

After about 15 minutes we were all ready to come down, to get out of the wind and slightly into the shelter of the mountain again. Pure relief began to take over as the main emotion now, relief that I was safe, that I would be able to return safely to my husband and to my children who, back in England, had feared I might never return. Knowing that I struggled more with going downhill because of dodgy knees, Ahmet proffered me his arm to hold onto while we descended the snow field in a straight line. I felt safe and determined not to let go at any cost. We strode ahead, overtaking the Armenian party again, taking huge steps and sometimes, as we got a little lower where the snow was less solid, sinking up to our waists in snow, laughing and having to dig each other out. By now it was close to 07.00 and the sky had cleared a lot, leaving views all around as well as back up to the summit. North and east is Armenia, south is Iran and west is Turkey: three countries from one summit. Being able to see for the first time what we had just climbed was an immense exhilaration and I marvelled at how on earth we had done it.

The speed of the descent in the better weather conditions was remarkable, and within what seemed like no time at all, we were at the point where the snow field ended and the boulder field that led down to Camp 2 began. We could see the tiny colourful tents way below us, and wondered whether anyone could see us, little specks on the snowy mountain.

At this point Ahmet gestured to me that we might descend a different way, avoiding the boulder field entirely. It involved me sliding down a huge snow ramp beside the boulder field, while he would run beside me, keeping me in check by holding onto one of my trekking poles. Mindful of the Iranian lady who had slid to her near fatal injuries just a few days earlier by attempting to do something similar, I was hesitant. He assured me it would be fine. With my crampons as brakes and him holding one end of my trekking pole so that I could never get ahead of him, I slid spectacularly down the final 400m to Camp 2. Safely down at Camp 2, my bum trail was clear on the snow field, the only mark on the virgin snow.

Day 4 At midnight your guides will bring a simple breakfast for which you have no appetite but which you force yourself to eat. The temperature is −10°C even at the height of summer. Getting ready to emerge from the tent in a fully equipped state with your daypack all ready is the first challenge in the pitch dark, strong wind and uneven terrain. Heavy rain is also common at night. On hearing fierce rain lash against the tent, we called out to Ahmet, our guide, with undisguised relief:

'So now we will not go?'

'No, it is normal,' came the reply.

Only thick fog would prevent an ascent, as visibility is critical. More people die on Ararat from losing their way and getting separated from their party than for any other reason.

The first three hours of the ascent are the hardest, up a very steep, slippery, icy boulder field. The rocks are huge and there is no obvious path. In the dark, wearing your head torch, you have no sense of where you are heading except up, and you would be unwise to try to look up and see ahead. Ahmet had said: 'Do not look up, or you will be finished.' The best strategy is to shrink your horizons and focus only on your own feet. Check that your footing is sound, then take the next step. Think no further ahead than that. The trekking poles are invaluable here, to help keep your balance on the extremely slippery surface. Depending on the amount of snow that has fallen the previous winter, the rocks will be more or less snow-covered. The more snow there is, the more difficult the ascent, and the sooner your crampons will be required. At such low temperatures, the snow obviously freezes over and is very slippery. This is also the point at which, if you feel you are suffering or going to suffer from altitude sickness, you should think carefully about turning back. Many people find this ascent of the boulder field the most difficult part of the whole climb, and it is here that many lose heart.

If you can persevere for the two to three hours it takes, your reward will be to climb off the boulder face and onto a snow field. This is usually the first place where a proper rest is taken, and where crampons are put on. It is a good idea to eat and drink something here too. It is still pitch dark.

From this point on the going is easier. Underfoot is soft snow and the gradient is much less than on the boulder field. It begins to seem almost straightforward at this point, especially as after another hour or two, the first signs of daylight begin to appear in the sky. Never has dawn seemed so welcome, removing one element of danger from the ascent.

Once there is enough light to see by, you will able to tell what the weather conditions really are, and whether it is foggy or not. Owing to the strong winds, fog and mist come and go very quickly and the weather is usually changing all the time. By this stage you may have allowed yourself to think you can reach the summit, that it is within striking distance, but it is still not a good idea to look up at what lies ahead, even assuming the weather conditions permit you to see. Best to still focus on the immediate few metres in front of you, concentrating fully on each step, making certain you are safe. This next phase lasts quite a long time and it would be unwise to get ahead of yourself. See the box on pages 308–9 for a description of the final approach to the summit. Once you have reached it and taken in the views, you begin the descent back to Camp 2.

By now it is usually about 10.00, and after a brief rest and snack at Camp 2, the descent begins straight down to Camp 1, where you can rest again and have a very welcome lunch. Depending on your joints, you can either stay here another night, or, as most do, continue with the descent all the way back to 2,200m where transport will be waiting to take you back to your hotel. For this section from Camp 1 to 2,200m you can also arrange to ride a horse down, though be warned that the resultant saddle sores after two hours' lurching about may well be worse than any joint pain from walking. My own took two weeks to heal (as did my lips from forgetting to use sun-block). Riding a horse on the steeper gradients from Camp 1 to Camp 2, either up or down, is too dangerous and the guides will not permit it. Expect to return by about 18.00 to your hotel, a hot shower, food and bed. Make sure you take a full day of rest to readjust before continuing your itinerary, as the extreme exertion will have taken its toll.

10

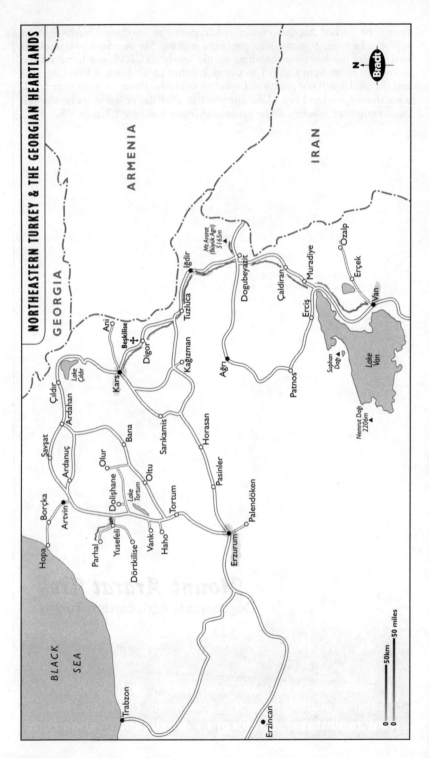

NORTHEASTERN TURKEY & THE GEORGIAN HEARTLANDS

11

Northeastern Turkey and the Georgian Heartlands

Harmony should be sought even in the blast of a trumpet.

This northeast corner of Turkey from Mount Ararat up to the Black Sea coast boasts some of the most spectacular scenery anywhere in Turkey, with magnificent, heavily forested mountains, serene lakes and beautifully green and lush valleys. Water gushes everywhere and this is the place for Turkey's white-water rafting fraternity. The Kaçkar Mountains offer fantastic trekking landscapes, and much of the scenery in the Georgian valleys is reminiscent of the high Alps in summer with green meadows covered in tiny brightly coloured flowers. The difference is the buildings, for nowhere in the Alps will you find the ruins of Armenian churches and monasteries tucked away in remote valleys, or castles in black basalt perched on hilltops. Allow a minimum of two nights in this area, if you plan to pass through quickly, staying one night at Kars while you visit Ani, the Armenian ghost town right on the Russian border, and one night in the Artvin area while you visit Georgian churches, before continuing your itinerary onwards to the Black Sea coast. To do it justice however, you could easily spend a week or more, especially if you want to do some trekking in the Kaçkar Mountains. The main city of the northeast, Erzurum, has some interesting Islamic monuments, but can be safely bypassed if these do not appeal.

FROM DOĞUBEYAZIT TO KARS

GETTING THERE AND AWAY There is no direct bus service and Doğubeyazıt has no airport (Van is the nearest) or train line. The only way by public transport is to catch a minibus from Doğubeyazıt to Iğdır (45 minutes, TL5), then change and catch another minibus to Kars (three hours, TL15). As ever in this part of Turkey, having your own transport makes life a lot simpler.

TO IĞDIR The journey to Kars from Doğubeyazıt takes between three and four hours on good roads which are being improved all the time. The stretch as far as Iğdır skirting the western flank of Ararat is very picturesque. The mountain is usually cloaked in cloud and mist, looking totally unreal, and the occasions when it stands unobscured in all its glory are few and far between. The most likely time is early morning. If you are fortunate enough to have such a view, try to spot the dramatic Ahora Chasm, a dramatic rift in the north face, where the massive earthquake of 1840 occurred. The village of Ahora had stood there, lived in by Armenians, servicing the monastery of St James some 700m above the village. The earthquake buried all the buildings, destroying the village and killing 1,900 people. The entire northern face remains uninhabited today. The mountain was always sacred to the Armenian monks, and ascents were never contemplated.

All around the foothills of Ararat are the nomad tents stretched over the circular stone walls with wooden struts for support like Mongolian yurts. These are the central Asian tents on which the Seljuk *türbe* is thought to be modelled, with its circular drum and conical dome. The nomads' flocks of sheep can be enormous.

IĞDIR *Telephone code: 476; altitude: 895m*

The city of Iğdır with a population of 76,500 looks like an oasis of sudden greenery, lined with tall poplar trees bending in the strong wind. In feel it is quite unlike anything else in eastern Turkey, and its proximity to the Armenian border clearly has an effect, for the town centre with its wide clean streets and proper pavements lined with modern shops and businesses, and even a Migros supermarket, gives a much more European feel and even the people in the streets are dressed more like Westerners. In the centre a roundabout has at its core a huge green apple with a bite taken out, and pedestrians can sit in the bitten-out hole like a bench. It has its own university and on the outskirts of town you can stop for half an hour to look over the **Anıt Müze (Tomb Museum)** (⊕ *08.00–17.00 Mon–Fri; entry free*), a Turkish Genocide Monument and museum built in 1999. The museum is built below the tall monument and is free to all comers. Inside photos of mass graves and mutilated bodies found in Van, Kars, Erzincan, Bayburt and Erzurum are on display as evidence of the Turkish genocide by Armenians in 1870 and 1920 supported by the West and Russia; up to one million of them. Of course the difficulty with such museums and such photos is that they all look the same, each ethnic group displaying photos of what they claim to be their massacred fellow men, and in all honesty they could be either Turkish or Armenian, as none of the photos show whether or not they are circumcised. All skeletons look alike. There is no doubt that both sides committed ghastly atrocities, and probably the only way forward is for both sides to acknowledge that and move on.

GETTING THERE Iğdır's minibuses stop on the main road close to the Hotel Azer. The exact location is different for Doğubeyazıt and for Kars, but they are only a few minutes' walk apart.

🏠 WHERE TO STAY

🏠 **Hotel Azer** (35 rooms) \ 4581314; www.icemtour.com/turkeyhotels_azer_hotel_igdir_turkey. Central location close to the bus stop. Restaurant, snack bar & en-suite bedrooms. $$
🏠 **Hotel Dedemin** (22 rooms) Gençler Sokak; \ 2273920; www.hoteldedemin.com. Sauna, hammam & restaurant. $$

🏠 **Hotel Olimpia** (25 rooms) Evren Paşa Caddesi; \ 2271866; www.olimpiateol.com. In the town centre, very clean & modern looking. $$
🏠 **Alkis Otel** (18 rooms) Kars Caddesi; \ 2271568. Basic place centrally located. $

BEYOND IĞDIR

From Iğdır the road continues towards Tuzluca, a dual carriageway of excellent quality, passing through a very green rich agricultural landscape with lots of poplar trees and rice fields. The soil around Tuzluca is very rich and red. Tuzluca has salt mines (*tuz* is Turkish for 'salt') and you can see the entrance to the mines cut in the cliff to the right of the road as you leave town. A few kilometres after Tuzluca there are a choice of routes to Kars either via Kağizman or via Digor, the former Armenian village of Tekor. This latter route is more direct but used to be avoided because it required a permit owing to its proximity to the Armenian border. Now however with your own transport it can be driven without qualms and is by far the more scenic route on near-empty roads. Armenian military

✓ camps can still be seen here on the other side of the gorge, as the river forms the border. In the area around Digor several ruined Armenian churches can be sought out, though they are not that easy to find.

BEŞKILISE (Five Churches, Armenian name *Khtskonk*) This is a very rewarding excursion which you can only do with your own transport, and involves a walk of about 40 minutes to reach the cluster of churches, dramatically situated on a ledge jutting out into a spectacular river gorge, miles from any habitation. There are no signposts and to reach it you must drive on the main road north from Digor for about 3km until you see a track leading to a white pumice quarry over to the left about 1km off the tarmac. The track ends in this quarry where you leave your vehicle. You will need good footwear as the terrain is sometimes rough underfoot, with small rocks embedded in the earth. From here you head in a northwest direction across the fields until you reach the edge of the gorge after about ten minutes, looking out for a small grassy path that runs down into the gorge and then twists out of view to the north. Follow that for a further 25–30 minutes and you will be rewarded suddenly after rounding a corner with the first view of the churches, one of them, St Sergius, still standing to its full height complete with conical roof. In its spectacular gorge setting it is one of the most dramatic locations in all of eastern Turkey, the more so for being so remote. It was built in the 11th century by a Bagratid king. St Sergius's walls are covered in delicate inscriptions in Armenian script, which identify it and give it the date of 1029. Collapsed remains of three more circular churches lie close beside St Sergius, and the fifth church is also a heap of stones, the first one you encounter beside the path, some 100m before the others. All five were restored in 1878, but according to local information they were destroyed either by explosives or by rolling large boulders down onto them from above sometime between 1920 and 1965.

Good maps of the area also show the site of **Mren**, an Armenian 7th-century cathedral (Mirini) with fine reliefs on its façade and a well-preserved dome, in the Arpaçay Gorge, very close to the Armenian border, but there are no signposts and villagers from the nearby village of Dolaylı will say it has since fallen down. If you approach instead from the village of Karabağ, which is signposted some 21km southeast of Digor, along a dirt track, the church comes into view after about 2km. Continue through the village itself in the direction of the church, until the track becomes undriveable. From here the church is still about 50 minutes' walk away, on the far side of the Digor Çayi (river) and can only be reached by descending into the valley, crossing the river on a narrow bridge, and winding up the other side. The rubble of the original town lies round the church standing on its desolate plateau, but the church itself, built in the characteristic red and black alternating stone blocks, still rises to its full height and even has most of its roof tiles. It was built in 639–40 by the Prince of Armenia, David Saharuni, and is therefore one of the earliest examples of Armenian architecture. Its octagonal dome is supported by four columns, and its ground plan, with three naves and cross-in-square, shows a very strong Byzantine influence, as do the reliefs on the exterior walls, showing angels above the Christ figure, St Peter and St Paul, and over the north door, the Restoration of the Cross in 630 at Jerusalem.

From Digor it is a further 40km across empty summer *yaylas* (high summer pastures) to reach Kars.

KARS *Telephone code: 474; altitude: 1,768m*

The province of Kars borders onto today's Armenia and between 1878 and 1917 it was part of Russia, something which is still apparent in the feel of the place.

The Siege of Kars is the title of a book (The Stationery Office, 2000) originally published in 1855 by General Williams, a British officer seconded to the Turkish army to train regiments in the war against Russia, and the town is also the setting for Orhan Pamuk's novel *Snow* (Kar), a complex story about a poet/journalist investigating local female suicides. Kars in dry weather is something of a rarity. Prepare yourself for wetness and a certain amount of mud. *Wd wevt bořkd*

GETTING THERE AND AWAY

By air Kars airport is 6km west of the centre, and Turkish Airlines (*www.anadolujet.com*) has a daily flight to and from Ankara (just under two hours, TL114) and to and from Istanbul (just over two hours, TL114), while Sun Express (*www.sunexpress.com.tr*) flies twice a week to and from Izmir (two hours, TL144). There are also flights direct from Kars run by Hamburg International (www.hamburg-international.de) flying weekly to and from Cologne/Bonn. Servis taxis run to the airport from the airline offices in the centre of town.

By train Kars's train station lies 1km to the southeast of the centre, and can be useful for the four-hour ride to Erzurum (TL10). The long-distance *Doğu Ekspresi* (Eastern Express) sets off every day for Istanbul at 07.10 via Erzurum, Kayseri and Ankara (TL40 to Istanbul), and there is also the *Erzurum Ekspresi* that heads for Ankara at 09.00 every day via Erzurum and Kayseri.

By bus Kars's *otogar* lies 2km southeast of the centre, and this is what you need for the long-haul destinations, such as Artvin (six hours, TL25), Erzurum (three hours, TL15, Trabzon (six hours, TL40) or Van (six hours, TL30). Services are far less frequent than in other parts of the country, sometimes only one a day, so it is worth double-checking before just turning up. The main bus companies, like **Doğu Kars**, **Turgutreis** and **Kafkas Kars**, have offices in the town centre.

By minibus The minibus terminal is 500m east of the main street Atatürk, on a road running east–west called Küçük Kazım Bey Caddesi.

TOURIST INFORMATION The tourist office (🕒 *08.00–12.00 & 13.00–17.00 Mon–Fri*) is on Lise Caddesi, a little to the west of the centre, and gives out maps and leaflets as usual. For tours to Ani the hotels are generally the best bet, or very often prospective guides will be lurking at the *otogar*.

WHERE TO STAY

Kar's Otel (8 rooms) Halitpaşa Caddesi; 2121616; www.karsotel.com. Amazing place to find in unlikely Kars, this small boutique hotel is the most expensive place in eastern Turkey. Set in a 19th-century converted black basalt Russian mansion, the contrasting modern interior design is white & minimalist, so not to everyone's taste. Its restaurant, the Ani, is likewise mega-pricey & very exclusive. Often booked solid, there is clearly money around these, so be sure to reserve ahead if you want to push the boat out. Good location within a short walk of the citadel & Church of the Apostles. $$$$$

Grand Ani Hotel (68 rooms) Ordu Caddesi 14; 2237500. A 6-storey modern new addition to Kars' accommodation, by itself a little southwest of the centre, close to the army base.

Wireless internet & free airport shuttle bus, but no restaurant, room service or bar. $$$

Hotel Karabağ (45 rooms) Faik Bey Caddesi; 2129304; www.hotel-karabag.com. Central location, a modern high-rise block with lots of flags flying outside, but rather overpriced as neither the rooms nor the b/fast is anything special. Mainly used by businessmen. $$$

Güngören Hotel (33 rooms) Millet Sokak; 2125630. Good location close to the citadel & Church of the Apostles. Spacious rooms with modern fittings. Good-value mid-range place with b/fast & its own restaurant, & men-only *hammam*. $$

Kent Otel (35 rooms) Hapan Mevkii; 2231929. Basic but cheap rooms with mainly shared bathrooms. Backs onto other hotels. No b/fast. $

WHERE TO EAT

Ani Restaurant (⊕ 12.00–15.00 & 18.00–22.00) Inside the Kar's Otel, a gastronomic extravaganza a million miles away from the local staple of kebabs & salad. You will need to dress up a little not to feel uncomfortable & make

sure you savour every mouthful to stomach the cost. $$$$

Fasil Ocakbaşı Faik Bey Caddesi; 2121714; ⊕ 09.00–23.00. Unlikely location on the 1st floor of a nondescript building, but this place is

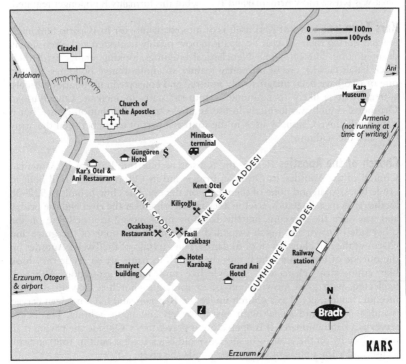

even licensed & has very good grills & *mezze*. At the w/ends there may be live music. $$
✗ Ocakbaşı Restaurant Atatürk Caddesi; ✎ 2120056; ⏰ 09.30–22.30. A good local restaurant in 2 parts with very good food. Pleasantly cosy feel, with its almost cave-like interior. No alcohol. $$

✗ Kiliçoğlu Faik Bey Caddesi; ✎ 2126039; ⏰ 09.00–21.00. This is basically a smart ice-cream parlour & *pastanhane* where you can select from a big range of puddings & sticky pastries at very reasonable prices. $

ENTERTAINMENT To get alcohol you can visit one of the many seedy-looking bars along Atatürk Caddesi towards the river end of the street. With their red lighting some of them look as if they might be brothels, but if you are desperate for a beer, this is where you will get it.

SHOPPING Kars is famous for its honey and its cheeses, and specialist shops selling just this can be found all along Atatürk Caddesi, the main street that runs towards the river and the citadel. Stock up here for picnics, and there are also excellent bakers along this street for wonderful fresh bread. Even these small shops stay open until about 20.30.

OTHER PRACTICALITIES Kars's ATMs, banks and internet cafés will all be found along the main street of Atatürk Caddesi.

WHAT TO SEE The main reason to come to Kars, and which does make it all worthwhile, is to visit the haunting Ani, a true Armenian ghost town, unlike Ahlat, on the Armenian (formerly Soviet) border 42km east. A special permit used to be required because of its sensitive location in the 700m of no-man's-land between what was Russia (now Armenia) and Turkey, but this formality is no longer required.

Kars Town The town of Kars itself is of interest mainly for its Russian buildings, erected during their 40-year occupation, now mainly neglected and often slowly disintegrating. The once-fine Neoclassical buildings, looking strange with their black basalt façades, are in use today mainly as administrative buildings, though one or two have been imaginatively restored and converted into boutique hotels, a trend that is likely to continue as tourism starts to increase. One Russian Orthodox church was formerly in use as an electricity distribution centre, but is now the Fethiye Camii, by itself in the southern part of town, between the army base and the stadium.

Church of the Apostles Besides the Russian architecture Kars has its Armenian Church of the Apostles, its Ottoman bridge and its Ottoman citadel, all built in crude black basalt and none of them easy on the eye. The church, built in 932–38 by the Armenian Bagratids, is set in a scruffy clearing near the river and the bridge and was once the museum, but this has now been moved to a new site on the other side of town and much extended. The church has none of the grace and charm of the Ani churches or of Akdamar. The carvings of the Twelve Apostles on the outside of the dome which give the church its name are so crude they look like comic-strip characters, gargoyle-like and faintly grotesque. Although neglected, with grass growing out of its roof, the church is now in use as a mosque, having served as a church under the Russians, and has a modern carved wooden *mimber* and *mihrab* with garish carpets and neon lighting. The belfry serves as a handy minaret. It is open around prayer times. Outside the paving is all new. Close by on the river is the attractive old black bridge, built in 1580 and still in use, and with a pleasant tea-garden beside the river.

Citadel (⏱ *08.00–17.00 daily; admission free*) The big black citadel dominates, glowering squatly over the town. Until recently it was in use as a military camp and not visitable, but the military have now left and it is open to the public. The first castle was built here in 1153 by the Saltuk Turks, then ravaged and torn down by the dreaded Tamerlane. The Ottomans built it up again in 1579, but it was destroyed once more in the siege of 1855 and had to be rebuilt. In World War I it was the scene of bitter fighting between the Russians and the Turks, and after the war it was given back to Turkey with the rest of the province in 1925. There is nothing to see inside except a park and the view back over the town. ✓ 2005

Beside the old black bridge are two Turkish baths recognisable by their domes, now disused, one to the right, one to the left of the bridge. Funds are said to have been allocated for their restoration.

Museum (*Cumhuriyet Caddesi;* ⏱ *08.00–17.00 Tue–Sun; adult TL3*) The new museum is on the eastern edge of town and is worth a quick visit if you want to see photos of some of the other Armenian churches in Kars Province apart from Ani. It also has photos of excavations at Ani. Upstairs is mainly an ethnographic section with some fine *kilims.*

Kars used to have some fine old steam engines that puffed their way to Erzurum in seven hours, but they have now been replaced with diesel locomotives that take just four hours.

ANİ 42km east of Kars

(⏱ *daily 08.00–18.00; adult TL5*)

HISTORY The name Ani comes from Anahid, an ancient Persian goddess identified with Aphrodite. Before Gregory the Illuminator, founder of the Armenian Church, she was one of the chief deities of the Armenians. The city grew up here on a major east–west caravan route, amassing great wealth which its Armenian rulers later used to endow the city with sumptuous churches. The **Bagratid kings** who transferred their capital here, claiming descent from kings David and Solomon of Israel, were one of the leading princely families to survive after 428 when Armenia was divided between the Byzantines and the Persians. It was such semi-autonomous families who preserved the Armenian and also the Georgian nationhood, for the Bagratid family and its various offshoots provided the rulers in both Armenia and Georgia for many hundreds of years.

In its size and magnificence in the mid 10th century, nothing in Europe could touch Ani, and in the East only Constantinople, Cairo and Baghdad were its rivals. In the superb architecture of Ani you have the inspiration for much that we now call Seljuk: the powerfully built walls and the graceful *türbe* shapes that became the standard mausoleum shape for the next few centuries. The Armenians were renowned stonemasons and the quality of workmanship of what remains at Ani bears witness to their technical virtuosity, the best in the world at that time.

The Mongol raids, combined with a severe earthquake in 1319, and the *coup de grâce* of Tamerlane, destroyed forever this town whose population at its height was said to number 200,000, some three times the current population of Kars.

GETTING THERE Taxi-minibuses taking a minimum of six people run to Ani from outside the Kars tourist office (TL30). To hire a private taxi (ordered via your hotel) costs around TL80 including the driver waiting while you look round. The excursion to Ani should be seen as a half-day trip from Kars, allowing about two hours to explore the site fully. The 42km approach is now a dual carriageway,

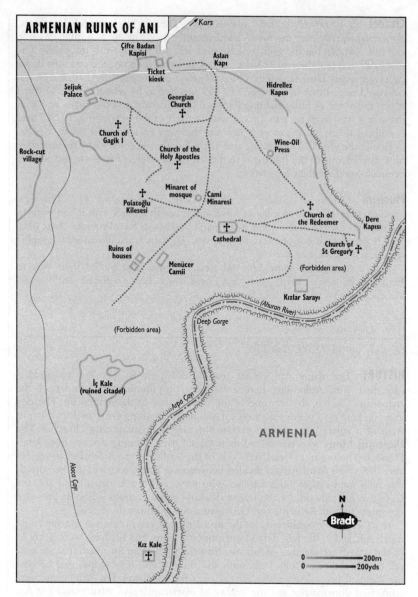

ARMENIAN RUINS OF ANI

↗ Kars

Çifte Badan Kapisi

Aslan Kapı

Ticket kiosk

Hidrellez Kapısı

Seljuk Palace

Georgian Church ✝

✝ Church of Gagik I

Wine-Oil Press

Rock-cut village

Church of the Holy Apostles ✝

Minaret of mosque ○ Cami Minaresi

✝ Poiatoğlu Kilesesi

✝ Church of the Redeemer

Dere Kapısı

✝ Cathedral

Church of St Gregory ✝

Ruins of houses

(Forbidden area)

Menücer Camii

Kızlar Sarayı

(Ahuran River)

(Forbidden area)

Deep Gorge

İç Kale (ruined citadel)

Arpa Çay

ARMENIA

Alaca Çay

N

Bradt

Kız Kale ✝

0 ———— 200m
0 ———— 200yds

whereas in the 1980s it was a narrow potholed road. It takes less than half an hour and the road passes through a couple of simple villages and an otherwise flat green landscape with deep red rich soil and fields full of grazing horses, cows, geese and chickens. The road ends at a car park by the walls where there is a small kiosk selling drinks, snacks and postcards, and tucked just by the huge gateway is the new ticket office.

PRACTICALITIES Photography used to be strictly forbidden here, but is unrestricted now. There are still a few areas at the far end of the site off towards the citadel which remain out of bounds, but they are clearly marked. Do not be tempted to ignore the signs, or you may find yourself shot at or arrested. There is no shade at the site apart from inside the remaining buildings themselves, so in summer make sure you have a hat, suncream and plenty of water. Local children try to sell you water for exorbitant prices if you run out. There are no WC facilities on site.

SITE VISIT The colossal sand-coloured walls are a triumph of Armenian architecture, and nowhere else in Turkey will you see an entire walled Armenian city like this. The walls form the third side of a triangle, the other two sides of which are the deep ravines of two rivers, the Arpaçay and the Alacaçay. The main double gate with its defensive dog-leg is now supported by metal girders. It is known as Aslan Kapısı (Lion Gate) because of the fine Seljuk sculpted lion that adorns it. This is the only one of Ani's original four gates to survive. Looking back up at the gate tower from the inside you will see the age-old swastika motif inset in the sandy walls.

Passing through the gate you see Ani for the first time. In front of you is an eerie scene of a destroyed city stretching ahead and to the sides over green grassy land towards the hills of Armenia. The Arpaçay Gorge that separates Turkey from Armenia can only be sensed from here. Of Ani, 'city of a hundred gates and a thousand churches', all that remains today is the rubble and shells of a few of its most robust churches.

The area has now been laid out in neat paths with signposts labelling the major landmarks. From the main gate you can take the right or the left path – it makes no odds as the path runs in a circuit that can be done in either direction. If you fork right, you can begin by walking towards the western walls, and get an interesting view into a small canyon where there are many caves cut into the reddish cliffs opposite, some of them used as rock churches. Built into the walls themselves is a rather over-restored **Seljuk Palace**, which has received so much attention it looks rather out of place. Much remains to be excavated at Ani, and it is to be hoped that future work is carried out sensitively.

Most people on organised tours take the left fork that leads on a wide path straight towards the semi-circular shell of the half-collapsed **Church of the Redeemer**. Built in 1034, the fact that one half stands intact while the other half has collapsed, not because of an earthquake centuries ago but because it was struck by lightning in 1957, adds to the curiously unreal scene. The half that remains carries Armenian inscriptions and carved Armenian crosses on the

SWASTIKA MOTIF

The origins of the swastika are unknown. It has been used for thousands of years as a symbol of the sun, of infinity and continuing recreation and fertility in Sumeria, China, India, Egypt, Greece, Scandinavia, the Americas and elsewhere. It has been found in the catacombs of Rome, on the textiles of the Incas and on relics unearthed at Troy. It is also one of the sacred signs of Buddhism. The word comes from the Sanskrit *svastika* meaning 'prosperity', and it was thought to bring good luck. As a decorative motif, it exists in many distorted forms on the doors of nearly all Seljuk and Ottoman buildings, notably on the gateways of Diyarbakır, and in the gateway of the Karatay Mosque in Konya. Some extremist Teutonic nationalists in Austria began to use it in the mistaken belief that the swastika was of Indian origin and therefore an Aryan motif symbolising their self-designated racial superiority. Hitler himself saw it as symbolising, in his own words: 'The fight for victory of Aryan man and of the idea of creative work, which in itself eternally has been anti-Semitic and eternally will be anti-Semitic.'

An Armenian poet on seeing Ani as it is now wrote this lament:

> Where are the thrones of our kings? They are seen nowhere. Where are the legions of soldiers that massed before them like dense cloud formations, colourful as the flowers of spring, and resplendent in their uniforms? They are nowhere to be seen. Where is our great and marvellous pontifical throne? Today it is vacant, deprived of its occupant, denuded of its ornaments, filled with dust and spiders' webs, and the heir to the throne removed to a foreign land as a captive and a prisoner. The voices and the sermons of the priests are silent now. The chandeliers are extinguished now and the lamps dimmed, the sweet fragrance of incense is gone, the altar of Our Lord is covered with dust and ashes. Now if all that we have related has befallen us because of our wickedness, then tell heaven and all that abide in it, tell the mountains and the hills, the trees of the dense woodlands, that they too may weep over our destruction.

outside wall about 3m above the ground. This frieze of crosses set in an elaborate rectangular background is the distinctive Armenian motif called *khatchkar*, meaning 'cross-stone', from which the Kaçkar Mountains have taken their name. Shortly before the church a sign labels a 12th-century oil press, with its huge grinding stone, though some scholars have speculated this is more likely to have been a wine press, the cultivation of grapes being more likely in these conditions and at this altitude than the cultivation of olive trees, which are only found much further south in the milder climate.

From here you now walk on towards the edge of the ravine and down some steps to **St Gregory's Church**, also known as Resimli Kilise (the Church with the Pictures), because of its beautifully coloured frescoes. Built in 1215 it is the loveliest and best preserved of Ani's remaining churches and has been undergoing heavy restoration in recent years, and is covered in scaffolding. All the murals are painted on the deep royal-blue background of the Sassanid tradition, and most of them depict scenes from the life of Gregory the Illuminator, *Tigran Honents*, apostle to the Armenians. On its south (riverside) wall is a sundial, a common Armenian feature. The dome and walls are delicately carved with animals like peacocks, stags and dragons amid garlands of foliage. Set on a lower terrace of the ravine, this is the closest you will come to the Armenian border that is formed by the Arpa Çayı itself. You can still see the guard posts on the other side, the ex-Russian ones green, the Turkish ones grey. Before the 1990s when all visits to Ani were conducted with a permit under military escort, the atmosphere here was totally silent, no children pestering you, no coach tours. Even now, if you are lucky, you can still enjoy this haunting atmosphere in quieter moments in some parts of the site.

From the Church of St Gregory you continue next towards the **Cathedral of Ani** itself. This late 10th-century building, superbly proportioned, still has its roof for the most part, but there are sections where you look through gaping holes to the sky. Its architect was the famous Trdat who rebuilt the Aya Sofya dome in Constantinople after it collapsed in the earthquake of 989. Like most Armenian architecture it is unusual in having a very high ceiling for its length and width, and its height is equal to its width (c22m) while its length is c40m. It is in fact by far the largest church left standing in Turkey. With no murals, its beauty lies totally in its bare style and its proportions. From the outside it has the characteristic blind arches. There is also superb use of two-coloured stone on the columns outside, black and red.

From here the path now leads on to an 11th-century mosque, the **Menüçer Camii**, with an octagonal minaret standing on the very edge of the ravine. This most unusual building feels inside more like a palace than a mosque. Built in 1072 just one year after the Battle of Manzikert where the Seljuks defeated the Byzantines, it is the first mosque built in Anatolia by the Seljuk Turks. Inside, its ceiling is beautifully decorated with the two red and black stones cut into geometric motifs and a 'stars in heaven' design as well as some *swastikas*. The patterning on the ceiling is reminiscent of the Mameluke *muqarnas* and this style is clearly the forerunner of the *ablaq* black and white stone contrasting patterning of the black basalt and white limestone so widely used in Syria in Mamluk times. The windows face directly out over the ravine, one with a pointed arch, the others curved. The foundations of the building are 8m deep, but the lower levels of the buildings are not accessible, though you can peer down into the deep hole. Sitting on the windowsill of the mosque you have a magnificent view over the gorge. In the total silence you can hear below the lovely rushing sound of the river in the ravine below. The steps leading up the minaret are very crumbling and a climb up is not advisable.

Down in the gorge to the right is what appears to be an island in the river, but which is in fact a peninsula jutting out from the Turkish side. On the summit of this hillock-shaped peninsula is a building with three vaulted arches, called the **Kızlar Sarayı**, literally Girls' Palace, thought to have been a convent. Above it, at the top of the ravine, is the citadel with its defence walls rising up the hillside. This whole section is out of bounds, and a large notice just past the Menüçer Camii prohibits access, though there is no actual fence blocking the area off. You can, however, explore the series of interesting houses here just past the mosque, recently excavated. They date to the 12th century and have curious circular holes cut into stone slabs in the ground and blackened areas like chimneys. The butterfly life here is wonderfully abundant, with clouded yellows, marbled whites and swallowtails.

From the mosque you now walk away from the ravine, first passing an excavated area of shops along a main street, complete with baker's oven, then towards the second Church of St Gregory, built in 994, labelled as **Polatoğlu Kilesesi** or the Pavlavi king of East Bulamir or Abu Gharents from Horosan. Its dome is still intact and its striking 12-sided exterior has 12 blind recessed windows. On its southeast exterior wall is a sundial that would have been used to help determine set prayer times, a practice that goes back to distant Christianity. The scallop shell symbol used in the exterior decoration is a symbol of pilgrimage. Inside, in the eastern apse there are traces of blue paint and several birds' nests. The nearby **Church of the Holy Apostles**, dated to 1031, looks at first to be heavily ruined, but is in fact an interesting hybrid because the Seljuks adapted it, after conquering Ani in 1064, to be a caravanserai. If you trouble to identify the church nave, however, you will notice the beautiful ceiling in two-colour stone patterns with ribbing arcs and a dome with *muqarnas* (stalactite) vaulting.

You come now towards the end of your circuit to the collapsed round **Church of Gagik I** (989–1019), not the same king as the earlier Gagik of Akdamar. Impressive because of its huge scale, this building has survived less well because of its roundness which made it an inherently weaker structure. Built in 1001 its circular style with an interior circle of columns is unique in Armenian architecture. Earthquakes got the better of the experiment. The fallen blocks still carry many Armenian crosses and scrolls. In its centre is a deep well, maybe some kind of sacred spring, an idea the Armenians were keen on.

Other Armenian remains In the vicinity of Ani there are several fine Armenian monasteries and a particularly fine Armenian castle, called Magazbert, of the 10th century, in almost perfect preservation, two hours' walk away to the southwest. All of these used to be out of bounds because of their closeness to the Russian border, but it is possible that today, things may have improved sufficiently for a guide to escort you.

ROUTES NORTH AND WEST

From Kars it is possible to drive direct to the Black Sea coast at Hopa, avoiding Erzurum altogether. This route passes through the highly scenic mountain region which was once the heartland of Georgia and is a very rewarding trip. Remote Georgian churches can still be visited here, along with beautiful and unexpected lakes, and now that roads have improved and there is a bit more accommodation available, it has become perfectly feasible to spend several days in the area, staying in simple but beautifully located pensions, high in the forested hills. The roads are almost empty and the region is quite sparsely populated.

For those who prefer the cities and want to see some fine urban Islamic architecture rather than rural Georgian churches, an alternative route is covered at the end of this chapter, from Kars via Erzurum to Trabzon.

NORTH VIA LAKE ÇILDIR, ARDAHAN AND ŞAVŞAT TO ARTVİN

There is now a new fast road from Kars north towards Susuz and the fork off from it towards Arpa Çayı and Çildir is clearly signposted. The road is dead straight and heads north across an attractive but treeless landscape of rolling grassland.

GETTING THERE AND AWAY Minibuses run from Kars to Sarıkamiş, Ardahan and Posof at the Georgian border, but not to Lake Çıldır. It may be possible to find a *dolmuş* taxi, but if not, you will need your own transport for this route.

✗ WHERE TO EAT There is no accommodation around the lake, but there is one simple fish restaurant, Balık Lokantasi ($), about 8km before Cildir Town on the shore of Lake Çıldır.

WHAT TO SEE

Lake Çıldır Lake Çıldır has a slight feel of a miniature Lake Van, wild and remote, but ringed with gentler mountains. At 1,950m it is 200m higher than Van and the land is under snow for eight months of the year. From November to April the lake is frozen over. In season large colonies of waterbirds can be seen. At the village of Doğruyol is an early 11th-century domed Armenian church, the Church of the Mother of God, not visible from the road. Getting to the actual lakeshore can be surprisingly difficult, as the road is always just that bit too far away and there are very few tracks down to the lake. The easiest place is where a brown sign points left to Akçakale and Ada Şehri, where you can drive down into the village and cross a causeway onto a small grassy island. On a hilltop here are the vestigial remains of a medieval fort with large stone blocks in its foundations, and a heavily ruined 11th-century Armenian church lower down the slope. The village football pitch is ranged beside a megalithic sanctuary. The spot is quite deserted except at weekends in the summer. Along the lakeshore are several monastery and church ruins, often difficult to reach. The road winds round the northern shore, and near the northwest tip of the lake is Gölbelen, with a domed Georgian 11th-century basilica used today as the village mosque. It still has a nave and triple apse and dome, with unusual carved capitals and vegetal motifs in its sculptured stonework. A road forks off south along the west shore of the lake but is very difficult for a saloon car. With a jeep or minibus, however, you could visit Pekresin with its ruins of a double church and a Kurdish cemetery.

Devil's Castle After leaving the town of Çildir to the north of the lake, the road starts to climb and soon after there is a brown sign pointing off to the right announcing Şeytan Kalesi, the Devil's Castle. You can just glimpse the medieval fortress from the road, dramatically perched on a cliff edge in the gorge to your right. To reach it, take the fork into the village of Yildirimtepe, and when you reach a second fork, bear left, staying up, rather than forking right and down into the village proper. The left track continues on the same level, running round the top of the village, to end in a cluster of simple houses with ducks and geese quacking about your feet. From here it is a further 20-minute walk along a very attractive grassy wide path that follows the left side of the gorge, with huge drops of over 300m below to a river. From a distance the castle looks totally inaccessible, but as you get closer you will see that the path in fact leads you right up to it. Once inside the wall you will see two cisterns, and a small path runs up to the keep. The spot is utterly isolated, one of the most dramatically sited castles in the country.

ARDAHAN *Telephone code: 478*

The road continues west, passing through very attractive heavily pine-forested hills, to reach Ardahan, set in an austere high steppeland on a riverbank opposite a mighty citadel rebuilt by the Ottoman sultan Selim the Grim in the 16th century. The town was occupied by Russia from 1873 until 1921 and in the heavy fighting many buildings were destroyed and rebuilt, giving the town quite a modern aspect with broad streets and pretty gardens. The castle (*kale*) can be visited when the gate is left open, but there is nothing inside. The walls have been restored and there are fine views over the river.

From Ardahan the road continues for 44km to Şavşat, a pretty drive that climbs over the Cam Pass at 2,640m and then makes a spectacular drop winding down in hairpin bends through heavily forested mountain slopes. Here for the first time you get a taste of the scenery of the Georgian valleys.

 WHERE TO STAY The **Büyük Ardahan Otel and Restoran** (*Kars Avenue;* \ *2116498; $$*) is a modern faceless four-storey block in the centre of town, but OK, with licensed restaurant, internet and garden.

THE GEORGIAN VALLEYS

The closest thing to these magnificent Georgian valleys are scenes in the remotest corners of the Pyrenees or the Alps. With the sudden superabundance of timber, the houses are all made of dark wood, with gables for the snow to slide off, rustic versions of Alpine chalets. In between the forest are grassy clearings and slopes, excellent pasture for cattle. There is very little habitation before you reach Şavşat, just a couple of camping spots, tucked away among the trees on the descent. You would need at least four days to see the main churches here, though most people just content themselves with seeing one or two as they pass through È to the Black Sea. Coach tours can only reach Öşk Vank and Dolişhane, so the remainder are barely visited and you are likely to have them to yourself. Alternative bases are Artvin and Yusufeli where there is adequate accommodation, or Parhal if you are going trekking in the Kaçkar Mountains. The villagers in this region, descendants of the Georgians, are like a different race from the inhabitants of Erzurum or Doğubeyazıt.

11

HISTORY Though ethnically distinct, the Armenians and the Georgians shared a similar history of invasions and counter-invasions, and through frequent intermarriage they became to some extent mixed. The Bagratid family for example featured large in Armenian history, as rulers of Ani and Kars, and also in Georgian history, as rulers of the upper Çoruh Valley at Bayburt, İspir and Ardanuç. There were many branches of the Bagratid family and rivalries were constant, with various barons controlling small sections independently of each other. The Seljuk conquest in the 11th century put an end to these little fiefdoms for a time, but by the early 12th century a new young king, David the Restorer, attempted to re-establish authority over the semi-independent barons, then drove the Seljuks out of the Georgian heartlands and recaptured Ispir and even Tiflis, the ancient Armenian capital in the east, now in the Armenian Republic.

In the 13th and 14th centuries Georgia suffered heavily under Mongol attacks, especially that of Tamerlane. He had singled out Georgia as the bulwark of Christianity in Asia, and inflicted an especially vicious series of invasions, leaving its cities, towns and villages in ruins. Georgia never really recovered from the onslaught. The land was depopulated, the remaining inhabitants exhausted and without central authority. A few semi-independent barons again set up small domains, but in this weakened condition Georgia could not withstand Ottoman power. When the Trebizond Comnene Empire fell to the Ottomans in 1461, it was the beginning of the end for Georgia. By 1552 a detachment of Janissaries was stationed in the ancient Bagratid fortress of Ardanuç.

In the 18th and 19th centuries the Georgians, like the Armenians, saw in the Russians a fellow Christian ally, and like the Armenians they were punished by their Turkish masters. The Ottomans held only loose control over Georgia, content to let the princes and barons squabble among themselves in their endless family feuding. Russian advances, however, were seen by the porte as attempts to extend her borders southwards using Georgia as a stepping stone, and this inevitably was to lead to war between Russia and Turkey; a series of wars in fact, each more horrible than the last, culminating in the bloody Battle of Sarıkamış during World War I.

THE GEORGIANS

The Georgians have had little influence on the history of Turkey. They speak a non-Indo-European language which belongs, like Laz (the language spoken on the Black Sea), to the Caucasian group. At the controversial Council of Chalcedon in the 5th century when the Armenian and Nestorian churches broke away from the Greek Orthodox Church, the Georgians sided with the Greeks, and there were always close links between Byzantium and Georgia. Byzantine emperors endowed churches here, sending craftsmen, architects and masons to build and decorate them. The Georgians themselves drew almost entirely on Armenian and Byzantine models, and though they provided little architectural inspiration of their own, they may well have been the channel through which Byzantine influence passed into Russia. The churches all have the Armenian drum and conical dome, later incorporating the basilical plan. The carving on the outer stonework of the walls, with animals and rich garlands, is also highly reminiscent of Armenian styles. There are some 50,000 Georgians in Turkey and the language is still spoken in the remoter valleys and mountains of the extreme northeast. Many still have ginger hair and freckles, and they are more dignified in manner and the children less pesky. You will not be made to feel here like a tourist curiosity to be peered and poked at, but like a guest who has taken the trouble to come and visit the remoter parts of the country.

GETTING THERE AND AROUND Public transport in the Georgian valleys is dependent on local minibuses, requiring lots of changes and timings are not that frequent. Since most of the Georgian churches are tucked up remote side valleys anyway, the best public transport can do is drop you at the turnings. Having your own transport, be it car, motorbike or bicycle, will transform matters from a time-consuming hassle into a pleasure.

WHERE TO STAY AND EAT

🏠 **Laşet Motel** (7 rooms) 8km east of Şavşat, on the Ardahan road; ✆ 466 5712136. Idyllic chalet-style place with a lovely wide terrace beside a rushing stream where the owners have made a couple of trout pools, & where trout is the main item on the menu. Quite a find in this part of the country, but also quite pricey for the small timber-lined rooms. The name Laset is the name of a nearby mineral spring & means 'bitter water' in Georgian. New in 2009, it has also opened a series of 10 wooden holiday bungalows designed for families of 4, with a double bedroom, a twin-bedded room & a living room. Excellent b/fast

with homemade jam & honey. Takes credit cards, unusually for this part of the country. $$$
🏠 **Saray Motel/Restaurant** ✆ (466) 2947. Simple place by the roadside between Şavşat & Artvin. $
🏠 **Yeşil Vadı Touristlik Otel** Şavşat; ✆ (466) 5171770. Basic stopping place on the road. $
⛺ **Camping** Available in several places around Şavşat, in green wooded valleys. Facilities are adequate but basic. $
✕ **Saman Yolu Restoran** ⏱ 10.00–21.00. Attractively situated, between Şavşat & the turn-off to Meydancik. Offering the local trout from the river. $$

WHAT TO SEE The Georgian valleys can be approached from three directions: east from Ardahan, north from Tortum and south from Hopa. All three routes converge at Artvin. The following description assumes what is probably the commonest starting point – north from Tortum, which is also the route most readily practicable by public transport, as a minibus runs once a day from Erzurum to Artvin, so you can ask to be dropped off. However you travel, simply pick and choose the ones that appeal most to you and the ones that can most readily be incorporated into your itinerary.

Leaving Erzurum on the Artvin road the first stretch of 50km or so to Tortum is on a good straight and relatively flat road. The town of Tortum is a small place engaged in the timber trade with many felled and sawn-up trees in stacks at the roadside.

From here the road now enters the beginning of a gorge with the muddy Tortum River running through it. The scenery as the gorge begins to narrow becomes very pretty with bright green trees and lush vegetation on the hillsides. The population throughout this valley is sparse, with just a few tiny villages appearing occasionally on the riverbanks. Most of the villages in fact lie up in the side valleys, approached by narrow roads, sometimes unsurfaced, from the main road. The main Georgian churches are generally signposted these days, and are either derelict ruins or renovated by the villagers and converted into their mosque.

Haho The first one you come to, off the road 26km north of Tortum, is the 10th-century Georgian church of Haho, signposted as *Taş Kilise, Meryemana Kilisesi*, and lies 8km off the main road. Begin by crossing the small hump-backed bridge, then bear left in the first village, then left again to İspir beside a modern mosque, to reach the centre of the village of Bağbaşı with a handful of shops, tea-houses and the Belediye building. Continue on through the village, bearing left whenever there is a choice, until you reach the church some 300m beyond the centre, identifiable by the little breeze-block ablution huts built just on the right of the road.

This interesting church with its typical but distinctive conical dome in the lovely soft yellow colour of the local sandstone was originally part of a monastic

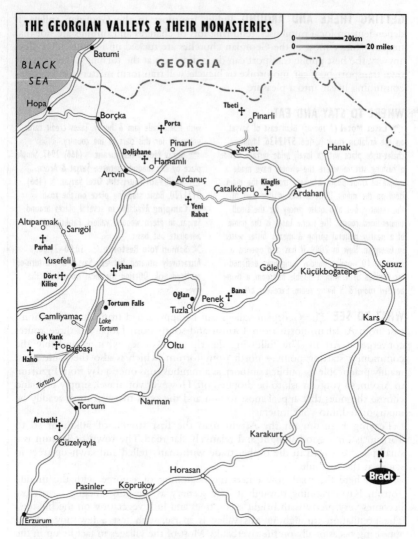

THE GEORGIAN VALLEYS & THEIR MONASTERIES

complex with a 9th-century chapel built by King David the Restorer and a 10th-century church of the Mother of God. It has been carefully restored by the locals and converted into their village mosque. Most of the Georgians in this area converted to Islam in the 17th century.

If you can contrive to get here shortly before noon you will be present to witness the arrival of the various male elders of the village staggering up here from the village to the noon-day prayer. The mosque is usually kept locked but will be opened at this time and you will gladly be invited to join the congregation. One toothless 90-year-old still proudly wears his medals from previous wars under his coat, while another, cupping his hands over his ears, eyes closed and swaying trancelike begins to wail the call to prayer into a loudspeaker.

The galleried entrance where he stands to wail is a later Muslim addition and is now used as a school for the children. You can still clearly see the join where this abuts the original nave. On either side of the entrance to the original church, stone reliefs can be seen. To the right of the entrance is a very comic relief of Jonah and the Whale, reminiscent of the monster in the Akdamar reliefs, looking like a pig with teeth. The Georgians had no more idea of what a whale looked like than the Armenians and simply copied the Armenian version: it was the blind leading the blind. Underneath this is a cockerel, and a little further to the right is a heavily blackened niche where a carving of the Virgin Mary once stood. To the left of the entrance a lion and a griffin-like beast are busy devouring some prey. Inside, a *mihrab* has been added, yet traces of blue paint and murals still remain in the apse and five Apostles are visible. The feel is still very much of a church, though whitewashed like a mosque. A wood-burning stove has been added where the altar would once have stood to make the winter prayers more comfortable. Walking around the church gardens you pass, at the back of the building, a semi-collapsed and now unused aisle. The part in use has had its roof replaced with corrugated iron in places. The tomb of some saint lies within railings and overgrown grass.

Öşk Vank Returning to the main road you now continue on through the valley for a further 15km until you reach a turn-off to the left signposted *Öşk Vank*. This is a colossal monastery church that lies 8km off the main road. The valley at this point is much wider than before, and the road leads across the flat open valley, passing through a curious ghost village and then on along the right-hand side of a valley. This used to be a two-hour walk from the main road, but now is just a straightforward drive with no confusing turn-offs, just climbing a little in the final kilometre.

The church is instantly visible as you approach, rising up with its conical dome from the houses and trees clustered round it. It is the finest example of Georgian Gothic in these valleys, and the scale and height of its dome are still very impressive, even though it is now a derelict hulk in the heart of the village. In the 1980s the porch was used as parking for a local Renault and its nave was a sheltered volleyball playground. In its porch a carefully shaped tree trunk had been ingeniously slotted in to replace one of the broken stone columns. To the left of the tree trunk notice the very fine and elaborately carved pillars and paintings of angels, Mary, Jesus and one other unknown figure. The faces of these are still very well preserved, and have been dated to the 11th century. Shrubs and greenery grow from the roof and there are reliefs of lions and bulls adorning the façade, with the archangels Michael and Gabriel high in the gable. Inside, it is no more than a huge shell, its roof having long ago collapsed. Within the front entrance are traces of murals. Like Haho, Vank too was originally part of a 10th-century monastery with only its church, dedicated to the Deisis (Christ, the Virgin and John the Baptist), now remaining.

Lake Tortum Returning to the main road you now come after just a few hundred metres to the southern tip of Lake Tortum, a fine blue sliver 10km long and 1km wide. It has a strangely manmade look, with sheer sides and no real shoreline, and was in fact formed by a landslip damming the Tortum River three centuries ago. A spectacular new road has now been built in the left cliff side of the lake, often very steep indeed, with sheer drops and dizzying views. The scenery here, with the lushly treed hillsides, the lake and the gorge, is in many ways the most dramatic stretch of landscape in eastern Turkey, certainly more attractive than the drive through the Zab Valley to Hakkâri.

Dropping down to the shore level about halfway along the length of the lake, a spit of land sticks out into the water with a track leading out onto it. This is one of the very few places where you can approach the lakeshore, and is a superb picnic spot where you can feast on strawberries and Turkish champagne bought in Erzurum. Camping and caravanning is popular here. The lake has a stillness that

11

is almost eerie and its colour ranges from a clear blue to an opaque green, depending on the angle of your gaze.

At the northern end of the lake you come upon a small settlement which has grown up as a result of the industrial development of the lake. The **Tortum Waterfalls** which once fell from the end of this lake were the tallest waterfalls in Turkey at 48m high, but have now been regulated by the construction of a dam completed in 1960. From May onwards for the summer months there are no waterfalls to be seen at all, but in the winter months you can follow the pebbled road which leads off to the right down into the new dam settlement with its whitewashed mosque, and then turn right to follow the road round to the falls, less than 1km away. Their setting is especially lovely, in wild and unspoilt scenery. Though you can hear the water thundering from a distance, the falls are not visible from the road, and you come upon them very suddenly.

As the main road north now drops down through a village flanked with leafy trees, some of them walnut, and lush greenery, you reach a section of road that has often caused problems. Landslips prompted by the extensive road construction here can often create delays and the road may be closed for periods of several hours while the blockage is cleared. The road winds on through the gorge which becomes narrower and much more dramatic, flanked with high cliffs.

İşhan Some 35km on from the Vank turn-off, you reach a fork to the right to Olur, crossing a bridge at the confluence of two rivers. The main road to Artvin continues straight on. This is the fork you must take to visit İşhan, the third of the Georgian churches, once a bishops' church, which has the most lovely setting of the three. From the tarmac road to Olur, a signposted rough track, difficult in places and with hairpin bends and vertiginous drops, leads left 9km (20 minutes' drive) up to a raised cliff terrace where the village stands. To reach the church, continue through the village and follow the track to drop down suddenly onto a magnificent open terrace where the church stands surrounded by trees. A simple tea-house/café sits tucked at the back of the terrace, selling drinks and snacks. Entry is charged at TL5 for a car and TL1 per person.

The original church here, the Church of the Mother of God, was 7th century, extended in the 11th century. The windows, as is usual in the Georgian tradition, are richly decorated with stone carving. The east façade has two fine blind niches. The roofs have fallen in, so the dome in the centre appears to float on the corner pillars. Inside in the dome and near the windows several murals of flying angels are still preserved. A famous solid-gold processional cross found here in the 19th century is now in the state museum of Tbilisi, ancient Tiflis, capital of the Republic of Georgia.

From Olur those with a lot of time and keen to explore the remoter churches can make a difficult 13km excursion, much of it on foot, to the interesting round church of Bana, by the village of Penek, which was not destroyed until 1877 in the Russian–Turkish wars. Just 2km further on up the valley is the heavily ruined Harap Kilise, and two hours' further hard climb leads up to Salamonkale (Solomon's Castle), with an 11th-century chapel and murals and frescoes in a cliff chapel.

YUSUFELI *Telephone code: 466; altitude 560m*

The main road towards Artvin continues north and 8km after the Olur turn-off, a road leads left 10km to Yusufeli, a picturesque mountain town, and two churches are signposted up the same turning: Dört Kilise (28km) and Parhal (38km). Yusufeli has grown a great deal in recent years and now offers a range of accommodation and can be used as a base to visit these two 10th-century churches. It has also become a popular base for white-water rafting and trekking tours from Europe, the USA, Turkey and even Israel, and boasts a tourist office as a result (⏱ *08.00–18.00 Mon–Sat*) close to the *otogar*.

WHAT TO SEE
Dört Kilise To reach Dört Kilise take the fork from Yusufeli to the left marked Ispir. The road is small and narrow, following the course of the Çoruh River. There are a few campsites along the river which offer simple but adequate facilities. Dört Kilise is reached after about 6km and stands raised up to the left on a terrace set back about 50m from the road. A large signpost shows a picture of the church to announce your arrival. Walk up the path a few metres then bend to the left through the gate. The huge church has runner beans growing round the side. Inside it has frescoes of the Apostles in a faded red colour round the central window. Outside there is still blue- and red-coloured decoration round the windows. A stream runs round the side where a picturesque ruined cloister stands.

PARHAL *Telephone code: 466; altitude: 1,300m*

Back at Yusufeli you can now take the right-hand fork that follows the course of the Parhal River to reach after an hour's drive, Parhal, an attractive village with its own Georgian church of Parhal, and base for treks into the Kaçkar Mountains. Even further up the road is Hevek, another starting point for treks.

The road is in bad condition and quite slow driving, but the scenery compensates, with the permanent sound of rushing water everywhere. Wooden houses are perched precariously in valleys with balconies overlooking vertiginous edges. Along the course of the rushing river there are various camping sites with lovely locations along the riverbanks. White-water rafting is also popular here in orange inflatable dinghies. Parhal village now has a number of pensions and the village shops offer fresh bread and a range of groceries. To reach the church either follow the road round to the end of the village, or take the concrete steps to walk up the more direct route, passing through hillsides of village orchards. The large church now sits with the village basketball pitch beside it and old women sitting knitting socks which they sell to passing tourists. Entry tickets are sold for TL3 into the church which is now used as the village mosque. Inside it has a balcony that was originally used for the choir and serves today as the carpeted women's balcony of the mosque.

GETTING THERE AND AWAY Minibuses run from Yusufeli twice a day to Parhal (Altıparmak), taking two hours (TL10). The road is narrow and winding and full

11

The whole range is available here on the Çoruh River, from skill level II to level V, and the river has now become recognised as one of the best in the world, with its excellent rapids and stunning scenery. The best months are May, June and July, when the snowmelt is at its best and the temperature is warming up. For beginners conditions are easier later in the season, July and even August, when the river levels have subsided and the current is weaker. A guide is also on board to help and give instructions, and a minibus follows by road to pick up the rafters at the end. Several companies based in Yusufeli offer tours of varying length. Two of the bigger outfits are **Water by Nature** (\ *Yorkshire (01226) 740444; www.waterbynature.com*), a UK-based company, and **Alternatif Outdoor** (\ *(252) 417272; www.alternatifraft.com*), based in Marmaris, western Turkey.

Local hotels in Yusufeli such as Otel Barcelona (*www.hotelbarcelona.com.tr*) can also organise trips, and the tourist office can advise. Yusufeli's future is uncertain however, as a dam project that is scheduled for completion in the next couple of years will flood the whole town and force it to relocate higher up the valley. The Turkish authorities have guaranteed that no churches will be submerged.

Çamlıhemsin is also a centre for white-water rafting in July and August, but the rafting itself is less exciting, though the scenery is possibly more beautiful. The contact there is www.dagraft.com.tr.

of potholes, at times more like an unsurfaced track than a tarmac road. The nearest airport is Erzurum, 230km away.

WHERE TO STAY

Kaçkar Pansiyon (15 rooms) Meretet (Olgunlar); \ 8322047; www.kackar.net; closed winter. Lying well beyond Parhal (about 25km further to the southwest) this place can only be reached on a rough track & takes 2–3hrs. The altitude here is 2,140m & is a perfect base for climbers & trekkers. Restaurant & Wi-Fi. From here it is a 2–3-day trek to Ayder & Çamlıhemsin on the other side of the Kaçkar mountain range, reaching a maximum height of 3,100m at the Caymakcur Pass. $$

Barhal Pension (7 rooms) \ 2646765; www.barhalpansiyon.com. This is the first place you come to on the right at the start of the village of Parhal. Basic wooden rooms with en suite are very simple, with the absolute minimum of comfort. The amount of water everywhere can mean everything is very muddy, though on clear days in summer everything looks so beautiful you soon forget the mud. B/fast & dinner inc. $

Karahan Pension (6 rooms & roof terrace sleeping 15) \ 8262071; closed Nov–Apr. Very close to Parhal Kilise, on a slope overlooking the valley, a large rambling house with small rooms & lots of twists & turns. Good food. $

WHERE TO EAT

There are several attractive places set with terraces right on the river, best for enjoying the lovely soothing sound of the rushing water. There are also village shops selling a range of groceries for picnics.

BACK ON THE ROAD TO ARTVİN

The road follows the dramatic gorge, quite narrow at times, with the river often muddy and brown in the spring months after the melting snows have swelled its waters. Attractive dark-timbered houses can be seen clustered in small villages on the steep slopes of the valley above the river, almost Swiss-chalet style, with gabled roofs and wooden overhanging balconies. At several points extraordinarily rickety wooden bridges are strung over the gorge: some are evidently disused and are slowly falling piece by piece into the rushing river below; others are intriguing as they appear to lead into a sheer rock face with no visible path or village on the far side.

ARTVİN *Telephone code: 466; altitude: 600m*

Shortly before Artvin the gorge widens out and you can see for the first time, high on the left, mists permitting, the houses of Artvin lying in a magnificent setting on the upper slopes of the valley, looking just like an Alpine ski resort in summer. An impressive 15th-century castle at its foot looms up on a jagged cliff with an enormous sheer drop to the river below. Sometimes described as 'where Turkey and the Caucasus meet', Artvin makes an excellent base for exploring these Georgian heartlands, and the name itself is Georgian, as are all the place names around prefixed with 'Ar', the equivalent of 'ville' or 'burg'. Both Russian- and Greek-style buildings can be seen. On the alpine-like meadows, spring flowers are very plentiful especially in June and July.

GETTING THERE AND AROUND Artvin's *otogar* is situated about 500m down the valley from the town centre and this is its only public transport link with the outside world. From here minibuses run fairly regularly to Ardanuç (one hour, TL8), Şavşat (90 minutes, TL12), Hopa on the Black Sea (90 minutes, TL15), Ardahan (2.5 hours, TL20) and Yusufeli (two hours, TL13). For further afield, buses run once a day to Trabzon (4.5 hours, TL20) and to Kars (five hours, TL25). Erzurum can be reached by both bus and minibus, taking five hours (TL25).

TREKKING IN THE KAÇKAR MOUNTAINS

The more commercialised side of the Kaçkar Mountains is to the north, approached from the Black Sea coast at Pazar, via Çamlıhemsin to the high mountain plateau of Ayder (1,300m) with its hot springs. Far more accommodation is available there, both in Çamlıhemsin and Ayder, as well as in a range of smaller more remote villages up on the *yaylas* (high summer pastures). (For further information, see page 349.)

For those who want a less commercialised spot, Parhal offers an alternative approach.

The Kaçkar themselves are quite a small range, running for about 30km, roughly from Artvin in the east to south of Rize in the west. The lower valleys are heavily forested but once you climb above 2,100m the landscape becomes like high alpine meadows covered in brightly coloured flowers, with mountain lakes and jagged peaks. The climbing season is from mid-May to mid-September from whichever side you approach. The highest point is Mount Kaçkar at 3,937m which has a glacier on its north face, and is a straightforward three-day ascent from the southern route, and may require crampons for the final stretches. The other popular area is the northeast ranges around the peak of Altıparmak at 3,310m, which requires a three–four-day trek to cross the range. From Parhal (Altıparmak) you can also trek for five hours to reach the Karagöl (Black Lake), camp and return next day. Another favourite is a week's trek from Çamlıhemsin up the Firtına Valley to Çat, reaching an altitude of 2,650m. There is a mountain hut at Kotencur which can be used as a base at 2,300m. See www.kackarmountains.com for full information.

TOURIST INFORMATION Artvin has its own tourist office (↘ *2123071;* e *artvin@ ttmail.com;* ☉ *08.00–17.00 Mon–Fri*). It hands out a useful map of the area marking all the Georgian churches, together with a few leaflets.

🏠 WHERE TO STAY

🏠 **Karahan Otel** (6 rooms) İnönü Caddesi; ↘ 2121800. A reasonable place with AC & en-suite bathrooms. $$

🏠 **Otel Kaçkar** (12 rooms) Hamam Sokak; ↘ 2129009. Up a side street off the main road, this place is quiet but rather basic. $

✗ WHERE TO EAT
There is a range of cheap places along the main street of İnönü Caddesi.

✗ **Teras Restaurant** Cumhuriyet Caddesi 42; ↘ 2128476. Simple place with homely wooden panelling offering traditional cooking in lovely surroundings. Outdoor seating & licensed. $

ENTERTAINMENT Every year in the last weekend of June the Caucasus **Culture and Arts Festival** (*Kafkasör Kultur ve Sanat Festivali;* ↘ *2123711*) takes place in the Kafkasör Yaylasi, the high summer pasture 7km above Artvin to the southwest of the village. This is where you must come to enjoy the extraordinary spectacle of bloodless bull-wrestling, *boğa güreşleri*, where the bulls are pitted against each other in a contest of strength, similar to bullfighting in Oman. There is no public transport to the *yayla*, so you would have to take a taxi or use your own transport.

WHAT TO SEE In the eastern valley opposite Artvin there was once such a wealth of monasteries that the area was called the Georgian Mount Athos. Some of these are still relatively well preserved and can be visited on driveable tracks. The first and most commonly visited of all the Georgian churches is **Dolishane**, which even some German coach tours now incorporate in their itinerary. Returning south to the Şavşat turn-off you follow this eastwards for some 10km, and then taking a left turn up a track for about 4km. The track is steep in parts. The village in which the church stands is called Hamamlikoy and the 10th-century church now serves as the village mosque, with the lower level in use as a stable.

Returning to the main Şavşat road, the next churches, Barta, Poiza and Porta, all lie in the hills to the left of the road and are heavily ruined: a visit is really only for enthusiasts. Shortly before Şavşat a turn-off left to Veliköy brings you after 6km to another left turn leading to the church of **Tbeti**. In wet weather the track is difficult for cars. The church stands in a fertile valley among the trees and is not visible from afar as a result. Although heavily ruined, the quality of construction was evidently very high. Inside, remains of fine frescoes are visible such as Christ on a throne with outstretched arms surrounded by angels and saints, still with strong colours.

Şavşat Şavşat itself is quite an ugly scruffy place with lots of modern multi-storey buildings. It has a castle, **Şavşat Kalesi**, about 2km out of town right on the road, in the process of being restored. A few kilometres beyond Şavşat a clearly signposted road leads off to Meydancık. As the road drops lower and lower the river gets bigger and bigger.

The ruins of the **10th-century Georgian church of Tbeti** can be found in the nearby village of Ciritduzu. Much damaged in recent years by treasure-seekers, it still has its south transept and east façade with finely carved windows.

🏠 Where to stay

🏠 **Karagöl Pansiyon** (6 rooms) Karagöl Mvk, Meseli, Şavşat; ↘ 466 5372137. 27km from Şavşat, head 2km towards Artvin then turn right to Veliköy on a poor road. This basic but comfortable pension is in a very remote & beautiful spot on the edge of the Karagöl Lake. The building used to belong to the Forestry Administration. Meals can be taken by arrangement. $

Ardanuç In the southern slopes of the Imerhevi Valley, a further excursion can be made to the town of Ardanuç, once a Bagratid stronghold, by taking a right turn off the Şavşat road opposite the Dolişhane. A huge dam is being built across the valley just before the Ardanuç turn-off. The road winds up a dramatic gorge and after about 3km a fine fortress called **Ferhatli Kalesi** appears perched high up on the rocks on the right. On the left a sign announces the Ardanuç Hell (Cehennem) Canyon, and steps and a ramp lead up into a narrow ravine. Ardanuç itself is not a very prepossessing place; it's rather scruffy. Shortly before and slightly apart from the new town a beaten-up sign points to the right to **Gehvernik Kalesi**, and standing on a mighty cliff above you can see the remains of a large fortification in a dramatic setting overlooking a gorge. At the foot of the cliff a smaller old village is huddled, but the inhabitants are increasingly moving to the new town as the rock above has been pronounced unstable. The cliff can be climbed by a steep twisting path and a flight of rickety steps, but apart from a few outer walls and towers, little is left on top, though its setting remains impressive.

Yeni Rabat Beyond Ardanuç a brown sign announces *Yeni Rabat Church/Mosque 17km*, and you can follow the dramatic road out beyond the town, through two tunnels, as it then begins to climb steeply, passing many potential picnic spots beside the road with permanently running springs piped into troughs. A second sign then announces *Yeni Rabat 6km*, forking left up on a dirt track to the village of Bulancik. The 9th-century ruined church lies high on a hillside in a wooded hollow and is therefore not visible from afar. Look out for the unusual wooden minaret in the village with its vertical planks. There are no more signs, but you fork left and continue through the village, then take the next fork left again. The forest track continues for 2–3km and is sometimes tricky and vertiginous, ending at a solitary house among the trees. The church rises behind the house, surrounded by walnut trees threatening to engulf it and even make it collapse. The elderly couple who live in the house are very friendly and welcoming and will insist on you joining them for *Türk mısafirlık*, ie: tea and their special homemade white mulberry jam. With richly decorated window frames and well-preserved dome, this monastery was once a school of book illustration for the monks.

TO THE BLACK SEA

Continuing from Artvin northwards to the Black Sea you come after 26km of driving along the valley to Borçka, a very Russian-looking town, not to be confused with the soup. Clinging to both sides of the river with a bridge linking it, it is heavily militarised as two roads lead off east from here to the border.

WHERE TO STAY Macahel Pansiyonları offers approximately 30 rooms spread over four pensions (see following list). Located beyond Borçka, to get there travel 5km towards Muratli, then turn right on a partly poor road. Set in a tiny valley tucked right up against the border with Georgia is this group of six tiny villages where the villagers still speak a dialect of Georgian and sing ancient Georgian songs. There are excellent hiking opportunities in the hills and valleys around, though because it is so close to the border, foreigners still need to get permission from the armed forces to visit, and passport details need to be submitted two months in advance. Credit cards are not accepted. The pensions, which are closed in winter, are:

⌂ Dedaena Pension (14 rooms) \ 466 4852096. Set in the remotest of the villages, Efeler, this place is a little larger & has a fabulous location, though the organisation is a touch chaotic. $$
⌂ Katamize Pension (7 rooms) \ 466 4852247. 10km from the centre in Maral village, this is the most beautifully situated place with a lovely garden & terrace & stunning views. The pretty rooms are spotless & the lady owner cooks wonderful meals. $$

⌂ Modi Pension (5 rooms) \ 466 4852013. In the main village of Camili, the charming wooden house used to belong to the village headman. Good village food is provided. $$
⌂ TEMA Foundation Guesthouse (14 rooms) \ 466 4852404. A purpose-built set of guesthouses on a ridge, this place is used by local tours for their groups, but lacks the character of the authentic village houses. $$

ON TO HOPA

From this point on the road begins to climb over the final range of the Pontic Mountains 37km to the coast at Hopa, leaving the Çoruh river valley behind. After dark or early in the morning this route is prone to extremely dense fog and visibility is so poor that it can take over an hour to drive this last stretch from Borçka. The road winds and snakes through heavily wooded hills, passing several pretty mountain villages with beautifully built stone hump-backed bridges over small rushing streams. You reach a small pass summit at 690m and as you descend towards Hopa through these rain-soaked northern-facing slopes, you pass through the first of the lush green tea plantations which characterise this coast. You also have your first view of the sea, and after weeks spent in the harsh interior you too can share the relief felt by Xenophon's Ten Thousand Greeks when, after their long retreat from Babylon, they saw the sea and shouted: 'Thalassa, thalassa!'.

Reaching the coast at a T-junction on the Hopa esplanade you turn right to reach the town proper, a charming small resort strung out along one main street. There are hotels to be found along this street, facing out to sea. You have now returned to the fringes of civilisation.

FROM KARS VIA ERZURUM TO TRABZON

From Kars the main road heads southwest to Sarıkamiş, once a resort of the Russian tsar, now a minor ski resort. A few kilometres beyond Kars you pass through the hamlet of Kumbetli which gets its name from the small Armenian *kümbet* standing off to the left in the ploughed fields looking as if it is on the verge of collapse. Shortly before Sarıkamiş the hills all around are heavily tree-covered, transforming the landscape into an almost Scandinavian scene. The trees appear to be continually cut down, so it is anyone's guess how long this pocket will last. Atatürk, as ever the forward thinker, made it a capital offence to cut down a tree, but even this drastic measure came too late to save Anatolia's once-beautiful and lush forests.

It was in these hillsides that a fierce three-day battle was fought in heavy snow in December 1914 between the Russians and the Turks under Enver Pasha. The Turkish Third Army, usually stationed at Erzurum, was virtually annihilated, and the blood of 75,000 men stained the white slopes of Sarıkamiş. The town's average annual temperature is the coldest in Turkey.

From Sarıkamiş the road on to Horasan is very pretty, passing through heavily wooded hillsides along the course of a river valley. Near Horasan a graceful six-arched bridge, the Çoban Köprü (Shepherd's Bridge), spans the river. It was constructed in the 16th century by the famous Sinan, architect of Istanbul's greatest mosques, and is the finest old bridge still in use in Turkey. From Horasan onwards the scenery becomes bleaker and flatter. A fair number of trucks travel along this route between Erzurum and Doğubeyazıt, transiting into Iran. Some 25km beyond Horasan you pass Pasinler and the village of Hasankale with its ruined Armenian castle, later used by the White Sheep Turcomans.

WHERE TO STAY The **Hotel Camkar** (*55 rooms; Cibiltepe Kayak Merkezi, Sarıkamış;* \ *474 4136565; www.camkar.com;* $$$) is a welcome stop at this winter ski resort 45km from Kars airport, slightly Swiss chalet-like in design and with a restaurant, sauna and essential central heating.

ERZURUM *Telephone code: 442; altitude: 1,853m*

Arriving in Erzurum from the east is like hitting a pocket of civilisation, for it is the finest proper city you are likely to have visited since Diyarbakır. Mercilessly cold in winter, high on its plateau, Erzurum is in many ways a bleak and godforsaken place, but it can still seem like a welcome haven of modernity with its streets of shops and bright lights. Set in a great bowl at nearly 2,000m, Turkey's highest provincial capital, it is ringed by broad eroded mountains rather than by dramatic peaks. The landscape is harsh and the dull grey stone of the buildings is in perfect harmony with the surroundings. Always in the past called a 'garrison town' on the route of armies marching to and fro across central Asia, today Erzurum is known for its university, the main one in eastern Turkey, chosen in 1958 over Van. Wolves have been seen roaming the campus in the winter months. It is said to be difficult to get teachers from Ankara and Istanbul as they are unwilling to come to the harsh climate and limited entertainment of Erzurum unless they are dedicated archaeologists or agricultural experimentalists, the two strongest faculties at the university. The destruction left by the Russians in the 19th century and by the earthquake of the late 1930s has now been replaced by wide new boulevards and tall white concrete buildings.

HISTORY The town was passed to and fro between Byzantines, Persian Sassanids, Arabs and Armenians until in 1071 after the Battle of Manzikert, the Seljuk Turks took it. The Mongols overwhelmed it in 1241 and it then passed to the Ottomans as their northern outpost in 1514. It was captured by the Russians in 1882 and in 1916, but not for long. In July 1919 Atatürk called the Congress of Erzurum where the outlines of post-Ottoman Turkish foreign policy and Turkey's modern boundaries were drawn up. It was the Arabs who first called it 'Arz Er-Rum' ('land of the Romans', ie: Byzantines), and the Seljuk Turks kept the name.

GETTING THERE AND AWAY

By air Erzurum's airport (*www.erzurum-erz-airport.webport.com*) is 15km out of town to the northwest. Turkish Airlines (*www.thy.com*) runs daily flights to and from Istanbul taking two hours (TL120) and to and from Ankara (90 minutes, TL115), while Sun Express (*www.sunexpress.com.tr*) flies to and from Antalya and Bursa (from TL120) as well as Istanbul and Izmir (from TL120). Onur Air (*www.onurair.com.tr*) also flies daily to and from Istanbul (two hours, TL115). Hamburg International (www.hamburg-international.de) also flies once a week to and from Cologne/Bonn. A taxi to or from the airport costs about TL30.

By train The train station [339 C1] is the most central public transport hub, just 1km north of Cumhuriyet Caddesi. Services from here run to and from Istanbul via Sivas, Kayseri and Ankara on the *Doğu Ekspresi*, and the *Erzurum Ekspresi* heads to and from Ankara also via Sivas and Kayseri and also to and from Kars (4.5 hours, TL10). Departures tend to be just once a day.

By bus The *otogar* [339 A1] is 2km from the centre to the northwest, towards the airport. This is the place for long-distance coaches and services run between all the following places in all directions including northeast to Kars, (three hours, TL15), east to Doğubeyazıt (4.5 hours, TL20), northwest to Trabzon (six hours, TL20), southeast to Van (6.5 hours, TL25) and south to Diyarbakır (eight hours, TL30).

For shorter-range places like Yusufeli (three hours, TL15), Artvin (four hours, TL20) and Hopa (five hours, TL25), the minibus terminal is where you must head, called Gölbaşi Semt Garaji, 1km northeast of Adnan Menderes Caddesi.

GETTING AROUND A taxi from the airport to the city centre costs about TL30, and minibuses run out to the *otogar* for TL1. Car hire is available from Avis on Terminal Caddesi (\ *2338088; www.avis.com.tr*) and from Sude-National Car Rental on Milletbahce Caddesi (\ *2343025*), fractionally cheaper than Avis.

TOURIST INFORMATION Erzurum's tourist office (⊕ *08.00–19.00 Mon–Fri, 10.00–17.00 Sat/Sun*) is on Cemal Gürsel Caddesi and hands out city maps and a few other leaflets.

🏠 **WHERE TO STAY** The luxury places are all up at the Palendöken ski resort, 5km to the south. Erzurum itself has nothing better than mid range.

🏠 **Hotel Dilaver** [339 C2] (75 rooms) Aşagi Mumcu Caddesi; \ 2350068; e dilaverotel@ superonline.com. Faceless modern block with 6 floors but in a good quiet location close to the main sights. B/fast is served in the rooftop restaurant with good views over the city. $$$
🏠 **Esadas Otel** [339 B2] (45 rooms) Cumhuriyet Caddesi; \ 2335425; www.erzurumesadas.com.tr. Probably Erzurum's best place in this price bracket. Can be noisy on the main street, so ask for a room at the back. Very good b/fast inc. $$
🏠 **Grand Hitit** [339 C1] (40 rooms) Kazım Karabekir Caddesi; \ 2835001; www.hitithotel.net.

Good value with well-tended rooms & convenient location. B/fast room & restaurant on the top floor with views. $$
🏠 **Otel Polat** [339 C1] (60 rooms) Kazım Karabeikr Caddesi; \ 2350363; www.otelpolat.com. Unprepossessing grey block 6-storeys tall but inside its rooftop restaurant has good views. Rooms are small but clean. $
🏠 **Yeni Çinar Oteli** [339 C1] (36 rooms) Ayazpasa Caddesi; \ 2136690. Erzurum's rock-bottom place for backpackers. No frills, but the location is close to the main sights & rooms are quiet & clean. No b/fast. $

✗ **WHERE TO EAT**

✗ **Erzurum Evleri** [339 C2] Cumhuriyet Caddesi; \ 2128372; ⊕ 09.30–23.30. Wonderfully atmospheric place just off the main street full of Ottoman memorabilia & with private alcove seating, low tables & cushions. Good food. Unlicensed. $$$
✗ **Güzelyurt Restaurant** [339 C2] Cumhuriyet Caddesi; \ 2345001; ⊕ 10.00–23.00. An Erzurum institution that has been going since 1928 &, unusually, is licensed, so make the most of it. The menu is also different, with some 20 varieties of *mezze*. The ambience has not changed for years, with bow-tied waiters who are truly expert at their work. $$
✗ **Çay Bahçesi** [339 C2] Cumhuriyet Caddesi; ⊕ 09.00–21.00. Very attractive & welcome tea-garden on the main street in a garden beside the Turkish-Islamic Arts & Ethnography Museum. $

✗ **Kiliçoğlu** [339 B2] Cumhuriyet Caddesi; \ 2353233; ⊕ 09.00–20.30. Erzurum's most irresistible *pastahane* with an astonishing range of ice creams (23 flavours) & *baklava* (27 types), on the main street. $
✗ **Kücükbey Konağı** [339 C2] Erzurum Dugun Salonu Karşışı; \ 2140381; ⊕ 10.00–23.30. Set in a little side street off the main road Cumhuriyet Caddesi, this place is a converted mansion that offers snacks with *nargile* (water-pipe) & with its slightly bohemian atmosphere is popular with local students. $
✗ **Vatan Lokantasi** [339 C1] İstasyon Caddesi; \ 2348191; ⊕ 09.30–23.00. On the road leading up to the railway station, a good reliable place serving dependable kebabs & other meat dishes. $

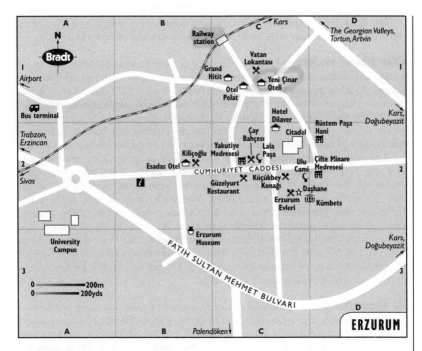

ERZURUM

Map labels:
A · B · C · D
N
Bradt
Kars
Railway station
The Georgian Valleys, Tortun, Artvin
Vatan Lokantası
Airport
Grand Hitit
Yeni Çınar Oteli
Otel Polat
Bus terminal
Hotel Dilaver
Kars, Doğubeyazit
Trabzon, Erzincan
Çay Bahçesi
Citadel
Rüstem Paşa Hani
Yakutiye Medresesi
Lala Paşa
Çifte Minare Medresesi
Kiliçoğlu
Esadas Otel
CUMHURIYET CADDESİ
Ulu Cami
Sivas
Güzelyurt Restaurant
Küçükbey Konağı
Daşhane
Erzurum Evleri
Kümbets
University Campus
Erzurum Museum
Kars, Doğubeyazit
FATİH SULTAN MEHMET BULVARI
0 ——— 200m
0 ——— 200yds
Palendöken

ENTERTAINMENT Under the same management as the Erzurum Evleri, **Daşhane** (\ 2137080) [339 C2] has live music on Friday and Saturday nights, but no alcohol.

The hotels at Palendöken (see page 341) have quite a buzzing disco scene if you fancy a bit of proper nightlife with dancing and alcohol.

SHOPPING Erzurum's *oltutaş* (a kind of black amber, like black onyx) jewellery is the unusual highlight here, for sale principally in the Rustem Paşa Hani [339 D2] (see page 341).

OTHER PRACTICALITIES Erzurum's ATMs, banks and internet cafés are clustered along the main street of Cumhuriyet Caddesi.

WHAT TO SEE Apart from the walls of the citadel there is nothing left in Erzurum which predates the Seljuk conquest in the 11th century. Severe earthquakes and years of wars have taken their toll but there are still some fine buildings to see near the centre of town.

Yakutiye Medresesi (Turkish-Islamic Arts and Ethnography Museum) [339 C2](*Cumhuriyet Caddesi;* ⊕ *08.00–12.00 & 13.00–17.00 Tue–Sun; adult TL3*)

Standing in an open park area in the centre of town, this *medrese* was built in 1310 by the Ilhan Mongol rulers of Persia, with its pretty turquoise tiling on the minaret and traces of green and yellow in the portal making it the most attractive building in Erzurum. On the sides of its portals two lions and an eagle stand astride a palm tree. The whole design of this façade shows marked Persian influence.

Until the 1990s the *medrese* was kept locked and used as a military depot, but now it serves as Erzurum's Turkish-Islamic Arts and Ethnography Museum. Inside, the *dome* has wonderful *muqarnas* (intricate stalactite carvings). The exhibits are mainly the local jet-black jewellery and various dervish items of clothing.

The **Lala Paşa Mosque** [339 C2] next door is very much in use, a typical 16th-century Ottoman–style building with no particular architectural merit.

Çifte Minare Medresesi [339 D2] Erzurum's most famous building, this twin-minareted *medrese* is set back about 20m from the main road, just off the main square. In photographs it looks larger than it is in reality, although it is still Anatolia's largest *medrese* at 35m x 48m with two storeys and four *iwans*. Founded in 1253 by the Seljuk sultan Aleddin Keykubad II, grandson of the great builder of the fortress of Alanya on the Mediterranean coast, it was built in honour of his daughter, Huant Hatun, whose mausoleum is part of the *medrese* at the back. Its fine vaulted portal with *muqarnas* carries bold designs with carved dragons and the Seljuk double-headed eagle, and the whole conception was quite ambitious, the largest of its time. For whatever reason, the external decoration was never finished. The brick-ribbed 30m-high minarets still have a few turquoise tiles. For years it was used as a military store, but has been restored more than once since the 1970s. Seen head on with its squat towers it is involuntarily reminiscent of Battersea Power Station, and lacks the grace of its half-sister of the same name in Sivas. The museum was moved from here in 1968 to a new building on the outskirts of town. The inside can still be visited and entrance is free. Opening hours are erratic.

Üç Kümbetler [339 C2] Behind the *medrese* you can walk past some old houses, some still inhabited, some derelict, and come after about 100m to an open scruffy park area with three conical Seljuk *kümbets* – Üç Kümbetler, similar to those seen in the Van area. The one on the left is in two-tone stone and differs from the others in that its cone appears circumcised. It is the oldest of the three, dating to the early 12th century, and its architecture is a blend of Georgian, Armenian and early Turkish. Entry into all three is blocked. A fourth midget *kümbet* has been constructed behind the circumcised one. An empty ornamental pool and chickens pecking around in the dirt complete the air of neglect.

Ulu Cami [339 C2] Returning to the main street the building immediately on your left is the Ulu Cami (1179), an austere squat building with little decoration inside or out. Six arched vaults supported by a forest of columns run its length, and in the centre is a stalactite dome carved with a central window. In the 1960s its roof fell in but has since been repaired. At the far end of the central aisle is an unusual wooden dome and a pair of even more unusual round windows. It can be visited anytime except during prayers.

Citadel [339 C2] (🕐 *daily 08.00–17.00; adult TL3*) Directly opposite, a road leads off towards the old citadel 300m from the main road. The high walls enclose a large area now used as a football pitch by local youths, with a couple of incongruous rusting cannon lying around. Originally of 5th-century Byzantine construction, it was rebuilt several times. Its curious clock tower began life as an 11th-century Seljuk minaret. The Russians are said to have run off with the clock in 1830, but this is a handy explanation for anything missing in Erzurum. In Ottoman times it was the eastern stronghold for many years of the dreaded Janissaries, the Ottoman SS. From its edge you can look down the hill over the houses below, with their filthy-looking corrugated iron roofs sprawling over the hillsides.

Rüstem Paşa Hanı [339 D2] Slightly down the hill from the Ulu Cami, 75m further on, you will come to a severe dark-stone 16th-century caravanserai on your right, called Rüstem Paşa Hanı, after the name of the great *vizir* of Süleyman the Magnificent. Still used today as a covered bazaar, it specialises exclusively in the sale of jewellery and worry beads made from the local *oltutaş*, meaning 'stone from Oltu', a small town to the north in the Georgian valleys. It is a kind of obsidian-like black jet, and is fashioned into all manner of ornaments, and often set in flashy gold and silver for rings, earrings and necklaces.

Erzurum Museum [339 B3] (*Yenişehir Caddesi;* 🕐 *08.00–17.00 Tue–Sun; adult TL3*) Well worth a visit is the purpose-built Erzurum Museum, now in the modern outskirts of town, with its own car park. Downstairs among the well laid-out exhibits are mammoth bones, fine Urartian drinking vessels in the shape of horses' or rams' heads, and a huge bronze bell, unlabelled, cast in Croydon, which once adorned the clock tower in the citadel. Many items of Ottoman jewellery and clothing are displayed with some fine Ottoman silver breastplates, quaintly translated as 'pinafores'. There is one exquisite set of Ottoman bed linen, beautifully embroidered with colourful flowers. To lie in a bed with these must have felt like sleeping in a spring meadow. Upstairs are weapons and coins, and also several highly decorated Korans. One is so tiny that the script and illuminations are almost microscopic. Various unlabelled items are scattered in the garden, and stone rams, possibly representing the Black Sheep or the White Sheep clan, stand near the entrance, along with several elaborately carved Seljuk tombstones.

PALENDÖKEN

South of Erzurum 5km out of town you can visit the winter ski resort of Palendöken. Facilities have improved hugely in recent years and Palendöken offers by far Turkey's best skiing. The slopes are mainly north-facing, from 2,300m up to 3,125m on Mount Ejder, and conditions are excellent with deep powder. There are currently seven chairlifts, two drag-lifts and a telecabin serving eight beginners' slopes, six intermediate, two advanced and four off-piste runs. The total piste length is 35km, with at least 10km more planned. The season runs from December to April.

 WHERE TO STAY

🏠 **Palan Otel** (160 rooms) 📞 442 3170707; www.palanotel.com. A large 5-storey red-brick block 15km from Erzurum airport with all mod cons, geared to skiing in winter, swimming & relaxation in summer. Outdoor pool in summer with children's section. Restaurant, sauna & disco. **$$$$**

🏠 **Ski Resort Dedeman Palandöken** (184 rooms) ☎ 442 3162414. Erzurum's ski resort's top place 12km from the airport, again with all mod- cons, which could have been lifted out of the Alps. Indoor swimming pool, sauna & disco. **$$$$**

PRACTICALITIES Skis and all the gear can be hired from the hotels for around TL40 per day.

FROM ERZURUM TO THE BLACK SEA

From Erzurum there are two major routes northwards to the Black Sea coast. The route via Aşkale, Bayburt and Gümüşhane to Trabzon is the most commonly used and is the way most coach tours take. The road is good and leads through the spectacular scenery of the Pontic Mountains over the Zigana Pass at 2,025m, the highest major road pass in Turkey. This route is described in detail in *Chapter 12* (see page 362).

The alternative, far less used and equally, if not more spectacular, is north via Lake Tortum and Artvin to the Black Sea at Hopa, a small resort and Turkey's easternmost port on the Black Sea, just 22km from the ex-Soviet border. This route can be driven in one long day from Erzurum to Hopa, stopping off to see several Georgian churches on the way. Alternatively you can overnight at Yusufeli or Artvin for a couple of nights if you want to explore more of the churches scattered in these remote but beautiful valleys (see pages 331 and 334).

12

The Black Sea Coast

Until you have seen the sea, commit yourself to nothing.

There are two main surprises about the Black Sea coast. The first is how green and lavishly vegetated it is, and the second is how built-up it is. The name 'Black Sea' has somehow always managed to conjure up for most people a drab bleak coastline and certainly not a heavily populated one. Yet in practice the coastline has a near-unbroken string of development along it, much of it recent and brought about to a large extent by the prosperity of the tea plantations. These deck the extensive slopes of the Pontic range all the way to the crest of the north, seaward-facing slopes, dropping right down in terraces like a gently descending staircase, to touch the edge of the road along the coast itself. This road, which runs the length of the coast from Hopa to Sinop, is now a major four–six-lane highway east of Samsun, following the water's edge for the most part, transforming the speed of journeys. Traffic here is quite heavy, far heavier than anything you will have been used to after the deserted roads of the east, consisting of an endless series of trucks, buses and vans.

The highpoints are Trabzon and the Sumela Monastery, but one or two nights will be enough for these and to satisfy your curiosity about the Black Sea coast, and the beaches and hotels are on the whole frankly disappointing. Otherwise, the other noteworthy places are the pretty Ottoman towns of Kastamonu and

WHY 'BLACK'?

Quite why the Turks (and the Arabs for that matter) call this the 'Black' Sea, Karadeniz, and the Mediterranean the 'White' Sea, Akdeniz, is not known for sure. The most plausible explanation is that the sun glinting on the Mediterranean gives it a white sheen whereas the rain of the north makes the water seem blacker here. In medieval Turkish kara (black) was also used to denote the north, and ak (white) was used to denote the south, as in the Karakoyyunlu and the Akkoyunlu empires. The difference in climate between Turkey's north and south coasts is also the explanation of why the north has been less favoured as a tourist destination. Even in the height of summer it can rain heavily any day and the temperature can fluctuate from a pleasant 30°C to a cool 18°C. There is often a breeze, and feasibility studies are currently being conducted on wind-driven power stations. While the coast is used by Turks and resident expatriates for holidays, this lack of reliability in the weather means that the Black Sea will never receive the attentions of developers and tour operators in the way that the Aegean and Mediterranean coasts have. The main resorts are within easy striking distance of Istanbul, west at Kilios, east at Şile, Akçafoca and Amasra, but the most attractive part of the coastline in fact does not begin until east of Samsun.

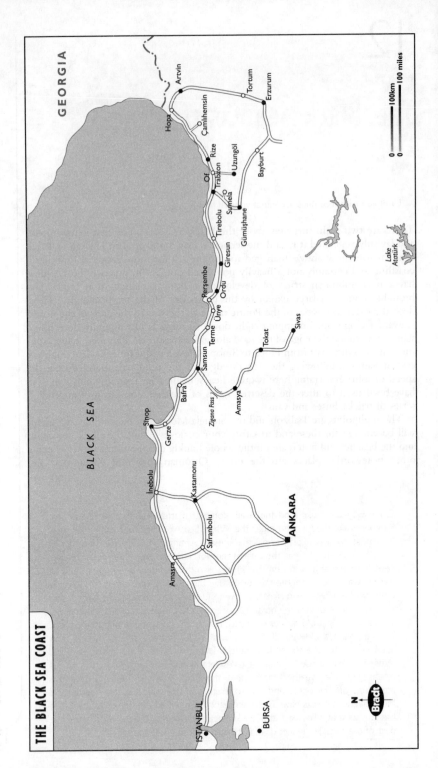

THE BLACK SEA COAST

GEORGIA

BLACK SEA

Artvin
Hopa
Çamlıhemşin
Rize
Of   Uzungöl
Trabzon
Sumela
Tirebolu   Gümüşhane
Giresun
Perşembe
Ordu
Ünye
Terme
Samsun
Bafra   Tokat   Sivas
Zigana Pass   Amasya
Sinop
Gerze

Tortum
Erzurum
Bayburt

İnebolu
Kastamonu
Amasra   Safranbolu
ANKARA

İSTANBUL
BURSA

Lake
Atatürk

N
Bradt

0   100km
0   100 miles

344

Safranbolu, inland from Inebolu and Amasra, memorable for the opportunity they offer to stay in genuine Ottoman wooden houses furnished in traditional style. The Kaçkar Mountains are another undeniable highpoint if you are a trekker looking for stunning scenery and simple living, but that will require a stay of several days to make the long journey up there worthwhile. They can be approached from Çamlıhemşin to the north or from Yusufeli/Parhal to the southeast.

Early June is the best time to visit the Black Sea. Summer temperatures rarely exceed 28°C. East of Ünye the rainfall is higher because of the mountains.

HISTORY

In historical terms the region has also lacked the dynamism of the Aegean and Mediterranean coasts, and the major events of history seem largely to have passed it by. For most people it is associated with Jason and the Argonauts who sailed along it in their search for the Golden Fleece.

The earliest-known foundations here made were in the 7th and 8th centuries BC by the enterprising colonists from Miletos, the greatest of the ancient Greek Ionian cities. These Milesians established the leading sea trade city of the Greek world, founding nearly 100 colonies on the shores of the Hellespont, the Sea of Marmara and the Black Sea coast. Sinop, Samsun, Ordu, Giresun and Trabzon were all Greek Milesian colonies. None of them ever attained much status or produced a famous citizen apart from Diogenes the Cynic, and the only really significant kingdom to rule here was that of the Pontic kings which sprang up after the confusion following Alexander's death in the 4th century BC. These kings, called Mithradates, were troublesome to the Romans for centuries, and the Roman legions finally managed to put an end to them.

When Xenophon and the Ten Thousand reached Trabzon after their tough retreat from Babylon, they took their time returning back along the coast before returning to Greece. As Sir Willian Ramsey has put it: 'Hardly any of these great armies has failed to leave behind some part of its numbers', and it all added to the already varied racial mix of Anatolia.

GETTING THERE AND AWAY

Sadly, Turkish Maritime Lines no longer run ferries along the Black Sea coast from Istanbul that used to hop slowly east along the ports, ending at Trabzon. This used to be a particularly relaxing way of returning to Istanbul at the end of a holiday touring eastern Turkey, but now the much-improved roads, especially the new highway east of Samsun, has made it redundant. There is also no train service along the coast, so buses are the only option, or flights into Trabzon or Samsun. Full details are given under each city later in this chapter.

GETTING AROUND

Once there, you can rent a car in Samsun or Trabzon (Avis is the most reliable; *www.avis.com*), or use the local buses to travel around, as listed under the relevant town entry.

WHERE TO STAY

Accommodation along the Black Sea coast is functional and unexciting. Even in Trabzon it is surprisingly difficult to find anywhere with real charm. A few of the smaller towns like Hopa, Perşembe and Amasra have some beach hotels which have a certain faded appeal, but most are not places where Westerners will feel that comfortable using the beach as they will be objects of curiosity.

✕ WHERE TO EAT

Food along the Black Sea coast is generally good, far better than in the inland areas of central eastern Turkey, but it is also more expensive. Fish varies with the season: in April there is turbot (*kalkan*), and from May onwards there is red mullet (*barbunya*), tuna (*palamut*) and anchovies (*hamsi*). Anchovies are the most abundant and the cheapest and are the staple diet of the fishing village. Many restaurants do not serve alcohol, and often you have to use hotel restaurants to get wine, *rakı* or beer.

HOPA *Telephone code: 466*

From Hopa it is only 22km east to the Georgian border and the town of Batumi at the mouth of the Çoruh, the river which will have been accompanying you on so much of your exploration in the Georgian valleys. The scenery on the way to the border has lush green vegetation on the steep hillsides tumbling down to the road.

GETTING THERE AND AWAY Hopa's *otogar* lies on the road to Artvin just outside town on the western bank of the Sundura River and buses run from here to and from Trabzon (3.5 hours, TL15), Artvin (90 minutes, TL12) and Rize (90 minutes, TL8). For the Georgian border however minibuses leave from the petrol station beside the Otel Cıhan.

🏠 WHERE TO STAY AND EAT

🏠 **Otel Cıhan** (35 rooms) Ortahopa Caddesi; ☏ 3514897; www.hotelcihan.com. Hopa's best offering beside a petrol station, a high-rise place with rooftop restaurant & bar. The rooms are small but well kitted-out, even with minibars. $$

🏠 **Otel Ustabaş** (27 rooms) Ortahopa Caddesi; ☏ 3514507. An OK budget choice with downstairs café. Locally it dubs itself 3-star. $

✕ **Green Kebap** Cumhuriyet Caddesi; ☏ 3514277; ⏰ 09.00–22.00. Set in a pleasant park this place has a couple of outdoor terraces & serves basic but edible kebabs & *pide* (filled Turkish pitta bread). $

OTHER PRACTICALITIES On the main street there is a post office, banks with ATMs and internet cafés. There is also an off-licence (*tekel bayii*), selling beer and *rakı*. The exchange offices give a poor deal on Georgian lari, knowing they have a captive market.

WEST FROM HOPA

From Hopa westwards the coastline begins to get more built-up with a fairly continuous stream of larger or smaller towns and villages sprawling along the roadside. A few of these only are in the old style with gables and wooden balconies. Most are rather ugly new blocks of flats, often looking half-finished, and those that are finished look as though they are starting to fall down. Washing adorns the windows and balconies on every day of the week. To judge from this sheer quantity of washing the inhabitants must be obsessed with cleanliness, but if this is the case, it is not evident in the streets and houses. Perhaps it is just a reflection of the size of the families, where seven to eight children is the norm. Over 40% of the population is under 15 and the government is hurriedly introducing birth control campaigns and dispensing free contraceptives. For many Turkish women giving birth is just a day off from the fields. Many of them want smaller families and surveys have shown that 80% of women do not want more than three children.

The women, dressed in quite colourful clothes and white headscarves, can be seen in the terraced tea plantations on the steep slopes working non-stop at all times of the day, clipping tea and collecting it into bags. These are then emptied into colossal baskets which they carry off to the store. Some of the older ones are bent double under the weight and from the back as you pass them on the road, all you can see is the bouncing basket and a pair of feet sticking out from the bottom.

Meanwhile the men can be seen at all times of day, strolling round the streets in small groups, chatting, twiddling with their worry beads and watching the passing traffic with the curiosity of people who have nothing better to do. Michael Pereira, when walking in this part of Turkey in the 1970s, observed how the seats of men's trousers were 'often highly polished from long contact with coffee-house chairs'. Life expectancy for the men in this area is far higher than

THE UNLAZY LAZ

The people in this part of Turkey are often Laz, a seafaring race of obscure Caucasian origins. They are like remote cousins of the Georgians, but with the important difference that they converted to Islam early and remained staunch Muslims. As such they were loyal to the Turks in the wars against Russia, while the Christian Georgians and Armenians were suspect. Their language too is related to Georgian and is still spoken in the villages, though not written. They are the indigenous inhabitants of the Rize area and the women do much of the work in the tea plantations. The women are self-contained and hard working and the men are fond of dancing and playing bagpipes. Their houses are unlike any others in Turkey, well made of timber and stone and always set in gardens. They are never clustered together in rows or terraces, but are spread out along ridges so that villages are often strung along the tops of ridges to ensure breathing space. The ancient Greeks wrote of them as being savage tribesmen and they have a reputation for being fiercely aggressive as enemies but generous as friends. Rather like most Turks, they are patient and good natured until pushed beyond a certain point. 'The Laz talks with a pistol', runs a local saying.

for the women. The latter are probably so crippled by heavy work that in their old age they can hardly move from the house, and it is certainly noticeable that far more old men than old women are to be seen out in the streets. These practices are not the same throughout Turkey, and in central Anatolia, for example, the men are much more in evidence working with the women in the fields.

ÇAMLIHEMSİN AND AYDER *(Telephone code: 464)*

Shortly before Pazar some 40km west from Hopa, a sign points off to Ayder Kaplicalari, thermal springs in the mountains near Çamlıhemsin. These are probably much in demand by the local women to ease their crippled limbs. At Çamlıhemsin itself you can still see a typical Laz village with all its neat wooden houses laid out in a row, each with its own garden. Close to Şenyuva village is the lovely stone single-arch bridge, **Şenyuva Köprüsü**, built in 1696. From the bridge the road continues for a further 9km to the romantic medieval castle of **Zil Kale** perched on a heavily forested hill with trees growing out of its turrets. It stands at a height of 750m overlooking the Fırtına Gorge 100m below. Thought to have been built in the 14th or 15th century, it protected the caravan route to Bayburt. Inside it still has garrison accommodation, a chapel and the head tower. Surrounded by rhododendron forests, it makes a spectacular walk along a rough road. Further on still is the tiny village of **Çat** at 1,250m with a small shop and a handful of pensions, used as a base for remoter treks, reached after another 15km. (For trekking details and accommodation, see opposite.)

Ayder is the most accessible of the mountain plateaux and as such has become the main centre for tourism in the Kaçkar Mountains, a touch overdeveloped and trendy. In an uncontrolled building splurge of the early 1990s, concrete blocks were rushed up, but later regulations meant they had to be clad in timber to at least make some attempt at conserving the feel of the place. All new buildings must be in the traditional wooden Alpine-chalet style, so at least they now predominate. There are souvenir shops clustered together and bars playing loud music. Every afternoon the fog descends and shrouds the place from view. When the weather is good and clear you can see the beautiful setting in a steep valley with a dozen or so waterfalls tumbling down the cliffs on all sides and evergreen trees growing unusually tall. The place is extremely popular with Turkish tourists, and numbers of western trekkers are also increasing, including lots of Israelis. As a result of the growing demand standards of accommodation are gradually rising, along with prices. In the centre there is now a supermarket, off-licence and even an internet café, but not yet an ATM or bank. The nearest is back in Çamlıhemsin. Things are only really busy during the trekking season which runs from mid-May to mid-September, and a lot of the places close for the winter. The whole area is now protected as the Kaçkar Dağları Milli Parki (Kaçkar Mountains National Park), and about 5km before reaching Ayder there is a gate at which private vehicles have to pay a charge of TL8. In the remoter parts of the park brown bears still live, along with salamanders and the rare Caucasian black grouse.

GETTING THERE AND AWAY In season (mid-May to mid-September) *dolmuşes* run regularly from Pazar on the Black Sea coast up to Ayder (one hour, TL6), stopping at Ardessen and Çamlıhemsin, and even in low season there are still four minibuses a day. Minibuses also run daily along the same route from Rize (two hours, TL10). Try to avoid Saturdays and Sundays as this is when the route gets really busy. During the summer *dolmuses* also run from Ayder to the other mountain villages up on the *yaylas*, such as Caymakçur, Avusör, Yukarı Kavron and Galer Duzu. A taxi from Çamlıhemsin up to Ayder will cost at least TL60.

TOURIST INFORMATION The second week of June is very busy with all accommodation bursting, thanks to the Çamlıhemsin Ayder Festival held here every year at that time. Emigrés from Hemsin often return home for this dose of their roots, with a type of dance called the *horon* accompanied by a kind of bagpipe called a *tulum*. The women are often very colourfully dressed with long skirts and fine headdresses.

For organised trekking tours, consult www.turkutour.com or www.middleearthtravel.com to book something in advance. Alternatively most of the pension owners can organise tours on the spot after you arrive. The minimum is two days, ideally a week. For full details see www.kackarmountains.com or buy the 2008 trekking guide *The Kaçkar* by Kate Clow, also author of the *Lycian Way* trekking guide. White-water rafting is available in July and August on the rapids west of Çamlıhemsin, with various grades from 1 to 4 (see www.dagraft.com.tr).

WHERE TO STAY

Kuşpuni (16 rooms, 2 suites) Ayder, Çamlıhemsin; ☎ 6572052; www.kuspuni.com; ⏱ all year. In Ayder village, 17km from Çamlıhemsin. Run by Dr Veziroğlu, a former surgeon, who became the local mayor & played a leading role in helping stem the uncontrolled building rush of the early 1990s. Excellent local specialities are served such as *muhlama* (a cheese fondue with cornmeal) & lots of unusual vegetables. Rooms in the main house are centrally heated, very welcome on cold nights, & 2 further rooms, unheated but full of charm, are available in the old *serender*, the timber storehouse built on stilts. Friendly & unpretentious. $$

Pokut Yaylaevi (4 rooms) Pokut Yaylası, Çamlıhemsin; ☎ 6517530; www.pokutyaylaevi.com; closed winter. 20km from Çamlıhemsin, on the Ayder Plateau, left from Şenyuva village, 1.5km from the tarmac road, but the owners will collect you from Çamlıhemsin in their own vehicle. Lovely views & landscapes just below the tree line. Restaurant, pretty garden. Shared bathrooms. $$

Serender Pansiyon (14 rooms) Ayder, Çamlıhemsin; ☎ 6572201; closed Dec–Apr. A homely timber chalet in Ayder village, 17km from Çamlıhemsin, with wood-panelled rooms in sauna style, some quite big & which can interconnect to make family suites. Excellent b/fast served by the owner & lovely terrace with views over the emerald pastures & contented cows. Meals by arrangement. $$

Cancık Hotel (7 rooms, 2 cabins for 4) Cat, Çamlıhemsin; ☎ 6544120; closed Nov–Mar. 28km from Çamlıhemsin, 16km beyond Zil Castle on a bad road. The village of Çat is at the end of the driveable road & has 20 houses & a mosque. Nearby are the 2 peaks of Tatos (3,560m) & Vercenik (3,711m), & the simple accommodation here is a popular stop for trekkers. Homely atmosphere. $

Fırtına Pansiyon (6 rooms, 2 apts, 2 bungalows) Senyuva (Sinciva) Köyü, Çamlıhemsin; ☎ 6533111; www.firtinavadisi.com; closed Nov–Feb. 6km from Çamlıhemsin. Converted from the old schoolhouse of Senyuva village is this pension, beside the rushing Firtına River where the tarmac road ends. The old classroom is the lounge & dining room, & the teacher's quarters are now 5 simple but cosy rooms. Fittingly the owner & his sister are both retired teachers. From here you can walk the 7km to Zil Castle, passing waterfalls in forest clearings & many abandoned timber houses built from chestnut wood scattered high in the foggy hills. Some rooms without bathroom. $

Kocira (7 rooms) Kito Yaylası, Çamlıhemsin; ☎ (gsm) (532) 6335748; www.kocira.com; closed winter. 20km from Çamlıhemsin, on the road from Pazar to Hemsin. At an altitude of 2,000m & reached on a slow & difficult track, a very pretty mountain lodge. The owner is a cook & guide. Pretty garden with stunning views, restaurant, shared bathrooms. $

WHERE TO EAT
Half board is the usual arrangement for people staying in their chalets and pensions, so there are not that many eateries. A couple deserve mention:

Dört Mevsim ☎ (464) 6572019. Situated right beside a waterfall 400m uphill from Ayder village centre. Serves cold beer. $$

Nazlı Çiçek ☎ 6572130. Specialising in fresh trout from the river & a few Black Sea favourites like *muhlama*, this place is set in a lovely old house in the centre of Ayder village. $$

Rize, the tea capital, some 60km further on, is the largest town on the coast east of Trabzon. It is a modern town, its prosperity built totally on tea, and there is nothing of particular interest to visitors. It has no deep-water harbour and larger ships have to anchor off the coast, using smaller boats to ferry cargo to a long pier.

GETTING THERE AND AWAY Bus is the only public transport available and Rize's *otogar* has minibuses that run to and from Trabzon (one hour, TL6) and Hopa (90 minutes, TL9), and in summer there are also daily services direct to and from Ayder (one hour 45 minutes, TL12), a good jumping-off point for treks into the Kaçkar Mountains.

TOURIST INFORMATION Rize has a tourist office on the main square next to the PTT (\ *2130408;* ⊕ *09.00–17.00 Mon–Fri*). It has a few leaflets to hand out.

WHERE TO STAY AND EAT

🏠 **Dedeman Hotel Rize** (82 rooms) Merkez Alipaşa Köyü; \ 2234444; www.dedemanhotels.com. The usual good standard of the Turkish Dedeman chain, on the shore with private beach, indoor pool, health & fitness club, sauna & massage facilities. $$$

🏠 **Otel Kaçkar** (35 rooms) Cumhuriyet Caddesi; \ 2131490; www.otelkackar.com. Good-value place situated just off the main square, recognisable by its mosaic façade. Clean, simple rooms. $$

✕ **Sevimli Konak** Cumhuriyet Caddesi; \ 2170895. Very attractive place about 300m north of the main square in a restored Ottoman house with a garden & serving traditional Laz food. Traditional music on Wed & Fri. Unlicensed. $$

✕ **Çaykur Tea & Botany Garden** Rize's wonderful tea-garden where you must stop for a memorable cup of tea, the freshest you are ever likely to have, situated above the town behind the Seyh Camii & with good views. $

TEA IN TURKEY

All of Turkey's tea grows in the Rize area, on slopes of up to 1,000m facing north towards the Black Sea, reaching inland as far as 30km. The tea-clipping and production season runs for six months from May to October, and the process is entirely natural with no chemical additives. Turkey today has the highest per-capita consumption of tea in the world, with the UK coming second, though in terms of production India, China, Kenya and Sri Lanka are all ahead of Turkey which is fifth in the world. Yet tea has only relatively recently become a popular drink in Turkey, largely because of the high cost of imported coffee. The Russians began planting tea in Georgia at the end of the 19th century, and it was first planted in Turkey in 1935, and the first tea factory opened here in 1947. The 1986 harvest had to be destroyed since it was irradiated to unacceptably high levels after the Chernobyl disaster. The tea farmers were compensated and the crop was buried at various sites in eastern Turkey. The 1987 harvest was pronounced safe. The tea is drunk black and is prepared in a double kettle called a samovar where the tea, one teaspoon per person, is prepared and boiled in the bottom kettle for 15 minutes, with plain water boiled in the upper kettle. When it is served in the small tulip-shaped glasses with sugar lumps in the saucer, the glass is only filled a third to a half full, then the boiling plain water added according to strength desired, *koyu* meaning 'dark' (strong) and *açık* meaning 'light' (weak). Apple tea and other fruit or herbal teas are nothing to do with traditional Turkish black tea and are caffeine-free, produced mainly for tourists.

UZUNGÖL

Some 25km west from Rize, at Of, a road heads inland towards Çaykara, following the course of the Solatli River. If you are interested in bridges you might like to make the 26km detour to see the remarkable old wooden-roofed bridge at Çaykara, unlike any other in Turkey, though rather heavily and obviously restored. Passing through Çaykara, you turn left towards Uzungöl (Long Lake) a beautiful spot about 45km inland from the coast. Uzungöl is now a small resort of about 25 chalets that have grown up around the lake, where people can enjoy the water, the fresh trout, the forest, the fresh air and the mountains.

Some 13km beyond the Çaykara turn-off you come to the town of Sürmene. Just 4km before Sürmene, hidden from the road by a high hedge, is the so-called Kestel Kale or Kastelli Mansion or even Memisağa Konağı, now derelict. This is a quite magnificent and unusual building, built in c1800 by local 'lords of the valley'. Its lower storey is in reddish brickwork and its two upper storeys are in white with timbered frames and elaborate wooden lattice windows. The whole is then capped by a spectacular wide overhanging roof on timbered supports which makes the building look like a gigantic mushroom. It also has interesting dungeons.

Back along the coast road, at 5km beyond Sürmene a sign announces the 13th-century Byzantine castle of Araklı, on an outcrop by the side of the sea. There is absolutely nothing to see beyond a few fragmentary walls; but the local province is so short of important places to signpost along this stretch that anything merits a sign.

 WHERE TO STAY The **Inan Hotel** (*18 rooms, 25 cabins; Uzungöl, Çaykara;* \ *6566021;* ☉ *all year;* $$) has a genuine feel and provides meals; the food is excellent. The villagers speak the Pontic dialect of Greek.

✖ **WHERE TO EAT**

✖ **Hancioglu Restaurant** Camburnu Mevkii; \ 7522650. Wooden panelled waterfront restaurant with fabulous views & expansive garden. Fresh fish & meat dishes, but unlicensed. $

TRABZON   *Telephone code: 462*

'Fabled Trebizond lies like a green Eden at the foot of the Pontic Mountains, a little Constantinople on the Black Sea coast.' If you have read anything like this about Trabzon you have read a fable indeed. Rose Macaulay's towers are equally illusory and you have to hunt long and hard to find a view of the walls that is even remotely impressive. The approach from the sea gives the best overall impression. That said, as long as you arrive with expectations suitably deflated, Trabzon does have some interesting things to offer and can even begin to grow on you after a couple of days. If the bustle of the city is all too much for you after the emptiness and quiet of the Georgian valleys, one option is to overnight at Maçka, so you can visit the two highlights of the Sumela Monastery and Ayia Sofya, then be on your way again.

HISTORY The Cathedral of Ayia Sophia [353 A3] 3km west of Trabzon's main square, Atatürk Alanı, is rightly the most famous site, outshining all the city's other architectural monuments. These include ten churches, a number of them converted to mosques by the Ottomans, a convent and an Armenian monastery, all relics of the Comnene dynasty which fled Constantinople just before its fall to the Fourth Crusade in 1204. Alexius Comnenus, 22-year-old son of the

Byzantine emperor Manuel I, established himself as king here with the help of Georgian queen Tamara (see page 330) to whom he was related.

Trebizond's Greek roots went back to the 7th century BC when it was founded by the great Ionian sea-trading city of Miletos in southwest Turkey. It was a typical site for a Greek colony, with a good harbour and an acropolis (which gave it its name Trapezus, meaning 'table'); its climate could support olives and, across difficult mountains, it managed a trade route to Persia. To Trebizond came camel caravans from Erzurum and Tabriz carrying silk and spices, and it even benefited during Byzantine times from Arab incursions into Anatolia which redirected the overland trade between Constantinople and the East through the Black Sea.

When Constantinople fell a second and final time, to the Ottomans in 1453, Trebizond and the Comnenes held out for a further eight years. As the last flickers of Byzantium it acquired a certain romantic mystique in Europe as the distant Christian outpost in Asia, still defiant against Islam. Despite being the birthplace of Süleyman the Magnificent in 1494, Trebizond fell into decline. The Ottomans made the overland trade routes secure and commerce passed the city by. In World War I it suffered when it was bombarded and occupied by the Russians. But the Turkish Republic's policy of reorienting the country towards Anatolia has brought some life back to Trabzon, its Turkish name, turning it into a major port.

GETTING THERE AND AWAY

By air Trabzon's airport is 5km east of the city centre. Turkish Airlines (*www.thy.com*) flies daily to and from Istanbul, Ankara and Izmir, and twice a week to and from Antalya and Bursa. Pegasus Airlines (*www.flypgs.com*) also flies twice a day to and from Istanbul's Asian airport of Sabiha Gökçen, and once a day to and from Ankara. OnurAir (*www.onurair.com.tr*) flies three times a day to and from Istanbul's main airport (Atatürk). In summer Sun Express (*www.sunexpress.com.tr*) flies to and from Istanbul five times a week, Bursa and Sivas twice a week, Adana and Antalya once a week. Azerbaijan Airways (*www.azal.az*) also flies once a week (30 minutes, KK155) to and from Baku. Taxis to and from the airport cost TL22, leaving from outside the terminal, *dolmuses* cost TL2 and leave from 500m away from the terminal entrance heading to the main square Atatürk Alanı, and buses with 'Park' or 'Meydan' on their fronts also run from the main square to the airport, costing TL1.5.

By train There is no train link to Trabzon, so the closest is to take the *Doğu Ekspresi* train to Erzurum and then catch a bus on to Trabzon.

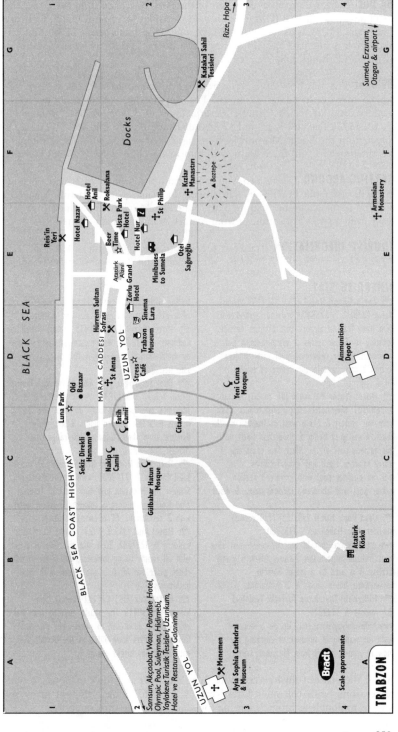

BLACK SEA

BLACK SEA COAST HIGHWAY

UZUN YOL

Docks

Rize, Hopa →

X Kadakal Sahil
Tesisleri

Hotel
Anil

X Roksafana

Hotel Nazar

Beer
☆ Time
Café

Usta Park
Hotel

✝ St Philip

Reis'in
Yeri X

Hotel Nur

Atatürk
Alanı

Minibuses
to Sumela

Otel
Sağıroğlu

✝ Kızlar
Manastırı

▲ Boztepe

Zorlu ☆
Grand
Hotel

Hürrem Sultan
Sofrası X

Sinema
Lara

Trabzon
Museum

Old
● Bazaar

☆ Luna Park

MARAS CADDESİ

UZUN YOL

☆ Stress
St Anna ✝ Café

☾ Yeni Cuma
Mosque

Sekiz Direkli
Hamamı ●

Nakıp ☾
Camii

☾ Fatih
Camii

Citadel

Gülbahar Hatun ☾
Mosque

Ammunition
Depot

*Sumela, Erzurum,
Otogar & airport* →

✝ Armenian
Monastery

UZUN YOL

*Samsun, Akçaabat, Water Paradise Hotel,
Olympic Pool, Suleyman, Hidirnebi,
Yaylakent Turistik Tesisleri, Uzunkum,
Hotel ve Restaurant, Galanima* →

✝ X Menemen

Ayia Sophia Cathedral
& Museum

🎗 Atatürk
Köşkü

Bradt

Scale approximate

TRABZON

By bus Trabzon's *otogar* lies 3km east of the port. Buses run from there to cities in all directions such as Rize (one hour, TL6), Artvin (4.5 hours, TL22), Erzurum (six hours, TL25), Kars (ten hours, TL35) and Sinop (nine hours, TL38). You can also catch a bus to Tbilisi in Georgia (20 hours, US$30) or even Yerevan in Armenia (25 hours, US$60).

By boat The only boat services run from Trabzon to Sochi in Russia, with twice-weekly departures taking 12 hours. The shipping agents are both on Iskele Caddesi, and are called Princess Victoria Lines (\ *3266674*) and Apollonia II (\ *3264842*). The cost is around $70–80 one way, though only $60 if you buy it direct from the Sochi Morport website (*www.morport-sochi.ru*). The website also has the timetable and there is a helpful information line on \ +7 (8622) 609603.

GETTING AROUND *Dolmuş* taxis run to and from the airport (TL2), and a private taxi will cost about TL20. They start around the main square of Atatürk Alanı and also run to the *otogar* (bus station) 3km to the east. Minibuses to Sumela [353 E2] leave from a point just southeast from Atatürk Alanı, the main square.

TOURIST INFORMATION Trabzon's tourist office is on Camii Sokak [353 E2] (\ *3264760*; ⊕ *08.00–17.30 Mon–Fri*) and hands out the usual maps and leaflets.

WHERE TO STAY

🏠 **Zorlu Grand Hotel** [353 D2] (157 rooms) Maraş Caddesi; \ 3268400; www.zorlugrand.com. 4km from Trabzon airport. Lots of flags outside, boasting its 5-star status. 2 restaurants, a pub & *hammam*. Indoor swimming pool with children's section, sauna, right in the centre of town. $$$$$

🏠 **Hotel Water Paradise** (86 rooms) Akcaabat; \ 2682701; www.hotelwaterparadise.com.tr. 25km from the airport & 21km west of Trabzon on the beach. A rarity in being a good-class hotel on this eastern part of the Black Sea coast, this 4-storey modern block has good facilities, along with an outdoor pool with children's section, indoor pool with children's section, sauna & disco. $$$$

🏠 **Usta Park Hotel** [353 E2] (120 rooms) Iskender Paşa Mahallesi; \ 3265700; www.ustaparkhotel.com. In the city centre just 3km from Trabzon airport, this 7-storey block is pretty faceless. It is used by a lot of Russian businessmen, has a sauna & 2 restaurants. $$$$

🏠 **Hidirnebi Yaylakent Turistik Tesisleri** (51 rooms) \ 3232323; www.hidirnebiyaylakent.com. Up on a summer *yayla* for walking in summer or enjoying the snow in winter, inland from Akcaabat. Lovely setting with forest & good mountain views. I restaurant, sauna, volleyball. Central heating. $$$

🏠 **Hotel Nazar** [353 E1] (35 rooms) Güzelhisar Caddesi; \ 3230081; www.nazarhotel.net. Favoured by middle-range businessmen, this place is also a safe bet. $$$

🏠 **Otel Sağiroğlu** [353 E2] (55 rooms) Taksim Ishani Sokak; \ 3232899; www.sagirogluotel.com. Trabzon's attempt at a '*butik otel*' but the closest it gets is a few wooden floors & a slightly demure atmosphere. Good middle-range place though. $$$

🏠 **Uzunkum Hotel ve Restaurant** (33 rooms) Sahil Caddesi; \ 2212021; www.oteluzunkum.com. Simpler beach option just 4km west of Trabzon & 7km from the airport, a colourful 3-storey hotel with 2 restaurants, AC & central heating. $$$

🏠 **Hotel Anil** [353 E1] (27 rooms) Güzelhisar Caddesi; \ 3267282. Built into the side of a hill with all rooms facing forwards, this lower–middle-range place has AC & is good value with clean bathrooms. $$

🏠 **Hotel Nur** [353 E2] (22 rooms) Camii Sokak; \ 3230445. The nearby mosque may wake you with its dawn call to prayer, but otherwise this place offers good value at the bottom end, with small but bright rooms. $

Along the seafront dual carriageway there are rows and rows of hotels, simple places, some with balconies. Otel Kent (\ *3280961*) looks OK, but many are known to double as brothels serving the sailors from the port opposite.

✗ WHERE TO EAT

There is nothing particularly special on offer in Trabzon, and most of the restaurants are pretty average. There is an expensive (**$$$$**) fish restaurant on the first floor of a shopping arcade, **Ipekyolu İş Merkesi**, off Maraş Caddesi, where you can select your own fish, and otherwise there are many standard kebab places around the main square of Atatürk Alanı and along Uzun Yol (Long Street). Uzun Yol is also blessed with many *pastahanes* and ice-cream parlours, as well as shops selling dried local fruit, Turkish delight (*lokum*) and the local chestnut honey (*kestane bali*).

For ambience, you can escape the city bustle and go to **Reis'in Yeri** [353 E1] down in the harbour, reached by crossing the road on the pedestrian bridge, in a little cove where you can even hire rowing boats. It also serves beer, has a garden and offers fish, chicken and *köfte*.

✗ **Galanima Restaurant** Adnan Kahveci Bulvarı, 2, Sogutlu; ☏ 2487127. Probably the best in the area, a licensed seaside fish restaurant located in an old mansion with a large garden. It uses much home-grown produce in its vegetable *meze* & serves local specialities. On Fri & Sat evenings it has live classical Turkish music. **$$$**

✗ **Hürrem Sultan Sofrası** [353 D2] Maraş Caddesi; ☏ 3218651. Frequented at lunchtimes by local businessmen & students alike, with plenty of local specialities. Good value. **$$**

✗ **Roksalana Restaurant** [353 E2] Iskenderpaşa Mahallesi, Siramagazalar; ☏ 3224008. Named after Roxelana, the Ukranian wife of Suleyman the Magnificent who was born in this area, this small homely place offers lots of anchovy specialities, as well as casseroles & grilled meat. Licensed. **$$**

✗ **Süleyman Restaurant** D Dere, 100 Yil Parki; ☏ 3250550. Near the Olympic pool, this seaside place has a good view & a bar with live Turkish music on Sat. It serves local specialities & also some Italian pasta & French dishes. **$$**

✗ **Balıkcı Dede Restaurant** Devlet Karayolları altı Akyazı Beldesi; ☏ 2210398. Licensed place on the waterfront known for its local anchovies – fried, grilled or casseroled – & its 15 different types of *meze*. Live classical Turkish music on Saturdays. **$**

✗ **Kadakal Sahil Tesisleri** [353 G3] Yali Mahallesi, Sahil Yolu Caddesi, Balıkcı Limanı yanı Faroz; ☏ 2298344. Popular family place where children can run round in the extensive garden. Huge selection of dishes including baked beans & savoy cabbage soup. Unlicensed. **$**

✗ **Menemen Café/Restaurant** [353 A3] Beside the ticket kiosk entrance to Ayia Sofya, an attractive place for a light lunch with good views over the church from its terrace. **$**

ENTERTAINMENT AND NIGHTLIFE

Sinema Lara [353 D2] Gazipaşa Mahallesi. Shows Hollywood films remarkably soon after their release. Tickets are around TL8.

Luna Park [353 C1] A large permanent fairground between the old & the new coast roads.

Sekiz Direkli Hamamı [353 C1] Direkli Hamamı Sokak; ⏲ men 07.00–17.00 Fri–Wed, women 08.00–17.00 Thu. Trabzon's best Turkish bath lies tucked away 600m west of the Çarşi Camii

(Bazaar Mosque). The only old elements remaining are the 8 Seljuk columns of the name *sekiz direkli*, but the baths are still quite atmospheric. A full sauna & massage costs around TL26.

♀ **Beer Time** Atatürk Alanı; ⏲ 12.00–23.00. A basic bar with an upstairs & downstairs.

☆ **Stress Café** [353 D2] Uzun Sokak. ⏲ 10.00–midnight. Trabzon's liveliest place for smoking a *nargile* & playing backgammon. It often has live music.

SHOPPING

Local handicrafts to look out for are the gold Trabzon bracelets, very broad and distinctive, usually fairly plain but with very elaborate clasps, copper workmanship, weaving and wooden-ship building. Most shops are concentrated in the area close to the main square and along Uzun Yol and Maraş Caddesi. The **Old Bazaar** [353 D1] close to the coastal highway is also worth a look.

OTHER PRACTICALITIES

Trabzon's ATMs, banks and internet cafés are all situated along Maraş Caddesi.

WHAT TO SEE

The town and citadel Setting off from the main square, Atatürk Alanı [353 E2], sometimes also known as Meydan Parki, you can begin by walking along Uzun Yol, Long Street, which heads towards the citadel. Distances are not long, so it is fun to do this on foot as you can peer in all the shops along the way, this being the main street of Trabzon. The leather shops here are particularly good for bags, belts and wallets, and the food shops are also interesting, many of them selling the thinly sliced *pastırma* (air-dried beef), a local speciality excellent for picnics.

The first little church you come to is up a small side street to the left, just as the road begins to go uphill. A compact stone building, this is **St Anna** [353 D2], Trabzon's oldest church, dating from the 7th century and restored in the 9th century. This is its only claim to fame however, for it is now kept locked, is devoid of decoration or frescoes, and is only of interest to experts in Byzantine architecture. (The Church of St Basil was on the other side of the street, used as a storehouse in the metalworking section of the bazaar. It recently collapsed and was razed to the ground.) The **Nakıp Camii** [353 C2], north of the citadel nearer the sea, is thought to have been the **Church of St Andrew**, who reputedly introduced Christianity to Trebizond. Today almost in ruins, it was built in the 10th or 11th century.

Returning to Uzun Yol from the Trabzon Museum [353 D2] (see below), you soon cross a road bridge with white railings over a gully to the citadel. Climbing uphill slightly on the other side of the bridge, you reach an open square with an elegant neo-classical government hall on the left, and in the centre, the unmistakeable **Fatih** or **Ortahisar Camii** [353 C2] with ochre walls. Until the Ottoman conquest this was the Byzantine church of Panaghia Chrysocephalus, the Golden-Topped Virgin, because of its copper dome. The principal church of Trebizond, it was built in the 10th century and much enlarged after 1204. For all its historical significance, its Islamic embellishments are a living testimony to tastelessness.

The 16th-century **Gülbahar Hatun Camii** [353 C2] beyond the narrow citadel on the far side is almost as ugly as the Fatih, with crass new colours, neon lighting and garish carpets. It was built in 1514 by Selim the Grim in honour of his mother, who was known in her later years as Gülbahar, the Rose of Spring.

The **Yeni Cuma Camii** [353 D3], difficult to find up a maze of streets, was also originally a church (St Eugenios), and does at least still look like one. It is kept shut except at prayer times when you could slip in to see its finely carved *mihrab*.

Returning to the Fatih Camii at the centre of the citadel, you can now walk up the long steep hill to the summit where there are still fragments of the keep. Little children will appear as you approach, to take you to the **kale**. This is no bad thing as you need to cross a few people's back gardens to reach the edge, and it would be difficult to find unaided. Here, you can walk along the battlements that look down 100m or so into the gulley below. Windows with some decoration are still visible in the taller fragments of walls, liberally covered now with ivy and creepers. It was in this high corner that the Palace of the Comnene emperors and their lovely princesses is thought to have been located, and it is from here that you get the best feel for what Trebizond must once have been like.

As you walk back towards the main square you can still notice the occasional grand Greek dwelling in the backstreets behind Uzun Yol, often four storeys high with attractive carving on the doors and windows. Until 1923 and the exchange of populations Trabzon had one of the largest Greek populations in Turkey. Many are now derelict, some with boarded or smashed windows.

Trabzon Museum [353 D2] (*Zeytinlik Caddesi;* ⊕ *09.00–12.00 & 13.00–18.00 Tue–Sun; adult TL3*) Just a short way south from Uzun Yol is a wonderful imposing Russian mansion built in 1912 which has now been adapted as the Trabzon

Museum, boasting magnificent late Ottoman interiors with fine ceilings and all its original furnishings. On display too are some interesting Islamic pieces and some ethnographic material. In the basement is a good archaeological section displaying local finds from Byzantine sites. Atatürk stayed here briefly.

Ayia Sophia Müzesi [353 A3] (🕐 Apr–Oct 09.00–18.00 Tue–Sun; Nov–Mar 09.00–17.00 Tue–Sun; adult: TL3)

A visit to the Ayia Sophia cathedral on the outskirts of town is best done by car or taxi as it is a good 3km to the west of the centre. In the 1960s it stood by itself on a terrace overlooking the sea where Hadrian had once built a temple to Apollo. Now the setting has been largely lost, as the sprawl of Trabzon has engulfed it, although the railinged garden surrounding it gives a little respite from the busy city and its traffic.

The cathedral was built in the mid 13th century as a monastery church in the heyday of the Comnene Empire and converted to a mosque after the Ottoman conquest of 1461. As is usual in this process, the walls were whitewashed and covered with hard plaster, and the rescue of these murals from under these layers was lengthy and involved, taking from 1957 until 1964 under the supervision of David Talbot Rice and David Winfield. The Turks also used it as a military storeroom and, at the turn of the 20th century, as a fever hospital. Now well lit and clearly labelled, it has been transformed into a fine museum.

As you approach from the ticket kiosk the tall grey building to the left is the old bell tower built in 1427. The small size of the church/cathedral compared to its namesake in Istanbul makes you realise how small this kingdom was in comparison with the real Byzantine Empire.

Kızlar Manastırı [353 F2]

The most pleasantly situated building in Trabzon is the Kızlar Manastırı, originally the Theokephastos Convent, set up on one of the hills overlooking the town and the sea. To reach it you follow the sign to Boztepe, a

FAMOUS FRESCOES

The magnificent frescoes for which the Ayia Sophia Cathedral is famous adorn the walls and ceiling of the narthex. Among the most beautiful is the Marriage at Cana, the colours vivid as Christ turns the water into wine. Among the other miracles depicted are the Feeding of the Five Thousand, Christ Walking on the Water and the Miracle of the Boy Possessed of a Demon. One of the labels on the frescoes has a delightful mistranslation in its English version: 'Angel adoring the Holy Towel' (instead of Shroud). These paintings were all executed in the late 13th century and are in the tradition of Constantinople with some Cappadocian influence: they are thought to have all been the work of one individual.

Inside the church are more frescoes and fragments of the original marble mosaic flooring with elaborate geometric designs, and marble columns are used within the church and in the arcaded porches. In the dome a huge half-effaced Christ Pantokrator looks down. In the south porch a frieze above the arches depicts the Garden of Eden, Adam and Eve and the Temptation. The style shows Armenian and Eastern influences, while much of the decorative carving of the church, especially the stalactite work in the porches, geometric medallions, the lotus flower and star motifs are Seljuk, were added when the church was converted to a mosque. Walking round the outside to the sea terrace on the northern side, the porch shows a heart-rending fresco labelled 'Jonah plagued by boils'. Restoration works began in 1957 and went on for six consecutive summers under the supervision of David Talbot Rice.

picnic and recreational area on a hill above the city. The road leads inland and winds on uphill for about 1.5km. Then, as you approach a right bend with a large pink hospital building on your right, you will notice a smaller tarmac road leading straight on from the bend, and an even smaller tarmac road leading steeply downhill. The first road is the one that leads to Boztepe, soon passing a football ground on the right, and the second is the road that leads steeply down for 20m and then forks off uphill for 10m to the convent entrance.

The guardian will soon materialise. He is the local primary school teacher and has been entrusted with the care of the convent in return for being allowed to grow his vegetables in its grounds. He says the convent is shortly to be restored and put firmly on the tourist map. For the moment, however, it is rarely visited and the atmosphere, once within the high walls, is beautifully peaceful, a welcome escape from the bustle of the town. Much remains, including a rock cave-church, a second church, a bell tower, a bathroom, the refectory and hall. Faint traces of 15th-century murals are still visible in the blackened walls of the rock church. A spring in the cave is associated with eternal youth. Walking up through the vegetable garden you come to a little folly, like an ornamental well. It is in fact a tomb. From here the views out across Trabzon with the convent in the foreground are memorable.

EXCURSIONS FROM TRABZON

From the Theokephastos Convent with a few hours to spare you can make an excursion further inland to the even more rarely visited Armenian monastery, **Kaymaklı Manastırı**, occupied by monks until 1923 and now used as a barn. As long as you behave respectfully and politely the family will let you poke around, as the part they live in is a modern breeze-block construction which will have no interest for you.

Continue uphill on the main road that you turned off to see the Kızlar Manastırı, and after about 1km when you reach a T-junction, turn right, and following the potholed road for about 2km as it runs between hazelnut groves and vineyards, 10m or so after a newly built mosque, an earth road runs obliquely left off down the hill. In wet weather this earth road is tricky for cars because the gradient is steep, so you are best advised to walk the remaining 500m down the hillside. Like the convent, the monastery has high walls punctuated with windows on two storeys facing out over the valley.

The church stands in a grassy courtyard. Beyond it is a little chapel, now a chicken coop. The farmyard animals, chickens, dogs and cows, will all set up a rumpus as you approach, and the mother yells things at you which sound like rather fierce abuse as she carries on with her heavy labour in the yard, but be assured that this is just her normal manner.

ATATÜRK KÖŞKÜ (⊕ *daily 08.00–17.00; adult TL2*) Another short excursion, definitely worthwhile, is to visit Atatürk's Summer House, Atatürk Köşkü, 4km inland behind Trabzon high up in heavily pine-wooded hills. This house is an attractive white stucco villa which could have been lifted straight out of any European riviera, set in its own extensive and beautifully tended gardens, now laid out as tea-gardens among the pine trees. It serves today as a museum of Atatürk memorabilia, and the ticket kiosk sells some suitable Atatürk souvenirs.

To reach Atatürk Köşkü you must drive from the main square off towards the citadel, as for Ayia Sofya. Having crossed the bridge over the gorge by the citadel turn left uphill and follow the signs to Atatürk Köşkü. It is in fact also from this stretch of road, both on the way up and the way down, that you will get the best views of the citadel walls, bringing the fable of Trebizond's towers closest to its reality.

By opening the doors of the Kaymaklı Manastırı wide there is enough light to see the astonishing frescoes on three walls. The most memorable is a fantastic depiction of hell, with the red river of hell-fire running the length of the wall. The devil crouches in various gleeful and beckoning postures along it as he lures people further and further down into the pit, and Cerebus, the black dog of Hades, and other typically Armenian fantastical creatures like griffins, lurk behind the bushes along the way. This painting is unlike anything to be seen in Cappadocian or Byzantine churches, which depict standard scenes from the Bible. The colours are still quite strong, protected from the light as they are in the darkened barn.

SUMELA MONASTERY (⏱ *daily 09.00–18.00; national park entry cars TL8, adult TL3; monastery entry adult TL8*) The excursion from Trabzon 48km inland to the superb mountain Sumela Monastery takes a full half day but is well worth the effort. It is its setting, clinging Tibetan-style to a sheer rock face above steep and heavily wooded slopes that makes the trip memorable, together with the stiff 30-minute walk from the car park below to reach it. Far from any village or habitation and often shrouded in mist, the monastery has a haunting quality despite the huge numbers of visitors who flock here in the summer months. East of Ankara, it is probably Turkey's most visited site after Nemrut Dağı.

Getting there and away From May until late August two bus companies, **Ulusoy** and **Metro** run a daily tour to Sumela leaving from outside their Trabzon offices on the main square of Atatürk Alanı at 10.00 and returning at 15.00. Both cost TL20 return.

The road follows the course of the river Değirmendere in a wide valley with wooded slopes rising either side. This is the main road to Erzurum, up over the Zigana Pass at the end of the Pontic Mountains and descending onto the plateau of the Anatolian hinterland. A busy road, carrying much truck traffic, this is also the main coach route for tours leaving Trabzon and having to reach Erzurum that night. Because of this, the tours depart very early from Trabzon, and so between 08.00 and 12.30 the monastery is at its most crowded, with continuous streams of people plodding up and down the mountain path. If you have your own transport it is well worth timing your arrival for 13.00 or later, as you will find the place much less populated, and as it stays open until 17.00 you can have lunch

The road winds higher than the Kızlar Manastırı, high enough in spring to be shrouded in mist. You then come quite suddenly on the elegant white house. Its gardens are well tended with roses and fountains and two gardeners are instructed by ten supervisors where to weed. Rubbish (*çöp*) containers are laid out every 5m, not that anyone would dare drop litter here, such is the atmosphere of reverence. Most visitors are Turkish, but it is, for the foreign tourist, delightfully obsessive, and all for a house that Atatürk graced for only three days, in 1921. Inside are photos of Atatürk in every conceivable pose and the desk drawers are stuffed full of further memorabilia that there is no room to display. Guards are on hand, not so much to check you do not steal anything, as to make sure you do not defile with your touch.

afterwards at one of the many restaurants around the car park beside the rushing stream, rather than making the ascent on a full stomach.

Where to stay There is good accommodation in Maçka if you want to avoid the scrum of Trabzon and make an early start visiting Sumela.

⌂ **Büyük Sumela Hotel** (115 rooms) \ (462) 5167553. Right at the entry to the town of Maçka, on the main square by the river, 12km from Sumela Monastery. All plush mod-cons here, with indoor pool, sauna, massage & jacuzzi, plus 2 restaurants, 1 on the roof. $$$$

⌂ **Vazelon Pansiyon** (25 rooms) \ (462) 5122040. Set beside the river as you first enter the town of Maçka from the main highway, a pleasant, clean & unpretentious place. For dinner there is a restaurant (unlicensed) next door with a terrace right on the river. B/fast inc. $$

Other practicalities Reaching Maçka on the main road south after 25km from Trabzon, the turn-off left to Sumela is clearly marked. For the next 17km this dead-end road winds through stunning scenery of heavy pine forests, following the course of the rushing river, until it reaches a ticket kiosk at the entrance to what announces itself as the Altındere Vadısı Milli Parkı (Altındere Valley National Park) where separate charges are levied for cars and individuals. You then arrive in an extended area of parking for coaches and cars. There are many souvenir shops, a post office and restaurants where you can eat anything from a small snack to a freshly caught trout from the river, and the setting is very lovely. There are even a few simple bungalows for rent, and many wooden picnic tables laid out in the forest, Alpine-style. From here it is only on an exceptionally clear day that you will see the monastery levitating above you in the cliff face – usually it is shrouded in mist and you will not see it until you are a lot closer.

What to see The idle can now drive on – as most coach tours do – on a specially constructed road that winds up to a point just a few minutes' walk from the monastery. The more virtuous approach, however, is to walk up the forest path from the main car park by the restaurants, crossing the river on the wooden bridge. In wet weather the path can be slippery so make sure you have suitable footwear. Many a tourist has been deterred from the ascent by open-toed sandals. It takes 25–30 minutes depending on your level of fitness. The monastery is 1,250m above sea level, and although the ascent only climbs through 250m of these, the distance of the path is 1,100m with 25 zigzags. An entry fee (*TL8*) is charged at the top, so make sure you have brought money along.

REMOTER MONASTERIES
Vazelon Monastery In dry weather you can visit a second and far more remote and unknown monastery nearby called Vazelon. To reach it you will need a full half day, as the road is not good and you then have to walk the final two hours, but if you want to escape the crowds and see a kind of mini Sumela, complete with frescoes, this may be the place for you. It also has the benefit of no entry fees for vehicles or people. In its heyday it was second only to Sumela in wealth, but the deterioration in its condition since the 1980s is shocking, the result of vandalism and campfire smoke. By the time you get there, you may wonder why you bothered.

Getting there and away From the Maçka turn-off to Sumela, follow the main road towards Erzurum for another 10km. As the road climbs along the left-hand slope of the valley, at a sharp hairpin bend to the left, a dirt track leads right, or rather straight on, quite steeply downhill. There is sometimes even a sign here pointing

Once inside, you can see how heavily ruined the monastery is behind its imposing heavily restored façade. Nowhere in Turkey, except perhaps in the Göreme churches of Cappadocia, is there anything to equal the degree of defacement found here. Great chunks of fresco have been gouged out over the years and the surfaces covered in graffiti. As in Cappadocia the names carved are mainly in Turkish and Greek, with just the odd German or French addition.

Founded in the 6th century to house the icon of the Virgin painted by St Luke (Panaghia tou Melas, Virgin of the Black Rock, corrupted in the Pontic dialect to Soumelas, then to Sumela), the monastery was inhabited until 1923 when the Greeks were expelled from the country in the exchange of populations. Alexius Comnenus III was crowned Emperor of Trebizond here in 1349. Most of the façade dates only from the 18th century, and the monastery's sorry state today is the result of a fire just after its monks were forced out in 1923. A historic mass was held here in August 2010 in a symbolic gesture.

Of what remains, the frescoes on the façade and, inside, on the ceiling of the cave-church are outstanding. On the façade, the top row of paintings are a fascinating Adam and Eve series to be read like a cartoon from left to right. In the top left Adam is lying down naked having a chat with God; next Adam and Eve stand together naked (Adam with his penis defaced) and a snake in the background; the middle picture is too defaced to make out; next Adam and Eve are standing with their fig leaves, looking guilty and ashamed next to God; finally, on the far right side, Adam and Eve are out in the world without God. On the right-hand side of the façade you can just make out a painting of St George killing the dragon. Inside the cave-church the frescoes are heavily defaced but the strong colours and the sheer numbers of paintings still makes them impressive. Where the later plaster has fallen off, it has revealed older frescoes beneath. Look for the particularly fine Virgin and Child seated on a magnificent gold throne.

to Vazelon Manastırı. The total distance from this point is 6km. The track can be very muddy after rain and is not then suitable for a saloon car. It leads down to the bottom of the valley, crosses the river, and then climbs back up the other side, winding round the hill to the monastery set above the road in the cliff face. The road passes a trout farm and saloon cars can be left in the car park here if you fear the remainder of the track is too tough. If you choose to do this, it then takes a further half hour to walk the remainder of the track as it heads east. All vehicles must stop 2km after the trout farm at a concrete culvert, and the monastery is visible from here. The access path begins 150m past the culvert, forking uphill, but can easily be missed.

What to see Founded in the 5th century, the monastery is dedicated to John the Baptist. The final approach staircase enters the monastery's entry hall on the first floor, the same as Sumela. Monks' cells lead off a corridor to either side. On the terrace a triple-nave church still has frescoes illustrating the Last Judgement, Hell and Paradise. It was abandoned in 1923 and its wooden roof has now fallen in. The side chapel outside the walls has fragmentary scenes of the Dormition, the Baptism and the Raising of Lazarus.

St George in Peristera A third and even remoter monastery, built in the time of Justinian, can be visited by keen walkers on the return to Trabzon from Sumela, or preferably as a day trip from Trabzon. This is the convent of St George in Peristera,

The Black Sea Coast EXCURSIONS FROM TRABZON 12

also called Hızır Ilyas Manastırı, near Kustul village. From Esiroglu, 19km from Trabzon on the main Sumela–Erzurum road, you fork left 4km to Sahinkaya/Liboda and then on to Kuştul village 14km further on. In dry weather the tracks are driveable with a car, but more usually it is a three-hour walk and you are advised to take a guide with you from Esiroğlu, as the maze of tracks is very confusing. Built on a rock, a 93-step stairway leads up to the monastery. It was once very wealthy, but in 1906 a severe fire badly destroyed the building and then the monks had to leave for good in 1923. It was later converted to a mosque and no frescoes are visible.

In these Pontic foothills, once an important monastic centre, there are many more little-known monasteries, never signposted and often very difficult to reach. The monks of course were never bothered by a few hours' walk; quite the contrary, remoteness from populated centres was a necessary prerequisite to meditation. Others, marked on the map for those who are real enthusiasts, are Oma, Seno, Charweli (all south of Sürmene) and Kızlar (just after Maçka).

TRABZON TO ERZURUM: THE ZIGANA PASS

From the Black Sea the commonest route inland is over the Zigana Pass towards Erzurum, following the first great caravan route overland to Persia that brought Trabzon its wealth. The climb through the valley beyond Maçka is impressive, winding up through heavily wooded conifer hillsides, though the scenery and mountains are in many ways less dramatic than the less-used route inland described earlier (see page 327), from Hopa through the Tortum Gorge. The most striking moment comes when you reach the abrupt transition from the lush green vegetation of the coastal zone to the bleakness of the central Anatolian Plateau. Today this moment comes when you emerge from a 2km-long tunnel recently built as part of the road improvements.

Some 15km after the Zigana Pass you reach the town of **Torul**, where a brown sign points off right to **Meryemana Taş Köprü**, a remarkable stone bridge. Then from Ikisu, about 15km before Gümüşhane, a sign points off left 24km to Imera Manastırı. In these hills both to the east and west of Torul and Gümüşhane, are well over 20 churches, all now in a ruined state. These two signposted ones are those in the best condition. The Meryemana Bridge was built in the 19th century in a single span, its arch made of ashlar blocks, the rest in stone rubble. You have to cross this bridge to reach the village of Yaylalı where the Meryemana Church still stands, with a dungeon on its east side, and the church entrance on the south, unusually. On the other side of the main Trabzon–Gümüşhane road, **Imera Monastery** is in the village of Olucak, and dates to 1350. Standing by itself 2km outside the village is the Imera Valley Church, still remarkably well preserved with its roof and central dome intact. The entrance is elaborately decorated and bears the date 1885.

XENOPHON'S ROUTE TO THE SEA

This was same route, carried out in reverse, which Xenophon and his Ten Thousand followed from Babylon in 400BC and from where, as they reached the summit, they caught their first glimpse of the sea: 'So Xenophon mounted on his horse and, taking Lycus and the cavalry with him, rode forward to give support and, quite soon, they heard the soldiers shouting out "The sea! The sea!" and began passing the word down the column. Then suddenly they all began to run, the rear guard and all, and drove on the baggage animals and the horses at full speed, and when they had all got to the top, the soldiers, with tears in their eyes, embraced each other and their generals and captives.'

Some 40km after the summit of the pass you reach Gümüşhane, at an altitude of 1,100m, a new town built after World War I. It takes its name (Silver Caravan) from the silver mines in the neighbourhood, now closed down. The Old Town, in ruins 4km away, although many of its fine old mansions are now being restored, was once a summer resort for the wealthy merchants of Trabzon and had a large Greek population. It was occupied by the Russians in 1916 and subsequently so thoroughly destroyed that a new town needed to be built. Shortly after Gümüşhane a sign points left to **Akçakale**, a castle perched up on a solid rock outcrop, which seems to have served more as an observation tower and storage than a castle. Its plan is circular and there is a cistern inside its tower.

About 17km southeast of Gümüşhane, instead of continuing to Erzurum, you can instead fork southwest to Kelkit, before heading on to Erzincan, 125km away to the south, where your itinerary can link up with *Chapter 5* and the drive through the gorges of the upper Euphrates (see page 124). This region around Kelkit is known as the Kelkit Basin, an attractive landscape of forested hills based around the Kelkit River, relatively unpopulated and with many camping possibilities if you are travelling under your own steam and can stop wherever you like. The route crosses a pass at 2,020m.

If instead, you decide to continue east to Erzurum, a further 80km brings you to **Bayburt**, a larger and more appealing town than modern Gümüşhane, dominated by impressive fortifications running along a high ridge to the north. Originally Armenian, it was rebuilt by the Romans, Seljuks and Ottomans. Marco Polo stayed there on his way to China. Despite the excellent state of the outer walls, little remains inside the castle. A river runs around the foot of the castle hill, and along its banks attractive houses have continuous wooden balconies on props overhanging the water.

Beyond Bayburt you climb over a second pass, Köpdaği at 2,390m, higher than the Zigana but nowhere near as spectacular. In winter it is notorious for its sudden blizzards when whole caravans used to be snowed in and frozen to death. Xenophon describes it: 'The snow was six feet deep and many of the animals and slaves perished in it, as did about 30 of the soldiers… Soldiers who had lost the use of their eyes through snow blindness or whose toes had dropped off from frostbite were left behind.'

A drive through uneventful scenery for the final 70km brings you then to Erzurum.

FROM TRABZON TO SAMSUN

Trabzon used to be the easternmost port of call for the car ferries of Turkish Maritime Lines from Istanbul, and back in the 1970s the ferries even went as far east as Hopa and stopped off at many more ports. However the importance of trade eastwards with Georgia and the former Soviet states now that the border is fully open again has seen a huge investment in the building of the Black Sea Coastal Highway.

The coast west from Trabzon still has the now familiar tea plantations covering the hillsides to the left, and beyond Akçaabat the beaches are black sand with black rocks along the shore. The anchovy caught in quantity all along this coast is very cheap and forms the staple diet of the fishing villages. Otherwise the commonest varieties of fish are red mullet, tuna, bluefish and turbot.

Shortly before Tirebolu a sign points inland up a valley just before crossing a river to **Bedrama Kalesi**, a castle built by the Genoese, who were active traders all along the Black Sea from Seljuk times onwards. At Tirebolu an imposing fortification on a promontory is **St Jean Castle**, with steps leading up to it. Below is an attractive

This four–six-lane highway runs from Samsun eastwards all the way to the Georgian border and has been under construction for many years. Whilst its economic benefit is not in doubt, the downside has been the decline of shipping traffic so that Turkish Maritime Lines no longer found it viable to run the ferry service that used to run from Istanbul all along the coast to Trabzon, but also the environmental and ecological cost has been considerable. Where the course of the highway follows the coast itself, whole towns and communities have been permanently cut off from their shoreline. Tunnelling, sea walls and breakwaters have disfigured the once sleepy coast, as heavy goods traffic thunders along towards the Georgian border. There is only one stretch between Trabzon and Samsun where it is still possible to get a feel for what this coastline used to be like, and that is between Bolaman and Ordu, where the highway cuts straight through the headland, but the old road can still be followed in an attractive detour as it wiggles round Cape Yason.

tea-house and restaurant on the pretty curve of Tirebolu Harbour. From Espiye, another sign points off inland to **Andoz Kalesi**, again built by the Genoese.

GİRESUN *Telephone code: 454*

You now reach Giresun, a bustling town with its own castle (Giresun Kalesi), which stands on the top of the wooded headland you passed, and was once the acropolis of the Milesian colony of Cerasus. It was from here that the Roman general Lucullus, who captured the town in the Pontic Wars in 69BC, brought back the first cherry trees to Europe. The name Cerasus is the origin of our words cerise and cherry. Just offshore is a small island with a second castle, where Jason and the Argonauts are said to have put in on their quest for the Golden Fleece and attacked by birds dropping feathered darts. Now called Büyük Ada (Big Island), it was once the ancient island of Aretias where an Amazon queen founded a temple to Ares, god of war. Inhabited today by fishermen, the island can be visited by boat.

GETTING THERE AND AWAY Buses run east to and from Trabzon (two hours, TL10) and west to and from Ordu (one hour, TL5) from the centre of town, Atapark, on the coastal road.

WHERE TO STAY

Hotel New Jasmin (86 rooms) GMK Bulvarı Cerkez Mevkii; ☎ 2141646; www.otelnewjasmin.com. Boasting an outdoor pool with children's section, sauna & 3 restaurants, this is Giresun's most comfortable place to break your journey, situated well out of town on the coast to the west, 190km from Trabzon airport. $$$

Kit-Tur Otel (50 rooms) Arifbey Caddesi 2; ☎ 2120245; www.otelkittur.com. Attractive place

with roof bar, fine views, good restaurant & sauna. In the centre of town, 140km from Trabzon airport. $$

Başar Hotel (54 rooms) Atatürk Bulvarı, Liman Mevkii; ☎ 2129920; www.hotelbasar.com.tr. Right on the coast with spectacular views. Simple rooms, good restaurant with local dishes. Unlicensed. $

WHERE TO EAT

✕ Çavuşlu Dinlenme Tesisleri Sahil Caddesi 10, Çavuşlu Görele; ☎ 5230031; ⊕ 24hrs. Halfway

between Trabzon & Giresun, right on the roadside, a good place to stop for a quick meal by the sea. Serves simple meat, fish & vegetable dishes. Outdoor seating. $

✗ **Cerkez Restaurant** Gemiler Cekeği Mahallesi; Cerkez Mevkii; ☎ 2163139. Seaside place opposite

a small island. Fish-based main courses with excellent *kadayıf* (sticky hazelnut pastry dessert) to follow, reputed to be the best in the area. Licensed. $

ORDU *Telephone code: 452*

Ordu is a pleasant city with palm trees lining its seafront and has a few older Ottoman houses tucked away in its backstreets. One of these has been converted to a museum, the **Pasha's Palace and Ethnography Museum** (*Tasocak Caddesi;* ⊕ *09.00–12.00 & 13.30–17.00 Tue–Sun; adult TL3*), and has interesting exhibits recreating life and furnishings in 19th-century Ottoman times. Its garden serves light snacks.

🏠 **WHERE TO STAY** The **Ikizevler Hotel** (*17 rooms; Kazım Karabekir Caddesi;* ☎ *2250081; www.karlibelhotel.com.tr; $$$*) is very rare for the Black Sea coast, an attractive hilltop boutique hotel in a gracious Ottoman mansion, complete with antique rugs, traditional furnishings and a garden café. It also has a sister hotel on the seafront, the **Karlıbel Atherina Otel** (*9 rooms with sea view; on the coast road near the Army Centre;* ☎ *2121616*).

✗ **WHERE TO EAT**

✗ **Vonalı Celal'in Yeri** Ordu-Samsun karayolu uzeri, Perşembe'nin Ramazan Köyü, Vona mevkii; ☎ 5872137. Renowned licensed place favoured by politicians & artists, famous for its 101 pickles & 30 local specialities, many based on anchovies. Cosy atmosphere, good views & outdoor seating. $$

PERŞEMBE

Perşembe, on a headland 16km beyond Ordu, is one of the most attractive towns and harbours along this coast, and now that it is bypassed by the Black Sea Coastal Highway, it is one of the few places that has kept its charm. The trees on the slopes

---

THE HABITS OF THE AMAZONS

The land around the Black Sea was associated in ancient times with the Amazons. These remarkably independent women were described by Strabo:

The Amazons spend ten months of the year off to themselves performing their individual tasks, such as ploughing, planting, pasturing cattle, or particularly in training horses, though the bravest engage in hunting on horseback and practice warlike exercises. The right breasts of all are seared when they are infants, so that they can easily use their right hands for any purpose, and especially that of throwing the javelin. They also use bows and arrows and light shields, and make the skins of wild animals serve as helmets, clothing and girdles. They have two months in spring when they go up into the neighbouring mountain which separates them from the Gagarians. The Gagarians, also in accordance with an ancient custom, go thither to offer sacrifice with the Amazons and to have intercourse with them for the sake of begetting children, doing this in secrecy and darkness, any Gagarian at random with any Amazon; and after making them pregnant they send them away; and the females that are born are retained by the Amazons, but the males are taken to the Gagarians to be brought up; and each Gagarian to whom a child is brought adopts the child as his own, regarding the child as his son because of the uncertainty.

are spectacular and cover the hillside right down to the edge of the road. The tea plantation region has been left behind; these trees are all either hazelnut (*findik*), an important Turkish export, or cherry. In early May the hills blossom.

The weather from here westwards is less prone to rain showers and gets more sunshine. When the sun is out along this coastline it transforms the colours of the scenery. The sea immediately becomes intensely blue and the greens of the coast become even greener. The occasional picnic area with wooden tables and benches is laid out on the shore by the roadside.

The road continues on to Bolaman where it picks up with the Black Sea Coastal Highway again, and between here and Fatsa, where large sulphur reserves have been found, there are a number of good comfortable hotels on the sea. Just before Ünye a road leads inland to Niksar, where 6km further on, the striking castle of **Çaleoğlu** stands on a volcanic hill. At a high point within its walls is the entrance to a tunnel of 400 steps down to the water, built by Mithradates, King of Pontus. Along the rocky shore near the town of Ünye there are caves inhabited by seals.

From Ünye onwards the road straightens out as it leaves the coast and then passes through the large fertile delta of the Yeşilırmak, a landscape suddenly very different from the hilly wooded coastline. The main cash crop here is the famous Turkish tobacco.

 WHERE TO STAY The **Difana Hotel** (*28 rooms; Sahil Yolu;* \ *3231602; www.difanahotel.com; $$*) is on the beach 8km from Ünye, 55km east of Samsun airport. It is a charming family-run hotel with a restaurant and central heating.

SAMSUN *Telephone code: 362*

Samsun, as ancient Amisos, was founded by Greeks from Miletos in the 7th century BC and was later ruled by the Pontic kings, the Romans, the Byzantines and the Seljuks, who gave it its present name. When it fell to the Ottomans in the 15th century, the Genoese, who were given trading privileges here by the Seljuks, burned the city down, which is why nothing of historical interest remains to be seen today.

In more recent history Samsun is the point where Atatürk disembarked on 19 May 1919 and began organising the defence against the Greek army which had landed at Izmir at about the same time. This date is therefore taken as the beginning of the Turkish War of Independence, and 19 May is a national holiday in Turkey as well as a frequent street name. Samsun welcomed Atatürk with bands and cheering crowds and has been staunchly republican ever since. The city commemorates the event with a colossal equestrian statue of Atatürk, surpassed in size only by that in Ankara. It is the Black Sea's biggest port, and people only stop here today because it is a major transport hub. In July the city has a regional Black Sea Fair which can make accommodation difficult to find.

GETTING THERE AND AWAY

By air Turkish Airlines (*www.thy.com*) flies five times a day to and from Istanbul and four times a day to and from Ankara. Onur Air (*www.onurair.com*) flies twice a day to and from Istanbul, Pegasus Airlines (*www.flypgs.com*) flies twice a week to and from Izmir and Sun Express (*www.sunexpress.com.tr*) flies to and from Izmir in summer only. The airport, known as Samsun-Çarşamba (\ *8448830*), lies 23km south of the city, and takes 30 minutes by taxi, costing TL30. Havaş buses (run by Turkish Airlines) do a shuttle every half hour between the airport and the city centre coach park close to the Kultur Sarayı.

By train The train station (✆ *2332293*) is only 500m southeast of Atatürk Parki on the coastal road, and daily services run to and from Sivas (8.5 hours, TL16) and Amasya (three hours, TL6).

By bus Samsun has a new *otogar* (✆ *2381706*) 3km inland which runs regular services between all local towns in all directions such as west to Sinop (three hours, TL20), east to Trabzon (six hours, TL30) and southwest to Ankara (seven hours, TL49).

By car Car rental is available from Avis (✆ *2316750; www.avis.com*) and Eleni (✆ *2300091*), the same agencies as at Trabzon.

TOURIST INFORMATION Samsun has a good tourist office on Atatürk Bulvarı (⊕ *08.00–12.00 & 13.00–17.00 Mon–Fri*) which will give you free maps and leaflets.

WHERE TO STAY

⌂ **Omtel Otel** (44 rooms) Kurupelit Kampusu; ✆ 4575481; www.omu.edu.tr. With a private beach 35km from Samsun airport & set on a university campus, this place offers reasonable & relaxing accommodation, with 2 restaurants. Good range of activities such as beach volleyball, billiards & table tennis. $$

⌂ **Tepe Otel** (120 rooms) Universite Kampusu ici Kurupelit; ✆ 4576074; e tepeotel@ ttnet.net.tr. Also on a university campus & close to the sea, this place also has 2 restaurants & is 25km from Samsun airport. $$

WHERE TO EAT

✗ **Samsun Balık Restaurant** Kazımpasa Caddesi; ✆ 4357550. Set in an attractive brick house, this is Samsun's most upmarket fish restaurant. $$$
✗ **Korfez Restaurant** Korfez Mahallesi, Atatürk Bulvarı 110, Kurupelit; ✆ 4575329; ⊕ 09.30–22.30. Popular with families at w/ends with a lively atmosphere & music, garden with seating up to 500 people. Good range of fish & meat dishes, with Turkish pizzas & various toppings. Sea view from roof-top bar. Licensed. $$

✗ **Canlı Balık Restaurant** Liman ici Mevkii, Yakakent; ✆ 6112362; ⊕ 09.00–23.00. There are many waterfront restaurants in this pretty harbour along a long stretch of sand, & this one is a good one to sit outside & relax with grilled fish, meze & salad. Unlicensed. $
✗ **Maide Et Lokantası** 19 Mayıs Sanayı Sitesi, Atatürk Bulvarı 25, Kutlukent; ✆ 2667472; ⊕ 09.30–22.30. Popular unlicensed place with a range of grilled meat, casseroles & Turkish pizzas (pide). $

WEST TO SINOP

The coast west of Samsun is generally not as attractive as the stretch to the east, with the exception of the stretch from Bafra to Sinop. The total drive to Sinop

DIOGENES THE CYNIC

The only citizen of any note produced by the Milesian colonies along the Black Sea was Diogenes the Cynic, born in Sinop in 413BC. It was not here, but at Corinth in Greece, that Alexander the Great encountered Diogenes who, shunning worldly pleasures, chose to live inside a barrel. Taking pity on this abject figure, Alexander asked if there was anything he wanted. 'Yes,' replied Diogenes, 'stand aside a little, for you are blocking the sun.' 'If I had not been Alexander,' came the reply, 'I would have wanted to be Diogenes.'

takes about two hours, following the coast for most of the way except where you cross the broad delta of the Kızılırmak. The road west first passes through Bafra, a tobacco-growing centre on the Kızılırmak. It is also famous for its caviar.

SİNOP *Telephone code: 368*

Sinop is the only natural harbour along the Black Sea. Situated on a peninsula easily defended from attack and protected from the west and north winds, Sinop is known to have served as a port as early as Hittite times for the capital of Hattuşaş due south of here. Because of its setting, it was chosen for the largest Milesian colony in the 8th century BC, and it was from here that the Greek colonists made sub-colonies to the east in Giresun and Trabzon. It remained prosperous under the Pontic kings, for whom it served as a capital city for a time, and later under the Romans. It passed from the Byzantines to the Seljuks in the 13th century, and then fell to the local emirs of Kastamonu in the hills inland, who allowed the Genoese to use it as the centre for their Black Sea trade. After being taken by the Ottomans in 1458, it became secondary to Samsun as a port.

The town still makes its living from the sea and a good meal can be had in the fish restaurants on the quayside. Little remains of its illustrious past beyond the ruined Genoese castle, the 13th-century Alaeddin Cami and the Alaiye Medrese, now a museum with a fine Seljuk portal. The town's name is said to come from an Amazon queen called Sinope. Zeus, attracted by her charms, came to court here and offered her any gift she desired. She chose everlasting virginity and lived happily ever after.

There are good swimming beaches outside Sinop, and at Aklıman, 15km from town, the forest comes down to the beach and the bay is dotted with attractive small islands ideal for camping. The scenery is attractive as far as Abana and Inebolu, where there are more good swimming beaches.

GETTING THERE AND AWAY

By bus Sinop has a new *otogar* about 5km west of town on the main road, linked by minibuses and *dolmuş* services to the centre (TL2). A taxi costs TL8. Services run regularly to and from Inebolu (for Kastamonu) (three hours, TL20), Karabuk (for Safranbolu) (six hours, TL30) and Trabzon (nine hours, TL50).

TOURIST INFORMATION There is a helpful tourist information office on Gazi Caddesi (⏱ *mid-Jun–mid-Sep 08.30–17.00 Mon–Fri*), giving out maps and booklets.

🏠 WHERE TO STAY

🏠 **Zinos Country Hotel** (14 rooms) Enver Bahadır Yolu; ✆ 2605600; www.zinoshotel.com. Located 2km to the east out of town on the road to Karakum this interesting place with its timbered exterior is on the black-sand beach, 10km from Sinop airport. It has 2 restaurants & AC. $$$

🏠 **Otel Mola** (24 rooms) Derinboğazağzi Sokak; ✆ 2611814; www.sinopmolaotel.com.tr. This is a new place close to the harbour with sea views & comfortable rooms. $$

🏠 **Sinop Turist Hotel** (36 rooms) Korucuk Köyü Denizler Mevkii; ✆ 2604945; www.sinopturistotel.com. Right on the beach, this simple place also boasts an outdoor pool & a basketball pitch. $$

🏠 **Otel Sarı Kadır** (18 rooms) Derinboğazağzi Sokak; ✆ 2601544. Right on the waterfront, the spacious rooms have balconies over the sea. Opposite is a tea-garden. $

✕ WHERE TO EAT
All along the waterfront there are many good restaurants serving fish and other meat dishes, with outdoor seating and almost all of them licensed.

✗ Deniz Restaurant Yalı Mahallesi, Omer Seyfettin 8, Iskele Meydanı; ☎ 6135106. Unpretentious licensed place on the waterfront with grilled fish & meat. Outdoor seating with good views of the pretty harbour. $

KASTAMONU *Telephone code: 366*

From Inebolu a good road leads inland to Kastamonu, an extremely picturesque town with typical Ottoman square half-timbered houses, one of them housing a museum with a good collection of Roman sculpture. The 13th-century Atabey Mosque is also worth a visit. Nearby Kasaba, 17km to the northwest, has a very rare entirely wooden mosque dating to 1366, and Pınarbaşı, a small town 97km northwest of Kastamonu is the main centre for the Kure Dağlari National Park (*www.ked.org.tr*), a wonderful area of undiscovered natural beauty with forests, waterfalls, canyons and cliff faces.

GETTING THERE AND AWAY Kastamonu has an *otogar* 7km north of the city centre and is reachable by taxi (TL10) or *dolmuş*. Services run regularly to and from the coast at Inebolu (minibuses) taking two hours (TL10), Sinop (three hours, TL20), Ankara (4.5 hours, TL25) and Istanbul (nine hours, TL40).

⌂ WHERE TO STAY

⌂ **Toprakcılar Konakları** (10 rooms, 1 suite) Ismailbey Mahallesi Alemdar; ☎ 2121812; www.toprakcilar.com; ◷ all year. In the centre of town near the Ismailbey Mosque this place has its own restaurant where *rakı* can be served with your meal. Pleasant garden. Restored by an art historian it was the first proper boutique hotel in Kastamonu. $$$$

⌂ **Park Ilica Turizm Tesisi** (6 cabins sleeping 5 or 4 people) ☎ 7712046; www.parkilica.com. The best base for looking round the National Park, this is a kind of simple wooden eco-lodge. $

⌂ **Paşa Konaği-Pınarbaşı** (8 rooms) ☎ 7713375; ◷ all year. 46km from Safranbolu, about midway between Kastamonu & Safranbolu, at 750m on the road between Cide on the coast & Eflani inland, this entirely timber house has downstairs storage for animals & small rooms upstairs, all with en-suite bathrooms. Pretty garden & its own restaurant. The local women still mainly wear traditional dress & headscarves. A nearby village has a natural thermal bath where one can still bathe inside the Roman ruins. $

AMASRA *Telephone code: 378*

Following the coast from Inebolu the road winds on to Amasra, a pretty resort. Founded by the Milesians and beautifully situated on its own well-treed peninsula, it has a Genoese castle on its citadel.

GETTING THERE AND AWAY Only minibuses run to and from Amasra, leaving from the PTT office to Bartin (30 minutes, TL3), from where buses run on to and from Safranbolu (two hours, TL12), Ankara (five hours, TL30) and Istanbul (seven hours, TL45).

⌂ **WHERE TO STAY** Amasra has many simple pensions and you can look out for signs along the seafront and around the *kale*. Among the best ones are **Kusna Pansiyon** ($$$), **Pansiyon Evi** ($$), just inside the *kale* gates, and **Carsi Pansiyon Evi** ($$) in the market near the *kale* entrance. They all tend to close from November to April.

✗ **WHERE TO EAT** Amasra has a range of eateries along its attractive harbour-front, specialising in fish.

✗ **Çeşm-i-Cihan Restaurant** Büyük Liman Caddesi 21; ☎ 3151062. This 3-storey restaurant has excellent views over the harbour & offers fried mussels & *calamar* (squid) among its delicacies. Outdoor seating. Licensed. **$$**

✗ **Öz Canlı Balık Restaurant** Küçük Liman Caddesi 8; ☎ 3152606. Amasra's oldest fish restaurant, in business since 1945, with a good atmosphere & a varied menu of fish, meat & chicken. Licensed & with outdoor seating. **$$**

SAFRANBOLU *Telephone code: 370*

From Amasra the road dips inland 23km to Bartin through splendid scenery. Here, and especially further inland at Safranbolu, the attractive black-timbered whitewashed houses with their overhanging balconies can be seen in profusion, similar in style to the houses around Bursa. There are three separate areas. The area you arrive in first is Kıranköy, the former Greek quarter, now very modern with all the banks, ATMs and shops; Bağlar, further uphill with many fine old houses; and downhill in Çarşi, where the heart of the Old City lies, full of the old timbered houses you have come to see, now an UNESCO World Heritage site.

GETTING THERE AND AWAY Bus is the only public transport option, and Ulusoy (*www.ulusoy.com*) runs daily services between Istanbul and Safranbolu (seven hours, TL30). Daily services also run from Ankara's ASTİ *otogar*.

TOURIST INFORMATION There is a helpful tourist office (🕒 *09.00–12.30 & 13.30–18.00 Mon–Fri*) just off the main square which hands out good leaflets and simple guides.

 WHERE TO STAY Nearly 50 historic Ottoman houses in Safranbolu have now been restored and converted to small traditional hotels, all under the supervision

---

OTTOMAN MANSIONS

Safranbolu has concentrated in its three districts, and especially in the Çarşi district, what is widely agreed to be the finest collection of beautiful old Ottoman mansions in the country. They date to the 19th century and are built of timber frames which were then filled in with *adobe* (mud brick) and then plastered over and usually painted white but with the timbers still showing. Most are two or even three storeys tall and quite square in shape, standing detached in their own gardens. The larger mansions had 10–12 rooms and often had internal courtyards and separate areas called *selamlik*, where the men received guests, and the *haremlik* where the women and children lived. The ceilings were often very beautifully carved and throughout the house there were decorative elements either of carved wood or plaster, according to the wealth of the owner. The Safranbolu houses also often had a revolving cupboard (*donme dolaplar*) between the *selamlik* and the *haremlik* so that the women could pass prepared food for guests without themselves being seen. The tiny cupboards around the rooms were designed to store the bedding during the day when the rooms doubled as living areas with seating on low benches (*sedirs*). Today ingenious conversions have managed to make these into tiny en-suite bathrooms, and you can see them properly if you stay in one of the hotels and pensions that many of the larger ones have now become. The household animals used to be kept downstairs in the courtyards overnight, while the living areas for the family were upstairs, often with attractive overhanging window areas supported on carved wooden corbels.

of the Monuments Commission. They are very popular places to stay among holidaying Turks themselves, so you will need to book ahead to guarantee securing a room.

Gülevi (9 rooms, I suite) Hükümet Sokak; ✆ 7254645; www.canbulat.com.tr; ⊕ all year. A delightful place in the middle of the Old Town with a pretty garden. Meals are served on demand. $$$$

Gökcuoğlu Konağı (8 rooms) Bağlarbasi Mahallesi, Bağlar; ✆ 7128153; www.gokcuoglukonagi.com. Sometimes closed in winter. Located in the summer quarter of Bağlar, 2km from Safranbolu, this magnificent house is wonderfully spacious with wood everywhere. Meals are available on demand. $$$

Rasitler Bağ Evi (5 rooms) Bağlar Mahallesi; ✆ 7251345; www.rasitlerbagevi.com. In the garden suburb of Bağlar (meaning 'orchards') 3km up the hill from Safranbolu, where the wealthy used to keep a winter home down in the town, & a summer home higher up where it was cooler. Standing beside the old public watermill, this fine old house has a large & peaceful garden, with small rooms & even smaller bathrooms fitted into cupboards. $$$

Cesmeli Konak (8 rooms, I suite) Çeşme Mahallesi; ✆ 7254455; www.cesmelikonak.com.tr; ⊕ all year. In the centre of Safranbolu, this 19th-century house is named after the fountain found in its garden. The Cinci *hammam* is next door & the market is close by. The house has many traditional features. Meals available on demand. $$

Degirmenci Konak (7 rooms, I suite) Cambaz Sokak; ✆ 7255045; www.degirmencikonak.com; ⊕ all year. Reached by turning right at a petrol station on entering Safranbolu, this is a 150-year-old Greek mansion. B/fast is wonderful with fresh walnuts & local jam & cheese. The interior is an unusual blend of traditional & modern. $$

Mehves Hanım Konaği (8 rooms) Hacihalil m Mescit Sokak; ✆ 7128787; www.mehveshanimkonagi.com.tr; ⊕ all year. A lovely mansion in a quiet street in the old centre of Safranbolu, it stands in a lovely romantic garden complete with roses, pergolas & marble pool. The authentic atmosphere has remained unchanged, with simple but beautifully furnished rooms (some without bathroom), with iron bedsteads, heavy linen & delicate lace. Meals available on demand. $$

Yoruk Pansiyon (4 rooms) Yorük Köyü; ✆ 7372153; closed winter. Yoruk is a small village 11km from Safranbolu consisting of about 140 beautiful Ottoman houses, some of them still semi-derelict with overgrown gardens. The name means 'Nomad Village' & the house was once lived in by dervishes of the Bektaşi sect. The rooms in this fine old house are basic but utterly authentic & they share I squat bathroom. Lovely garden. The village has a handful of simple places to eat & a small grocer's shop. $

✗ WHERE TO EAT Most of the hotels offer food, and as a result there are not too many restaurants in town. One memorable place is **Havuzlu Köşk** (✆ 7252168; $$$) in Bağlar, in a lovely setting with garden seating round the historic 300-year old house and a licensed bar.

SHOPPING Locally made textiles are particular specialities, such as lace. Safranbolu's name comes from the precious spice saffron which is used to flavour the Turkish delight (*lokum*). Many local shops all around the main square in Çarşi sell local sweets like the sticky *yaprak helvasi* (*halva*) with ground walnuts mixed in.

Appendix 1

LANGUAGE

COPING WITH TURKISH
Pronunciation

Vowels and consonants are pronounced as in English, except for: ö = oe (Göreme); ü = as in French *tu*; ı = the dotless i which is peculiar to Turkish and is pronounced as the initial 'a' in away (Topkapı); c = j (*cami*, meaning 'mosque' = jami); ç = ch (Çamlıhemsin); ş = sh (Maraş); ğ is unpronounced, but lengthens the preceding vowel (*dağ*, meaning mountain = daa); h is always pronounced; e on the end of a word is always pronounced, so Rize has two syllables. Stress falls evenly over the syllables in Turkish rather than being concentrated on one syllable as tends to be the case in English. The following English words as spelt in Turkish will help you get the idea: *ketcap* (ketchup), *taksi* (taxi), *futbol* (football), *kuaför* (coiffeur, hairdresser), *söför* (chauffeur, driver), *gişe* (ticket booth) and *büfe* (snack bar). There is no 'q', 'w' or 'x' in Turkish.

Greetings For simple greetings in Turkey, the easiest thing to say on arrival is: *Merhaba* (from the Arabic *marhaba*, welcome), to which the reply is the same. Sometimes you will also hear: *Hoş geldeniz* (you have come well), to which you reply *Hoş bulduk* (we find ourselves here well). When you leave, those staying behind may say *Güle güle* (may you go smilingly, smilingly), to which you as the person leaving reply either *Hoşça kal* or *Allaha ısmarladık* (we have committed ourselves to God), a bit of a mouthful but worth practising as it goes down very well. Other words and phrases you may find useful are:

The basics

Good morning	*Günaydin* (said on meeting)
Good day	*Iyi Günler* (said on meeting or parting in the daytime)
Good evening	*Iyi akşamlar* (said on meeting or parting in the evening)
Please	*lütfen*
Thanks	*teşekkürler, sağ ol*
Goodbye	*hoş çakal*
Yes	*evet*
No	*hayır*
I want...	*istiyorum...*
My name is...	*benim adım...*
What's your name?	*adınız ne?*

Food and drink

breakfast	*kahvaltı*	coffee	*kahve*
eggs	*yumurta*	milk	*süt*
tea	*çay*	sugar	*şeker*
more tea	*daha çay, lütfen*	coffee with sugar	*şekerli kahve*

bread	ekmek	cake	pasta
butter	tereyağ	packed lunch	piknik
jam	reçel	salt	tuz
honey	bal	pepper	biber
cheese	peynir	water	su
soup	çorba	mineral water	maden suyu
salad	salata	hot water	sıcak su
tomato	domates	fruit juice	meyva suyu
fish	balık	beer	bira
chicken	tavuk, piliç	wine	şarap
fried	kızatma	red wine	kırmızı şarap
grilled	grill	white wine	beyaz şarap
roast	rost	dry	sek
chips	patates	sweet	tatlı
fruit	meyva	the bill, please	hesab, lütfen
ice cream	dondurma		

Shopping

very beautiful	çok güzel	No problem	problem yok
How much?	Ne kadar?	shop	dukkan
cheap	ucuz	market	çarşi, pazar
expensive	pahalı	open	acık
money	para	shut, closed	kapalı
a lot, much, very	çok		

Places

bank	banka	hotel	otel
post office	postane	restaurant	restoran/lokanta/
chemist	eczane		tesisler
hospital	hastahane	police	polis
museum	müze	ticket office	gişe

Hotels

room	oda	bathroom	banyo
Do you have a		towel	havlu
room?	oda varmı?	soap	sabun
For one person	bir kişilik	Gents	baylar
For two people	iki kişilik	Ladies	bayanlar
toilet	tuvalet		

Travel

airport	havaalanı	unleaded	kursunuz
bus	otobus	leaded	kursunlu
bus station	otogar	diesel	dizel
train	tren	good road	iyi yol
station	tren istasyonu	bad road	bozuk yol
small boat	sandal/kayak	Road closed	yol kapalı
	(ie: caique)	Is this road possible	Bu yol arabamla
ship/ferry	vapur/feribot	for my car?	gitmeye musait midir?
motorboat	motorbot	No entry	girilmez
shared taxi	dolmuş	Attention	dikkat
private car	özel oto/araba	Stop	dur
petrol	benzin	right	sağ

left	sol	near	yakın
straight on	doğru	petrol	benzin
far	uzak	Where is …?	…nerede?

General

I don't know	bilmiyorum	Head man, mayor	kaymakam
I don't understand	anlamiyorum	Director, manager	müdür
Do you speak	Ingilizce/ Türkçe	Primary school	ilkokul
English/Turkish?	konusuyoruz?	Pharmacy	eczane
To let/hire	kıralık	Docks, jetty	iskele
For sale	satılık	Railway station	istasyon
Forbidden	yasak	Bus station	otogar
Forbidden zone	yasak bölge	England	Ingiltere
Photography	Fotograf çekmek	Ireland	Irlanda
forbidden	yasaktir	Scotland	Iskoçya
No smoking	sigara içilmez	Wales	Galler
Broken, not working	bozuk	France	Faransa
Entrance	giriş	Germany	Almanya
Exit	çikiş	Italy	Italya
Information	danışma	Canada	Kanada
Municipality	belediye	Australia	Avustralya
Governor	vali	USA	Amerika Birlesik
(of a province)			Devletleri
Province	vilayet		

Numbers

1	bir	6	altı
2	iki	7	yedi
3	üç	8	sekiz
4	dört	9	dokuz
5	beş	10	on

Days of the week

Monday	Pazartesi	Friday	Cuma
Tuesday	Salı	Saturday	Cumartesi
Wednesday	Çarşamba	Sunday	Pazar
Thursday	Perşembe		

IMPROVING YOUR TURKISH If you want to take your language a bit further, the best serious book is *Turkish in Three Months* (Dorling Kindersley Ltd 1998) by Bengisu Rona, not always easy to find in bookshops but sometimes available on Amazon. Otherwise Lonely Planet produces a handy Turkish phrasebook that has a small dictionary at the back, along with some really quite complicated sentences grouped according to subject matter, such as *Kredi kartımla para çekebilir miyim?* meaning 'Can I use my credit card to withdraw money?' and at customs, *Bunu ulkeden çıkaramiyacağımı bilmiyorudum* meaning 'I didn't realise I couldn't take this out of the country', which are frankly unrealistic for any beginner to master. There are also one-day Turkish audio CDs, such as the one produced by Teach Yourself, which also has an eight-page booklet, and says you only have to learn 50 words. Certainly it's good to hear the language properly before going, so that you at least get used to the concept of the dotless i and the silent g, and the Turkish c being pronounced as the English j. One thing you will notice time and again is the appearance of an ı or dotless i or other vowel at the end of words, such as Nemrut Dağı. This is the omnipresent Turkish genitive case ending showing possession, so meaning in this case 'Nemrut his Mountain'.

Another example is *Atatürk Caddesi* where the Turkish *cadde* means street, but it acquires the genitive ending *–si* because the literal meaning is 'Atatürk his street'. If you are really serious about mastering Turkish, the Turkish & Foreign Language Research & Application Center (TOMER), which is part of the University of Ankara, runs courses for foreigners wanting to learn Turkish throughout Turkey and has recently launched an online learning centre; see www.tomer.ankara.edu.tr or www.turkishcenter.com.

Appendix 2

GLOSSARY

This glossary includes Turkish words you may see on notices or signs; where an extra (i) or (si) is shown in brackets after the word, this is how it may appear in signs, and simply shows the genitive case ending, having no effect on the main meaning of the word, eg: Sultanhanı, the *han* of the sultan; Atatürk Meydanı, Atatürk's Square.

Ablaq	patterned stonework of alternate dark and light colours
Acanthus	artichoke-like stylised leaves carved as decoration on Corinthian capitals
Aile salonu	family dining room, where women and children (accompanied by their menfolk or not) eat in traditional Turkish restaurants
Anatolia	the Asian part of Turkey, known as Asia Minor by the Romans
Baraj	dam
Baraka	Arabic for blessing, used to imply gaining God's blessing
Bedesten	similar to *han* where merchants stored valuable goods for sale and trading
Belediye	municipality, town hall
Bey	Turkish polite form of address, put after the name, ie: Ali Bey
Bimaristan	hospital and school of medicine in the Muslim world
Caliph	from the Arabic *khalifa* meaning successor
Cami(i)	mosque
Caravanserai	fortified stopping place for merchants' camel caravans with inn facilities
Çardak	huge metal or wooden cot raised up on stilts (often on the roofs of houses) where people sleep on hot summer nights, especially in the southeast of Turkey
Cardo maximus	main street running north–south in a Roman city
Çay bahçesi	tea-garden
Çeşme	fountain, spring
Cilician Gates	major pass used since antiquity to descend from the Anatolian Plateau to the Mediterranean through the Taurus mountains
Cornucopia	horn of plenty, a curved goat's horn from whose mouth fruit and grain overflow, symbol of fertility and abundance
Dağ(i)	mountain
Decumanus	main street running east–west in a Roman city
Dervish	from the Persian meaning beggar, the term has now come to be used for a member of any Sufi Muslim religious fraternity, known for extreme poverty and austerity, similar to a mendicant friar
Dolmuş	shared taxi, literally Turkish for 'stuffed'
Emanet	left-luggage office

Emir	from the Arabic *amir*, meaning 'tribal chieftain'
Ev pansiyonu	pension that is a private house
Eyvan	Arabic *iwan*, a roofed but open, usually north-facing room with an arch giving directly onto the courtyard of a traditional Ottoman house or *medrese*
Ezan	Arabic *idhan*, meaning 'Muslim call to prayer'
GAP	Turkish acronym for Southeastern Anatolia Project, based around a series of dams on the Euphrates
Gazino	Turkish nightclub, usually serving alcohol (not a casino)
Geçit	mountain pass
Göl(ü)	lake
Guilloche	pattern of interlacing bands forming a plait
Hammam	Turkish bath-house with steam room, adapted from the Roman baths but with no pool, as Muslims believe water must flow freely and not sit stagnant, as this is considered unhygienic
Hanafi	belonging to the Hanafite School of Islamic Law (as opposed to the Hanbali, Malaki and Shafa'i schools of law). Most Ottomans were Hanafis, from their belief that ablutions needed to be conducted under running water, not stagnant water in a basin like the Shafa'is – *hanafia* is Arabic for 'tap'.
Han(ı)	from the Persian *khan*, an inn or caravanserai set round a courtyard where merchants could stay in upstairs rooms, while their goods and animals were kept in the downstairs rooms
Hanim	polite form of Turkish address for a woman, like *bey* for men
Haremlik	Ottoman term for the women's quarters of a house
Hittites	indigenous Anatolian people who ruled in the 2nd millennium BC
Iconostasis	screen in an Orthodox church separating the nave from the choir, inset with icons
Imam	same as the Arabic, meaning 'prayer leader' or 'Muslim cleric'
Iwan	three-sided roofed recess opening onto a courtyard
Indirim	discount
Iskele	jetty, quay
Jandarma	Turkish police, gendarmerie
Jeton	token for travel
Kale(si)	castle, citadel
Kaplıca	thermal springs
Karagöz	traditional Turkish shadow-puppet theatre
KDV	Turkey's equivalent of VAT
Kervanseray	caravanserai
Khatchkar	Armenian cross
Kilim	flat-weave rug
Kilise(si)	church
Konak(ği)	mansion, grand hall
Köprü(sü)	bridge
Kosk(u)	villa, pavilion
Kufic	oldest form of Arabic calligraphic script, from Kufa in Iraq, recognisable by its square and straight angular forms
Külliye(si)	Ottoman mosque complex, with religious college, hospital and soup kitchen
Kümbet	dome or tomb with a dome, often pointed
Lokanta	traditional restaurant serving ready-made food on display for customers to choose

Maenad	literally 'madwoman'. Female follower of the wine god Dionysus, usually shown participating in orgiastic Dionysian rites.
Mahalle(si)	neighbourhood or district, often occurring in addresses, from the Arabic *mahall*.
Medrese	from the Arabic *madrasa* meaning school; the earliest ones were always religious, teaching the Koran and religious law
Mescit	small mosque, prayer room
Meydan(ı)	public square in a town, from the Arabic *maydan*
Mezze	selection of starters, hot and cold, which comprise a typical Arab meal
Mihrab	prayer niche facing Mecca in a mosque
Milli parkı	national park
Mimber	raised pulpit in a mosque reached by a flight of steps, from which the Friday sermon is preached by the *imam*
Muezzin	man who calls to prayer from the mosque minaret
Muqarnas	'stalactite' decoration in wood or stone, usually above portals or arches, sometimes also called 'beehive' decoration
Müze(si)	museum
Nargile	from the Persian word for water-pipe, also called hubble-bubble or hookah in Arab countries
Narthex	vestibule or entrance hall to the nave of a Byzantine church usually running the whole width of a building
Nave	central rectangular hall of a church or basilica, usually lined with colonnades to separate it from the side aisles
Nereid	sea nymph fathered by Nereus, a sea god
Otobus	bus
Otogar	bus station
Paşa	Turkish title of respect, usually a governor or general
Pastane	Turkish for patisserie, also sometimes *pastahane*
Pazar	weekly market or bazaar
Peribacalar	fairy chimneys
Pestimal	thin cotton towel/wrap issued to clients in a Turkish bath
Petrol ofisi	petrol station
Qibla	the direction of Mecca
Ramazan	Islamic holy month of fasting
Şadırvan	fountain in a mosque courtyard where ritual ablutions are performed before prayer
Saray(ı)	palace
Şehir	city
Selamlik	Ottoman term for the men's quarter in a traditional home, also where guests were received
Seljuk	of the Seljuk Turks, the first Turkish state that ruled Anatolia between the 11th and 13th centuries.
Sema	ceremony of the Whirling Dervishes
Servis	Turkish name for the minibus shuttle service going to and from the *otogar* (bus station)
Shi'a	the branch of Islam that split off from the Sunni orthodoxy, believing 'Ali was Muhammad's rightful successor
Sufi	Muslim mystic
Sultan	Muslim ruler
Sunni	Orthodox Islam that follows the 'Sunna', the tradition
Souk	Arab market
Tekke	dervish lodge

Tesserae	tiny and usually square-cut pieces of stones, usually limestone or marble or glass
Triclinium	literally 'three couches', a term for a Roman dining room with three couches, arranged along three sides of the room, on which diners reclined to eat
Türbe(si)	tomb, grave, mausoleum
Vizir	adviser to the ruler
Vilayet	provincial government headquarters
Waqf/Vekif	system of Islamic trusts
Yayla	summer highland pastures

Appendix 3

FURTHER INFORMATION

BOOKS
Bookshops

In London Stanfords (*12–14 Long Acre, London WC2E 9LP; www.stanfords.co.uk*) and Daunts (*83 Marylebone High St, London W1M 3DE; www.dauntbooks.co.uk*) are the travel bookshop specialists, where you will find the biggest range of books and maps in stock. Hatchards (*187 Piccadilly, London SW1; www.hatchards.co.uk*) too has a very good travel section. You can also order direct from www.amazon.co.uk. There are also three publishers who have large Turkish/Middle Eastern lists: I B Tauris (*www.ibtauris.co.uk*), The Eothen Press (*www.theeothenpress.com*) and Saqi Books (*www.saqibooks.com*). For rarer or out-of-print books the best places to start looking are the following websites: www.abe.com/.co.uk and www.bookfinder.com.

Travel writing and biography

Berlitz, Charles *The Lost Ship of Noah* W H Allen, 1988. The myths examined.

Burnaby, Frederick *On Horseback Through Asia Minor* (1877) Oxford Paperbacks, 1996

Byron, Robert *The Road to Oxiana* Penguin Travel Library, 1937. Classic travelogue.

Childs, W J *Across Asia Minor on Foot* Budge Press, 1917. Compulsive reading.

Dalrymple, William *From the Holy Mountain: A Journey in the Shadow of Byzantium* Flamingo, 1998. Readable account following in the footsteps of two Byzantine monks, starting in Mount Athos in Greece and moving via monasteries in Turkey, Syria, Palestine and finishing in Egypt, looking at and analysing the remnants of eastern Christianity *en route*.

Glazebrook, Philip *Journey to Kars* Henry Holt & Co, 1984. Some interesting insights.

Halid, Halil *The Diary of a Turk* A&C Black, 1972. A fascinating 1903 diary, republished.

Irwin, James B *More than an Ark on Ararat* Broadman Press, 1985. Scary stuff.

La Haye, Tim and Morris, John *The Ark on Ararat* Creation-Life, 1976. Even scarier.

Orga, Irfan *Portrait of a Turkish Family* Eland, 1950. Tragic and haunting childhood memories.

Macaulay, Rose *The Towers of Trebizond* Collins, 1956. Amusing account of travel in the 1950s in eastern Turkey in the company of Father Chantry-Pigg and Aunt Dot, as they explore the possibility of setting up a High Anglican mission here. Wonderfully eccentric.

Pamuk, Orhan *Snow* Faber & Faber, 2004. Set in Kars, this novel by Turkey's best-known novelist deals with previously taboo subjects like political Islam and Kurdish nationalism, causing a stir in intellectual circles of Istanbul but barely a ripple in the east itself, where hardly anyone read it.

Pereira, Michael *East of Trebizond* Bles, 1971. History blended with a travelogue along the Black Sea coast and in the northeast of Anatolia.

Seal, Jeremy *A Fez of the Heart* Picador, 1995. Glib but entertaining in places.

Stark, Freya *Riding to the Tigris* John Murray, 1959. Stark's inimitable style and travel musings mingled with ancient history always make her an entertaining travel companion.

Turkish Culture for Americans Intl Concepts Ltd, 1989. Unintentionally hilarious book full of examples of cultural misunderstandings aimed at Americans living in Turkey.

History
Classical

Herodotus *The Histories* 5th century BC. Edited by Robert B Strassler, trans. Andrea L Purvis, Quercus, 2008. Written by the father of history and anthropology, with many descriptions of the tribes and nations of Anatolia. He was born in Halicarnassus (modern Bodrum) and lived from 484–c425BC.

Strabo *Geography* translated by Horace Leonard Jones, Bibliolife, 2009. Born in Amasya, Strabo (64BC–24AD), Greek historian, geographer and philosopher who travelled widely and wrote about Roman Anatolia.

Xenophon *Anabasis* or *The March Up-Country* translated by H G Dakyns, EPN Press, 2007. Account of the Athenian leader of the Ten Thousand and the long retreat from Mesopotamia to the Black Sea.

Ancient history and archaeology

Akurgal, Ekrem *Ancient Civilisations and Ruins of Turkey* Kegan Paul, 2002. Comprehensive survey of Anatolian sites from prehistoric times.

Bryce, Trevor *Life and Society in the Hittite World* OUP, 2004. Lucid and scholarly study, with fascinating insights into Hittite festivals, gods, law, medicine, myth and death.

Gurney, O R *The Hittites* Penguin, 1991. Authoritative history of the first great Anatolian civilisation.

Lloyd, Seton *Ancient Turkey – a Traveller's History of Anatolia*. Excellent readable account of the ancient civilisations, by the head of the British Archaeological Institute in Ankara.

MacQueen, J G *The Hittites and their Contemporaries in Asia Minor* Thames & Hudson, 1990. Easier reading than Gurney's work, and well illustrated.

Byzantine history

Mango, Cyril *Byzantium: The Empire of the New Rome* Weidenfeld & Nicholson, 1994. Interesting and easy-to-read account of the Byzantine Empire, also covering some unusual aspects like cosmology and superstition, universities and scholarship, economic policy and daily life.

Runciman, Steven *Byzantine Style and Civilisation* Plume, 1974. A complete account of Byzantine art, full of fascinating detail, yet in a small handy paperback.

Ottoman history

Finkel, Caroline *Osman's Dream* Basic Books, 2007. Excellent, highly readable overview.

Inalcık, Halil *The Ottoman Empire: The Classical Age, 1300-1600* Reprint Phoenix 2000 (1973). Very highly regarded, the standard work.

Kinross, Patrick Balfour *The Ottoman Centuries* William Morrow, 1979. Covering the whole period from the 14th to the 20th century, very readable and balanced account.

Modern history

Hotham, David *The Turks* John Murray, 1972. Entertaining insights from *The Times* correspondent.

Kinross, Lord Patrick *Atatürk: The Rebirth of a Nation* (1964) Reprint Phoenix, 2001. Rightly seen as the definitive biography, with everything covered in a balanced and thorough way.

Lewis, Geoffrey *Modern Turkey* Ernest Benn, 1974. Ground-breaking book by this self-taught Oxford professor who introduced Turkish Studies as a degree course. Originally a classicist, his works mix scholarship with humour.

Mango, Andrew *The Turks Today* John Murray, 2004. Focusing on the period from Atatürk's death in 1938 until 2004, the author is a seasoned Turkey observer and fluent Turkish-speaker, and gives a comprehensive account of Turkey's complexities over the last 70 years.

Mango, Andrew *Atatürk* Overlook, 2007. The most recent biography of Atatürk, highly acclaimed and clearly sympathetic to the ideology of the man and the Turkish national project. Very little mention of the Greek/Turkish exchange of populations or of the Armenian question.

Pope, Nicole and Hugh *Turkey Unveiled: A History of Modern Turkey* Overlook Press, 2004. This is a series of essays by this husband-and-wife duo who are both foreign correspondents based in Istanbul for over 20 years, who clearly love the country but remain objective.

Robins, Philip *Turkey and the Middle East* Continuum, 1999. A thought-provoking study.

Toynbee, Arnold *Turkey: A Past and a Future* Hodder & Stoughton, 1917. Classic of its time.

Walker, Christopher J *Visions of Ararat Writings on Armenia* I B Tauris, 1997. Enlightening.

Warkworth, Lord *Asiatic Turkey* London, 1898. A fascinating early diary.

Williams, Gwyn *Eastern Turkey* Faber and Faber, 1972

Art, literature and architecture

Goodwin, Godfrey *A History of Ottoman Architecture* Thames & Hudson, 1987. A thorough and definitive guide to the subject.

Hillenbrand, Robert *Islamic Art and Architecture* Thames and Hudson, 1999. Wide-ranging guide to the arts of Islam, including architecture, calligraphy, ceramics and textiles, covering the whole geographic scope over a 1,000-year period.

Hull, Alastair *Kilims: The Complete Guide* Thames & Hudson, 1995. Thoroughly illustrated and comprehensive survey of Turkish *kilims*.

Krautheimer, Richard *Early Christian and Byzantine Architecture* (1992). From the Yale University Press Pelican 'History of Art' series, an excellent overview, now recognised as a classic.

Kritzeck, James *Anthology of Islamic Literature* Penguin, 1987. Comprehensive and clear account of everything Islamic literature has to offer, from pre-Islamic poetry, through the developments of the Umayyad and Abbasid caliphates, the Ottoman times, to the present day.

Mango, Cyril *Byzantine Architecture* Electa/Rizzoli, 1985. Only around a quarter of these fall within modern Turkey's boundaries, but it is still a very good overview.

Önal, Mehmet *Mosaics of Zeugma* A Turizm Yayinlari, 2005

Robinson, Francis (ed) *Islamic World: Cambridge Illustrated History* CUP, 1996. Lavishly illustrated cultural history of the Islamic world from Muhammad to the present day, demystifying Muslim civilisation and celebrating its achievements, whilst putting its role in the world today into perspective.

Sinclair, Tom *Eastern Turkey: An Archaeological and Architectural Study* (four vols) Pindar Press, 1987–90. Incredibly detailed, cataloguing pretty much every pile of stones from Cappadocia eastwards, with good plans. Available in university or specialist libraries.

Talbot Rice, David *Islamic Art* Thames & Hudson, 1975. Covering a huge area, but includes interesting perspectives on Ottoman and Seljuk art compared to Persia and Muslim Spain. His *The Church of Hagia Sophia in Trebizond* Edinburgh University Press, 1968 is still the best work on this, as he headed the team that restored its frescoes.

Religion and ethnic minorities

Akcam, Taner *From Empire to Republic: Turkish Nationalism and the Armenian Genocide* Zed Books, 2004. Convincing study by a Turkish academic resident in the USA showing how the ethnic cleansing of the Armenians was necessary to the beginnings of the Turkish Republic, based on thorough examination of the official Turkish archives.

Arberry, A J *The Koran* Oxford World Classics, Oxford Paperbacks, 1998. Generally seen as the best English translation, along with N J Dawood's version. Arberry was Professor of Arabic at London and Cambridge universities.

Armstrong, Karen *Islam: A Short History* Phoenix, 2000. Engaging and provocative corrective to the hostile caricatures of Islam that circulate in the English-speaking world.

Livingstone, E A *Concise Dictionary of the Christian Church* OUP, 2000

McDowall, David *The Kurds: A Nation Denied* Harry Ransom Humanities Research Center, 1992 and *A Modern History of the Kurds* IB Tauris, 2004. The author has devoted his life to the study of this problem, and gives a very detailed and authoritative exposition of the problems.

Pelikan, Jaroslav *Christian Tradition: A History of the Development of Doctrine: The Spirit of Eastern Christendom 600-1700* University of Chicago Press, 1977. Masterpiece of exposition which explains the divisions between Eastern and Western Christendom, the linguistic barriers, political divisions and liturgical differences which combine to isolate the two cultures from each other.

Rogerson, Barnaby *The Prophet Muhammad: A Biography* Abacus, 2003. Fascinating, thoughtful and open-minded biography, giving insights into the life of the man, leader and visionary. The book will probably change the way you think about Islam.

Zernov, Nicolas *History of Religion: Eastern Christendom* Weidenfeld & Nicholson, 1961. An overview of the history of the Eastern Orthodox Church; thorough and comprehensive.

Mountaineering and trekking

Clow, Kate *The Kaçkar* Upcountry Ltd, 2008. The first of its kind, with map and guide describing 32 routes in the Kaçkar Mountains (Pontic Alps), ranging from half-day walks to multi-day treks, following traditional footpaths or paved packhorse routes that have been in use for centuries.

Parrot, Friedrich *Journey to Ararat* Elibron Classics, 2005 (1855). A wonderful classic, by the first person to climb it in 1829, a German professor.

Tüzel, O B *The Ala Dag* Cicerone, 1993. Quite technical, for serious climbers.

WEBSITES

www.gototurkey.co.uk The Turkish Tourist Office in London, with comprehensive general information.

www.tourismturkey.org Turkish information offices abroad.

www.exploreturkey.com Good background on the historical monuments, though weaker east of Cappadocia.

www.kackarmountains.com Good coverage of all mountains and trekking opportunities in Turkey, as well as Ararat and the Ala Dagları. Maintained by the Turkish trekking agency Middle Earth, but also giving lots of useful information for those trekking on their own.

www.turkishdailynews.com Abridged version of the English-language daily.

www.aa.com.tr Anadolu Ajansi, information on museums and other news.

www.mymerhaba.com General information on Turkish culture and background.

www.tcdd.gov.tr The official website of Turkish State Railways, now much easier to use since April 2010. Train tickets can be booked and paid for online.

www.seat61.com Very helpful, bang up-to-date website on train travel in Turkey (and onwards into Syria or Iran). Tickets can be booked through the travel agents they recommend in Istanbul, Tur-ISTA (\ *(212) 5277085;* e *erdemir@tur-ista.com*).

www.turkeytravelplanner.com Useful website giving all sorts of advice to help travel planning in Turkey, put together by Tom Brosnahan, who wrote the first (and rather poor) *Lonely Planet* to *Turkey* back in the 1980s.

WIN A FREE BRADT GUIDE
READER QUESTIONNAIRE

**Send in your completed questionnaire and enter our monthly draw
for the chance to win a Bradt guide of your choice.**

To take up our special reader offer of 40% off, please visit our website at
www.bradtguides.com/freeguide or answer the questions below and return to us
with the order form overleaf.

(Forms may be posted or faxed to us.)

Have you used any other Bradt guides? If so, which titles? . . . .
. . . .

What other publishers' travel guides do you use regularly? . . . .
. . . .

Where did you buy this guidebook? . . . .

What was the main purpose of your trip to Turkey (or for what other reason did
you read our guide)? eg: holiday/business/charity . . . .
. . . .

How long did you travel for? (circle one)

weekend/long weekend   1–2 weeks   3–4 weeks   4 weeks plus

Which countries did you visit in connection with this trip? . . . .
. . . .

Did you travel with a tour operator?' If so, which one? . . . .
. . . .

What other destinations would you like to see covered by a Bradt guide?
. . . .

If you could make one improvement to this guide, what would it be?
. . . .

Age (circle relevant category) 16–25   26–45   46–60   60+

Male/Female (delete as appropriate)

Home country . . . .

Please send us any comments about this guide (or others on our list).
. . . .
. . . .
. . . .

Bradt Travel Guides
23 High Street, Chalfont St Peter, Bucks SL9 9QE, UK
☎ +44 (0)1753 893444 f +44 (0)1753 892333
e info@bradtguides.com
www.bradtguides.com

TAKE 40% OFF YOUR NEXT BRADT GUIDE!
Order Form

To take advantage of this special offer visit www.bradtguides.com/freeguide
and enter our monthly giveaway, or fill in the order form below, complete the
questionnaire overleaf and send it to Bradt Travel Guides by post or fax.

Please send me one copy of the following guide at 40% off the UK retail price

No	Title	Retail price	40% price
1	....	....	....

Please send the following additional guides at full UK retail price

No	Title	Retail price	Total
...	....	....	....
...	....	....	....
...	....	....	....

Sub total ....
Post & packing ....
(Free shipping UK, £1 per book Europe, £3 per book rest of world)
Total ....

Name ....

Address..

Tel .... Email ....

☐ I enclose a cheque for £........ made payable to Bradt Travel Guides Ltd

☐ I would like to pay by credit card. Number: ....

   Expiry date: ... / ...   3-digit security code (on reverse of card) .....

   Issue no (debit cards only) .....

☐ Please sign me up to Bradt's monthly enewsletter, Bradtpackers' News.

☐ I would be happy for you to use my name and comments in Bradt
   marketing material.

Send your order on this form, with the completed questionnaire, to:

Bradt Travel Guides
23 High Street, Chalfont St Peter, Bucks SL9 9QE
☏ +44 (0)1753 893444   f +44 (0)1753 892333
e info@bradtguides.com   www.bradtguides.com

Index

INDEX OF HIGHLIGHTED BOXES